DATE DUE

		DISCARD	
GAYLORD			PRINTED IN U.S.A.

WRITTEN WORDS

The written word, unlike the spoken word, is something which every person examines privately and judges calmly by his own intellectual standards . . . .

E. B. WHITE

Pablo Picasso: The Old
Guitarist (oil, 1903)
*Courtesy of The Art Institute
of Chicago. Helen Birch
Bartlett Memorial Collection.*

WRITTEN WORDS

A Literary Introduction to English Composition

ARTHUR NORMAN
UNIVERSITY OF CHICAGO

and

LEWIS SAWIN
UNIVERSITY OF COLORADO

RANDOM HOUSE
NEW YORK

Third Printing, April 1964

© Copyright, 1962, by Random House, Inc.

All rights reserved under International and Pan-American Copyright
Conventions. Published in New York by Random House, Inc., and
simultaneously in Toronto, Canada, by Random House of Canada, Limited.
Library of Congress Catalog Card Number: 62-10669
Manufactured in the United States of America by George McKibbin and Son

Design by Jacqueline Schuman

TO C. D. L. AND L. C. H.

THROUGH THICK, AND OFTEN THROUGH THIN

Acknowledgments

"A Noiseless Flash" from *Hiroshima* by John Hersey. Copyright 1946 by John Hersey. Reprinted
by permission of Alfred A. Knopf, Inc.

"Dr. Parkman Takes a Walk" from the book *The Proper Bostonians* by Cleveland Amory. Copyright © 1947 by Cleveland Amory. Reprinted by permission of the publishers, E. P. Dutton &
Co., Inc.

"Marrakech" from *Such, Such Were the Joys* by George Orwell. Copyright, 1945, 1952, 1953,
by Sonia Brownell Orwell. Reprinted by permission of Harcourt, Brace & World, Inc., and Martin
Secker & Warburg Ltd.

"Prologue: 1933" from Arthur M. Schlesinger, Jr., *The Crisis of the Old Order*, © 1957, is reprinted by permission of and arrangement with Houghton Mifflin Company, the authorized
publishers.

Selection from *Mark Twain's Autobiography*, edited by Albert Bigelow Paine. Copyright 1924 by
Clara Gabrilowitsch. Reprinted by permission of Harper & Brothers.

"The Old Guitarist" by Pablo Picasso. Reproduced by permission of The Art Institute of Chicago.

"Bores" from *Guests* by Russell Lynes. Copyright 1951 by Harper & Brothers. Reprinted by permission.

Definition of *dog* from the *American College Dictionary*. Copyright 1947, © 1962, by Random
House, Inc. Reprinted by permission.

Definition of *dog* from *Webster's Third New International Dictionary*, copyright 1961 by G. & C.
Merriam Co., Publishers of the Merriam-Webster Dictionaries. By permission.

Definition of *dog* from *Webster's New World Dictionary of the American Language*, College Edition, copyright 1962 by the World Publishing Company. Reprinted by permission.

Definition of *dog* from the *Oxford English Dictionary*. Reproduced by permission of The Clarendon Press, Oxford.

Preface

Written Words reflects a philosophy of teaching which has grown from our joint experience at several universities. We have always thought that the beginning writer must first be a reader, and his ears ought to ring with great and mighty prose. Before he can write, the student must have something to say, and this means knowledge, which is most easily gotten from books, and wisdom, which the student himself must bring to the course. As he writes, the student must have an awareness of the forms which give order to prose and the qualities which give it vigor and grace. All of this is reflected in our selection of writers and ideas, our emphasis upon style, and above all in the stress we place on rhetoric.

It is a pleasure to thank the many good people who have helped us with this volume. To Anthony Amberg, L. Duane Ball, J. Wallace Donald, Sylvan Karchmer, John L. Murphy, Norval Rindfleisch, William Smith, A. Lewis Soens, Raymond Walters, Arthur Norman Wilkins, and to Captain and Mrs. David D. Zink II, our thanks for their generous advice and encouragement. To Marilynn Sawin, for her long hours with typewriter and gluepot and in the library, to Raven I. McDavid, Jr., and to Joe Howard of the University of Colorado Libraries, we owe special debts of gratitude. To all the writers and publishers who have permitted us to use their work, our sincere thanks, but we are especially beholden to Charles Lieber and Leonore C. Hauck of Random House, and to John Harvey, Allen McNab, Robert Odess, Robert Osborn, Philip Roth, R. C. Stephenson, E. B. White, Napier Wilt, and to Gene Tunney, our favorite prizefighter. The weight of tradition forbids us to list anyone we are not grateful to.

Of all the people and institutions to whom we are indebted, our greatest debt, and the one least easily paid, is to the College Composition Staff of the University of Chicago. The philosophy of rhetoric which is to be found at the University of Chicago and the experience of teaching with this Staff have helped more than anything else to fashion and mould this book. We are grateful.

If in any way we are remiss, and for faults of every kind, we can only ask forgiveness.

A. N.
L. S.

Introduction: To The Student

A first course in English at most American colleges and universities is a course in writing. More than that, it is a service course; your English Department is attempting to teach you the skills that will enable you to write papers for your other studies with the greatest success and the least misery and heartache. Since this is the chief purpose of the course, it follows that your textbook should be a tool that will further this purpose.

During the next few months you will concentrate on a number of valuable ways to organize and discuss information: narration and description—which you should find easy, since you have had some experience with these patterns before—and classification, definition, comparison and contrast, and cause and effect—which are more abstruse and much less familiar. You will study the devices of argumentation, including induction and deduction, and you will inquire into the nature of that elusive, baffling thing called style.

As you study and discuss the major techniques of organization, you will read essays which illustrate them, in whole or in part. It is necessary to isolate them so, to study them under the literary magnifying glass, and you will find this a difficult and intellectually demanding task. Then, when you have mastered these techniques by study and by writing essays of your own, you will turn your attention to the essays in the last section of this book, which are arranged by subject rather than by principles of organization.

In studying these essays, you will be interested not in one isolated technique of organization but in all the principles, devices, and tricks of the trade that the author uses to explain an idea or argue a point. In the first three sections of this volume, you will be learning to walk; in the fourth section, it will be time to run. You will also find that the last section of this book will provide you with information and ideas that should lead to essays of your own about some of the great topics of our world.

Because you have first practiced the important rhetorical maneuvers one by one, you will find yourself using them more successfully once it is time to bring them together, like units of a well-disciplined army, in support of an idea.

Of the selections in this volume, some will be easy, others rigorous. But all should be interesting, and working through a tough, sinewy piece of writing is good exercise: you will get in the habit of reading critically, and you will demand more of yourself in your own thinking and writing. Through these essays you will also encounter some of the best minds and some of the noblest writing produced in almost four hundred years of English and American letters. A good first course in English should not only teach you how to write, it should offer you the chance to get acquainted with great writers and outstanding literature.

As you do your weekly papers, keep in mind the five requirements of all good writing: It must have something to say. It must be clear. It must be orderly. It must be graceful and interesting to read. Last—and most important—good writing is always a search for truth. (Needless to say, it must also be a literate search, but one should not wait until college to acquire literacy.)

A combination of careful reading, class discussion, and controlled writing is probably the best method there is for teaching someone how to write. But ultimately no one can teach you this or any other skill. The only way a person learns to write is by writing, and it may take many years of painful practice.

Contents

Part IV　*IN SEARCH OF IDEAS*

Part One

EXPOSITION

The Written Word

Before a person can attempt to master the craft of the essay, he must bring to his work a certain awareness of what the word, the sentence, and the paragraph can do if well used—or if abused.

Unhappily, there is no easy advice or proverbial wisdom that will tell a student how to choose his words. The writer must possess a feeling for words—a kind of word sense—that will help him to put the right word in the right place. To some extent this can be cultivated. Once a person becomes aware of the variety and richness of expression which the English vocabulary offers so prodigally, he has taken the first step towards mastering an instrument of unbelievable range and sensitivity. Consider any common word, such as *food*—so common that it can be found at least a hundred times in every million words of prose. Without straining the average vocabulary, we can think of rather learned synonyms like *nourishment* or *sustenance*, learned and fairly uncommon terms like *aliment* or *pabulum*, and jocular or highly informal synonyms like *chow* or *grub*. A word like *chow* would be as much out of place in an address before the Congress of the United States as *aliment* would be in an Army mess hall. Both would stick out like sore thumbs. The sloppy writer is one who puts down the first word that comes to mind; the pretentious writer, who is even worse, is forever showing off his Latinity; but the competent writer tries to find the right word for the occasion (which is probably *food* more often than not).

The synonyms for *food* illustrate pretty clearly the levels at which we can pitch a discourse and some of the innuendoes that words are capable of. An even greater source of rhetorical effectiveness is the specificity with which we talk or write. Suppose that the writer is describing some artwork. In ordinary conversation he would probably translate the word as *picture*, but in careful speech or writing he would hunt for the term that describes the picture with the greatest precision. If it is a painting rather than a print or drawing, he would tell us so. But the good writer is likely to go a step further and call the painting a landscape (or a still life, or whatever it is), pinning the most specific label on it that he can find in his word hoard.

A feeling for specifics, a talent for seeing things in detail—for prose, these abilities spell the difference between vigor and lifelessness. Sometimes it is a simple matter of cramming information into a well-turned sentence: "Our present interest in Cuba began in 1898, when the battleship *Maine* was blown up in Havana Harbor." A less skillful writer would have said that our interest in Cuba dates from the Spanish-American War, perhaps adding the year; this writer tells *what*, *where*, *when*, and *how*—all in eighteen words. The student who habitually answers these unasked questions (along with *who* and *why*) is prepared to grapple with the essay.

Facts are details, and details make good writing; but not all details are facts. Details have their source in the ability to visualize things, actions, and qualities— the pores on a gentleman's bald scalp; the snap in a newly commissioned officer's salute; the bronze tones of a well-bred Japanese chrysanthemum—and to report them. While we most often encounter this talent in descriptive writing, it finds employment everywhere. Take this sentence as an example: "As soon as the sheepskin is clenched in hand, a graduate may breathe the fresh air and go his way, no better, and not very much worse, for his four years of regimentation." If the writer had talked about a diploma instead of the sheepskin held in hand, or if the graduate had merely left instead of taking in the fresh air and then depart- ing, the sentence would have been acceptable enough but flaccid, ordinary, and lacking in punch. As it stands, it is literally *vivid*; the young graduate has motion and life.

Good detail is often the result of good fancy, a God-given talent akin to genius but much more entertaining: "There are enough bombs now to destroy the earth in a day—less than the time it took to make it Biblically." By cultivating details, examples, and illustrations as he would a garden, the writer makes his generali- zations clear and his presentation effective.

EXERCISE

In the following sentences, what synonyms can be substituted for the italicized words? Would they be equally appropriate to essay writing? Which of the syno- nyms are neutral; which have favorable connotations; which are disparaging?

1. The old *man* was eating an orange.
2. The old man was *eating* an orange.
3. He *talked* for hours on end.
4. He *died* very suddenly.
5. The *car* wasn't very good.
6. The car wasn't very *good*.

Are there any restrictions on our choice of words if we supply synonyms for *man* and *eating* in the first sentence and *car* and *good* in the last sentence simul- taneously?

Take the following sentences, which are factual but not overwhelmingly inform- ative, and expand them by telling what, when, where, who, why, and how. At what point does the sentence become so unwieldy that it needs to be broken in two?

1. Washington was our first President.
2. Tokyo is the world's biggest city.
3. Teddy Roosevelt won fame with the Rough Riders.
4. Edison has been elected to the Hall of Fame.
5. Texas became a republic in 1836.
6. Because of Jonas Salk, polio is no longer a threat.

The very opposite of specificity is vagueness—a firm reliance upon uninformative generalities—and many amateur writers possess this as a kind of negative talent: "Private conversations after the meeting revealed a number of fears in the audience, as well as a more amenable communication." Up to the comma the sentence can be understood; it could even serve as a topic sentence for a paragraph. But as it appears here (and in the essay from which it was excised), it is deficient in content, airy, nebulous, and ineffective. It needs to be anchored to immediacy by the use of precise details. H. L. Mencken, a man who could make nonfiction read like a novel, once said that anyone who thinks clearly can write clearly. The student who suffers from vagueness is afflicted with one of the milder forms of woolly-mindedness, the final stage of which is total gibberish, such as: "An examination of a proposed plan for putting the welfare state into action reveals a peculiar problem of circumstance now facing any evaluations of its actual infringement upon the individual."

These are by no means the only weeds that flourish in muddled thought. The fuzzy-minded writer has a habit of writing around his ideas, wasting valuable words, and getting his point across only by extreme indirection. A sentence like "People admit the existence of the need for more and better schools and museums and cleaner cities" shows a little deadwood, but it is easily pruned. This sentence is worse because it can be improved only by ditching it completely and writing another: "The only way in which we can hope to solve the problem of averting total destruction to the world is by the negotiation of all the world powers to find methods of dealing with the problem before it becomes unmanageable." Germans, behavioral scientists, and entirely too many writers of government documents seem to glory in prose run wild, emphasizing circumlocution and sesquipedalian jargon as if they were genuinely ornamental: "Such preparations shall be made as will completely obscure all Federal buildings and non-Federal buildings occupied by the Federal Government during an air-raid for any period of time from visibility by reason of internal and external illumination. Such obscuration may be obtained either by blackout construction or by termination of the illumination."

The competent writer needs a clear head, but a good ear is equally important. The structure of English is so complex and the opportunities for mistreating it so many that few of us ever develop a completely intellectual understanding of the errors we make. It is possible for the teacher to mark a particular sentence as awkward or clumsy or to tell the student to use more subordinate clauses in his prose. It is possible to take an individual blunder like "The grade is based on a completely anonymously marked examination only" and point to the graceless repetitions of -ly, to take phrases like "U. S. Latin American policy goal" or "farm legislation recommendations" and complain about too many nouns being piled on top of one another. These things are difficult to teach and considerably harder to learn, but they can be heard! The person who reads to himself, listening to the silent music of words in combination, is aware of the cacophonous phrase as soon as it is committed to paper. He may not know why a particular sentence clumps along with elephantine ponderousness, but he will hear the noise. All of us can listen to a tune and proceed to hum it, though we may be ignorant of music; it is much the same with the speech tunes underlying phrase and sentence.

The written word may be memorable for many reasons—for its quality of thought or its felicity of expression—but all prose having the ring of greatness is pleasant to the ear. Its cadences are varied and harmonious but full of strength. It may be as simple and direct as Churchill's "Give us the tools, and we will finish the job" or as embellishedly noble as Hugh Latimer's words at the stake: "Play the man, Master Ridley; we shall this day light such a candle, by God's grace, in England, as I trust shall never be put out." It may condense into a few words the troubles of an era, as when Franklin D. Roosevelt said to the nation, "The only thing we have to fear is fear itself," or it may thunder an idea forth, as when Elizabeth I spoke to her soldiers at Tilbury on the approach of the Armada: "I know I have the body of a weak and feeble woman, but I have the heart and stomach of a king, and a king of England too; and think foul scorn that Parma or Spain, or any prince of Europe should dare to invade the borders of my realm." The good ear is indispensable to the writer, and it is cultivated by reading and listening to fine prose.

EXERCISE

The following sentences, most of them from student essays, show a variety of ailments: flatulence, circuitousness, clumsiness, murkiness of thought, and miscellaneous errors of diction, idiom, and parallelism. For each sentence, explain the student's trouble as precisely as possible and then revise the sentence to make it respectable.

1. Our freedom of expressed written opinion and fact would be injured.
2. To disprove the syllogism is so trivial any logical thinking person can see the fallacies within the premises.
3. Her American image is unjustly distorted.
4. The editors claim that the coveted authors of top-selling post-war literature have for the most part presented America as ugly and arid.
5. It certainly seems apparent that their deliberate omission of these facts renders them, if nothing else, narrow-minded.
6. These people have maintained their position of being opposed to its presence [i.e., fluorine's] in drinking water.
7. In a reactionary-like manner the editors suggest that American novelists "defy a trend and return to a richer tradition," instead of suggesting that they look ahead to create a new and better than ever tradition.
8. Agreements on disarmament, the banning of nuclear tests, and the consequential aversion of atomic war are before this assembly at every session.
9. *Look Homeward, Angel*, about Thomas Wolfe's own life, was a communication of the author's glimpsed portion of reality for its own sake.
10. If an inter-collegiate schedule was again set up, it is highly improbable that any acceptance of football would occur.
11. This is conceived as a genuine *work*shop, utilizing a variation of the 'in-basket' teaching-learning technique, and undergirded by a solid theoretical foundation of learning theory.

12. This is a device which has encroached the freedom and liberty of the American people. It has caused a self-reliant citizenry to become dependent to a welfare state. This word has of course taken an odious connotation.

13. This class of people makes itself unaware of the material needs of some and the, equally important, spiritual needs of all.

14. This novel is not representative of American life because it depicts only the worst conditions (war life), which reflects American conventions at home.

15. It seems likely that governmental control of the monetary support of education will bring about increased control of the methods by which, and the extents to which unpopular doctrines can be taught, and increased governmental determination of the areas of education in which the major part of its money should be spent.

16. All people to whom we feel are important enough to leave a good impression of the United States, will I am sure, form their opinions of our country through means other than fictional works.

17. If we allow them to surpass us, if we sit by and hopefully watch our meager economic growth, our country is doomed to a doctrine of slavery.

18. The contest . . . was decided by two Patterson rights, one of which landed on Johansson's neck, the final bouncing off the Swede turned Swiss' jaw as he was half turned around. —Warren Brown in the Chicago *American*.

19. Thirdly, the attitude inherent in the reaction which our system of social welfare is evoking from a portion of the public, viz., an indifferent, lazy attitude of "Let the others work, the government will feed me," is being carried over into many other aspects of our daily lives.

20. To accomplish this goal, you will learn to sharpen your eyeballs to a lawyer-like point.

21. We must halt our present lethargy.

22. Let us look at this matter of the usurpation of freedom as it would manifest itself in concrete terms.

23. Membership in the American Philatelic Society is limited to high type men and women of honorable standing in their communities.

24. Students cannot talk loudly, scuffle, be rowdy, or have careless conduct in the buildings.

25. Provided one has a mature work which observes some unity and has some correlation of ideas and tone, some progress of enfolding meaning, be it intellectual, or emotional, a degree of certainty exists in interpretation.

26. These novels had powerful themes of social correction and public elucidation of conditions which needed correction.

27. I have insisted upon the fact of his being an intense American. —Henry James.

28. The areas in which my interests are presently involved, and in which most of my reading has been done, are rather general, and I believe that increased knowledge and understanding in these and other areas is necessary to a determination of any research projects, as well as to more extensive clarification of my academic objectives.

29. It is impossible either to deny bitterness or to deduce immunity from suffer-

ing from the two instances where Griselda speaks to her husband after her second child is to be taken away, and after she knows that she too, is to be cast away.

30. The subject which I am about to discuss is quite lengthy. However, I will attempt, through a rather short discussion, to arrive at some logical conclusion.

31. The characters behave naturally until the crucial moments in the tale when their actions being determined by the plot become bizarre.

32. The "happy" person has a repertoire of behavior patterns which are maximally adequate as responses to the stimuli created by his environment.

Richness of detail, clarity of thought, and sentence harmony are three of the four most valuable skills a writer can develop. The fourth, an orderly mind, enables the writer to mold sentences into coherent paragraphs and then build these paragraphs into purposeful essays, for paragraphs *are* building blocks and should be as carefully manufactured as the bricks that go into a house or office building.

The paragraph should have a unity and integrity that only careful planning can provide. The most familiar type of paragraph is built around a single important idea expressed by the topic sentence, a generalization that the writer proceeds to illustrate and make convincing by supplying specifics, examples, and full details. It is nothing less than induction on a small scale. In fact all the devices of exposition and argument, whether narration, deduction, comparison and contrast, or cause and effect, can be used to order the paragraph and give it coherence.

Consider this paragraph by Daniel J. Boorstin, from *The Americans: The Colonial Experience:*

> The American language has indeed shown a spectacular uniformity. Only after we have looked at polyglot nations like India, the Soviet Union, and China, or when we remind ourselves that Europe, with an area of less than four million square miles, possesses at least a dozen major languages, can we appreciate our advantage. The people of the United States, spread over three million square miles, speak only one language. There is more difference between the speech of Naples and Milan, or of Canterbury and Yorkshire, or of a Welsh coal-miner and an Oxford undergraduate, or of a Provençal peasant and a Paris lawyer than there is between the language of Maine and California, or between the speech of a factory-worker and a college president in the United States.

First the writer makes his point, clearly and plainly: American English shows great uniformity. He then develops the idea by a series of contrasts, comparing America first with the huge "polyglot nations" and then with the smaller states of Europe. The point of comparison shifts, and Boorstin shows with concrete examples that neither location nor education affects American English, whereas extreme variations of speech are found in Europe. With great unobtrusiveness he works into the paragraph a wealth of convincing information, at the same time imposing order and movement upon his writing.

While Federal prose is seldom good enough to read for pleasure, some writers of government documents take pains to write understandably:

> When high explosives are set off, their change from a natural to a gaseous state is extremely rapid; this reaction is called *detonation*. When a high explosive is exploded by heat or shock, a wave called the detonating wave is set up and runs through the whole mass of explosive, changing its particles to gases almost instantaneously. In expanding they overcome the resistance of anything which opposes expansion: the effect is a sudden, shattering blow on the immediate surroundings.

Here the paragraph is ordered by a group of cause-and-effect statements explaining the nature of an explosion. Like Boorstin, the anonymous writer is able to pack a number of ideas—including definitions—into a few short sentences.

Even a simple description of the Black Forest may prove anything but simply organized:

> Those woods stretch unbroken over a vast region; and everywhere they are such dense woods, and so still, and so piney and fragrant. The stems of the trees are trim and straight, and in many places all the ground is hidden for miles under a thick cushion of moss of a vivid green color, with not a decayed or ragged spot in its surface, and not a fallen leaf or twig to mar its immaculate tidiness. A rich cathedral gloom pervades the pillared aisles; so the stray flecks of sunlight that strike a trunk here and a bough yonder are strongly accented, and when they strike the moss they fairly seem to burn. But the weirdest effect, and the most enchanting, is that produced by the diffused light of the low afternoon sun; no single ray is able to pierce its way in, then, but the diffused light takes color from moss and foliage, and pervades the place like a faint, green-tinted mist, the theatrical fire of fairyland. The suggestion of mystery and the supernatural which haunts the forest at all times is intensified by this unearthly glow.

The paragraph manages to suggest a complicated set of visual impressions. Like a motion-picture camera, it pans in on the forest, moving up close enough to examine the trunks of the trees, then down to the blanket of moss and back for a look at the ground from a distance. A shift comes with the third sentence. From here to the end of the paragraph, it is light that dominates the description. But even as he begins to comment on the "cathedral gloom" of the forest, Twain yokes the two halves of the paragraph together by describing the light—almost like a character in a drama—at play on the tree trunks, moss, and leaves—the setting which Twain has already established. He caps the description by drawing from it the epitome which ends the paragraph.

Examine this paragraph from "Some Remarks on Humor" by E. B. White:

> In a newsreel theatre the other day I saw a picture of a man who had developed the soap bubble to a higher point than it had ever before reached. He had become the ace soap bubble blower of America, had perfected the business of blowing bubbles, refined it, doubled it, squared it, and had even

worked himself up into a convenient lather. The effect was not pretty. Some of the bubbles were too big to be beautiful, and the blower was always jumping into them or out of them, or playing some sort of unattractive trick with them. It was, if anything, a rather repulsive sight. Humor is a little like that: it won't stand much blowing up, and it won't stand much poking. It has a certain fragility, an evasiveness, which one had best respect. Essentially, it is a complete mystery. A human frame convulsed with laughter, and the laughter becoming hysterical and uncontrollable, is as far out of balance as one shaken with the hiccoughs or in the throes of a sneezing fit.

Not many people have White's talent for making abstract statements interesting. An ordinary mortal writing on the nature of humor would probably do so in the saddest and dullest of prose. But by seizing upon the "ace bubble blower of America," describing his art, and then comparing it to humor, White is able to tie his abstractions to something similar and immediate, something in the here and now. And therein lies its effectiveness.

EXERCISE

1. Analyze this paragraph from the *Engineer Soldier's Handbook*:

You are an engineer. You are going to build bridges and blow them up. You are going to stop tanks and destroy them. You are going to build roads, airfields, and buildings. You are going to construct fortifications. You are going to fight with many kinds of weapons. *You are going to make sure that our own troops move ahead against all opposition, and you are going to see to it that enemy obstacles do not interfere with our advance. You are an engineer.*

What device(s) give(s) order and unity to the excerpt? Is it possible to shift the arrangement of any of the sentences and still have a decent paragraph? Is it possible to change the order of any of the sentences and improve the paragraph?
2. Analyze the paragraph structure in some of your own essays and in the student papers quoted in "What Johnny Don't Know" and "What Johnny Needs to Know."
3. Clip a one-paragraph editorial from your newspaper and analyze it.
4. Analyze a paragraph by a writer of nonfiction whose work you enjoy.

Do you find that paragraphs which show a high degree of organization are also high in the other qualities that make for good writing?

The abilities that go to make a good writer are nothing less than gifts (though even writers of modest talent can exercise and develop what ability they have). Too many students feel that inspiration is on a level with talent, that if the muse doesn't appear the essay cannot be written. Writing is an art, very definitely, but a craft as well, and the workmanlike student will approach his essays with the same care and forethought that a carpenter or any fine craftsman brings to his work. When an assignment is made for an essay, the student should head for the library. He may be brimming with ideas about football, free love, nickel beer, and other topics of great moment, but he has to know something about the subject before he can start an essay. Even if the assignment calls only for personal experience, the student should begin by making notes which he can later organize into something more coherent.

After reading comes the writing of an outline or some scheme for ordering the discussion. Then and only then should the student attempt his first draft, and he must write it with love. When the first version is finished, it should be read over quickly and put on the shelf. After a night's sleep, even the worst draft looks better than it did immediately after composition. It is now time to revise it—fleshing out generalizations, tightening up paragraphs, editing away turgidity —and perhaps to rewrite great chunks of it completely.

The second draft should be treated in the same way as the first: it must be left to age a while until the writer has his perspective back and can judge it fairly, and then it is ready for the finishing touches—the little bits of polishing and burnishing that every good craftsman gives to his work. Finally the student is ready to make a fair copy of the essay (with a carbon), but even this final copy should be put away overnight and proofread the next day for errors of typing, spelling, and quotation. Most essays do not spring like Minerva, full grown from the head of Jove; they are built and shaped by slow, careful, successive steps.

ESSAY SUGGESTIONS

1. Write a carefully ordered paragraph telling what career you hope to study for and why.
2. Write a paragraph explaining the nature of the profession you want to go into.
3. Write a paragraph comparing your intended profession with another that you have considered. Tell why one has won out over the other.
4. Describe in one paragraph the most interesting sight on your campus.
5. Write a paragraph telling about some comic incident in your life.

All these paragraphs should exhibit unity and have a plenitude of lively, immediate details.

FURTHER READING

Charles Sears Baldwin, A *College Manual of Rhetoric*. Fourth edition, revised. New York: Longmans, Green, and Company, 1909. Especially Chapters I and IV.

Jim W. Corder and Lyle H. Kendall, Jr., A *College Rhetoric*. New York: Random House, Inc., 1962. Especially Chapters II through V.

James Bradstreet Greenough and George Lyman Kittredge, *Words and Their Ways in English Speech*. New York: Macmillan Company, 1901.

Porter G. Perrin, *Writer's Guide and Index to English*. Revised edition. Chicago: Scott, Foresman and Company, 1950. Especially Chapters 7 through 12.

Sir Arthur Quiller-Couch, *On the Art of Writing*. New York: G. P. Putnam's Sons, 1916. Especially Chapters II, V, and VII.

Herbert Read, *English Prose Style*. London: G. Bell & Sons, Ltd., 1928. Especially Chapters I, IV, V, and VI.

NOTE:

Full information about the suggested readings is given only the first time a book is mentioned. Most of these books have gone through countless editions, often on both sides of the ocean, so that there is nothing particularly sacrosanct about the editions we cite.

Many of the readings we suggest are old and hoary with age, for we seek always for the good ways, which are often the old ways:

> For out of olde feldes, as men seyth,
> Cometh al this newe corn from yer to yere,
> And out of olde bokes, in good feyth,
> Cometh al this newe sciénce that men lere.

Narration

How does a writer tell a story? The simplest approach—and the most direct one—is to relate events in a straightforward chronological order. A student telling about a day at the beach might first want to jot down an hour-by-hour account of what happened: up at 7:00 A.M.; left home at 8:00; arrived at beach house at 9:00; changed clothes and went swimming, 9:00 to 10:30; rested on beach, 10:30 to 12:00; lunch at noon; went crabbing, 12:30 to 2:00 P.M.; rested, 2:00 to 4:00; cleaned and barbecued crabs, 4:00 to 5:30; dinner from 5:30 to 6:30; washed dishes and cleaned up, 6:30 to 7:00; left beach house at 7:00; home at 8:00, via drugstore to buy sunburn lotion; to bed at 9:30.

But this is only the raw material from which a narration might be shaped. Before the student can begin to write, he must ask himself what dominant point he wants to get across to his reader. Even if his purpose is nothing more complicated than to give a picture of a lazy, leisurely, carefree day full of swimming and sunshine, the writer must choose and edit the details which he plans to include in the essay. From his choices will come the essay's focus and emphasis. If the student begins his account by telling the reader that he got up at seven o'clock and if he concludes it by saying that he went to sleep at nine-thirty, the essay will have a fairly natural beginning and end; its focus will be clear and well chosen. But this feeling of completeness would be lost if the essay started with our adventurer getting up at seven, only to end with an account of what he had for lunch. We would want to know what happened to the rest of his day. Did he go home after lunch? Or have we missed some hidden but clever point that the writer wanted to make about his remarkable adventures from seven o'clock until noon?

Out of this basic stuff of everyday experience there might come any number of strikingly different essays. The interests of a city dweller who has to suffer through an entire year, waiting for his summer vacation before he can satisfy his craving for beach, sun, and water, may be quite unlike the interests of a country boy to whom nature is familiar, tame, and maybe a little monotonous. These different interests can result in essays that present the same details, more or less, but leave the reader with anything but the same impression.

Given the huge accumulation of events and details that come from a day at the beach, one student might want to write only about the people he met; another might want to ignore everything but the crabs and explain the mysteries of catching, storing, killing, cleaning, and cooking crustaceans. Still another student might want to subtly emphasize the hour and a half spent in the water and the time spent crabbing under a fierce summer sun. By stressing the beach activities rather than the siestas or the barbecue, the writer can describe a very full day at the beach while preparing the reader for an emphatic conclusion: sunburn.

All these essays would be narrations, and all would make use of chronological order. But there are other ways of telling a story. Suppose, for instance, that the writer's purpose is to relate how his inordinate stupidity got him a good case of sunburn. He might then decide to begin his essay with the sunburn itself—with its redness, fever, blisters, pain, and skin peeling off like strips of old wallpaper. He would start not at the beginning but at the end, with the sunburn in its full glory. And once he has aroused the reader's interest by this minuscule bit of drama, he can switch to the beginning and proceed to tell his story in simple chronological order. If the writer can win the reader's interest in the first paragraph, fine; if he can also narrate the story with increasing excitement, leading to a climax of interest and a strong conclusion, admirable!

Often the writer's purpose and emphasis will dictate the order in which he handles certain events. If, for example, he is writing a history of the atomic bomb, he might want to start with Einstein's famous letter to President Roosevelt. But if the writer's purpose is only to chronicle the events immediately preceding Hiroshima and Nagasaki, his main narrative might begin with the surrender ultimatum delivered by the Allies at the Potsdam Conference; the earlier history of the bomb could then form a minor narrative digression within the larger framework of the story. But whatever techniques the writer decides to use, his aim is to produce an interesting, well-written, and highly unified essay. And a unified essay must have a point and it must have order; without these it is little more than a tangle of facts and ideas, the kind of haphazard association that characterizes the essays of clever grade-school children.

ESSAY SUGGESTIONS

1. Write a biographical sketch of Thomas A. Edison, Helen Keller, Babe Ruth, or Harry S Truman. To which events in the lives of these great people would you want to give your chief emphasis?
2. Write a narrative paper about your most embarrassing experience.
3. Write an essay telling what happened in your dormitory last Saturday evening.
4. Write an account of a typical day in your life at college. Deal with the events of one day as they actually occurred. Do not blend or fictionalize.
5. Use the reference materials in your library to write an account of the Battle of Leyte Gulf, the sinking of the *Titanic*, the Battle of the Alamo, the Boston Tea Party, or the first hundred days of the New Deal.
6. Closely related to the narrative—since it deals with events taken in chronological order—is the process. Explain in nontechnical terms how the gasoline engine works. How does the body digest food? Explain how the heart operates. Give simple and clear directions for playing tennis, poker, or chess.
7. Read a story, play, or novel and then summarize the action in an entertaining manner.
8. How do you train dogs? Quarter horses? If you have no first-hand information on these subjects, where would you seek it?

FURTHER READING

Charles Sears Baldwin, *A College Manual of Rhetoric*, Chapter V.
Jim W. Corder and Lyle H. Kendall, Jr., *A College Rhetoric*, Chapter IX.
Herbert Read, *English Prose Style*, Chapter VIII.
L. A. Sherman, *How to Describe and Narrate Visually*. New York: George H. Doran Company, 1925.

JOHN HERSEY

A Noiseless Flash

At exactly fifteen minutes past eight in the morning, on August 6, 1945, Japanese time, at the moment when the atomic bomb flashed above Hiroshima, Miss Toshiko Sasaki, a clerk in the personnel department of the East Asia Tin Works, had just sat down at her place in the plant office and was turning her head to speak to the girl at the next desk. At that same moment, Dr. Masakazu Fujii was settling down cross-legged to read the Osaka *Asahi* on the porch of his private hospital, overhanging one of the seven deltaic rivers which divide Hiroshima; Mrs. Hatsuyo Nakamura, a tailor's widow, stood by the window of her kitchen, watching a neighbor tearing down his house because it lay in the path of an air-raid-defense fire lane; Father Wilhelm Kleinsorge, a German priest of the Society of Jesus, reclined in his underwear on a cot on the top floor of his order's three-story mission house, reading a Jesuit magazine, *Stimmen der Zeit*; Dr. Terufumi Sasaki, a young member of the surgical staff of the city's large, modern Red Cross Hospital, walked along one of the hospital corridors with a blood specimen for a Wassermann test in his hand; and the Reverend Mr. Kiyoshi Tanimoto, pastor of the Hiroshima Methodist Church, paused at the door of a rich man's house in Koi, the city's western suburb, and prepared to unload a handcart full of things he had evacuated from town in fear of the massive B-29 raid which everyone expected Hiroshima to suffer. A hundred thousand people were killed by the atomic bomb, and these six were among the survivors. They still wonder why they lived when so many others died. Each of them counts many small items of chance or volition—a step taken in time, a decision to go indoors, catching one streetcar instead of the next—that spared him. And now each knows that in the act of survival he lived a dozen lives and saw more death than he ever thought he would

see. At the time, none of them knew anything.

The Reverend Mr. Tanimoto got up at five o'clock that morning. He was alone in the parsonage, because for some time his wife had been commuting with their year-old baby to spend nights with a friend in Ushida, a suburb to the north. Of all the important cities of Japan, only two, Kyoto and Hiroshima, had not been visited in strength by *B-san*, or Mr. B, as the Japanese, with a mixture of respect and unhappy familiarity, called the B-29; and Mr. Tanimoto, like all his neighbors and friends, was almost sick with anxiety. He had heard uncomfortably detailed accounts of mass raids on Kure, Iwakuni, Tokuyama, and other nearby towns; he was sure Hiroshima's turn would come soon. He had slept badly the night before, because there had been several air-raid warnings. Hiroshima had been getting such warnings almost every night for weeks, for at that time the B-29s were using Lake Biwa, northeast of Hiroshima, as a rendezvous point, and no matter what city the Americans planned to hit, the Superfortresses streamed in over the coast near Hiroshima. The frequency of the warnings and the continued abstinence of Mr. B with respect to Hiroshima had made its citizens jittery; a rumor was going around that the Americans were saving something special for the city.

Mr. Tanimoto is a small man, quick to talk, laugh, and cry. He wears his black hair parted in the middle and rather long; the prominence of the frontal bones just above his eyebrows and the smallness of his mustache, mouth, and chin give him a strange, old-young look, boyish and yet wise, weak and yet fiery. He moves nervously and fast, but with a restraint which suggests that he is a cautious, thoughtful man. He showed, indeed, just those qualities in the uneasy days before the bomb fell. Besides having his wife spend the nights in Ushida, Mr. Tanimoto had been carrying all the portable things from his church, in the close-packed residential district called Nagaragawa, to a house that belonged to a rayon manufacturer in Koi, two miles from the center of town. The rayon man, a Mr. Matsui, had opened his then unoccupied estate to a large number of his friends and acquaintances, so that they might evacuate whatever they wished to a safe distance from the probable target area. Mr. Tanimoto had had no difficulty in moving chairs, hymnals, Bibles, altar gear, and church records by pushcart himself, but the organ console and an upright piano required some aid. A friend of his named Matsuo had, the day before, helped him get the piano out to Koi; in return, he had promised this day to assist Mr. Matsuo in hauling out a daughter's belongings. That is why he had risen so early.

Mr. Tanimoto cooked his own breakfast. He felt awfully tired. The effort of moving the piano the day before, a sleepless night, weeks of worry and unbalanced diet, the cares of his parish—all combined to make him feel hardly adequate to the new day's work. There was another thing, too; Mr. Tanimoto had studied theology at Emory College, in Atlanta, Georgia; he had graduated in 1940; he spoke excellent English; he dressed in American clothes; he had corresponded with many American friends right up to the time the war began; and among a people obsessed with a fear of being spied upon—perhaps almost obsessed himself—he found himself growing increasingly uneasy. The police had questioned him several times, and just a few days before, he had heard that an influential acquaintance, a Mr. Tanaka, a retired officer of the Toyo Kisen Kaisha steamship line, an anti-Christian, a man famous in Hiroshima for his showy philanthropies and notorious for his personal tyrannies, had been telling people that Tanimoto should not be trusted. In compensation, to show himself publicly a good Japanese, Mr. Tanimoto had taken on the chairmanship of his local *tonarigumi,* or Neighborhood Association, and to his other duties and concerns this position had added the business of organizing air-raid defense for about twenty families.

Before six o'clock that morning, Mr. Tanimoto started for Mr. Matsuo's house. There he found that their burden was to be a *tansu,* a large Japanese cabinet, full of clothing and household goods. The two men

set out. The morning was perfectly clear and so warm that the day promised to be uncomfortable. A few minutes after they started, the air-raid siren went off—a minute-long blast that warned of approaching planes but indicated to the people of Hiroshima only a slight degree of danger, since it sounded every morning at this time, when an American weather plane came over. The two men pulled and pushed the handcart through the city streets. Hiroshima was a fan-shaped city, lying mostly on the six islands formed by the seven estuarial rivers that branch out from the Ota River; its main commercial and residential districts, covering about four square miles in the center of the city, contained three-quarters of its population, which had been reduced by several evacuation programs from a wartime peak of 380,000 to about 245,000. Factories and other residential districts, or suburbs, lay compactly around the edges of the city. To the south were the docks, an airport, and the island-studded Inland Sea. A rim of mountains runs around the other three sides of the delta. Mr. Tanimoto and Mr. Matsuo took their way through the shopping center, already full of people, and across two of the rivers to the sloping streets of Koi, and up them to the outskirts and foothills. As they started up a valley away from the tight-ranked houses, the all-clear sounded. (The Japanese radar operators, detecting only three planes, supposed that they comprised a reconnaissance.) Pushing the handcart up to the rayon man's house was tiring, and the men, after they had maneuvered their load into the driveway and to the front steps, paused to rest awhile. They stood with a wing of the house between them and the city. Like most homes in this part of Japan, the house consisted of a wooden frame and wooden walls supporting a heavy tile roof. Its front hall, packed with rolls of bedding and clothing, looked like a cool cave full of fat cushions. Opposite the house, to the right of the front door, there was a large, finicky rock garden. There was no sound of planes. The morning was still; the place was cool and pleasant.

Then a tremendous flash of light cut across the sky. Mr. Tanimoto has a distinct recollection that it travelled from east to west, from the city toward the hills. It seemed a sheet of sun. Both he and Mr. Matsuo reacted in terror—and both had time to react (for they were 3,500 yards, or two miles, from the center of the explosion). Mr. Matsuo dashed up the front steps into the house and dived among the bedrolls and buried himself there. Mr. Tanimoto took four or five steps and threw himself between two big rocks in the garden. He bellied up very hard against one of them. As his face was against the stone, he did not see what happened. He felt a sudden pressure, and then splinters and pieces of board and fragments of tile fell on him. He heard no roar. (Almost no one in Hiroshima recalls hearing any noise of the bomb. But a fisherman in his sampan on the Inland Sea near Tsuzu, the man with whom Mr. Tanimoto's mother-in-law and sister-in-law were living, saw the flash and heard a tremendous explosion; he was nearly twenty miles from Hiroshima, but the thunder was greater than when the B-29s hit Iwakuni, only five miles away.)

When he dared, Mr. Tanimoto raised his head and saw that the rayon man's house had collapsed. He thought a bomb had fallen directly on it. Such clouds of dust had risen that there was a sort of twilight around. In panic, not thinking for the moment of Mr. Matsuo under the ruins, he dashed out into the street. He noticed as he ran that the concrete wall of the estate had fallen over—toward the house rather than away from it. In the street, the first thing he saw was a squad of soldiers who had been burrowing into the hillside opposite, making one of the thousands of dugouts in which the Japanese apparently intended to resist invasion, hill by hill, life for life; the soldiers were coming out of the hole, where they should have been safe, and blood was running from their heads, chests, and backs. They were silent and dazed.

Under what seemed to be a local dust cloud, the day grew darker and darker.

At nearly midnight, the night before the bomb was dropped, an announcer on the city's radio station said that about two hun-

dred B-29s were approaching southern Honshu and advised the population of Hiroshima to evacuate to their designated "safe areas." Mrs. Hatsuyo Nakamura, the tailor's widow, who lived in the section called Nobori-cho and who had long had a habit of doing as she was told, got her three children—a ten-year-old boy, Toshio, an eight-year-old girl, Yaeko, and a five-year-old girl, Myeko—out of bed and dressed them and walked with them to the military area known as the East Parade Ground, on the northeast edge of the city. There she unrolled some mats and. the children lay down on them. They slept until about two, when they were awakened by the roar of the planes going over Hiroshima.

As soon as the planes had passed, Mrs. Nakamura started back with her children. They reached home a little after two-thirty and she immediately turned on the radio, which, to her distress, was just then broadcasting a fresh warning. When she looked at the children and saw how tired they were, and when she thought of the number of trips they had made in past weeks, all to no purpose, to the East Parade Ground, she decided that in spite of the instructions on the radio, she simply could not face starting out all over again. She put the children in their bedrolls on the floor, lay down herself at three o'clock, and fell asleep at once, so soundly that when planes passed over later, she did not waken to their sound.

The siren jarred her awake at about seven. She arose, dressed quickly, and hurried to the house of Mr. Nakamoto, the head of her Neighborhood Association, and asked him what she should do. He said that she should remain at home unless an urgent warning—a series of intermittent blasts of the siren—was sounded. She returned home, lit the stove in the kitchen, set some rice to cook, and sat down to read that morning's Hiroshima *Chugoku*. To her relief, the all-clear sounded at eight o'clock. She heard the children stirring, so she went and gave each of them a handful of peanuts and told them to stay on their bedrolls, because they were tired from the night's walk. She had hoped that they would go back to sleep, but the man in the house directly to the south began to make a terrible hullabaloo of hammering, wedging, ripping, and splitting. The prefectural government, convinced, as everyone in Hiroshima was, that the city would be attacked soon, had begun to press with threats and warnings for the completion of wide fire lanes, which, it was hoped, might act in conjunction with the rivers to localize any fires started by an incendiary raid; and the neighbor was reluctantly sacrificing his home to the city's safety. Just the day before, the prefecture had ordered all able-bodied girls from the secondary schools to spend a few days helping to clear these lanes, and they started work soon after the all-clear sounded.

Mrs. Nakamura went back to the kitchen, looked at the rice, and began watching the man next door. At first, she was annoyed with him for making so much noise, but then she was moved almost to tears by pity. Her emotion was specifically directed toward her neighbor, tearing down his home, board by board, at a time when there was so much unavoidable destruction, but undoubtedly she also felt a generalized, community pity, to say nothing of self-pity. She had not had an easy time. Her husband, Isawa, had gone into the Army just after Myeko was born, and she had heard nothing from or of him for a long time, until, on March 5, 1942, she received a seven-word telegram: "Isawa died an honorable death at Singapore." She learned later that he had died on February 15th, the day Singapore fell, and that he had been a corporal. Isawa had been a not particularly prosperous tailor, and his only capital was a Sankoku sewing machine. After his death, when his allotments stopped coming, Mrs. Nakamura got out the machine and began to take in piecework herself, and since then had supported the children, but poorly, by sewing.

As Mrs. Nakamura stood watching her neighbor, everything flashed whiter than any white she had ever seen. She did not notice what happened to the man next door; the reflex of a mother set her in motion toward her children. She had taken a single step (the house was 1,350 yards, or three-quarters of a mile, from the center of the explosion) when something picked her up and she

seemed to fly into the next room over the raised sleeping platform, pursued by parts of her house.

Timbers fell around her as she landed, and a shower of tiles pommelled her; everything became dark, for she was buried. The debris did not cover her deeply. She rose up and freed herself. She heard a child cry, "Mother, help me!," and saw her youngest—Myeko, the five-year-old—buried up to her breast and unable to move. As Mrs. Nakamura started frantically to claw her way toward the baby, she could see or hear nothing of her other children.

In the days right before the bombing, Dr. Masakazu Fujii, being prosperous, hedonistic, and at the time not too busy, had been allowing himself the luxury of sleeping until nine or nine-thirty, but fortunately he had to get up early the morning the bomb was dropped to see a house guest off on a train. He rose at six, and half an hour later walked with his friend to the station, not far away, across two of the rivers. He was back home by seven, just as the siren sounded its sustained warning. He ate breakfast and then, because the morning was already hot, undressed down to his underwear and went out on the porch to read the paper. This porch—in fact, the whole building—was curiously constructed. Dr. Fujii was the proprietor of a peculiarly Japanese institution: a private, single-doctor hospital. This building, perched beside and over the water of the Kyo River, and next to the bridge of the same name, contained thirty rooms for thirty patients and their kinfolk—for, according to Japanese custom, when a person falls sick and goes to a hospital, one or more members of his family go and live there with him, to cook for him, bathe, massage, and read to him, and to offer incessant familial sympathy, without which a Japanese patient would be miserable indeed. Dr. Fujii had no beds—only straw mats—for his patients. He did, however, have all sorts of modern equipment: an X-ray machine, diathermy apparatus, and a fine tiled laboratory. The structure rested two-thirds on the land, one-third on piles over the tidal waters of the Kyo. This overhang, the part of the building where Dr. Fujii lived, was queer-looking, but it was cool in summer and from the porch, which faced away from the center of the city, the prospect of the river, with pleasure boats drifting up and down it, was always refreshing. Dr. Fujii had occasionally had anxious moments when the Ota and its mouth branches rose to flood, but the piling was apparently firm enough and the house had always held.

Dr. Fujii had been relatively idle for about a month because in July, as the number of untouched cities in Japan dwindled and as Hiroshima seemed more and more inevitably a target, he began turning patients away, on the ground that in case of a fire raid he would not be able to evacuate them. Now he had only two patients left—a woman from Yano, injured in the shoulder, and a young man of twenty-five recovering from burns he had suffered when the steel factory near Hiroshima in which he worked had been hit. Dr. Fujii had six nurses to tend his patients. His wife and children were safe; his wife and one son were living outside Osaka, and another son and two daughters were in the country on Kyushu. A niece was living with him, and a maid and a manservant. He had little to do and did not mind, for he had saved some money. At fifty, he was healthy, convivial, and calm, and he was pleased to pass the evenings drinking whiskey with friends, always sensibly and for the sake of conversation. Before the war, he had affected brands imported from Scotland and America; now he was perfectly satisfied with the best Japanese brand, Suntory.

Dr. Fujii sat down cross-legged in his underwear on the spotless matting of the porch, put on his glasses, and started reading the Osaka *Asahi*. He liked to read the Osaka news because his wife was there. He saw the flash. To him—faced away from the center and looking at his paper—it seemed a brilliant yellow. Startled, he began to rise to his feet. In that moment (he was 1,550 yards from the center), the hospital leaned behind his rising and, with a terrible ripping noise, toppled into the river. The Doctor, still in the act of getting to his feet, was thrown forward and around and over; he

was buffeted and gripped; he lost track of everything, because things were so speeded up; he felt the water.

Dr. Fujii hardly had time to think that he was dying before he realized that he was alive, squeezed tightly by two long timbers in a V across his chest, like a morsel suspended between two huge chopsticks—held upright, so that he could not move, with his head miraculously above water and his torso and legs in it. The remains of his hospital were all around him in a mad assortment of splintered lumber and materials for the relief of pain. His left shoulder hurt terribly. His glasses were gone.

Father Wilhelm Kleinsorge, of the Society of Jesus, was, on the morning of the explosion, in rather frail condition. The Japanese wartime diet had not sustained him, and he felt the strain of being a foreigner in an increasingly xenophobic Japan; even a German, since the defeat of the Fatherland, was unpopular. Father Kleinsorge had, at thirty-eight, the look of a boy growing too fast—thin in the face, with a prominent Adam's apple, a hollow chest, dangling hands, big feet. He walked clumsily, leaning forward a little. He was tired all the time. To make matters worse, he had suffered for two days, along with Father Cieslik, a fellow-priest, from a rather painful and urgent diarrhea, which they blamed on the beans and black ration bread they were obliged to eat. Two other priests then living in the mission compound, which was in the Nobori-cho section—Father Superior LaSalle and Father Schiffer—had happily escaped this affliction.

Father Kleinsorge woke up about six the morning the bomb was dropped, and half an hour later—he was a bit tardy because of his sickness—he began to read Mass in the mission chapel, a small Japanese-style wooden building which was without pews, since its worshippers knelt on the usual Japanese matted floor, facing an altar graced with splendid silks, brass, silver, and heavy embroideries. This morning, a Monday, the only worshippers were Mr. Takemoto, a theological student living in the mission house; Mr. Fukai, the secretary of the diocese; Mrs. Murata, the mission's devoutly Christian housekeeper; and his fellow-priests. After Mass, while Father Kleinsorge was reading the Prayers of Thanksgiving, the siren sounded. He stopped the service and the missionaries retired across the compound to the bigger building. There, in his room on the ground floor, to the right of the front door, Father Kleinsorge changed into a military uniform which he had acquired when he was teaching at the Rokko Middle School in Kobe and which he wore during air-raid alerts.

After an alarm, Father Kleinsorge always went out and scanned the sky, and in this instance, when he stepped outside, he was glad to see only the single weather plane that flew over Hiroshima each day about this time. Satisfied that nothing would happen, he went in and breakfasted with the other Fathers on substitute coffee and ration bread, which, under the circumstances, was especially repugnant to him. The Fathers sat and talked awhile, until, at eight, they heard the all-clear. They went then to various parts of the building. Father Schiffer retired to his room to do some writing. Father Cieslik sat in his room in a straight chair with a pillow over his stomach to ease his pain, and read. Father Superior LaSalle stood at the window of his room, thinking. Father Kleinsorge went up to a room on the third floor, took off all his clothes except his underwear, and stretched out on his right side on a cot and began reading his *Stimmen der Zeit.*

After the terrible flash—which, Father Kleinsorge later realized, reminded him of something he had read as a boy about a large meteor colliding with the earth—he had time (since he was 1,400 yards from the center) for one thought: A bomb has fallen directly on us. Then, for a few seconds or minutes, he went out of his mind.

Father Kleinsorge never knew how he got out of the house. The next things he was conscious of were that he was wandering around in the mission's vegetable garden in his underwear, bleeding slightly from small cuts along his left flank; that all the buildings round about had fallen down except the Jesuits' mission house, which had long before been braced and double-braced by a priest named Gropper, who was terrified of earthquakes; that the day had turned dark; and that Murata-*san,* the housekeeper, was nearby, crying over and over, "*Shu Jesusu, awaremi tamai!* Our Lord Jesus, have pity on us!"

On the train on the way into Hiroshima from the country, where he lived with his mother, Dr. Terufumi Sasaki, the Red Cross Hospital surgeon, thought over an unpleasant nightmare he had had the night before. His mother's home was in Mukaihara, thirty miles from the city, and it took him two hours by train and tram to reach the hospital. He had slept uneasily all night and had awakened an hour earlier than usual, and, feeling sluggish and slightly feverish, had debated whether to go to the hospital at all; his sense of duty finally forced him to go, and he had started out on an earlier train than he took most mornings. The dream had particularly frightened him because it was so closely associated, on the surface at least, with a disturbing actuality. He was only twenty-five years old and had just completed his training at the Eastern Medical University, in Tsingtao, China. He was something of an idealist and was much distressed by the inadequacy of medical facilities in the country town where his mother lived. Quite on his own, and without a permit, he had begun visiting a few sick people out there in the evenings, after his eight hours at the hospital and four hours' commuting. He had recently learned that the penalty for practicing without a permit was severe; a fellow-doctor whom he had asked about it had given him a serious scolding. Nevertheless, he had continued to practice. In his dream, he had been at the bedside of a country patient when the police and the doctor he had consulted burst into the room, seized him, dragged him outside, and beat him up cruelly. On the train, he just about decided to give up the work in Mukaihara, since he felt it would be impossible to get a permit, because the authorities would hold that it would conflict with his duties at the Red Cross Hospital.

At the terminus, he caught a streetcar at

once. (He later calculated that if he had taken his customary train that morning, and if he had had to wait a few minutes for the streetcar, as often happened, he would have been close to the center at the time of the explosion and would surely have perished.) He arrived at the hospital at seven-forty and reported to the chief surgeon. A few minutes later, he went to a room on the first floor and drew blood from the arm of a man in order to perform a Wassermann test. The laboratory containing the incubators for the test was on the third floor. With the blood specimen in his left hand, walking in a kind of distraction he had felt all morning, probably because of the dream and his restless night, he started along the main corridor on his way toward the stairs. He was one step beyond an open window when the light of the bomb was reflected, like a gigantic photographic flash, in the corridor. He ducked down on one knee and said to himself, as only a Japanese would, "Sasaki, *gambare!* Be brave!" Just then (the building was 1,650 yards from the center), the blast ripped through the hospital. The glasses he was wearing flew off his face; the bottle of blood crashed against one wall; his Japanese slippers zipped out from under his feet— but otherwise, thanks to where he stood, he was untouched.

Dr. Sasaki shouted the name of the chief surgeon and rushed around to the man's office and found him terribly cut by glass. The hospital was in horrible confusion: heavy partitions and ceilings had fallen on patients, beds had overturned, windows had blown in and cut people, blood was spattered on the walls and floors, instruments were everywhere, many of the patients were running about screaming, many more lay dead. (A colleague working in the laboratory to which Dr. Sasaki had been walking was dead; Dr. Sasaki's patient, whom he had just left and who a few moments before had been dreadfully afraid of syphilis, was also dead.) Dr. Sasaki found himself the only doctor in the hospital who was unhurt.

Dr. Sasaki, who believed that the enemy had hit only the building he was in, got bandages and began to bind the wounds of those inside the hospital; while outside, all over Hiroshima, maimed and dying citizens turned their unsteady steps toward the Red Cross Hospital to begin an invasion that was to make Dr. Sasaki forget his private nightmare for a long, long time.

Miss Toshiko Sasaki, the East Asia Tin Works clerk, who is not related to Dr. Sasaki, got up at three o'clock in the morning on the day the bomb fell. There was extra housework to do. Her eleven-month-old brother, Akio, had come down the day before with a serious stomach upset; her mother had taken him to the Tamura Pediatric Hospital and was staying there with him. Miss Sasaki, who was about twenty, had to cook breakfast for her father, a brother, a sister, and herself, and—since the hospital, because of the war, was unable to provide food—to prepare a whole day's meals for her mother and the baby, in time for her father, who worked in a factory making rubber earplugs for artillery crews, to take the food by on his way to the plant. When she had finished and had cleaned and put away the cooking things, it was nearly seven. The family lived in Koi, and she had a forty-five-minute trip to the tin works, in the section of town called Kannonmachi. She was in charge of the personnel records in the factory. She left Koi at seven, and as soon as she reached the plant, she went with some of the other girls from the personnel department to the factory auditorium. A prominent local Navy man, a former employee, had committed suicide the day before by throwing himself under a train—a death considered honorable enough to warrant a memorial service, which was to be held at the tin works at ten o'clock that morning. In the large hall, Miss Sasaki and the others made suitable preparations for the meeting. This work took about twenty minutes.

Miss Sasaki went back to her office and sat down at her desk. She was quite far from the windows, which were off to her left, and behind her were a couple of tall bookcases containing all the books of the factory library, which the personnel department had organized. She settled herself at her desk, put some things in a drawer, and shifted papers. She thought that before she began to make entries in her lists of new employees, discharges, and departures for the Army, she would chat for a moment with the girl at her right. Just as she turned her head away from the windows, the room was filled with a blinding light. She was paralyzed by fear, fixed still in her chair for a long moment (the plant was 1,600 yards from the center).

Everything fell, and Miss Sasaki lost consciousness. The ceiling dropped suddenly and the wooden floor above collapsed in splinters and the people up there came down and the roof above them gave way; but principally and first of all, the bookcases right behind her swooped forward and the contents threw her down, with her left leg horribly twisted and breaking underneath her. There, in the tin factory, in the first moment of the atomic age, a human being was crushed by books.

QUESTIONS FOR STUDY AND DISCUSSION

1. "A Noiseless Flash" employs the technique of multiple points of view, presenting the routine existences of a number of people who are related only by their participation in a catastrophic event. Why is this technique effective here? In what other ways could a narrative of the Hiroshima bombing be told?

2. Quite obviously the essay is unified by the atom-bomb explosion. Hersey provided some "guideposts" by which the reader can identify the approach of the "event." What are they? How does he prevent these "guideposts" from seeming merely repetitious?

3. This essay is full of precise detail: the clothing worn, the exact position of each person at the time of the explosion, the food eaten, the mental preoccupations of each, even the hand (the left) in which Dr. Sasaki was carrying the blood specimen. What purposes do these details accomplish in the narrative?

4. Is suspense maintained after the first description of the explosion? If so, why and by what means? If not, why not?

5. What does the last sentence of the essay "mean"? Does it make an effective conclusion?

WRITING ASSIGNMENTS

1. Write a short narrative employing the multiple point of view of "A Noiseless Flash," choosing some event you have some knowledge about from several points of view: the reported reactions of a number of people involved in an automobile accident; the "sides" taken by parents, children, relatives, and outsiders in a family argument.

2. Write a short account of a small incident—not necessarily a highly dramatic one—in which you attempt to reproduce the details of the scene and the action.

CLEVELAND AMORY

Dr. Parkman
Takes a Walk

To the student of American Society the year 1849 will always remain a red-letter one. In that year two events occurred at opposite ends of the country, both of which, in their own way, made social history. At one end, in Sutter's Creek, California, gold was discovered. At the other, in Boston, Massachusetts, Dr. George Parkman walked off the face of the earth.

The discovery of gold ushered in a new social era. It marked the first great rise of the Western *nouveau riche*, the beginning of that wonderful time when a gentleman arriving in San Francisco and offering a boy fifty cents to carry his suitcase could receive the reply, "Here's a dollar, man—carry it yourself," and when a poor Irish prospector suddenly striking it rich in a vein near Central City, Colorado, could fling down his pick and exclaim, "Thank God, now my wife can be a lady!"

Dr. Parkman's little walk did no such thing as this. It must be remembered, however, that it occurred some three thousand miles away. Boston is not Sutter's Creek or Central City or even San Francisco. There has never been a "new" social era in the Western sense in Boston's rock-ribbed Society, and it remains very doubtful if there ever will be one. The best that could be expected of any one event in Boston would be to shake up the old. Dr. Parkman's walk did this; it shook Boston Society to the very bottom of its First Family foundations. Viewed almost a hundred years later it thus seems, in its restricted way, almost as wonderful as the Gold Rush and not undeserving of the accidental fact that it happened, in the great march of social history, in exactly the same year.

The date was Friday, November 23rd. It was warm for a Boston November, and Dr.

Parkman needed no overcoat as he left his Beacon Hill home at 8 Walnut Street. He wore in the fashion of the day a black morning coat, purple silk vest, dark trousers, a dark-figured black tie, and a black silk top hat. He had breakfasted as usual, and he left his home to head downtown toward the Merchants Bank on State Street. Dr. Parkman was quite a figure as he moved along. His high hat and angular physique made him seem far taller than his actual five feet nine and a half inches. He was sixty years old and his head was almost bald, but his hat hid this fact also. To all outward appearances he was remarkably well-preserved, his most striking feature being a conspicuously protruding chin. Boston Parkmans have been noted for their chins the way Boston Adamses are noted for their foreheads or Boston Saltonstalls are noted for their noses, and the chin of old Dr. Parkman was especially formidable. His lower jaw jutted out so far it had made the fitting of a set of false teeth for him a very difficult job. The dentist who had had that job had never forgotten it. He was proud of the china-white teeth he had installed. He had even kept the mold to prove to people that he, little Dr. Nathan Keep, had made the teeth of the great Dr. George Parkman.

Although he had studied to be a physician and received his degree Dr. Parkman had rarely practiced medicine in his life. He was a merchant at heart, one of Boston's wealthiest men, and he spent his time in the Boston manner keeping sharp account of his money—and a sharp eye on his debtors. He had many of the traits of character peculiar to the Proper Bostonian breed. He was shrewd and hard, but he was Boston-honest, Boston-direct and Boston-dependable. Like so many other First Family men before his time and after Dr. Parkman was not popular but he was highly respected. It was hard to like a man like Dr. Parkman because his manners were curt and he had a way of glaring at people that made them uncomfortable. Without liking him, however, it was possible to look up to him. People knew him as a great philanthropist and it was said he had given away a hundred thousand dollars in his time. The phrase "wholesale charity and retail penury" as descriptive of the Proper Bostonian breed had not yet come into the Boston lingo, though the day was coming when Dr. Parkman might be regarded as the very personification of it. Certainly he had given away large sums of money with wholesale generosity—even anonymously—yet with small sums, with money on a retail basis, he was penny-punctilious. "The same rule," a biographer records, "governed Dr. Parkman in settling an account involving the balance of a cent as in transactions of thousands of dollars."

Children in the Boston streets pointed out Dr. Parkman to other children. "There goes Dr. Parkman," they would say. People always seemed to point him out after he had passed them. There was no use speaking to Dr. Parkman before he went by. If you weren't his friend, Dr. George Shattuck, or his brother-in-law, Robert Gould Shaw, Esq., or a Cabot or a Lowell, or perhaps a man who owed him money—and then, as someone said, God help you—the doctor would ignore you. Dr. Parkman had no need to court favor from anybody. The Parkmans cut a sizeable chunk of Boston's social ice in 1849, and they still do today. Like other merchant-blooded First Families they were of course economically self-sufficient. They hadn't yet made much of an intellectual mark on their city, but a nephew of the doctor, Francis Parkman, had just published his first book and was on his way to becoming what Van Wyck Brooks has called "the climax and crown" of the Boston historical school. The Parkmans were in the Boston fashion well-connected by marriages. Dr. Parkman's sister's marriage with Robert Gould Shaw, Boston's wealthiest merchant, was a typical First Family alliance. As for Dr. Parkman's own wealth, some idea of its extent may be gathered from the fact that his son, who never worked a day in his life, was able to leave a will which bequeathed, among other things, the sum of five million dollars for the care and improvement of the Boston Common.

On the morning of that Friday, November 23rd, Dr. Parkman was hurrying. He walked with the characteristic gait of the Proper Bostonian merchant—a gait still practiced by such notable present-day First Family footmen as Charles Francis Adams and Godfrey Lowell Cabot—measuring off distances with long, ground-consuming strides. Dr. Parkman always hurried. Once when riding a horse up Beacon Hill and unable to speed the animal to his satisfaction he had left the horse in the middle of the street and hurried ahead on foot. On that occasion he had been after money, a matter of debt collection.

This morning, too, Dr. Parkman was after money. He left the Merchants Bank and after making several other calls dropped into a grocery store at the corner of Blossom and Vine Streets. This stop, the only non-financial mission of his morning, was to buy a head of lettuce for his invalid sister. He left it in the store and said he would return for it on his way home. The time was half past one and Dr. Parkman presumably intended to be home at 2:30, then the fashionable hour for one's midday meal. Ten minutes later, at 1:40, Elias Fuller, a merchant standing outside his counting room at Fuller's Iron Foundry at the corner of Vine and North Grove Streets, observed Dr. Parkman passing him headed north on North Grove Street. Fuller was later to remember that the doctor seemed particularly annoyed about something and recalled that his cane beat a brisk tattoo on the pavement as he hurried along. What the merchant observed at 1:40 that day is of more than passing importance, for Elias Fuller was the last man who ever saw the doctor alive on the streets of Boston. Somewhere, last seen going north on North Grove Street, Dr. George Parkman walked off the face of the earth.

At 8 Walnut Street Mrs. Parkman, her daughter Harriet and Dr. Parkman's invalid sister sat down to their two-thirty dinner long after three o'clock. Their dinner was ruined and there was no lettuce, but Mrs. Parkman and the others did not mind. They were all worried about the master of the house. Dr. Parkman was not the sort of man who was ever late for anything. Right after dinner they got in touch with Dr. Parkman's agent, Charles Kingsley. Kingsley was the man who looked after the doctor's business affairs, usually some time after the doctor had thoroughly looked after them himself. Almost at once Kingsley began to search for his employer. First Family men of the prominence of Dr. Parkman did not disappear in Boston—and they do not today —even for an afternoon. By night-fall Kingsley was ready to inform Robert Gould Shaw. Shaw, acting with the customary dispatch of the Proper Bostonian merchant, went at once to Boston's City Marshal, Mr. Tukey. Marshal Tukey did of course what Shaw told him to do, which was to instigate an all-night search.

The next morning the merchant Shaw placed advertisements in all the papers and had 28,000 handbills distributed. The advertisements and the handbills announced a reward of $3,000 for his brother-in-law alive and $1,000 for his brother-in-law dead. The prices, considering the times, were sky-high but Shaw knew what he was doing in Yankee Boston. Before long virtually every able-bodied man, woman and child in the city was looking for Dr. Parkman. They beat the bushes and they combed the streets. Slum areas were ransacked. All suspicious characters, all persons with known criminal records, were rounded up and held for questioning. Strangers in Boston were given a summary one-two treatment. An Irishman, it is recorded, attempting to change a twenty-dollar bill, was brought in to the police headquarters apparently solely on the assumption that no son of Erin, in the Boston of 1849, had any business with a bill of this size in his possession.

Every one of Dr. Parkman's actions on the previous day, up to 1:40, were checked. At that time, on North Grove Street, the trail always ended. Police had to sift all manner of wild reports. One had the doctor "beguiled to East Cambridge and done in." Another had him riding in a hansom cab, his head covered with blood, being driven at "breakneck speed" over a Charles River bridge. Of the papers only the Boston *Transcript* seems to have kept its head. Its reporter managed to learn from a servant in the Parkman home that the doctor had received a caller at 9:30 Friday reminding

him of a 1:30 appointment later in the day. The servant could not remember what the man looked like, but the *Transcript* printed the story in its Saturday night edition along with the reward advertisements. Most people took the caller to be some sort of front man who had appeared to lead Dr. Parkman to a dastardly death. By Monday foul play was so thoroughly suspected that the shrewd merchant Shaw saw no reason to mention a sum as high as $1,000 for the body. Three thousand dollars was still the price for Dr. Parkman alive but only "a suitable reward" was mentioned in Shaw's Monday handbills for Dr. Parkman dead. Monday's handbills also noted the possibility of amnesia but the theory of a First Family man's mind wandering to this extent was regarded as highly doubtful. Dr. Parkman, it was stated, was "perfectly well" when he left his house.

All that the Parkman case now needed to make it a complete panorama of Boston's First Family Society was the active entry of Harvard College into the picture. This occurred on Sunday morning in the person of a caller to the home of Rev. Francis Parkman, the missing doctor's brother, where the entire Family Parkman in all its ramifications had gathered. The caller was a man named John White Webster, Harvard graduate and professor of chemistry at the Harvard Medical School. He was a short squat man, fifty-six years old, who had a mass of unruly black hair and always wore thick spectacles. He had had a most distinguished career. He had studied at Guy's Hospital, London, back in 1815, where among his fellow students had been the poet John Keats. He was a member of the London Geological Society, the American Academy of Arts and Sciences, and during his twenty-five years as a Harvard professor had published numerous nationally noted scientific works. His wife, a Hickling and aunt of the soon-to-be-recognized historian William Hickling Prescott, was "well-connected" with several of Boston's First Families.

The Rev. Parkman was glad to see Professor Webster and ushered him toward the parlor expecting that his desire would be to offer sympathy to the assorted Parkmans there assembled. But Webster, it seemed, did not want to go into the parlor. Instead he spoke abruptly to the minister. "I have come to tell you," he said, "that I saw your brother at half past one o'clock on Friday." The minister was glad to have this report. Since Webster also told him he had been the caller at the Parkman home earlier that day it cleared up the mystery of the strange appointment as recorded in the *Transcript.* Webster explained he should have come sooner but had been so busy he had not seen the notices of Dr. Parkman's disappearance until the previous night. The minister was also satisfied with this. Webster further declared that, at the appointment shortly after 1:30 which took place in his laboratory at the Medical School, he had paid Dr. Parkman the sum of $483.64 which he had owed him. This, of course, explained why the doctor had last been seen by the merchant Fuller in such a cane-tattooing hurry. It had indeed been a matter of a debt collection.

When Professor Webster had left, Robert Gould Shaw was advised of his visit. Shaw was intimate enough in his brother-in-law's affairs to know that Webster had been owing Dr. Parkman money for some time. He did not, however, know the full extent of Webster's misery. Few men have ever suffered from the retail penury side of the Proper Bostonian character as acutely as John White Webster.

The professor received a salary from Harvard of $1,200 a year. This, augmented by income from extra lectures he was able to give, might have sufficed for the average Harvard professor in those days. But Webster was not the average. His wife, for all her connections with Boston's First Families, was still a socially aspirant woman, particularly for her two daughters of debutante age. Mrs. Webster and the Misses Webster entertained lavishly at their charming home in Cambridge. Professor Webster went into debt. He borrowed money here and he borrowed money there. But mostly he borrowed from Dr. George Parkman.

Who better to borrow from? Dr. Parkman, man of wholesale charity, Proper Bostonian merchant philanthropist. He had given Harvard College the very ground on which at that time stood its Medical School. He had endowed the Parkman Chair of Anatomy, then being occupied by the great Dr. Oliver Wendell Holmes. He had himself been responsible for Webster's appointment as chemistry professor. There were no two ways about it. When Webster needed money the doctor was his obvious choice. As early as 1842 he had borrowed $400. He had then borrowed more. In 1847 he had borrowed from a group headed by Dr. Parkman the sum of $2,000. For the latter he had been forced to give a mortgage on all his personal property. He knew he had little chance to pay the debt but he was banking on the generosity of the "good Dr. Parkman." A year later, in 1848, he even went to Dr. Parkman's brother-in-law, the merchant Shaw, and prevailed upon him to buy a mineral collection for $1,200. This was most unfortunate. The mineral collection, like the rest of Webster's property, in hock to Dr. Parkman and his group, was not Webster's to sell. By so doing he had made the doctor guilty of that cardinal sin of Yankeeism—the sin of being shown up as an easy mark. No longer was there for Webster any "good Dr. Parkman." "From that moment onward," says author Stewart Holbrook, "poor Professor Webster knew what it was like to have a Yankee bloodhound on his trail. His creditor was a punctilious man who paid his own obligations when due and he expected the same of everybody else, even a Harvard professor."[1]

Dr. Parkman dogged Professor Webster in the streets, outside his home, even to the classrooms. He would come in and take a front-row seat at Webster's lectures. He would not say anything; he would just sit and glare in that remarkable way of his. He wrote the professor notes, not just plain insulting notes but the awful, superior, skin-biting notes of the Yankee gentleman. He spoke sternly of legal processes. Meeting

[1] "Murder at Harvard," by Stewart Holbrook, *The American Scholar,* 1945.

Webster he would never shout at him but instead address him in clipped Proper Bostonian accents. It was always the same question. When would the professor be "ready" for him?

Dr. Parkman even bearded Professor Webster in his den, in the inner recesses of the latter's laboratory at the Medical School. He had been there, in the professor's private back room—according to the janitor of the building—on Monday evening, November 19th, just four days before he had disappeared.

The janitor was a strange man, the grim New England village type, a small person with dark brooding eyes. His name was Ephraim Littlefield. He watched with growing interest the goings-on around him. Following Webster's call on Rev. Francis Parkman, which established the farthest link yet on the trail of Dr. Parkman's walk, it had of course been necessary to search the Medical School. Littlefield wanted this done thoroughly, as thoroughly for example as they were dragging the Charles River outside. He personally led the investigators to Webster's laboratory. Everything was searched, all but the private back room and adjoining privy. One of the party of investigators, which also included Dr. Parkman's agent Kingsley, was a police officer named Derastus Clapp. Littlefield prevailed upon this officer to go into the back room, but just as Clapp opened the door Professor Webster solicitously called out for him to be careful. There were dangerous articles in there, he said. "Very well, then," said Officer Clapp, "I will not go in there and get blowed up." He backed out again.

The whole search was carried on to the satisfaction of even Robert Gould Shaw who, after all, knew at firsthand the story of Webster's duplicity via the mineral collection. And who was the little janitor Ephraim Littlefield to dispute the word of the great merchant Robert Shaw? As each day went by the theory of murder was becoming more and more generally accepted, but in a Boston Society eternally geared to the mesh of a Harvard A.B. degree the idea of pinning a homicide on a Harvard man—

and a professor at that—was heresy itself. One might as well pry for the body of Dr. Parkman among the prayer cushions of the First Family pews in Trinity Church.

But Littlefield was not, in the socially sacrosanct meaning of the words, a "Harvard man." He was a Harvard janitor. Furthermore he was stubborn. He wanted the Medical School searched again. When it was, he was once more prodding the investigators to greater efforts. He told them they should visit the cellar of the building, down in the section where the Charles River water flowed in and carried off waste matter from the dissecting rooms and privies above. The agent Kingsley took one gentlemanly sniff from the head of the stairs and refused to accompany the janitor and the other investigators any farther. The others, however, went on. As they passed the wall under Webster's back room the janitor volunteered the information that it was now the only place in the building that hadn't been searched. Why not, the men wanted to know. The janitor explained that to get there it would be necessary to dig through the wall. The men had little stomach left for this sort of operation and soon rejoined Kingsley upstairs.

Littlefield, however, had plenty of stomach. He determined to dig into the wall himself. Whether he was by this time, Monday, already suspicious of Professor Webster has never been made clear. He had, it is true, heard the Webster-Parkman meeting of Monday night the week before. He had distinctly overheard the doctor say to the professor in that ever-insinuating way, "Something, Sir, must be accomplished." Just yesterday, Sunday, he had seen Professor Webster enter the Medical School around noontime, apparently shortly after he had made his call on Rev. Francis Parkman. Webster had spoken to him and had acted "very queerly." Come to think of it, Littlefield brooded, Sunday was a queer day for the professor to be hanging around the School anyway. "Ephraim," writes Richard Dempewolff, one of the Parkman case's most avid devotees, "was one of those shrewd New England conclusion-jumpers who, unfortunately for the people they victimize, are usually right. By putting two and two together, Mr. Littlefield achieved a nice round dozen."[2]

The janitor's wife was a practical woman. She thought little of her husband's determination to search the filthy old place under the private rooms of the Harvard professor she had always regarded as a fine gentleman. Her husband would lose his job, that would be what would happen. Just you wait and see, Mr. Littlefield.

Mr. Littlefield deferred to Mrs. Littlefield and did wait—until Tuesday, five days after Dr. Parkman's disappearance. On Tuesday something extraordinary happened. At four o'clock in the afternoon he heard Professor Webster's bell jangle, a signal that the janitor was wanted. He went to Webster's laboratory. The professor asked him if he had bought his Thanksgiving turkey yet. Littlefield did not know what to say. He replied he had thought some about going out Thanksgiving.

"Here," said Webster, "go and get yourself one." With that he handed the janitor an order for a turkey at a near-by grocery store.

John White Webster had here made a fatal error. The call he had paid on Rev. Francis Parkman had been bad enough. It had aroused the searching of the Medical School and had brought Littlefield actively into the case. But as Webster later admitted he had been afraid that sooner or later someone would have found out about his 1:30 Friday rendezvous with Dr. Parkman and felt that his best chance lay in making a clean breast of it. For this action in regard to the janitor's Thanksgiving turkey, however, there could be no such defense. If he hoped to win the janitor over to "his side," then he was a poor judge of human nature indeed. Harvard Janitor Ephraim Littlefield had worked for Harvard Professor John Webster for seven years—curiously the same length of time Professor John Webster had been borrowing from Dr. Parkman—without

[2] *Famous Old New England Murders,* by Richard Dempewolff (Brattleboro, Vt.: Stephen Daye Press, 1942).

ever receiving a present of any kind. And now, a Thanksgiving turkey. Even the deferentially dormant suspicions of Mrs. Littlefield were thoroughly aroused.

Janitor Littlefield had no chance to begin his labors Wednesday. Professor Webster was in his laboratory most of the day. On Thanksgiving, however, while Mrs. Littlefield kept her eyes peeled for the professor or any other intruder, the janitor began the task of crow-barring his way through the solid brick wall below the back room. It was slow work and even though the Littlefields took time off to enjoy their dinner—the janitor had characteristically not passed up the opportunity to procure a nine-pound bird—it was soon obvious he could not get through the wall in one day. That evening the Littlefields took time off again. They went to a dance given by the Sons of Temperance Division of the Boston Odd Fellows. They stayed until four o'clock in the morning. "There were twenty dances," Littlefield afterwards recalled, "and I danced eighteen out of the twenty."

Late Friday afternoon, after Professor Webster had left for the day, Littlefield was at his digging again. This time he had taken the precaution of advising two of the School's First Family doctors, Doctors Bigelow and Jackson, of what he was doing. They were surprised but told him since he had started he might as well continue. But they were against his idea of informing the dean of the School, Dr. Holmes, of the matter. It would, they felt, disturb the dean unnecessarily.

Even a half-hearted First Family blessing has always counted for something in Boston, and Janitor Littlefield now went to work with renewed vigor. Again his wife stood watch. At five-thirty he broke through the fifth of the five courses of brick in the wall. "I held my light forward," he afterwards declared, "and the first thing which I saw was the pelvis of a man, and two parts of a leg . . . It was no place for these things."

It was not indeed. Within fifteen minutes Doctors Bigelow and Jackson were on the scene. Later Dr. Holmes himself would view the remains. Meanwhile of course there was the matter of a little trip out to the Webster home in Cambridge.

To that same police officer who had been so loath to get himself "blowed up" in Webster's back room fell the honor of making the business trip to Cambridge and arresting the Harvard professor. Once bitten, Derastus Clapp was twice shy. There would be no more monkeyshines, Harvard or no Harvard. He had his cab halt some distance from the Webster home and approached on foot. Opening the outer gate he started up the walk just as Webster himself appeared on the steps of his house, apparently showing a visitor out. The professor attempted to duck back inside. Officer Clapp hailed him. "We are about to search the Medical School again," he called, moving forward rapidly as he spoke, "and we wish you to be present." Webster feigned the traditional Harvard indifference. It was a waste of time; the School had already been searched twice. Clapp laid a stern hand on his shoulder. Webster, escorted outward and suddenly noting two other men in the waiting cab, wanted to go back for his keys. Officer Clapp was not unaware of the drama of the moment. "Professor Webster," he said, "we have keys enough to unlock the whole of Harvard College."

Boston was in an uproar. Dr. Parkman had not walked off the face of the earth. He had been pushed off—and by the authoritative hands of a Harvard professor! Even the *Transcript*, calm when there was still a hope the Parkman case was merely a matter of disappearance, could restrain itself no longer. It threw its genteel caution to the winds. There were two exclamation marks after its headline, and its editor called on Shakespeare himself to sum up the situation:

Since last evening, our whole population has been in a state of the greatest possible excitement in consequence of the astounding rumor that the body of Dr. Parkman has been discovered, and that Dr. John W. Webster, Professor of Chemistry in the Medical School of Harvard College, and a gentleman connected by marriage with some of our most distinguished families, has been arrested and imprisoned, on suspicion of being the murderer. Incredulity, then amazement, and then blank, unspeakable horror have been the emotions, which have agitated the public mind as the rumor has gone on, gathering countenance and confirmation. Never in the annals of crime in Massachusetts has such a sensation been produced.

In the streets, in the market-place, at every turn, men greet each other with pale, eager looks and the inquiry, "Can it be true?" And then as the terrible reply, "the circumstances begin to gather weight against him," is wrung forth, the agitated listener can only vent his sickening sense of horror, in some expression as that of Hamlet,— "O, horrible! O, horrible! most horrible!"

There is irony in the fact that proud, staid Boston chose the time it did to provide American Society with the nineteenth century's outstanding social circus. Boston was at the height of its cultural attainments in 1849. In that year a scholarly but hardly earth-shaking book by a rather minor Boston author, *The History of Spanish Literature* by George Ticknor, was the world literary event of the year and the only book recommended by Lord Macaulay to Queen Victoria. Yet just three months later, on March 19, 1850, Boston put on a show which for pure social artistry Barnum himself would have had difficulty matching. The Boston courtroom had everything. It had one of Boston's greatest jurists, Judge Lemuel Shaw, on its bench; it had the only Harvard professor ever to be tried for murder, John White Webster, as its defendant; it had promised witnesses of national renown, from Dr. Oliver Wendell Holmes on down; and in the offing, so to speak, it had the shades of Dr. George Parkman, perhaps the most socially distinguished victim in the annals of American crime.

Nobody wanted to miss such a sight. Trains and stages from all parts of the East brought people to Boston. They wanted tickets. Everybody in Boston wanted tickets, too. Consequences of revolutionary proportions were feared if they could not be accommodated. Yet what to do? There was only a small gallery to spare, it having been decreed in typical Boston fashion that the main part of the courtroom would be reserved on an invitation basis. Finally, Field Marshal Tukey hit on the only possible solution, which was to effect a complete change of audience in the gallery every ten minutes during the proceedings. It took elaborate street barricades and doorway defenses to do the job, but in the eleven days of the trial, to that little gallery holding hardly more than a hundred souls, came a recorded total of sixty thousand persons. Considering that the constabulary of Boston assigned to the job numbered just fifteen men, this feat ranks as a monumental milestone in police annals.

From the suspense angle the trial, which has been called a landmark in the history of criminal law, must have been something of a disappointment. By the time it began, despite Webster's protestations of innocence, there was little doubt in the minds of most of the spectators as to the guilt of the professor. A few days after his arrest a skeleton measuring 70½ inches had finally been assembled from the grisly remains found lying about under the professor's back room, and while the sum total of this was an inch taller than Dr. Parkman had been in happier days, there had been no question in the minds of the coroner's jury, of Dr. Holmes, and of a lot of other people, but that Dr. Parkman it was. The case against the professor was one of circumstantial evidence of course. No one had seen Webster and Parkman together at the time of the murder; indeed, during the trial the time of the murder was never satisfactorily established. But the strongest Webster adherents had to admit that it was evidence of a very powerful nature, as Chief Justice Shaw could not fail to point out in his famous charge to the jury, an address which lawyers today still consider one of the greatest expositions of the nature and use of circumstantial evidence ever delivered.

There were a number of pro-Websterites. Harvard professor though he may have been, he was still the underdog, up against the almighty forces of Boston's First Families. Many of the Websterites had undoubtedly had experiences of their own on the score of Proper Bostonian retail penury and were ready to recognize that Dr. Parkman had been so importunate a creditor that he had quite possibly driven the little professor first to distraction and then to the deed. They went to Rufus Choate, Boston's great First Family lawyer, and asked him to undertake the defense. After reading up on the case Choate was apparently willing to do so on the condition that Webster would admit the killing and plead manslaughter. Another First Family lawyer, old Judge Fay, with whom the Webster family regularly played whist, thought a verdict of manslaughter could be reached.

But Webster would not plead guilty. From the beginning he had made his defense an all but impossible task. He talked when he shouldn't have talked and he kept quiet when, at least by the light of hindsight, he should have come clean. On his first trip to the jail he immediately asked the officers about the finding of the body. "Have they found the *whole* body?" he wanted to know. This while certainly a reasonable question in view of the wide area over which the remains were found was hardly the thing for a man in his position to be asking. Then, while vehemently protesting his innocence, he took a strychnine pill out of his waistcoat pocket and attempted to kill himself, an attempt which was foiled only by the fact that, though the dose was a large one, he was in such a nervous condition it failed to take fatal effect. At the trial Webster maintained through his lawyers that the body he was proved to be so vigorously dismembering during his spare moments in the week following November 23rd had been a Medical School cadaver brought to him for that purpose. This was sheer folly, and the prosecution had but to call upon the little dentist, Nathan Keep, to prove it so. Tooth by tooth, during what was called one of the "tumultuous moments" of the trial, Dr. Keep fitted the fragments of the false teeth found in Webster's furnace into the mold he still had in his possession. Charred as they were there could be no doubt they had once been the china-white teeth of Dr. Parkman.

The spectators were treated to other memorable scenes. The great Dr. Holmes testified twice, once for the State on the matter of the identity of the reconstructed skeleton and once for the defense as a character witness for the accused. Professor Webster's character witnesses were a howitzer battery of First Family notables, among them Doctors Bigelow and Jackson, a Codman and a Lovering, the New England historian John Gorham Palfrey and Nathaniel Bowditch, son of the famed mathematician—even Harvard's president Jared Sparks took the stand for his errant employee. All seemed to agree that Webster, if occasionally irritable, was basically a kindhearted man, and President Sparks was thoughtful enough to add one gratuitous comment. "Our professors," he said, "do not often commit murder."

Credit was due Webster for his ability as a cadaver carver. He had done the job on Dr. Parkman, it was established, with no more formidable instrument than a jackknife. A Dr. Woodbridge Strong was especially emphatic on this point. He had dissected a good many bodies in his time, he recalled, including a rush job on a decaying pirate, but never one with just a jackknife. Ephraim Littlefield was of course star witness for the prosecution. The indefatigable little janitor talked for one whole day on the witness stand, a total of eight hours, five hours in the morning before recess for lunch and three hours in the afternoon. Only once did he falter and that on the occasion when, under cross-examination with the defense making a valiant attempt to throw suspicion on him, he was asked if he played "gambling cards" with friends in Webster's back room. Four times the defense had to ask the question and four times Littlefield refused to answer. Finally, his New England conscience stung to the quick, he replied in exasperation, "If you ask me if I played cards there *last winter*, I can truthfully say I did not."

In those days prisoners were not allowed to testify, but on the last day of the trial Professor Webster was asked if he wanted to say anything. Against the advice of his counsel he rose and spoke for fifteen minutes. He spent most of those precious moments denying the accusation that he had written the various anonymous notes which had been turning up from time to time in the City Marshal's office ever since the disappearance of Dr. Parkman. One of these had been signed CIVIS and Webster's last sentence was a pathetic plea for CIVIS to come forward if he was in the courtroom. CIVIS did not, and at eight o'clock on the evening of March 30th the trial was over.

Even the jury seems to have been overcome with pity for the professor. Before filing out of the courtroom the foreman, pointing a trembling finger at Webster, asked: "is that all? Is that the end? Can nothing further be said in defense of the man?" Three hours later the foreman and his cohorts were back, having spent, it is recorded, the first two hours and fifty-five minutes in prayer "to put off the sorrowful duty." When the verdict was delivered, "an awful and unbroken silence ensued, in which the Court, the jury, the clerk, and the spectators seemed to be absorbed in their own reflections."

Webster's hanging, by the neck and until he was dead, proceeded without untoward incident in the courtyard of Boston's Leverett Street jail just five months to the day after he had been declared guilty. Before that time, however, the professor made a complete confession. He stated that Dr. Parkman had come into his laboratory on that fatal Friday and that, when he had been unable to produce the money he owed, the doctor had shown him a sheaf of papers proving that he had been responsible for getting him his professorship. The doctor then added, "I got you into your office, Sir, and now I will get you out of it." This, said Webster, so infuriated him that he seized a stick of wood off his laboratory bench and struck Dr. Parkman one blow on the head. Death was instantaneous and Webster declared, "I saw nothing but the alternative of a successful removal and concealment of the body, on the one hand, and of infamy and destruction on the other." He then related his week-long attempt to dismember and burn the body. Even the clergyman who regularly visited Webster in his cell during his last days was not able to extract from the professor the admission that the crime had been premeditated. He had done it in that one frenzy of rage. "I am irritable and passionate," the clergyman quoted Webster as saying, "and Dr. Parkman was the most provoking of men."

The late Edmund Pearson, recognized authority on nonfictional homicide here and abroad, has called the Webster-Parkman case America's classic murder and the one which has lived longest in books of reminiscences. Certainly in Boston's First Family Society the aftermath of the case has been hardly less distinguished than its actual occurrence. To this day no Proper Bostonian grandfather autobiography is complete without some reference to the case. The Beacon Hill house at 8 Walnut Street from which Dr. Parkman started out on his walk that Friday morning almost a hundred years ago is still standing, and its present occupant, a prominent Boston lawyer, is still on occasion plagued by the never-say-die curious.

Among Boston Parkmans the effect was a profound one. For years certain members of the Family shrank from Society altogether, embarrassed as they were by the grievous result of Dr. Parkman's financial punctiliousness and all too aware of the sympathy extended Professor Webster in his budgetary plight. In the doctor's immediate family it is noteworthy that his widow headed the subscription list of a fund taken up to care for Webster's wife and children. Dr. Parkman's son, George Francis Parkman, was five years out of Harvard in 1849. He had been, in contrast to his father, a rather gay blade as a youth and at college had taken part in Hasty Pudding Club theatricals; at the time of the murder he was enjoying himself in Paris. He returned to Boston a marred man. He moved his mother and sister from 8 Walnut Street and took a house at 33 Beacon Street. From the latter house he buried his mother and aunt, and there he and his sister lived on as Boston Society's most distinguished recluses. His solitary existence never included even the solace of a job. Describing him as

he appeared a full fifty years after the crime a biographer records:

> Past the chain of the bolted door on Beacon Street no strangers, save those who came on easily recognised business, were ever allowed to enter. Here George Francis Parkman and his sister Harriet, neither of whom ever married, practised the utmost frugality, the master of the house going himself to the market every day to purchase their meager provisions, and invariably paying cash for the simple supplies he brought home.
>
> The windows of his house looked out upon the Common but he did not frequent it . . . He always walked slowly and alone, in a stately way, and attracted attention by his distinguished though retiring appearance . . . In cool weather he wore a heavy coat of dark cloth and his shoulders and neck were closely wrapped with a wide scarf, the ends of which were tucked into his coat or under folds. He sheltered himself against the east winds of Boston just as he seemed, by his manner, to shelter his inmost self from contact with the ordinary affairs of men.[3]

Tremors of the Parkman earthquake continued to be felt by Boston Society often at times when they were least desired. Twenty years later, when Boston was privileged to play proud host to Charles Dickens, there was a particularly intense tremor. Dickens was asked which one of the city's historic landmarks he would like to visit first. "The room where Dr. Parkman was murdered," he replied, and there being no doubt he meant what he said, nothing remained for a wry-faced group of Boston's best but to shepherd the distinguished novelist out to the chemistry laboratory of the Harvard Medical School.

A Webster-Parkman story, vintage of 1880, is still told today by Boston's distinguished author and teacher, Bliss Perry. He recalls that for a meeting of New England college officers at Williamstown, Massa-

[3] *Famous Families of Massachusetts*, by Mary Caroline Crawford (Boston: Little Brown) © 1930.

chusetts, his mother had been asked to put up as a guest in her house Boston's First Family poet laureate, diplomat and first editor of the *Atlantic*, James Russell Lowell. Unfortunately Lowell was at that time teaching at Harvard and for all his other ac-complishments Mrs. Perry would have none of him. He had to be quartered elsewhere.

"I could not sleep," Mrs. Perry said, "if one of those Harvard professors were in the house."

QUESTIONS FOR STUDY AND DISCUSSION

1. Though "Dr. Parkman Takes a Walk" contains elements of a "true crimes" story, it is a chapter of a book entitled *The Proper Bostonians*. Why is this account of a murder included? How does it differ from a "true crimes" story? from detective fiction? How long is suspense—doubt as to the identity of the murderer—maintained? Is all real doubt dispelled only with Webster's confession, or earlier? After disposing of Webster, Amory goes on to describe long-term effects of the murder. To what extent does the inclusion of this material violate good "detective-story" practice? What other materials introduced into the account are extraneous to the story of the murder? Do these point to Amory's real purposes?

2. Is this essay in any sense a satire on detective fiction?

3. What is the general point-of-view of this narrative? In other words, from what vantage-point is the narrator viewing events?

WRITING ASSIGNMENTS

1. Write an essay on "The Proper Bostonian of 1849," using only the information given in Amory's chapter.

2. Write a short narrative in which an untoward event reveals an unsuspected aspect of a person's character, a family's pretensions, a community's surface atmosphere, or the "corporate image" of a business concern.

3. Taking into account only the "facts" presented—not Amory's particular purpose —make a list of possible points-of-view from which the narrative could be told.

4. From the list in No. 3 above, choose one point-of-view. Then write an essay analyzing the effects such a point-of-view would have on the telling of the story and compare them with the effects Amory produces by means of his point-of-view.

Description

Description is such a familiar process that it scarcely needs comment. When a writer describes something, he tells his reader what he sees, or perhaps what he feels. This is easy enough in theory, but a great many people—men especially—fail to observe carefully. How many of us can sit down and write a description of our father or mother? Before the writer can describe anything well, he must first get in the habit of looking and, next, remembering what he has seen.

The hardest part of the writer's job is to make his reader visualize what the writer himself has seen. Generally this can be done by lavishing the reader with sharp, lively details. If the student is describing his cabin in the Rockies and he writes that there are aspen trees in his back yard, well and good; this is a descriptive note. But if he elaborates this bare statement, perhaps by saying that there is a grove of young aspens, some of them reaching up thirty feet into the air, then the reader begins to picture the scene himself. And if the writer has a keen eye and can develop the description further—by telling the reader about the aspen's straight, skinny trunk, or its greenish-tan bark broken by horizontal growth welts, or its thin heart-shaped leaves that tremble furiously in the slightest wind—then the responsive reader may see, in his mind's eye, the island of quivering trees that has so impressed the writer. He begins to feel that he has shared an experience with the writer, and the scene in the Rockies comes alive.

People can be described as well as trees. But what about personality and character, a person's likes and dislikes, the way he drinks his coffee or sneezes? Where do these fit in? In the sense that a writer describes whatever he can observe, we can say that a character sketch is a description too. By the same reasoning, we can also say that a brief portrait of the ideas and manners of an age is a description. Certainly the techniques used to describe a person, place, or thing can be applied with advantage to a personality or an epoch.

Needless to say, the exact, literal description is not the only one. The emotions may also be brought into play, and figurative language—especially the simile—may prove strongly effective in writing a description. We know that our aspen trees are straight and thin; but they could also be described as straight as a telephone pole; one might exclaim over their beanpole straightness; and their leaves, instead of just trembling, might fidget nervously like so many expectant fathers. Whereas one writer might want to photograph them with words, another might use the poetry of association to interpret them to his reader. Both are important techniques, but the latter must be used judiciously when the purpose of writing is to report, to inform, or to argue the truth of an issue (as in all good journalistic and academic prose). In the essays that the student will be asked to do in college, he must be accurate and

objective—to the extent that this is possible for one who is only a human being
—and the alluring but subjective language of poetry, if ill handled, may obscure
accuracy or truth; the student may produce propaganda instead of thoughtful,
honest writing. But no one should think that objectivity and accuracy are
synonymous with dullness.

The student has observed and noted; he is now ready to write the essay.
But where does he start? With a narration he could always begin at the beginning. But what is the beginning of an aspen tree, or a picture, or a sunrise?
If the student squirms in his chair and feels uneasy once he is about to set
pen to paper, there is good reason, for he cannot afford to plop down a mass
of casually related details and call them an essay. A description, like any essay,
must be a deliberate, well-planned, and highly ordered piece of writing.

There are many ways of ordering the details that make up a description,
but all of them have one thing in common: movement. A description may be
patterned, for instance, after the natural movements of the eye as it views a
scene. Perhaps there is a dominant mass or figure that arrests the eye; if so,
the writer should begin with that and proceed to describe everything else of
importance in the same order that the eye naturally turns to it. A good variation on this method is to write an introduction that barely lists or hints at
the principal figures or masses and then, in the body of the essay, describe
each figure in detail, following the order in which it was mentioned in the
introduction.

Perhaps the object being described does not force the eye to move in some
special way. The writer's problem then is to impose an order upon his details
that will permit his reader to absorb them easily. Suppose that I am told to
describe the bookshelves nearest me. The books and the objects on the shelves
are a random lot, ranging from *Inside U. S. A.* to *Blood of the West*, from dried
pine cones to *The National Geographic Magazine*. To describe them in such
a haphazard fashion is to increase the confusion and boredom that any reader
will feel when burdened with someone's intellectual laundry list. A better way
to handle the assignment would be to describe the bookshelves and their contents from left to right and from top to bottom. The books and objects will
still be as miscellaneous as ever, but the reader will enjoy a feeling of orderliness and purpose in the description.

In all these techniques of description, the movement has been that of the
eye, both the observer and the object standing still. Occasionally the thing
being described will move (as a parade), thereby providing the writer with a
natural order for his essay. Still another useful device is for the observer to
move about and to use this movement as a thread with which to string his
observations together. Paintings, for example, sometimes present one aspect
from fifteen feet and quite another from five. The continuous rhythm of a
statue, since it exists in three dimensions, can be captured by walking around
it and describing what is to be seen. A town, a city, and even a state can be
described by moving through it and telling what is there. But whatever the
technique, it should bring coherence and orderliness to the experience that the
writer wishes to pass on to the reader.

ESSAY SUGGESTIONS

1. Visit an art museum and write a paragraph describing one of the paintings you most liked. Write a second paragraph describing one of the paintings you least cared for. Keep your choice of words precise and neutral.

2. Rewrite the two descriptions, using words that connote your feelings toward the painting. Then compare the two exercises. Which would be more appropriate for publication in a magazine or a book of art criticism? Which is better suited to a letter home?

3. Locate a full-sized reproduction of a painting by Georges Seurat. Describe it from a distance of twenty feet, ten feet, five, then one.

4. Describe a statue by walking around it.

5. Take a walk through some interesting street; then describe what you have seen.

6. Describe the room you live in.

7. If you are interested in the natural sciences, describe the brain, heart, or lungs of some mammal. Describe the microscopic flora and fauna that you have studied.

8. Describe your roommate. (Note that the word *describe* when applied to a person can be a request for a character sketch as well as a physical description.)

9. Write a character sketch of a fascinating person you know.

10. Describe Hamlet and his character. What does he look like? How much does he weigh? How old is he? What kind of clothes does he wear? What are his interests in life? His abilities? What are his inner tensions? Does he love his mother? Does he believe in ghosts? Is Hamlet a drinking man? Does Shakespeare portray him consistently?

11. Write a description of a milieu: for instance, the Depression years of the 1930s, the "Fabulous Fifties," or the Civil War years in the Confederacy.

12. Describe "The Old Guitarist" by Pablo Picasso, which is printed as the frontispiece to this book.

FURTHER READING

Charles Sears Baldwin, *A College Manual of Rhetoric*, Chapter VI.
Jim W. Corder and Lyle H. Kendall, Jr., *A College Rhetoric*, Chapter VIII.
L. A. Sherman, *How to Describe and Narrate Visually*.

GEORGE ORWELL

Marrakech

As the corpse went past the flies left the restaurant table in a cloud and rushed after it, but they came back a few minutes later.

The little crowd of mourners—all men and boys, no women—threaded their way across the market-place between the piles of pomegranates and the taxis and the camels, wailing a short chant over and over again. What really appeals to the flies is that the corpses here are never put into coffins, they are merely wrapped in a piece of rag and carried on a rough wooden bier on the shoulders of four friends. When the friends get to the burying-ground they hack an oblong hole a foot or two deep, dump the body in it and fling over it a little of the dried-up, lumpy earth, which is like broken brick. No gravestone, no name, no identifying mark of any kind. The burying-ground is merely a huge waste of hummocky earth, like a derelict building-lot. After a month or two no one can even be certain where his own relatives are buried.

When you walk through a town like this —two hundred thousand inhabitants, of whom at least twenty thousand own literally nothing except the rags they stand up in— when you see how the people live, and still more how easily they die, it is always difficult to believe that you are walking among human beings. All colonial empires are in reality founded upon that fact. The people have brown faces—besides, there are so many of them! Are they really the same flesh as yourself? Do they even have names? Or are they merely a kind of undifferentiated brown stuff, about as individual as bees or coral insects? They rise out of the earth, they sweat and starve for a few years, and then they sink back into the nameless mounds of the graveyard and nobody notices that they are gone. And even the graves themselves soon fade back into the soil. Sometimes, out for a walk, as you break your way through the prickly pear, you notice that it is rather bumpy underfoot, and only a certain regularity in the bumps tells you that you are walking over skeletons.

I was feeding one of the gazelles in the public gardens.

Gazelles are almost the only animals that look good to eat when they are still alive, in fact, one can hardly look at their hind-quarters without thinking of mint sauce. The gazelle I was feeding seemed to know that this thought was in my mind, for though it took the piece of bread I was holding out it obviously did not like me. It nibbled rapidly at the bread, then lowered its head and tried to butt me, then took another nibble and then butted again. Probably its idea was that if it could drive me away the bread would somehow remain hanging in mid-air.

An Arab navvy working on the path nearby lowered his heavy hoe and sidled slowly towards us. He looked from the gazelle to the bread and from the bread to the gazelle, with a sort of quiet amazement, as though he had never seen anything quite like this before. Finally he said shyly in French:

"I could eat some of that bread."

I tore off a piece and he stowed it gratefully in some secret place under his rags. This man is an employee of the Municipality.

When you go through the Jewish quarters you gather some idea of what the medieval ghettoes were probably like. Under their Moorish rulers the Jews were only allowed to own land in certain restricted areas, and after centuries of this kind of treatment they have ceased to bother about overcrowding. Many of the streets are a good deal less than six feet wide, the houses are completely windowless, and sore-eyed children cluster everywhere in unbelievable numbers, like clouds of flies. Down the centre of the street there is generally running a little river of urine.

In the bazaar huge families of Jews, all dressed in the long black robe and little black skull-cap, are working in dark fly-infested booths that look like caves. A carpenter sits cross-legged at a prehistoric lathe, turning chair-legs at lightning speed. He works the lathe with a bow in his right hand and guides the chisel with his left foot, and thanks to a lifetime of sitting in this position his left leg is warped out of shape. At his side his grandson, aged six, is already starting on the simpler parts of the job.

I was just passing the coppersmiths' booths when somebody noticed that I was lighting a cigarette. Instantly, from the dark holes all round, there was a frenzied rush of Jews, many of them old grandfathers with flowing grey beards, all clamouring for a cigarette. Even a blind man somewhere at the back of one of the booths heard a rumour of cigarettes and came crawling out, groping in the air with his hand. In about a minute I had used up the whole packet. None of these people, I suppose, works less than twelve hours a day, and every one of them looks on a cigarette as a more or less impossible luxury.

As the Jews live in self-contained communities they follow the same trades as the Arabs, except for agriculture. Fruit-sellers, potters, silversmiths, blacksmiths, butchers, leatherworkers, tailors, water-carriers, beggars, porters—whichever way you look you see nothing but Jews. As a matter of fact there are thirteen thousand of them, all living in the space of a few acres. A good job Hitler wasn't here. Perhaps he was on his way, however. You hear the usual dark rumours about the Jews, not only from the Arabs but from the poorer Europeans.

"Yes, mon vieux, they took my job away from me and gave it to a Jew. The Jews! They're the real rulers of this country, you know. They've got all the money. They control the banks, finance—everything."

"But," I said, "isn't it a fact that the average Jew is a labourer working for about a penny an hour?"

"Ah, that's only for show! They're all moneylenders really. They're cunning, the Jews."

In just the same way, a couple of hundred years ago, poor old women used to be burned for witchcraft when they could not even work enough magic to get themselves a square meal.

All people who work with their hands are partly invisible, and the more important the work they do, the less visible they are. Still, a white skin is always fairly conspicuous. In northern Europe, when you see a labourer ploughing a field, you probably give him a second glance. In a hot country, anywhere south of Gibraltar or east of Suez, the chances are that you don't even see him. I have noticed this again and again. In a tropical landscape one's eye takes in everything except the human beings. It takes in the dried-up soil, the prickly pear, the palm tree and the distant mountain, but it always misses the peasant hoeing at his patch. He is the same colour as the earth, and a great deal less interesting to look at.

It is only because of this that the starved countries of Asia and Africa are accepted as tourist resorts. No one would think of running cheap trips to the Distressed Areas. But where the human beings have brown skins their poverty is simply not noticed. What does Morocco mean to a Frenchman? An orange-grove or a job in Government service. Or to an Englishman? Camels, castles, palm trees, Foreign Legionnaires, brass trays, and bandits. One could probably live there for years without noticing that for nine-tenths of the people the reality of life is an endless, back-breaking struggle to wring a little food out of an eroded soil.

Most of Morocco is so desolate that no wild animal bigger than a hare can live on it. Huge areas which were once covered with forest have turned into a treeless waste where the soil is exactly like broken-up brick. Nevertheless a good deal of it is cultivated, with frightful labour. Everything is done by hand. Long lines of women, bent double like inverted capital L's, work their way slowly across the fields, tearing up the prickly weeds with their hands, and the peasant gathering lucerne for fodder pulls it up stalk by stalk instead of reaping it, thus saving an inch or two on each stalk. The plough is a wretched wooden thing, so frail that one can easily carry it on one's shoulder, and fitted underneath with a rough iron spike which stirs the soil to a depth of about four inches. This is as much as the strength of the animals is equal to. It is usual to plough with a cow and a donkey yoked together. Two donkeys would not be quite strong enough, but on the other hand two cows would cost a little more to feed. The peasants possess no harrows, they merely plough the soil several times over in different directions, finally leaving it in rough furrows, after which the whole field has to be shaped with hoes into small oblong patches to conserve water. Except for a day or two after the rare rainstorms there is never enough water. Along the edges of the fields channels are hacked out to a depth of thirty or forty feet to get at the tiny trickles which run through the subsoil.

Every afternoon a file of very old women passes down the road outside my house, each carrying a load of firewood. All of them are mummified with age and the sun, and all of them are tiny. It seems to be generally the case in primitive communities that the women, when they get beyond a certain age, shrink to the size of children. One day a poor old creature who could not have been more than four feet tall crept past me under a vast load of wood. I stopped her and put a five-sou piece (a little more than a farthing) into her hand. She answered with a shrill wail, almost a scream, which was partly gratitude but mainly surprise. I suppose that from her point of view, by taking any notice of her, I seemed almost to be violating a law of nature. She accepted her status as an old woman, that is to say as a beast of burden. When a family is travelling it is quite usual to see a father and a grown-up son riding ahead on donkeys, and an old woman following on foot, carrying the baggage.

But what is strange about these people is their invisibility. For several weeks, always at about the same time of day, the file of old women had hobbled past the house with their firewood, and though they had registered themselves on my eyeballs I cannot truly say that I had seen them. Firewood was passing—that was how I saw it. It was only that one day I happened to be walking behind them, and the curious up-and-down motion of a load of wood drew my attention to the human being beneath it. Then for the first time I noticed the poor old earth-coloured bodies, bodies reduced to bones and leathery skin, bent double under the crushing weight. Yet I suppose I had not been five minutes on Moroccan soil before I noticed the overloading of the donkeys and was infuriated by it. There is no question that the donkeys are damnably treated. The Moroccan donkey is hardly bigger than a St. Bernard dog, it carries a load which in the British Army would be considered too much for a fifteen-hands mule, and very often its pack-saddle is not taken off its back for weeks together. But what is peculiarly pitiful is that it is the most willing creature on earth, it follows its master like a dog and does not need either bridle or halter. After a dozen years of devoted work it suddenly drops dead, whereupon its master tips it into the ditch and the village dogs have torn its guts out before it is cold.

This kind of thing makes one's blood boil, whereas—on the whole—the plight of the human beings does not. I am not commenting, merely pointing to a fact. People with brown skins are next door to invisible. Anyone can be sorry for the donkey with its galled back, but it is generally owing to some kind of accident if one even notices the old woman under her load of sticks.

As the storks flew northward the Negroes were marching southward—a long, dusty column, infantry, screw-gun batteries, and then more infantry, four or five thousand men in all, winding up the road with a clumping of boots and a clatter of iron wheels.

They were Senegalese, the blackest Negroes in Africa, so black that sometimes it is difficult so see whereabouts on their necks the hair begins. Their splendid bodies were hidden in reach-me-down khaki uniforms, their feet squashed into boots that looked like blocks of wood, and every tin hat seemed to be a couple of sizes too small. It was very hot and the men had marched a long way. They slumped under the weight of their packs and the curiously sensitive black faces were glistening with sweat.

As they went past a tall, very young Negro turned and caught my eye. But the look he gave me was not in the least the kind of look you might expect. Not hostile, not contemptuous, not sullen, not even inquisitive. It was the shy, wide-eyed Negro look, which actually is a look of profound respect. I saw how it was. This wretched boy, who is a French citizen and has therefore been dragged from the forest to scrub floors and catch syphilis in garrison towns, actually has feelings of reverence before a white skin. He has been taught that the white race are his masters, and he still believes it.

But there is one thought which every white man (and in this connection it doesn't matter twopence if he calls himself a socialist) thinks when he sees a black army marching past. "How much longer can we go on kidding these people? How long before they turn their guns in the other direction?"

It was curious, really. Every white man there had this thought stowed somewhere or other in his mind. I had it, so had the other onlookers, so had the officers on their sweating chargers and the white N.C.O.'s marching in the ranks. It was a kind of secret which we all knew and were too clever to tell; only the Negroes didn't know it. And really it was like watching a flock of cattle to see the long column, a mile or two miles of armed men, flowing peacefully up the road, while the great white birds drifted over them in the opposite direction, glittering like scraps of paper.

QUESTIONS FOR STUDY AND DISCUSSION

1. Though "Marrakech" is a great deal more than a simple description of the town and the surrounding countryside, it offers excellent examples of certain descriptive techniques. Orwell is noted, among other things, for his interest in and use of vivid metaphor and simile, e.g. "The burying-ground is merely a huge waste of hummocky earth, like a derelict building-lot"; or "boots that looked like blocks of wood." See how many you can find. What conclusions can you draw from the number employed? from the kinds of things used for comparison?

2. Selection of details is one of the most important considerations in writing effective description. What details does Orwell select in each of the "scenes" he presents? Are these sufficient? What might he have included that he did not? Would more detail spoil or improve any particular description? Why?

3. Carefully handled description can set the "tone" of a piece of writing. What details of landscape, people's faces, dress, actions does Orwell focus upon? What are their predominant colors?

4. How do Orwell's descriptions support the statement, made in the third paragraph of the essay, that "when you walk through a town like this . . . it is always difficult to believe that you are walking among human beings"?

WRITING ASSIGNMENT

After close observation of a "scene"— landscape, figures in action, buildings, or some combination of these—write a description of it from each of these mental points-of-view: (a) a typical tourist in a foreign country; (b) a man in a hurry to keep an appointment; (c) a man who has lost his way.

ARTHUR M.
SCHLESINGER, JR.

Prologue: 1933

The White House, midnight, Friday, March 3, 1933. Across the country the banks of the nation had gradually shuttered their windows and locked their doors. The very machinery of the American economy seemed to be coming to a stop. The rich and fertile nation, overflowing with natural wealth in its fields and forests and mines, equipped with unsurpassed technology, endowed with boundless resources in its men and women, lay stricken. "We are at the end of our rope," the weary President at last said, as the striking clock announced the day of his retirement. "There is nothing more we can do."

Saturday, March 4, dawned gray and bleak. Heavy winter clouds hung over the city. A chill northwest wind brought brief gusts of rain. The darkness of the day intensified the mood of helplessness. "A sense of depression had settled over the capital," reported the *New York Times*, "so that it could be felt." In the late morning, people began to gather for the noon ceremonies, drawn, it would seem, by curiosity as much as by hope. Nearly one hundred thousand assembled in the grounds before the Capitol, standing in quiet groups, sitting on benches, watching from rooftops. Some climbed the bare, sleet-hung trees. As they waited, they murmured among themselves. "What are those things that look like little cages?" one asked. "Machine guns," replied a woman with a nervous giggle. "The atmosphere which surrounded the change of government in the United States," wrote Arthur Krock, "was comparable to that which might be found in a beleaguered capital in war time." The colorless light of the cast-iron skies, the numb faces of the crowd, created almost an air of fantasy. Only the Capitol seemed real, etched like a steel engraving against the dark clouds.

On the drive from the White House to the Capitol, the retiring President, his eyes lowered, his expression downcast, did not try to hide his feelings. The nation which had helped him rise from a poor Iowa farm to wealth and power, which he had repaid with high-minded and unstinted service, had rejected him. "Democracy is not a polite employer," Herbert Hoover later wrote. "The only way out of elective office is to get sick or die or get kicked out."

It was customary for the retiring President to ask his successor for dinner on the night of the third of March; but Hoover had declined to issue the usual invitation. At length, the White House usher insisted that the President-elect must be given the opportunity to pay his respects. Instead of the traditional dinner, a tea was arranged for the afternoon of the third. It had been a strained occasion in the Red Room, complicated by fruitless last-minute discussions about the banking crisis. Finally the President-elect, recognizing that Hoover was not in the mood to complete the round of protocol, politely suggested that the President need not return the visit. Hoover looked his successor in the eye. "Mr. Roosevelt," he said coldly, "when you are in Washington as long as I have been, you will learn that the President of the United States calls on nobody." Franklin Delano Roosevelt, hurrying his family from the room, returned to the Mayflower Hotel visibly annoyed. "It was . . ." a close friend later reported, "one of the few times I have ever seen him really angry."

Now Hoover sat motionless and unheeding as the car moved through crowded streets toward the Capitol. Doubtless he assumed the occasional cheers from the packed sidewalks were for Roosevelt and so not his to acknowledge. But for Roosevelt, sitting beside him in the open car, these last moments belonged to the retiring President; it was not for the President-elect to respond to the faint applause. On they drove in uncomfortable silence. Passing the new Commerce Building on Constitution Avenue, Roosevelt hoped that at least this sight might tempt the former Secretary of Commerce into an exchange of amiabilities.

When a friendly remark produced only an unintelligible murmur in reply, the President-elect suddenly felt that the two men could not ride on forever like graven images. Turning, he began to smile to the men and women along the street and to wave his top hat. Hoover rode on, his face heavy and expressionless.

The fog of despair hung over the land. One out of every four American workers lacked a job. Factories that had once darkened the skies with smoke stood ghostly and silent, like extinct volcanoes. Families slept in tarpaper shacks and tin-lined caves and scavenged like dogs for food in the city dump. In October the New York City Health Department had reported that over one-fifth of the pupils in public schools were suffering from malnutrition. Thousands of vagabond children were roaming the land, wild boys of the road. Hunger marchers, pinched and bitter, were parading cold streets in New York and Chicago. On the countryside unrest had already flared into violence. Farmers stopped milk trucks along Iowa roads and poured the milk into the ditch. Mobs halted mortgage sales, ran the men from the banks and insurance companies out of town, intimidated courts and judges, demanded a moratorium on debts. When a sales company in Nebraska invaded a farm and seized two trucks, the farmers in the Newman Grove district organized a posse, called it the "Red Army," and took the trucks back. In West Virginia, mining families, turned out of their homes, lived in tents along the road on pinto beans and black coffee.

In January, Edward A. O'Neal, an Alabama planter, head of the Farm Bureau Federation, bluntly warned a Senate committee, "Unless something is done for the American farmer we will have revolution in the countryside within less than twelve months." Donald Richberg, a Chicago lawyer, told another Senate committee a few weeks later, "There are many signs that if the lawfully constituted leadership does not soon substitute action for words, a new leadership, perhaps unlawfully constituted, will arise and act." William Green, the ordinarily benign president of the ordinarily conservative American Federation of Labor, told a third committee that if Congress did not enact a thirty-hour law, labor would compel employers to grant it "by universal strike." "Which would be class war, practically?" interrupted Senator Hugo Black. "Whatever it would be," said Green, "it would be that. . . . That is the only language that a lot of employers ever understand—the language of force." In the cities and on the farms, Communist organizers were finding a ready audience and a zealous following.

Patrick J. Hurley, Hoover's Secretary of War, ordered a transfer of troops from a small Texas post to Kentucky. Tom Connally of Texas, rising in the Senate, accused the War Department of deliberately concentrating its armed units near the larger cities. "The Secretary of War, with a glitter of fear in his eye," Connally reported, "referred to Reds and possible Communists that may be abroad in the land." The mayor of New York, newly inaugurated, sought to reassure his city: "You're going to have a Mayor with a chin and fight in him. I'll preserve the Metropolis from the Red Army." But the next week a group of Communists shoved their way through a police line before the brownstone house on East 65th Street where Franklin D. Roosevelt was making his plans for the future. Eleven Democratic leaders were having their picture taken on the front steps; they stepped nervously into the house as the Communists shook their fists and shouted, "When do we eat? We want action!" (Among the politicians were Cordell Hull and James F. Byrnes; they would have more to do with Communists before they were through.) The police with a flourish of nightsticks cleared the street.

Elmer Davis reported that the leading citizens of one industrial city—it was Dayton, Ohio—had organized a committee to plan how the city and the country around could function as an economic unit if the power lines were cut and the railroads stopped running. Over champagne and cigars, at the Everglades in Palm Beach, a banker declared the country on the verge of revolution; another guest, breaking the startled silence, advised the company to "step without the territorial boundaries of the United States of America with as much cash as you can carry just as soon as it is feasible for you to get away." "There'll be a revolution, sure," a Los Angeles banker said on a transcontinental train. "The farmers will rise up. So will labor. The Reds will run the country—or maybe the Fascists. Unless, of course, Roosevelt does something."

But what could he do? In February 1933, the Senate Finance Committee summoned a procession of business leaders to solicit their ideas on the crisis. Said John W. Davis, the leader of the American bar, "I have nothing to offer, either of fact or theory." W. W. Atterbury of the Pennsylvania Railroad: "There is no panacea." Most endorsed the thesis advanced by the permanent elder statesman Bernard Baruch: "Delay in balancing the Budget is trifling with disaster." And, as they spoke their lusterless pieces, the banks began to close their doors. "Our entire banking system," said William Gibbs McAdoo in exasperation, "does credit to a collection of imbeciles."

But bankruptcy of ideas seemed almost as complete among the intellectuals. "My heartbreak at liberalism," wrote William Allen White, "is that it has sounded no note of hope, made no plans for the future, offered no program." On the eve of the inaugural, a leading American theologian pronounced an obituary on liberal society. His essay was written, said Reinhold Niebuhr, on the assumption that "capitalism is dying and with the conviction that it ought to die." Let no one delude himself by hoping for reform from within. "There is nothing in history to support the thesis that a dominant class ever yields its position or its privileges in society because its rule has been convicted of ineptness or injustices." Others, in their despair, could only yearn for a savior. Hamilton Fish, the New York congressman, spoke for millions when he wrote to Roosevelt late in February that in the crisis we must "give you any power that you may need."

The images of a nation as it approached zero hour: the well-groomed men, baffled and impotent in their double-breasted suits before the Senate committee; the confusion and dismay in the business office and the university; the fear in the country club; the angry men marching in the silent street; the scramble for the rotting garbage in the dump; the sweet milk trickling down the dusty road; the noose dangling over the barn door; the raw northwest wind blasting its way across Capitol plaza.

In the Capitol, the President-elect waited in the Military Affairs Committee Room. Sober and white-faced, he sat in silence, glancing at the manuscript of his inaugural address. Huey Long, the senator from Louisiana, glimpsed him and started to sweep into the room; then paused at the threshold and tiptoed away. Ten minutes before noon Roosevelt started down the corridor toward the Senate, only to be stopped. "All right," he said, "we'll go back and wait some more." When the moment arrived, he was to ride in his wheelchair to the east door; then walk thirty-five yards to the speaker's stand.

A few moments before, in the Senate Chamber, the new Vice-President, John Nance Garner of Texas, had taken his oath of office. There followed a rush from the Senate to the inaugural stand outside. The mass of people, swarming into the narrow exit from the east doors of the Capitol, blocked the runway. In a moment the congestion was hopeless. Garner and the retiring Vice-President, Charles Curtis of Kansas, had meanwhile reached the stand. The Texan, with no overcoat, shivered in the harsh wind; he borrowed a muffler and wrapped it around his neck. Near him Curtis disappeared into the depth of his fur coat, looking steadily at the floor, apparently lost in memory. Gradually, invited guests began to force their way through the jam: members of the new cabinet, half a dozen senators, the new President's wife, his mother, his tall sons. Eventually Charles Evans Hughes, the Chief Justice of the United States, made his appearance, erect and stately, a black skullcap on his head, his white beard stirred by the wind and his black robe fluttering about his legs. In a leather-upholstered chair to the left of the lectern sat Herbert Hoover.

The tension in the crowd mounted steadily with the delay. Presently a Supreme Court attendant arrived bearing the family Bible of the Roosevelts. Then, at last, the bugle sounded; and Franklin Delano Roosevelt, intensely pale, leaning on the arm of his eldest son James, walked slowly up the maroon-carpeted ramp. The Marine Band, in its scarlet jackets and blue trousers, finished the last bars of "Hail to the Chief." There was a convulsive stir in the crowd, spread over forty acres of park and pavement; then cheers and applause. Mrs. Woodrow Wilson waved a handkerchief. Bernard Baruch leaped upon a bench and swung his black silk hat. Josephus Daniels, the new President's old chief, his eyes wet with tears, pounded vigorously with his cane. A few rays of sunshine broke for a moment through the slate clouds upon the inaugural stand.

The Chief Justice read the oath with dignity and power. Instead of returning the customary "I do," Roosevelt repeated the full oath. ("I am glad," Hughes had written when the President-elect suggested this. ". . . I think the repetition is the more dignified and appropriate course.") The family Bible lay open to the thirteenth chapter of the First Corinthians. "For now we see through a glass, darkly; but then face to face: now I know in part; but then shall I know even as also I am known. And now abideth faith, hope, charity, these three; but the greatest of these *is* charity."

Six days before, Roosevelt in his Hyde Park study, writing with pencil on a lined, legal-sized yellow pad, had made a draft of his inaugural address. Waiting in the Senate committee room on inauguration day, he added a new opening sentence to his reading copy: "This is a day of consecration." But, as the great crowd quieted down, the solemnity of the occasion surged over him; he said, in ringing tones, "This is a day of national consecration."

Across the country millions clustered around radio sets. The new President stood bareheaded and unsmiling, his hands gripping the lectern. The moment had come, he said, to speak the truth, the whole truth, frankly and boldly. "Let me assert my firm belief that the only thing we have to fear is fear itself—nameless, unreasoning, unjustified terror which paralyzes needed efforts to convert retreat into advance." The speaker flung back his head. "In every dark hour of our national life a leadership of frankness

and vigor has met with that understanding and support of the people themselves which is essential to victory."

The bounty of nature, he continued, was undiminished. "Plenty is at our doorstep, but a generous use of it languishes in the very sight of the supply." Why? Because the rulers of the exchange of mankind's goods "have failed through their own stubbornness and their own incompetence, have admitted their failure, and have abdicated. . . . They have no vision, and when there is no vision the people perish. The money changers have fled from their high seats in the temple of our civilization." The crowd delivered itself of its first great applause. "There must be an end," Roosevelt went on, "to a conduct in banking and in business which too often has given to a sacred trust the likeness of callous and selfish wrong-doing." Again the crowd shouted.

"This Nation asks for action, and action now. . . . We must act and act quickly. . . . We must move as a trained and loyal army willing to sacrifice for the good of a common discipline, because without such discipline no progress is made, no leadership becomes effective." "It may be," he said, "that an unprecedented demand and need for undelayed action may call for temporary departure from that normal balance of public procedure." If Congress should fail to enact the necessary measures, if the emergency were still critical, then, added Roosevelt solemnly, "I shall ask the Congress for the one remaining instrument to meet the crisis—broad Executive power to wage a war against the emergency, as great as the power that would be given to me if we were in fact invaded by a foreign foe." The crowd thundered approval in a long, continuing demonstration—the loudest applause of the day.

Roosevelt—"his face still so grim," reported Arthur Krock, "as to seem unfamiliar to those who have long known him" —did not acknowledge the applause. Nor, indeed, did all share the enthusiasm. Some who watched the handsome head and heard the cultivated voice mistrusted what lay behind the charm and the rhetoric. "I was thoroughly scared," the retiring Secretary of State, Henry L. Stimson, wrote in his diary. ". . . Like most of his past speeches, it was full of weasel words and would let him do about what he wanted to." Edmund Wilson, covering the inaugural for the *New Republic*, saw "the old unctuousness, the old pulpit vagueness," the echoes of Woodrow Wilson's eloquence without Wilson's glow of life behind them. "The thing that emerges most clearly," wrote Wilson, "is the warning of a dictatorship."

But the unsmiling President showed no evidence of doubt. "We do not distrust the future of essential democracy," he said in summation. "The people of the United States have not failed. In their need they have registered a mandate that they want direct, vigorous action. They have asked for discipline and direction under leadership. They have made me the present instrument of their wishes. In the spirit of the gift I take it." Herbert Hoover stared at the ground.

The high clear note of the cavalry bugles announced the inaugural parade. Franklin Roosevelt, in the presidential car, waved greetings to the crowd along the way—men and women now curiously awakened from apathy and daze. The horsemen wheeled into line, and the parade began.

In Washington the weather remained cold and gray. Across the land the fog began to lift.

QUESTIONS FOR STUDY AND DISCUSSION

1. Writers of fiction are often tempted to describe their scenes in such a way as to make them match the emotions of the characters or the mood of the story. This technique, branded the "pathetic fallacy," has been condemned by many modern critics, although it is an effective device for communicating and intensifying mood. Is Schlesinger guilty of the "pathetic fallacy"? If he is, can the technique be justified, in this essay or in any piece of writing? Might Schlesinger have any special excuse for employing it?

2. What are the pervasive colors in this essay?

3. A skillful writer helps the reader to visualize the scene by furnishing him specific details: the direction of the wind, the kind of hat a character is wearing, the number of steps a character takes between two points. How often and how well does Schlesinger employ such concrete details? Point to specific examples.

4. Specific details of another sort also actualize description, particularly descriptions of a general state or condition (considered as a technique of exposition these would constitute development of a topic by means of examples). Study how Schlesinger supports such generalizations as "The fog of despair hung over the land." (Par. 6).

5. Details may also function to help establish a writer's attitude toward the events and people he is describing. If a description of poverty in France before the Revolution prominently featured Marie Antoinette's "Let them eat cake," one would suspect the writer's sympathy lay with the peasants. Can you find any examples of Schlesinger's presentation of details which suggest that he is sympathetic or unsympathetic toward certain people or attitudes?

WRITING ASSIGNMENTS

1. Write an essay on some meaningful event (a wedding, graduation ceremony, funeral) about which you had—or have—a clear personal attitude (formal weddings are useless, graduation symbolizes an end of carefree adolescence, the deceased was an evil man). Do not *state* your attitude but try to imply it in the way you handle the description.

2. Write a (shorter) version of Roosevelt's first inauguration from the Republican point of view.

MARK TWAIN

from

The Autobiography

My uncle, John A. Quarles, was a farmer, and his place was in the country four miles from Florida. He had eight children and fifteen or twenty negroes, and was also fortunate in other ways, particularly in his character. I have not come across a better man than he was. I was his guest for two or three months every year, from the fourth year after we removed to Hannibal till I was eleven or twelve years old. I have never consciously used him or his wife in a book, but his farm has come very handy to me in literature once or twice. In *Huck Finn* and in *Tom Sawyer, Detective* I moved it down to Arkansas. It was all of six hundred miles, but it was no trouble; it was not a very large farm—five hundred acres, perhaps—but I could have done it if it had been twice as large. And as for the morality of it, I cared nothing for that; I would move a state if the exigencies of literature required it.

It was a heavenly place for a boy, that farm of my uncle John's. The house was a double log one, with a spacious floor (roofed in) connecting it with the kitchen. In the summer the table was set in the middle of that shady and breezy floor, and the sumptuous meals—well, it makes me cry to think of them. Fried chicken, roast pig; wild and tame turkeys, ducks, and geese; venison just killed; squirrels, rabbits, pheasants, partridges, prairie-chickens; biscuits, hot batter cakes, hot buckwheat cakes, hot "wheat bread," hot rolls, hot corn pone; fresh corn boiled on the ear, succotash, butter-beans, stringbeans, tomatoes, peas, Irish potatoes, sweet potatoes; buttermilk, sweet milk, "clabber"; watermelons, muskmelons, cantaloupes—all fresh from the garden; apple pie, peach pie, pumpkin pie, apple dumplings, peach cobbler—I can't remember the rest. The way that the things were cooked was per-haps the main splendor—particularly a certain few of the dishes. For instance, the corn bread, the hot biscuits and wheat bread, and the fried chicken. These things have never been properly cooked in the North—in fact, no one there is able to learn the art, so far as my experience goes. The North thinks it knows how to make corn bread, but this is mere superstition. Perhaps no bread in the world is quite so good as Southern corn bread, and perhaps no bread in the world is quite so bad as the Northern imitation of it. The North seldom tries to fry chicken, and this is well; the art cannot be learned north of the line of Mason and Dixon, nor anywhere in Europe. This is not hearsay; it is experience that is speaking. In Europe it is imagined that the custom of serving various kinds of bread blazing hot is "American," but that is too broad a spread; it is custom in the South, but is much less than that in the North. In the North and in Europe hot bread is considered unhealthy. This is probably another fussy superstition, like the European superstition that ice-water is unhealthy. Europe does not need ice-water and does not drink it; and yet, notwithstanding this, its word for it is better than ours, because it describes it, whereas ours doesn't. Europe calls it "iced" water. Our word describes water made from melted ice—a drink which has a characterless taste and which we have but little acquaintance with.

It seems a pity that the world should throw away so many good things merely because they are unwholesome. I doubt if God has given us any refreshment which, taken in moderation, is unwholesome, except microbes. Yet there are people who strictly deprive themselves of each and every eatable, drinkable, and smokable which has in any way acquired a shady reputation. They pay this price for health. And health is all they get for it. How strange it is! It is like paying out your whole fortune for a cow that has gone dry.

The farmhouse stood in the middle of a very large yard, and the yard was fenced on three sides with rails and on the rear side with high palings; against these stood the smoke-house; beyond the palings was the orchard; beyond the orchard were the negro quarters and the tobacco fields. The front yard was entered over a stile made of sawed-off logs of graduated heights; I do not remember any gate. In a corner of the front yard were a dozen lofty hickory trees and a dozen black walnuts, and in the nutting season riches were to be gathered there.

Down a piece, abreast the house, stood a little log cabin against the rail fence; and there the woody hill fell sharply away, past the barns, the corn-crib, the stables, and the tobacco-curing house, to a limpid brook which sang along over its gravelly bed and curved and frisked in and out and here and there and yonder in the deep shade of overhanging foliage and vines—a divine place for wading, and it had swimming pools, too, which were forbidden to us and therefore much frequented by us. For we were little Christian children and had early been taught the value of forbidden fruit.

In the little log cabin lived a bedridden white-headed slave woman whom we visited daily and looked upon with awe, for we believed she was upward of a thousand years old and had talked with Moses. The younger negroes credited these statistics and had furnished them to us in good faith. We accommodated all the details which came to us about her; and so we believed that she had lost her health in the long desert trip coming out of Egypt, and had never been able to get it back again. She had a round bald place on the crown of her head, and we used to creep around and gaze at it in reverent silence, and reflect that it was caused by fright through seeing Pharaoh drowned. We called her "Aunt" Hannah, Southern fashion. She was superstitious, like the other negroes; also, like them, she was deeply religious. Like them, she had great faith in prayer and employed it in all ordinary exigencies, but not in cases where a dead certainty of result was urgent. Whenever witches were around she tied up the remnant of her wool in little tufts, with white thread, and this promptly made the witches impotent.

All the negroes were friends of ours, and with those of our own age we were in effect comrades. I say in effect, using the phrase as a modification. We were comrades, and yet not comrades; color and condition inter-posed a subtle line which both parties were conscious of and which rendered complete fusion impossible. We had a faithful and affectionate good friend, ally, and adviser in "Uncle Dan'l," a middle-aged slave whose head was the best one in the negro quarter, whose sympathies were wide and warm, and whose heart was honest and simple and knew no guile. He has served me well these many, many years. I have not seen him for more than half a century, and yet spiritually I have had his welcome company a good part of that time, and have staged him in books under his own name and as "Jim," and carted him all around—to Hannibal, down the Mississippi on a raft, and even across the Desert of Sahara in a balloon—and he has endured it all with the patience and friendliness and loyalty which were his birthright. It was on the farm that I got my strong liking for his race and my appreciation of certain of its fine qualities. This feeling and this estimate have stood the test of sixty years and more, and have suffered no impairment. The black face is as welcome to me now as it was then.

In my schoolboy days I had no aversion to slavery. I was not aware that there was anything wrong about it. No one arraigned it in my hearing; the local papers said nothing against it; the local pulpit taught us that God approved it, that it was a holy thing, and that the doubter need only look in the Bible if he wished to settle his mind—and then the texts were read aloud to us to make the matter sure; if the slaves themselves had an aversion to slavery, they were wise and said nothing. In Hannibal we seldom saw a slave misused; on the farm, never.

There was, however, one small incident of my boyhood days which touched this matter, and it must have meant a good deal to me or it would not have stayed in my memory, clear and sharp, vivid and shadowless, all these slow-drifting years. We had a little slave boy whom we had hired from some one, there in Hannibal. He was from the eastern shore of Maryland, and had been brought away from his family and his friends, halfway across the American continent, and sold. He was a cheery spirit, innocent and gentle, and the noisiest creature that ever was, perhaps. All day long he was singing, whistling, yelling, whooping, laughing—it was maddening, devastating, unendurable. At last, one day, I lost all my temper, and went raging to my mother and said Sandy had been singing for an hour without a single break, and I couldn't stand it, and *wouldn't* she please shut him up. The tears came into her eyes and her lip trembled, and she said something like this:

"Poor thing, when he sings it shows that he is not remembering, and that comforts me; but when he is still I am afraid he is thinking, and I cannot bear it. He will never see his mother again; if he can sing, I must not hinder it, but be thankful for it. If you were older, you would understand me; then that friendless child's noise would make you glad."

It was a simple speech and made up of small words, but it went home, and Sandy's noise was not a trouble to me any more. She never used large words, but she had a natural gift for making small ones do effective work. She lived to reach the neighborhood of ninety years and was capable with her tongue to the last—especially when a meanness or an injustice roused her spirit. She has come handy to me several times in my books, where she figures as Tom Sawyer's Aunt Polly. I fitted her out with a dialect and tried to think up other improvements for her, but did not find any. I used Sandy once, also; it was in *Tom Sawyer.* I tried to get him to whitewash the fence, but it did not work. I do not remember what name I called him by in the book.

I can see the farm yet, with perfect clearness. I can see all its belongings, all its details; the family room of the house, with a "trundle" bed in one corner and a spinning-wheel in another—a wheel whose rising and falling wail, heard from a distance, was the mournfulest of all sounds to me, and made me homesick and low spirited, and filled my atmosphere with the wandering spirits of the dead; the vast fireplace, piled high, on winter nights, with flaming hickory logs from whose ends a sugary sap bubbled out, but did not go to waste, for we scraped it off and ate it; the lazy cat spread out on the rough hearthstones; the drowsy dogs braced against the jambs and blinking; my aunt in one chimney corner, knitting; my

uncle in the other, smoking his corn-cob pipe; the slick and carpetless oak floor faintly mirroring the dancing flame tongues and freckled with black indentations where fire coals had popped out and died a leisurely death; half a dozen children romping in the background twilight; "split"-bottomed chairs here and there, some with rockers; a cradle —out of service, but waiting, with confidence; in the early cold mornings a snuggle of children, in shirts and chemises, occupying the hearthstone and procrastinating— they could not bear to leave that comfortable place and go out on the wind-swept floor space between the house and kitchen where the general tin basin stood, and wash.

Along outside of the front fence ran the country road, dusty in the summertime, and a good place for snakes—they liked to lie in it and sun themselves; when they were rattlesnakes or puff adders, we killed them; when they were black snakes, or racers, or belonged to the fabled "hoop" breed, we fled, without shame; when they were "house snakes," or "garters," we carried them home and put them in Aunt Patsy's work basket for a surprise; for she was prejudiced against snakes, and always when she took the basket in her lap and they began to climb out of it it disordered her mind. She never could seem to get used to them; her opportunities went for nothing. And she was always cold toward bats, too, and could not bear them; and yet I think a bat is as friendly a bird as there is. My mother was Aunt Patsy's sister and had the same wild superstitions. A bat is beautifully soft and silky; I do not know any creature that is pleasanter to the touch or is more grateful for caressings, if offered in the right spirit. I know all about these coleoptera, because our great cave, three miles below Hannibal, was multitudinously stocked with them, and often I brought them home to amuse my mother with. It was easy to manage if it was a school day, because then I had ostensibly been to school and hadn't any bats. She was not a suspicious person, but full of trust and confidence; and when I said, "There's something in my coat pocket for you," she would put her hand in. But she always took it out again, herself; I didn't have to tell her. It was remarkable, the way she couldn't learn to like private bats. The more experience she had, the more she could not change her views.

I think she was never in the cave in her life; but everybody else went there. Many excursion parties came from considerable distances up and down the river to visit the cave. It was miles in extent and was a tangled wilderness of narrow and lofty clefts and passages. It was an easy place to get lost in; anybody could do it—including the bats. I got lost in it myself, along with a lady, and our last candle burned down to almost nothing before we glimpsed the search party's lights winding about in the distance.

"Injun Joe," the half-breed, got lost in there once, and would have starved to death if the bats had run short. But there was no chance of that; there were myriads of them. He told me all his story. In the book called *Tom Sawyer* I starved him entirely to death in the cave, but that was in the interest of art; it never happened. "General" Gaines, who was our first town drunkard before Jimmy Finn got the place, was lost in there for the space of a week, and finally pushed his handkerchief out of a hole in a hilltop near Saverton, several miles down the river from the cave's mouth, and somebody saw it and dug him out. There is nothing the matter with his statistics except the handkerchief. I knew him for years and he hadn't any. But it could have been his nose. That would attract attention.

The cave was an uncanny place, for it contained a corpse—the corpse of a young girl of fourteen. It was in a glass cylinder inclosed in a copper one which was suspended from a rail which bridged a narrow passage. The body was preserved in alcohol, and it was said that loafers and rowdies used to drag it up by the hair and look at the dead face. The girl was the daughter of a St. Louis surgeon of extraordinary ability and wide celebrity. He was an eccentric man and did many strange things. He put the poor thing in that forlorn place himself.

Beyond the road where the snakes sunned themselves was a dense young thicket, and through it a dim-lighted path led a quarter of a mile; then out of the dimness one emerged abruptly upon a level great prairie which was covered with wild strawberry plants, vividly starred with prairie pinks, and walled in on all sides by forests. The strawberries were fragrant and fine, and in the season we were generally there in the crisp freshness of the early morning, while the dew beads still sparkled upon the grass and the woods were ringing with the first songs of the birds.

Down the forest slopes to the left were the swings. They were made of bark stripped from hickory saplings. When they became dry they were dangerous. They usually broke when a child was forty feet in the air, and this was why so many bones had to be mended every year. I had no ill luck myself, but none of my cousins escaped. There were eight of them, and at one time and another they broke fourteen arms among them. But it cost next to nothing, for the doctor worked by the year—twenty-five dollars for the whole family. I remember two of the Florida doctors, Chowning and Meredith. They not only tended an entire family for twenty-five dollars a year, but furnished the medicines themselves. Good measure, too. Only the largest persons could hold a whole dose. Castor oil was the principal beverage. The dose was half a dipperful, with half a dipperful of New Orleans molasses added to help it down and make it taste good, which it never did. The next standby was calomel; the next, rhubarb; and the next, jalap. Then they bled the patient, and put mustard plasters on him. It was a dreadful system, and yet the death rate was not heavy. The calomel was nearly sure to salivate the patient and cost him some of his teeth. There were no dentists. When teeth became touched with decay or were otherwise ailing, the doctor knew of but one thing to do—he fetched his tongs and dragged them out. If the jaw remained, it was not his fault. Doctors were not called in cases of ordinary illness; the family grandmother attended to those. Every old woman was a doctor, and gathered her own medicines in the woods, and knew how to compound doses that would stir the vitals of a cast-iron dog. And then there was the "Indian doctor"; a grave savage, remnant of his tribe, deeply read in the mysteries of nature and the secret properties of herbs; and most backwoodsmen had high faith in his powers and could tell of wonderful cures achieved by him. In Mauritius, away off yonder in the solitudes of the Indian Ocean, there is a person who answers to our Indian doctor of the old times. He is a negro, and has had no teaching as a doctor, yet there is one disease which he is master of and can cure and the doctors can't. They send for him when they have a case. It is a child's disease of a strange and deadly sort, and the negro cures it with a herb medicine which he makes, himself, from a prescription which has come down to him from his father and grandfather. He will not let anyone see it. He keeps the secret of its components to himself, and it is feared that he will die without divulging it; then there will be consternation in Mauritius. I was told these things by the people there, in 1896.

We had the "faith doctor," too, in those early days—a woman. Her specialty was toothache. She was a farmer's old wife and lived five miles from Hannibal. She would lay her hand on the patient's jaw and say,

"Believe!" and the cure was prompt. Mrs. Utterback. I remember her very well. Twice I rode out there behind my mother, horseback, and saw the cure performed. My mother was the patient.

Doctor Meredith removed to Hannibal, by and by, and was our family physician there, and saved my life several times. Still, he was a good man and meant well. Let it go.

I was always told that I was a sickly and precarious and tiresome and uncertain child, and lived mainly on allopathic medicines during the first seven years of my life. I asked my mother about this, in her old age —she was in her eighty-eighth year—and said:

"I suppose that during all that time you were uneasy about me?"

"Yes, the whole time."

"Afraid I wouldn't live?"

After a reflective pause — ostensibly to think out the facts — "No — afraid you would."

QUESTIONS FOR THOUGHT AND DISCUSSION

1. This description of Uncle Quarles's farm from Mark Twain's *Autobiography* is not merely a "set-piece" description but a part of his mature reflections on his childhood. What matters are clearly not pertinent to a physical description of the Quarles farm? Do they destroy the unity of the selection? What would you cut out if you were excerpting this selection?

2. Before making a final judgment on the first question, ask yourself which portions are clearly relevant. What would you certainly include? In making these decisions you will be able to discover just how thoroughly the farm is described. What portions of the farm does Twain visualize? Is there any "method" in (a) the sequence of the details? (b) the details selected? Are the sketches of people like "Aunt" Hannah, "Uncle Dan'l," the little slave boy Sandy, Twain's mother, and Aunt Patsy in any sense relevant to a comprehensive "picture" of the farm? What of the winter scene in the family room? The lengthy discussion of food?

3. How does Twain employ the resources of the language to vivify and clarify his descriptions? Analyze one paragraph carefully to determine (1) the extent to which adjectives and adverbs are used, (2) the ratio of specific nouns (names of particular objects) to more abstract ones.

4. How does Twain achieve wit and humor in this selection?

WRITING ASSIGNMENTS

1. Rewrite Twain's physical description in your own words, starting at a point at the edge of the farm and working in to the house.

2. Choose a place which you enjoyed visiting and write a description of it, taking care not to inject your own feelings into your writing. Or do the same with one which disgusted you or in which you were very unhappy.

Material for an Essay

PABLO PICASSO
The Old Guitarist

(see Frontispiece)

Classification and Division

Classification is the process by which individual items—whether people, things, or ideas—are brought together in significant groupings. Division is essentially the same process, but in division we start with a major grouping and break it down into its important varieties. Classification and division are at the same time a science and an art.

As a homely illustration of classification, suppose that a restaurant offered its patrons a choice of salmon, beef, oysters, chicken, pheasant, trout, red snapper, lobster, and deer. Into what groups or classes can we combine these? Salmon, trout, and red snapper are obviously in the fish class. Lobster and oysters are shellfish. Chicken and pheasant are types of fowl. Beef is the flesh of cattle, and cattle like deer are four-footed mammals.

But someone could point out that fish and shellfish might be spoken of together as fish since they are all members of the animal kingdom that live in water, they are all cold-blooded, and they all obtain their oxygen by means other than lungs. Similarly, both fowl and quadrupeds like cattle and deer could be grouped together as warm-blooded vertebrates. On the other hand, someone might want to distinguish between oysters and lobster, which are soft, pulpy creatures protected by an outer shell, and each of the other animals on our list, which have been blessed with backbones.

The important thing to notice from these examples is that it is often possible to classify the same material in more than one way. The writer's choice will depend upon his knowledge of the subject and the purposes for which he is making his classification or division. A biologist might argue that the salmon, since it has a backbone, is closer to the pheasant than it is to the oyster; someone preparing the daily menu for a restaurant might think it more sensible to list both salmon and oysters as sea food.

In all these groupings we used our knowledge of the animal kingdom to claim that certain creatures share certain traits, that they are enough alike in one way or another for us to yoke them together in large classes. (These likenesses are not just a matter of having a name handy; while we could speak of the trout, red snapper, and salmon as being fish, we had no word for the class that contained both cattle and deer, only makeshift terms like "quadruped mammals.")

When we make such groupings as these, we may use a technical expression and say that our trout is a species of the genus fish and that the deer is a species of the genus quadruped mammals. Both fish and quadrupeds, as we noted, might be thought of as species of the genus vertebrate animals. And with ample justification, our fish, shellfish, fowl, and four-footed mammals might all be considered species of the genus food. (Note that the word *species* is both singular and plural. The plural of *genus* is *genera*.) Classification, in other words, is the process of combining species into genera.

As an illustration of division, let us take the English consonants as our genus and partition them into species. We might first set up a group of consonants called stops, which would include *p, b, t, d, k,* and *g;* with each of these the breath is literally stopped or blocked by the lips or the tongue. Another group of consonants could be called fricatives; these would include *f, v, th* (as in *thistle*), *th* (as in *this'll*), *s, z, sh* (as in *Confucian*), *zh* (as in *confusion*), and *h.* With these consonants the stream of air coming from the throat is narrowed by lips, teeth, tongue, or glottis (either singly or in combination), producing a hissing sound. By noticing that some consonants are made by blocking the breath in the mouth while letting the air vibrate through the nose, we can establish a group of nasals: *m, n,* and *ng* (as in *sing*). A pair of affricates— *ch* (as in *church*) and *j* (as in *judge*)—might be distinguished, and the consonants *r, l, w,* and *y* form even smaller groupings.

It is at this point, probably, that the student begins to wonder whether the process of classification helps us to discover the true reality of things or whether it is simply a pragmatic tool, something we use because it gets results. The classification of foods offered by the imaginary restaurant argues for the pragmatic side of the issue, but many students—remembering their high-school biology—will contend that what they learned of the animal and vegetable kingdoms is not only useful classification but a taxonomy based upon reality itself. But the ancient classification of animals into those of the land and those of the air and those of the sea is also based on reality. It is a fine classification, despite the objection that it does not account for amphibians like the frog. Its only trouble is that it doesn't do enough for us; it's too coarse a sieve to be of much use. Perhaps the whole question (a classic argument) is at fault, since it implies that all classifications are either grounded in reality or arbitrarily established for some useful purpose, but never both. Perhaps the truth is that some taxonomies have their basis in the true nature of things, while others are merely helpful arrangements of facts.

An ideal classification or division is one that uses only one principle of classification at a time in grouping its facts. That is, if someone were to classify all students as very good, very bad, and athletes, he would be using two principles of classification (academic goodness and athletic ability) simultaneously, purposelessly, and poorly.

This rule is only an appeal to good sense, and it does not prohibit elaborate classifications. For example, students could be classified in successive steps by such diverse and unrelated principles as sex, athletic ability, interests, academic standing, color of eyes, color of hair, and academic major. It would take only a jiffy for an IBM sorter to make such a classification and list each possibility in order, giving, for instance, the name and address of every girl tennis player with an "A" average, blue eyes, and blonde hair who is majoring in physics.

The ideal classification should also account for all the facts. Our division of students into very good, very bad, and athletes fails to do this, obviously. Most of us know students who are neither terribly good nor terribly bad, and it would be impossible to list the ones who are unathletic. But while a classification needs to account for the facts, it must not accomplish this by over-simplifying matters. Our division of the consonants into stops, fricatives, nasals, and affricates took care of only twenty of the twenty-four English consonants. The rule reminds us that we cannot go off and forget about the remaining four. They must be listed as a residue or remainder (actually they can be accounted for by setting up other, smaller categories). The rule does not tell us that our classification needs improving.

Last, the ideal classification is one that does not set up overlapping classes or false oppositions between classes. The division of students into very good, very bad, and athletes conceivably does both. Inasmuch as athletes—like other students—can make high grades, and low ones, the classes overlap one another. And to some, such a classification may imply that athletes are exempt from having to earn grades, which is not entirely true.

"Everyone who is not for us is against us." This is another false opposition. Some may be for us and some against, but most people probably don't give a hoot. Between black and white come all sorts of shades of gray, and between logical classes there are often any number of fine transitions. This love for "either-or" thinking, which often leads to fallacious conclusions in exposition as well as argument, is an ingrained part of our very nature, and possibly has to do with the binary character of thought itself.

ESSAY SUGGESTIONS

1. Read Russell Lynes's "Highbrow, Lowbrow, Middlebrow" (published in *Harper's Magazine*, February, 1949) and jot down the traits you share with each of these three abstractions. Which "brow" are you most nearly like? Discuss. Is it possible to be neither highbrow, lowbrow, or middlebrow but an amalgam of all three? If this is so, we have to view classification as a kind of intellectual chemistry. We try, first of all, to isolate the ultimate elements, but we must remember that these elements do not always occur pure in nature. They are found in mixtures, and they can enter into chemical compounds. And the compounds, of course, can be as different from their basic constituents as salt is unlike the sodium and chlorine of which it is formed.

2. How can we classify the languages spoken throughout the world? (You will need to use the library in working out this problem. A good book to start with is H. L. Gleason's *An Introduction to Descriptive Linguistics*.)

3. Classify people according to how they drive a car.

4. How may poetry be classified?

5. Women sometimes enjoy classifying men according to the lines they use on dates.

6. Explain how animals and plants are classified by biologists. To whom do we owe this scheme? Compare the scientific classification with the simple division into animals of the land, sea, and air. Both are sound classifications, but the latter is a crude and uninformative attempt to explain a complex matter. A classification is only as good as the amount of enlightenment it brings.

7. How many ways are there to classify colors?
8. Study an illustrated survey of the paintings of Pablo Picasso. Can Picasso's work be divided into periods? What would be the principles of division?
9. Classify the races of the world.
10. Classify jazz into its subtypes and varieties.
11. Obtain copies of the lyrics of all the songs that have made the local "Top Twenty" in the last three months. Can the lyrics be classified into types?

FURTHER READING

Morris R. Cohen and Ernest Nagel, *An Introduction to Logic and Scientific Method.* New York: Harcourt, Brace and Company, 1934. Chapter XII.

John Stuart Mill, *A System of Logic Ratiocinative and Inductive.* This great work was first published in 1843. It is kept in print by Longmans, Green and Company, Ltd. See Book I, Chapter VII; and Book IV, Chapters VII and VIII.

RUSSELL LYNES

Bores

It was not until long after my first encounter with guests as a child that I realized that some guests were boring and some were not. The comings and goings in the rectory were constant, and some of the people who came I liked and other I didn't. Sometimes I was told to "run along," as I have said; sometimes when callers came I was allowed to stay and "sit quietly" or even go on with my games on the floor. What it was that set up hostility in me toward some adults and made me a little social menace or a sullen lump and what warmed me toward others was something I did not understand for a long while. Now I can say that some of those adults were bores and some were not.

Let me explain what I mean. We select our friends because they are not bores; or, to put it another way, because they do not think that we are bores. Some of the adults who invaded the rectory were not in the least interested in me, no matter how polite their protestations to the contrary, and I felt it, even if I didn't know it. Others, however, seemed to share my world in spite of their size. My world did not bore them; so I liked them.

More often than not a bore is merely a convenient label we give to a person whom we do not fascinate, and just as often these bores are socially essential to us. If it weren't for them, we should have nothing against which to measure our sophistication, and we should be compelled to admit that we are bores ourselves.

It is probably this that explains why everyone entertains boring guests at some time or other, and why one constantly encounters them in other people's houses. We don't invite them just out of social duty (though we may tell ourselves that we do); we invite them because they do something for our self-esteem.

It also explains the large (and often un-manageable) party as an institution. At a cocktail party, for instance, the host is the only individual who never gets trapped. It is his duty, recognized by everyone, to move about the room, to bestow his favors everywhere but never long in any one place. Cocktail shaker in hand he fills a glass here, makes a polite inquiry there, says a few words of greeting, gets a forlorn guest attached to a conversational group, and moves on, his social duty being for once to spread himself as thin as possible. If he sees a woman carefully examining the *bibelots* on the table, or thumbing a magazine, or looking at a drawing on the wall with complete absorption, he will know that she is teeming inside with feelings of neglect. No matter what her social gifts, no matter whether she is a bore or not, he can easily manipulate her into conversation with her opposite number, a male who for some unaccountable reason has taken an intense interest in reading the titles on the backs of the record albums. Whether they bore each other once the host has got them face to face is their business. The host moves on to other matters with a sense of accomplishment, with a feeling of satisfied generalship which reminds him of Horace's comment: "A host is like a general: it takes a mishap to reveal his genius."

Unfortunately, however, the cocktail party, which is more blessed to give than to receive, often has to be attended in somebody else's house, and it is there that the whole business takes on quite a different complexion. There you may easily find yourself (having momentarily forgotten the only essential rule of cocktail party behavior: never sit down on a sofa) trapped by a bore from whom nothing short of overt rudeness can save you.

I have studied the bore at a great many parties, dinner parties, literary teas, wedding receptions, and other sociable gatherings, including conventions, testimonial luncheons, and church "socials," and I have found that some can be distinguished by facial types, some by the cut of their clothes, and some by their eagerly roving eyes which are so obviously searching for a quarry. These methods of distinguishing

which people to avoid are, however, too subjective to pass along, and are only partially
reliable even after long practice. The sad
thing about most bores is that they cannot
be distinguished at a distance: it is only
when one is face to face with them (or side
by side with them) in a situation from
which it is next to impossible to withdraw
that one is aware, too late, of their special
alchemy for turning golden moments into
lead.

The common varieties of bores are well
known to everyone. Ambrose Bierce said
that a bore is "a person who talks when you
want him to listen," but as apt as the definition is, the species is a good deal more
complicated than that. There are, for example, many gradations of boredom, such
as the Crashing Bore whose conversation
weighs on you like an actual physical burden
that you want to throw off because it is
stifling you, and quite a different kind, the
Tinkling Bore whose conversation bothers
you in the way that an insistent fly does,
annoying but not dangerous. There are such
types as the Still Waters Run Deep variety
who defy you to say anything that will
change the expression on their faces much
less elicit an encouraging word from them.
There you are on the sofa with them, their
intense eyes peering at you with something
between hopelessness and scorn, impressing
on you the deep reservoir of their self-
sufficiency and challenging you to ruffle the
waters that lurk there. I cite this merely as
an example of the passive as opposed to the
militant type (both the Crashing and the
Tinkling are militant), for it is those who
make you feel like a bore who are the most
boring of all.

But let us get to more specific types that
one is likely to encounter at a strawberry
festival, cocktail party, wedding reception,
or other carnival. You have arrived early . . .
not before the time for which you were
invited, of course, but less than an hour
after the appointed hour, so that the party
is not yet in full swing. There are just a
few people; not yet as many people as there
are chairs, so you have no choice but to sit
down next to or at least near someone.
There is a better than even chance that you

may be rooted for the next half hour, though
as the place fills up you will be able to plant
a lady in your chair and slip away on the
pretext of getting yourself another drink.

For the moment, however, you are
planted; your party smile pulls your lips
back in a pose of amiability, and you are
prepared for whatever line the conversation
may take. You may even be ready to establish a line yourself, once the feeling-out
process has been got through, but the
chances are that the lady, for you are next
to a lady, will, according to custom, take
the initiative. She may, indeed, try to "draw
you out," in which case she has indicated
that she is quite willing to be on the receiving end, and if anyone is going to be bored,
she is prepared to accept the burden.

The risk, of course, is that you may fall
for her pretty bait and embark on a line of
conversation that is more involved or more
serious than is generally considered suitable
to a party, and slowly you become aware
that your voice is beginning to drone. While
the lady's polite smile continues to egg you
on, her eyes look beyond you to the group
that is standing in front of the fireplace at
the far side of the room. You are aware, all
at once, that you are being a bore, and that
you have been put in this position by a
species known as a Good Listener.

It is customary to think of the Good
Listener as a "social asset," and many children are taught by their parents, at an early
age, as I was, how to be a Good Listener.
But a Good Listener's ultimate social contribution is to make bores out of other
people. His bright eyes and inviting smile
mask a profound indifference to what anyone else says, and his basic rule of behavior
is that it pays better to cock an ear than to
cock a snook. In that sense he is a bore
himself, just as much of a bore as that other
social "asset," the Fascinating Conversationalist.

It is difficult to assemble a gaggle of people without including at least one Fascinating Conversationalist. He naturally gravitates
to large parties because he is strictly an audience man and anecdotalist, and he is easy
to distinguish in any gathering. He talks in
a voice filled with the authority of complete

self-possession and with a volume a trifle louder than most of the other guests, as he likes to project himself beyond his immediate circle of listeners and, if possible, to increase it to encompass the entire company. His dress is inclined to exhibit some minor eccentricity which sets him slightly but not outlandishly apart from other people, such as a flower in the lapel, or tremendous moonstone cuff links, or a long cigarette holder, or possibly even a monocle hung around his neck on a black thread. His conversation is entirely anecdotal with innuendoes of a slightly scandalous nature, carefully gauged to exhibit his urbanity and wide acquaintance among well-known personages. He refers to celebrities by their first names, or even better, by their nicknames. Once he has started on a story about his good friend "Willie" Maugham, he will embroider it until it is as encrusted with ornament as a bishop's chasuble and about as suitable to a cocktail party.

The fact that he is often the hostess's delight should not dim one to the fact that he is the bane of other guests. He is not a conversationalist at all but a monologist, and I contend he is one of the more virulent species of party bore.

The cocktail party is not, of course, the only social device for gathering bores together, but it is one of the most common. It is more than likely to be a one-fell-swoop party at which one repays an overdue accumulation of social obligations. And so it is apt to be made up of the people one "ought to do something about," which is another name for the people one doesn't want to have for dinner but should. A dinner has to be planned with some attention to whether the guests are going to like each other or not, or as some unscrupulous hosts plan them, with an eye to whether the guests are such an unlikely mixture that there are bound to be fireworks. The cocktail party, as good a symbol of the informality of modern entertaining as any, is, in a sense, a display of social irresponsibility.[1] A host and hostess usually invite a nucleus of

close friends who can be depended on to keep the liquor flowing and the *canapés* in circulation and perhaps even to rescue the most flagrantly miserable strays who are unable to fend for themselves. Beyond that, it is every man and woman for him- or herself.

It is not that the people one invites to a cocktail party are bores; it is the necessity that each one feels to get the most out of the ordeal somehow that makes them such. Not long ago I found myself mustered into service at a party given by close friends, and I was busily making martinis in a large pitcher at a table in the corner of the dining room. A few people, besides myself, had taken refuge there from the crush in the living room, and one of them, a man I hadn't met before began to tell me a long story about a nursery that was supposed to deliver some lilac bushes to his place in Salisbury, Connecticut, and had planted them by mistake in his neighbor's front yard so that the neighbor, who was very proud of his lawn and didn't like having holes dug in it, had ripped up the bushes in a rage and had planted them across his (the first man's) driveway so that he couldn't get his car in. He would get out a sentence and a half and be frustrated by someone asking me for a drink. Each time he would take up where he left off. Not a detail was sacrificed. I was forced to examine every sap-filled twig of those bushes and every damp handful of dirt from the holes, until finally, many interruptions later, we arrived at the point which was intended to illustrate something I had said casually about bad temper but by that time could no longer remember.

I was, however, reminded of a doctrine of social behavior impressed on me by my mother. If you are interrupted in the course of telling a story, never try to finish it unless you are asked to. It is a difficult rule to practice, and if I don't observe it, I am at least aware of its virtues.

This sort of Total Recall Bore is one of the commonest types, but it takes one of Spartan endurance to perform adequately in the late stages of a cocktail party. By that time other types have taken over—the Hilarious Laugher, the Lapel Hanger, and

---

[1] To T. S. Eliot, who wrote a play about it, it is something much more serious than that, though I am not quite sure what.

other Life of the Party types[2] familiar enough to anyone who stays beyond the moment when those who have plans for dinner have gone about their business, and those who haven't, haven't.

The cocktail party emerged as a social institution at just about the moment when the lavish dinner party with its ten or twelve courses and five or six wines went into eclipse. It was also the moment at which the books of etiquette were giving up the battle for chaperones for all unmarried women up to the age of twenty-five and when social arbiters ceased to be shocked by young ladies applying powder and lipstick in public. Naturally enough, the older generation felt with grave concern that such marked relaxation of the standards of behavior signaled a general decline in public morality. But if their rigid rules of deportment now seem to us to have been oppressive, we must admit that they at least had some formulas for taking care of the bores. As we look back upon such devices as the dance card and the "fifteen-minute formal call," it is apparent that the avoidance of being stuck for long with a bore was a primary concern of social planning. We have no such devices today.

When the buffet supper supplanted the formal dinner, the problem of who talks with whom was transferred from the hostess to the guests. A clever hostess could frequently arrange the seating at her table so that everyone was assured of being next to someone he or she might enjoy. Now both food and partners have become a matter of potluck. At a dinner party the chances are that the person with whom you have been conversing over cocktails will not be next to you when you get to the table. At a buffet it is your duty to get food for the lady you have been talking with, and it is conceivable that you might put in three hours struggling for conversation with someone with whom you have nothing in common but the fact that you are both balancing plates on your knees.

Some types of bores have no opportunity

[2] Especially those types who, when you say, "Oh, don't go," stay.

to show their true colors at a cocktail party; it takes a long evening to give them a chance to perform, and in this respect the dinner, whether buffet or not, is their most congenial medium. There are too many long-evening bores to mention them all, but there are a few typical ones which everyone encounters.

The first of these is the Noncommittal type who when asked his opinion about anything invariably exposes the fact that he hasn't any by insisting that "I always reserve judgment until I know all the facts." Conversation with this type is nearly impossible, which is just as well, and it is a good deal less risky than with his opposite, the Know All the Answers type. He can never let the conversation get beyond the first few sentences without at least figuratively taking you by the lapel and saying, "Now listen to me." He rarely leads the conversation, but wherever it goes, whether it has to do with Asiatic politics or modern painting, or national parks, or the life cycle of the salmon, he is right with it. "Listen, fellow," he will say, "you don't know what you're talking about." When you skewer him with an irrefutable argument or a precisely applied statistic, he wriggles free with, "That's not what my sources tell me." If the going really gets rough for him, he takes to imputing motives. "Why, man, that's Red talk," he'll fling at you, or if that is too farfetched, he'll raise his eyebrows quizzically and ask, "What's your angle? You got money in this?"

The opposite of this type is likely to be a woman of the Poor Stupid Little Me sort who hasn't an opinion about anything. She can mangle any conversational gambit by declaring, "Oh, I wouldn't know anything about *that*." There is a male variation of this type who acts from quite different motives but produces much the same effect. He is the kind who says "I wouldn't know about that" in such a deprecating way as to imply that he is much too busy with the really important matters of life to bother with such frivolities as those which concern you. "I haven't time to read a book or get to a show. Too busy. Haven't read a book in years."

These sorts are all on the defensive, unlike such types as the Travel Bores, who are always just back from somewhere you wish they had stayed, or the Statistical Bores, who regale you with facts and figures about such subjects as the mean temperature of July and the recent variations from it, or the familiar Post-Mortem kind who replay their golf game for you divot by divot. Potentially none of these types are bores. It is only that you make them so by not having traveled where they have, not caring about weather statistics or not playing golf. Their enthusiasm, even though you cannot share it, has a somewhat infectious quality, and you are at least eager to interrupt them so that you can steer their enthusiasm to something that might interest you more.

This is not true of the Bored Bore, whose attempt at sophistication takes the form of letting you know that everything bores him. If you have any enthusiasms of your own which you have been unguarded enough to mention, the Bored Bore will do his best to make you feel naïve about them. He has a sour word to say for the book you had thought was clever, the play you thought entertaining, or the woman you have found enchanting. His own boredom is all-encompassing. He listens to you as though he has heard everything you have to say before and better said; he refuses your offer of a drink with the disdain of a reformed alcoholic, and he looks at your wife as though he has known hundreds of her sort and thought them all tiresome. His kind is often emulated by teen-agers who believe his pose to be one of true sophistication.

It is not unusual to be saddled with this type by a hostess who uses the most enervating of all introductions: "I want you two to meet each other. You have so much in common." This is a cliché that inevitably sows the seeds of mutual suspicion, ruffles the poise of both and tends to dry up the conversational wells. It is second only in obtuseness to another substandard and wholly unsportsmanlike gambit: "I want you to meet Mrs. Green. Mrs. Green always says such witty things." Mrs. Green hates you on sight because she can't think of anything witty to say, and you hate yourself for not

being able to give Mrs. Green a lead that will restore her composure. For putting you in such an awkward spot, you both think that your hostess is not only a bore but a social cripple as well.

This business of pairing guests is sometimes carried to an extreme in which whole parties are built around the concept that if you get two "very interesting" people together they are going to make a fascinating evening for everybody. This is assumed to be particularly true of authors, yet nothing could be further from the truth. Authors are very likely to elbow their way to the center of the floor (since they are always hoping to be lionized) and they are not in the least prone to share it with anyone else. There is nothing essentially wrong with two authors at a party if they can be kept apart, each with his own circle of listeners. But if you get them face to face, you will find that they will spend the evening telling each other about the reviews of their latest books, how many copies they have sold, and the amount of advertising space their respective publishers have bought for them. If their conversation doesn't take this turn, and they both assume a modest pose (not uncommon among really successful writers), they spend their time patting each other gently on the back in one of the coldest kinds of love feasts one is ever likely to witness. There is a third turn that such an encounter may take. Some time ago in Paris several young literary lion-hunters managed to arrange a meeting between James Joyce and Marcel Proust, who had never encountered each other before. The young hunters waited breathlessly to see what these literary giants would say, pencils figuratively poised to record the meeting of these two great minds. Both men were ill; Joyce nearly blind, Proust suffering from acute asthma. They spent the evening talking about their symptoms; literature was never mentioned. A biographer and a novelist may often put on an entertaining show since they are not competitors; two novelists, two poets, two biographers almost never.

Sometimes the pairing of bores, however, has definite advantages. If you can get the Oversympathetic Bore with the Pathos Bore, you have made them both happy. The former is the sort who is so terribly kind and understanding that she (for it is usually a woman) quite literally looks for trouble so that she can be soothing. If you have been ill, the oversympathetic type can quickly make you bored with your own illness—something of a feat. The Pathos Bore, on the other hand, is the type to whom everything dreadful happens and who has always either come straight from the bedside of a sick friend or has been up all night with someone who has lost a "dear one," or has just dragged herself (she only moves by dragging herself) out of bed where she has been suffering "the tortures of the damned" from a headache, backache, or other psychosomatic or traumatic experience. If the Oversympathetic and Pathos types can be maneuvered into a corner with a third type, a threatened evening can sometimes be saved from destruction. This third bore, the Stiff Upper Lip kind, makes the obvious final addition to the triumvirate. This is the sort who makes the gay gesture calculated to expose (not conceal) his unhappy lot. "Oh, it was nothing," he'll say. "The tooth wasn't badly impacted. They only had to take out one good one besides the bad one to stop the pain."

My wife's grandmother insisted that there were five forbidden subjects of conversation, forbidden, that is, on the grounds that they were boring. They were known to her and propounded to her family as the "Five D's" and they reflect not only the language but the social amenities of her time. They were: Domiciles, Domestics, Dress, Diseases, and Descendants.[3] It is a good, rule-of-thumb list, though I believe that there is no topic of conversation that is boring per se. It takes a bore to make it boring, and being a bore is usually the mere calamity of miscalculating one's audience, a thing for which some people have a more marked talent than others.

Miscalculation of this sort makes bores of even the most brilliant men and the most charming women, and it is the very qualities that make them fascinating to some people in some circumstances that make them dull or obtuse to other people in other circumstances. George Bernard Shaw was once voted the greatest bore in England at a time when his countrymen found his acidity out of date and his warnings unnecessary. There is a simple way to explain this. La Rochefoucauld in his *Maxims* said, "We often pardon those who bore us, but never those whom we bore," and presumably the British could not forgive Mr. Shaw for being bored with them.

It is a wise man who knows whom he bores. But by this same token there is no such thing as a boring person, and there is no person who is not a bore. The bore, like beauty, exists only in the eye of the beholder, for the bore, alas, is from within.

[3] A variant of this cliché described the woman whose conversation was "bounded on the north by her servants, on the west by her children, on the south by her ailments, and on the east by her clothes."

QUESTIONS FOR STUDY AND DISCUSSION

1. Early in the essay, Russell Lynes offers a definition of *bore*, as "a convenient label we give to a person whom we do not fascinate." How adequate is this definition? Can you find some of the elements of other definitions in the essay? How adequate are they?

2. What is the principle of classification Lynes employs? Is it satisfactory? Is more than one principle used?

3. How many varieties of bores does Lynes mention? Is each a unique "species," or are there sub-species of certain types?

4. How does this essay differ from a "scientific" classification? In exhaustiveness? In style and tone?

WRITING ASSIGNMENT

Draw up a thoroughgoing classification of "bores" or some other type of individual who is distinguished by a pleasant or objectionable trait. Then write an essay explaining the classification.

SIR FRANCIS BACON

Of Simulation and Dissimulation

Dissimulation is but a faint kind of policy or wisdom; for it asketh a strong wit and a strong heart to know when to tell truth, and to do it. Therefore it is the weaker sort of politics that are the great dissemblers.

Tacitus saith, *Livia sorted well with the arts of her husband and dissimulation of her son;* attributing arts or policy to Augustus, and dissimulation to Tiberius. And again, when Mucianus encourageth Vespasian to take arms against Vitellius, he saith, W*e rise not against the piercing judgment of Augustus, nor the extreme caution or closeness of Tiberius.* These properties, of arts or policy and dissimulation or closeness, are indeed habits and faculties several, and to be distinguished. For if a man have that penetration of judgment as he can discern what things are to be laid open, and what to be secreted, and what to be shewed at half lights, and to whom and when, (which indeed are arts of state and arts of life, as Tacitus well calleth them,) to him a habit of dissimulation is a hinderance and a poorness. But if a man cannot obtain to that judgment, then it is left to him generally to be close, and a dissembler. For where a man cannot choose or vary in particulars, there it is good to take the safest and wariest way in general; like the going softly, by one that cannot well see. Certainly the ablest men that ever were have had all an openness and frankness of dealing; and a name of certainty and veracity; but then they were like horses well managed; for they could tell passing well when to stop or turn; and at such times when they thought the case indeed required dissimulation, if then they used it, it came to pass that the former opinion spread abroad of their good faith and clearness of dealing made them almost invisible.

There be three degrees of this hiding and veiling of a man's self. The first, Closeness, Reservation, and Secrecy; when a man leaveth himself without observation, or without hold to be taken, what he is. The second, Dissimulation, in the negative; when a man lets fall signs and arguments, that he is not that he is. And the third, Simulation, in the affirmative; when a man industriously and expressly feigns and pretends to be that he is not.

For the first of these, Secrecy; it is indeed the virtue of a confessor. And assuredly the secret man heareth many confessions. For who will open himself to a blab or babbler? But if a man be thought secret, it inviteth discovery; as the more close air sucketh in the more open; and as in confession the revealing is not for worldly use, but for the ease of a man's heart, so secret men come to the knowledge of many things in that kind; while men rather discharge their minds than impart their minds. In few words, mysteries are due to secrecy. Besides (to say truth) nakedness is uncomely, as well in mind as body; and it addeth no small reverence to men's manners and actions, if they be not altogether open. As for talkers and futile persons, they are commonly vain and credulous withal. For he that talketh what he knoweth, will also talk what he knoweth not. Therefore set it down, *that an habit of secrecy is both politic and moral.* And in this part, it is good that a man's face give his tongue leave to speak. For the discovery of a man's self by the tracts of his countenance is a great weakness and betraying; by how much it is many times more marked and believed than a man's words.

For the second, which is Dissimulation; it followeth many times upon secrecy by a necessity; so that he that will be secret must be a dissembler in some degree. For men are too cunning to suffer a man to keep an indifferent carriage between both, and to be secret, without swaying the balance on either side. They will so beset a man with questions, and draw him on, and pick it out of him, that, without an absurd silence, he must shew an inclination one way; or if he do not, they will gather as much by his silence as by his speech. As for equivocations, or oraculous speeches, they cannot hold out long. So that no man can be secret, except

he give himself a little scope of dissimulation; which is, as it were, but the skirts or
train of secrecy.

But for the third degree, which is Simulation and false profession; that I hold more
culpable, and less politic; except it be in
great and rare matters. And therefore a general custom of simulation (which is this last
degree) is a vice, rising either of a natural
falseness or fearfulness, or of a mind that
hath some main faults, which because a man
must needs disguise, it maketh him practise
simulation in other things, lest his hand
should be out of ure.

The great advantages of simulation and
dissimulation are three. First, to lay asleep
opposition, and to surprise. For where a
man's intentions are published, it is an
alarum to call up all that are against them.
The second is, to reserve to a man's self a
fair retreat. For if a man engage himself by a
manifest declaration, he must go through or
take a fall. The third is, the better to discover
the mind of another. For to him that opens

himself men will hardly shew themselves
adverse; but will fair let him go on, and
turn their freedom of speech to freedom of
thought. And therefore it is a good shrewd
proverb of the Spaniard, *Tell a lie and find
a troth.* As if there were no way of discovery but by simulation. There be also three
disadvantages, to set it even. The first, that
simulation and dissimulation commonly
carry with them a shew of fearfulness, which
in any business doth spoil the feathers of
round flying up to the mark. The second,
that it puzzleth and perplexeth the conceits
of many, that perhaps would otherwise co-
operate with him; and makes a man walk
almost alone to his own ends. The third and
greatest, is, that it depriveth a man of one
of the most principal instruments for action;
which is trust and belief. The best composition and temperature is to have openness
in fame and opinion; secrecy in habit; dissimulation in seasonable use; and a power
to feign, if there be no remedy.

QUESTIONS FOR STUDY AND DISCUSSION

1. From what property, habit, or faculty
does Bacon, in his first two paragraphs,
separate "dissimulation or closeness"? Why
is this first step necessary?

2. Into what categories does Bacon classify
"dissimulation or closeness"? What are the
attributes of each?

3. Is there any confusion in terminology?
Is the word *dissimulation* used at more than

one level? How can you clear up any possible confusion?

4. What is Bacon's judgment about each
category?

5. What does Bacon conclude about a
man's use of each?

6. To what extent does Bacon subscribe
to the view that "honesty is the best
policy"?

WRITING ASSIGNMENT

Taking the point of view of a "practical man," write an essay in which you (1)
classify the varieties of one of the activities
or habits of mind listed below, and (2) explain when and where each may be expedi-

ently employed (if at all):

a. Lying	e. Purity
b. Cheating	f. Might
c. Stealing	g. Anger
d. Piety	h. Greed

Definition

The study of classification inevitably touches upon the identity of the classes being talked about and thus foreshadows a discussion of definition. In classification we use a limited number of principles to distinguish between classes. In definition we are interested in showing as closely as we can the nature of the classes themselves.

It may be illuminating to start by going to the tenth edition of Dr. Johnson's *Dictionary*, a stripped-down version of the great two-volume work—what we would call a collegiate dictionary today. In this edition of 1794, Johnson defines *dog* as a "domestic [*sic*] animal remarkably various in his species," which hardly identifies the dog with any certainty. How, using this definition, can we exclude cats (except by consulting Dr. Johnson again and learning that the cat is a "domestick [*sic*] animal that catches mice")? The double-folio edition of 1755, as the student will see from the definitions which follow this introduction, contains a more adequate statement. Here the dog is successfully identified by listing some of its breeds. Johnson's definition of *cat* is better still, for it ranks the "domestick animal that catches mice" in the "lowest order of the leonine species."

Thanks to the labors of such men as Samuel Johnson, dictionary making has come a long way, and the definitions provided by modern desk dictionaries like the *American College Dictionary*, *Webster's Collegiate Dictionary*, *Webster's New World Dictionary of the American Language*, the big *Webster's Third New International Dictionary*, and the greatest among the great, the *New English Dictionary* (called the *Oxford*), contain enough information to enable even the uninformed to identify the dog successfully. But, as the student will notice, the dictionaries rely upon a biological classification of the dog as a means of placing him in his proper niche among the animals; only the *American College Dictionary* and *Webster's New World Dictionary* manage to relate the dog without too much esoteric lingo to the class which includes the fox, wolf, and jackal. The scientific classification certainly ought to be brought in for sheer technical accuracy, but it is too remote from the experience of most of us to be meaningful. If someone honestly needs to look up a word like *dog*, it is not likely that he will be any better informed about zoology. This objection becomes a major one when we consider how the dictionaries handle definitions of other plants and animal names. From time to time we *do* need to find out what *yucca, Spanish bayonet, turkey buzzards,* and *mockingbirds* are, and a good definition must help by establishing whenever it can a class of familiar animals or plants of which the yucca (or any of the rest) is a member.

The definition, in other words, must start by considering the word being defined as a species of some larger genus and then give the differentiae, the traits that distinguish the species from this larger class. It is not enough to describe a dog and call that a definition. The dog remains undefined until we manage to relate it to its genus and explain how it differs from every other species within that genus. A full definition of *dog* would then go on to consider *dog* as genus and discuss its many species, as the dictionary definitions do.

A definition, according to Aristotle, tells us "a thing's essence." It is thus analogous to an axiom in mathematics or logic, and just as theorems can be inferred from an axiom, certain properties often follow from the "essence" of a definition. To use Aristotle's illustration, "if A be a man, then he is capable of learning grammar." We know better, but the example does not refute the theory. The President of our nation might be defined as the chief executive of the American Republic. The term being defined, *President,* becomes our species, and we place it in the genus of chief executives; obviously enough, the trait differentiating the President from the chief executives of other nations is that only he is chief executive of the United States. But the President is also Commander-in-Chief of our armed forces, and this duty may be considered a property that follows from the essence of the Presidency. In this case the property is convertible: that is, if anyone is President, he is Commander-in-Chief; if anyone is Commander-in-Chief, he is also President. But to define the President as Commander-in-Chief is to miss the central idea; the two are not exact equivalents; it is like defining *cat* as an "animal that catches mice."

A theory of definition is not complete unless it calls attention to accidents, which are just that—qualities of individuality which must be noted but which do not follow as the theorem follows from the axiom. It is thus an accident that all the Presidents of the United States have been men.

In writing we use at least three kinds of definitions. There is the real definition, which tries to establish a thing's true nature or essence, to show where it belongs in the scheme of things. There is the nominal definition, which is simply an agreement as to the sense with which we are using a certain word. There is the definition by example, which we use to identify the things that we cannot fully explain. And there is the extended definition, used to inform, clarify, and explain anything from an object to an idea. An extended definition may deal with a thing's origin or cause, its use or purpose, its composition or construction, its types or kinds, and it may describe the thing it defines. But it will always tell what it is most like and how it differs from that thing.

A few guideposts can be set up to direct the student in framing his definitions. First, a definition is successful only if it states the true essence of the thing being defined; the definition must list attributes so precisely that the word under definition is clearly marked off from all other species within its genus. The definition of *dog* in the 1794 version of Dr. Johnson's *Dictionary* fails pretty badly on this count since it does not permit us to distinguish between dogs and members of completely unrelated genera, such as cats. Just as a definition must never be too broad, it must also avoid becoming too narrow. If *inoculation* is defined as a means of preventing tetanus, the rule has again been violated.

A definition must not be circular; that is, it must not be couched in derivatives of the word being defined. If in an essay we define *linguist* as a "person versed in linguistics," we are being circular. Dictionaries do this sometimes for compactness, but they always go on, if they make any pretense to being a respectable reference tool, to give a true definition of *linguistics*.

A definition is not considered good if it relies upon figurative, obscure, or fanciful language. Thus "Religion is the opiate of the people" fails as definition. And Dr. Johnson's famous explanation of *network* as "any thing reticulated or decussated, at equal distances, with interstices between the intersections" or his treatment of *cough* as "a convulsion of the lungs, vellicated by some sharp serosity" are less than successful (which is the case with most definitions of plants and animals in dictionaries today; we have not come that far since 1755).

As a corollary to this rule, we must avoid needless subjectivity and editorializing when writing definitions. Dr. Johnson's explanation of *doggerel* as "mean, despicable, worthless verses" is thus open to question. Eliminating subjectivity does not mean that the student cannot praise or blame, that he cannot judge an institution as good or bad. But opinion and argument must follow the definition itself, which tries to be a neutral and analytic process.

Last, a definition should not be phrased in negative terms when this can be avoided or unless negation is part of the essence of the word being defined. Dr. Johnson's definition of *peace* as "Respite from war" is questionable, while *maid* ("An unmarried woman") is not.

EXERCISE

Define in one sentence of twenty-five words or less: book, paper, life (that is, living things), democracy, liberty, house, influenza, duty, poetry, chair. After you have written your definitions compare them with the definitions given by the five dictionaries mentioned in this introduction, the great *Century Dictionary*, and any others that you find in your library.

ESSAY SUGGESTIONS

1. Write a paper explaining the nature of hi-fi equipment. What makes it hi-fi?
2. Write an essay explaining the nature and techniques of skin diving, technical climbing, spelunking, or some other outdoor activity.
3. Define and explain a major political system. Cite your sources of information.
4. Read a good anthology of English and American verse and then define poetry, drawing upon the anthology for your examples and illustrations.
5. Define chess, or any other game or sport. What is its object? How is it played? What are its tactics in offense or defense? Describe its history.
6. Explain the nature of any fad or movement—for instance, that of the beatniks. What is a beatnik? What does he believe in? What does he want?
7. Explain the nature of any popular form of mass entertainment, for example the soap opera on radio or TV, the Western, the detective story, or the science fiction story. Be sure to develop your essay out of specific shows that you have seen or stories and books that you have read.

8. Write an essay on a major disease. What are its symptoms? What are its types or kinds? What are its causes? How is it treated?
9. What is liberal education? What does it consist of? How is it acquired?
10. Explain the nature and types of humor. What kinds of things make us laugh? Why?

FURTHER READING

Since modern ideas about definition derive from Aristotle, the student should consult the Topica, Book I. A convenient anthology of Aristotle's *Works* has been edited by Richard McKeon. New York: Random House, Inc., 1941.

Morris R. Cohen and Ernest Nagel, *An Introduction to Logic and Scientific Method*, Chapter XII.

John Stuart Mill, *A System of Logic*, Book I, Chapter VIII.

W. H. Werkmeister, *An Introduction to Critical Thinking*. Lincoln: Johnsen Publishing Company, 1948. Chapter VI.

Five Definitions of Dog

From *Dictionary of the English Language*, Samuel Johnson:

DOG. *n. s.* [*dogghe*, Dutch.]

1. A domestick animal remarkably various in his species; comprising the mastiff, the spaniel, the buldog, the greyhound, the hound, the terrier, the cur, with many others. The larger sort are used as a guard; the less for sports.

> Such smiling rogues as these sooth every passion:
> Renege, affirm, and turn their halcyon beaks
> With ev'ry gale and vary of their masters,
> As knowing nought, like *dogs*, but following.   *Shakesp.*

> Why should we not think a watch and pistol as distinct species one from another, as a horse and a *dog*.   *Locke.*

> The clamour roars of men and boys, and *dogs*,
> Ere the soft fearful people, to the flood
> Commit their woolly sides.   *Thomson.*

2. A constellation called Sirius, or Canicula, rising and setting with the sun during the canicular days, or dog days.

> Among the southern constellations two there are who bear the name of the *dog*; the one in sixteen degrees latitude, containing on the left thigh a star of the first magnitude, usually called Procyon, or Anticanus.   *Brown's Vulgar Errours.*

> It parts the twins and crab, the *dog* divides,
> And Argo's keel that broke the frothy tides.   *Creech.*

A reproachful name for a man.

> I never heard a passion so confus'd,
> So strange, outrageous, and so variable,
> As the *dog* Jew did utter in the streets.   *Shakespeare.*

> Beware of *dogs*, beware of evil workers.   *Phil.* iii. 2.

4. *To give or send to the* DOGS; to throw away. *To go to the* DOGS; to be ruined, destroyed, or devoured.

> Had whole Colepeper's wealth been hops and hogs,
> Could he himself have sent it to the *dogs?*   *Pope.*

5. It is used as the term for the male of several species; as, the *dog* fox, the *dog* otter.

> If ever I thank any man, I'll thank you; but that they call compliments is like the encounter of two *dog* apes.   *Shakesp.*

6. *Dog* is a particle added to any thing to mark meanness, or degeneracy, or worthlesness; as, *dog* rose.

To DOG. *v. a.* [from the noun.] To hunt as a dog, insidiously and indefatigably.

> I have *dogg'd* him like his murtherer.   *Shakespeare.*

> His taken labours bid him me forgive;
> I, his despiteful Juno, sent him forth
> From courtly friends, with camping foes to live,
> Where death and danger *dog* the heels of worth.   *Shakesp.*

> Sorrow *dogging* sin,
> Afflictions sorted.   *Herbert.*

> These spiritual joys are *dogged* by no such sad sequels as are the products of those titillations, that reach no higher than fancy and the senses.   *Glanville.*

> I have been pursued, *dogged*, and way-laid through several nations, and even now scarce think myself secure.   *Pope.*

> Hate *dogs* their rise, and insult mocks their fall.
>   *Vanity of Human Wishes.*

From *The Oxford English Dictionary*:

Dog (dǫg), *sb.* Forms: 1 **docga**, 3–7 **dogge**, (3, 6 **doggue**, 6 *Sc.* **doig**), 6–8 **dogg**, 3– **dog**. [late OE. *docga* (once in a gloss); previous history and origin unknown. (The generic name in OE., as in the Teutonic langs. generally, was *hund*: see HOUND.) So far as the evidence goes, the word appears first in English, as the name of a powerful breed or race of dogs, with which the name was introduced into the continental languages, usually, in early instances, with the attribute 'English'. Thus mod. Du. *dog*, late 16th c. *dogge* ('een dogghe, vn gros matin d'Engleterre, *canis anglicus*', Plantijn *Thesaur.* 1573), Ger. *dogge*, in 16–17th c. *dock, docke, dogg* ('englische Dock', *Onomast.* 1582, 'eine englische Docke', 1653), LG. *dogge*, Da. *dogge*, Sw. *dogg*; F. *dogue* ('le genereux dogue anglais', Du Bellay 15..), It., Sp., Pg. *dogo*, Pg. also *dogue*; in all the languages applied to some variety or race of dog.]

I. The simple word.

1. A quadruped of the genus *Canis*, of which wild species or forms are found in various parts of the world, and numerous races or breeds, varying greatly in size, shape, and colour, occur in a domesticated or semi-domesticated state in almost all countries. These are referred by zoologists to a species *C. familiaris*; but whether they have a common origin is a disputed question.

c **1050** *Prudentius Glosses* (Recd. 148/1) [Gloss to] *canum* [gen. pl.] docgena. *a* **1225** *Ancr. R.* 288 His [the devil's] teð beoð attrie, ase of ane wode dogge. *Ibid.* 290 Þet tes dogge of helle kumeð. *c* **1290** *S. Eng. Leg.* I. 307/281 A teie doggue. *a* **1300** *Cursor M.* 13658 (Cott. & G.) Þai scott him als a dog Right vte o þair synagog. **1393** LANGL. *P. Pl.* C. x. 261 Thi dogge dar nat berke. **1460** CAPGRAVE *Chron.* (1858) 281 Thei seide pleynly that it was no more trost to the Pope writing than to a dogge tail. **1568** TILNEY *Disc. Mariage* D viij b, Dogs barke boldely at their owne maisters doore. **1586** B. YOUNG *Guazzo's Civ. Conv.* IV. 179 Like the Sheepheards good Dog. **1601** SHAKS. *Twel. N.* II. iii. 154 If I thought that, Ide beate him like a dogge. **1686** HORNECK *Crucif. Jesus* xxii. 682 The dog teaches thee fidelity. **1732** POPE *Ess. Man* I. 112 His faithful dog shall bear him company. **1869** W. P. MACKAY *Grace & Truth* viii, The dog in the East is not as here domesticated, but .. outside the cities, is more like a wolf prowling for prey.

† b. Used *spec.* as the name of some particular variety; see quots. *Obs.*

1398 TREVISA *Barth. De P. R.* XVIII. xxvi. (1495) 786 A gentyll hounde..hath lesse flesshe than a dogge and shorter heere and more thynne. *c* **1440** *Promp. Parv.* 125/1 Dogge, shyppe-herdys hownde, *gregarius*. **1530** PALSGR. 214/2 Dogge, a mischevous curre, *dogue*.

c. *esp.* A dog used for hunting; a hound.

a **1307** *Pol. Songs* (Camden) 239 A doseyn of doggen Ne myhte hyre drawe. **1398** TREVISA *Barth. De P. R.* XVIII. ciii. (1495) 847 Brockes..ben huntyd and chassyd wyth hunters dogges. *? c* **1475** *Hunt. Hare* 26 Ychon of hus hase a dogge or too; For grehowndes have thou no care. **1649** BP. REYNOLDS *Hosea* iii. 38 The Dogge in hunting of the Deere. **1748** N. SALMON *Comp. Univ.* 14 Some gentlemen of the Town always keep a Pack of Dogs.

d. *fig.*; *esp.* in Shaksperian phr. *the dogs of war.*

a **1225** [see 1]. **1601** SHAKS. *Jul. C.* III. i. 273 Caesars Spirit ranging for Reuenge, With Ate by his side..Shall in these Confines..Cry hauocke, and let slip the Dogges of Warre. **1667** MILTON *P. L.* X. 616 See with what heat these Dogs of Hell advance. **1842** S. LOVER *Handy Andy* ii, Let loose the dogs of law on him. **1860** TROLLOPE *Framley P.* xliii, The dogs of war would be unloosed.

e. With qualifications denoting variety or use, as BANDOG, BULL-DOG, CUR-DOG, etc., q.v. in their alphabetical places or under the first element. Also *buck-, cattle-, field-, parlour-, shore-, toy-dog.*

a **1225** Kur-dogge [see CUR 1 c.]. **1633** T. JAMES *Voy.* 93 Bucke Dogs, of a very good race. **1672** JOSSELYN *New Eng. Rarities* 15 The Indian Dog is a Creature begotten 'twixt a Wolf and a Fox. **1813** COL. HAWKER *Diary* (1893) I. 89 My Newfoundland dog..had decamped. **1870** B. CLAYTON *Dog-Keeper's Guide* 6 Field dogs are used for field purposes only. **1889** ST. J. TYRWHITT in *Univ. Rev.* 15 Feb. 253 Society kept him..painting toy dogs. **1893** EDITH CARRINGTON *Dog* vi. 52 Very famous cattle dogs.

2. In distinguishing sex, the male of this species; a male hound; opp. to BITCH. Also, a male fox, DOG-FOX.

1577 B. GOOGE *Heresbach's Husb.* III. (1586) 154 b, The Dogge is thought better than the Bitche. **1768** G. WASHINGTON *Writ.* (1889) II. 248 Four puppys, that is 3 dogs and a bitch. **1882** *Society* 21 Oct. 19/2 If this is your fox, Jack, he s an unmistakable old dog. **1890** *Sat. Rev.* 1 Feb. 134/2 The man who knows and loves his hound only uses the word dog, as he does the word bitch, to denote sex.

3. Applied to a person; **a.** in reproach, abuse, or contempt: A worthless, despicable, surly, or cowardly fellow. (Cf. CUB 1 b.)

c **1325** *Coer de L.* 4518 Jhon Doyly..slowgh hym..And sayde: 'Dogge, ther thou ly!' **1382** WYCLIF 2 *Sam.* xvi. 9. *c* **1440** *York Myst.* xix. 106 A! dogges, þe deuell ȝou spede. **1591** SHAKS. 1 *Hen. VI*, I. ii. 23. **1596** — *Merch. V.* I. iii. 129 You spurn'd me such a day; another time You cald me dog. **1653** H. COGAN tr. *Pinto's Trav.* xx. 72 Such feeble slaves, as these Christian Dogs. **1712** ADDISON *Spect.* No. 530 ₱ 4 Had not my dog of a steward run away as he did, without making up his accounts. **1820** SCOTT *Ivanhoe* vii, Dog of an unbeliever..darest thou press upon a Christian? **1880** TENNYSON *Revenge* ii, If I left them..To these Inquisition dogs and the devildoms of Spain.

b. playfully (usually in humorous reproof, congratulation, or commiseration): A gay or jovial man, a gallant; a fellow, 'chap'. Usually with *adj.* such as *cunning, jolly, lucky, sad, sly*, etc. *To be dog at*: see *to be old dog at*, 15 i.

a **1618** Q. ANNE *Let. to Buckingham* in Ellis *Orig. Lett.* Ser. I. III. 101 My kind Dog..You doe verie well in lugging the Sowes eare [Jas. 1], and I .. would have yow doe so still upon condition that yow continue a watchfull dog to him. **1711** BUDGELL *Spect.* No. 67 ₱ 9 An impudent young Dog bid the Fiddlers play a Dance called Mol. Patley. **1719** DE FOE *Crusoe* I. vi, I was an unfortunate dog. **1814** J. HUNT *Feast Poets* 14 Poems (1832) 144 The dog had no industry. **1884** W. E. NORRIS *Thirlby Hall* ix, A sad dog.

c. = BULL-DOG 2.

1847 TENNYSON *Princ.* Prol. 113 He had climb'd across the spikes..he had breath'd the Proctor's dogs.

4. *Astron.* **a.** The name of two constellations, the Great and Little Dog (*Canis Major* and *Minor*) situated near Orion; also applied to their principal stars Sirius and Procyon: see DOG-STAR. **b.** *The Hunting Dogs*, a northern constellation (*Canes Venatici*) near the Great Bear.

1551 RECORDE *Cast. Knowl.* (1556) 268 Northe almost from this Dogge is there a constellation of 2 only starres named Canicula, the lesser Dogge. **1577** B. GOOGE *Heresbach's Husb.* I. (1586) 210 b, The greate heate of the Sunne ..is most extreame at the rysyng of the lesser Dogge. **1611** BEAUM. & FL. *Maid's Trag.* IV. i, The burnt air, when the Dog reigns. **1718** ROWE tr. *Lucan* 428 'Till the hot Dog inflames the Summer Skies. **1890** C. A. YOUNG *Uranogr.* § 41 Canes Venatici (The Hunting Dogs). These are the dogs with which Bootes is pursuing the Great Bear.

5. Applied, usually with distinctive prefix, to various animals allied to, or in some respect resembling, the dog:

e. g. **Burrowing dog**, the COYOTE or prairie-wolf, *Canis latrans*; **hunting-dog**, a kind of hyena (see HUNTING-DOG); **pouched dog**, a dasyurine marsupial of Tasmania, *Thylacinus cynocephalus*, also called *zebra-wolf*; **prairie-dog** (also *colloq.* called simply *dog* in Western U. S.), a North American rodent (see PRAIRIE-DOG).

6. Short for DOGFISH.

1674 RAY *Words..(Sea) Fishes* 98 Picked Dogs, *Catulus spinax*. **1848** C. A. JOHNS *Week at Lizard* 241, I..fished in five or six different spots..there were 'dogs', as they are called, everywhere..but nothing else. **1860** WOOD *Reptiles, Fishes, Insects* 71 The destructive..fish..known by the names of..Penny Dog, or Miller's Dog. **1861** COUCH *Brit. Fishes* I. 49 The Picked Dog is the smallest but far the most abundant of the British Sharks.

7. A name given to various mechanical devices, usually having or consisting of a tooth or claw, used for gripping or holding. Among these are :
a. A clamp for supporting something (*e. g.* part of a building), or fastening or holding it in place. † **b.** An instrument for extracting teeth (*obs.*). **c.** An implement for drawing poles out of the ground (see also HOP-DOG), or for extracting roots of broom, furze, etc. (cf. DOG *v.* 6 b, and see *broom-dog*, BROOM *sb.* 6). **d.** A grappling-iron for raising the monkey of a pile-driver, or clutching and withdrawing tools used in well-boring or mining. **e.** A grappling-iron with a fang which clutches an object, as a log, barrel, etc. to be hoisted, or a log to be secured in position for sawing. **f.** *pl.* Nippers used in wire-drawing. **g.** At the Mint, a device consisting of two levers mounted on a small carriage running on wheels along the draw-bench, and so arranged as to constitute a pair of pincers which seize the fillet and draw it through the opening at the head of the draw-bench. One of 'the converging set screws which establish the bed-tool of a punching-press in direct coincidence with the punch' (Knight *Dict. Mech.*). **i.** A projection or tooth acting as a detent, *e. g.* in a lock ; a catch or click which engages the teeth of a ratchet-wheel. **j.** In a fire-arm = DOG-HEAD 2 b [cf. F. *chien*, snaphaunce (Cotgr.) ; so It. *cane* (Florio), Sp. *can* (Minsheu)]. **k.** A drag for the wheel of a vehicle. **l.** ' A clamp fastened to a piece suspended on the centres of a lathe, by which the rotation of the chuck or face-plate is imparted to the piece to be turned' (= CARRIER 1 d). **m.** An adjustable stop placed in a machine to change direction of motion. (Webster 1864.) **n.** *Ship-building* = DOG-SHORE. (Smyth *Sailor's Word-bk.*) **o.** 'A lever used by blacksmiths in hooping cart-wheels' (Jamieson 1825). **p.** A kind of spike used on railways for fastening flat-bottomed or bridge rails to the sleepers : = DOG-NAIL. **q.** An appliance for toasting bread, etc. : cf. CAT *sb.*[1] 9, and see Brockett *N. C. Gloss.*

a. **1458** *Churchw. Acc. St. Andrews, East Cheap* in *Brit. Mag.* XXXI. 249 To Barnard the Smyth for x doggs of Iryn for the Steple weying lxx lb. **1552** HULOET, Dogge of yron to claspe a house from fletyng, *retinaculum, trabalis clauus uel hamus.* **1649** BLITHE *Eng. Improv. Impr.*(1653) 212 As a Buttress to support it, and may be as serviceable as an Iron dog as many use. **1892** *Law Times Rep.* LXV. 582/1 The posts of the gantry stand on planks, and are fixed thereto by iron dogs and dowels.
b. **1611** COTGR., *Pelican*..a Snap, or Dog, the toole wherewith Barbers pull out teeth.
c. **1727** BRADLEY *Fam. Dict. s.v.*, An instrument called a Dog for the more easy drawing the Poles out of the ground. **1893** C. A. MOLLYSON *Parish of Fordoun* xxv. 290 The dog, we presume, is still extant .. We will quote .. a description of the broom-dog..'It operates somewhat like a toothdrawer and eradicates the broom in an instant.'
d. **1747** HOOSON *Miner's Dict. s. v. Boring*, For drawing up the Rods, we have..an Iron Instrument called a Bitch, and, for unscrewing them, two more we call Dogs.
e. **1740** DYCHE & PARDON, *Dog* .. also an utensil for coopers to carry large casks between two persons. **1750** BLANCKLEY *Nav. Expos.* 51 *Timber Doggs*, Are drove into Timber for Horses to draw it about the Yard, or to the Sawpits. **1825** JAMIESON, *Dogs*, pieces of iron, having a zig-zag form, for fixing a tree in the saw-pit. **1840** R. H. DANA *Bef. Mast* xxix. 99 One [block] hooked to the strap on the end of the steeve, and the other into a dog, fastened into one of the beams.
g. **1859** *All Year Round* No. 10. 239 This dog is a small thin carriage, travelling upon wheels over a bench, under which revolves an endless chain. **1875** *Ure's Dict. Arts* III. 342 The chain..in its onward motion drags the dog, and causes it to bite the fillet and draw it through the opening.
i. **1853** C. TOMLINSON in *Ure's Dict. Arts* III. 142 There is a dog or lever..which catches into the top of the bolt, and thereby serves as an additional security against its being forced back. **1857** COLQUHOUN *Comp. Oarsman's Guide* 32 The dog, or catch, prevents its running down.
j. *c*1660 *Monckton Papers* (1884) 36, I immediately.. clapt hold of the dog of the blunderbus. *a*1684 LAW *Mem.* (1818) 225 (Jam.) He lets fall the dog, the pistoll goes off. **1846** *Archæologia* XXXI. 492 (D.) A contrivance..for producing fire by the friction of the grooved edges of a steel wheel..against a piece of iron pyrites .. held in a cock or dog which pressed upon it.
k. **1795** *Trans. Soc. Arts* XIII. 255 This simple and useful contrivance, called here a Dog, or Wheel-Drag.
l. **1833** J. HOLLAND *Manuf. Metal* II. 134 A contrivance called the dog and driver, the former being a sort of clutch screwed upon the end of the work. **1884** F. J. BRITTEN *Watch. & Clockm.* 168 A lathe furnished with dogs.
o. **1735** *Crt. Bk. Barony Urie* (1892) 156 He saw the defenders throw a dogg at each other.

p. **1883** *Proc. Philol. Soc.* 21 Dec., *Dog* (spike used on railways), from form of head which resembles a dog's. **1892** *Labour Commission* Gloss., *Dogs*, a class of nails used for fastening down rails on sleepers. Each nail consists of a long spike, with ears on the side of the head, by means of which the nail may be wrenched up and re-used.

8. One of a pair of iron or brass utensils placed one on each side of a fireplace to support burning wood; = ANDIRON ; (more fully called *fire-dogs.*); **b.** a similar support for a dog grate or stove ; **c.** a rest for the fire-irons.

1596 *Unton Invent.* 5 One paire of dogges in the Chymly. *a* **1661** FULLER *Worthies* ix. (R.), The iron doggs bear the burthen of the fuel, while the brazen-andirons stand only for state. **1663** PEPYS *Diary* 7 Sept., Buying several things at the ironmonger's—dogs, tongs, and shovels. **1762** FRANKLIN *Remarks* Wks. 1887 III. 184 The iron dogs, loggerhead, and iron pot were not hurt. **1862** H. AÏDÉ *Carr of Carrlyon* I. 140 The wood fire .. burnt cheerfully on great brass dogs upon the hearthstone. *Mod. Ironfounders' Catal.*, Dog stoves .. fine polished brass dogs .. fire basket sloping forward at the top. *Ibid.*, Fire Dogs.. All Brass.

† 9. An early kind of fire-arm. *Obs.*
1549 *Compl. Scot.* vi. 41 Mak reddy 3our cannons..bersis, doggis, doubil bersis, hagbutis of croche. **1650** *Art. Reddition Edin. Castle*, 28 short brasse munkeys alias dogs.

10. Name given to various atmospheric appearances. **a.** A luminous appearance near the horizon; also *fog-dog, sea-dog.* **b.** *Sun-dog*, a luminous appearance near the sun, a parhelion. **c.** *Water-dog*, a small dark floating cloud, indicating rain.

1825–80 JAMIESON, *Dog, Sea-dog*, a name given by mariners to a meteor seen, immediately above the horizon, generally before sunrise, or after sunset..viewed as a certain prognostic of the approach of bad weather..If this be seen before sunrise, it is believed that (as they express themselves) it will bark before night ; if after sunset, that it will bark before morning..The *dog* has no variety of colours, but is of a dusky white. **1847–78** HALLIWELL, *Water-dogs*, see *Mares'-Tails*. **1867** SMYTH *Sailor's Word-bk.*, *Stubb*, or *Dogg*, the lower part of a rainbow visible towards the horizon, and betokening squally weather..On the banks of Newfoundland they are considered precursors of clearer weather, and termed *fog-dogs*. **1869** *Lonsdale Gloss.*, *Dog*, a partial rainbow. 'A dog at night is the farmer's delight.' **1876** *Surrey Provincialisms* (E. D. S.), *Water-dogs*, dark clouds that seem to travel through the air by themselves, and indicate a storm. **1892** W..PIKE *Barren Ground N. Canada* 97 Often a sun-dog is the first thing to appear, and more or less of these attendants accompany the sun during his short stay above the horizon.

11. Name given to a copper coin used in some islands in the West Indies ; also to ' a small silver coin' (Smyth) ; see also BLACK DOG 1.

1797 W. BULLOCK in *Naval Chron.* X. 128 Negro money called stampees, or black dogs. **1811** KELLY *Univ. Cambist* (1835) I. 362 There are here [Leeward Islands] small copper coins, called Stampes, Dogs, and Half Dogs. **1888** *Star* 18 Feb. 1/4 Fees .. are paid in old Spanish dollars .. and in 'dogs' or French coppers struck in the reign of Louis XVI. for Cayenne.

12. Short for DOG-WATCH.
1893 PEMBERTON *Iron Pirate* 151 Towards the second bell in the second ' dog' there was a change.

† 13. = *Dog-chance, dog-throw* at dice : see 18.
1671 H. M. tr. *Erasm. Colloq.* 441 That the throw *Cous* was a lucky one, and the *dog* was unfortunate.

II. Phrases and Proverbs.

14. *To the dogs* : to destruction or ruin ; as in *to go, send, throw to the dogs. So not to have a word to throw at a dog.*

1565–73 COOPER *Thesaurus, Addicere aliquem canibus*, to bequeath hym to dogs. **1600** SHAKS. *A. Y. L.* i. iii. 3 *Cel.* Why Cosen, why Rosaline : Cupid haue mercie, Not a word? *Ros.* Not one to throw at a dog. **1604** — *Oth.* iv. i. 147. **1605** — *Macb.* v. iii. 47 Throw Physicke to the Dogs, Ile none of it. **1619** R. HARRIS *Drunkard's Cup* Epist. A ij b, One is coloured, another is foxt, a third is gone to the dogs. **1732** POPE *Ep. Bathurst* 66 Had Cole-pepper's whole wealth been hops and hogs, Could he himself have sent it to the dogs? **1770** FOOTE *Lame Lover* ii. Wks. 1799 II. 78, I should not have thought he had a word to throw to a dog. **1809** W. IRVING *Knickerb.* vii. iv. (1849) 398 He .. threw diplomacy to the dogs. **1857** HUGHES *Tom Brown* I. vi, Rugby and the School-house are going to the dogs.

Reproduced by permission of The Clarendon Press, Oxford.

72

From *Webster's Third New International Dictionary:*

¹dog \'dȯg *sometimes* 'dȯg\ *n* -s [ME *dog, dogge,* fr. OE *docga*] **1 a :** a carnivorous mammal (*Canis familiaris*) of the family Canidae that has been kept in a domesticated state by man since prehistoric times, is undoubtedly descended from some unknown wild member of the genus Canis possibly the common wolf, varies in its artificially produced breeds far more than any other mammal (as in form, size, color, and length and character of coat), and is kept chiefly for sporting use or as a guard or companion or esp. formerly for light draft and other labor;

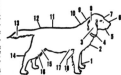

dog: *1* pastern, *2* chest, *3* leather, *4* dewlap, *5* flews, *6* muzzle, *7* stop, *8* occiput, *9* crest, *10* withers, *11* loin, *12* rump, *13* feather, *14* hock, *15* stifle, *16* knee, *17* brisket, *18* elbow

broadly **:** any animal of the family Canidae **b :** a male dog — opposed to *bitch* **2 a :** a mean worthless fellow **:** CUR, WRETCH, RASCAL ⟨~ of an unbeliever —Sir Walter Scott⟩ **b :** a sportive or roguish fellow **:** BIRD, CHAP ⟨a gay old ~⟩ **c :** FELLOW — used with a qualifying adj. ⟨a lazy ~⟩ ⟨a very sad ~⟩ **3 :** any of various usu. simple mechanical devices for holding, gripping, or fastening something: as **a :** any of various devices consisting essentially of a spike, rod, or bar of metal with a ring, hook, claw, or lug at the end used in various ways (as by driving or embedding in an object or hooking to an object) **b :** either of the hooks of a pair of sling dogs **c :** an iron for holding wood in a fireplace **:** FIREDOG, ANDIRON **d :** a clamp in a lathe for gripping the piece of work and for communicating motion to it from the faceplate **e :** STOP, DETENT, CLICK **f :** a drag for the wheel of a vehicle **g :** a short heavy sharp-pointed steel hook with a ring at one end **h :** a steel projection on a log carriage or on an endless chain that conveys logs into a sawmill **i :** the hammer in a gunlock **4 a** (1) **:** DOGFISH (2) **:** DOG SALMON (3) **:** PRAIRIE DOG **b** (1) **:** SUN DOG (2) **:** WATER DOG **4** (3) **:** FOGBOW **c** (1) **:** DOGSHORE (2) **:** DOGWATCH **d :** HOT DOG **5 :** ostentatious display **:** affected stylishness or dignity ⟨there was a lot of ~ about the affair⟩; *often* **:** dress and behavior not characteristic of or suited to one's station — used esp. in the phrase *pu on the dog* **6 :** dogskin used as fur **7 dogs** *pl, slang* **:** FEET **8 :** something inferior of its kind ⟨you call your agent but the only scripts available are real ~s —Paul Newman⟩ **9 dogs** *pl* **:** RUINATION, DESTRUCTION — used with *the* ⟨it's enough to drive anyone to the ~s⟩ ⟨everything is going to the ~s around here⟩ **10 :** PROMISSORY NOTE **11 a :** a poor investment; *usu* **:** a stock or bond not worth its price **b :** a domestic animal of inferior quality or performance **c :** a sluggish horse or a racehorse that does not do well in competition **d :** a low-grade beef animal **e :** a slow-moving or undesirable piece of merchandise — compare RUNNER **f :** a poor-quality motor vehicle **:** LEMON; *esp* **:** a badly worn used car **g** *slang* **:** a woman inferior in looks, character, or accomplishments; *sometimes* **:** PROSTITUTE **h** *slang* **:** a theatrical or musical flop **:** a poor, hackneyed, or outmoded presentation **12** *usu cap* **:** any of certain American Indian peoples: as **a :** CHEYENNE **b :** FOX **13 dogs** *pl* **:** dog racing **14 :** one of the wooden sawhorses placed on a racetrack near the rail when the track is soft to keep horses out of the mud during workouts

²dog \"\ *vb* **dogged** \-gd\ **dogged** \"\ **dogging; dogs** *vt* **1 a :** to hunt or track like a hound **:** follow insidiously or indefatigably ⟨she *dogged* him until he gave in and married her⟩ **b :** to chase with a dog **c :** to worry as if by dogs **:** HOUND ⟨he was *dogged* by financial worries⟩ **2 :** to fasten with a dog — sometimes used with *down* ⟨a sailor *dogged* down the hatch⟩ **3** *South & Midland* **:** DAMN, DARN ⟨well ~ my boot⟩ ⟨~ it all⟩ ~ *vi, archaic* **:** to follow slavishly or pertinaciously — **dog it 1** *slang* **:** to run away **2** *slang* **:** to fail to try one's best **:** loaf on the job **:** GOLDBRICK — **dog the watches :** to change the order of night watches by means of dogwatches

³dog \"\ *adv* **:** EXTREMELY, VERY, UTTERLY — often used in combination ⟨*dog*-poor⟩ ⟨*dog*-tired⟩ ⟨*dog*-lame⟩

⁴dog \"\ *adj* **1 :** of or for dogs ⟨~ diseases⟩ ⟨~ breeders⟩ ⟨a ~ collar⟩ **:** CANINE **2 :** MALE — used chiefly of carnivorous mammals ⟨a ~ otter⟩ **3 :** MONGREL, SPURIOUS, INFERIOR ⟨~ rhyme⟩; *esp* **:** unlike that used by native speakers or writers ⟨~ Latin⟩ ⟨~ French⟩

⁵dog \"\ *usu cap* — a communications code word for the letter *d*

dog alley *n, Midland* **:** DOGTROT

From *The American College Dictionary:*

dog (dôg, dŏg), *n., v.,* **dogged, dogging.** —*n.* **1.** a domesticated carnivore, *Canis familiaris,* bred in a great many varieties. **2.** any animal belonging to the same family, *Canidae,* including the wolves, jackals, foxes, etc. **3.** the male of such an animal (opposed to *bitch*). **4.** any of various animals suggesting the dog, as the prairie dog. **5.** a despicable fellow. **6.** a fellow in general: *a gay dog.* **7.** (*cap.*) *Astron.* either of two constellations, Canis Major (**Great Dog**) and Canis Minor (**Little Dog**), situated near Orion. **8.** *Mech.* any of various mechanical devices, as for gripping or holding something. **9.** an andiron. **10.** *Meteorol.* a sundog or fogdog. **11. go to the dogs,** *Colloq.* to go to ruin. **12. put on the dog,** *U.S. Colloq.* to behave pretentiously; put on airs. —*v.t.* **13.** to follow or track like a dog esp. with hostile intent; hound. **14.** to drive or chase with a dog or dogs. [ME *dogge,* OE *docga;* orig. unknown]

Mechanical dogs (def. 8)
A, Bench dog; B, Ring dog; C, Sling dog

From *Webster's New World Dictionary of the American Language:*

dog (dôg), *n.* [*pl.* DOGS (dôgz), DOG; see PLURAL, II, D, 1], [ME. *dog, dogge;* generalized in sense < rare AS. *docga, dogga* (usual AS. *hund;* see HOUND), dog of native breed (whence Fr. *dogue,* G. *dogge,* Eng. *dog, mastiff*); akin to or borrowed in ON. *dugga,* headstrong, intractable person; the form *dog* instead of *dog* (< AS. *docga*) suggests ON. transmission; IE. base *dheugh-,* to be strong, be of use, avail; cf. DOUGHTY], **1.** any of a large and varied group of domesticated animals related to the fox, wolf, and jackal. **2.** the male of any of these animals. **3.** a low, contemptible fellow. **4.** a prairie dog, dogfish, or animal thought of as resembling a dog. **5.** [< orig. shape; cf. Fr. *chenet*], an andiron; firedog. **6.** [Colloq.], a boy or man: as, lucky *dog, gay dog.* **7.** *pl.* [Slang], feet. **8.** [D-], in *astronomy,* either of two constellations near Orion, separated from each other by the Milky Way; the Great Dog (*Canis Major*) or the Little Dog (*Canis Minor*). **9.** in *mechanics,* any of several devices for holding or grappling. **10.** in *meteorology,* a parhelion; sundog, seadog, or fogdog. *v.t.* [DOGGED (dôgd), DOGGING], **1.** to follow, hunt, or track down like a dog. **2.** to hold down with a mechanical dog. *adv.* very; completely: used in combination, as, *dog*-tired.
a dog's age, [Colloq.], a long time.
a dog's life, a wretched existence.
dog eat dog, ruthless and savage competition.
dog in the manger, a person who keeps others from using something which he has but cannot or will not use: from the fable of the dog that kept the ox from eating the hay.
every dog has his day, something good or lucky happens to everyone at one time or another.
go to the dogs, [Colloq.], to deteriorate; degenerate.
let sleeping dogs lie, to let well enough alone; not disturb things as they are for fear of something worse.
put on the dog, [Slang], to make a show of being very elegant, wealthy, etc.
teach an old dog new tricks, to induce a person of settled habits to adopt new methods or ideas.

MARKHAM HARRIS

JAZZ (from The Encyclopedia Americana)

JAZZ, jăz, an omnibus term for various 20th century styles of popular music historically and commercially linked with social dancing. When lumped together and regarded nontechnically, these styles are characterized by melodies shaped to standard lengths, syncopated and often complex rhythms, eclectic harmony and instrumentation, and standards of execution that range from inept formula to inventive virtuosity. As viewed by the devotee, jazz is a unique Afro-American music whose freshness and expressiveness are indebted to a free use of the human voice and the fullest possible exploitation of instrumental resources, plus an emphasis upon improvisation. Jazz, to the historian, is a musical compound whose initial synthesis is considered to have taken place under Negro and/or white auspices in the United States during World War I or thereabouts, but whose constituent elements can be traced to the Negro and Creole music of New Orleans as far back as the turn of the century and beyond to ever more remote and speculative origins in Latin America, Europe, and West Africa.

For the initiated, jazz cannot be wholly transferred to music paper. The true idiom is more a matter of how the material is rendered than what it may superficially look like, whether march, stomp, blues, popular song, or, if translatable into the jazz manner, an importation from the classical repertory. Good jazz musicians share a highly developed rhythmic sense anchored to the fundamental beat, considerable powers of improvisation, ample technique, and a group spirit marked by freedom and spontaneity, together with as relaxed an approach as is consistent with energized, intuitive, and hair-trigger responsiveness. It is, therefore, performance, as distinguished from composition or even elaborate arrangement, that often creates, upon the spot, the real jazz.

Etymology.—The etymology of the word is uncertain at best, yet what may well have been the original climate of jazz music is suggested by such a proposed source as the French verb, *jaser*, which literally means to chat, to chatter, and presumably, by extension, to gossip (in tones). Early spellings in actual use were jas, jass, and jaz. Lafcadio Hearn reported that he encountered one form or another of the term in the Creole patois of New Orleans as far back as 1880. He said that the Louisiana Creoles had it from the Negroes and that it meant "to speed things up" as applied to music of a syncopated nature. Less polite meanings also have been suggested.

Ragtime.—One of the two immediate ancestors of jazz was ragtime, which, in turn, drew upon the march and such minstrel show sources as the buck and wing, cakewalk, and jig. The majority of rags had no text and were more instrumental than vocal in character. The basic rhythmic patterns of ragtime were Negroid and may be divided into two principal types known as primary and secondary rag. A common type of primary rag places a short note in what is normally a position of stress in the measure, a longer note in what is normally an unstressed position. This is a typical device of syncopation, which is essentially a deliberate shifting or displacement of normal metrical accent. Primary rag likewise suppresses accents proper to the established rhythmic pulse and by various means anticipates and postpones them. Secondary rag goes farther, in that it creates two independent rhythm patterns, whereby the melody may be in triple time, while the accompaniment remains in double time. Extended over several measures, secondary rag is often considered to exceed the limits of simple syncopation and becomes what is termed polyrhythm. (Consult Winthrop Sargeant's *Jazz: Hot and Hybrid* for a detailed analysis of jazz polyrhythm.)

Blues.—The second immediate ancestor

73

of jazz was the blues, a type of vocal music now thought to have been developed by the southern Negro from the "cry" and "holler" in the first instance, with later influences from the work song (ensemble) and the spiritual (harmony). The blues took its character not only from a predominantly melancholy emotional content but also from the so-called blue (slightly flatted) notes characteristic of its melodies when sung by ear. These flatted notes, falling particularly on the third and seventh degrees of the scale, gave an unstable intonation to the normally major or minor pitch of these intervals. Unlike ragtime, the blues usually had a text, the bittersweet nature of which dictated a more or less declamatory style of rendering, less staccato rhythm, and a tempo frequently slower (New Orleans and St. Louis blues) than that of ragtime. The blues also made use of barbershop harmonies (highly chromatic chordal progressions) and an additional feature that later became prominent in jazz—the break. The break is a brief, improvised instrumental cadenza containing much syncopation.

Jazz emerged as a synthesis of certain elements of ragtime and the blues. It retained ragtime's rhythmic patterns, particularly secondary rag, while from the blues it acquired melodic resources (particularly "blue" tonality) which were wanting in ragtime. From the blues jazz likewise assimilated the expressive possibilities of a moderate tempo (slow blues) and the potential for freedom and variety afforded by the break.

Hot Jazz.—Early jazz tended to be "hot" jazz, a relatively unrestrained, largely improvised style (except for basic chordal progression) which, although based upon popular tunes, was played with little or no dependence upon written parts. An early jazz band, which might consist of cornet or trumpet, trombone, clarinet, guitar or banjo, tuba or string bass, piano (if not a wagon band), and drums, would select a tune, perhaps announce it once in order to establish a point of departure, and then proceed to develop it freely under the inspiration of the moment. The development was of at least two kinds: a free-for-all in which each instrument went its own way in melodic and rhythmic competition with the others (New Orleans style); a take-your-turn scheme by which most of the instruments took solos in rotation, the others supplying a supportive background for them (Chicago style).

Sweet Jazz.—A more or less commercialized reaction to "hot" jazz started with the appearance of "sweet" jazz. This type sacrificed spontaneity and power and individual freedom in favor of milder, more conventional appeals. Where the "hot" band played without written parts, the "sweet" band often employed a full score, the players adhering to their parts as written. Suavity, close coordination, and considerable prettiness resulted. The "sweet" band also introduced a number of mild instruments, such as the harp, chimes, and celeste, meanwhile sharing with "hot" bands the violin (quite often to be found in pioneering, "hot" aggregations) and the subsequently adopted saxophone. Certain "sweet" bands, although maintaining among their personnel a nucleus of "hot" players, were ultimately expanded to a point where they approached the small symphony orchestra in numbers and precalculated discipline ("symphonic" jazz).

"Sweet" jazz meanwhile adopted the portamento style characteristic of spontaneous vocal blues and exaggerated it into the well-nigh perpetually sliding manner of the early crooner. "Sweet" jazz likewise reached out to various non-Negroid features of contemporary music: for example, melodic material of the sentimental ballad or Viennese light opera species and harmonic devices adapted from 19th century romanticism and 20th century impressionism. The essential jazz idiom was thus carried so far afield that it threatened to remain jazz only by virtue of the fact that it preserved the duple time (4/4) of the fox trot which, during World War I, superseded the one-step and the two-step. At no time, however, did the jazz tradition, even at its widest and loosest, embrace the triple time (3/4) of the waltz, although it did assimilate, during their periods of popular favor, such Afro-American dances as the shimmy and Charleston, such Latin-American dances as the tango, rhumba, conga, samba, and mambo.

Swing and Boogiewoogie.—Jazz was refreshened in the mid-1930's by the rise of swing. While none too precise a term, swing may be described as a renascence of "hot" jazz plus an added measure of premeditation, virtuosity, and, in some instances, slickness. A byproduct of this return to the past was boogiewoogie, heard at private gatherings (Negro) more than a decade prior to its public appearance about 1935–1936. Boogiewoogie is a type of piano blues that consists of a fixed, eight-beat rhythmic figure for the left hand, above which the right hand improvises freely.

Bebop and Cool Jazz.—The 1940's witnessed the emergence of bebop or "bop," upon which several critics elected to look askance, finding it no more than overstrained "hot" jazz whose accompanying lyrics stressed the bawdy and the nonsensical. But other analysts arrived at far different conclusions, claiming to find in bebop a coolness, lightness, softness, and, despite its leaning toward the use of short phrases, a contrapuntal elaboration, which were a welcome change from what they regarded as the heat, weight, noise, and harmonic rigidity of crystallized swing.

"Cool" jazz, with its concern for a "lagalong" beat and pure instrumental tone and its reconsideration of the working relationship between naive heat and a restrained sophisticated intensity, came to prominence as a successor to bebop from about 1948 onward.

Rock 'n' Roll and Calypso.—A species of strongly rhythmic blues, developed at the outset by Negro musicians for the Negro market in the 1920's and revived in the 1940's, was eventually taken up by white bands, which modified it and popularized it during the mid-1950's under the name of rock 'n' roll. The same decade also proved hospitable to calypso, an importation from Trinidad. A hybrid form, it is said to have emerged under the influence of the West African song of ridicule. Its elements include melodic-harmonic borrowings from the French folk song, texts in a polyglot vocabulary, and African rhythmic infusions. American adaptations often feature lyrics that have lost their satirical bite and rhythms that have lost their indigenous interest.

History.—The history of ragtime is not too well documented, yet there are a few landmarks of tolerable accuracy. Making its appearance near the close of the 19th century with such an early example as *Harlem Rag* (1897) by the pianist Thomas M. Turpin and *Maple Leaf Rag* (1899) by W. Scott Joplin, ragtime was featured by the pioneering band of Buddy "King" Bolden at New Orleans from about 1895 onward, and by the pianist Ben R. Harney, who began a series of New York appearances at Tony Pastor's Variety Theatre in 1896. The first New York stage presentation of ragtime is said to have taken place at Proctor's Theatre in 1905, when Will Marion Cook's Memphis Students played a number of rags. *Alexander's Rag Time Band* by Irving Berlin, who did much to popularize ragtime, was published in 1911.

The recorded history of the blues is introduced by the now famous *Memphis Blues* composed by the cornetist and band leader, William Christopher Handy, and published in 1912, although written three years earlier. His equally well-known *St. Louis Blues* dates from 1914. At the outset intended to be sung, the blues had a great exponent in Bessie Smith and remained essentially vocal until the advent of exclusively instrumental blues, such as Edward "Duke" Ellington's *Blue Light*, and boogiewoogie (Jimmy Yancey, "Pine Top" Smith, Thomas "Fats" Waller).

Although the word jazz as applied to a species of popular music is considered to have entered the language (oral) circa 1914–1916 in Chicago, at least partial anticipations of the musical style thus labeled have been traced to examples that pre-date World War I. These anticipations of the "hot" jazz manner are credited to such precursors as Freddie Keppard and the Original Creoles, reported by "Jelly Roll" Morton to have been playing powerful jazz in New Orleans well before 1914 (1908); Joseph "King"

Oliver, cornetist, bandleader, and New Orleans contemporary of Keppard; and Ferdinand "Jelly Roll" Morton himself, composer of *King Porter Stomp* (1906), and arranger of *Tiger Rag*, based on a French quadrille and performed in various "hot" versions under various titles long before it was first recorded in 1917 as *Tiger Rag*. From about 1912 onward, jazz began to fan out from its reputedly original locus in New Orleans (Storyville). Not necessarily in strict chronological order (claims to priority remain in dispute), it is said to have been carried to Chicago by, among others, Tom Brown's Band from Dixieland; to New York by the same band and also by the Original Dixieland Jass (*sic*) Band; to Los Angeles (Keppard and the Original Creoles) and to San Francisco, where Art Hickman introduced a sweetened variety at the St. Francis Hotel as early as 1914.

"Sweet" jazz and "symphonic" jazz received stimulus from Paul Whiteman, who is credited with the first playing of jazz from fully scored parts at Los Angeles in 1920. Whiteman's pianist and arranger, Ferde Grofé, became widely known for his scoring of jazz music through which it reached semisymphonic proportions. Whiteman toured the United States and Europe, particularly during the 1920's, establishing landmarks by his jazz concerts, first in Aeolian Hall, then in the much larger Carnegie Hall, New York City. The Aeolian performance, which occurred on Feb. 12, 1924 and was attended by the first-string music critics of the metropolitan newspapers, purported to be the first jazz concert ever given. The program was highlighted by the debut performance of George Gershwin's *Rhapsody in Blue* (1924), an impressionistic work for piano and orchestra employing jazz elements.

Continuing his interest in jazz, Gershwin followed the *Rhapsody in Blue* with the *Concerto in F Major* (1926) for piano and orchestra; the tone poem *An American in Paris* (1928); *Second Rhapsody* (1932; originally *Rhapsody in Rivets*); a Negro folk opera, *Porgy and Bess* (1935), which was revived for a long run on Broadway in 1942;

and *Jazz Piano Preludes* (1936), later scored for orchestra. By means of what was considered their freshness and originality, these works made Gershwin the first prominent example of simultaneous recognition in both tin-pan alley and the concert room.

Although preoccupation on the part of serious composers with jazz music and jazz performers may be said to have reached a peak in America and Europe about the mid-1920's, ragtime and jazz influences can be found in their output as far back as 1908, the publication year of *The Golliwog's Cake Walk* from *The Children's Hour* by Claude Debussy. Three additional early contributions were made by Igor Feodorovich Stravinsky with his *Ragtime* for 11 instruments (1918), *The Soldier's Tale* (1918) and *Piano Rag-Music* (1919).

Apart from Gershwin and by way of supplement to the above-mentioned contributions to at least nominal jazz music by Stravinsky and Debussy, the following representative list of European and United States composers and their compositions which employ ragtime and jazz will serve to indicate the extent to which these musical forms invaded the art music of the 20th century.

John Alden Carpenter, *Concertino* (1915) for piano and orchestra, featuring ragtime; also his ballet *Krazy Kat* (1922), containing sections labeled "Fox-Trot" and "Blues"; likewise his ballet *Skyscrapers* (1926), using fox-trot rhythms and blues melodies.

Erik Satie, *Parade* (1917), a ballet written for the Russian impresario Sergei Diaghilev and carrying the subtitle *Rag-time du paquebot*.

Darius Milhaud, *Le boeuf sur le toit* (1919), ballet with jazz rhythms; and his *La création du monde* (1923), a ballet based on a scenario by Blaise Cendrars, treating the creation of the world, according to African Negro legends, and including a fugue on a jazz subject, a blues section, and an extended melodic passage with a barbershop harmonic accompaniment.

Paul Hindemith, *1922 Suite for Piano* (1922) with movements designated "Shimmy" and "Ragtime."

Louis Gruenberg, *The Daniel Jazz* (1924), scored for small ensemble and solo voice, text by the poet Vachel Lindsay.

Arthur Honegger, *Concertino* (1925) for piano and orchestra, with jazz rhythms.

Aaron Copland, *Concerto* (1926) for piano and orchestra, which employs Charleston rhythms and special jazz mutes for trombone.

Ernst Křenek, *Jonny spielt auf* (1927), an opera with a Negro bandleader as hero and with sections marked "Shimmy," "Blues," and "Spiritual."

Maurice Ravel, *Sonata* (1927) for violin and piano, of which the second movement is a blues.

Constant Lambert, *Rio Grande* (1929), a composition for voices and orchestra, containing jazz rhythms.

Morton Gould, *Chorale and Fugue in Jazz* (1936).

Serious composers have been attracted to jazz by its rhythmic possibilities, by the uncommon tonal qualities to be had from special jazz handling of familiar instruments, and, above all, by the spirit of freedom and crisp candor rarely absent from genuine "hot" jazz and its performers. Composers have presumably been less interested in the emotional gamut of jazz, because it is thought to generate only a few fundamental moods—the melancholy protest or resignation of the blues, for example, and the headlong exhilaration of "jump." The commercial moonlight and roses of such songs as *My Blue Heaven* or *I'll Buy That Dream* stem from the sentimental ballad (as in songs by such composers as Jerome David Kern and Sigmund Romberg) rather than from jazz.

The interest of tin-pan alley commercialism in classical music has likewise been conspicuous and persistent. Early borrowings —such as a theme from Frédéric Chopin's *Fantasie-Impromptu* as the melodic basis of

I'm Always Chasing Rainbows, and the considerable thematic assistance rendered to *Yes, We Have No Bananas* by the "Hallelujah Chorus" in George Frederic Handel's oratorio, *Messiah*—sired a numerous progeny. Various classics have from time to time been swung, prominent examples including a theme from a Mozart piano sonata which was turned into a fox trot and renamed *In An Eighteenth Century Drawing Room*; also Ignace Jan Paderewski's *Menuet à l'antique*; and Franz Liszt's *Liebestraum*. Other standard instrumental works have been treated more radically, emerging from the tune factory as popular songs. Among these may be cited the transformation of the opening theme of a Peter Ilich Tchaikovsky piano concerto into *Tonight We Love* and the yet more drastic metamorphosis of one of Chopin's polonaises into the sentimental ballad ("sweet" jazz type) *Till the End of Time*.

The evolution of more or less pure jazz, as distinguished from numerous hybrid forms, has acquired momentum from the playing and recordings of carefully selected, highly expert although relatively large, combinations led by jazz musicians of the caliber of Louis "Satchmo" Armstrong, Fletcher Henderson, Edward "Duke" Ellington, Benny Goodman, William "Count" Basie, Gene Krupa, Woody Herman, Dizzy Gillespie, Stan Kenton, and Lennie Tristano— to name a representative few. Their leadership has proved significant, in that it has consistently affirmed the importance to any art of imagination, innovation, a high order of technical skill, and a following. The best jazz has also helped to keep alive the practice of improvisation, a musical capacity that had reached high levels by Ludwig van Beethoven's time (1770–1827), but suffered a decline in Western music thereafter, until a fresh impetus was supplied by that unassuming pioneer, the Negro folk musician.

That jazz will one day emerge as *the* American music remains a subject of perennial debate. Proponents urge its unremitting search for freshness, depth, and mastery. Opponents cannot forget its dubious origins, its uncommon susceptibility to box office, its comparatively narrow range of intellectual and emotional expression. Meanwhile, however, neither side denies to honest and gifted jazz music a continuing place alike among the enthusiasms of the specialist and in the favor of a large public.

Bibliography.—Whiteman, Paul, and McBride, Mary Margaret, *Jazz* (New York 1926); Armstrong, Louis, *Swing That Music* (New York 1936); Panassié, Hugues, *Hot Jazz* (New York 1936); Goodman, Benny, and Kolodin, Irving, *The Kingdom of Swing* (Harrisburg 1939); Hobson, Wilder, *American Jazz Music* (New York 1939); Ramsey, Frederic, and Smith, Charles E., *Jazzmen* (New York 1939); Copland, Aaron, *Our New Music* (New York 1941); Handy, William Christopher, *Father of the Blues; An Autobiography* (New York 1941); Howard, John Tasker, *This Modern Music* (New York 1942); Panassié, Hugues, *The Real Jazz* (New York 1942); Sargeant, Winthrop, *Jazz: Hot and Hybrid* (New York 1946); Delaunay, Charles, *New Hot Discography: The Standard Directory of Recorded Jazz* (New York 1948); Ulanov, Barry, *A History of Jazz in America* (New York 1952); Stearns, Marshall, *The Story of Jazz* (New York 1956).

QUESTIONS FOR STUDY AND DISCUSSION

1. In this article, what is the genus into which jazz is placed?

2. What differentiae distinguish jazz from other species in the same genus?

3. What are the principal types or subgroups into which jazz may be divided? How do they differ from one another?

4. Even though this is a technical article, it is clear and readable. What devices does Harris use to make his discussion lively? Pay particular attention to his use of words.

RUSSELL LYNES

The Part-Time Lady

There is probably no subject that consumes more journalistic print today than what is known as "the woman's problem." It is conveniently faceted with thousands of glittering questions and complaints, and there is an audience of untold millions of women who wear their problems like costume jewelry—big, gaudy, and more often than not simulated. The "man's problem," by comparison does not exist; you will find no books about men that are comparable to *Modern Woman: the Lost Sex* or *The Second Sex*, nor will you find magazine articles devoted to the plight of the male in our society. If he has a plight, it is assumed, it must be his own fault. The plight of women, on the other hand, would seem, if the amount of space devoted to it is a reasonable measure, to consume the reading hours of more than half the adult population. The simple fact seems to be that the woman's problem is separate from the human problem, but that the man's problem is not.

It is not my intention to argue the merits of this situation; I have just devoted myself briefly, if not altogether sympathetically, to the male, and I would now like to turn my attention to an aspect of the female in America that gets very little attention. There is a good reason why it doesn't. It can scarcely be called part of the woman's problem; it can scarcely be called a problem at all. It is simply the matter of what, in our new society, is a lady, if indeed there is any such thing.

One evening not long ago I called to my sixteen-year-old daughter, who was doing her homework, and she came into the room where I was sitting.

"Do you know what a lady is?" I asked her.

"Gee," she said, "*now* what have I done?"

That wasn't the answer I expected, and it made me laugh. She looked surprised.

"That's not what I mean," I said. "When you think of a lady, who comes to mind?"

She thought for a moment: "I don't think I know any ladies."

"Oh, come on," I said. "Not any?"

"Well, maybe Mummy's a lady."

"What do you mean, *maybe*?"

"Well," she avoided my question. "Granny's a lady from the top of her head to her toes."

It took a few minutes to pin her down. She thought of none of her contemporaries as ladies; it was an ideal of behavior that seemed to be of no immediate concern; it had to do with older women, off there in the future somewhere.

If you were to ask the same question, I believe that you would find that it sets women, even young ones, slightly on edge. In our day it puzzles men, as it would not have a generation ago. The old concept of a lady as an upper-class, straight-spined, and rather useless (if ornamental) creature whose standards were social rather than human has fortunately disappeared.

I have asked quite a number of men and women what a lady is. I asked my secretary, for instance. She accepted the question amiably, if a little startled, and went about asking some of her friends. I trust my daughter's judgment where her contemporaries are concerned—up to a point. I asked her to ask her classmates what a lady is. I have also asked members of my mother's generation. I have asked my colleagues. I have asked my wife. There has never been a less scientific or more inconclusive opinion poll than mine, but it does, I hope, throw a glimmer of light on the position of women in our society, if not on the woman's problem.

My question was simply and abruptly: "What is a lady?" All of the answers started much the same way: "What is a lady? Why, a lady is . . . well, let's see . . . what *is* a lady? You know, that's a very interesting question."

That is as far as some people ever got. Most of my respondents, to use a pollster's word, launched on their answers and could not stop. Before pinning the ladies down, let me first give you a few broad generalizations that emerged from the answers.

A lady is nothing very specific. One man's lady is another man's woman; sometimes one man's lady is another man's wife. Definitions overlap but they almost never coincide. A great many women, I discovered, do not think of themselves as ladies; they are modest and they know themselves too well. On the other hand they expect to be taken for ladies by other people. Most men think of their mothers as ladies, since mothers in most cases set their sons' standards of feminine deportment. Teen-age boys are likely to divide all women over twenty into two broad categories—"ladies" and "babes." To most men in their twenties ladies are women over forty. To many working women (a category which here includes over-busy housewives as well as office workers) ladies are women who have the time to be immaculately groomed, to smell good, and to sit and listen while others talk. To most women, and this I suppose is significant, few women have time to be more than part-time ladies; the larger part of their time is spent picking up after other people—children, husbands, or bosses.

As you can see from these generalizations the word "lady" has no exact meaning today, but it does contain consistent overtones of admiration. It is a state of grace that women would like to achieve and that men would like to be able to take for granted.

My researches have led me to several rather out-of-the-way sources, and some rather obvious conclusions. The first and unavoidable source merely proves that all women in America are ladies. You have never heard of a lady going to the women's room. It is always vice versa. It is "ladies' day" at the ball park. Women who used to be called "sales girls" are now "sales ladies." There are also "ladies of the evening," which seems to me to be pushing the word a little further than is absolutely necessary. I have checked the listings in the New York (Manhattan) telephone book, and I have found that ladies out-number women almost two to one. Under *women*, for example, I found such organizations as Woman for President & Other Public Offices Inc. and Woman's Apparel Shoulder Pad Assn Inc. Under *ladies* there was a brighter note: Lady Joy Undies, Lady Bountiful Salon, and most interesting (and rather puzzling to the his-

torically minded) the Lady Godiva Undergarment Corp. One of the soundest, and also most progressive, labor unions in America is the ILGWU (International *Ladies* Garment Workers Union), and surely the ladies who make the garments also wear them.

Before we make an assault on the bastion of the contemporary lady and try to define her as she exists today, I should like to try to put the American lady in context. That is, I should like to give you some background of the lady as she has been regarded by somewhat earlier generations.

When Harriet Martineau, the first distinguished newspaper woman of London, visited America in 1834, she arrived at a time when a good many Americans were putting on airs. It was the first era of the common man; that is, it was the first opportunity that the common man had in America to become as uncommon as he pleased. Andrew Jackson was President, and he had brought with him to Washington a new kind of society that made the old aristocracy turn pale with shock. "Respectability" became everybody's quarry, not just the quarry of the few. It was then that all American women became ladies. Miss Martineau was surprised to hear a preacher say from the pulpit: "Who were the last at the Cross? Ladies. Who were the first at the Sepulchre? Ladies." But she was even more surprised when she visited the jail in Nashville and asked if she might visit the women's cells. "We have no ladies here at present, madam," the turnkey said. "We've never had but two ladies, who were convicted for stealing a steak; but as it appears that they were deserted by their husbands, and in want, they were pardoned." The ladies, it appears, had a woman's problem.

But there were ladies everywhere. "By 1845," Dixon Wecter wrote in *The Saga of American Society*, "New York boasted a Ladies' Oyster Shop, a Ladies' Reading Room, and a Ladies' Bowling Alley elegantly equipped with carpets and ottomans and girls to set the pins." And a writer in 1855 (a woman) complained of the number of "females in their ambition to be considered 'ladies'" who used their hands entirely "in playing with their ringlets, or touching the piano or guitar." John H. Gregory, an Irish prospector who struck gold in Colorado in 1859, threw down his pick and cried, "Thank God, *now* my wife can be a lady!"

But there was another aspect of the position of women in America that is more important, and to foreign visitors, has always seemed very strange. This is the deference accorded to women here. One traveler remarked: "From the captain of a western steamboat to the roughest miner in California, from the north, south, east, and west we hear but one voice. Women are to be protected, respected, supported and petted." That was a century ago. Just recently another Englishman, Sir Harold Nicolson, commented in his book *Good Behavior* that he could not understand "the position of power and privilege claimed by, and accorded to, the American woman." He wrote: "It is not merely that American mothers and grandmothers expect and obtain a level of worship comparable only to that established among primitive matriarchal societies of the Malabar coast. It is that American wives assume a contemptuous attitude towards their husbands, whom they exploit economically and to whom they adopt an attitude of cultural superiority."

These are hard words, but they are not unfamiliar ones. The position enjoyed by women in America came about for good and sufficient reasons, even though those reasons have worn out their usefulness by now. In frontier America there was a shortage of women. Short supply leads to hoarding and protection, and often to the assumption that the object that is hoarded has remarkable virtues. So it was with women in America. In the dust-blown and fly-blown villages of the prairies in the last century a woman "was absolutely safe both in fact and in reputation," as James Truslow Adams wrote in *The Epic of America.* "The conditions of frontier life often compelled a man to be away from home and perhaps take refuge for the night in another house where the man was also absent. For the sake of protection of each man's own wife, a sort of unwritten law came to be universally and absolutely observed. No man would think of approach-

ing an honest woman, and so rigidly was the rule observed that even when men and women, perhaps absolute strangers to one another, thus spent the night under the same roof, no whisper of scandal would be breathed because it was felt there would be no foundation for it." There is no longer a shortage of women in America; women outnumber men today, but the fact remains that the tradition is so ingrained that men act today as though the shortage had not been alleviated.

It is not my purpose to engage in an argument about whether American women take advantage of men or not. I am talking about ladies, which is, or ought to be, a quite different subject, and I do not want to lose my historical theme quite yet. It was really men who made American women into ladies, and not women themselves, by putting them on an elaborate pedestal. It was a convenient way not only of flattering them into thinking that they were very special, but of lording it over other men. The American man's dream in the last century was to make enough money so that his wife could be as useless as possible, to surround her with servants and luxuries, to hire somebody else to bring up her children, and to house her in something like a full jewel box. In other words to make her into a lady he could be proud of and not have to worry about. If he could do this, he considered himself a success. He left all cultural matters to her, all matters of taste and education, while he pursued the dollars for her to spend. The result was, according to Henry Adams, that "the American woman of the nineteenth century was much better company than the American man." And according to Henry James, "Nothing . . . is more concomitantly striking than the fact that women over the land—allowing for every element of exception—appear to be of a markedly finer texture than the men. . . ."

It would be interesting to know what Henry James would say about American women today; it would probably not be greatly different, though the American woman has changed tremendously in the last half century and so has the American man. The American man has concerned himself a great deal more with matters of culture and taste and the American woman has given up the pursuit of being a lady. She decided some time ago that there are much more interesting ways to spend her time and employ her talents than cultivating the feminine graces and charms with all their subtleties for their own sake. She not only went to work in a man's world, and finally captured her political equality, but she gave up her long skirts, flexed her muscles, cut her hair to look like a boy, and took up men's sports.

So much for history.

"A lady," said Sinclair Lewis in a debate, "is a woman so incompetent as to have to take refuge in the secluded class, like kings and idiots, who have to be treated with special kindness because they can't take it."

It was not so very long ago that Lewis said this, only about fifteen years, and yet it is already as out of date as bloomers on a girl's basketball team, and smacks of that same era. Today there are no secluded classes, and there is no place in our society for the woman who "can't take it." The problem of the woman who wants to be a lady today (and I think we can assume that in some sense every woman does want to be considered a lady) is how to be a lady and, at the same time, all things to all men, women, and children. To her role of glamour girl, career woman, mother, housewife, chauffeur for the children, Den Mother for a litter of Cub Scouts, one must also add the battle of the supermarket, her avidity to hold her own culturally and to do her share of "good works." Her life is a full, if not necessarily a rich, one. Lillian Day said in *Kiss and Tell* that a "lady is one who never shows her underwear unintentionally." The problem of the busy modern woman almost seems to be when she would ever have time to show her underwear on purpose.

Today's woman is expected to maintain her poise at the same time that she is pulled to the north, south, east, and west by demands which she has, in fact, asked for. It was women, not men, who inaugurated the feminist movement that was intended to liberate women from their domestic and matrimonial bondage and to give them a

chance to be not just chattels but whole people, to realize their intellectual potentialities, and assume responsibilities. It is true, as we have already noted, that they have shunted some of their womanly jobs onto their husbands. However, it remains their province to be women, for, as James Branch Cabell said, "No lady is ever a gentleman."

This does not contradict the assertion that part of the lady's problem today is how to cope with gentlemen on their own ground. More and more women are not only in business but are assuming positions of authority which have traditionally belonged to men. They are, of course, executives in department stores and advertising agencies; they are also, according to the *Wall Street Journal*, increasingly sought out by corporations for "high calibre sales jobs." The demand for women trained in the Harvard Business School (under the watchful eye of Radcliffe College) far exceeds the annual supply of bright young things; they might, without pushing the word unnecessarily far, be called the "ladies of the morning." The fact is that the ambitious woman of the last century worked at being a lady, for that was how she gained influence and position for herself and advantages for her children. The ambitious woman of today works at being a part-time man. The time she has left over is devoted to being a lady, and sometimes to being that part of a woman which is a drudge.

It is for this reason, I believe, that the term "lady" is taken for granted by the older generation, who remember when as few women as possible tried to be anything but ladies. It also explains why my generation (the middle one) looks upon the term as having connotations of snobbishness, of pretentious gentility, and of being unwilling to face the facts of economic and social change. The young are so far removed from their grandparents that they know the word "lady" only as "ladylike," and they therefore distrust it, as they very well should.

My secretary, after pursuing the investigation I suggested to her, put it this way: "The twenty-year-old group seemed startled and confused when asked to define a lady.

Those in their thirties have definite ideas about what a lady does or doesn't do (and each rather diffidently assumes she is one); those over forty are shocked that one should have to ask."

We still have not defined what a lady is today, but while almost everyone I asked has a definition of a lady, a great many of them seemed uneasy about using the word at all. For all its being bandied about as a general substitute for the word "woman," it is old-fashioned. It is all very well to speak of "ladies," meaning any woman over twenty, but when you call a woman a lady, smile.

One evening at dinner recently I asked an editor of a very well-known woman's magazine what a lady is, and she said, "I hate that word." To her it implied class consciousness. You may have noticed that in the title on the cover of the *Ladies' Home Journal* the word "Ladies" is in such small type that it is almost unnoticeable. Not long ago that same magazine published an article called "What Makes Grace Kelly Different?" and in it Jimmy Stewart of the movies is quoted as saying: "Grace is good. She has class. Not just the class of a lady—I don't think that has anything to do with it—but she'll always have the class you find in a really great race horse." It is, it appears, better to be compared to a horse than to a lady.

Her Serene Highness, however, does seem to have had some standing as a lady in a good many eyes, especially the eyes of the young, who, I have found, put Audrey Hepburn (especially for her performance as a princess in *Roman Holiday*) in the same category. Why? Largely because they both have a somewhat aloof and reserved dignity which, while it gives the impression of friendliness, seems almost to defy intimacy. By their presence and persons they make it quite clear that one should keep his distance and mind his manners. Alec Guinness said of Grace Kelly in the same article in the *Ladies' Home Journal* in which Jimmy Stewart mentioned the horse: "Around her, one finds oneself being careful of language and things like that." One friend whom I asked to define a lady said: "A lady is a

woman to whom you apologize when you tell her a dirty joke." And Don Marquis once wrote: "There are three kinds of limericks: limericks to be told when ladies are present; limericks to be told when ladies are absent but clergymen are present—and limericks." It is interesting that in many eyes Grace Kelly should have tarnished her attractions as a "lady" when she married Prince Rainier. In the nineteenth century rich American mothers, like Mrs. Bradley Martin and Mrs. William K. Vanderbilt (who captured the Duke of Marlborough for her daughter) were in constant pursuit of European titles for their marriageable daughters, and though many people were amused, some of them very wryly, they also took it for granted as one of the eccentricities of the upper classes. When a movie "queen" who is also thought to be a "lady" marries a minor prince with all the attendant folderol today, one almost feels that it should not be mentioned in the presence of ladies without an apology.

But who are the ladies in whose presence one does not say such things? Not so very long ago there were many convenient rules for the behavior of a lady and many aphorisms to describe her. They do not apply today, but in 1900 a lady lived by such tidy rules as these:

> A *lady never raises her hands above her shoulders in public.*
>
> A *lady never smokes. Only actresses and foreign women smoke.*
>
> A *lady never crosses her knees.*
>
> A *lady never uses lip rouge.*
>
> A *lady never calls a new acquaintance by her Christian name, unless requested to do so.*
>
> A *lady never engages in argument at a social gathering.*
>
> A *lady always sits with the base of her spine against the back of the chair.*
>
> A *young lady never ventures out unchaperoned in the evening, even when she is with a group of her contemporaries.*
>
> A *lady never goes into the street without her hat and gloves and she never walks rapidly.*
>
> A *lady never discusses her children,*

servants, clothes, ailments, or house except with her intimates. These are the five forbidden "D's"—Descendants, domestics, dress, diseases, and domiciles.

Any book of etiquette of the day listed a great many "ladies never" but such easy commandments do not apply today. The question of how to define a lady is now a different matter for different generations. The young define her in one way, the middle-aged in another, and the older generation in still another.

When the young speak of their contemporaries as "ladies," there is likely to be venom in their hearts. They mean prissy. They mean "genteel" with its common overtones of affectation. They mean being snobbish and upstage and too proper and too clean and too fussy. But when they apply the word "lady" to their elders the words "charming" and "gracious" come easily. Clothes play an unsurprisingly important part in their concept of a lady. "Modest, unpretentious clothing," one sixteen-year-old said, and another: "Above all a lady is neat." Still another said: "A man may not want to spend his life with a lady, but he certainly enjoys them as refreshing balm." This same girl added (and I catch only a glimmer of what she means): "She may not have morals, but she has high ethics." The teenager's need to be listened to is evident in the remark, "A lady is interested in what you say," and her optimism in ". . . being a lady is something that comes with maturity. It's a quality that comes unconsciously out of a person's character." There seems to be a consensus among the teenagers that "it's hard to get to be a real lady, especially in modern society." The most constantly used adjective was "calm" or its equivalents "at ease" and "poised." Finally a lady is "sincere."

When you move up a decade or two and inquire of the middle-aged you find different adjectives which betray different attitudes. You find that "self-sufficiency" and "perceptiveness" become important. Intelligence also counts for more. "A lady," one lady said to me, "is a woman who creates an atmos-phere in which people behave their best." And another: ". . . a woman who can rise to any situation." Worldliness and sophistication count for a good deal. "A lady is a woman who has accepted her disciplines." Not bad. But perhaps more important: "There is no trace of snobbishness in a lady." Another woman said: "I discovered early that you could go anywhere in New York if you dressed and behaved 'like a lady'—it was like an invisible shield." And a man said: "A lady is a well-adjusted but not over-adjusted woman." Freud was bound to get into the middle-aged attitude somehow.

When you come to the older generation another dimension is added; the definition of a lady includes "breeding." It is a word little used now because of its class-conscious overtones, but it was common enough thirty years or so ago. We have dropped it just as we have dropped the word "common" as it used to be applied to people who were loud and rude and pushed themselves forward. We have also dropped the word "vulgar" in this same connotation. "Breeding" was meant to be the antithesis of "common," and it implied that it took several generations to make a lady or a gentleman. Lady to the older generation not only had implications of social standing but of idleness; women worked and so did "ladies in reduced circumstances," who displayed "gallantry" in so doing.

To us this seems to be an attitude reminiscent of nineteenth-century novels of manners, of the days when ladies had fainting spells and men had legs but ladies had limbs. Our notions of what a lady is have changed and are still changing. It is a better word than it used to be. It no longer bears any relation to idleness or the command over the services of others. The implication of social parasite has gone and so has every trace of snobbishness. No lady is ever rude or overbearing to the people who serve her, for she does not think of them as her inferiors. The wives of the men who occupy the positions at the top of the social pyramids may look down on the wives of men who rank below their husbands, but they do not regard them as lesser ladies than themselves.

A lady has no position; she has only her self-esteem. "The great secret," Shaw says in *Pygmalion,* "is not having bad manners or good manners or any other particular sort of manners, but having the same manner for all human souls: in short, behaving as if you were in Heaven, where there are no third-class carriages, and one soul is as good as another." He also says: "The difference be- tween a lady and a flower girl is not how she behaves, but how she's treated."

If our society is becoming increasingly classless, then Shaw's "great secret" of man- ners becomes increasingly apt, and the only definition of a lady that applies to our egali- tarian concept of society is, it seems to me, this: *A lady is a woman who makes a man behave like a gentleman.*

QUESTIONS FOR STUDY AND DISCUSSION

1. Re-read the first half-dozen paragraphs of this essay. What purpose do they serve in Lynes's definition of *lady?*

2. How have our ideas about the lady changed over the years?

3. Consider Lynes's list of "tidy rules" which a lady would have observed in 1900. Can you make a list that might apply to many ladies today? You should compare your observations about ladies with com- ments made by Emily Post and other writers on modern etiquette.

4. Evaluate the definition with which Lynes ends his discussion. How well does it fit the rules of thumb that you have learned about definition?

SAMUEL TAYLOR COLERIDGE

from

Biographia Literaria

During the first year that Mr. Wordsworth and I were neighbors, our conversations turned frequently on the two cardinal points of poetry, the power of exciting the sympathy of the reader by a faithful adherence to the truth of nature, and the power of giving the interest of novelty by the modifying colors of imagination. The sudden charm which accidents of light and shade, which moonlight or sunset diffused over a known and familiar landscape, appear to represent the practicability of combining both. These are the poetry of nature. The thought suggested itself—(to which of us I do not recollect)—that a series of poems might be composed of two sorts. In the one, the incidents and agents were to be, in part at least, supernatural; and the excellence aimed at was to consist in the interesting of the affections by the dramatic truth of such emotions, as would naturally accompany such situations, supposing them real. And real in this sense they have been to every human being who, from whatever source of delusion, has at any time believed himself under supernatural agency. For the second class, subjects were to be chosen from ordinary life; the characters and incidents were to be such as will be found in every village and its vicinity, where there is a meditative and feeling mind to seek after them, or to notice them, when they present themselves.

In this idea originated the plan of the LYRICAL BALLADS; in which it was agreed, that my endeavors should be directed to persons and characters supernatural, or at least romantic; yet so as to transfer from our inward nature a human interest and a semblance of truth sufficient to procure for these shadows of imagination that willing suspension of disbelief for the moment, which constitutes poetic faith. Mr. Wordsworth, on the other hand, was to propose to himself as his object, to give the charm of novelty to things of every day, and to excite a feeling analogous to the supernatural, by awakening the mind's attention to the lethargy of custom, and directing it to the loveliness and the wonders of the world before us; an inexhaustible treasure, but for which, in consequence of the film of familiarity and selfish solicitude we have eyes, yet see not, ears that hear not, and hearts that neither feel nor understand.

With this view I wrote THE ANCIENT MARINER, and was preparing among other poems, THE DARK LADIE, and the CHRISTABEL, in which I should have more nearly realized my ideal than I had done in my first attempt. But Mr. Wordsworth's industry had proved so much more successful, and the number of his poems so much greater, that my compositions, instead of forming a balance, appeared rather an interpolation of heterogeneous matter. Mr. Wordsworth added two or three poems written in his own character, in the impassioned, lofty, and sustained diction, which is characteristic of his genius. In this form the LYRICAL BALLADS were published; and were presented by him, as an experiment, whether subjects, which from their nature rejected the usual ornaments and extra-colloquial style of poems in general, might not be so managed in the language of ordinary life as to produce the pleasurable interest, which it is the peculiar business of poetry to impart. To the second edition he added a preface of considerable length; in which, notwithstanding some passages of apparently a contrary import, he was understood to contend for the extension of this style to poetry of all kinds, and to reject as vicious and indefensible all phrases and forms of speech that were not included in what he (unfortunately, I think, adopting an equivocal expression) called the language of real life. From this preface, prefixed to poems in which it was impossible to deny the presence of original genius, however mistaken its direction might be deemed, arose the whole long-continued controversy. For from the conjunction of perceived power with supposed heresy I explain the inveteracy and in some instances, I grieve to say, the acrimonious passions, with which the controversy has been conducted by the assailants.

Had Mr. Wordsworth's poems been the silly, the childish things, which they were for a long time described as being; had they been really distinguished from the compositions of other poets merely by meanness of language and inanity of thought; had they indeed contained nothing more than what is found in the parodies and pretended imitations of them; they must have sunk at once, a dead weight, into the slough of oblivion, and have dragged the preface along with them. But year after year increased the number of Mr. Wordsworth's admirers. They were found too not in the lower classes of the reading public, but chiefly among young men of strong sensibility and meditative minds; and their admiration (inflamed perhaps in some degree by opposition) was distinguished by its intensity, I might almost say, by its religious fervor. These facts, and the intellectual energy of the author, which was more or less consciously felt, where it was outwardly and even boisterously denied, meeting with sentiments of aversion to his opinions, and of alarm at their consequences, produced an eddy of criticism, which would of itself have borne up the poems by the violence with which it whirled them round and round. With many parts of this preface in the sense attributed to them and which the words undoubtedly seem to authorize, I never concurred; but on the contrary objected to them as erroneous in principle, and as contradictory (in appearance at least) both to other parts of the same preface, and to the author's own practice in the greater part of the poems themselves. Mr. Wordsworth in his recent collection has, I find, degraded this prefatory disquisition to the end of his second volume, to be read or not at the reader's choice. But he has not, as far as I can discover, announced any change in his poetic creed. At all events, considering it as the source of a controversy, in which I have been honored more than I deserve by the frequent conjunction of my name with his, I think it expedient to declare once for all, in what points I coincide with the opinions supported in that preface, and in what points I altogether differ. But in order to render myself intelligible I must previously, in as few words as possible, explain my views, first, of a Poem; and secondly, of Poetry itself, in kind, and in essence.

The office of philosophical disquisition consists in just distinction; while it is the privilege of the philosopher to preserve himself constantly aware, that distinction is not division. In order to obtain adequate notions of any truth, we must intellectually separate its distinguishable parts; and this is the technical process of philosophy. But having so done, we must then restore them in our conceptions to the unity, in which they actually co-exist; and this is the result of philosophy. A poem contains the same elements as a prose composition; the difference therefore must consist in a different combination of them, in consequence of a different object being proposed. According to the difference of the object will be the difference of the combination. It is possible, that the object may be merely to facilitate the recollection of any given facts or observations by artificial arrangement; and the composition will be a poem, merely because it is distinguished from prose by metre, or by rhyme, or by both conjointly. In this, the lowest sense, a man might attribute the name of a poem to the well-known enumeration of the days in the several months;

"Thirty days hath September,
   April, June, and November," &c.

and others of the same class and purpose. And as a particular pleasure is found in anticipating the recurrence of sounds and quantities, all compositions that have this charm superadded, whatever be their contents, *may* be entitled poems.

So much for the superficial form. A difference of object and contents supplies an additional ground of distinction. The immediate purpose may be the communication of truths; either of truth absolute and demonstrable, as in works of science; or of facts experienced and recorded, as in history. Pleasure, and that of the highest and most permanent kind, may result from the attainment of the end; but it is not itself the immediate end. In other works the communication of pleasure may be the immediate purpose; and though truth, either moral or intellectual, ought to be the ultimate end, yet this will distinguish the character of the author, not the class to which the work belongs. Blest indeed is that state of society, in which the immediate purpose would be baffled by the perversion of the proper ultimate end; in which no charm of diction or imagery could exempt the BATHYLLUS even of an Anacreon, or the ALEXIS of Virgil, from disgust and aversion!

But the communication of pleasure may be the immediate object of a work not metrically composed; and that object may have been in a high degree attained, as in novels and romances. Would then the mere superaddition of metre, with or without rhyme, entitle these to the name of poems? The answer is, that nothing can permanently please, which does not contain in itself the reason why it is so, and not otherwise. If metre be superadded, all other parts must be made consonant with it. They must be such, as to justify the perpetual and distinct attention to each part, which an exact correspondent recurrence of accent and sound are calculated to excite. The final definition then, so deduced, may be thus worded. A poem is that species of composition, which is opposed to works of science, by proposing for its *immediate* object pleasure, not truth; and from all other species—(having *this* object in common with it)—it is discriminated by proposing to itself such delight from the *whole*, as is compatible with a distinct gratification from each component *part*.

Controversy is not seldom excited in consequence of the disputants attaching each a different meaning to the same word; and in few instances has this been more striking, than in disputes concerning the present subject. If a man chooses to call every composition a poem, which is rhyme, or measure, or both, I must leave his opinion uncontroverted. The distinction is at least competent to characterize the writer's intention. If it were subjoined, that the whole is likewise

entertaining or affecting, as a tale, or as a series of interesting reflections, I of course admit this as another fit ingredient of a poem, and an additional merit. But if the definition sought for be that of a *legitimate* poem, I answer, it must be one, the parts of which mutually support and explain each other; all in their proportion harmonizing with, and supporting the purpose and known influences of metrical arrangement. The philosophic critics of all ages coincide with the ultimate judgment of all countries, in equally denying the praises of a just poem, on the one hand, to a series of striking lines or distiches, each of which, absorbing the whole attention of the reader to itself, becomes disjoined from its context, and forms a separate whole, instead of a harmonizing part; and on the other hand, to an unsustained composition, from which the reader collects rapidly the general result unattracted by the component parts. The reader should be carried forward, not merely or chiefly by the mechanical impulse of curiosity, or by a restless desire to arrive at the final solution; but by the pleasurable activity of mind excited by the attractions of the journey itself. Like the motion of a serpent, which the Egyptians made the emblem of intellectual power; or like the path of sound through the air:—at every step he pauses and half recedes, and from the retrogressive movement collects the force which again carries him onward. *Præcipitandus est liber spiritus,** says Petronius most happily. The epithet, *liber,* here balances the preceding verb; and it is not easy to conceive more meaning condensed in fewer words.

But if this should be admitted as a satisfactory character of a poem, we have still to seek for a definition of poetry. The writings of Plato and Jeremy Taylor, and Burnet's Theory of the Earth, furnish undeniable proofs that poetry of the highest kind may exist without metre, and even without the contradistinguishing objects of a poem. The first chapter of Isaiah—(indeed a very large proportion of the whole book)—is poetry in the most emphatic sense; yet it would be not less irrational than strange to assert, that pleasure, and not truth was the imme-

* The free spirit must be swept onward.

diate object of the prophet. In short, whatever specific import we attach to the word, Poetry, there will be found involved in it, as a necessary consequence, that a poem of any length neither can be, nor ought to be, all poetry. Yet if an harmonious whole is to be produced, the remaining parts must be preserved in keeping with the poetry; and this can be no otherwise effected than by such a studied selection and artificial arrangement, as will partake of one, though not a peculiar property of poetry. And this again can be no other than the property of exciting a more continuous and equal attention than the language of prose aims at, whether colloquial or written.

My own conclusions on the nature of poetry, in the strictest use of the word, have been in part anticipated in some of the remarks on the Fancy and Imagination in the first part of this work. What is poetry?— is so nearly the same question with, what is a poet?—that the answer to the one is involved in the solution of the other. For it is a distinction resulting from the poetic genius itself, which sustains and modifies the images, thoughts, and emotions of the poet's own mind.

The poet, described in ideal perfection, brings the whole soul of man into activity, with the subordination of its faculties to each other according to their relative worth and dignity. He diffuses a tone and spirit of unity, that blends, and (as it were) *fuses*, each into each, by that synthetic and magical power, to which I would exclusively appropriate the name of Imagination. This power, first put in action by the will and understanding, and retained under their irremissive, though gentle and unnoticed, control, *laxis effertur habenis*,† reveals itself in the balance or reconcilement of opposite or discordant qualities: of sameness, with dif-

† It is carried along with loose reins.

ference; of the general with the concrete; the idea with the image; the individual with the representative; the sense of novelty and freshness with old and familiar objects; a more than usual state of emotion with more than usual order; judgment ever awake and steady self-possession with enthusiasm and feeling profound or vehement; and while it blends and harmonizes the natural and the artificial, still subordinates art to nature; the manner to the matter; and our admiration of the poet to our sympathy with the poetry. Doubtless, as Sir John Davies observes of the soul—(and his words may with slight alteration be applied, and even more appropriately, to the poetic Imagination)—

> Doubtless this could not be, but that she turns
> Bodies to *spirit* by sublimation strange,
> As fire converts to fire the things it burns,
> As we our food into our nature change.
>
> From their gross matter she abstracts *their* forms,
> And draws a kind of quintessence from things;
> Which to her proper nature she transforms
> To bear them light on her celestial wings.
>
> *Thus* does she, when from *individual states*
> She doth abstract the universal kinds;
> *Which then re-clothed in divers names and fates*
> *Steal access through the senses to our minds.*

Finally, Good Sense is the Body of poetic genius, Fancy its Drapery, Motion its Life, and Imagination the Soul that is everywhere, and in each; and forms all into one graceful and intelligent whole.

QUESTIONS FOR STUDY AND DISCUSSION

1. How important, in Coleridge's view, is the distinction which separates a poem from a prose composition on the grounds of the presence or absence of rhyme and metre?

2. What is the principle which distinguishes a poem from works of science?

3. What principle distinguishes a poem from other classes of works which have the

same immediate object?

4. In Coleridge's definition, is it possible for a work not written in rhyme or in metre to be a poem?

5. How does "poetry" differ from "poem"? What are the attributes of "poetry"?

WRITING ASSIGNMENTS

1. After careful study of Coleridge's definition, attempt your own paraphrase of his definition of "a poem."

2. See if you can work out your own definition of "poem" or "poetry"; then present it in a logical essay.

3. Work out a definition of some other literary genre—the essay, the short story, the novel, for example—and present it in a logical essay.

Comparison and Contrast

Like classification and definition, comparison and contrast has its basis in the belief that experience and reality can to some degree be organized into classes or genera. When we compare the performance of two cars or the merit of two historical novels, we are doing nothing more than to examine the likenesses and differences of two species of the same genus. Unless the entities being compared have enough features in common so that we can relate them to one genus, there is no point in the comparison. It would be like debating the merits of the flower against the leaf.

In any comparison the species are similar in that they share the same generic traits. But similar does not mean identical. Suppose a comparison is made of the Caucasian race with the Oriental. We would consider as generic traits such qualities as pigmentation of skin, color of eyes, color and texture of hair, and shape of head, nose, and lips; they are features common to mankind—our genus—but the actual form that these features take varies from race to race, and it is the configuration of these variables which best identifies a race. In preparing a comparison and contrast, the writer must first consider how each species modifies generic similarities.

After the generic similarities come the differences, which are not qualities of the parent genus but of the species. These are the differentiae, properties, and accidents which give each species its individuality. As an example, if modern American homes are compared with homes a hundred years ago (both of them species of the genus domicile), we would find that both have some kind of heating —a generic trait—though the actual form might vary from a fireplace in the older home to a heat pump in the basement of the modern. The modern home, though, would sport a number of conveniences—electricity, indoor plumbing, and the like —unknown to the older species. These are the differences, and a comparison is not complete without them.

The theory of comparison and contrast suggests a natural and effective means of organizing the essay, namely a comparison of likenesses followed by a comparison of differences. A comparison of teachers in high school and college might lend itself to such a treatment. The many similarities might first be ticked off, leading the reader to the differences, the really interesting part of such a comparison.

But there are other useful techniques for ordering the same material. In a whole-to-whole comparison, the writer thoroughly explores one species, then a second, and so on. In an essay on homes, he might write first about the characteristics of American houses in 1862, and only then would he turn to a discussion of the modern home. (Such a comparison is more effective for paragraphs and short passages than for full essays, which run the risk of being fragmented by this technique.)

In a part-to-part comparison, the writer singles out the characteristic traits of the genus and takes them up one by one, showing what form each trait assumes in the species being compared. A comparison of two races which is organized by this technique would take up, one after another, such generic traits as color of skin, color of eyes, and the rest, discussing each one separately. These are all useful devices, but their application depends upon the subject, and it is not unusual to find writers working with all three techniques in the same essay.

ESSAY SUGGESTIONS

1. Select a magazine, such as the *Atlantic*, which has been in business for some time, and write a comparison of the advertisements used to sell automobiles, insurance, or women's clothes now and forty years ago.
2. Read *Hours of Idleness* and compare Byron's juvenilia with his mature lyrics.
3. Select two novels set in a future time (for instance, Aldous Huxley's *Brave New World* and George Orwell's *1984*) and contrast the authors' views of the shape of things to come.
4. Compare cars forty, thirty, twenty, or ten years ago with the automobiles manufactured today.
5. Contrast TV soap operas, or other shows which are aimed at women, with the evening shows which are directed to the whole family.
6. Read Dryden's *All for Love* and compare it with Shakespeare's treatment of the theme in *Antony and Cleopatra*.
7. Contrast the advertising in a man's magazine, such as *True*, with that found in a woman's magazine, such as *Good Housekeeping*.
8. Contrast the chief theories about the origin of the universe.
9. Compare basketball as it is played today with the game as played twenty years ago.
10. Compare and contrast the four versions of the "Flight into Egypt" by Dürer, Rembrandt, Tiepolo, and Bresdin, which end this section. Compare the four prints for their content, first of all. How do they interpret the account of the Flight given in the second chapter of Matthew? Compare them also for their composition and technique. How does each artist group and balance his figures? How does he represent light and shade? How does he use lines?

EDMUND WILSON

from A Piece of My Mind

A certain kind of European overrates the comparative importance, in the present age of the world, of a good deal of his cultural tradition, and often of his own real interest in it. For myself, as an American, I have not the least doubt that I have derived a good deal more benefit of the civilizing as well as of the inspirational kind from the admirable American bathroom than I have from the cathedrals of Europe. I do not, of course, deny the impressiveness or the many varied beauties of these monuments, nor their usefulness to the people in their time; I have enjoyed their delightful coolness and their shade from the glare of the sun on broiling days in France and Italy—though in cold weather they are likely to be unbearable. But I have had a good many more up-lifting thoughts, creative and expansive visions—while soaking in comfortable baths or drying myself after bracing showers—in well-equipped American bathrooms than I have ever had in any cathedral. Here the body purges itself, and along with the body, the spirit. Here the mind becomes free to ruminate, to plan ambitious projects. The cathedrals, with their distant domes, their long aisles and their high groinings, do add stature to human strivings; their chapels do give privacy for prayer. But the bathroom, too, shelters the spirit, it tranquillizes and reassures, in surroundings of a celestial whiteness, where the pipes and the faucets gleam and the mirror makes another liquid surface, which will render you, shaved, rubbed and brushed, a nobler and more winning appearance. Here, too, you may sing, recite, refresh yourself with brief readings, just as you do in church; and the fact that you do it without a priest and not as a member of a congregation is, from my point of view, an advantage. It encourages self-dependence and prepares one to face the world, fortified, firm on one's feet, serene and with a mind like a diamond.

QUESTIONS FOR STUDY AND DISCUSSION

1. Cathedrals and bathrooms seem unlikely objects for comparison. Wherein lie the similarities which make them comparable? In what ways, according to Edmund Wilson, do they both serve the same purposes?

2. What makes the American bathroom, in Wilson's view, superior to the cathedral for carrying out the functions they both share?

3. To what extent are the contrasts between cathedrals and bathrooms illustrated in this essay?

ROBERT LOUIS
STEVENSON

Crabbed Age
and Youth

"You know my mother now and then
argues very notably; always very warmly
at least. I happen often to differ from
her; and we both think so well of our
own arguments, that we very seldom are
so happy as to convince one another. A
pretty common case, I believe, in all
vehement debatings. She says, I am *too
witty*; Anglicè, *too pert*; I, that she is
too wise; that is to say, being likewise
put into English, *not so young as she
has been.*"—Miss Howe to Miss Har-
lowe, *Clarissa*, vol. ii. Letter xiii.

There is a strong feeling in favour of cowardly and prudential proverbs. The sentiments of a man while he is full of ardour
and hope are to be received, it is supposed,
with some qualification. But when the same
person has ignominiously failed and begins
to eat up his words, he should be listened
to like an oracle. Most of our pocket wisdom
is conceived for the use of mediocre people,
to discourage them from ambitious attempts,
and generally console them in their medi-
ocrity. And since mediocre people constitute
the bulk of humanity, this is no doubt very
properly so. But it does not follow that the
one sort of proposition is any less true than
the other, or that Icarus is not to be more
praised, and perhaps more envied, than Mr.
Samuel Budgett the Successful Merchant.
The one is dead, to be sure, while the other
is still in his counting-house counting out
his money; and doubtless this is a consideration. But we have, on the other hand, some
bold and magnanimous sayings common to
high races and natures, which set forth the
advantage of the losing side, and proclaim it
better to be a dead lion than a living dog.

It is difficult to fancy how the mediocrities
reconcile such sayings with their proverbs.
According to the latter, every lad who goes
to sea is an egregious ass; never to forget
your umbrella through a long life would
seem a higher and wiser flight of achievement than to go smiling to the stake; and
so long as you are a bit of a coward and
inflexible in money matters, you fulfil the
whole duty of man.

It is a still more difficult consideration for
our average men, that while all their teachers, from Solomon down to Benjamin
Franklin and the ungodly Binney, have in-
culcated the same ideal of manners, caution,
and respectability, those characters in history
who have most notoriously flown in the face
of such precepts are spoken of in hyper-
bolical terms of praise, and honoured with
public monuments in the streets of our
commercial centres. This is very bewildering
to the moral sense. You have Joan of Arc,
who left a humble but honest and reputable
livelihood under the eyes of her parents, to
go a-colonelling, in the company of rowdy
soldiers, against the enemies of France;
surely a melancholy example for one's daughters! And then you have Columbus, who
may have pioneered America, but, when all
is said, was a most imprudent navigator.
His life is not the kind of thing one would
like to put into the hands of young people;
rather, one would do one's utmost to keep it
from their knowledge, as a red flag of adventure and disintegrating influence in life.
The time would fail me if I were to recite
all the big names in history whose exploits
are perfectly irrational and even shocking
to the business mind. The incongruity is
speaking; and I imagine it must engender
among the mediocrities a very peculiar attitude towards the nobler and showier sides
of national life. They will read of the
Charge of Balaclava in much the same
spirit as they assist at a performance of the
Lyons Mail. Persons of substance take in the
Times and sit composedly in pit or boxes according to the degree of their prosperity in
business. As for the generals who go gallop-
ing up and down among bomb-shells in absurd cocked hats—as for the actors who
raddle their faces and demean themselves

for hire upon the stage—they must belong, thank God! to a different order of beings, whom we watch as we watch the clouds careering in the windy, bottomless inane, or read about like characters in ancient and rather fabulous annals. Our offspring would no more think of copying their behaviour, let us hope, than of doffing their clothes and painting themselves blue in consequence of certain admissions in the first chapter of their school history of England.

Discredited as they are in practice, the cowardly proverbs hold their own in theory; and it is another instance of the same spirit, that the opinions of old men about life have been accepted as final. All sorts of allowances are made for the illusions of youth; and none, or almost none, for the disenchantments of age. It is held to be a good taunt, and somehow or other to clinch the question logically, when an old gentleman waggles his head and says: "Ah, so I thought when I was your age." It is not thought an answer at all, if the young man retorts: "My venerable sir, so I shall most probably think when I am yours." And yet the one is as good as the other: pass for pass, tit for tat, a Roland for an Oliver.

"Opinion in good men," says Milton, "is but knowledge in the making." All opinions, properly so called, are stages on the road to truth. It does not follow that a man will travel any further; but if he has really considered the world and drawn a conclusion, he has travelled as far. This does not apply to formulæ got by rote, which are stages on the road to nowhere but second childhood and the grave. To have a catchword in your mouth is not the same thing as to hold an opinion; still less is it the same thing as to have made one for yourself. There are too many of these catchwords in the world for people to rap out upon you like an oath and by way of an argument. They have a currency as intellectual counters; and many respectable persons pay their way with nothing else. They seem to stand for vague bodies of theory in the background. The imputed virtue of folios full of knockdown arguments is supposed to reside in them, just as some of the majesty of the British Empire dwells in the constable's truncheon.

They are used in pure superstition, as old clodhoppers spoil Latin by way of an exorcism. And yet they are vastly serviceable for checking unprofitable discussion and stopping the mouths of babes and sucklings. And when a young man comes to a certain stage of intellectual growth, the examination of these counters forms a gymnastic at once amusing and fortifying to the mind.

Because I have reached Paris, I am not ashamed of having passed through Newhaven and Dieppe. They were very good places to pass through, and I am none the less at my destination. All my old opinions were only stages on the way to the one I now hold, as itself is only a stage on the way to something else. I am no more abashed at having been a red-hot Socialist with a panacea of my own than at having been a sucking infant. Doubtless the world is quite right in a million ways; but you have to be kicked about a little to convince you of the fact. And in the meanwhile you must do something, be something, believe something. It is not possible to keep the mind in a state of accurate balance and blank; and even if you could do so, instead of coming ultimately to the right conclusion, you would be very apt to remain in a state of balance and blank to perpetuity. Even in quite intermediate stages, a dash of enthusiasm is not a thing to be ashamed of in the retrospect: if St. Paul had not been a very zealous Pharisee, he would have been a colder Christian. For my part, I look back to the time when I was a Socialist with something like regret. I have convinced myself (for the moment) that we had better leave these great changes to what we call great blind forces: their blindness being so much more perspicacious than the little, peering, partial eyesight of men. I seem to see that my own scheme would not answer; and all the other schemes I ever heard propounded would depress some elements of goodness just as much as they encouraged others. Now I know that in thus turning Conservative with years, I am going through the normal cycle of change and travelling in the common orbit of men's opinions. I submit to this, as I would submit to gout or gray hair, as a concomitant of growing age or else of failing animal heat; but I do not acknowledge that it is necessarily a change for the better—I daresay it is deplorably for the worse. I have no choice in the business, and can no more resist this tendency of my mind than I could prevent my body from beginning to totter and decay. If I am spared (as the phrase runs) I shall doubtless outlive some troublesome desires; but I am in no hurry about that; nor, when the time comes, shall I plume myself on the immunity. Just in the same way, I do not greatly pride myself on having outlived my belief in the fairy tales of Socialism. Old people have faults of their own; they tend to become cowardly, niggardly, and suspicious. Whether from the growth of experience or the decline of animal heat, I see that age leads to these and certain other faults; and it follows, of course, that while in one sense I hope I am journeying towards the truth, in another I am indubitably posting towards these forms and sources of error.

As we go catching and catching at this or that corner of knowledge, now getting a foresight of generous possibilities, now chilled with a glimpse of prudence, we may compare the headlong course of our years to a swift torrent in which a man is carried away; now he is dashed against a boulder, now he grapples for a moment to a trailing spray; at the end, he is hurled out and overwhelmed in a dark and bottomless ocean. We have no more than glimpses and touches; we are torn away from our theories; we are spun round and round and shown this or the other view of life, until only fools or knaves can hold to their opinions. We take a sight at a condition in life, and say we have studied it; our most elaborate view is no more than an impression. If we had breathing space, we should take the occasion to modify and adjust; but at this break-neck hurry, we are no sooner boys than we are adult, no sooner in love than married or jilted, no sooner one age than we begin to be another, and no sooner in the fulness of our manhood than we begin to decline towards the grave. It is in vain to seek for consistency or expect clear and stable views in a medium so perturbed and fleeting. This

is no cabinet science, in which things are tested to a scruple; we theorise with a pistol to our head; we are confronted with a new set of conditions on which we have not only to pass a judgment, but to take action, before the hour is at an end. And we cannot even regard ourselves as a constant; in this flux of things, our identity itself seems in a perpetual variation; and not infrequently we find our own disguise the strangest in the masquerade. In the course of time, we grow to love things we hated and hate things we loved. Milton is not so dull as he once was, nor perhaps Ainsworth so amusing. It is decidedly harder to climb trees, and not nearly so hard to sit still. There is no use pretending; even the thrice royal game of hide and seek has somehow lost in zest. All our attributes are modified or changed; and it will be a poor account of us if our views do not modify and change in a proportion. To hold the same views at forty as we held at twenty is to have been stupefied for a score of years, and take rank, not as a prophet, but as an unteachable brat, well birched and none the wiser. It is as if a ship captain should sail to India from the Port of London; and having brought a chart of the Thames on deck at his first setting out, should obstinately use no other for the whole voyage.

And mark you, it would be no less foolish to begin at Gravesend with a chart of the Red Sea. *Si Jeunesse savait, si Vieillesse pouvait*, is a very pretty sentiment, but not necessarily right. In five cases out of ten, it is not so much that the young people do not know, as that they do not choose. There is something irreverent in the speculation, but perhaps the want of power has more to do with the wise resolutions of age than we are always willing to admit. It would be an instructive experiment to make an old man young again and leave him all his *savoir*. I scarcely think he would put his money in the Savings Bank after all; I doubt if he would be such an admirable son as we are led to expect; and as for his conduct in love, I believe firmly he would out-Herod Herod, and put the whole of his new compeers to the blush. Prudence is a wooden Juggernaut, before whom Benjamin Franklin walks with the portly air of a high priest, and after whom dances many a successful merchant in the character of Atys. But it is not a deity to cultivate in youth. If a man lives to any considerable age, it cannot be denied that he laments his imprudences, but I notice he often laments his youth a deal more bitterly and with a more genuine intonation.

It is customary to say that age should be considered, because it comes last. It seems just as much to the point, that youth comes first. And the scale fairly kicks the beam, if you go on to add that age, in a majority of cases, never comes at all. Disease and accident make short work of even the most prosperous persons; death costs nothing, and the expense of a headstone is an inconsiderable trifle to the happy heir. To be suddenly snuffed out in the middle of ambitious schemes, is tragical enough at best; but when a man has been grudging himself his own life in the meanwhile, and saving up everything for the festival that was never to be, it becomes that hysterically moving sort of tragedy which lies on the confines of farce. The victim is dead—and he has cunningly overreached himself: a combination of calamities none the less absurd for being grim. To husband a favourite claret until the batch turns sour, is not at all an artful stroke of policy; and how much more with a whole cellar—a whole bodily existence! People may lay down their lives with cheerfulness in the sure expectation of a blessed immortality; but that is a different affair from giving up youth with all its admirable pleasures, in the hope of a better quality of gruel in a more than problematical, nay, more than improbable, old age. We should not compliment a hungry man, who should refuse a whole dinner and reserve all his appetite for the dessert, before he knew whether there was to be any dessert or not. If there be such a thing as imprudence in the world, we surely have it here. We sail in leaky bottoms and on great and perilous waters; and to take a cue from the dolorous old naval ballad, we have heard the mermaidens singing, and know that we shall never see dry land any more. Old and young, we are all on our last cruise. If there is a fill of tobacco among the crew, for God's sake pass it round, and let us have a pipe before we go!

Indeed, by the report of our elders, this nervous preparation for old age is only trouble thrown away. We fall on guard, and after all it is a friend who comes to meet us. After the sun is down and the west faded, the heavens begin to fill with shining stars. So, as we grow old, a sort of equable jog-trot of feeling is substituted for the violent ups and downs of passion and disgust; the same influence that restrains our hopes, quiets our apprehensions; if the pleasures are less intense, the troubles are milder and more tolerable; and in a word, this period for which we are asked to hoard up everything as for a time of famine, is, in its own right, the richest, easiest, and happiest of life. Nay, by managing its own work and following its own happy inspiration, youth is doing the best it can to endow the leisure of age. A full, busy youth is your only prelude to a self-contained and independent age; and the muff inevitably develops into the bore. There are not many Doctor Johnsons, to set forth upon their first romantic voyage at sixty-four. If we wish to scale Mont Blanc or visit a thieves' kitchen in the East End, to go down in a diving dress or up in a balloon, we must be about it while we are still young. It will not do to delay until we are clogged with prudence and limping with rheumatism, and people begin to ask us: "What does Gravity out of bed?" Youth is the time to go flashing from one end of the world to the other both in mind and body; to try the manners of different nations; to hear the chimes at midnight; to see sunrise in town and country; to be converted at a revival; to circumnavigate the metaphysics, write halting verses, run a mile to see a fire, and wait all day long in the theatre to applaud *Hernani*. There is some meaning in the old theory about wild oats; and a man who has not had his green-sickness and got done with it for good, is as little to be depended on as an unvaccinated infant. "It is extraordinary," says Lord Beaconsfield, one of the brightest and best preserved of youths up to the date of his last novel, "it is extraordinary how hourly and how violently change the feelings of an inexperienced young man." And this mobility is a special talent entrusted to his care; a sort of indestructible virginity; a magic armour, with which he can pass unhurt through great dangers and come unbedaubed out of the miriest passages. Let him voyage, speculate, see all that he can, do all that he may; his soul has as many lives as a cat, he will live in all weathers, and never be a halfpenny the worse. Those who go to the devil in youth, with anything like a fair chance, were probably little worth saving from the first; they must have been feeble fellows—creatures made of putty and pack-thread, without steel or fire, anger or true joyfulness, in their composition; we may sympathise with their parents, but there is not much cause to go into mourning for themselves; for to be quite honest, the weak brother is the worst of mankind.

When the old man waggles his head and says, "Ah, so I thought when I was your age," he has proved the youth's case. Doubtless, whether from growth of experience or decline of animal heat, he thinks so no longer; but he thought so while he was young; and all men have thought so while they were young, since there was dew in the morning or hawthorn in May; and here is another young man adding his vote to those of previous generations and rivetting another link to the chain of testimony. It is as natural and as right for a young man to be imprudent and exaggerated, to live in swoops and circles, and beat about his cage like any other wild thing newly captured, as it is for old men to turn gray, or mothers to love their offspring, or heroes to die for something worthier than their lives.

By way of an apologue for the aged, when they feel more than usually tempted to offer their advice, let me recommend the following little tale. A child who had been remarkably fond of toys (and in particular of lead soldiers) found himself growing to the level of acknowledged boyhood without any abatement of this childish taste. He was thirteen; already he had been taunted for dallying overlong about the playbox; he had to blush if he was found among his lead soldiers; the shades of the prison-house were closing about him with a vengeance. There

is nothing more difficult than to put the thoughts of children into the language of their elders; but this is the effect of his meditations at this juncture: "Plainly," he said, "I must give up my playthings, in the meanwhile, since I am not in a position to secure myself against idle jeers. At the same time, I am sure that playthings are the very pick of life; all people give them up out of the same pusillanimous respect for those who are a little older; and if they do not return to them as soon as they can, it is only because they grow stupid and forget. I shall be wiser; I shall conform for a little to the ways of their foolish world; but so soon as I have made enough money, I shall retire and shut myself up among my playthings until the day I die." Nay, as he was passing in the train along the Esterel mountains between Cannes and Fréjus, he remarked a pretty house in an orange garden at the angle of a bay, and decided that this should be his Happy Valley. Astrea Redux; childhood was to come again! The idea has an air of simple nobility to me, not unworthy of Cincinnatus. And yet, as the reader has probably anticipated, it is never likely to be carried into effect. There was a worm in the bud, a fatal error in the premises. Childhood must pass away, and then youth, as surely as age approaches. The true wisdom is to be always seasonable, and to change with a good grace in changing circumstances. To love playthings well as a child, to lead an adventurous and honourable youth, and to settle when the time arrives, into a green and smiling age, is to be a good artist in life and deserve well of yourself and your neighbour.

You need repent none of your youthful vagaries. They may have been over the score on one side, just as those of age are probably over the score on the other. But they had a point; they not only befitted your age and expressed its attitude and passions, but they had a relation to what was outside of you, and implied criticisms on the existing state of things, which you need not allow to have been undeserved, because you now see that they were partial. All error, not merely verbal, is a strong way of stating that the current truth is incomplete. The follies of youth have a basis in sound reason, just as much as the embarrassing questions put by babes and sucklings. Their most antisocial acts indicate the defects of our society. When the torrent sweeps the man against a boulder, you must expect him to scream, and you need not be surprised if the scream is sometimes a theory. Shelley, chafing at the Church of England, discovered the cure of all evils in universal atheism. Generous lads irritated at the injustices of society, see nothing for it but the abolishment of everything and Kingdom Come of anarchy. Shelley was a young fool; so are these cocksparrow revolutionaries. But it is better to be a fool than to be dead. It is better to emit a scream in the shape of a theory than to be entirely insensible to the jars and incongruities of life and take everything as it comes in a forlorn stupidity. Some people swallow the universe like a pill; they travel on through the world, like smiling images pushed from behind. For God's sake give me the young man who has brains enough to make a fool of himself! As for the others, the irony of facts shall take it out of their hands, and make fools of them in downright earnest, ere the farce be over. There shall be such a mopping and a mowing at the last day, and such blushing and confusion of countenance for all those who have been wise in their own esteem, and have not learnt the rough lessons that youth hands on to age. If we are indeed here to perfect and complete our own natures, and grow larger, stronger, and more sympathetic against some nobler career in the future, we had all best bestir ourselves to the utmost while we have the time. To equip a dull, respectable person with wings would be but to make a parody of an angel.

In short, if youth is not quite right in its opinions, there is a strong probability that age is not much more so. Undying hope is co-ruler of the human bosom with infallible credulity. A man finds he has been wrong at every preceding stage of his career, only to deduce the astonishing conclusion that he is at last entirely right. Mankind, after centuries of failure, are still upon the eve of a thoroughly constitutional millennium. Since we have explored the maze so long without

result, it follows, for poor human reason, that we cannot have to explore much longer; close by must be the centre, with a champagne luncheon and a piece of ornamental water. How if there were no centre at all, but just one alley after another, and the whole world a labyrinth without end or issue?

I overheard the other day a scrap of conversation, which I take the liberty to reproduce. "What I advance is true," said one. "But not the whole truth," answered the other. "Sir," returned the first (and it seemed to me there was a smack of Dr. Johnson in the speech), "Sir, there is no such thing as the whole truth!" Indeed, there is nothing so evident in life as that there are two sides to a question. History is one long illustration. The forces of nature are engaged, day by day, in cudgelling it into our backward intelligences. We never pause for a moment's consideration, but we admit it as an axiom. An enthusiast sways humanity exactly by disregarding this great truth, and dinning it into our ears that this or that question has only one possible solution; and your enthusiast is a fine florid fellow, dominates things for a while and shakes the world out of a doze; but when once he is gone, an army of quiet and uninfluential people set to work to remind us of the other side and demolish the generous imposture. While Calvin is putting everybody exactly right in his *Institutes*, and hot-headed Knox is thundering in the pulpit, Montaigne is already looking at the other side in his library in Perigord, and predicting that they will find as much to quarrel about in the Bible as they had found already in the Church. Age may have one side, but assuredly Youth has the other. There is nothing more certain than that both are right, except perhaps that both are wrong. Let them agree to differ; for who knows but what agreeing to differ may not be a form of agreement rather than a form of difference?

I suppose it is written that any one who sets up for a bit of a philosopher, must contradict himself to his very face. For here have I fairly talked myself into thinking that we have the whole thing before us at last; that there is no answer to the mystery, except that there are as many as you please, that there is no centre to the maze because, like the famous sphere, its centre is everywhere; and that agreeing to differ with every ceremony of politeness, is the only "one undisturbed song of pure concent" to which we are ever likely to lend our musical voices.

QUESTIONS FOR STUDY AND DISCUSSION

1. In this essay, how does Stevenson employ the three chief methods for organizing a comparison and contrast?

2. Consider Stevenson's many casual references—from Icarus and Mr. Samuel Budgett to "the ungodly Binney" and Atys. How great are the demands that he makes upon his readers? Are they justifiable? Where does a person look for information about these allusions?

3. Compare Stevenson's style of writing with an essay that you consider typical of good current prose. What are their similarities? Their differences?

4. Robert Louis Stevenson's comparison of the young and the old is carried on to serve a thesis well beyond the comparison in and for itself. Try to formulate a statement of his purpose. Perhaps the questions below will help you.

In what ways, according to Stevenson, do young and old differ?

Should the young pay attention to their elders' cautionary admonitions? Why?

Should youth be a time of preparation for maturity and old age?

Are the young nearer the truth than the old? Further from it? Or are their opinions merely different?

Is truth ascertainable?

5. Comment on Stevenson's use of metaphor in this essay.

Materials for an Essay

*Four Versions of the Flight into Egypt**

* Reproduced by courtesy of The Art Institute of Chicago.

Albrecht Dürer (woodcut, published in 1511)

Rodolphe Bresdin (etching)

Rembrandt van Rijn (etching, ca. 1653)

Giovanni Tiepolo (etching, 1753)

Cause and Effect, and the Hypothesis

Causal analysis is difficult enough under laboratory conditions, and outside the laboratory it is sometimes impossible to do more than talk about it. But the human need to hunt causes is so great that we frequently abandon caution, discrimination, and good common sense in dealing with problems of this kind. Guesswork and proof are so often confused that causal reasoning tends to be the least critical kind of thinking that the human race engages in. Yet everyone does it. Every centenarian is invited to give his recipe for a long life, and does so without hesitation.

Hard as it is to analyze causes accurately, the writer who has a little systematic knowledge of cause-and-effect theory can work more prudently and avoid some of the pitfalls which trap the unwary. The fundamental task of any causal investigation is to show that if X occurs, Y will follow; and that if X does not take place, Y will not occur either. To illustrate: the fuse blows one stormy night, and not having a spare or the inclination to go out and face the elements, we foolishly slip a penny into the fuse box. The lights go back on, though we are in danger of burning the house down, and we conclude that if copper is present between two terminals, the current will flow. This much is true: we have proved that if X, then Y—that a copper wire or strip is a *sufficient* condition for transmitting electricity between two points. But we have not proved that if X is not present, Y will not occur; for electricity can travel with even greater ease through silver than it does through copper. All that is needed is a medium of sufficiently great conductivity for the strength of the current; this is the *necessary* condition for the flow of electricity. The job of the writer who treats causes is to find both necessary and sufficient conditions.

John Stuart Mill attempted to reduce the procedures for studying and proving causal relationships to five methods or canons. The method of agreement states:

> *If two or more instances of the phenomenon under investigation have only one circumstance in common, the circumstance in which alone all the instances agree is the cause (or effect) of the given phenomenon.*

Suppose, for instance, that a state agricultural agent receives a number of complaints from people all over the state whose trees and shrubs look yellow and sickly. Trees and shrubs, location and climate, soil and precipitation vary considerably within the state. Apparently there are no circumstances common to any of these factors, but the agricultural agent runs tests on the many samples of soil he has gathered and finds that they are alike in lacking iron. Iron, of course, is necessary to plants for growth and verdure. With the method of agreement as a guide, the agricultural agent suspects that the deficiency of iron is responsible for the trouble.

The method of difference—perhaps the biggest gun of them all—states:

> *If an instance in which the phenomenon under investigation occurs, and an instance in which it does not occur, have every circumstance in common save one, that one occurring only in the former; the circumstance in which alone the two instances differ is the effect, or the cause, or an indispensable part of the cause, of the phenomenon.*

The agricultural agent knows that iron can't be added to the soil in just any form and he wishes to test the effectiveness of iron sulphate, which seems like a good bet, before recommending it to his clients. He decides to experiment by treating one each of his two pecan trees, magnolias, redbuds, and fig trees with the chemical. All four pairs of trees apparently have every relevant circumstance in common except the iron sulphate. Then, if the fertilized trees respond to treatment while the control group remains unchanged, the agent knows that the iron sulphate is responsible for the improvement.

The joint method of agreement and difference attempts to handle still more intricate causal situations:

> *If two or more instances in which the phenomenon occurs have only one circumstance in common, while two or more instances in which it does not occur have nothing in common save the absence of that circumstance, the circumstance in which alone the two sets of instances differ is the effect, or the cause, or an indispensable part of the cause, of the phenomenon.*

A young man of good health and some cleverness had cereal, blueberries, milk, sugar, and black coffee for breakfast. Shortly thereafter he experienced an extreme discomfort in the belly, which lasted about two hours. For lunch he had only weak tea, but by evening he was himself again and ate a supper of steak, potatoes, salad, and beer. The next morning he continued to feel well and had a breakfast of scrambled eggs and black coffee, after which there was a return of the illness. Employing the joint method of agreement and difference, the young man reasoned that the coffee was in some way connected with his sickness. But more than that—whether the trouble was coffee in general, or the brand he used, or the particular can of coffee in his pantry, or the way he fixed it—he could not know without further experimentation.

The fourth canon is called the method of residues:

> *Subduct from any phenomenon such part as is known by previous inductions to be the effect of certain antecedents, and the residue of the phenomenon is the effect of the remaining antecedents.*

In its simplest form, the method of residues helps to pinpoint an unknown by subtraction. For example, a certain apartment in a typical Chicago slum must operate on not more than 15 amperes of current. The refrigerator runs on gas; the air conditioner in the bedroom uses 7.5 amps; the fan in the living room, 3.5 amps; each of the light bulbs, .9 amps; and the hi-fi rig, an unknown amount. On an especially bad night, the occupant is in the living room with the fan on to draw the cold air out of the bedroom. Three light bulbs are burning, and he wants to turn on the hi-fi. He does so and the fuse does not blow. The occupant, utilizing the method of residues, knows that the hi-fi uses under 1.3 amperes of current. In one of its more striking applications, the method of residues led to the discovery of the planet Neptune.

The last of the canons is the method of concomitant variation:

> *Whatever phenomenon varies in any manner whenever another phenomenon varies in some particular manner, is either a cause or an effect of that phenomenon, or is connected with it through some fact of causation.*

Suppose that we notice a display of the aurora borealis at the same time that we are having trouble with the radio. We observe that as the aurora intensifies, the static on the radio becomes worse. The method of concomitant variation suggests that the two are in some way connected, but it does not tell us that the aurora is the cause of the static. To assume such is to be misled by the hidden cause, sunspot activity, of which both aurora and static are effects.

A similar error is to match up two sets of data, notice that there is a correlation in the way they vary, and proclaim one as the cause of the other. It requires no great cleverness to show that between 1952 and 1959 the total admissions to mental hospitals correlate suspiciously with the average wages earned by farm hands during those years. Before we can invoke the canon of concomitant variation, we must be able to explain the actual mechanism of causal relationship. Until someone shows how increasing salaries on the farm can send people to the insane asylum, or vice versa, we have no business matching figures and calling it cause and effect.

Mill is inevitably chastised because his canons do not offer the foolproof method that the world needs for discovering and proving causes. The student of causality must still determine for himself what the relevant factors are in any situation and also the mechanism by which any cause produces its effect. Mill's canons, though, are the nearest thing to a rigorous statement of causal reasoning that we have, and they can be exceedingly helpful in deciding which factors are not real causes.

Causal reasoning is inescapably hazardous. There are not only the perils of hidden causes and accidental co-variation, but the danger of calling one thing the cause of another simply because it precedes it in time. ("The tumor was undoubtedly caused by the board that struck my client on the arm, and I therefore ask that your company pay damages.") There are other monkey wrenches ready and waiting to foul up the neatest analysis: reciprocal causes (such as wax and wick in a burning candle) and multiple causes (an effect resulting from one of several causes, or several causes acting in concert to create one effect). Sufferers from hay fever, if they have tried to chart their physical distress against the monthly pollen count and analysis, know about multiple causes. In studying causality we must know precisely what the causal agent is acting upon; after the same amount of exposure to infection, the person in bad health is more likely to catch a disease than one in top physical condition. Nor can the analyst of causes ever be sure that he has all the relevant information. Complicated situations—wars and cold wars, culture and civilization—are certainly the result of many causes, not all of them knowable. Causal reasoning is so perilous that the writer who attempts to treat causes must approach his subject with unfeigned humility.

The chains of causation running through life are so entwined and interdependent that for any one link we can find a cause and then a cause of the cause, working our way back indefinitely along the causal chain. What caused the Civil War: The firing on Fort Sumter? The secession of a few unhappy states? The question of slavery? Or the simple inability of a cantankerous human race to live in peace with itself? A certain effect may not only be the result of multiple causes but a chain of causes, and our analysis of these is relative to our interest and point of view. The social historian writing on the Civil War is not likely to have the same interpretation of events as the Constitutional lawyer. His problem will be as different as his viewpoint. The relativity of causes is beautifully illustrated by William McFee's "The Peculiar Fate of the *Morro Castle*."

Causal analysis, induction, and deduction are hardly isolated forms of reasoning. We employ them all, conjointly, to work out the simplest problems of everyday existence. And in finding the answer to our problems, we build hypotheses. To illustrate, suppose that we are awakened one midnight by the ghastly shrieking of tomcats under the house. We turn on the lamp by the bed, but it doesn't light so we flick on the ceiling light instead. The wailing outside has subsided, but before we go back to bed we put a new light bulb in the lamp. It still doesn't work. Something, we suspect, is wrong with the lamp; but in a burst of scientific curiosity we decide to plug the lamp into another socket, and here it does work. If the lamp is eliminated as the source of trouble and if the other lights in the house are working, the problem must be the outlet by the bed, to which the lamp was connected. We then remember that this outlet was not installed in the usual fashion; it connects to a wire running under the house instead of through the wall. Suddenly the ululations that awakened us have significance, and we hypothesize that in their overdone heroics the cats broke the wire leading to the outlet by the bed. We call the electrician the next morning, and at a cost of $16.50 the outlet is repaired and the hypothesis confirmed. "Such reasoning is used by every man in every hour of his life," as Henry Sturt put it.

In seeking causes we are obliged to construct hypotheses, but one hypothesis is not necessarily as good as another. The hypothesis itself must be evaluated. For one thing, it must be self-consistent and physically possible. (Our notions of what is physically possible change, of course. A century ago the idea that time can slow down or that one element could be transmuted into another or that there might be a continuous creation of matter would have been dismissed as outrageous.)

A good hypothesis should be verifiable. We should be able to prove it or disprove it by checking. Otherwise, like Einstein's unified field theory at the present time, it belongs to a different order of knowledge—one which may be valuable speculation or philosophy, but which cannot be incorporated into the body of man's established knowledge, as the theory of relativity has been.

A good hypothesis must be based on all the relevant information, or it is guilty of special pleading. A familiar Russian boast is the progress made by communism since the Russian revolution. But the Russians do not boast that their greatest progress came only after World War II, when Russia had reaped the advantages of wartime aid from the United States and had absorbed the factories and skills of eastern Europe into its economy.

A good hypothesis accounts for all the phenomena—or at least for a significant part of the phenomena. Some would regard the hypothesis only as a handy model for bringing order to a complicated reality and would thus be content to note a small percentage of variation and worry no more. Often such variation can be explained by a slight modification of the original theory, if it is essentially sound. Thus Copernican theory was not discredited when it was found that planets travel in ellipses rather than circles; it was merely improved.

A good hypothesis should be relatively simple—that is, it should make no more assumptions than necessary to explain the phenomena it deals with. If two hypotheses explain the same phenomena equally well, we choose the one that is less complicated. The simpler of two theories in modern physics may not be simple to understand and it may have a great many parts to it, but Occam's razor—as this principle is called—still applies. Copernican astronomy in the time of Copernicus explained nothing more about the solar system than did the Ptolemaic system, but anyone equipped with Occam's razor should have chosen it because it explained the known universe without the elaborate machinery of cycles and epicycles of the Ptolemaic theory.

A good hypothesis, finally, is often predictive. It does more than explain the facts it was set up to handle: it has consequences as well. Einstein's theory of relativity was established to explain certain problems of nineteenth-century physics; but in so doing, it predicted a number of observable phenomena which—when investigated—helped to prove the theory itself.

EXERCISE

1. Make a list of folk beliefs that you know. How would you apply Mill's canons in order to test them? You might consider these among others:

   A ring around the moon means rain.
   If it rains when the sun is still shining, it will rain again tomorrow.
   In winter, if the sun is bright when it goes down, the next day will be cold.
   A quarter moon upside down means rain.
   A broken mirror means seven years' bad luck.

2. List the common reasons given to explain the rise of various societies to greatness and their later decline. Can these causes be *proved* for the cultures to which they have been applied? Do they have application to other cultures? That is, are the conditions involved necessary or sufficient?

3. Who was William Ockham (or Occam)? What is John Stuart Mill known for besides his great work on logic? For information, go to the *Dictionary of National Biography*.

4. A popular notion that shows both causal thinking and induction, after a fashion, is that the Democratic Party is a war party because there has been war during the Wilson, Roosevelt, and Truman administrations. (Cf. the letter by F. L. Stack to the editors of *Time*, July 25, 1960.) Evaluate.

5. Evaluate as causal analysis: "This vitamin [inositol] is a by-product of corn-

starch manufacture; tons of it are added to the gray paint used by our Navy. Since inositol is not cheap, this paint may account for part of our high taxes." Adelle Davis, *Let's Eat Right to Keep Fit*.

6. Evaluate as causal analysis: "Statistics, again, prove that the expectation of life has been longer since the introduction of tobacco and its use by the ordinary man. Taking the example of France: in 1830 the average duration of life was no more than twenty-eight years; in 1953 it is forty-five years, the consumption of tobacco in proportion to the population having trebled in that period." Georges Herment, *The Pipe*, translated by Arthur L. Hayward.

ESSAY SUGGESTIONS

1. Explain the causes of World War I.
2. What were the reasons for the defeat of the Confederacy?
3. Write a critical report on the studies that have been made on smoking and lung cancer.
4. Evaluate the studies that try to relate animal and other saturated fats to cardiovascular disease.
5. How great can radioactive fallout be before it becomes a menace?
6. Read Sigmund Freud's psychoanalysis of Michelangelo and evaluate it as reasoning and as proof.

These essays are not to be undertaken lightly. They require critical reading and knowledge. The following topics require critical perception:

7. Following Mark Twain, write an essay on the turning point of your life. What was it, more than anything else, that has caused your life to take its present course?
8. Make a list of friends whom you consider likely to succeed in life. What reasons can you give for your belief? Next, take your rough notes and work them into a coherent, polished essay.
9. List the people to whom you are especially attracted and those for whom you feel antipathy. What are the reasons for your likes and dislikes? Rewrite your notes in essay form.
10. Various people have claimed that movies, comic books, and now television exert considerable influence upon growing minds. Can you show from your own experience whether or not this is so? Discuss in essay form.

FURTHER READING

The serious student will want to read Francis Bacon's *Novum Organum* since it marks the beginning of modern thinking about cause and effect and also induction. A handy reprint of the translation by James Spedding, *et al.*, has been edited by Fulton H. Anderson. New York: The Liberal Arts Press, 1960.

Morris R. Cohen and Ernest Nagel, *An Introduction to Logic and Scientific Method*, Chapters XI and XIII.

John Stuart Mill, *A System of Logic*, Book III, Chapters V through X, also Chapters XV and XXI.

W. H. Werkmeister, *An Introduction to Critical Thinking*, Chapters XXI and XXII.

MARK TWAIN

The Turning-Point
of My Life

I

If I understand the idea, the *Bazar* invites
several of us to write upon the above text.
It means the change in my life's course
which introduced what must be regarded by
me as the most *important* condition of my
career. But it also implies—without intention, perhaps—that that turning-point *itself*
was the creator of the new condition. This
gives it too much distinction, too much
prominence, too much credit. It is only the
last link in a very long chain of turning-
points commissioned to produce the cardinal
result; it is not any more important than
the humblest of its ten thousand predecessors. Each of the ten thousand did its appointed share, on its appointed date, in
forwarding the scheme, and they were all
necessary; to have left out any one of them
would have defeated the scheme and brought
about *some other* result. I know we have a
fashion of saying "such and such an event
was the turning-point in my life," but we
shouldn't say it. We should merely grant
that its place as *last* link in the chain makes
it the most *conspicuous* link; in real importance it has no advantage over any one
of its predecessors.

Perhaps the most celebrated turning-point
recorded in history was the crossing of the
Rubicon. Suetonius says:

> Coming up with his troops on the
> banks of the Rubicon, he halted for a
> while, and, revolving in his mind the
> importance of the step he was on the
> point of taking, he turned to those
> about him and said, "We may still
> retreat; but if we pass this little bridge,
> nothing is left for us but to fight it out
> in arms."

This was a stupendously important moment. And all the incidents, big and little,
of Cæsar's previous life had been leading up
to it, stage by stage, link by link. This was
the *last* link—merely the last one, and no
bigger than the others; but as we gaze back
at it through the inflating mists of our
imagination, it looks as big as the orbit of
Neptune.

You, the reader, have a *personal* interest
in that link, and so have I; so has the rest
of the human race. It was one of the links
in your life-chain, and it was one of the
links in mine. We may wait, now, with
bated breath, while Cæsar reflects. Your fate
and mine are involved in his decision.

While he was thus hesitating, the following incident occurred. A person remarked
for his noble mien and graceful aspect appeared close at hand, sitting and playing
upon a pipe. When not only the shepherds,
but a number of soldiers also, flocked to
listen to him, and some trumpeters among
them, he snatched a trumpet from one of
them, ran to the river with it, and, sounding the advance with a piercing blast, crossed
to the other side. Upon this, Cæsar exclaimed: "Let us go whither the omens of
the gods and the iniquity of our enemies call
us. *The die is cast.*"

So he crossed—and changed the future of
the whole human race, for all time. But
that stranger was a link in Cæsar's life-chain,
too; and a necessary one. We don't know
his name, we never hear of him again; he
was very casual; he acts like an accident; but
he was no accident, he was there by compulsion of *his* life-chain, to blow the electrify-
ing blast that was to make up Cæsar's mind
for him, and thence go piping down the
aisles of history forever.

If the stranger hadn't been there! But he
was. And Cæsar crossed. With such results!
Such vast events—each a link in the *human
race's* life-chain; each event producing the
next one, and that one the next one, and
so on: the destruction of the republic; the
founding of the empire; the breaking up of
the empire; the rise of Christianity upon its
ruins; the spread of the religion to other
lands—and so on: link by link took its appointed place at its appointed time, the dis-

covery of America being one of them; our Revolution another; the inflow of English and other immigrants another; their drift westward (my ancestors among them) another; the settlement of certain of them in Missouri, which resulted in *me*. For I was one of the unavoidable results of the crossing of the Rubicon. If the stranger, with his trumpet blast, had stayed away (which he *couldn't*, for he was an appointed link) Cæsar would not have crossed. What would have happened, in that case, we can never guess. We only know that the things that did happen would not have happened. They might have been replaced by equally prodigious things, of course, but their nature and results are beyond our guessing. But the matter that interests me personally is that I would not be *here* now, but somewhere else; and probably black—there is no telling. Very well, I am glad he crossed. And very really and thankfully glad, too, though I never cared anything about it before.

II

To me, the most important feature of my life is its literary feature. I have been professionally literary something more than forty years. There have been many turning-points in my life, but the one that was the last link in the chain appointed to conduct me to the literary guild is the most *conspicuous* link in that chain. *Because* it was the last one. It was not any more important than its predecessors. All the other links have an inconspicuous look, except the crossing of the Rubicon; but as factors in making me literary they are all of the one size, the crossing of the Rubicon included.

I know how I came to be literary, and I will tell the steps that led up to it and brought it about.

The crossing of the Rubicon was not the first one, it was hardly even a recent one; I should have to go back ages before Cæsar's day to find the first one. To save space I will go back only a couple of generations and start with an incident of my boyhood. When I was twelve and a half years old, my father died. It was in the spring. The summer came, and brought with it an epidemic of measles. For a time, a child died almost every day. The village was paralyzed with fright, distress, despair. Children that were not smitten with the disease were imprisoned in their homes to save them from the infection. In the homes there were no cheerful faces, there was no music, there was no singing but of solemn hymns, no voice but of prayer, no romping was allowed, no noise, no laughter, the family moved spectrally about on tiptoe, in a ghostly hush. I was a prisoner. My soul was steeped in this awful dreariness—and in fear. At some time or other every day and every night a sudden shiver shook me to the marrow, and I said to myself, "There, I've got it! and I shall die." Life on these miserable terms was not worth living, and at last I made up my mind to get the disease and have it over, one way or the other. I escaped from the house and went to the house of a neighbor where a playmate of mine was very ill with the malady. When the chance offered I crept into his room and got into bed with him. I was discovered by his mother and sent back into captivity. But I had the disease; they could not take that from me. I came near to dying. The whole village was interested, and anxious, and sent for news of me every day; and not only once a day, but several times. Everybody believed I would die; but on the fourteenth day a change came for the worse and they were disappointed.

This was a turning-point of my life. (Link number one.) For when I got well my mother closed my school career and apprenticed me to a printer. She was tired of trying to keep me out of mischief, and the adventure of the measles decided her to put me into more masterful hands than hers.

I became a printer, and began to add one link after another to the chain which was to lead me into the literary profession. A long road, but I could not know that; and as I did not know what its goal was, or even that it had one, I was indifferent. Also contented.

A young printer wanders around a good deal, seeking and finding work; and seeking again, when necessity commands. N. B. Necessity is a *Circumstance*; Circumstance is man's master—and when Circumstance commands, he must obey; he may argue the matter—that is his privilege, just as it is the honorable privilege of a falling body to argue with the attraction of gravitation—but it won't do any good, he must *obey*. I wandered for ten years, under the guidance and dictatorship of Circumstance, and finally arrived in a city of Iowa, where I worked several months. Among the books that interested me in those days was one about the Amazon. The traveler told an alluring tale of his long voyage up the great river from Para to the sources of the Madeira, through the heart of an enchanted land, a land wastefully rich in tropical wonders, a romantic land where all the birds and flowers and animals were of the museum varieties, and where the alligator and the crocodile and the monkey seemed as much at home as if they were in the Zoo. Also, he told an astonishing tale about *coca*, a vegetable product of miraculous powers, asserting that it was so nourishing and so strength-giving that the native of the mountains of the Madeira region would tramp up hill and down all day on a pinch of powdered coca and require no other sustenance.

I was fired with a longing to ascend the Amazon. Also with a longing to open up a trade in coca with all the world. During months I dreamed that dream, and tried to contrive ways to get to Para and spring that splendid enterprise upon an unsuspecting planet. But all in vain. A person may *plan* as much as he wants to, but nothing of consequence is likely to come of it until the magician *Circumstance* steps in and takes the matter off his hands. At last Circumstance came to my help. It was in this way. Circumstance, to help or hurt another man, made him lose a fifty-dollar bill in the street; and to help or hurt me, made me find it. I advertised the find, and left for the Amazon the same day. This was another turning-point, another link.

Could Circumstance have ordered another dweller in that town to go to the Amazon and open up a world-trade in coca on a fifty-dollar basis and been obeyed? No, I was the only one. There were other fools there— shoals and shoals of them—but they were not of my kind. I was the only one of my kind.

Circumstance is powerful, but it cannot work alone; it has to have a partner. Its partner is man's *temperament*—his natural disposition. His temperament is not his invention, it is *born* in him, and he has no authority over it, neither is he responsible for its acts. He cannot change it, nothing can change it, nothing can modify it—except temporarily. But it won't stay modified. It is permanent, like the color of the man's eyes and the shape of his ears. Blue eyes are gray in certain unusual lights; but they resume their natural color when that stress is removed.

A Circumstance that will coerce one man will have no effect upon a man of a different temperament. If Circumstance had thrown the bank-note in Cæsar's way, his temperament would not have made him start for the Amazon. His temperament would have compelled him to do something with the money, but not that. It might have made him advertise the note—and *wait*. We can't tell. Also, it might have made him go to New York and buy into the Government, with results that would leave Tweed nothing to learn when it came his turn.

Very well, Circumstance furnished the capital, and my temperament told me what to do with it. Sometimes a temperament is an ass. When that is the case the owner of it is an ass, too, and is going to remain one. Training, experience, association, can temporarily so polish him, improve him, exalt him that people will think he is a mule, but they will be mistaken. Artificially he *is* a mule, for the time being, but at bottom he is an ass yet, and will remain one.

By temperament I was the kind of person that *does* things. Does them, and reflects afterward. So I started for the Amazon without reflecting and without asking any questions. That was more than fifty years ago. In all that time my temperament has not changed, by even a shade. I have been punished many and many a time, and bitterly, for doing things and reflecting afterward, but these tortures have been of no value to me: I still do the thing commanded by Circumstance and Temperament, and reflect afterward. Always violently. When I am reflecting, on those occasions, even deaf persons can hear me think.

I went by the way of Cincinnati, and down the Ohio and Mississippi. My idea was to take ship, at New Orleans, for Para. In New Orleans I inquired, and found there was no ship leaving for Para. Also, that there never had *been* one leaving for Para. I reflected. A policeman came and asked me what I was doing, and I told him. He made me move on, and said if he caught me reflecting in the public street again he would run me in.

After a few days I was out of money. Then Circumstance arrived, with another turning-point of my life—a new link. On my way down, I had made the acquaintance of a pilot. I begged him to teach me the river, and he consented. I became a pilot.

By and by Circumstance came again—introducing the Civil War, this time, in order to push me ahead another stage or two toward the literary profession. The boats stopped running, my livelihood was gone.

Circumstance came to the rescue with a new turning-point and a fresh link. My brother was appointed secretary to the new Territory of Nevada, and he invited me to go with him and help him in his office. I accepted.

In Nevada, Circumstance furnished me the silver fever and I went into the mines to make a fortune, as I supposed; but that was not the idea. The idea was to advance me another step toward literature. For amusement I scribbled things for the Virginia City *Enterprise*. One isn't a printer ten years without setting up acres of good and bad literature, and learning—unconsciously at first, consciously later—to discriminate between the two, within his mental limitations; and meantime he is unconsciously acquiring what is called a "style." One of my efforts attracted attention, and the *Enterprise* sent for me and put me on its staff.

And so I became a journalist—another link. By and by Circumstance and the Sacramento *Union* sent me to the Sandwich Islands for five or six months, to write up sugar. I did it; and threw in a good deal of extraneous matter that hadn't anything to do with sugar. But it was this extraneous matter that helped me to another link.

It made me notorious, and San Francisco invited me to lecture. Which I did. And profitably. I had long had a desire to travel and see the world, and now Circumstance had most kindly and unexpectedly hurled me upon the platform and furnished me the means. So I joined the "Quaker City Excursion."

When I returned to America, Circumstance was waiting on the pier—with the *last* link—the conspicuous, the consummating, the victorious link: I was asked to *write a book*, and I did it, and called it *The Innocents Abroad*. Thus I became at last a member of the literary guild. That was forty-two years ago, and I have been a member ever since. Leaving the Rubicon incident away back where it belongs, I can say with truth that the reason I am in the literary profession is because I had the measles when I was twelve years old.

III

Now what interests me, as regards these details, is not the details themselves, but the fact that none of them was foreseen by me, none of them was planned by me, I was the author of none of them. Circumstance, working in harness with my temperament, created them all and compelled them all. I often offered help, and with the best intentions, but it was rejected—as a rule, uncourteously. I could never plan a thing and get it to come out the way I planned it. It came out some other way—some way I had not counted upon.

And so I do not admire the human being —as an intellectual marvel—as much as I did when I was young, and got him out of books, and did not know him personally. When I used to read that such and such a general did a certain brilliant thing, I believed it. Whereas it was not so. Circumstance did it by help of his temperament. The circumstance would have failed of effect with a general of another temperament: he might see the chance, but lose the advantage by being by nature too slow or too quick or too doubtful. Once General Grant was asked a question about a matter which had been much debated by the public and the newspapers; he answered the question without any hesitancy. "General, who planned the march through Georgia?" "The enemy!" He added that the enemy usually makes your plans for you. He meant that the enemy by neglect or through force of circumstances leaves an opening for you, and you see your chance and take advantage of it.

Circumstances do the planning for us all, no doubt, by help of our temperaments. I see no great difference between a man and a watch, except that the man is conscious and the watch isn't, and the man *tries* to plan things and the watch doesn't. The watch doesn't wind itself and doesn't regulate itself—these things are done exteriorly. Outside influences, outside circumstances, wind the *man* and regulate him. Left to himself, he wouldn't get regulated at all, and the sort of time he would keep would not be valuable. Some rare men are wonderful watches, with gold case, compensation balance, and all those things, and some men are only simple and sweet and humble Waterburys. I am a Waterbury. A Waterbury of that kind, some say.

A nation is only an individual multiplied. It makes plans and Circumstance comes and upsets them—or enlarges them. Some patriots throw the tea overboard; some other patriots destroy a Bastille. The *plans* stop there; then Circumstance comes in, quite unexpectedly, and turns these modest riots into a revolution.

And there was poor Columbus. He elaborated a deep plan to find a new route to an old country. Circumstance revised his plan for him, and he found a new *world*. And *he* gets the credit of it to this day. He hadn't anything to do with it.

Necessarily the scene of the real turning-point of my life (and of yours) was the Garden of Eden. It was there that the first link was forged of the chain that was ultimately to lead to the emptying of me into the literary guild. Adam's *temperament* was the first command the Deity ever issued to

a human being on this planet. And it was the only command Adam would *never* be able to disobey. It said, "Be weak, be water, be characterless, be cheaply persuadable." The later command, to let the fruit alone, was certain to be disobeyed. Not by Adam himself, but by his *temperament*—which he did not create and had no authority over. For the *temperament* is the man; the thing tricked out with clothes and named Man is merely its Shadow, nothing more. The law of the tiger's temperament is, Thou shalt kill; the law of the sheep's temperament is, Thou shalt not kill. To issue later commands requiring the tiger to let the fat stranger alone, and requiring the sheep to imbue its hands in the blood of the lion is not worth while, for those commands *can't* be obeyed. They would invite to violations of the law of *temperament*, which is supreme, and takes precedence of all other authorities. I cannot help feeling disappointed in Adam and Eve. That is, in their temperaments. Not in *them*, poor helpless young creatures—afflicted with temperaments made out of butter; which butter was commanded to get into contact with fire and *be melted*. What I cannot help wishing is, that Adam and Eve had been postponed, and Martin Luther and Joan of Arc put in their place—that splendid pair equipped with temperaments not made of butter, but of asbestos. By neither sugary persuasions nor by hell fire could Satan have beguiled *them* to eat the apple.

There would have been results! Indeed, yes. The apple would be intact to-day; there would be no human race; there would be no *you*; there would be no *me*. And the old, old creation-dawn scheme of ultimately launching me into the literary guild would have been defeated.

QUESTIONS FOR STUDY AND DISCUSSION

1. "The Turning-Point of My Life" is itself an essay on cause and effect; Twain's discussion of events in his own life provides an extended example of the process in action. What kind of cause and effect relationship does Twain concentrate on?

2. How far back does Twain trace the chain of cause and effect which produced the "turning-point" in his life?

3. What, according to Twain, are the two elements which control man's destiny? What can man do to alter them?

4. Where does Twain seem to stand on the argument of necessity *vs.* free will?

5. Do you feel that Twain is irreligious or anti-religious, so far as his comments about Adam and Eve are concerned?

6. Read John Donne's "Devotion XVII" in this book. How does it contribute to your understanding of causation?

WRITING ASSIGNMENTS

1. You have probably experienced more than once the feeling that a particular decision you are being called on to make will have a dramatically significant effect on your life. Recalling such a situation, explain what actually did happen—whether your feeling at the time was proved correct.

2. If Cæsar had not crossed the Rubicon, the history of Rome, the history of the world, would have been different, Twain asserts. To what extent do you agree with this view of cause and effect? Write an essay embodying your own opinion on this matter.

WILLIAM MC FEE

The Peculiar Fate
of the Morro Castle

"It is not enough, to exonerate all persons who are interested in the boat from all just blame, to say they have no direct agency in any accident that may happen. They should be considered as tied together by the cord of a common interest—as sharers in the profits and losses—and as moral participants in all acts pertaining to the business in which she may be used, and the law should hold them accountable."

Senate report, in the State of New York, on the loss of the steamboat Swallow, *1845.*

Saturday, September 8, 1934, was a blustery autumn day along the Atlantic coast. There was some rain, the leaves were falling, and so was the barometer. It was the kind of day on shore which indicates dirty weather at sea. September is the hurricane month.

Three days earlier, September 5, the twin-screw turbo-electric liner *Morro Castle*, of the Ward Line, sailed from Havana on her homeward run to New York. September 8, in a storm of wind and rain, she was three miles east of Barnegat, heading for the Ambrose Channel, where she would pick up her pilot. It was nearly three o'clock in the morning. Her 318 passengers and most of the crew of 231 men and women were asleep.

The usual Friday night conviviality, the "farewell dinner," the paper hats and toy balloons, the drinking, dancing, and love-making, the traditional culmination of a pleasure cruise in the West Indies, had been clouded by an unusual event. Captain R. Willmott was taken ill at dinner and died within a few hours.

It was a grave psychological strain for the chief officer, Mr. William F. Warms, who had come off watch at eight o'clock. He was about to turn in, for he had a strenuous day ahead of him in New York, when he made the discovery. To find his captain dead in his bunk, to face the sudden responsibility of taking over the command of the ship, would impose a burden on the strongest of men.

Mr. Warms, moreover, had another anxiety.

The gap between chief officer and master of any ship is wide enough, but in this particular case much of the executive authority usually assumed by a chief officer by custom and tradition had been retained in his own hands by the dead captain. We have to keep this in mind when we come to the actions of Captain Warms, suddenly confronted with the most terrifying emergency to be faced by the master of a vessel crowded with helpless, sleeping passengers.

At five minutes to three Mr. Hackney, acting second officer, saw smoke issuing from the stokehole fiddley. He called down from the bridge to the engine room to know "if there was a fire in the engine room." Cadet Engineer William F. Tripp, an eighteen-year-old Massachusetts Institute of Technology student, who was on duty near the telegraph and telephone, for they were about to pick up the pilot, replied in the negative. He knew of no fire. This is a highly important detail which, for some reason, was not emphasized by the experts. One minute later, at 2:56, Mr. Hackney pulled the fire alarm, which would be relayed all over the ship.

By this time, of course, Captain Warms was on the bridge. Accepting the above official record, confirmed by Mr. Tripp's log sheet, we face the extraordinary facts that (1) some eighteen minutes elapsed before the captain ordered a radio call for assistance; (2) the radio operator, Mr. Rogers, whose cabin, fifty feet aft of the navigating bridge, was on fire, sent three times to ask for instructions; (3) other ships near by saw the fire and sent calls before the *Morro Castle* call went out; (4) the ship was kept at nineteen knots, into a twenty-mile wind, in darkness, pouring rain, and pounding seas, before being stopped.

117

By that time, around half past three, the fire had made such headway that the ship's upper structure, from the forward funnel to the mizzenmast, which rose abaft the deck ballroom and the veranda, was a furnace. The passengers were crowding to the tourist section of the ship, right on the stern rails, on B and C decks. They were pouring through the passageways. Some, who were later seen at portholes, screaming for help, had been trapped in their cabins and were to die horribly there. Six young ladies, who had been carried by stewardesses from the bar to their cabins at the end of the evening's festivities, were not seen again. Some, of course, probably less fuddled, more athletic, and more enterprising, squirmed their way through their portholes and dropped into the sea, and were lucky enough to be picked up by the boats.

Most of the passengers, however, suddenly awakened by the raucous loud-speakers, frightened by the roaring of the flames and the running of men who had lost their wits and had no one to command them, surged aft through the smoke-filled passages. In such a case the word "panic" is inadequate. It conveys nothing of the actuality. These people, running through corridors of a burning ship, half-clothed and many of them half-demented, were in a bad way. When they came out on the after rail it was raining in torrents. There was no light save the lurid flames leaping at them from the superstructure. Below them was the dark turbulence of the sea, dotted with crying people in life belts, calling to the boats dimly seen, standing off fearfully from the heat of the burning ship. Desperation came to these people, and a measure of courage too. Down they went, jumping, or sliding down ropes, and, being inexpert at such business, scorching their soft hands, so that some of them were forever incapacitated for their professional work. There were many women there too, and they threw off their flimsy shoes by the rail, discarding their lipsticks and compacts, their lighters and cigarettes and girdles, as though, when faced with the final, grim, eternal verities of the sea, they instinctively abandoned the nonessentials.

It is logical and even inevitable now to regard the events of that fatal morning off Barnegat, in a storm of wind and rain, as the classic modern example of a marine disaster. Nothing was wanting to complete the picture. There was incompetence, panic, evasion, ignorance, credulity, and avarice. And from the first moment of alarm, when the C.Q. signal went out (the radio call for immediate assistance), legend and myth began to crystallize around the stark facts of the tragedy.

There was, for instance, the rumor which inland radio listeners heard early on Saturday, that the *Morro Castle* had been struck by lightning and had blown up, with a loss of five hundred lives. So incredible did it appear to the ordinary landsman for a fast modern liner, known to thousands who had made the cruise to Havana and to many more who hoped to make it, a liner with 173 voyages successfully and joyously completed, a liner often described as the safest ship afloat, to be destroyed by fire at sea, within sight of land, and surrounded by ships rushing to her assistance, that many people instinctively credited the disaster to natural causes and an "act of God." They thought it must be due to an unavoidable malignancy of the elements, or to sabotage, to spontaneous combustion of cargo—to anything, in fact, but what it was, panic and incompetence.

There was nothing remarkable about so many ships being on hand on this occasion. Every ship south-bound from New York, every ship coming up from the Americas, is on this course, to or from Ambrose Channel. What was remarkable was their inability to get a clear notion of what was going on, on board the *Morro Castle*. It must have seemed to some of those commanders, peering through the rain, that there were lunatics on board. How otherwise explain a ship in flames driving full speed into a twenty-mile gale? How explain the delay in sending out a call?

How explain the inexplicable?

There were the boats, which were rendered largely useless by the delay in getting them swung out, because they were all amidships or nearly so, and were burning on their chocks. There was the speed with which the fire, discovered in a locker in the writing room, upstairs on B deck, abeam of the forward funnel, became a roaring furnace. This speed the New York *Times* on the following Monday morning described as "a mystery." It remains a mystery if we accept the official contention that the fire started between two and three o'clock. There is reason to believe it began long before that, and did not originate in the locker. And when Mr. Hackney asked Mr. Tripp, down at the engine-room telegraph, if there was a fire down there, he may not have been so far off the track after all.

Soon after, then, with his ship in flames twenty miles south of Scotland Light, where the voyage officially ends, Captain Warms authorized C.Q. signals to all ships. He was only fifty feet away from Mr. Rogers in his wireless cabin, but they might as well have been strangers who had not been introduced. Captain Warms, who had not had a command before, and whose predecessor lay dead in the master's cabin, was under a strain. You can go to sea in command for forty years and never face a crisis such as he confronted inside forty minutes, almost, from the time he took charge. For a while he was rattled. He took too long to make his decisions. For many years it has been an unwritten law that a ship in trouble should avoid at all costs calling for assistance to outside ships. She should, if possible, get help from another ship of the company. It was a cruel predicament for Captain Warms. He seems never to have had the executive authority and responsibility a chief officer should possess. And his bosun was reported drunk at 2:30 A.M.

Among those who have had experience of ships like the *Morro Castle*, the natural re-action to the extraordinary lethargy of the personnel would be, Where was the watch-man? What was he doing all this time? Why was "a fire in the writing room," a public space on B deck, only a few feet away from the bridge, not reported? And why did not the automatic fire-detection system warn the officer of the watch?

Shrewd questions, but they have the simplest answers. The watchman, it was revealed at the inquiry, had so many other duties he had little time to watch. In ships under discipline the watchman makes his rounds, as in a factory or store on land. He has a key which he plugs into the system at various points on his itinerary, to record his vigilance. This is his duty, and he has no others. But on the *Morro Castle*, he said, he had many other duties, so that he was not really a watchman at all, in the legal sense.

The writing room, where the watchman, if he made his rounds, had noticed nothing unusual, had no fire-detection apparatus. Nor had any of the public rooms on the ship. The Darby system was installed in the private cabins, where fires sometimes start because women plug in electric toilet appliances and forget them, or drop cigarette butts into wastebaskets full of tissues, and these conflagrations would have given a warning in the wheelhouse. But writing letters, however passionate or inflammatory, was not considered by the builders or the naval architect to be a fire hazard. Moreover, although the United States signed the 1929 Convention for Safety at Sea in London, the august United States Senate had not ratified that Convention in 1930, when the *Morro Castle* was launched. So she was neither built nor operated in compliance with the Convention. Yet she was publicized as "the safest ship afloat."

So we have the picture of a splendid, modern ship, of fifteen thousand tons' displacement, steaming at nineteen knots toward the Ambrose Channel, to pick up her pilot, and dock early on Saturday morning, suddenly bursting into flames which roar along the alleyways and trap sleepers in their beds, and nobody seems to know what to do. The stories told by passengers sound like fiction of an unusually lurid type, yet they were corroborated so often, and they fit so closely into each other, that there can be no controversy. For a short time the ship had no direction at all. Members of the crew declared that the fire alarm in the crew quarters was feeble, "like an alarm clock." When the fire pumps were going and the hoses were brought into operation, we have the evidence of a passenger, an expert professional fire fighter, that the crew did not know how to lay them out. He had other things to say, this particular passenger, of great importance. He will be quoted again.

One of the wireless operators of the *Morro Castle*, having come out of the affair with credit, went on a barnstorming tour as a hero. Anyone on that ship who did his simple duty was hailed as a hero by an uncritical press and public. But not Captain Warms. It was an appalling crisis, but shipmasters have been facing appalling crises for centuries, and many of them have left records of greater glory than Captain Warms. Why was this? Why did his chief engineer, Mr. Eben S. Abbott, instead of staying with his commander, go off in Lifeboat 1? Why did Boat 3 get away with sixteen of the crew but no passengers? A boat certified to carry seventy persons!

These questions are not so personal and particular as they may seem at first glance. The *Morro Castle* affair was part of the general picture of the United States Merchant Marine. "The Ward Liner *Morro Castle*" and "the Ward Liner *Oriente*," her sister ship, were phrases which gave a misleading impression. So did "the Ward Liner *Mohawk*." All were part of a picture which had been getting darker and gloomier for a number of years.

More than one Congress had been bedeviled by the problem of how to have an American Merchant Marine without emptying the Treasury. It had been tried over and over again. Millions of dollars had been poured into the industry, and the industry had sooner or later reached a state of receivership and disintegration. Forty-five years ago a member of Congress declared, "The moment a man invests his capital, or any portion of it, in ships or ship-building interests, he blossoms into a full-grown patriot and insists on having the Treasury of the United States opened for his benefit." Thirty years ago William Gibbs McAdoo, Secretary of the Treasury, complained that "every shipowner and every ship monopolist wants subsidies." The Shipping Board became the greatest pork barrel in the history of the country. And still there was no Merchant Marine. In spite of a closely protected coastwise service, in spite of the denial of American registry to foreign-built ships, in spite of high wages (100 per cent more than Great Britain), in spite of long-term building loans at small interest and generous operational subsidies, in spite of mail contracts which could hardly be distinguished from charitable bequests, there was no Merchant Marine, and almost no shipbuilding. Capitalists were no longer interested in risking their capital in American ships. Shippers did not permit their patriotism to interfere with their business. They patronized any firm under any flag—British, German, Dutch, Danish, Norwegian, Swedish, or Japanese—which delivered cargoes on fast, dependable schedules.

Something had to be done and something was done, but not what the shipping interests were asking. They had grandiose schemes for competing in the transatlantic trade by inaugurating four-day crossings. Congress decided on a more balanced Merchant Marine. The Jones-White Bill of 1928, as the new Merchant Marine Act was called, authorized a construction fund of $250,000,000. Approved companies could get twenty-year loans covering 75 per cent of the cost of a ship. Mail subsidies were based on tonnage and speed. For example, a sixteen-thousand-ton vessel doing twenty knots earned a subsidy of ten dollars a mile on the outward voyage.

This legislation authorized the construction of, among others, the Ward Line sister ships *Morro Castle* and *Oriente*. They were designed by Theodore F. Ferris of New York, an eminent naval architect, and built by the Newport News Shipbuilding Company, one of the largest and best yards in America. The firm applying for the loan was the Atlantic, Gulf, and West Indies Steamship Lines, a merger of a number of smaller companies, including the Ward Line, under whose house flag the ships sailed. They were cruise ships. They carried mails and cargo. They maintained a fast service for bona-fide passengers between New York and Cuba, but their primary function, the function which made them pay, was taking round-trip cruise passengers from New York. Their cost was around four millions apiece. The United States Government held a first mortgage of $3,422,181 on each ship, with very low interest charges.

The *Morro Castle*, then, was a first-class ship of the most modern design, and in spite of the fact that certain requirements of the 1929 Convention for Safety at Sea were not included, it is reasonable to accept her as one of the safest ships of her day as to structural design. The defects of the *Morro Castle* lay in her personnel, afloat and ashore.

She was of 11,520 tons register, 6,449 tons net. She was 508 feet in length between perpendiculars, 70.9 feet beam and 39 feet draft. She was a twin-screw, oil-fired ship with six Babcock and Wilcox water-tube boilers, General Electric turbo-electric generators driving electric motors on the two shafts. She developed 16,000-shaft horsepower, and her service speed was 20 knots. She was built to the highest classification of the American Bureau of Shipping, and she had been approved by the United States Navy as a naval auxiliary. It seems strange we should have heard that talk, after the disaster, of her "faulty construction."

She had nine water-tight, transverse bulkheads extending to the shelter deck, and her water-tight doors were electrically operated. Her superstructure was three decks in depth, with a combined forecastle and bridge. All decks were of steel and laid with teak.

Her fire-fighting equipment was the best of its kind in 1930. The Darby system was installed everywhere except in the public rooms, as we have noted. Down below the cargo space was equipped with the Rich smoke-detecting apparatus. Twenty-seven lines of piping connected the holds to a box on the bridge, where the officer of the watch could at once detect the origin of smoke. There was also a Lux carbon-dioxide system for smothering fires in the engine room and boiler rooms. There were nearly a hundred fire extinguishers on brackets all over the ship. There were 2,100 feet of canvas fire hose.

There was criticism in some quarters because no sprinklers were installed. Sprinklers, as we find them on shore, are not the answer to marine risks. In any case they would have been useless in the *Morro Castle* fire.

What more was needed? What more could any steamship owner provide for the protection of his patrons? The answer is, Nothing except personnel of the same quality as his ship. There was nothing the matter with the *Morro Castle* that night except personnel.

By comparing, in *Lloyd's Register of Shipping*, the *Morro Castle* and *Oriente* with the company's other vessels, such as the *Mohawk* (5,896 tons, single-screw freighter with some passengers, 387 feet in length), we get the impression that there had not been a development of discipline on board and organization in the office to cope with liners of the *Morro Castle* class, ships carrying several hundred passengers and a crew of 230. The voyage was short; the turnover in personnel 20 per cent, which would have given any management with intelligence uneasy nights. The ship was of course adequately serviced in New York by shore staffs, but the time at sea was so short that it was almost impossible, remembering that 20-per-cent turnover, to develop any sense of solidarity. It was not, in a seaman's sense, a voyage at all, but a high-speed junket to a tropical port, where liquor was plentiful, potent, and cheap. The ship was a constant headache to the Narcotics Squad, Havana being what it was. Andrew Furuseth, then head of the Seaman's Union, said that *Morro Castle* "seamen" actually paid for their jobs instead of receiving wages, their profits on smuggled dope were so high.

There was, then, a musty odor of slackness in running the ship. According to Section 2 of the Seaman's Act, the crew should have been divided into day and night watches. There were only seven men on duty at night, out of a total of 231 on board, when the fire started. If Captain Willmott tolerated this arrangement for his own reasons, nobody else was likely to make complaint.

Another astonishing feature of the way the ship was operated was that there was no list of rules, no book of company regulations, to which an officer could turn (if he did not already know them from long service) for guidance. This was so extraordinary that the question was put to the vice-president in charge of operations more than once. No, there were no printed regulations.

Now here was something which might be listed under the heading "faulty construction." In all first-class lines the traditions, experience, and policy, accumulated by generations of management, are crystallized, distilled, condensed, reduced to a set of rules and regulations, which have the authenticity and prestige of Holy Writ. In one company in which the writer served it was actually known as "the Bible," without any intention of being irreverent. The captain and his heads of departments each had a numbered copy. In the hands of a literal-minded and possibly malevolent commander such a code of laws could be used to further his own ends, exactly as other codes on land have been misapplied. The point is that a company of any quality almost inevitably evolves such a code, and prints it, and insists on its observance at sea.

But on the *Morro Castle*, according to the first vice-president, there was nothing of this at all.

Allusion has already been made to the suspicion that Captain Warms, as chief officer, lacked the usual authority of that rank. Captain Willmott, in fact, had been a long time in the company, and he seems to have run the ship by rule of thumb and word of mouth. It worked all right from his point of view. He was able to keep down expenses. Printed rules would have had to adhere to the law regarding ships, so perhaps it was better to have no such hard-and-fast instructions issued. Captain Willmott told his chief mate what to do. But when Captain Willmott suddenly was not there, the defects of his system became obvious enough. Right on down the line, to the stewards and bellhops who swarmed into a boat and rowed away, there was no company "principle" at work.

So, the skeptics may say, the ship caught fire because there was no principle, no discipline? They could not handle the fire because there was a lack of discipline? You want us to believe that?

Let us go back a little. We have it from Andrew Furuseth, a man not given to reckless libeling of seamen, that the crew on these New York-Havana runs paid for their jobs, to smuggle narcotics. This writer has been at his breakfast in the messroom after such a run, and the messman, an intensely respectable, pious, efficient, and (to us) valuable person, in the very act of serving our ham and eggs, has been taken away by government agents, under arrest, to be seen no more by us. Nothing unusual in this. It was going on all the time. They had found narcotics in his bunk.

We have, moreover, the statement of the night watchman that he had so many other duties he could not do much watching. There were not enough men on duty to comply with the law. We may ask here, What sort of men? Who chose them for their work? What were their qualifications?

Here we come to grips with the relations between the shipowners and the Bureau of Navigation and Steamboat Inspection. The *Morro Castle* had been inspected for Voyage 174, which was her last, in May, 1934. She was reinspected on August 4, a month before the disaster. This meant, probably, that the May inspection had not been completed before she sailed. Anyway, she was inspected, just as the ill-fated *Vestris* was inspected, and the excursion steamer *Mackinac*, whose boilers were inspected in New York not long before they blew up and killed forty-seven people.

These inspections had become largely routine, formal, and in the nature of gentlemen's agreements. It was assumed that the master and his officers would not knowingly go to sea with defects likely to jeopardize their own lives and ships, or at any rate their professional reputations. With a ship like the *Morro Castle* the inspection was perfunctory. She was new; she was a first-class job; she was approved by the Navy, and she was underwritten by Lloyd's of London.

Another thing. The Inspection Service was the Cinderella of the government services bureaus. To quote Mr. Howard S. Cullman, who in 1936 was on President Roosevelt's Committee for Safety of Life at Sea, and who was becoming a thorn in the side of the Department of Commerce, "The Bureau was shockingly undermanned and underpaid. There were not enough clerks or surveyors. . . . Innumerable reports by competent investigators were quietly buried." Mr. Cullman and the Committee were also quietly buried soon after, so far as any results could be discerned, and Mr. Cullman, whose interests ranged from tobacco wrappers to financing Broadway shows, from New York hospitals to the receivership of the Roxy Theater, decided that reform of the American Merchant Marine was not his destiny.

The Bureau was part of the Department of Commerce, whose Secretary at the time of the *Morro Castle* disaster was a smooth, Southern lawyer-politician, Mr. Daniel Roper. His grasp of realities, incredible as it seems today, was such that, when the *Morro Castle* suddenly revealed the stagnation and obsolescence of his regime, he appointed a *naval* officer to sail on each merchant ship, to prevent accidents. At no time did Mr. Roper become aware of the Gilbert-and-Sullivan situation of his Bureau when accidents did happen. If the Bureau was negligent, the Bureau investigated itself, and of course the Bureau discovered that the Bureau had no flaw.

The Bureau, for instance, had been issuing what were called lifeboat certificates to seamen, as well as certifying those seamen as "able" or otherwise. These documents were pieces of paper, quite small; easily lost or stolen; easily sold, like the official American discharges. In the new legislation of 1936 discharge-books for seamen were authorized. Every other maritime nation on earth used these books. The continuous-discharge-book corresponded to the passports carried by passengers. But American seamen would have none of it. To have their records permanent and inviolable was, in their view, "un-American."

In 1934, however, it was common knowledge that these paper discharges and certificates were sold outside the Seamen's Institute on South Street to any who wanted to ship out. No chief officer or first assistant regarded them as having any meaning. He took what he could get, and if the men were no good he fired them and tried again. Or, in the case of the *Morro Castle*, the crew were engaged by the Ward Line's shipping master.

Here again we float off into cloud-cuckoo-land. The United States Government, through the Bureau of Navigation and Steamboat Inspection, was trying to lift some of the curse on American shipping. Part of that curse was the large number of native and alien incompetents who were buying their credentials in South Street. Another was the peril involved in so many aliens, unidentifiable and unable to speak, write, or read English. Many of them could not read or write any language. It was highly desirable, to say the least, that the official responsible for engaging seamen should scrutinize their credentials before hiring.

But the Ward Line shipping master, a Greek gentleman, could neither read nor write English. If the American discharges had been printed in Greek it may be doubted whether this modern Ulysses would have been any the wiser. Perhaps he spoke Cuban Spanish, for many of the deck hands were Cubans. We do not know. What we do know is that he was the employee of the Ward Line appointed to select the crews for American-flag ships, and the law of the land, to put it mildly, was interpreted in an elastic manner.

So much for the crew. There could not have been much "inspection" of *them*, and they acted very much as an uninspected crew would act. What about the boats?

Lifeboats are for saving life, though there have been times in recent years when American shipowners gave the impression that they were designed for rowing races and publicity. To chief officers lifeboats are a headache, a clumsy apparatus for painting the ship's sides and boot-topping.

The *Morro Castle's* steel boats would have been adequate if kept in condition. Like the ship, they were only four years old, yet it was stated by crew members that Boats 3, 9, and 10 had buoyancy tanks rusted into holes. Boat 1 had a motor which would not work, and the boat had to be rowed.

The general public is ill informed on the

subject of lifeboats. Indignation surges up white hot when it transpires that lifeboats are not regularly lowered, operated, inspected, revictualed, and maintained. If you ask, When is this to be done? there is a certain lack of unanimity in the answers. The ship ties up at her pier in New York. The boats on the dock side cannot be lowered. Often neither can those on the off side, for the dock, as often as not, is full of lighters. The crew are mostly off their articles and will not rejoin until sailing morning. Is the chief officer supposed to do this job single-handed?

At the other end of the voyage it is not much better. You say, the law demands it. The ship should lie off in the river or the harbor, and go through boat inspection and drill.

It sounds quite simple. But in a world where ships are run to make money and keep schedules, and government subsidies are earned only on the number of sea-miles they cover, a world in which wages go on all the time and passengers are irked over an hour's delay, these are counsels of perfection. Lifeboats are heavy. Motor lifeboats are extremely heavy. The present writer, taking over as engineer on a New York-Havana liner twenty-five years ago, discovered that the motor of the lifeboat (Number 1) had never worked in all the ten years of the ship's running. The valves were rusted solid in their seats and the timing had never been adjusted. On arrival in Havana it took several quarrels with the chief officer and an interview with the master to get the boat into the water for a test. Suppose we had needed that motorboat in a crisis!

Steel boats, moreover, are the very devil to keep in good condition. Sea air and water corrode mild steel like magic. The average clinker-built wooden lifeboat costs around $250 a year to maintain in condition, but it can be so kept. The steel boat is rusting internally all the time. It is fair without, but within it is full of minute corrosions. You cannot have copper buoyancy tanks, as in a wooden boat, for the salt water sets up electrolytic action between the steel hull and the copper tank.

But boats are only part of the story. Those members of the crew, with their lifeboat certificates, are the main thing. With that personnel turnover of 20 per cent, what chance had the *Morro Castle* of boat crews trained and experienced? The answer is, She had no chance at all.

This accounts for the bizarre fact that Boat 3 (with her rusted tanks) got away with sixteen of the crew, but no passengers. She was certified to carry seventy persons. Boat 1 went off with three passengers (evidently resourceful and agile fellows) and twenty-nine of the crew. The general impression we gather from these facts is that the crew had only one thought in mind, which was to save their own skins, and there seemed to be nobody in command to correct that thought. At last, off Sea Girt, all power having failed, the anchor was dropped by the new acting chief officer, Mr. Freeman, and the *Morro Castle* lay swathed in dense smoke and fumes, shot by the flames consuming the interior of the upper decks, while passengers, huddled by the after rail, dropped into the sea or shinned down ropes. They saw the more resourceful members of the crew rowing away as hard as they could. This is one of the most terrible features of a terrible disaster. Nothing impresses the student of this marine casualty more than the complete disintegration of all conscience in the crew of the ship. Many of the passengers were in a panic, a fact which we can sympathize with and condone. But the crew exhibited an ignoble panic which deprives them of all human forgiveness. Many of them were, quite simply, despicable in their behavior.

Captain Warms, who was to be master for the shortest time on record, followed the immemorial tradition of the sea by being the last man to leave the doomed ship. He and fourteen of the crew of two hundred and thirty remained on the forecastle, which was untouched by the fire. When the Coast Guard cutter *Tampa* arrived it was decided to tow the burning hulk to New York. Two tugs were also in attendance, and the dreary procession, moving slowly through heavy seas, reached Asbury Park, when the hawsers parted. The *Morro Castle* drifted broadside on a sand bar, a few yards off the huge, lacustrine Convention Hall, at the foot of Sixth Avenue. Here she stuck fast. The two powerful salvage tugs failed to shift her. This was Saturday evening.

Then began one of the most amazing episodes in American maritime history. It was a Saturday in early September, and Asbury Park is a "resort." It lives on tourists, weekenders, conventions, beauty contests of bathing girls, and suchlike "attractions." And here was the nation's latest sensation, a glittering cruise liner, full of exactly the kind of people who patronized Asbury Park, catching fire at sea and coming to rest right off Convention Hall Pier. Dead bodies were already washing ashore on the beach. Lifeboats were coming in. Authorities were coming down posthaste from New York. It was an incredible, a stupendous, a miraculous "attraction."

Asbury Park had a commission government headed by a city manager, a gentleman named Carl Bischoff. Mr. Bischoff saw the smoldering *Morro Castle* from one point of view and one only. To him she was an "attraction," a gold mine for Asbury Park. As thousands of cars streamed through the September night on all the roads of New Jersey, heading for Asbury Park, Mr. Bischoff decided to cash in. Beach and Convention Hall were fenced off and a charge of twenty-five cents a head was made for admission, to stand on the outer galleries of the structure and gape at the still-burning vessel, where people like themselves had been caught in luxurious cabins and burned alive as in furnaces, while the ship fled through the night.

This was understandable enough. Showmanship is part of the American scene. But Mr. Bischoff had other ideas. It struck his forward-looking but simple mind with great force that, since Providence had brought the *Morro Castle* to beach herself in his front yard, so to speak, finders were keepers. To him she was no tragedy at all, but a gold mine, and he saw no reason why, as city manager, or mayor, of Asbury Park, he should not take possession of her. He was a humane man and a public-spirited citizen. He would have been angry and outraged if

he had seen the ghouls that night dragging the bodies of the dead ashore and hacking off their fingers to get the rings. He was sorry for those who had lost their lives or their loved ones in the disaster. But it was hardly likely that another burning liner would ever come ashore in Asbury Park and lie in such a miraculously good location for commercial exploitation. He saw the jam of cars in the streets, the land-office business at the pier, and he wanted to keep the *Morro Castle* where she was, as a permanent "attraction," a museum as well as a mausoleum for the charred dead.

This attitude of Asbury Park's leading citizen was a symptom. It expressed in dramatic form the prevailing lack of understanding in the public mind concerning ships. When Frank B. Conover, of the New York Board of Underwriters, arrived on the scene, he found Mr. Bischoff in possession. The Board of the Steamboat Inspection Bureau, headed by Mr. Dickerson N. Hoover, and the United States Attorney, all had urgent business on board the *Morro Castle*. Mr. Bischoff had never heard of such people. He claimed—and this is perhaps the oddest note in a very odd affair—"riparian rights" over the ship. He even threatened to arrest Mr. Conover, the representative of the Federal Government, for disorderly conduct, unlawful entry, and (note this) insubordination. Mr. Bischoff became so much of a deterrent to official business that it was necessary to remove him from the scene. He would have found a kindred spirit in the mortician who joined the crowd of anxious relatives outside the Ward Line offices and handed around his business cards.

The inquiry which sought to discover the cause of this terrible disaster afforded a field day for cranks and headline hunters. Captain Willmott was pictured as a commander afraid of and suspicious of his second wireless operator, Mr. George Alagna. Shipmasters are traditionally conservative. To Captain Willmott, Alagna was a "radical" because he had the fortitude to head a protest against conditions of labor on the ship. Mr. Alagna was promptly arrested and handcuffed to a deputy United States mar-

shal as a material witness. Later he was released with what was almost an apology,
and then immediately rearrested and released on bail.

All through the inquiry there ran a vein
of hysteria, and another vein of stubborn
though clandestine wishful thinking, to
ascribe the *Morro Castle* fire to arson. There
are four hundred pages of maritime laws in
the federal statute book, and one of them,
the Harter Act, defines arson on a ship as
"an act of God," thereby releasing the own-
ers from civil liability.

Captain Warms, asked what motive would
inspire anyone to sabotage the *Morro Castle*
by arson, replied, "God knows what the
motive was."

Others, however, were less modest. Not
only God, but they, knew. It was all due to
"Reds." Major Cayetano Fraga, head of the
Havana detective force, announced his conviction that a liquid-fire bomb was planted
on the *Morro Castle* by Communists, members of a secret international maritime sabotage ring who shipped as members of the
crews. These fiends in human form, the
Major insisted, received direct instructions
from the Third International in Moscow.
And Captain Oscar Hernandez, chief of
Havana harbor police, was convinced that
"Communists and terrorists," directed by
"the Caribbean Bureau" of the Third International, had set fire to the ship.

Reading through the evidence, the arson
note is like a refrain. Most of it is hearsay,
conjecture, prejudice, and downright lunacy.
Nobody, for instance, asked these people
what motive Moscow would have in destroying a cruise liner. It could not even be
agreed on that the labor troubles in Havana
had any bearing on the disaster. Scores of
ships entered and left Havana unscathed.
But a "Red" scare was the universal explanation of anything unusual at that time.
For a while, after the *Morro Castle* fire,
every fire in a ship's hold was blamed on
"Reds" or sabotage, as though ships had
never had any fires in their holds before
the Russian Revolution.

There were some witnesses, however, who
were sane and contributed useful evidence.
Mr. William M. Tripp, the young M.I.T.

student already mentioned, impressed everybody with the clarity and honesty of his
statements. There was no getting away from
the bell sheet, the log he kept of the orders
coming down from the bridge. But he could
let no light into the darkness surrounding
the main question—What set the ship on
fire?

It was discovered, you will recall, in a
locker in the writing room, on B deck, a
locker which normally held stationery, ink,
and suchlike equipment for writing. This is
the classic official explanation of where the
fire originated. Nobody seems to have questioned it for a moment. So far as can be
determined from the blueprints, the writing
room extended across the ship, part of it
being known as the library. In any case the
funnel passed up through B deck at that
point. Just forward of the funnel were the
main first-class staircase and elevator, both
of which were to act as flues for the fire.
Above the boilers was the first-class dining
room, with its mezzanine, then the lounge
and ballroom, also with a mezzanine, and
then the writing room and library. Above
these public rooms were staterooms on
either side, on A deck. The fact that the
funnel carrying the gases from six oil-fired
boilers passed through this passenger structure was not mentioned by anybody.

But it started in the locker, we are assured, and Captain Warms knew of it
shortly before 3 A.M. The call went out at
3:15. At 3:29 the lights went out in the
engine room, which was filling with smoke.
Nobody inquired how smoke was getting
through steel bulkheads from the writing
room. Second Officer Hackney, promoted
from third when Captain Willmott died,
saw smoke coming *out* of the ventilators in
the fiddley at 2:55. These must have been
the fire-room ventilators, but Mr. Tripp assured him at that time that there was no
fire in the engine room. Here is a point
which should have been narrowly cross-examined by the board of inquiry.

Unsatisfactory as most of the witnesses
were, there were two who not only agreed,
and who were innocent of collusion, but
whose evidence disposed of the sedulously
cultivated fiction that the ship took fire with

miraculous suddenness and was as quickly destroyed as if she were constructed of celluloid. One was a cruise passenger, Mr. John Kempf, by profession a city fireman of Maspeth, Long Island, who was on vacation. He was presumably an expert witness as regards fires. The other was Harriet B. Brown, a stewardess. Mr. Kempf stated that he smelled smoke *soon after midnight.* Mrs. Brown confirmed this.

Mr. Kempf had a number of uncomplimentary things to say about the skill, discipline, and courage of the ship's crew. He made a special point of the fact that there was no officer visible anywhere to tell the crew what to do or where to go. If it were possible to attribute the fire to arson, the crew rendered first aid to the arsonists by knowing nothing about their duty in an emergency. So did Captain Warms, for that matter, when he kept the ship at 19 knots into a twenty-mile gale. Of course there were exceptions. In several hundred men and women we are bound to find exceptions. Third Engineer Arthur Stamper remained on watch until driven from his post by smoke and fumes. Dr. DeWitt Van Zyle, the ship's surgeon, died with the women and children he attempted to save. His body was picked up by a fishing boat.

Who, then, was to blame? It is a tradition in American transportation, deriving from the bad old days, when American railroads were less safe than now, to blame the dead engineer. The engineer was generally dead. The Ward Line, however, did not have this consolation. Their engineer, Mr. Eben S. Abbott, was very much alive. He left in Number 1 boat. Captain Warms stated that the engineer appeared on the bridge, suffering from smoke and fumes, and said he could do no more and was leaving the ship. What Captain Warms, who sorely needed sustaining at such a moment, must have thought of his engineer we have no means of learning, but those of us who have been to sea can hazard a guess. We are told, by members of the crew in the boat, that the engineer tore off the braid from his sleeves, with a view to preserving his anonymity when he got ashore.

Obviously such a tragic figure did not create a very favorable impression at the inquiry. His good fortune was that there was no one conducting the interrogations technically competent to ask leading questions.

There was no one, for instance, to correct the public notion that the chief engineer should have been "at his post" in the engine room. His post was on deck. So far as we know, he was doing what he was supposed to do, supervising the fire-fighting equipment. We are told that he was ordered by the captain to abandon the ship, which might have a number of differing interpretations, but they would all be conjectures now.

What did emerge from the sorry business was that neither Warms as master nor Abbott as engineer was an inspiring figure. While Warms was chief officer, the reigning authority was evidently Willmott, who by long service, and possibly financial interest in the Line, kept everything in his own hands, including fire and boat drills.

Now, if you take from a lieutenant the authority which properly belongs to his rank, you injure his self-respect and render him indifferent to discipline and efficiency. This point was not made by anyone at the inquiry. The point was not made that a shipmaster of immense seniority and with stock in the company usually keeps things in his own hands. It used to be a commonplace in the old British Mercantile Marine, when shipmasters invested in shipping. But in the frenzied hunt for sabotage and arson, in the attempt to detect the sinister hand of the Third International, vital questions such as the above were never raised.

Mr. Martin Conboy, United States Attorney, complained that the Ward Line's officials and lawyers did all they could to frustrate and interfere with the inquiry. The Ward Line's legal representatives denied the charge. In the opinion of the present writer the charge is not sustained. A defendant is not supposed to assist in his own indictment, and the Ward Line knew very well that they were, in the eyes of the public at any rate, defendants. The lawyers of a steamship line in trouble are perfectly justified in coaching the crew, not in what to say under oath, but in what not to say to reporters. Men who have just escaped a horrible death, who are under mental and physical strain from shock and exposure, are not fit subjects for newspaper interviews.

The aim of the Ward Line was, of course, to evade responsibility for a most shocking disaster. They did not succeed, because negligence was nakedly exposed. All we can be sure of now is that they would have created a better impression in the public mind if they had revealed even common humanity toward the victims of that disaster. But while they were collecting $4,186,000 hull insurance from Lloyd's, $263,000 more than the ship's book value, they attempted to limit their liability to the value of the freight and passenger fares—around $13,000—plus the value of the ship, which was nothing. A year after the tragedy the claims of over four hundred survivors were still pending. Another Ward Liner, the *Mohawk*, had by that time made history by going mysteriously haywire while passing the tanker *Talisman*, and had been rammed and sunk. By September, 1936, the Ward Line had experienced a change of heart. The sum of $890,000 was allocated to the *Morro Castle* case, and most of the claimants accepted the settlement.

It would be easy to lay undue stress, in a history of this character, on the trial, conviction, and sentences imposed on the captain, chief engineer, and the vice-president in charge of operations in the office. Four years in prison for Chief Engineer Abbott and suspension of his license, two years for Captain Warms, and temporary suspension of his master's license, and one year's suspended sentence, with a fine of five thousand dollars, for Mr. Cabaud. In addition a fine of ten thousand dollars was imposed on the Line. Warms and Abbott appealed, and the United States Circuit Court of Appeals, after wading through nearly five thousand pages of "transcript of record," reversed the judgment against them.

The whole business was a gesture. It is difficult to believe that the judge who imposed the prison sentences, or the defendants, believed that any time would be served

behind bars. It was simply that, when it became obvious that Moscow was not responsible for the destruction of the *Morro Castle*, public opinion demanded scapegoats. The gesture was made of sending the ship's officers to jail. The Secretary of Commerce made the gesture of placing naval officers on merchant ships, to render them safe. Less spectacular but more important, Congress made the gesture of improving the obsolete, understaffed, underpaid Bureau of Navigation and Steamboat Inspection. It could no longer be permitted to imperil human lives. The incompetence of the Bureau was dramatized by appointing Captain George Fried, who had made some highly publicized rescues at sea, as head of a new department of inspection. But by the middle of 1937 the United States Senate reported that "it seems clear . . . no further activity may be expected in connection with the *Morro Castle* fire."

By that time the captain and engineer had regained their licenses and were again at sea. The name "Ward Line" was permitted to fade from the public memory, and the *Morro Castle*'s sister ship, the *Oriente*, continued a successful career as a cruise liner.

The historian is left groping through the records for an answer to the original conundrum—What caused the fire? Why did a modern ship burn with such inconceivable rapidity? The reply at first was "arson." We were asked to believe that the criminal, with fiendish ingenuity, after poisoning the master, selected the locker in the writing room (1) because the writing room had no electric fire alarm, (2) he knew the stewards kept illegal and inflammable polishing liquid in the locker (this was never established as a fact), and (3) he chose the hour for his crime when most people on board were either drunk or asleep, or both.

This was the sensational yarn elaborated after the Red scare passed. Nobody asked the simple question, What was behind the writing room locker?

The present writer was at one time chief engineer of oil-fired steamers. The popular notion that fuel oil is a dangerous element is incorrect. Fuel oil is about as volatile and inflammable at room temperature as the oil spread on roads in the fall and spring. It has its hazards, chief of which is explosive gas given off from the oil, gas which is heavy and hangs around in bilges and tanks. Another is the danger of overheating the long uptakes which lead from the furnaces to the funnel, if the burners are neglected.

Like most modern, medium-sized, medium-speed steamers, the *Morro Castle* had only one real funnel. The after funnel was partly ornament, partly a ventilator. If, through neglect of the burners in the furnaces, the funnel base had become overheated, the heat would have been most intense where the funnel passed through the writing room, behind the cupboard. The writer once discovered his funnel red-hot just above the uptakes, owing to negligence. The ship was a freighter. There was a wide space between the funnel and the accommodation, and only minor damage ensued.

The validity of a theory is based on the number of observed facts it can account for. Most of the theories advanced for the *Morro Castle* fire were merely fantastic. They flourished on the obvious unfamiliarity of the interrogators with the actual operation of modern oil-fired turbo-electric ships. The present hypothesis assumes that parts of the steel structure around the funnel had been red-hot for hours and were charring the woodwork, disintegrating the insulation, giving off that smell of smoke which Mr. John Kempf and Mrs. Brown, the stewardess, declared they smelled soon after midnight. Remember that Mr. Hackney, the second officer, saw smoke coming up from the fiddley grating and inquired if there was a fire in the engine room, receiving a negative reply from Mr. Tripp. Then, at three o'clock, according to Mr. Hackney, smoke was seen in the writing room, and the door of the locker burst open, belching flames. And from then on they could do nothing to stem the conflagration.

Does anyone believe that a fire generated in a locker with steel bulkheads behind it could be of such fierceness, even if it had contained a "time bomb"? Does anyone believe that such a source could consume a large part of the ship with such speed? The flames roared up stairways and elevator shafts. It made the passageways impassable. But if you assume that the interior structure of the funnel casing, passing up through the ship behind the writing room walls, had been reddening for hours (through negligence), sending the heat along the steel deck beams, plates, and stanchions, all was set for the holocaust, while the ship drove on through the night.

Only a hypothesis, but it does attempt to explain something, which the fumbling, prejudiced conjectures of the day did not.

Who, then, was to blame? As regards the particular instance, we shall never know. As regards the general picture of the American Merchant Marine, of which the *Morro Castle* fire was the incandescent center, we may apportion the responsibility. There was the haphazard system of permitting, without adequate supervision, the amalgamation of numerous small lines, each with its special traditions and loyalties, and consigning their operation to an impersonal office management, without sea experience, and controlled by a "holding company." There was the slow ossification of the Bureau of Navigation, whose inspections were in such low repute that underwriters ignored them. And there was the complete absence, among legislators, of any interest in the integrity and character of the men who demanded such lavish generosity when they proposed to build and operate a merchant marine.

Another factor, less immediate but of great importance in the long, lugubrious deterioration of the industry, was the attitude of the American Federation of Labor toward marine unions. The A.F.L. had and has a tradition of craft unionism, but instead of fostering that tradition in seafaring, the A.F.L., through ignorance, indolence, and unintelligence, ignored the great champion of the seamen, Andrew Furuseth, and allowed the craft of the sailor to slide into the depths. Going to sea became the last resource of the dregs of the waterfront, the vicious, the improvident, the incompetent, and the irresponsible.

A further indictment can be made against the American public in general. Until disaster followed disaster, and bludgeoned it into paying attention to realities, that public had consistently failed to take any interest at all in its own merchant marine. Capital would not invest in it, the average citizen would not sail in it, and the working, native-born American would not accept employment in it. Not even the first World War, when American troops had to be ferried to France in British transports and defended by British warships, made any lasting impression on the inland populations. American newspapers, from coast to coast, placed all possible emphasis on such trivia as "the Blue Riband of the Atlantic," so that their readers were conditioned to believe that a merchant marine consisted of very large, very fast, very luxurious passenger vessels. Those same newspapers, moreover, publicized and overemphasized every mishap and accident to an American ship. The wages of able seamen and junior officers, and the social prestige of the calling, were so low that parents shied away from the sea as a possible profession for their sons.

It took another great war to change all that. The United States now has an enormous merchant marine. Nothing like the *Morro Castle* tragedy can ever happen again —ships will take fire on occasion, but there will never recur the staggering incompetence of that fatal Saturday in September, 1934. Or so we hope. It depends on the public, which in the past has been quick to anger, quick to forgive, quick to forget, but slow to do anything about it. The lesson of the *Morro Castle* is so simple that it may quite possibly be misunderstood. It is that the price of a merchant marine, like the price of liberty, is eternal vigilance.

QUESTIONS FOR STUDY AND DISCUSSION

1. What is the "effect" whose causation is analyzed in "The Peculiar Fate of the *Morro Castle*"? Is more than one effect analyzed? Are the questions "What caused the fire?" and "What caused the disaster?" really the same question or different ones?

2. Mark Twain's "The Turning-Point of My Life" described a linkage of cause and effect in a temporal sequence. To what extent is temporal sequence employed in "The Peculiar Fate of the *Morro Castle*" to demonstrate causation?

3. How far back is the linkage of events carried?

4. What causal relationship besides the temporal sequence of relevant events is employed in this essay?

5. In "The Turning-Point of My Life" Twain concentrates on the linking of a single series of events in his own life. How many series of linkages of different kinds can you distinguish in "The Peculiar Fate of the *Morro Castle*"?

WRITING ASSIGNMENTS

1. The causes of academic failure.
2. Why do I value success?
3. The effects of television viewing on my family.

4. Why I like (a person, an activity, a book, a musical composition).
5. What causes automobile accidents?

RACHEL CARSON

The Global Thermostat

Out of the chamber of the south
cometh the storm,
And cold out of the north.

THE BOOK OF JOB

When the building of the Panama Canal was first suggested, the project was severely criticized in Europe. The French, especially, complained that such a canal would allow the waters of the Equatorial Current to escape into the Pacific, that there would then be no Gulf Stream, and that the winter climate of Europe would become unbearably frigid. The alarmed Frenchmen were completely wrong in their forecast of oceanographic events, but they were right in their recognition of a general principle—the close relation between climate and the pattern of ocean circulation.

There are recurrent schemes for deliberately changing—or attempting to change—the pattern of the currents and so modifying climate at will. We hear of projects for diverting the cold Oyashio from the Asiatic coast, and of others for controlling the Gulf Stream. About 1912 the Congress of the United States was asked to appropriate money to build a jetty from Cape Race eastward across the Grand Banks to obstruct the cold water flowing south from the Arctic. Advocates of the plan believed that the Gulf Stream would then swing in nearer the mainland of the northern United States and would presumably bring us warmer winters. The appropriation was not granted. Even if the money had been provided, there is little reason to suppose that engineers then—or later—could have succeeded in controlling the sweep of the ocean's currents. And fortunately so, for most of these plans would have effects different from those popularly expected. Bringing the Gulf Stream closer to the American east coast, for example, would make our winters worse instead of better. The Atlantic coast of North America is a lee shore, with the prevailing winds from the west. The air masses that have lain over the Gulf Stream seldom reach us. But the Stream, with its mass of warm water, does have something to do with bringing our weather to us. The cold winds of winter are pushed by gravity toward the low-pressure areas over the warm water. The winter of 1916, when Stream temperatures were above normal, was long remembered for its cold and snowy weather along the east coast. If we could move the Stream inshore, the result in winter would be colder, stronger winds from the interior of the continent—not milder weather.

But if the eastern North American climate is not dominated by the Gulf Stream, it is far otherwise for the lands lying 'downstream.' From the Newfoundland Banks, as we have seen, the warm water of the Stream drifts eastward, pushed along by the prevailing westerly winds. Almost immediately, however, it divides into several branches. One flows north to the western shore of Greenland; there the warm water attacks the ice brought around Cape Farewell by the East Greenland Current. Another passes to the southwest coast of Iceland and, before losing itself in arctic waters, brings a gentling influence to the southern shores of that island. But the main branch of the Gulf Stream or North Atlantic Drift flows eastward. Soon it divides again. The southernmost of these branches turns toward Spain and Africa and re-enters the Equatorial Current. The northernmost branch, hurried eastward by the winds blowing around the Icelandic 'low,' piles up against the coast of Europe the warmest water found at comparable latitudes anywhere in the world. From the Bay of Biscay north its influence is felt. And as the current rolls northeastward along the Scandinavian coast, it sends off many lateral branches that curve back westward to bring the breath of warm water to the arctic islands and to mingle with other currents in intricate whirls and eddies. The west coast of Spitzbergen, warmed by one of these lateral streams, is bright with flowers in the arctic summer; the east coast, with its polar current, remains barren and forbidding. Passing around the North Cape,

131

the warm currents keep open such harbors as Hammerfest and Murmansk, although Riga, 800 miles farther south on the shores of the Baltic, is choked with ice. Somewhere in the Arctic Sea, near the island of Novaya Zemlya, the last traces of Atlantic water disappear, losing themselves at last in the overwhelming sweep of the icy northern sea.

It is always a warm-water current, but the temperature of the Gulf Stream nevertheless varies from year to year, and a seemingly slight change profoundly affects the air temperatures of Europe. The British meteorologist, C. E. P. Brooks, compares the North Atlantic to 'a great bath, with a hot tap and two cold taps.' The hot tap is the Gulf Stream; the cold taps are the East Greenland Current and the Labrador Current. Both the volume and the temperature of the hot-water tap vary. The cold taps are nearly constant in temperature but vary immensely in volume. The adjustment of the three taps determines surface temperatures in the eastern Atlantic and has a great deal to do with the weather of Europe and with happenings in arctic seas. A very slight winter warming of the eastern Atlantic temperatures means, for example, that the snow cover of northwestern Europe will melt earlier, that there will be an earlier thawing of the ground, that spring plowing may begin earlier, and that the harvest will be better. It means, too, that there will be relatively little ice near Iceland in the spring and that the amount of drift ice in the Barents Sea will diminish a year or two later. These relations have been clearly established by European scientists. Some day long-range weather forecasts for the continent of Europe will probably be based in part on ocean temperatures. But at present there are no means for collecting the temperatures over a large enough area, at frequent enough intervals.

For the globe as a whole, the ocean is the great regulator, the great stabilizer of temperatures. It has been described as 'a savings bank for solar energy, receiving deposits in seasons of excessive insolation and paying them back in seasons of want.' Without the ocean, our world would be visited by un-thinkably harsh extremes of temperature. For the water that covers three-fourths of the earth's surface with an enveloping mantle is a substance of remarkable qualities. It is an excellent absorber and radiator of heat. Because of its enormous heat capacity, the ocean can absorb a great deal of heat from the sun without becoming what we would consider 'hot,' or it can lose much of its heat without becoming 'cold.'

Through the agency of ocean currents, heat and cold may be distributed over thousands of miles. It is possible to follow the course of a mass of warm water that originates in the trade-wind belt of the Southern Hemisphere and remains recognizable for a year and a half, through a course of more than 7000 miles. This redistributing function of the ocean tends to make up for the uneven heating of the globe by the sun. As it is, ocean currents carry hot equatorial water toward the poles and return cold water equator-ward by such surface drifts as the Labrador Current and Oyashio, and even more importantly by deep currents. The redistribution of heat for the whole earth is accomplished about half by the ocean currents, and half by the winds.

At that thin interface between the ocean of water and the ocean of overlying air, lying as they do in direct contact over by far the greater part of the earth, there are continuous interactions of tremendous importance.

The atmosphere warms or cools the ocean. It receives vapors through evaporation, leaving most of the salts in the sea and so increasing the salinity of the water. With the changing weight of that whole mass of air that envelops the earth, the atmosphere brings variable pressure to bear on the surface of the sea, which is depressed under areas of high pressure and springs up in compensation under the atmospheric lows. With the moving force of the winds, the air grips the surface of the ocean and raises it into waves, drives the currents onward, lowers sea level on lee shores, and raises it on windward shores.

But even more does the ocean dominate the air. Its effect on the temperature and humidity of the atmosphere is far greater than the small transfer of heat from air to sea. It takes 3000 times as much heat to warm a given volume of water 1° as to warm an equal volume of air by the same amount. The heat lost by a cubic meter of water on cooling 1° C. would raise the temperature of 3000 cubic meters of air by the same amount. Or to use another example, a layer of water a meter deep, on cooling .1° could warm a layer of air 33 meters thick by 10°. The temperature of the air is intimately related to atmospheric pressure. Where the air is cold, pressure tends to be high; warm air favors low pressures. The transfer of heat between ocean and air therefore alters the belts of high and low pressure; this profoundly affects the direction and strength of the winds and directs the storms on their paths.

There are six more or less permanent centers of high pressure over the oceans, three in each hemisphere. Not only do these areas play a controlling part in the climate of surrounding lands, but they affect the whole world because they are the birthplaces of most of the dominant winds of the globe. The trade winds originate in high-pressure belts of the Northern and Southern hemispheres. Over all the vast extent of ocean across which they blow, these great winds retain their identity; it is only over the continents that they become interrupted, confused, and modified.

In other ocean areas there are belts of low pressure, which develop, especially in winter, over waters that are then warmer than the surrounding lands. Traveling barometric depressions or cyclonic storms are attracted by these areas; they move rapidly across them or skirt around their edges. So winter storms take a path across the Icelandic 'low' and over the Shetlands and Orkneys into the North Sea and the Norwegian Sea; other storms are directed by still other low pressure areas over the Skagerrak and the Baltic into the interior of Europe. Perhaps more than any other condition, the low-pressure area over the warm water south of Iceland dominates the winter climate of Europe.

And most of the rains that fall on sea and land alike were raised from the sea.

They are carried as vapor in the winds, and then with change of temperature the rains fall. Most of the European rain comes from evaporation of Atlantic water. In the United States, vapor and warm air from the Gulf of Mexico and the tropical waters of the western Atlantic ride the winds up the wide valley of the Mississippi and provide rains for much of the eastern part of North America.

Whether any place will know the harsh extremes of a continental climate or the moderating effect of the sea depends less on its nearness to the ocean than on the pattern of currents and winds and the relief of the continents. The east coast of North America receives little benefit from the sea, because the prevailing winds are from the west. The Pacific coast, on the other hand, lies in the path of the westerly winds that have blown across thousands of miles of ocean. The moist breath of the Pacific brings climatic mildness and creates the dense rain forests of British Columbia, Washington, and Oregon; but its full influence is largely restricted to a narrow strip by the coast ranges that follow a course parallel to the sea. Europe, in contrast, is wide open to the sea, and 'Atlantic weather' carries hundreds of miles into the interior.

By a seeming paradox, there are parts of the world that owe their desert dryness to their nearness to the ocean. The aridity of the Atacama and Kalahari deserts is curiously related to the sea. Wherever such marine deserts occur, there is found this combination of circumstances: a western coast in the lee of the prevailing winds, and a cold coastwise current. So on the west coast of South America the cold Humboldt streams northward off the shores of Chile and Peru—the great return flow of Pacific waters seeking the equator. The Humboldt, it will be remembered, is cold because it is continuously being reinforced by the upwelling of deeper water. The presence of this cold water offshore helps create the aridity of the region. The onshore breezes that push in toward the hot land in the afternoons are formed of cool air that has lain over a cool sea. As they reach the land they are forced to rise into the high coastal mountains—the ascent cooling them more than the land can warm them. So there is little condensation of water vapor, and although the cloud banks and the fogs forever seem to promise rain, the promise is not fulfilled so long as the Humboldt rolls on its accustomed course along these shores. On the stretch from Arica to Caldera there is normally less than an inch of rain in a year. It is a beautifully balanced system—as long as it remains in balance. What happens when the Humboldt is temporarily displaced is nothing short of catastrophic.

At irregular intervals the Humboldt is deflected away from the South American continent by a warm current of tropical water that comes down from the north. These are years of disaster. The whole economy of the area is adjusted to the normal aridity of climate. In the years of El Niño, as the warm current is called, torrential rains fall—the downpouring rains of the equatorial regions let loose upon the dust-dry hillsides of the Peruvian coast. The soil washes away, the mud huts literally dissolve and collapse, crops are destroyed. Even worse things happen at sea. The cold-water fauna of the Humboldt sickens and dies in the warm water, and the birds that fish the cold sea for a living must either migrate or starve.

Those parts of the coast of Africa that are bathed by the cool Benguela Current also lie in the lee of high land. The easterly winds are dry, descending winds, and the cool breezes from the sea have their moisture capacity increased by contact with the hot land. Mists form over the cold waters and roll in over the coast, but in a whole year the rainfall is the meagerest token. The mean rainfall at Swakopmund in Walvis Bay is 0.7 inches a year. But again this is true only as long as the Benguela holds sway along the coast, for there are times when the cold stream falters as does the Humboldt, and here also these are years of disaster.

The transforming influence of the sea is portrayed with beautiful clarity in the striking differences between the Arctic and Antarctic regions. As everyone knows, the Arctic is a nearly land-locked sea; the Antarctic, a continent surrounded by ocean. Whether this global balancing of a land pole against a water pole has a deep significance in the physics of the earth is uncertain; but the bearing of the fact on the climates of the two regions is plainly evident.

The ice-covered Antarctic continent, bathed by seas of uniform coldness, is in the grip of the polar anticyclone. High winds blow from the land and repel any warming influence that might seek to penetrate it. The mean temperature of this bitter world is never above the freezing point. On exposed rocks the lichens grow, covering the barrenness of cliffs with their gray or orange growths, and here and there over the snow is the red dust of the hardier algae. Mosses hide in the valleys and crevices less exposed to the winds, but of the higher plants only a few impoverished stands of grasses have managed to invade this land. There are no land mammals; the fauna of the Antarctic continent consists only of insects—a wingless mosquito, a few flies, a microscopic mite.

In sharp contrast are the arctic summers, where the tundra is bright with many-colored flowers. Everywhere except on the Greenland icecap and some of the arctic islands, summer temperatures are high enough for the growth of plants, packing a year's development into the short, warm, arctic summer. The polar limit of plant growth is set not by latitude, but by the sea. For the influence of the warm Atlantic penetrates strongly within the Arctic Sea, entering, as we have seen, through the one large break in the land girdle, the Greenland Sea. But the streams of warm Atlantic water that enter the icy northern seas bring the gentling touch that makes the Arctic, in climate as well as in geography, a world apart from the Antarctic.

So, day by day and season by season, the ocean dominates the world's climate. Can it also be an agent in bringing about the long-period swings of climatic change that we know have occurred throughout the long history of the earth—the alternating periods of heat and cold, of drought and flood? There is a fascinating theory that it can. This theory links events in the deep, hidden places of the ocean with the cyclic changes of climate and their effects on human history. It was developed by the distinguished Swedish oceanographer, Otto Pettersson, whose almost century-long life closed in 1941. In many papers, Pettersson presented the different facets of his theory as he pieced it together, bit by bit. Many of his fellow scientists were impressed, others doubted. In those days few men could conceive of the dynamics of water movements in the deep sea. Now the theory is being re-examined in the light of modern oceanography and meteorology, and only recently C. E. P. Brooks said, 'It seems that there is good support for Pettersson's theory as well as for that of solar activity, and that the actual variations of climate since about 3000 B.C. may have been to a large extent the result of these two agents.'

To review the Pettersson theory is to review also a pageant of human history, of men and nations in the control of elemental forces whose nature they never understood and whose very existence they never recognized. Pettersson's work was perhaps a natural outcome of the circumstances of his life. He was born—as he died 93 years later —on the shores of the Baltic, a sea of complex and wonderful hydrography. In his laboratory atop a sheer cliff overlooking the deep waters of the Gulmarfiord, instruments recorded strange phenomena in the depths of this gateway to the Baltic. As the ocean water presses in toward that inland sea it dips down and lets the fresh surface water roll out above it; and at that deep level where salt and fresh water come into contact there is a sharp layer of discontinuity, like the surface film between water and air. Each day Pettersson's instruments revealed a strong, pulsing movement of that deep layer—the pressing inward of great submarine waves, of moving mountains of water. The movement was strongest every twelfth hour of the day, and between the 12-hour intervals it subsided. Pettersson soon established a link between these submarine waves and the daily tides. 'Moon waves,' he called them, and as he measured their height and timed their pulsing beat through the months and years, their relation to the ever-changing cycles of the tides became crystal clear.

Some of these deep waves of the Gulmar-fiord were giants nearly 100 feet high. Pettersson believed they were formed by the impact of the oceanic tide wave on the submarine ridges of the North Atlantic, as though the waters moving to the pull of the sun and moon, far down in the lower levels of the sea, broke and spilled over in mountains of highly saline water to enter the fiords and sounds of the coast.

From the submarine tide waves, Pettersson's mind moved logically to another problem—the changing fortunes of the Swedish herring fishery. His native Bohuslan had been the site of the great Hanseatic herring fisheries of the Middle Ages. All through the thirteenth, fourteenth, and fifteenth centuries this great sea fishery was pursued in the Sund and the Belts, the narrow passageways into the Baltic. The towns of Skanor and Falsterbo knew unheard-of prosperity, for there seemed no end of the silvery, wealth-bringing fish. Then suddenly the fishery ceased, for the herring withdrew into the North Sea and came no more into the gateways of the Baltic—this to the enrichment of Holland and the impoverishment of Sweden. Why did the herring cease to come? Pettersson thought he knew, and the reason was intimately related to that moving pen in his laboratory, the pen that traced on a revolving drum the movements of the submarine waves far down in the depths of Gulmarfiord.

He had found that the submarine waves varied in height and power as the tide-producing power of the moon and sun varied. From astronomical calculations he learned that the tides must have been at their greatest strength during the closing centuries of the Middle Ages—those centuries when the Baltic herring fishery was flourishing. Then sun, moon, and earth came into such a position at the time of the winter solstice that they exerted the greatest possible attracting force upon the sea. Only about every eighteen centuries do the heavenly bodies assume this particular relation. But in that period of the Middle Ages, the great underwater waves pressed with unusual force into the narrow passages to the Baltic, and with the 'water mountains' went the herring shoals. Later, when the tides became weaker, the herring remained outside the Baltic, in the North Sea.

Then Pettersson realized another fact of extreme significance—that those centuries of great tides had been a period of 'startling and unusual occurrences' in the world of nature. Polar ice blocked much of the North Atlantic. The coasts of the North Sea and the Baltic were laid waste by violent storm floods. The winters were of 'unexampled severity' and in consequence of the climatic rigors political and economic catastrophes occurred all over the populated regions of the earth. Could there be a connection between these events and those moving mountains of unseen water? Could the deep tides affect the lives of men as well as of herring?

From this germ of an idea, Pettersson's fertile mind evolved a theory of climatic variation, which he set forth in 1912 in an extraordinarily interesting document called *Climatic Variations in Historic and Prehistoric Time*. Marshalling scientific, historic, and literary evidence, he showed that there are alternating periods of mild and severe climates which correspond to the long-period cycles of the oceanic tides. The world's most recent period of maximum tides, and most rigorous climate, occurred about 1433, its effect being felt, however, for several centuries before and after that year. The minimum tidal effect prevailed about A.D. 550, and it will occur again about the year 2400.

During the latest period of benevolent climate, snow and ice were little known on the coast of Europe and in the seas about Iceland and Greenland. Then the Vikings sailed freely over northern seas, monks went back and forth between Ireland and 'Thyle' or Iceland, and there was easy intercourse between Great Britain and the Scandinavian countries. When Eric the Red voyaged to Greenland, according to the Sagas, he 'came from the sea to land at the middle glacier— from thence he went south along the coast to see if the land was habitable. The first year he wintered on Erik's Island . . .' This was probably in the year 984. There is no mention in the Sagas that Eric was hampered by drift ice in the several years of his

exploration of the island; nor is there mention of drift ice anywhere about Greenland, or between Greenland and Wineland. Eric's route as described in the Sagas—proceeding directly west from Iceland and then down the east coast of Greenland—is one that would have been impossible during recent centuries. In the thirteenth century the Sagas contain for the first time a warning that those who sail for Greenland should not make the coast too directly west of Iceland on account of the ice in the sea, but no new route is then recommended. At the end of the fourteenth century, however, the old sailing route was abandoned and new sailing directions were given for a more southwesterly course that would avoid the ice.

The early Sagas spoke, too, of the abundant fruit of excellent quality growing in Greenland, and of the number of cattle that could be pastured there. The Norwegian settlements were located in places that are now at the foot of glaciers. There are Eskimo legends of old houses and churches buried under the ice. The Danish Archaeological Expedition sent out by the National Museum of Copenhagen was never able to find all of the villages mentioned in the old records. But its excavations indicated clearly that the colonists lived in a climate definitely milder than the present one.

But these bland climatic conditions began to deteriorate in the thirteenth century. The Eskimos began to make troublesome raids, perhaps because their northern sealing grounds were frozen over and they were hungry. They attacked the western settlement near the present Ameralik Fiord, and when an official mission went out from the eastern colony about 1342, not a single colonist could be found—only a few cattle remained. The eastern settlement was wiped out some time after 1418 and the houses and churches destroyed by fire. Perhaps the fate of the Greenland colonies was in part due to the fact that ships from Iceland and Europe were finding it increasingly difficult to reach Greenland, and the colonists had to be left to their own resources.

The climatic rigors experienced in Greenland in the thirteenth and fourteenth centuries were felt also in Europe in a series of unusual events and extraordinary catastrophes. The seacoast of Holland was devastated by storm floods. Old Icelandic records say that, in the winters of the early 1300's, packs of wolves crossed on the ice from Norway to Denmark. The entire Baltic froze over, forming a bridge of solid ice between Sweden and the Danish islands. Pedestrians and carriages crossed the frozen sea and hostelries were put up on the ice to accommodate them. The freezing of the Baltic seems to have shifted the course of storms originating in the low pressure belt south of Iceland. In southern Europe, as a result, there were unusual storms, crop failures, famine, and distress. Icelandic literature abounds in tales of volcanic eruptions and other violent natural catastrophes that occurred during the fourteenth century.

What of the previous era of cold and storms, which should have occurred about the third or fourth century B.C., according to the tidal theory? There are shadowy hints in early literature and folklore. The dark and brooding poetry of the Edda deals with a great catastrophe, the Fimbul-winter or Götterdämmerung, when frost and snow ruled the world for generations. When Pytheas journeyed to the seas north of Iceland in 330 B.C., he spoke of the *mare pigrum*, a sluggish, congealed sea. Early history contains striking suggestions that the restless movements of the tribes of northern Europe —the southward migrations of the 'barbarians' who shook the power of Rome—coincided with periods of storms, floods, and other climatic catastrophes that forced their migrations. Large-scale inundations of the sea destroyed the homelands of the Teutons and Cimbrians in Jutland and sent them southward into Gaul. Tradition among the Druids said that their ancestors had been expelled from their lands on the far side of the Rhine by enemy tribes and by 'a great invasion of the ocean.' And about the year 700 B.C. the trade routes for amber, found on the coasts of the North Sea, were suddenly shifted to the east. The old route came down along the Elbe, the Weser, and the Danube, through the Brenner Pass to

Italy. The new route followed the Vistula, suggesting that the source of supply was then the Baltic. Perhaps storm floods had destroyed the earlier amber districts, as they invaded these same regions eighteen centuries later.

All these ancient records of climatic variations seemed to Pettersson an indication that cyclic changes in the oceanic circulation and in the conditions of the Atlantic had occurred. 'No geologic alteration that could influence the climate has occurred for the past six or seven centuries,' he wrote. The very nature of these phenomena— floods, inundations, ice blockades—suggested to him a dislocation of the oceanic circulation. Applying the discoveries in his laboratory on Gulmarfiord, he believed that the climatic changes were brought about as the tide-induced submarine waves disturbed the deep waters of polar seas. Although tidal movements are often weak at the surface of these seas, they set up strong pulsations at the submarine boundaries, where there is a layer of comparatively fresh, cold water lying upon a layer of salty, warmer water. In the years or the centuries of strong tidal forces, unusual quantities of warm Atlantic water press into the Arctic Sea at deep levels, moving in under the ice. Then thousands of square miles of ice that normally remain solidly frozen undergo partial thawing and break up. Drift ice, in extraordinary volume, enters the Labrador Current and is carried southward into the Atlantic. This changes the pattern of surface circulation, which is so intimately related to the winds, the rainfall, and the air temperatures. For the drift ice then attacks the Gulf Stream south of Newfoundland and sends it on a more easterly course, deflecting the streams of warm surface water that usually bring a softening effect to the climate of Greenland, Iceland, Spitsbergen, and northern Europe. The position of the low-pressure belt south of Iceland is also shifted, with further direct effect on European climate.

Although the really catastrophic disturbances of the polar regime come only every eighteen centuries, according to Pettersson, there are also rhythmically occurring periods that fall at varying intervals—for example, every 9, 18, or 36 years. These correspond to other tidal cycles. They produce climatic variations of shorter period and of less drastic nature.

The year 1903, for instance, was memorable for its outbursts of polar ice in the Arctic and for the repercussions on Scandinavian fisheries. There was 'a general failure of cod, herring, and other fish along the coast from Finmarken and Lofoten to the Skagerrak and Kattegat. The greater part of the Barents Sea was covered with pack ice up to May, the ice border approaching closer to the Murman and Finmarken coasts than ever before. Herds of arctic seals visited these coasts, and some species of the arctic whitefish extended their migrations to the Christiana Fiord and even entered into the Baltic.' This outbreak of ice came in a year when earth, moon, and sun were in a relative position that gives a secondary maximum of the tide-producing forces. The similar constellation of 1912 was another great ice year in the Labrador Current—a year that brought the disaster of the *Titanic*.

Now in our own lifetime we are witnessing a startling alteration of climate, and it is intriguing to apply Otto Pettersson's ideas as a possible explanation. It is now established beyond question that a definite change in the arctic climate set in about 1900, that it became astonishingly marked about 1930, and that it is now spreading into sub-arctic and temperate regions. The frigid top of the world is very clearly warming up.

The trend toward a milder climate in the Arctic is perhaps most strikingly apparent in the greater ease of navigation in the North Atlantic and the Arctic Sea. In 1932, for example, the *Knipowitsch* sailed around Franz Josef Land for the first time in the history of arctic voyaging. And three years later the Russian ice-breaker *Sadko* went from the northern tip of Novaya Zemlya to a point north of Severnaya Zemlya (Northern Land) and thence to 82° 41' north latitude—the northernmost point ever reached by a ship under its own power.

In 1940 the whole northern coast of Europe and Asia was remarkably free from ice

during the summer months, and more than 100 vessels engaged in trade via the arctic routes. In 1942 a vessel unloaded supplies at the west Greenland port of Upernivik (latitude 72° 43' N) during Christmas week 'in almost complete winter darkness.' During the 'forties the season for shipping coal from West Spitsbergen ports lengthened to seven months, compared with three at the beginning of the century. The season when pack ice lies about Iceland became shorter by about two months than it was a century ago. Drift ice in the Russian sector of the Arctic Sea decreased by a million square kilometers between 1924 and 1944, and in the Laptev Sea two islands of fossil ice melted away completely, their position being marked by submarine shoals.

Activities in the nonhuman world also reflect the warming of the Arctic—the changed habits and migrations of many fishes, birds, land mammals, and whales.

Many new birds are appearing in far northern lands for the first time in our records. The long list of southern visitors—birds never reported in Greenland before 1920—includes the American velvet scoter, the greater yellowlegs, American avocet, black-browed albatross, northern cliff swallow, ovenbird, common crossbill, Baltimore oriole, and Canada warbler. Some high-arctic forms, which thrive in cold climates, have shown their distaste for the warmer temperatures by visiting Greenland in sharply decreasing numbers. Such abstainers include the northern horned lark, the grey plover, and the pectoral sandpiper. Iceland, too, has had an extraordinary number of boreal and even subtropical avian visitors since 1935, coming both from America and Europe. Wood warblers, skylarks, and Siberian rubythroats, scarlet grosbeaks, pipits, and thrushes now provide exciting fare for Icelandic bird watchers.

When the cod first appeared at Angmagssalik in Greenland in 1912, it was a new and strange fish to the Eskimos and Danes. Within their memory it had never before appeared on the east coast of the island. But they began to catch it, and by the 1930's it supported 'so substantial a fishery in the area that the natives had become dependent upon it for food. They were also using its oil as fuel for their lamps and to heat their houses.

On the west coast of Greenland, too, the cod was a rarity at the turn of the century, although there was a small fishery, taking about 500 tons a year, at a few places on the southwest coast. About 1919 the cod began to move north along the west Greenland coast and to become more abundant. The center of the fishery has moved 300 miles farther north, and the catch is now about 15,000 tons a year.

Other fishes seldom or never before reported in Greenland have appeared there. The coalfish or green cod is a European fish so foreign to Greenland waters that when two of them were caught in 1831 they were promptly preserved in salt and sent to the Copenhagen Zoological Museum. But since 1924 this fish has often been found among the cod shoals. The haddock, cusk, and ling, unknown in Greenland waters until about 1930, are now taken regularly. Iceland, too, has strange visitors—warmth-loving southern fishes, like the basking shark, the grotesque sunfish, the six-gilled shark, the swordfish, and the horse mackerel. Some of these same species have penetrated into the Barents and White seas and along the Murman coast.

As the chill of the northern waters has abated and the fish have moved poleward, the fisheries around Iceland have expanded enormously, and it has become profitable for trawlers to push on to Bear Island, Spitsbergen, and the Barents Sea. These waters now yield perhaps two billion pounds of cod a year—the largest catch of a single species by any fishery in the world. But its existence is tenuous. If the cycle turns, the waters begin to chill, and the ice floes creep southward again, there is nothing man can do that will preserve the arctic fisheries.

But for the present, the evidence that the top of the world is growing warmer is to be found on every hand. The recession of the northern glaciers is going on at such a rate that many smaller ones have already disappeared. If the present rate of melting continues others will soon follow them.

The melting away of the snowfields in the Opdal Mountains in Norway has exposed wooden-shafted arrows of a type used about A.D. 400 to 500. This suggests that the snow cover in this region must now be less than it has been at any time within the past 1400 to 1500 years.

The glaciologist Hans Ahlmann reports that most Norwegian glaciers 'are living only on their own mass without receiving any annual fresh supply of snow'; that in the Alps there has been a general retreat and shrinkage of glaciers during the last decades, which became 'catastrophic' in the summer of 1947; and that all glaciers around the Northern Atlantic coasts are shrinking. The most rapid recession of all is occurring in Alaska, where the Muir Glacier receded about 10½ kilometers in 12 years.

At present the vast antarctic glaciers are an enigma; no one can say whether they also are melting away, or at what rate. But reports from other parts of the world show that the northern glaciers are not the only ones that are receding. The glaciers of several East African high volcanoes have been diminishing since they were first studied in the 1800's—very rapidly since 1920—and there is glacial shrinkage in the Andes and also in the high mountains of central Asia.

The milder arctic and sub-arctic climate seems already to have resulted in longer growing seasons and better crops. The cultivation of oats has improved in Iceland. In Norway good seed years are now the rule rather than the exception, and even in northern Scandinavia the trees have spread rapidly above their former timber lines, and both pine and spruce are making a quicker annual growth than they have for some time.

The countries where the most striking changes are taking place are those whose climate is most directly under the control of the North Atlantic currents. Greenland, Iceland, Spitsbergen, and all of northern Europe, as we have seen, experience heat and cold, drought and flood in accordance with the varying strength and warmth of the eastward and northward-moving currents of the Atlantic. Oceanographers who have been studying the matter during the 1940's have discovered many significant changes in the temperature and distribution of great masses of ocean water. Apparently the branch of the Gulf Stream that flows past Spitsbergen has so increased in volume that it now brings in a great body of warm water. Surface waters of the North Atlantic show rising temperatures; so do the deeper layers around Iceland and Spitsbergen. Sea temperatures in the North Sea and along the coast of Norway have been growing warmer since the 1920's.

Unquestionably, there are other agents at work in bringing about the climatic changes in the Arctic and sub-Arctic regions. For one thing, it is almost certainly true that we are still in the warming-up stage following the last Pleistocene glaciation—that the world's climate, over the next thousands of years, will grow considerably warmer before beginning a downward swing into another Ice Age. But what we are experiencing now is perhaps a climatic change of shorter duration, measurably only in decades or centuries. Some scientists say that there must have been a small increase in solar activity, changing the pattern of air circulation and

causing the southerly winds to blow more frequently in Scandinavia and Spitsbergen; changes in ocean currents, according to this view, are secondary effects of the shift of prevailing winds.

But if, as Professor Brooks thinks, the Pettersson tidal theory has as good a foundation as that of changing solar radiation, then it is interesting to calculate where our twentieth-century situation fits into the cosmic scheme of the shifting cycles of the tides. The great tides at the close of the Middle Ages, with their accompanying snow and ice, furious winds, and inundating floods, are more than five centuries behind us. The era of weakest tidal movements, with a climate as benign as that of the early Middle Ages, is about four centuries ahead. We have therefore begun to move strongly into a period of warmer, milder weather. There will be fluctuations, as earth and sun and moon move through space and the tidal power waxes and wanes. But the long trend is toward a warmer earth; the pendulum is swinging.

QUESTIONS FOR STUDY AND DISCUSSION

1. What is the main thesis of "The Global Thermostat"?

2. The same cause can produce different effects. Why? Can you cite examples from the essay to support this statement?

3. In what way do air and ocean affect each other?

4. This essay interestingly illustrates how history and literature can contribute to scientific inquiry. Can you think of any other areas of scientific study which are interpenetrated by art, literature, philosophy, or history?

5. What unusual and unexpected results

of the action of wind and water are described? Is this revelation of the difference between the apparent and the real characteristic of scientific inquiry? To what extent is it the purpose of all intellectual inquiry? Why?

6. Is this article only a series of speculations about causes, or can it be considered proof? Discuss.

7. How does Miss Carson bring interest and life to a technical discussion? What are the chief characteristics of her style of writing?

Part Two

THE ARGUMENT

Induction

Induction is the art of making sound generalizations. It is the art of making abstractions, of recognizing patterns. It is the foundation of modern science.

Several kinds of generalizations can be made. A statement such as "Triangles have three sides" applies to all triangles, certainly, but most people would want to call it a loose definition rather than an induction. The statement identifies the class of triangles, but a genuine induction moves from the particular to the abstract, from the known to the unknown.

Another kind of generalization is often referred to as the "perfect induction," though a philosopher like John Stuart Mill would not be willing to call it induction at all. In a generalization of this type, such as "All the Presidents of the United States have been men," we are not so much moving from the known to the unknown as bundling together certain facts about our past Presidents, much as an IBM punch-card sorter would do. The essence of the "perfect induction" is a sorting and counting operation performed upon *all* the members of a class and their known characteristics. If the class should grow or change, the "perfect induction" based upon an earlier class membership has low predictive value. We cannot say that because all the Presidents of the United States have been men all future Presidents will be men and not women.

More likely the result of real induction is a statement such as "The dog is man's best friend." It asserts that a characteristic which is known to be true of many members of the class is true of the entire class. Of course, the class may also consist of the repeated actions of only one member, as in the statement "The sun rises in the east and sets in the west." These two generalizations raise the question of proof. How do we show that any one generalization is true? The proof for an induction consists of testing a sample that is both fair and representative of the class. A person seeking to prove that dog is definitely man's best friend would probably do so by citing examples of all the noble, selfless canines who have sacrificed themselves to protect their masters, life and limb; who have remained loyally behind when all others, friends and family alike, have deserted; who have poured forth love and affection unrivaled by human emotion; and who by countless demonstrations from Adam until the present have shown that dogs more than any other earthly creature merit the title of man's best friend. Basically, this is the most familiar of the inductive techniques.

How much, though, is a fair sample? The problem has vexed logicians since the philosophy of induction began. As Mill points out, it would take only "one unexceptionable witness" who had found a gray crow to make us willing to believe that not all crows are black, but we are considerably more hesitant to believe that there are men whose heads grow beneath their shoulders, despite the "testimony of the naturalist Pliny." There is no magic number to guide the student in obtaining a fair sample. But his confidence in an induction will be greater if he can show that the material he has gathered is highly representative of the entire class —that the class, in other words, is homogeneous. If the student can prove that despite the variety of shapes and sizes all dogs are very much alike, he will have an easier time of convincing his audience that the dog is indeed man's best friend. In the physical sciences, where generalizations tend to support and reinforce one another in a tightly woven fabric of theory, it is still easier to prove the truth of any particular generalization.

But what about proof for "All men are mortal" or "The sun rises in the east and sets in the west" or "Two and two is four" or "Two plus three equals three plus two"? To many people these generalizations are self-evident, or intuitive, the truth being apparent from the universal experience of mankind itself. To some, who are inclined to overstate their case, the mathematical statements would constitute nothing more than arbitrary axioms upon which a logical system is grounded. The best advice when dealing with intuitive statements of any kind is to remember that what seems intuitively true to one age may not to another. People spent many hundreds of years observing that the earth is flat.

Shifting from the physical world to the world of ideas, we often encounter intuitive statements which take the form of judgments and philosophical outlooks. To some the world is essentially a good place; to others it is more tragic and evil than anything else. All of us are full of metaphysical assumptions of this kind, and except for divine revelation they are largely beyond ordinary proof. The same facts in any history of the human race could be used to argue that man is just a little lower than the angels or hardly better than the beasts of the field. The wise man does not scorn a metaphysical axiom because it cannot be proved to everyone's satisfaction, but he does recognize that the same set of facts can sometimes be interpreted in more than one way. Least of all does he regard an intuitive axiom as self-evident to all men. He attempts to examine the metaphysical assumptions that guide his interpretation of facts so that his arguments will be clearer for knowing exactly why he takes any particular stand. By knowing what his assumptions are, the writer can avoid one of the most tragic abuses of the human intellect: the selecting of facts to prove a thesis, mentioning only those which support his argument and ignoring the rest. It is a mistake made by the most learned and best intentioned of men.

We must keep in mind that generalizations do not have to be universal statements; though often they apply to *all* members of a class, they may equally well apply to *some* members of the class. A generalization to the effect that a great many millions of Americans like baseball and coffee is the result of legitimate induction, and the more precisely the statement can be qualified, the more reliable it is. One of the commonest mistakes people make in reasoning is to overgeneralize —to insist that every American likes coffee, every Englishman tea, every Frenchman wine, and every German beer.

The actual mechanism of induction is elusive. Logicians can tell us how to gather our data and remind us to be sure that we get a fair sample and a representative one, but after that we are on our own. We can only scrutinize the information and hope to make the "inductive leap"—a sudden flash of insight suggesting to us that some characteristics of individual members of a class are also characteristics of the class as a whole. The real mechanism of induction, then, is not so much the gathering of information as pattern recognition, a remarkable ability of the human mind to find orderly systems underlying an outward maze of facts. It is the same ability that enables us to identify something as a circle whether it is two inches in radius or three feet—even to recognize it as a circle if part of it is missing or bent out of shape. Pattern recognition enables us to identify as the same letter, type faces as different as A, ᴀ, **A**, or A. It enables us to look at a series of numbers like 1, 2, 3, 4, spot the pattern that orders them, and predict 5 as the next number in the series. It enables us to identify a person from a caricature in the newspaper or to recognize the voice of a friend even when distorted by low-fidelity telephone lines. It enables us to say that one painting is a Rembrandt and another a Botticelli, even if we have never seen them before. This is the inductive leap—the ability to recognize patterns (or *Gestalten* as they are called), a process of abstraction quite separate from the gathering of information which usually precedes it and which is cited as proof to confirm it.

Since this is the case, why call induction a type of argumentation? We do so because the processes of induction and deduction are most often used for argumentative purposes. But a cause-and-effect essay could well be an argument, and a purely deductive paper might not be. Rather than ask whether induction is really a kind of argument, it would be better to inquire what the argument itself is. An argument contends for something different from what people generally believe or accept, and often this new contention will invite attack. An essay favoring democracy, as we understand it, is hardly an argument in this country, but it would be in Russia.

EXERCISE

1. Find the pattern underlying each of the following sets of numbers and predict the fifth number:

1	4	9	16	?
1	8	27	64	?
1	9	25	49	?
1	0	1	4	?

2. A folk idea observes that since 1840 every President to be elected in a year divisible by twenty has either been assassinated or has died while still in office. (Cf. the letter by J. C. House to the editors of *Time*, July 25, 1960.) Evaluate as induction.

3. Make a list of generalizations often heard about Americans, Englishmen, Frenchmen, and Germans, or other national or ethnic groups. How far can any of these generalizations be supported?

4. Suppose that Random House asked you to write definitions of current slang words for a revision of the *American College Dictionary*. Study a number of entries in the *ACD* to see how the parts within the definition are arranged;

then write a style sheet, explaining what part goes where, the kind of type each part is printed in, the style of writing used in definitions, etc.

5. Assuming that Shakespeare's sixty-fourth sonnet is typical of the sonnet form as he used it, generalize upon the nature of this form:

> WHEN I have seen by Time's fell hand defaced
> The rich-proud cost of outworne buried age;
> When sometime loftie towers I see downe-rased,
> And brasse eternall slave to mortall rage:
> When I have seene the hungry ocean gaine
> Advantage on the kingdome of the shoare,
> And the firme soile win of the wat'ry maine,
> Increasing store with losse, and losse with store,
> When I have seen such interchange of state,
> Or state it selfe confounded to decay;
> Ruine hath taught me thus to ruminate,
> That Time will come and take my love away.
> This thought is as a death, which cannot choose
> But weepe to have that which it feares to loose.

6. The dining room of a home in Dallas, Texas, is paneled in wood. The panels are of three different widths, which may be represented by the numbers 1, 2, and 3. The arrangement of panels along one wall is as follows: 1-3-1-3-3-2-1-2-1-3-1-3-3-2-1-2-1-3-2-1-2-1-3-1-3-2-1-2. Is there a pattern to this arrangement?

7. The greatest number of English nouns form their written plurals by adding -s or -es, though these written forms represent no less than three plurals in the spoken language: /ɨz/ as in *watches*, /s/ as in *bats*, and /z/ as in *toes*. Draw up a long list of nouns (excluding such minor groups as *foot: feet; deer: deer; child: children*; etc.) and examine their spoken plurals. What is it that determines the plural ending for these nouns? Can you state a "rule"— that is, a very precise description—for forming plurals?

8. The regular verbs form their past tense and past participle in spoken English by adding /ɨd/ as in *batted*, /t/ as in *watched*, and /d/ as in *watered*. Analyze a long list of these verbs as you did the nouns and formulate another "rule" describing the past tense and past participle.

9. Thomas Speght's second edition of *The Workes of Our Ancient and learned English Poet, Geffrey Chaucer*, published in 1602, employs both the "insular s" [ʃ] and the "two r" [ɹ], as in the portrait of the Squire in the General Prologue:

¶ The Squire.   ii.

With him there was his son a yong squire,
A louer and a lusty Bachelere,
With his locks crull as they were laid in presse,
Of twenty yeare of age he was as I gesse:
Of his stature he was of euen length,
And wonderly deliuer, and of great strength.
And he had be sometime in chiuauchie,
In Flaunders, in Artois, and Picardie,
And borne him well, as of so little space,
In hope to stand in his ladies grace.
Embrouded was he, as it weren a mede,
All full of fresh floures, both white and rede:
Singing he was, or floiting all the day,
He was fresh, as is the moneth of May.
Short was his gown, with sleues long & wide
Well coud he sitte on a horse, and faire ride:
He coud songs make, and eke well endite,
Iust and eke daunce, portray and well write.
So hote he loued, that by nighter tale,
He slept no more than doth the Nightingale.
Curteis he was, lowly, and seruisable,
And kerfte before his fader at the table.

Can you construct an hypothesis that will explain how the variants of *s* and *r* were used by the printer, Adam Islip? You do not have enough material for a proof, but plenty for some good guesses, which you should test by going to the library and examining more of Islip's work, as well as other early printed books.

10. The First Folio of *Mr. William Shakespeares Comedies, Histories, & Tragedies*, printed in 1623, employs *u*, *v*, and *i* as in this excerpt from Portia's speech in *The Merchant of Venice*:

Though Iustice be thy plea, consider this,
That in the course of Iustice, none of vs
Should see saluation : we do pray for mercie,
And that same prayer, doth teach vs all to render
The deeds of mercie. I haue spoke thus much
To mittigate the iustice of thy plea :

Can you state tentatively how *u*, *v*, and *i* were used by Isaac Jaggard and Edward Blount, the printers? Assuming that pronunciation has not changed significantly, what sounds do these letters stand for?

11. What generalizations can you make from the following three tables drawn from *The World Almanac?*

FARM POPULATION OF THE UNITED STATES

Year (April)	Farm Population	Total U. S. Population
1910	32,077,000	91,972,266
1920	31,974,000	105,710,620
1930	30,529,000	122,775,046
1940	30,547,000	131,669,275
1950	25,058,000	150,697,361
1959	21,172,000	177,103,000

NUMBER OF TORNADOES IN U. S. SINCE 1916, DEATHS

Year	No.	Deaths	Year	No.	Deaths	Year	No.	Deaths	Year	No.	Deaths
1916	90	150	1929	197	274	1942	167	384	1955	593	125
1917	121	509	1930	192	179	1943	152	58	1956	532	83
1918	81	135	1931	94	36	1944	169	275	1957	864	191
1919	64	206	1932	151	394	1945	121	210	1958	565	66
1920	87	498	1933	258	362	1946	106	78	1959	589	58
1921	105	202	1934	147	47	1947	165	313	Total	9,756	9,299
1922	108	135	1935	180	70	1948	183	140			
1923	102	109	1936	151	552	1949	249	212	Avg	221.7	211.3
1924	130	376	1937	147	29	1950	199	70			
1925	119	794	1938	213	183	1951	272	34	Median	158	147
1926	111	144	1939	152	87	1952	236	230			
1927	163	540	1940	124	65	1953	437	516			
1928	203	92	1941	118	53	1954	549	35			

AVERAGE WEIGHT OF AMERICANS BY HEIGHT AND AGE

Source: Society of Actuaries; from its 1959 report on a 4-year study of 5,000,000 persons. The figures represent weights in ordinary indoor clothing and shoes, and heights with shoes.

Average Weight of Men

Height	Age Groups							
	15–16	17–19	20–24	25–29	30–39	40–49	50–59	60–69
5′ 0″	98	113	122	128	131	134	136	133
5′ 1″	102	116	125	131	134	137	139	136
5′ 2″	107	119	128	134	137	140	142	139
5′ 3″	112	123	132	138	141	144	145	142
5′ 4″	117	127	136	141	145	148	149	146
5′ 5″	122	131	139	144	149	152	153	150
5′ 6″	127	135	142	148	153	156	157	154
5′ 7″	132	139	145	151	157	161	162	159
5′ 8″	137	143	149	155	161	165	166	163
5′ 9″	142	147	153	159	165	169	170	168
5′ 10″	146	151	157	163	170	174	175	173
5′ 11″	150	155	161	167	174	178	180	178
6′ 0″	154	160	166	172	179	183	185	183
6′ 1″	159	164	170	177	183	187	189	188
6′ 2″	164	168	174	182	188	192	194	193
6′ 3″	169	172	178	186	193	197	199	198
6′ 4″	*	176	181	190	199	203	205	204

ESSAY SUGGESTIONS

1. Study the advertising in a number of issues of any man's magazine. Can you show that the ads are deliberately slanted to the male reader?

2. Analyze the newspaper you usually read for the amount of space it gives to

international, national, state, and local news; to features, columns, editorials, and pictures; to sports, financial news, comics, and advertising. How much real news is there in your newspaper? (You might use *The New York Times* as a point of comparison.)

3. Analyze your newspaper for the kinds of stories that it emphasizes. To what extent does it play up the sensational?

4. Study the advertising in a number of issues of a magazine with large circulation. What kinds of appeals does this advertising make to its readers?

5. If your experience is sufficiently great, write an inductive essay about horse operas on TV.

6. If you have read enough to do the job well, write a paper generalizing upon the major themes found in modern science fiction short stories.

7. Using the cartoons which follow this section, write an essay generalizing upon the nature of Charles Addams' humor. For further materials, see the following collections of Addams' work: *Drawn and Quartered, Monster Rally, Addams and Evil, Homebodies.*

In writing essays such as these, you must always assess the reliability of your data. Your generalizations may hold good for the material you have studied, but how much data would you need in order to make statements that are true for your newspaper, magazine, etc., as a continuing publication? If you feel that your statements have limited reliability, say so! Never push a generalization further than what you know to be accurate. And remember that a generalization is only as convincing as the evidence you give in order to prove it.

FURTHER READING

Francis Bacon, *Novum Organum.*

Morris R. Cohen and Ernest Nagel, *An Introduction to Logic and Scientific Method,* Chapter XIV.

Bernard F. Huppé and Jack Kaminsky, *Logic and Language.* New York: Alfred A. Knopf, 1956. Chapter 5.

John Stuart Mill, *A System of Logic,* Book III, Chapters I through IV.

The relationship between induction and Gestalt psychology has not before been recognized, so far as we know. The student might want to consult:

Willis Davis Ellis, *A Source Book of Gestalt Psychology.* London: Kegan Paul, Trench, Trubner, & Company, Ltd., 1938.

D. W. Hamlyn, *The Psychology of Perception.* New York: Humanities Press, 1957.

David Katz, *Gestalt Psychology, Its Nature and Significance,* translated by Robert Tyson. New York: Ronald Press Company, 1950.

NAPIER WILT

There Will Always Be a Camille

It is with some trepidation I begin this talk.*
Not only am I about to bring before you a
large company of women whose reputations
were not even questionable, but I shall have
to talk in some detail about the nature of
their transgressions. And while I am sure
each of you has seen one or two of them
across the safe gulf of the footlights, you have
probably never before been confronted with
so large a company of what one critic of the
90's called "soiled doves." But let me hasten
to assure you that all of them saw and be-
wailed—usually at some length—the error
of their ways.

Perhaps the best excuse I can give for
this paper is the one often given by the
dramatists who created the plays in which
these women appeared. Admitting their heroines were frail, and the details of their plays
were often sordid, the dramatists insisted
they were presented only for the common
good. Their plays, they affirmed, were highly
moral, and I assure you so is my talk.

For many years I have been interested in
the popular theatre, and, by popular theatre,
I mean only that theatre whose support
comes from the general public, and, roughly
speaking, from all classes of people. This
kind of theatre, for practical purposes, developed late in the Eighteenth Century and
has continued with varying fortunes down
to the present day. It developed in England
and the United States, in France and in
Germany, and also in other European countries. The popular successes of one country
were usually quickly adapted to the stage of
the others. In fact, the popular play has for
the last 150 years been one of the few real
international bonds. While in this paper I

shall be dealing mainly with the American
stage, I shall at the same time be dealing
with plays which were internationally popular.

One of the most noticeable characteristics
of these enormously popular plays is, after a
relatively short and happy life, they seem
silly and superficial. I'm sure each of you
has seen some old-time favorite, some play
which was, at one time, seriously received,
and now only revived to be laughed at.
When one reads some play like, say, Augus-
tin Daly's *Under the Gaslight*, one wonders
at the naiveté of the millions who were
thrilled by it. But when one reads many of
the old favorites and also many of the current favorites, he begins to see, if he is at
all perceptive, that the success of 1862 and
that of 1962 have a great deal in common,
far more, in fact, than they have differences.
One notices too that these very popular
plays fall into relatively few patterns and,
to repeat, within the pattern, the admired
play of today is basically like the scorned
play of yesterday.

Of these popular patterns none has been
more successful than that of the unhappy
woman whose plight allows the audience to
indulge in an orgy of tears. A Chicago reviewer of the 80's said it makes no difference whether the heroine was "a ten-cent
Sunday School heroine of unprecedented virtue, or a highly immoral one, so long as she
gives the audience ample opportunity to
weep." With this I cannot quite agree. It is
true that while the heroine of unprecedented
virtue, sorely tried but in the end triumphant, has been the center of many a tearful
popular drama, these plays have never been
as popular as those whose heroine sins and
repents. Female virtue triumphant is always
rewarded with a good and financially sound
husband, but while her erring and repentant
sister is usually rewarded with only a tearful
death, the public, alas, prefers her. Just
what this proves about the public I don't
know.

All of the plays I am going to talk about
to you have, first, a common history. Each
of them was an immediate and great success in the country of its origin, each was
adapted for the stage of many other coun-

---

* "There Will Always Be a Camille" was
originally written as a talk for the Fortnightly
Club of Chicago.

tries and became an international success. Each play was taken seriously by the critics as well as the public, and although some of the critics attacked each play as being immoral, degrading, and vicious, other critics praised it for its frankness, its pathos, and for what we now call its social significance. Each play provoked a hot controversy in the press. Some of the plays retained their popularity longer than others, but, except for the most recent of them, they have come to be regarded as not only naive and quaint, but worst of all, entirely harmless. And the chances are that the most recent successes will before long take their place with the others.

The center of each of these plays is a woman who either before the play opens or in the course of the play sins, shall I say, as only a woman can sin. She may be a wife who, in a moment of weakness, listens to, as Lady Isabel described her seducer, "a bold bad man." In this case, the woman soon repents her folly and leaves her lover. Eventually, she again meets her noble husband, who when he hears at some length her story, forgives her. But, except in one case, the forgiveness is followed almost immediately by the death of the repentant woman.

Or the center of the play may be a woman who when young and innocent was seduced, and has drifted into a life of shame. But she too repents, usually through the agency of pure love, and seeks a return to a decent life. But again, with one exception and even that an equivocal one, there is no return. In all of these plays the women are, of course, exceptionally attractive, glamorous, and charming. And, except for their one weakness, they are all very good, kind, charitable, generous, and understanding.

Among the many characteristics these plays have in common, the most important is that no opportunity is missed to produce an emotional reaction from the audience. They were, in fact, until the end of the Nineteenth Century, called simply and formally "emotional plays." Why this useful and amazingly accurate term was dropped from our critical vocabulary, I don't know.

To get down to cases, Kotzebue's *Menschenhass und Reue* had already been a great and scandalous success in Germany when no less a person than Richard Brinsley Sheridan presented in London, in 1798, his own adaptation of the play, called *The Stranger.*

That *The Stranger* was fortunate in having the famous Mrs. Siddons portray Mrs. Haller, its lachrymose heroine, and Charles Kemble its morose hero, the stranger, there is no doubt. But the success of the play was not tied up to their portrayals for, as the record attests, hundreds of other actors and actresses were to charm English and American audiences with *The Stranger* for over half a century. Every important actress on the English-speaking stage in the first half of the Nineteenth Century portrayed Mrs. Haller. When Charlotte Cushman made her only visit to Chicago she portrayed Lady Macbeth, Romeo—yes, Romeo, and Mrs. Haller.

The general atmosphere of *The Stranger* is one of refinement, elegance, noble sentiments, and general enlightenment. Faith in the essential goodness of human nature is in the air. The scene of the play is the country estate of a nobleman, and the action takes place while the count, his wife, children, and his wife's brother are visiting there. As the count's entourage arrives, being greeted by a very superior housekeeper, Mrs. Haller, the children rush off to play in the park. Soon there is a cry, some confusion, and servants report that the children had fallen into the lake and were about to drown, when, suddenly jumping from the shrubbery, a mysterious stranger had rescued them and had rushed away refusing even to be thanked. Mrs. Haller is sure the man must be the gentleman who, it is reported, living just outside of the estate, avoids all contacts and seems to be laboring under a great sorrow. The countess' young brother is at once attracted to Mrs. Haller and in no time at all, and to the lady's great consternation, makes genteel advances to her. Soon the audience from a conversation between Mrs. Haller and the countess learn that not long ago the countess had found Mrs. Haller in despair and on the verge of suicide, and had given her her present position; and we eventually learn that Mrs. Haller, once the honored wife of a great baron, had eloped with another man, but had soon realized the enormity of her action and had left him before the countess found her. Why had she left her noble husband? Here we get the first of an oft-repeated tale. She was young and inexperienced. Her husband had neglected her, had been stingy with money, and, she believed, had given his affections to another woman—or so at least her seducer told her.

When the young man in love with Mrs. Haller seeks out the stranger to insist on thanking him for rescuing the children, he finds the stranger to be an old friend, a man who after his wife had left him had disappeared from society. This man, now become a melancholy hater of mankind, was devoting his life to the care of his abandoned children. The young man, however, persuades the old friend to come to the house to see and advise him about Mrs. Haller, the woman he so admires.

The scene now is the drawing room. All except Mrs. Haller are there talking about and awaiting "the stranger." As he enters the door, on the other side of the room, Mrs. Haller enters. The two for a moment freeze into immobility, staring at each other. Then Mrs. Haller screams and faints, and the stranger almost fainting turns and rushes from the room. The stranger is, of course, the noble husband and Mrs. Haller the erring wife. Now we hear again in detail Mrs. Haller's story, and the stranger tells his story to his friend. It seems that a man professing to be his friend had robbed him and left him poor, but he had been too proud to tell his wife. His neglect was due to the time he had to spend repairing his fortune. While innocent of any wrong doing, he admits he should have acted differently. He now understands how his wife misunderstood him. He realizes he, not she, was to blame. In fact there is more than enough self-accusation on both sides. Finally the two are brought together. He has forgiven her. This makes Mrs. Haller, as I shall continue to call her, indulge in new statements of her unworthiness. He will give her custody of their children. He will give her most of his fortune. Here I cannot refrain from direct quotation. Mrs. Haller: "Never will I

take your money. To the labor of my hands alone will I owe my sustenance. A morsel of bread moistened with my tears will suffice my wishes and exceed my merit."

The husband next returns his wife's jewels, and in this scene we have a wonderfully simple example of how to arouse emotion. The husband, instead of simply giving the large jewel case to his wife, opens it and takes out a bracelet. "This," he says, "I gave you when we were engaged." And so on. Each jewel is a memento of some happy occasion of their life together. By the end of this scene the audience was drowned in tears. But now the time has come to part, for, while all is forgiven, they cannot live together. As they say goodbye for the last time, the door opens and their two children rush in. The girl throws her arms about her father's legs; the boy kneels by the mother. Both weep. And then all really *is* forgiven and the husband and wife are reconciled, and will begin a new life.

It was the reconciliation that caused the fracas. "Adultery condoned," cried one newspaper. And while the public flocked to see the play, the press, although approving much of the play, generally attacked the ending. Sheridan, for a short time, altered the ending, leaving it ambiguous. You could believe what you wanted. But soon he returned to the old ending.

In the United States, occasionally, the ambiguous ending was given. But over here another dodge was usually used to placate outraged moralists. And it was done by simply altering a few lines. When Mrs. Haller tells the story of her flight from her husband, she makes it very plain that before she and the villain reached the inn where they were to spend the night, she had repented, and that she jumped from the carriage and fled just as the inn came into sight. Hence, there was no adultery to be condoned.

There is every evidence that *The Stranger* made a tremendous effect in England and the United States. Newspapers give accounts of audiences that listened, hushed and tense for a while, and then suddenly burst into mass weeping. Letters, diaries, and memoirs speak of the deep emotional impact the play had on the writers. But by 1866 a critic in New York wrote that the only virtue he could see in that dull, pious play was that it was "useful to sober up on after a three-day drunk."

Although *not* the next successful play about a fallen woman, *East Lynne* in the early sixties was the real successor of *The Stranger*. As soon as Mrs. Henry Wood's novel, *East Lynne*, appeared, many dramatic versions of it came out, and for the next half century Lady Isabel's pathetic story was a popular favorite. While it was not attacked as vehemently as *The Stranger*, it was thought a questionable play; and while the greatest actresses of the time seldom played Lady Isabel, the play, as I have said, was very popular, probably more so in the less high-brow theatres than any of the others. It was revived as late as 1920. It is, in all of its features, a truly mid-Victorian play. The intensely domestic atmosphere, the pious sentiments, the acute sense of propriety, are all there. Moreover, its rapid action, its short scenes, its black and white characters, and its "tell all the story" structure are typical of the plays of the period.

In *East Lynne*, Lady Isabel, the orphan daughter of an impoverished earl, married a rising young lawyer, Mr. Carlyle, who has bought her old home. An embittered sister of her husband makes her life unhappy from the beginning, and monopolizes Isabel's children when they arrive. Her husband's attention, strictly for business reasons, to a young and beautiful client, makes her jealous, and so she is an easy victim of the villain, Francis Levison, who is so perfectly the stage villain that I suspect many later ones were modeled after him. Once when the husband meets his fair client, for the best of reasons, mysteriously and at night in the park, the villain, of course, completely misrepresenting the case, shows them to Lady Isabel, and she, now convinced of her husband's guilt, cries out, "Take me away from this accursed place, Francis Levison. I am faint—ill—wretched—mad." And he does take her away, to France, of course. But when Isabel's husband divorces her, Francis Levison, now Sir Francis, refuses to marry Isabel saying, "I am now the representative of a respected and ancient baron-

etcy. To make you my wife would offend my family." And when Isabel mentions their sin, Sir Francis says, "Ah, sin. You ladies should think of that beforehand," to which Isabel replies, "I pray Heaven they may. May Heaven help all those tempted as I was."

Isabel's uncle, the Earl of Mt. Severn, traces Isabel to her hideaway in France and comes to take her away. While talking to her he hears in the next room the cry of a baby. He listens a moment, looks sadly at Isabel, and says, "Oh Isabel, and you an Earl's only daughter."

The next scene is again at East Lynne. The former husband now learns through the newspaper of a train wreck in France in which it is reported Lady Isabel and her child were killed. He immediately married —oddly enough—his fair client. In the proper time, there are children. Then the young Mrs. Carlyle advertises for a governess to take care of Lady Isabel's children. In answer to this comes Madame Vine, a heavily veiled woman under whose veil one catches a glimpse of deep scars. When she is hired she shows unusual devotion to the children, especially the boy who is delicate. The boy soon dies, very much in the fashion of little Eva in *Uncle Tom's Cabin*, in the arms of Madame Vine. Then Madame Vine herself becomes ill. Hearing of this, Mr. Carlyle goes to see her, and discovers that she is none other than Lady Isabel. All is cleared up. She is forgiven and, as she dies she says, "No, it is not faintness. It is death. Farewell once more my always loved husband, farewell until eternity." It was always, from now on, "until eternity" for the erring wife. Incidentally, you will be happy to learn that before the end of the play, Sir Francis Levison is convicted of murdering a former mistress and is led off to be hanged.

In the last half of the nineteenth century, the stage was filled with these erring but repentant wives. Always they sinned, always they repented, always they returned, always they were forgiven, and always they died. But none of them achieved the popular fame of Lady Isabel. The last erring and repentant wife to attain great popular success was Madame X. *Madame X*, translated from the French of Alexander Bisson, appeared in New York and Chicago in 1910. In it, early in the play a repentant wife is refused forgiveness by a stern husband, turned from his door, and not allowed even to see her son. Years later we see the woman sunk very low indeed, living in a vile hotel with a criminal lover. But all decency has not left her, we see, when she shoots a man who threatens to blackmail her husband. At her trial, refusing to give her name, and called Madame X, she is defended, and nobly defended, by a young lawyer trying his first case. I trust I won't surprise you too much when I tell you this young lawyer is none other than her own son. Of course, he gets her set free, of course he discovers she is his mother, and she, of course, dies in his arms. Although there were many other repentant wives to follow poor Madame X, none attained great popular favor.

In fact, the erring wife has been replaced in popular favor by the scarlet woman seeking rehabilitation. It was not until 1852, when Dumas fils presented *La Dame aux Camélias* to a startled Parisian public that we have—as the French so nicely say—a demi-mondaine as the heroine of a play. And if the play startled Paris, you can well imagine the effect it had, even in watered-down versions, on New York, Chicago, and St. Louis. So accustomed are we to think of *Camille* as a romantic and sentimental costume play, we forget, that when first presented, it was strictly contemporary, that it was in many ways regarded both as a highly pertinent problem play, and as a condemnation of the society of the time. Its success was overwhelming. Its scandal was greater. In no time at all it was "adapted"—not translated, but "adapted" into other languages. New York saw it in 1853, Chicago in 1854. And no actress of the second half of the nineteenth century, who wanted to be considered a great actress, failed to try out in the role of the lovely lady who always wore a camellia. Verdi's operatic version of the play, *La Traviata*, increased its popularity—and continues to charm us. Not only did Chicago see the original version with Bernhardt, with Rejane, and Rhea, but saw

Matilda Heron, Fanny Davenport, Helena Modjeska, Laura Keene, Ethel Barrymore, and innumerable other actresses each do her own version of the play. Chicago has also seen German, Swedish, and Italian versions, the Italian Camille being played by the great Eleonora Duse. Garbo's movie version was highly successful, and just recently I saw *Camille* on TV. Camille is still dying. In Willa Cather's *My Antonia* (the "Lena Lengard" section), there is a charming description of a performance of *Camille* in Lincoln, Nebraska. The account ends "wherever and whenever that piece (*Camille*) is put on, it is April."

As Dumas fils wrote the play, much emphasis is placed on the fact that Marguerite has been a member of the demi-monde, but because she had resembled his dead daughter, a respectable duke had rescued her and tried to have her accepted by society. Society had refused. And when the play opens, Marguerite—I think I'll call her Camille—has returned to her old life. Then as you know, she meets young Armand, and true love blossoms. As she says in one of the famous arias in the opera, "*Ah, fors e lui qui l'anima.*" And so, sacrificing her place and money, she retires to the country with Armand. But the father of Armand, for very French reasons, persuades her to leave him, and leave him in such a way that Armand believes Camille has thrown him over for a former lover. She returns a second time to her old life, and Armand, meeting her by chance, publicly insults her. But later, Armand learns the truth, realizes her real nobility and returns to her—returns too late, for, of course, Camille is dying. Probably sentiment has never been so elaborately anatomized or prolonged as in the last act of this play. Every heart-wringing device is used.

While there are many versions of *Camille* in English, each follows closely one of two patterns. A few versions stick fairly closely to the original and do not gloss over some of the facts; and actresses, like Matilda Heron, using this version, have usually played Camille as a fairly vulgar and sensuous woman. But usually in English the more demi-mondaine side of Camille's life is played down. In one of them, she is not even a fallen woman, only a coquette. (Incidentally, in the Garbo picture, it was made very clear that Armand and Camille occupied different houses when they were in the country.) Modjeska was noted for her refined Camille. Laura Keene, and later Ethel Barrymore, briefly used a very, very moral version of the play. This was managed quite simply. There were added to the play two new short scenes, one at the beginning, one at the end. In the first we see a young girl sorely tempted by a worthless villain. As she ponders her plight she goes to sleep. And in the last scene, this same innocent girl awakens. All the play was a dream. This is the way to eat your cake and have it too.

So great was the popularity of *Camille* that while there were many plays on the same theme, none of them replaced it until the early 90's, when Pinero's *Second Mrs. Tanqueray* raised again the old fuss over the morals of such a play. While this play never reached the heights of *Camille* in popularity, it was a great international success. Mrs. Pat Campbell rose to fame with it. Chicago saw her, Mrs. Kendall, Olga Nethersole and Ethel Barrymore play the suffering Paula. Here was, as a critic said, "a modern problem play." Could a woman with a past, even if redeemed by true love and married to a good man, be reinstated in society. No, she couldn't. True, society was blamed, but had Pinero attempted to give Paula a happy life, there would have been a real scandal. In 1893, when *The Second Mrs. Tanqueray* was first performed here, two Chicago reviews gave nice illustrations of the divided attitude toward the morals of the play.

The Chicago *Tribune* said, "No wonder it was a sensation in London—and not women alone, but men, men of fashion, will shrink beneath its lash, and to save themselves, will brand it immoral.

"Mrs. Grundy whines, holds up her hands in horror. But Chicago received it with less hypocritical whining than did New York."

The Chicago *Inter Ocean*'s reviewer wrote, "Why should one weep for the too lightly repentant jade when she pleaded in vain for the embraces that were a profanation to a pure nature. Defensible from no

possible standpoint of morals or social ethics, a piece of sociological effrontery, and a thing necessarily repugnant to the sensibilities of higher refinement, it is both as a literary composition and a dramatic production, the best play of any contemporary Englishman."

In *The Second Mrs. Tanqueray*, Aubrey Tanqueray, a widower with a grown daughter, married, deliberately and with his eyes open, "a woman with a past," a beautiful and cultured woman, who was well known in London as a high-class professional. He tells his friends of his intentions and asks their aid. But "country society," after the wedding, does not "call" on the second Mrs. Tanqueray, and Tanqueray's daughter by his first marriage, even though she does not know all of the facts, cannot give her love to her stepmother. Paula, repulsed by everyone, turns bitter. But for a moment, when her stepdaughter falls in love, she and Paula come close together, and Paula has, like all of her erring sisters, a moment of hope. But when the daughter's fiancé appears, he turns out to be one of Paula's former lovers. The play, as you know, ends with Paula's suicide.

The years 1909 and 1913 respectively saw the birth of the first successful American Camilles. The first of these, Laura Murdock, appeared in *The Easiest Way*, written by Eugene Walter, and with Francis Starr playing the lead. The play was received much as Mrs. Tanqueray was received, but the play itself is something of a variation from the usual pattern.

In Act One, Laura Murdock, a minor actress, is vacationing in Colorado, where she meets and falls in love with Jim Madison, a young, but very experienced and noble western newspaper man. When he proposes to her, she, amidst much weeping, tells him of her past. As a young actress she had been seduced by her manager, and she later became the mistress of the rich and vulgar Mr. Brockton, who has just come to take her back to New York.

Jim, a noble western type, understands, and says her past does not worry him. Her future does. He asks her to break with Brockton at once, return to New York alone, and live for a year as a respectable woman. As the end of the year he will come to her and they will be married. Laura agrees, and also promises to write to Jim and frankly tell him if she returns to her old life. In a very strange scene between Laura, Jim, and Brockton, Brockton also promises to write to Jim if Laura returns to him.

In Act Two, Laura is in New York living in a cheap rooming house and trying unsuccessfully to find a job. But she doesn't find any and soon learns that Brockton is always there ready to receive her again. (Brockton has prevented any theatre from hiring Laura.) Later an old friend, a vulgar woman, persuades Laura to see Brockton. She does see him and returns to him. Now Brockton insists she write to Jim. This she does, but she will not give the letter to Brockton to mail, and of course, she does not mail it.

The third act takes place in a vulgarly elegant apartment where Laura is living with Brockton. She has never told Jim the truth, and now he is coming to claim her. Not only that, but he is rich. He has struck gold.

The last act shows us the same apartment, but with several trunks packed, ready for the expressman. Laura has, she thought, managed to get Brockton out of the way, and is ready to leave New York as soon as Jim arrives. He does arrive, she lies to him, and just as Jim and Laura are leaving, Brockton enters. After Jim learns the truth, he turns on Laura and says, "You don't know what a decent sentiment is. You'll sink till you've hit the bedrock of degradation." When Laura threatens suicide, Jim calls the maid to come in, calls upon her to witness the threat, and walks out. Laura sinks to the floor weeping. But she soon arises and calls the maid.

"Open these trunks," Laura says. "Get out my new hat. Dress up my body and paint my face. That's all they've left me. They've taken my soul."

The maid, somewhat unnecessarily, asks, "You goin' out?"

And Laura says, "Yes. I'm going to Rector's to make a hit, and to hell with the rest."

At this moment, a grind organ outside the window begins to play a rag-time tune. In the printed text of the play, we read:

"There is something about the tune which is particularly and peculiarly suggestive of the low life, the prostitution, the criminality of the New York tenderloin night life. The tune—its associations—spreads before Laura's eyes a panorama of the inevitable depravity that awaits her. She is torn now from the ideal she so weakly embraced. She listens to the tune, and then with infinite grief, resignation, and hopelessness totters towards the bedroom, saying, 'Oh, God. Oh, my God.' "

The eternal Camille has never been more harshly treated than in *The Easiest Way*.

In 1913, an ex-Chicagoan, by then a successful New York dramatist, saw launched in New York his new play, *Romance*. This play, with Doris Keene as its star, was to run for over a thousand nights, the longest initial run any play had at that time achieved. A new *Camille* was born. This play had, one might say, everything to guarantee its popular appeal. In the opening scene a kindly bishop is faced with his grandson who wants to marry an actress. The bishop is against it, and when the grandson accuses his grandfather of not knowing anything about love and life, the older man smiles and says he will tell the boy a story about himself. And then, elaborately acted, we have the bishop's story. As a young rector, he meets at the home of his wealthiest parishioner the fabulous Italian opera star, Mme. Cavallini, and they at once fall in love. He proposes, she hesitates and hints of "a past." She talks of how difficult it was for a young girl in the theatrical world to withstand the various pressures, but, she implies all of that is long over. The fact, however, is that Mme. Cavallini is then the mistress of the rich parishioner. But she goes to him, tells him of her new love, and breaks with him. However, the young rector learns something of the truth and forces her to confess it, whereupon he "rushes out into the night." But later he returns, now mad with passion, and asks her for one night with him. She, now purified by love, denies him and brings him to his senses. (You see, here we have not only Camille, but Thaïs, and Sadie Thompson, too.) Finally, the rector and Mme. Cavallini part, with many tears, forever. Then we return to the present. The grandson will, in spite of the bishop's story, marry his actress, and the bishop promises to perform the ceremony. But we aren't through yet. The bishop learns from the afternoon paper that Mme. Cavallini has just died. The paper also states that after retirement, Mme. Cavallini spent her time in charitable works and that she had founded a home in Paris for poor girls. Wiping a tear from his eye, the good bishop, as the curtain comes down, has started to play on his phonograph an aria from *Mignon*, the aria he had most loved to hear her sing.

One does not wonder at the play's success. It had everything, sin—conveniently in the romantic past—passion, repentance, plus successful young love and a happy ending.

The 1920's were much given to reversing the values of the past and interpreting life according to new formulas, especially by those vaguely related to Freud. For example, in *Rain* the 1920's saw Sadie Thompson victorious in her struggle with the Rev. M. Davidson. And in *They Knew What They Wanted*, saw a waitress from a cheap restaurant succeed where Isolde and Guinevere had failed.

But the two plays of the 1920's closest to our theme were Michael Arlen's *The Green Hat* and O'Neill's *Anna Christie*. Iris March, in Michael Arlen's *Green Hat*, was the more popular of the two heroines, but Anna Christie in O'Neill's play of that name, outlived her. Iris March, a member of the British aristocracy and of the lost generation, had, since her first and very unhappy marriage was dissolved, been as they said, "gallant." But love now comes to her in the form of a man already married. The lovers decide they must, at any cost, have each other—must, as they said, live their own lives. And, in honest British fashion, the husband tells his wife this. She, like "a mature person and a sportsman," gives him up. But Iris learned the wife was pregnant. Then, gallantly, and in a way so as to cause as little trouble as possible, Iris got into her car and deliberately—off stage, of course—wrecked it and killed herself. Many of you, like me, have very tender memories of Katharine Cornell and Leslie Howard as the

lovers. But even though I secretly liked the play, I was then of the new generation, and openly scorned it. But I, and others like me, *really* admired *Anna Christie*. Here we said was no romantic nonsense, but the real thing. When, in the low waterfront saloon, Anna told her sordid and pathetic story to an old prostitute who, although Anna didn't know it, is her father's mistress, we felt the American drama was at last growing up. But only the details of Anna's story were new. Camille, Paula, and Mme. Cavallini had had exactly the same kind of experience as Anna. Fate and Society had been against them too. When Anna, through her new life on her father's boat, felt "the cleansing influence of the sea," and when the shipwrecked sailor was brought aboard the barge and Anna, for the first time, felt true love, we should have seen Camille meeting Armand and Mme. Cavallini meeting her rector. The ending was, however, a little different, but just a little. Anna and Matt would, it is true, marry, but even O'Neill was careful to point out their marriage was not likely to be a happy one.

And now for our latest Camille. *A Streetcar Named Desire* started the same newspaper row the older plays had. It was violent, indecent, immoral, and inexcusable. It was also a great play, tense, vivid, moving, and profound. It was a success everywhere. At one time it was running in New York, Chicago, Paris, London, Stockholm, and many other European cities. The sordid background of Anna Christie had become more sordid, the language and action more "frank." Details of the play would have shocked even an "advanced" audience of the 20's. And everywhere there was violence, the violence to which we have become accustomed in the world of fascism and communism. By the time *Streetcar* was produced, we had, through the works of William Faulkner and Erskine Caldwell, and William March, become familiar with the world of southern decadence. And so the new Camille came, almost inevitably, from an aristocratic and decayed southern family. We had become so used to terms like homosexual and nymphomania, that it was not surprising to hear poor pathetic Blanche

Dubois tell of her marriage to a boy who was homosexual and to have it implied that her own subsequent, extensive sexual activity was only a kind of compensation for her unhappy marriage. Undoubtedly, Blanche's story is a harrowing and pathetic one. So was Paula's and Camille's, Anna's and Laura's. And like the others, Blanche too seeks acceptance and rehabilitation. And Blanche too is denied even the pathetic security which for a moment was held out to her. I wonder how future generations will feel about the ending of the play. Will they feel, as one New York critic felt, that "he had never seen anything in the theatre so moving as the pathetic yet dignified Blanche being led away to an asylum"? Or will they feel as most people today feel about the prolonged death scene in *Camille* or the melodramatic suicide in *The Second Mrs. Tanqueray?*

You can see well illustrated by these plays what Bronson Howard, this country's first professional dramatist, stated in a lecture at Harvard in 1880. Talking about what he called "satisfactory plays," that is, plays the public liked and supported, he said, "In England and America at least the death of a pure woman on the stage is not satisfactory. The death of an ordinary woman who is not pure . . . is perfectly satisfactory in that it is inevitable. The woman who has once taken the step from purity to impurity can never reinstate herself this side of the grave."

Yes, I am sure there always will be a Camille in the theatre, though her name may be Mrs. Haller, Lady Isabel, Paula, Mme. Cavallini, Anna Christie, or Blanche Dubois, and although her clothes and manner change with the times, she is always the same fatally charming, good hearted, pathetic, and frail, but repentant, woman. And always the audience—that is, you and I—will sympathize with her sad fate, weep whatever kind of tears are currently fashionable, but then refuse to allow her to be "reinstated this side of the grave."

It is not wise to be too specific in one's prophecies, and I shall not venture to speculate on the exact form Camille's next reincarnation will take. I only know that she will appear again before long.

QUESTIONS FOR STUDY AND DISCUSSION

1. Induction moves from the particular to the general, from the known to the unknown. In "There Will Always Be a Camille," the technique of presentation is to make a generalization or series of generalizations and illustrate with full examples. Why is this an effective technique? Consider the material being handled and the problem of communicating it clearly to an audience.

2. This article is full of good humor and funny to read, even though the topic itself is hardly comical. How does the writer achieve this effect?

3. Notice the quotations that Napier Wilt uses in this article. Why does he select them? What is their effect?

4. If the writer had begun his article with *A Streetcar Named Desire*, asserting that Blanche Dubois is merely "our latest Camille," would the reader be startled by his argument? Would he be convinced?

JOHN HARVEY

The Content Characteristics of Best-Selling Novels

"What makes a best seller?" is a perennial question to which countless answers have been offered by publishers, booksellers, librarians, and authors. However, none of their hypotheses and opinions have demonstrated why one book sells better than another, nor is it yet possible to predict the sales of any book on the basis of tested criteria.

The study on which this article is based confined itself to best-selling novels.[1] The popularity of these novels might be explained in terms of their timeliness, their authors, their sales promotion, or the prestige attached to having read them. By contrast, the present study concentrated on the content of novels in an attempt to isolate content characteristics differentiating best sellers from similar novels which failed to sell so well.

PREVIOUS APPROACHES TO THE PROBLEM

There have been numerous approaches to the "why?" of best sellers. The historical approach is best illustrated by Frank Luther Mott's history of American best sellers, which contains two chapters on causation.[2] Mott found sensationalism, themes of religion and adventure, and a sentimental treatment of subject matter recurring frequently in best sellers. His major thesis, however, was the frequently encountered one that there is no "best seller formula" and

consequently that lists of important variables are of little value.

George Stevens, of J. B. Lippincott Company, sought to explain sales in terms of publicity advantages.[3] He detailed figures on advertising appropriations, discussed the promotional techniques used with several well-known best sellers, and mentioned the importance of such advantages as publicity off the book page, condensation in the *Reader's Digest*, distribution by a book club, and a controversial theme.

Emanuel Haldeman-Julius, with a somewhat different approach because of differing marketing problems, found that many of his "Little Blue Books" sold much better when given new titles.[4] His re-titling played up themes of love, sex, religion, self-improvement, and humor.

Literary critics have made numerous contributions to the best seller literature. As examples, we might mention the articles by Granville Hicks and Edward Weeks.[5] Hicks read forty novels from the period 1930 through 1934 before arriving at his conclusions. The formula he recommended included ". . . a lively story, largely romantic in theme and setting with conventional characters and plot and some pretention to a message or thesis, apparently profound but really commonplace."[6]

Weeks, instead of studying a group of novels, studied only *Gone With the Wind*. He estimated its success to be due to the following factors in the proportions indicated: timeliness, 45 per cent; emotion, 25 per cent; characterization, 15 per cent; invention, 10 per cent; and advertising, 5 per cent. His interpretation of the novel's appeal emphasized the vitality of the major characters, the necessity of including an im-

[1] Harvey, John F., *The Content Characteristics of Best-Selling Novels,* unpublished Ph.D. dissertation, Graduate Library School, University of Chicago, 1949.
[2] Mott, Frank Luther, *Golden Multitudes; The Story of Best Sellers in the U.S.,* New York: Macmillan, 1947.

[3] Stevens, George, *Lincoln's Doctor's Dog, and Other Famous Best Sellers,* Philadelphia: J. B. Lippincott Company, 1938.
[4] Haldeman-Julius, Emanuel, *The First Hundred Million,* New York: Simon and Schuster, 1928, pp. 138–178.
[5] Hicks, Granville, "The Mystery of the Best Seller," *The English Journal,* Vol. 23 (October 1934), pp. 621–629; Weeks, Edward, "What Makes a Book a Best Seller?" *New York Times Book Review,* Vol. 41 (December 20, 1936), pp. 2, 15.
[6] Hicks, *op. cit.,* p. 626.

pressively large number of minor characters, the use of superlatives, and the use of over-long scenes to hold the reader's interest. His one sentence formula ran as follows: ". . . the novelist captures the ideas in the air at the time and puts them into words. . . ."[7]

The limitations of the above studies are readily apparent. They either failed to examine the books with sufficient thoroughness, conducted analyses which were too subjective, or else examined too few books for any sensible generalizations to be made. The studies by Joseph Kappel and J. V. M. Berreman are more important because these pitfalls were avoided and reliable analyses obtained. Joseph Kappel studied the literary quality of the best sellers and book club selections of the last twenty years.[8] He used *Book Review Digest* plus and minus ratings of reviews as his measure of literary quality and obtained from them annual index numbers showing the degree of favorability shown by the reviews. These index numbers were obtained for all Book of the Month Club and Literary Guild selections, for a random sample of each year's new books, and for all best sellers (both fiction and non-fiction) of the years 1926 through 1941. The annual favorability index numbers were then plotted on charts to show comparisons among the groups of books for each year. These charts showed that from a literary standpoint, best sellers as well as Book of the Month Club and Literary Guild selections ranked above the random sample (or average) each year. Kappel's study thus tended to suggest that neither the best sellers nor the book clubs have reduced the general quality of books in recent years.

In a study, entitled *Factors Affecting the Sale of Modern Books of Fiction*, J. V. M. Berreman examined the role of both content and non-content.[9] This study merits careful

[7] Weeks, *op. cit.*, p. 2.
[8] Kappel, Joseph W., "Book Clubs and the Evaluation of Books," *Public Opinion Quarterly*, Vol. 12 (1948), No. 2, pp. 243–252.
[9] Berreman, Joel Van Meter, *Factors Affecting the Sale of Modern Books of Fiction; a Study of Social Psychology*, unpublished Ph.D. dissertation, Department of Economics, Stanford University, 1940.

TABLE 1
BERREMAN'S CORRELATIONS BETWEEN
PUBLICITY FACTORS AND SALE

Publicity Factors	1935 Random Sample From Publishers Lists		1933–1938 Best Seller Titles	
	N	r	N	r
Advertising	77	+.79	50	+.28
Author prestige	228	.65	71	.48
Review wordage	77	.52	50	.10
Review favorability	77	.12	50	.09

consideration because of its thoroughness and objectivity, as well as for its close relation to the present study. Berreman's purpose was the prediction of book sales. He examined 234 best- and poor-selling novels published between 1933 and 1938. Their sales were measured by the frequency of their appearances in the weekly best seller charts of the *New York Herald Tribune* book review section.[10] Berreman found close relationships between several of the non-content (or publicity) factors and sales, although no causal relationships were established. These relationships were sufficiently close, however, to allow him to combine all of the important factors into a formula which yielded a correlation of +.77 with the sale of a selected group of novels.

Table 1 shows Berreman's correlations to be high only when he was distinguishing between best and poor sellers, as in his 1935 group. He could successfully predict a best or a poor seller from known differences in its publicity factors, but he could not equally predict differences between the sales of the top best sellers (the "super" best sellers) and those lower on the best seller lists. In short, his publicity factors explained only gross differences in sales.

Berreman devoted but little attention to content differences. On the basis of reviews, he grouped sixty novels into twelve classes by setting, theme, and treatment of theme. He concluded that content probably affected the sale of poor sellers which were well-marketed as well as best sellers which sold well despite feeble efforts to market them. He also pointed out the probable usefulness

[10] The validity of this measure of sale was tested successfully.

of content in any attempt to improve the correlations with sale shown in Table 1.

The present study is essentially an extension and supplement to the Berreman study. It begins where Berreman stopped; namely, with the analysis of differences in the content of novels and with the relating of such differences to their sales. Berreman's findings were accepted for what they were worth so that the present study arbitrarily excluded publicity factors from consideration and concentrated its attention on content.

THE VARIABLES

The core of the present study was a comparison of books in terms of certain variables. The purpose of the analysis was to discover recurring differences between the scores of best and poor sellers on each variable and on each group of variables. The variables used for the analysis are best described in terms of the six main groups into which they naturally fall. The groups and the numbers of variables included are as follows:

    a. Action—15 different variables
    b. Emotion—50 different variables
    c. Personalities of the Major Characters —750 different variables
    d. Plot Themes—350 different variables
    e. Romanticization—50 different variables
    f. Simplicity—32 different variables

Action. Action referred to any change or movement of the plot, setting, or characters. An action was shown whenever the plot themes changed, part of the setting moved (as for instance a door slammed), the scene of action changed, or a character moved. Such measures as the following were used: frequency of movement by each major character per 100 character lines, the frequency with which the reader's attention was shifted from character to character, and the frequency per page with which the scene shifted to a new location.

Emotion. The pattern of emotion referred to the amount, kind, and use of the emotion expressed in each novel. It included the amount of certain basic emotions shown by each character, the frequency of change from one emotion to another, and the percentage of the lines with an emotional charge.

Personalities of the Major Characters. This group of variables included many different aspects of each character's life: for example, the character's age, occupation, education, nationality, social status, social traits, morals, and prominence in the novel.

Plot Themes. The pattern of the plot themes referred to the inevitably differing themes used in different novels. The list of themes was taken from the table of contents of Elbert Lenrow's *Readers Guide to Prose Fiction,* which contains approximately 350 different themes.[11] The coverage of this list is indicated by the following outline: entertainment and escape, the individual and his personal environment (people and their personal problems), and the individual and his social environment (social, political, economic, vocational, religious, and philosophical problems).

Romanticization. Examples of variables in this category included extremes of each character's wealth or poverty, the contrast between income level at the beginning and end of the novel, the physical attractiveness of each character, his moral perfection, the luxury or poverty of the setting, and fortuitous events (such as receiving a million dollars without warning). It was the combination of unusually high or low scores for several of these variables that revealed the degree of romanticization.

Simplicity. The variables measuring simplicity tested the ease with which the average reader could move through the novel. These variables were related either to (a) the novel's style, (b) its plot, (c) its major characters, or (d) its setting. Simplicity of style was measured by such variables as the total wordage of the novel, the average chapter length, the frequency of abstract idea words, the number of lines and paragraphs per 100 words, and the readability of the novel. The principal measure of plot

[11] Lenrow, Elbert, *Readers Guide to Prose Fiction,* New York: Appleton-Century, 1940, pp. vii–xi.

simplicity was the number of Lenrow themes in each novel.

Variables relating to the major characters included the number of such characters in the novel, the number of goals for each character, the derivation of their names, and the allotment of lines between setting and characters. The five most important categories of major characters were the central male character and his best friend, the central female character and her best friend, and the villain.

The variables related to the setting included the degree of luxury, the number of geographical locations per 1000 words, and the frequency of changes of setting.

Sources of the Variables. The variables were taken from a variety of sources. However, three kinds of sources predominated: subjective analyses of best sellers by literary critics (such as the Weeks, Hicks, and Bennett[12] studies); general outlines for analyzing fiction (such as the Krieg[13] and Muller[14] outlines and the Lenrow classification of themes); and, finally, the observations of the writer as the analysis progressed.

The literary critics were a somewhat barren source. Nevertheless, Katherine Fullerton Gerould (in criticizing the leading female novelists) pointed out the importance to the female reader of detailed descriptions of social rituals, such as dinners, introductions, parties, and dressing scenes;[15] Edward Weeks contributed such variables as the frequency of shifts in character and setting and the importance of numerous minor characters;[16] George Orwell, in discussing popular boys' magazines, stressed the importance

of action;[17] and Granville Hicks contributed an important theme—the moralizing theme—and suggested the importance of the novel's length.[18]

Most of the variables were supplied by the second source, viz., the Krieg, Muller, and Lenrow outlines. The Krieg outline contained many variables used in analyzing the major characters—for example, the characters' social and character traits, their attitudes toward themselves, toward others, and toward social institutions. Muller suggested sociological variables relating to the major characters, such as social and economic status, ethicality, social perspective, age, and occupation. The use of Lenrow's list of themes has already been described.

There were certain problems to be solved before the first two groups of sources could be used satisfactorily. The chief problem with the literary critic's contributions was that of selecting variables which could be clearly defined and reliably measured. Since the Krieg and Muller outlines, on the other hand, were developed for other purposes, the chief concern was to select variables which would fit the present problem.

Finally, the variables originated by the present study were derived directly from the novels' content—whether, for example, the novel was written in the first or third person; relative amounts of space devoted to author description, character thought, and character conversation; the recency of events; lines of emotion for each major character; and the frequency of profanity.

It will be recognized that the sources were used in any way that would benefit the study. Variables were lifted out of context whenever they could be made to serve the present purposes. The final list contained as many variables as could be supported by plausible hypotheses and analyzed objectively.

THE SAMPLING PROBLEM

Sampling for Certain Variables. Some of the variables could be measured feasibly only

[12] Bennett, E. Arnold, *Fame and Fiction: An Inquiry into Certain Popularities,* London: G. Richards, 1901.

[13] Krieg, Laurel Lee, *A Suggested Method of Analysing Children's Fiction Reading,* unpublished M.A. thesis, Graduate Library School, University of Chicago, 1943, pp. 13–32.

[14] Muller, Hans, *Social Stratification in Magazine Fiction and its Relation to the Socio-Economic Status of Readers,* unpublished Ph.D. dissertation, Graduate Library School, University of Chicago, 1942, pp. 59–65.

[15] Fullerton, Katherine Gerould, "Feminine Fiction," *Saturday Review of Literature,* Vol. 13 (April 11, 1936), pp. 3–4.

[16] Weeks, *op. cit.,* p. 2.

[17] Orwell, George, *Dickens, Dali, and Others; Studies in Popular Culture,* New York: Reynal and Hitchcock, 1946, pp. 100–101.

[18] Hicks, *op. cit.,* pp. 626–629.

TABLE 2
RELIABILITY OF THE METHOD OF SAMPLING THE NOVELS

Factors	Mann: *Joseph the Provider*	Marshall: *Duchess Hotspur*	Remarque: *All Quiet on the Western Front*	Stribling: *The Store*	Warren: *All the King's Men*
1. Lines of central male character's level 1 emotion					
a. Unhappiness	97%	96%	92%	96%	97%
b. Love	100	100	100	99	100
c. Anger	98	99	100	97	96
2. Number of major characters toward whom central male character's attitude is					
a. Affectionate	100	100	100	100	89
b. Respectful	100	89	100	100	89
3. Sentimental theme	90	93	97	90	93

EXPLANATION: This table shows the results of rating 30 new sample pages from each of five novels for six of the variables found to be good discriminators. The percentages show the proportion of lines, pages, or characters which were rated the same way, or produced the same ratings, for the new sample as for the original sample. In other words, the table shows the percentage of agreement between the new and original samples for each of the six factors. Totals of 4850 lines and 29 characters were rated on 150 new sample pages.

by sampling each novel; trying to measure them for the entire novel would have required a prohibitive expenditure of time and labor. Readability, for instance, required measurement only on a small proportion of the novel's sentences. Consequently, some 510 of the variables were measured by sampling, while the remainder were measured for the novel as a whole.

Thirty pages of each novel were sampled with the page numbers selected from the Tippett tables of random sampling numbers.[19] The Tippett tables were developed to provide a list of 10,000 numbers which had been selected by a completely random method. The numbers in the tables were followed in order until thirty were picked up which were within the page limits of the novel being analyzed. The pages corresponding to these numbers were then analyzed for the variables in question.

Reliability of the Sampling Method. Two methods were used to check the reliability of the sampling. The first involved an at-

[19] Tippett, Leonard Henry Caleb, *Random Sampling Numbers* (Department of Applied Statistics (Computing Section), University of London, University College. Tracts for Computers . . . no. 15) London: Cambridge University Press, 1927.

tempt to prove statistically whether or not all the variables were adequately sampled in thirty pages, while the second involved the use of new thirty page samples from several novels. The attempt to prove whether or not all variables could be adequately sampled on thirty pages of a novel yielded results indicating only that a random sample of 400 words should be adequate.

It would obviously be impossible to rate more than a few of the variables on the basis of a random sample of 400 isolated words, because there would be no continuity, no story to follow. The alternative of analyzing every word on a random sample of thirty pages would seem satisfactory, although this method would require more than 400 words to sample the novel as well as could be done with 400 randomly selected words. Since it was impossible to say how many more words would be needed, it was necessary to assume that thirty randomly selected pages, usually containing about 10,000 words, was enough.

In the second test, another randomly selected thirty-page sample was drawn from the Tippett tables for each of five novels. No pages were duplicated between the two samples. Table 2 shows the per cent of correct out of total ratings to be satisfactorily high for all six variables. This means that the six variables occurred with the same frequency in the new sample as in the original sample, thereby encouraging confidence in the reliability of the original sample.

Reliability of the Variables. The objectivity of the present description of content was also proven for the above six variables in tests of their reliability. The tests indicated whether these variables were being measured objectively or subjectively—whether they could be measured consistently by the same and other raters or whether they were ill-defined and the measurement was erratic.

The reliability of the ratings could be tested by two methods: by examining the consistency of the original rater, and by comparing the observations of several raters. Both methods were employed in the present tests. The test of internal consistency—testing the percentage of lines classified the same way several months later by the original rater—indicated a fairly high degree of agreement between the two ratings. This is summarized in Table 3.

For the test of consistency among several raters, samples of the six variables were selected by the original rater on seven pages in one of the novels analyzed early in the study, Bottome's *Mortal Storm*. Definitions were then explained to three additional raters and their ratings obtained for the

TABLE 3
RELIABILITY OF SIX IMPORTANT VARIABLES

(1) Variables	(2) Total Ratings	Original Rater (3) Agreement	(4) % Agreement	(5) Total Ratings	Four Raters Combined (6) Agreement	(7) % Agreement
1a	2000	1983	99%	28	28	100%
1b	2000	1996	100	28	24	86
1c	2000	1981	99	28	26	93
2	35	31	88	28	27	96
3	46	40	87	28	25	89
4	90	83	92	28	26	93

Code

1. Central male character's level 1 emotion
    a. Unhappiness (level 1)
    b. Love (level 1)
    c. Anger (level 1)
2. Number of major characters toward whom central male character's attitude is affectionate
3. Number of major characters toward whom central male character's attitude is respectful
4. Sentimental theme

EXPLANATION: Columns 2 and 5 show the total agreement or "correct" ratings plus the total disagreement ratings; disagreement ratings included both errors of commission—when a variable was added where it did not belong—and omission—where a variable was not found in its proper place.

Columns 3 and 6 show the number of agreement ratings.

Columns 4 and 7 show the percentage which columns 3 and 6 are, of columns 2 and 5, respectively.

The original rater re-rated forty pages for variables 1a, 1b, and 1c, ninety pages for variable 4, and eight novels involving the attitudes of fourteen major characters toward eighty-one other major characters for variables 2 and 3. The four student raters rated seven pages for each of the variables.

In columns 2 and 3 the ratings should be read in this manner: for variables 1a, 1b, and 1c, the figures represent numbers of lines rated; for variables 2 and 3 the figures represent the numbers of major characters rated; for variable 4 the figures represent numbers of sample pages.

In columns 5 and 6 the ratings should be read in this manner: For all six variables the figures represent the total numbers of pages on which each variable was rated by the summed ratings of all four raters.

seven pages. Table 3 indicates that the six variables showed a high degree of reliability.

Pearson's *Chi-Square* (χ^2) test of the dispersion of individual scores about an expected score was also applied to the observations of the four raters. This test measured the likelihood that the differences between raters in the scores for each variable were actually significant. If the scores were not significantly different, then the variations were due to chance factors alone.

The mean score for all four raters was used as the "expected" score for each variable. The mean was used for this purpose because there was no expected score in the sense that one rating or one rater was necessarily correct and all others incorrect. For each of the six variables tested, results indicated that there was a probability of from .60 to 1.00 that the differences shown between the raters were due to chance. When the variables were lumped together and their total tested results were equally favorable and the ratings reliable. There was a probability of .80 to .90 that the differences were due only to chance factors; these variables, therefore, were rated reliably in this test.

THE NOVELS

A best-selling novel was defined as any novel which ranked among the top ten novels in sale for a year, as reported in Alice Hackett's book, *Fifty Years of Best Sellers, 1895–1945,*[20] or in her annual summary articles in *Publishers' Weekly.* A poor-selling novel was one which did not appear on these lists.

Sampling the Best and Poor Seller Universes. The time required for analyzing each novel (100 to 150 hours at the beginning of the analysis) made prohibitive the use of all eligible best and poor sellers; some method was required for sampling the best and poor seller universes. Berreman's findings indicated that a random sample would not be desirable for this purpose; he showed that sales differences were positively correlated with differences in the amounts of

[20] *Fifty Years of Best Sellers, 1895–1945,* New York: Bowker, 1945.

money, ingenuity, and other resources used to promote books and publicize them. Hence, a random sample of novels would not allow identification of the content elements influencing sale unless publicity factors were eliminated, neutralized, or held constant in the sampling operation. It was, therefore, required that the poor sellers used in the sample be as well endowed with publicity advantages as were the best sellers; in other words, best and poor sellers were equated or matched on publicity factors so that the influence of content on sale could be studied directly. In addition to the influence of publicity factors, it seemed probable that such factors as the novels' themes, wordages, publication dates, and perhaps even favorability of reviews were also involved. Consequently, these factors were matched for best and poor sellers in the same way that publicity factors were matched.

This matching of novels constituted a "matched sample" from the best and poor seller universes. Use of the matched sample suggested the desirability of matching and analyzing best and poor sellers, title by title. Accordingly, each best seller was closely matched with a poor seller to form a pair for purposes of analysis.

Selecting the Matched Sample: Publicity Factors. The closest feasible matching of publicity factors required use of the weights which Berreman developed for his formula. Berreman did not explain his weights in detail, nor how he arrived at his values, nor did he define his categories. It was therefore necessary to adapt his procedure (as it could be understood) to the present study, and in some cases even to modify the original weights. Each novel was scored on each publicity factor separately and a weight assigned; then all the weights were summed for the novel and the total taken as the novel's final score on publicity. A criterion was adopted for each pair of novels which stated that the total of the poor seller scores on publicity must always equal, if not exceed, that of the best seller. Pairs in which this criterion was not met were eliminated before the analysis started. The publicity factors, sources of information on them, and the

TABLE 4
SCORE CARD FOR WEIGHTING ON PUBLICITY FACTORS

Factor	Source	Weighting
A. Book club selection:		
Book-of-the-Month Club	*Publishers' Weekly*	
1926–1930		1.0
1931–1946		3.0
Literary Guild		
1927–1936		0.0
1937–1943		1.0
1944–1946		3.0
B. Pulitzer Prize	*World Almanac*	2.0
C. Pre-publication and first month advertising in the following journals:	Direct measurement	
New York Herald Tribune Sunday book review section		
New York Times Sunday book review section		
Publishers' Weekly		
Saturday Review of Literature		
1. Total of more than eight pages		1.5
2. Total of five to seven and nine-tenths pages		1.0
3. Total of three to four and nine-tenths pages		0.5
D. Author popularity: Inclusion of author on Hackett lists during the preceding ten years for best selling novels with similar themes	Hackett: *Fifty Years of Best Sellers*	1.0
E. Wordage of reviews in the following journals:	Direct measurement	
Nation		
New York Herald Tribune Sunday book review section		
New York Times Sunday book review section		
New Yorker		
Saturday Review of Literature		
Springfield Republican		
Time		
1. Total of more than 5500 words		1.0
2. Total of 3500 to 5499 words		0.5
F. Serialization or condensation in a national periodical	*Fiction Catalog* and *Readers Guide*	0.5
G. Other publicity factors aiding sale:		
1. Author reputation in some other field, or	*Twentieth Century Authors*	
2. Total of ten or more references, exclusive of reviews, in *Readers Guide* and *New York Times Index*	Direct measurement	0.5

weighting used in the present study are given in Table 4; total possible score is 9.5 points.

Matching Novels by Major Theme. To obtain closely matched samples of best- and poor-selling novels, it was also necessary to control the major theme; matching two novels with different major themes would have defeated the present plan of comparison and invited the criticism that the novels were not written with the same purpose or to appeal to the same audience. On the other hand, it was recognized that major theme might be important in influencing sale and that it was unfortunate to lose this possibly good discriminator. But it was assumed to be more desirable to evaluate the many other characteristics with major theme controlled than to restrict the comparisons to major theme alone. Accordingly, the rule was adopted that the novels of each pair have similar major themes, similar geographic and historic settings, and similar major characters.

Limitations on Publication Dates. In order to insure a degree of homogeneity among the novels and to increase uniformity of taste among the readers, time limitations on publication dates were adopted, both for the novels as a whole and for the novels in each pair. The limitation adopted for the entire group of novels required that they be published between 1930 and 1946, inclusive, while the time span between the novels of each pair was limited to five years.

Additional Factors. Three other factors were considered in the matching procedure: wordage of the novel, order of publication of the novels in each pair, and favorability of reviews. The first two factors were found to have a positive relation to sale. There was some advantage associated with a large wordage and with being published prior to the other novel in a pair. However, Berreman did not report these factors, and their importance was not discovered until after the matching procedure was under way, so it was possible to control them for only the first eight pairs. These were so selected that neither best nor poor seller was heavily favored on either factor. To have carried the matching beyond these first eight pairs would have seriously reduced the number of pairs remaining, so no further control was possible. The third factor, review favorability, was checked for all pairs of novels, and the best and poor sellers were found to be equally benefited by it.

Sales Ratio in Each Pair. The final factor to be controlled was the sales levels of the novels in each pair. The foregoing definition of best and poor sellers merely specified that the best seller be on the annual Hackett lists of the top ten novels and that the poor seller not be on them. This would allow matching a best seller in tenth place with a poor seller in eleventh place, just off the list. Such a pairing would scarcely serve to compare a best with a poor seller because their sales would have been so nearly the same. It was accordingly decided that the

best and poor seller in each pair should be separated by at least a 4:1 ratio in sale.

In the absence of any reliable figures on actual sale, an approximation was obtained by summing the monthly decimal scores for each novel in the *Publishers' Weekly* and converting them to whole numbers; the total thus obtained (hereafter referred to as the *PW* score) served as an estimate of the sale of each novel in relation to other novels. These monthly decimals or percentages were collected for the duration of each novel's stay on the lists, but not exceeding two years following its publication date; the two year limit gave every novel the same chance to make its score.

Examples of the Pairing and Analysis Procedures. An example of this scoring for a pair of novels would be in order here. One pair was Langley's *A Lion Is in the Streets* (the best seller), and Warren's *All the King's Men* (the poor seller). Langley's book appeared on the *Publishers' Weekly* charts for six months, from June through November of 1945. During this period its monthly percentages were 43, 65, 65, 44, 37, and 26. When these scores are summed, the total, 280, is the final *PW* score for this novel. Warren's novel appeared on the charts for only one month, September, 1946; its score for this month was 20 per cent. Therefore, the best seller scoring 280 and the poor seller scoring 20 make a ratio of 14:1 which is sufficiently high to meet the criterion.

To clarify the pairing procedure, Table 5 shows the raw scores of the two novels on all of the matching factors. Comparison of the raw scores in Table 5 to the weights in Table 4 will allow calculation of the scores on the publicity factors. Langley scored as follows: advertising, 1.0; and reviewing, 0.5; while Warren scored 2.0 on the Pulitzer prize, 0.5 on advertising, 1.0 on reviewing, and 0.5 on references. These totals are then 1.5 for Langley and 4.0 for Warren, thereby meeting the criterion that the poor seller score equal if not exceed that of the best seller. In general, the Langley-Warren pair was well matched on all factors. Figure 1 summarizes the gamut which all the pairs

TABLE 5
SCORES OF LANGLEY'S A *Lion Is in the Streets* AND WARREN'S *All the King's Men*
ON THE MATCHING FACTORS

Langley (the best seller)	Factors	Warren (the poor seller)
	Publicity Factors	
Not a selection	Book club selection	Not a selection
No	Pulitzer prize	Won prize for 1946
	Advertising pages:	
4 pages	*Publishers' Weekly*	2 pages
1½ pages	*New York Herald Tribune*	¾ page
1 page	*New York Times*	1 page
1 page	*Saturday Review of Literature*	1 page
Total pages: 7½		Total pages: 4¾
Never	Author prestige	Never
	(on previous Hackett lists)	
	Review wordage:	
0 words	*Nation*	1400 words
1200 words	*New York Herald Tribune*	1900 words
1050 words	*New York Times*	1150 words
200 words	*New Yorker*	100 words
950 words	*Saturday Review of Literature*	850 words
500 words	*Springfield Republican*	800 words
0 words	*Time*	750 words
Total words: 3900		Total words: 6950
Never	Serialization	Never
Never	Condensation	Never
None	Author reputation in another field	None
	References to novel:	
0 references	*New York Times Index*	5 references
3 references	*Readers Guide*	8 references
Total references: 3		Total references: 13
	Non-Publicity Factors	
6th in 1945	Hackett list	On no lists
Huey Long biography	Major theme	Huey Long biography
May, 1945	From 1930–1946 period	August, 1946
15 month interval	Five-year interval	. . . . .
150,000 words	Wordage in novel	230,000 words
Published in 1945	Order of publication	Published in 1946
280 *PW* score	4:1 ratio in *PW* score	20 *PW* score
	Review favorability:	
5 reviews	+	7 reviews
3 reviews	+ −	3 reviews
0 reviews	− +	0 reviews
0 reviews	−	1 review

were forced to run and the steady decline in the number of pairs still acceptable after each requirement was put forth.

The Analysis Procedure. The analysis procedure consisted principally of coding the variables on each sample page, totaling and transferring them to coding sheets, and transcribing the final scores (usually expressed as frequencies per 100 words or a percentage) to the result sheets. It was by comparing the final scores of each pair on each variable on the result sheets and then applying the 50 per cent criterion that the retention or elimination of the variable was judged at frequent intervals during the analysis.[21]

[21] The 50 per cent criterion stated that, to be retained for further analysis, a variable should have scored significantly higher or lower on the best seller in at least half of the pairs already analyzed.

FIGURE 1

SUMMARY OF MATCHING PROCEDURE WHICH YIELDED
TWENTY-TWO PAIRS OF NOVELS[b]

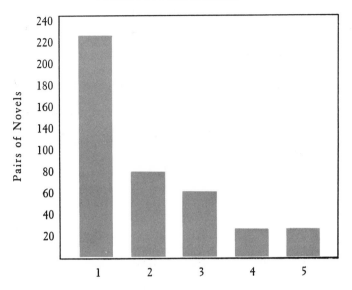

Control factors on which novels were matched[a]

[a] Code

(1) Limitation to 1930–1946 period

(2) Thematic matching

(3) 4:1 ratio in *PW* scores (sale), and
Five-year interval in dates of publication

(4) Publicity factors:
Book club selection
Winning the Pulitzer Prize
Advertising
Author popularity
Review wordage
Serialization
Condensation
Author reputation in another field
References in periodicals and newspapers

(5) Wordage of the novels
Order of publication
Review favorability

[b] Figure 1 indicates the number of pairs remaining *after* each limiting factor was brought forward. For example, there were 100 pairs remaining after the thematic matching (2).

FINDINGS: THE IMPORTANT VARIABLES

Table 6 presents the major findings of the study and shows that only sixteen variables survived all eliminations. These variables were therefore the best single-variable pre- dictors of sale. On the basis of these find- ings the following generalizations seem warranted for the novels in this study:

1. Emotion is a major ingredient of the best seller. This generalization is warranted because the best seller shows:

a. More sentimentality (variable 4)

b. More central male character sensationalism (variable 6)

c. More central male character affection toward other characters (variable 7)

d. More central male character level 1 emotion (variable 9)

e. More of the specific emotions listed in variables 10 through 14

2. Certain characteristics of the central male character (variables 6 through 14) are either positively or negatively associated with sale.

3. There are certain stylistic and thematic differences between best and poor sellers (variables 1 through 5).

TABLE 6

VARIABLES STILL IMPORTANT AT THE END
OF THE ANALYSIS

Code Number and Variable	Final Score[a]		
	+	0	−
Style			
1. Readability (Flesch)	1	12	9
2. Average chapter wordage	11	5	6
3. Recency of events in the novel	8	4	10
4. Sentimental theme	9	8	5
5. Moralizing theme	7	15	0
The Central Male Character			
6. Sensationalism as measured by exclamation points	11	2	9
7. Affectionate attitude toward other characters	9	10	3
8. Respectful attitude toward other characters	6	3	13
9. Total of level 1 emotion[b]	12	4	6
10. Total unhappiness (including both levels of intensity)	12	3	7
11. Unhappiness at level 1 (less intense)	11	3	8
12. Total anger (including both levels of intensity)	11	4	7
13. Anger at level 2 (more intense)	6	15	1
14. Anger at level 1 (less intense)	9	6	7
Non-Content Variables[c]			
15. Prior publication date	18	0	6
16. Wordage of the novel	9	9	4

[a] These scores are to be interpreted as follows: a score of 1–12–9 means that in one pair of novels the best seller's score was significantly larger than that of the poor seller, in twelve pairs the scores were even, and in nine pairs the poor seller's score was significantly larger than that of the best seller.

Retention of Variables Failing to Meet the 50 per cent Criterion. After twenty-two pairs of novels had been analyzed, the 50 per cent criterion was a plus or minus score of eleven. This meant that a variable's scores had to show a significant plus or a significant minus difference between best and poor seller in eleven of the twenty-two pairs. Table 6 shows that seven of the fourteen acceptable variables did not meet this criterion. Why were they retained? The reason for retention was primarily one of anticipated value: It was anticipated that they might be good discriminators when used in the formulas. Each was retained for at least one of three reasons: that the variable's scores showed a strong tendency in either a "plus" or a "minus" direction (i.e., that the direction of the variable's influence was clear); that the variable measured part of a spectrum, or series of variables which, as a series, was worth retaining; or that the variable's scores were pooled, along with those

[b] Specific emotions were scored in five different ways: level 2 indicated very strong emotion with the character in an extreme emotional state; level 1 indicated emotion of some strength but not at an extremely high level; total emotion of each kind (unhappiness, love, anger, etc.) contained a summation of the amount of emotion shown in both levels 1 and 2; all emotion at level 1 and all emotion at level 2 were summed; and finally the totals for level 1 and level 2 were summed to obtain a score for all emotion displayed in the 30 page sample of each novel.

[c] Variables 15 and 16 were segregated from the other variables because they were only partially related to content; they contained both content and non-content elements and therefore did not meet the rigorous interpretation of a content variable used in this study.

Regarding prior publication, it was hypothesized that, of two novels on the same theme, the first to be published probably "soaked up" all of the market for that particular theme or treatment of it and left the second novel with little or no market at all. This involved the content of the novel in that it involved its theme, but publication date itself had nothing to do with content.

Wordage involved the amount of the content in a novel, but non-content factors were present because a large wordage apparently encouraged readers to buy with the idea that they were getting more for their money, without regard to the ingredients of the novel. The readers seemed to believe that their pleasure would last longer with a long novel than with a short one.

of several other variables, to make up the scores of another variable which was a better discriminator.

The Important Groups of Variables. Table 7 summarizes the status of the six groups of variables at the beginning and end of the analysis. These groups, described earlier, were generalized categories based on a large number of individual variables. Most of the variables were represented in one or another of the groups. Table 7 shows the most important groups to be those of emotion, the personalities of the major characters, the plot themes, and simplicity. It must be recognized, however, that one of these groups, that related to emotion, stood out above all the others in importance.

TABLE 7

STATUS OF THE GROUPS OF VARIABLES AT THE
BEGINNING AND END OF THE ANALYSIS*

Groups	Number of Variables at Beginning of Analysis	Number of Variables at End of Analysis
Action	15	0
Emotion	54	10
Personalities	75	9
Plot themes	350	2
Romanticization	50	0
Simplicity	32	1

* Since several of the variables belonged to more than one group, the sums of the two columns equal more than the sums of the different variables included.

FINDINGS: THE FORMULAS

One of the purposes of the study was to find a combination of variables which would allow prediction of sale more accurately than could be done with one variable alone. Consequently, the sixteen variables in Table 6 were combined in various ways to ascertain which combination would correctly classify the highest percentage of the forty-four novels as best or poor sellers. The fewer variables used, the easier it would be to apply the formula. No attempt was made to predict the actual sale or even the *PW* score of a novel; a correct prediction meant only that a book was classified correctly as a best or poor seller.

The statistical technique used in develop-

ing the formulas was the discriminate functions technique. This was developed only a few years ago by R. A. Fisher to aid in separating the members of two groups on the basis of certain of their characteristics.[22] It has previously been employed in botanical, anthropological, personnel, and financial work; applications have ranged from separating two species on the basis of petal length[23] or bone dimension,[24] to distinguishing between good and poor salesmen,[25] or between good and poor loan risks in the consumer installment finance business.[26]

The Two-Variable Formulas. All of the sixteen variables were used at least once in the two-variable combinations. Readability (variable 1) was recognized as one of the best discriminators, so was tried once with all other variables. This provided a comparison of the discrimination obtained with each variable; it pointed to certain variables and combinations as worth trying in additional formulas, and to others as of no value because of high intercorrelations.

Formulas With Three or More Variables. After the two-variable combinations had been worked out, three-variable combinations were tried. The variables showing up well in the two-variable formulas were tried in three-variable combinations in an attempt to raise the level of successful prediction. Following the calculation of the three-variable formulas, four- and five-variable combinations were tried. They were developed on the same basis as the three-variable for-

[22] Fisher, R. A., "The Use of Multiple Measurements in Taxonomic Problems," *Annals of Eugenics,* Vol. 7 (September, 1936), 179–186; and R. A. Fisher, "The Statistical Utilization of Multiple Measurements," *Annals of Eugenics,* Vol. 8 (August, 1938), pp. 376–386.

[23] Smith, H. Fairfield, "A Discriminant Function for Plant Selection," *Annals of Eugenics,* Vol. 7 (December, 1936), pp. 240–250.

[24] Barnard, M. M., "The Secular Variations of Skull Characters in Four Series of Egyptian Skulls," *Annals of Eugenics,* Vol. 6 (March, 1935), pp. 352–371.

[25] Wallace, N., and R. M. W. Trevers, "A Psychometric Sociological Study of a Group of Specialty Salesmen," *Annals of Eugenics,* Vol. 8 (April, 1938), pp. 266–302.

[26] Durand, David, *Risk Elements in Consumer Installment Finance,* New York: National Bureau of Economic Research, 1941.

mulas; i.e., from the best combinations discovered previously. The improvement of the four- and five-variable combinations did not seem sufficient to warrant trying any combination with more than five variables.

Of all the combinations worked out, Table 8 shows the best one (of those which did not require use of variables 15 and 16) to be the 1-4-7-9 formula (readability, central male character's total of level 1 emotion, an affectionate attitude by the central male character toward other major characters, and a sentimental theme). It will be noted that only one of these variables (central male character's total of level 1 emotion) had enough plus or minus scores to meet the 50 per cent criterion. The other three variables, which proved to be among the four best when used in combination, would have been eliminated if the 50 per cent criterion had been applied indiscriminately in the latter part of the analysis.

Formulas Using Variables 15 and 16. The best formula based on content variables alone classified 77 per cent of the novels correctly. Table 8 shows that when their non-content nature was ignored and they were tried in combination with content variables, variables 15 (prior publication date)

and 16 (wordage of the novel) produced high percentages of correct prediction and in fact produced the five best formulas in the study. The two best formulas developed with them included four different variables: readability, a sentimental theme, an affectionate attitude by the central male character toward the other major characters, and prior publication date.[27] These formulas made it obvious that the percentage of correct prediction could be raised by using the two non-content variables.

Testing the Significance of the Discrimination. For each formula it was necessary to test the hypothesis that its percentage of correct prediction was actually due to chance factors rather than a real and reliable ability to discriminate between best and poor sellers. For the discrimination to be accepted as a real, rather than a chance discrimination, it had to meet the usual 95 per cent standard for level of significance, i.e., there had to be at least 95 chances out of 100 that the discrimination was real and reliable. This test eliminated approximately a third of the combinations.

A second test of significance was designed to test the value of new variables which might be added to a formula. This test was intended to show whether or not the addition of a variable to a particular formula significantly increased the percentage of correct prediction. Several formulas were eliminated by this test.

Testing the Reliability of the Best Formula. In any statistical study, it is necessary to test the reliability of the results. The ideal method for this in the present study would have been to apply the formula to additional pairs of novels matched in the same manner as the original group, but, the lack of good pairs which had not been used in the original group made it impossible to carry out this method. Themes, publicity factors, and sales totals would not have been matched as closely in the additional pairs as they were in the original pairs, and, consequently, the two groups—the original and

TABLE 8

BEST COMBINATIONS

Variables[a]	Percentage of Correct Prediction[b]
1–4–15	82%
4–7–15	82
1–4–7–9–15	82
1–4–7–15	80
1–3–4–7–15	80
4–15	77
1–4–7–9	77
4–7–9–16	77
4–9–15	75
1–3–7–15	75

[a] Code

1. Readability
3. Recency of the events in the novel
4. Sentimental theme
7. Central male character's affectionate attitude toward other characters
9. Central male character's total of level 1 emotion
15. Prior publication date
16. Wordage of the novel

[b] All discriminations in this table were significant at or below the five per cent confidence level.

[27] The 1–4–7–9–15 formula had an equally high percentage of correct prediction (82 per cent correct) but did not have the advantage of simplicity since it required five variables instead of three.

the test groups—would not have been quite comparable. Therefore, another method of testing reliability, the split-half method, was employed.

In the split-half method, results from half of the original data are compared with results from the remaining half of the data; this measures the data's internal consistency and is a partial measure of reliability. In the present study, the reliability of the best content formula (the 1-4-7-9 formula) was tested by comparing the eleven "better matched" with the eleven "poorer matched" pairs of novels. The better matched pairs were those in which themes, *PW* scores, and publicity factors were closely matched, while the poorer matched pairs were those not matched quite so closely on these factors. A new formula was worked out with the data for the four variables from the eleven poorer matched pairs; this formula was called the "1-4-7-9 poor" formula. This new formula was then applied to all the novels. It classified correctly 77 per cent of the poorer matched pairs and 73 per cent of the better matched pairs. Since these scores were so close, we may safely assume that there was a high degree of internal consistency and reliability in the 1-4-7-9 formula.

CONCLUSIONS

In the Berreman study and the research here reported, two of the important areas of consideration—the best seller's publicity and its content—have, for the first time, been studied carefully and correlated positively with sale. But while these studies have brought a certain amount of understanding of the problem, this understanding has not yet advanced beyond its elementary stages. It is not yet possible to state categorically just what the relations are between the conclusions of the two studies themselves. To understand their relationships it will be necessary to weigh the relative value of the factors they found important, and to find out when and under what conditions each is operative. Nor is it yet possible to state the conclusions of the two studies more than hypothetically for the novels they did not include. More evidence is needed before it will be possible to predict the effect on any one particular novel of its publicity and content factors.

The causal factors behind the sale of best sellers are sufficiently complex and are imbedded so deeply in the psychological and sociological aspects of modern culture that their description cannot be attempted, although the correlative factors found important in the two studies obviously suggest avenues of approach to the problem. Other areas which must be studied before all the correlative factors can be assembled are those relating to the author, the publisher, the "society," and the individual reader. Perfect prediction of sale cannot be accomplished before all have been analyzed.

QUESTIONS FOR STUDY AND DISCUSSION

1. Compare this article with the ones by Napier Wilt and C. Northcote Parkinson. Are the problems of proof faced by John Harvey essentially different from those of Wilt and Parkinson? What differences do you see in the way the three writers present their evidence? Are the three inductions equally convincing?

2. Compare Harvey's style of writing with Wilt and Parkinson. What specific differences do you see? Is the manner of writing influenced by the content of the articles? By the audience for which the authors are writing?

WRITING ASSIGNMENT

Write an essay generalizing upon the "content characteristics" of recent novels which you have read. Notice that it is easy enough to assert the presence of these characteristics, but how do ·you persuade the reader that your observations are sound? How much evidence must you present in order to *prove* your case?

C. NORTHCOTE PARKINSON

Plans and Plants, or the Administration Block

Every student of human institutions is familiar with the standard test by which the importance of the individual may be assessed. The number of doors to be passed, the number of his personal assistants, the number of his telephone receivers—these three figures, taken with the depth of his carpet in centimeters, have given us a simple formula that is reliable for most parts of the world. It is less widely known that the same sort of measurement is applicable, *but in reverse*, to the institution itself.

Take, for example, a publishing organization. Publishers have a strong tendency, as we know, to live in a state of chaotic squalor. The visitor who applies at the obvious entrance is led outside and around the block, down an alley and up three flights of stairs. A research establishment is similarly housed, as a rule, on the ground floor of what was once a private house, a crazy wooden corridor leading thence to a corrugated iron hut in what was once the garden. Are we not all familiar, moreover, with the layout of an international airport? As we emerge from the aircraft, we see (over to our right or left) a lofty structure wrapped in scaffolding. Then the air hostess leads us into a hut with an asbestos roof. Nor do we suppose for a moment that it will ever be otherwise. By the time the permanent building is complete the airfield will have been moved to another site.

The institutions already mentioned—lively and productive as they may be—flourish in such shabby and makeshift surroundings that we might turn with relief to an institution clothed from the outset with convenience and dignity. The outer door, in bronze and glass, is placed centrally in a symmetrical façade. Polished shoes glide quietly over shining rubber to the glittering and silent elevator. The overpoweringly cultured receptionist will murmur with carmine lips into an ice-blue receiver. She will wave you into a chromium armchair, consoling you with a dazzling smile for any slight but inevitable delay. Looking up from a glossy magazine, you will observe how the wide corridors radiate toward departments A, B, and C. From behind closed doors will come the subdued noise of an ordered activity. A minute later and you are ankle deep in the director's carpet, plodding sturdily toward his distant, tidy desk. Hypnotized by the chief's unwavering stare, cowed by the Matisse hung upon his wall, you will feel that you have found real efficiency at last.

In point of fact you will have discovered nothing of the kind. It is now known that a perfection of planned layout is achieved only by institutions on the point of collapse. This apparently paradoxical conclusion is based upon a wealth of archaeological and historical research, with the more esoteric details of which we need not concern ourselves. In general principle, however, the method pursued has been to select and date the buildings which appear to have been perfectly designed for their purpose. A study and comparison of these has tended to prove that perfection of planning is a symptom of decay. During a period of exciting discovery or progress there is no time to plan the perfect headquarters. The time for that comes later, when all the important work has been done. Perfection, we know, is finality; and finality is death.

Thus, to the casual tourist, awestruck in front of St. Peter's, Rome, the Basilica and the Vatican must seem the ideal setting for the Papal Monarchy at the very height of its prestige and power. Here, he reflects, must Innocent III have thundered his anathema. Here must Gregory VII have laid down the law. But a glance at the guidebook will convince the traveler that the really powerful Popes reigned long before the present dome was raised, and reigned not infrequently somewhere else. More than that, the later Popes lost half their authority while the work was still in progress. Julius II, whose decision it was to build, and Leo X, who approved Raphael's design, were dead long before the buildings assumed their present shape. Bramante's palace was still building until 1565, the great church not consecrated until 1626, nor the piazza colonnades finished until 1667. The great days of the Papacy were over before the perfect setting was even planned. They were almost forgotten by the date of its completion.

That this sequence of events is in no way exceptional can be proved with ease. Just such a sequence can be found in the history of the League of Nations. Great hopes centered on the League from its inception in 1920 until about 1930. By 1933, at the latest, the experiment was seen to have failed. Its physical embodiment, however, the Palace of the Nations, was not opened until 1937. It was a structure no doubt justly admired. Deep thought had gone into the design of secretariat and council chambers, committee rooms and cafeteria. Everything was there which ingenuity could devise— except, indeed, the League itself. By the year when its Palace was formally opened the League had practically ceased to exist.

It might be urged that the Palace of Versailles is an instance of something quite opposite; the architectural embodiment of Louis XIV's monarchy at its height. But here again the facts refuse to fit the theory. For granted that Versailles may typify the triumphant spirit of the age, it was mostly completed very late in the reign, and some of it indeed during the reign that followed. The building of Versailles mainly took place between 1669 and 1685. The king did not move there until 1682, and even then the work was still in progress. The famous royal bedroom was not occupied until 1701, nor the chapel finished until nine years later. Considered as a seat of government, as apart from a royal residence, Versailles dates in part from as late as 1756. As against that, Louis XIV's real triumphs were mostly before 1679, the apex of his career reached in 1682 itself and his power declining from about 1685. According to one historian, Louis, in coming to Versailles "was already sealing the doom of his line and race." Another says of Versailles that "The whole thing . . . was completed just when the decline of Louis's power had begun." A third tacitly supports this theory by describing the period 1685–1713 as "The Years of Decline." In other words, the visitor who

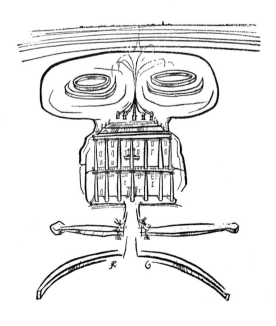

thinks Versailles the place from which Tu-
renne rode forth to victory is essentially
mistaken. It would be historically more correct to picture the embarrassment, in that
setting, of those who came with the news
of defeat at Blenheim. In a palace resplend-
ent with emblems of victory they can hardly
have known which way to look.

Mention of Blenheim must naturally call
to mind the palace of that name built for
the victorious Duke of Marlborough. Here
again we have a building ideally planned,
this time as the place of retirement for a
national hero. Its heroic proportions are
more dramatic perhaps than convenient,
but the general effect is just what the architects intended. No scene could more fittingly
enshrine a legend. No setting could have
been more appropriate for the meeting of
old comrades on the anniversary of a battle.
Our pleasure, however, in picturing the
scene is spoiled by our realization that it
cannot have taken place. The Duke never
lived there and never even saw it finished.
His actual residence was at Holywell, near
St. Alban's, and (when in town) at Marlborough House. He died at Windsor Lodge
and his old comrades, when they held a re-
union, are known to have dined in a tent.
Blenheim took long in building, not because
of the elaboration of the design—which was
admittedly quite elaborate enough—but because the Duke was in disgrace and even,
for two years, in exile during the period
which might otherwise have witnessed its
completion.

What of the monarchy which the Duke
of Marlborough served? Just as tourists now
wander, guidebook in hand, through the
Orangerie or the Galerie des Glaces, so the
future archaeologist may peer around what
once was London. And he may well incline
to see in the ruins of Buckingham Palace a
true expression of British monarchy. He
will trace the great avenue from Admiralty
Arch to the palace gate. He will reconstruct
the forecourt and the central balcony, thinking all the time how suitable it must have
been for a powerful ruler whose sway extended to the remote parts of the world.
Even a present-day American might be
tempted to shake his head over the arrogance

of a George III, enthroned in such impressive state as this. But again we find that the
really powerful monarchs all lived somewhere else, in buildings long since vanished
—at Greenwich or Nonesuch, Kenilworth
or Whitehall. The builder of Buckingham
Palace was George IV, whose court architect, John Nash, was responsible for what
was described at the time as its "general
feebleness and triviality of taste." But George
IV himself, who lived at Carlton House or
Brighton, never saw the finished work; nor
did William IV, who ordered its completion. It was Queen Victoria who first took
up residence there in 1837, being married
from the new palace in 1840. But her first
enthusiasm for Buckingham Palace was relatively short-lived. Her husband infinitely
preferred Windsor and her own later preference was for Balmoral or Osborne. The
splendors of Buckingham Palace are therefore to be associated, if we are to be accurate, with a later and strictly constitutional
monarchy. It dates from a period when
power was vested in Parliament.

It is natural, therefore, to ask at this
point whether the Palace of Westminster,
where the House of Commons meets, is
itself a true expression of parliamentary rule.
It represents beyond question a magnificent
piece of planning, aptly designed for debate
and yet provided with ample space for everything else—for committee meetings, for quiet
study, for refreshment, and (on its terrace)
for tea. It has everything a legislator could
possibly desire, all incorporated in a building of immense dignity and comfort. It
should date—but this we now hardly dare
assume—from a period when parliamentary
rule was at its height. But once again the
dates refuse to fit into this pattern. The
original House, where Pitt and Fox were
matched in oratory, was accidentally destroyed by fire in 1834. It would appear to
have been as famed for its inconvenience
as for its lofty standard of debate. The
present structure was begun in 1840, partly
occupied in 1852, but incomplete when its
architect died in 1860. It finally assumed its
present appearance in about 1868. Now, by
what we can no longer regard as coincidence, the decline of Parliament can be

traced, without much dispute, to the Reform Act of 1867. It was in the following year that all initiative in legislation passed from Parliament to be vested in the Cabinet. The prestige attached to the letters "M.P." began sharply to decline and thenceforward the most that could be said is that "a role, though a humble one, was left for private members." The great days were over.

The same could not be said of the various Ministries, which were to gain importance in proportion to Parliament's decline. Investigation may yet serve to reveal that the India Office reached its peak of efficiency when accommodated in the Westminster Palace Hotel. What is more significant, however, is the recent development of the Colonial Office. For while the British Empire was mostly acquired at a period when the Colonial Office (in so far as there was one) occupied haphazard premises in Downing Street, a new phase of colonial policy began when the department moved into buildings actually designed for the purpose. This was in 1875 and the structure was well designed as a background for the disasters of the Boer War. But the Colonial Office gained a new lease of life during World War II. With its move to temporary and highly inconvenient premises in Great Smith Street—premises leased from the Church of England and intended for an entirely different purpose—British colonial policy entered that phase of enlightened activity which will end no doubt with the completion of the new building planned on the site of the old Westminster Hospital. It is reassuring to know that work on this site has not even begun.

But no other British example can now match in significance the story of New Delhi. Nowhere else have British architects been given the task of planning so great a capital city as the seat of government for so vast a population. The intention to found New Delhi was announced at the Imperial Durbar of 1911, King George V being at that time the Mogul's successor on what had been the Peacock Throne. Sir Edwin Lutyens then proceeded to draw up plans for a British Versailles, splendid in conception, comprehensive in detail, masterly in design, and

overpowering in scale. But the stages of its progress toward completion correspond with so many steps in political collapse. The Government of India Act of 1909 had been the prelude to all that followed—the attempt on the Viceroy's life in 1912, the Declaration of 1917, the Montagu-Chelmsford Report of 1918 and its implementation in 1920. Lord Irwin actually moved into his new palace in 1929, the year in which the Indian Congress demanded independence, the year in which the Round Table Conference opened, the year before the Civil Disobedience campaign began. It would be possible, though tedious, to trace the whole story down to the day when the British finally withdrew, showing how each phase of the retreat was exactly paralleled with the completion of another triumph in civic design. What was finally achieved was no more and no less than a mausoleum.

The decline of British imperialism actually began with the general election of 1906 and the victory on that occasion of liberal and semi-socialist ideas. It need surprise no one, therefore, to observe that 1906 is the date of completion carved in imperishable granite over the British War Office doors. The campaign of Waterloo might have been directed from poky offices around the Horse Guards Parade. It was, by contrast, in surroundings of dignity that were approved the plans for attacking the Dardanelles.

The elaborate layout of the Pentagon at Arlington, Virginia, provides another significant lesson for planners. It was not completed until the later stages of World War II and, of course, the architecture of the great victory was not constructed here, but in the crowded and untidy Munitions Building on Constitution Avenue.

Even today, as the least observant visitor to Washington can see, the most monumental edifices are found to house such derelict organizations as the Departments of Commerce and Labor, while the more active agencies occupy half-completed quarters. Indeed, much of the more urgent business of government goes forward in "temporary" structures erected during World War I, and shrewdly preserved for their stimulating effect on administration. Hard by the Capitol, the visitor will also observe the imposing marble-and-glass headquarters of the Teamsters' Union, completed not a moment too soon before the heavy hand of Congressional investigation descended on its occupants.

It is by no means certain that an influential reader of this chapter could prolong the life of a dying institution merely by depriving it of its streamlined headquarters. What he can do, however, with more confidence, is to prevent any organization strangling itself at birth. Examples abound of new institutions coming into existence with a full establishment of deputy directors, consultants and executives; all these coming together in a building specially designed for their purpose. And experience proves that such an institution will die. It is choked by its own perfection. It cannot take root for lack of soil. It cannot grow naturally for it is already grown. Fruitless by its very nature, it cannot even flower. When we see an example of such planning—when we are confronted for example by the building designed for the United Nations—the experts among us shake their heads sadly, draw a sheet over the corpse, and tiptoe quietly into the open air.

QUESTIONS FOR STUDY AND DISCUSSION

1. Why does "Plans and Plants" exemplify inductive reasoning?

2. Where is the clearest statement of Mr. Parkinson's conclusion to be found? Restate that conclusion in your own words.

3. Enumerate the instances which provide the material for Mr. Parkinson's generalization.

4. How serious is the author? Are you amused at his discussion? If so, does this amusement render invalid the conclusion he arrives at?

5. Can you supply examples from your own experience to support Mr. Parkinson's conclusion?

6. Can this conclusion be challenged? If so, on what grounds?

7. Does Mr. Parkinson's conclusion surprise you? If so, do you feel that an element of surprise is an essential ingredient in the essay's effectiveness?

Materials for an Essay

CHARLES ADDAMS

Five Cartoons

"Tell me more about your husband, Mrs. Briggs."

"Oh, speak up, George! Stop mumbling!"

"Now, let's see—one sashweight, one butcher's
cleaver, one galvanized-iron tub, fifty feet of half-inch rope,
one gunny sack, one electric torch, one pickaxe, one shovel,
twenty pounds of quicklime, a box of cigars, and a beach chair."

"You have the wrong cell, Chaplain. HE's just serving
a short term for a traffic violation."

Deduction and the Handling of Arguments

No introduction to the argument can ignore traditional logic, yet nothing less than a full textbook could do justice to this most valuable tool. As with cause and effect, induction, and the hypothesis, we have been using deductive logic all our lives, but this is no guarantee that we can play it right because we play it by ear.

In making an induction, we try to prove the truth of a statement, or proposition. Sometimes we start with the generalization itself (for instance, "Red heads have bad tempers") and attempt to verify it by numerous examples; at other times we begin at the beginning, with a collection of case histories that leads us to the conclusion that people with red hair do indeed suffer from anger, as well as other deadly sins. But however we go about it, induction always tests for truth.

Deduction, though, is a process of consistent reasoning. It is a means of relating one statement to another. In using deductive reasoning, we test for consistency, or validity. Consider these:

All men are immortal	Some men marry shrews
Socrates is a man	Socrates is a man
Therefore Socrates is immortal.	Therefore Socrates is married to a shrew.

All men are mortal
Socrates is a man
Therefore Socrates is mortal.

The first syllogism, as such a group of statements is called, is manifestly untrue, but the reasoning involved is consistent, or valid. The second set of statements is quite true but devoid of consistency and totally invalid. Only the third set of propositions meets the requirement of a sound deduction: *it must be both valid and true*. Failure to realize this double-pronged requirement explains why induction and deduction to some people appear to be antithetical processes. Chaucer has Symkin, the scornful miller of the Reeve's Tale, say to his two young guests from Cambridge:

Myn hous is streit but ye han lerned art
Ye kan by argumentz make a place
A myle brood of twenty foot of space.

Deduction is a method for relating one class to another, and the language of logical classes is a considerably restricted form of language as we normally use it. Of the categorical propositions, which we must consider first, there are four and only four kinds:

183

All **X** is Y
All **men** are mortal

No **X** is Y
No **men** are **immortal**

Some X is Y
Some men are fools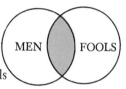

Some X is not **Y**
Some men are not **fools**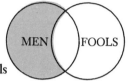

Each of the propositions contains a subject term (symbolized by X), a predicate term (here called Y), a quantifier (*all, no,* or *some*), and a copula (*is, are; is not, are not*) which links the terms together. When we say that all X is Y, we are saying that the whole class of X is part of the class of Y. Whenever a proposition refers to an entire class (all X, no X) and not just a part of that class (some X), we say that it is distributed. In the propositions listed above, the distributed terms are shown in bold print.

When we say that all X is Y, we mean that X is included in Y, that it is a member of the class of Y; but we are not saying that X equals Y. (It is fairly easy to show that all men are mortal, but quite another matter to prove that all mortals are men.) When we attempt to infer something from a proposition by switching subject and predicate terms, we convert it. If we try to derive a new statement by a modification of quality and predicate term, we obvert the proposition (as in changing "All men are mortal" to "No men are non-mortal," which may be translated as "No men are immortal"). Failures to convert and obvert properly are among our commonest errors. For categorical propositions, these are the possibilities for conversion and obversion:

All X is Y All men are mortal	No X is Y No men are immortal
CONVERSE: Some Y is X Some mortals are men	CONVERSE: No Y is X No immortals are men
OBVERSE: No X is non-Y No men are non-mortal	OBVERSE: All X is non-Y All men are non-immortal (= mortal)
Some X is Y Some men are fools	Some X is not Y Some men are not fools
CONVERSE: Some Y´ is X Some fools are men	NO CONVERSE
OBVERSE: Some X is not non-Y Some men are not non-fools	OBVERSE: Some X is non-Y Some men are non-fools

Once we establish the truth of any proposition, certain implications arise. If we can show that all men are mortal, we have also disproved that no men are mortal or that some men are not mortal. These implications are easily summed up:

		then ALL X IS Y is	then NO X IS Y is	then SOME X IS Y is	then SOME X IS NOT Y is
If ALL X IS Y	is True		False	True	False
	is False		Unknown	Unknown	True
If NO X IS Y	is True	False		False	True
	is False	Unknown		True	Unknown
If SOME X IS Y	is True	Unknown	False		Unknown
	is False	False	True		True
If SOME X IS NOT Y	is True	False	Unknown	Unknown	
	is False	True	False	True	

EXERCISE

Rewrite the following sentences in strict propositional form.

1. No one wants another war.
2. Only people who are willing to work will get ahead in this world.
3. Not all of his students know how to spell.
4. *I don't know half of you half as well as I should like; and I like less than half of you half as well as you deserve.*—J. R. R. Tolkien.
5. *These are the times that try men's souls.*—Tom Paine.
6. Handsome is as handsome does.
7. Water is a compound of hydrogen and oxygen.
8. He certainly isn't a good listener.
9. None but the brave deserve the fair.—John Dryden.
10. Everyone is against inflation except boobs.

Are the following inferences valid? If not, why?

1. If it is true that some people don't get enough to eat, it must also be true that some people do get enough to eat.
2. If some people do get enough to eat, it follows that there are some people who do not get enough to eat.
3. Everyone knows that the communists say they want racial equality. Therefore these people who are demanding racial equality must be communists.
4. No patriotic person would fail to sign up in time of war. Therefore everyone who fails to sign up in time of war is unpatriotic.
5. All patriotic men sign up in time of war. Therefore everyone who signs up in time of war is patriotic.

6. Every patriot loves his country. No one who does not love his country is a patriot.
7. It is true that the family that prays together stays together, which means that every family that stays together is a church-going family.
8. Since it is true that a wise man never shuts his mind to the facts, it follows that some people who shut their minds to the facts are not wise.
9. Some men do not deceive themselves as to their motives. It follows, then, that there are people who do deceive themselves as to their motives.
10. If some members of the lower-income groups are not in debt, we may safely conclude that some of the people who are in debt must come from the lower-income groups.
11. Originality in literature is quite a good thing, which means that a lack of originality is one of the marks of poor literature.

In our arguments we attempt to show the truth of individual statements by several means. Most propositions we prove by induction, though sometimes we may appeal to inductions already made and accepted as common knowledge ("Whales are mammals"). Some statements we claim are self-evident ("Two plus three equals three plus two"). Others ("Triangles have three sides") are a matter of definition. The word *triangle* is the name we bestow upon three-sided figures, and there is no problem of truth here (though there might well be in defining *beauty, aggressor, goodness,* or other terms). There is yet another way of proving the truth of a proposition: namely, by valid inference from other propositions that we know to be true. Once we show that it is true that all men are mortal and that Socrates was indeed a man, we have also proved the truth of our conclusion, if it follows validly from the premises. This would be so even if we lacked historical testimony as to Socrates' mortality.

In discussing truth and validity, we have already encountered the syllogism, which is a set of two propositions having one term in common and so arranged that we may draw a conclusion from them. In the familiar syllogism about Socrates, the statement "All men are mortal" is called the major premise (and it furnishes the predicate term of the conclusion); the proposition "Socrates is a man" is known as the minor premise (and provides the subject term of the conclusion); the term held in common, *man/men,* is the middle term.

A very few rules equip us to deal with all categorical syllogisms: Affirmative conclusions follow from affirmative premises, and a negative conclusion follows if one of the premises is negative. (There can be no syllogism if both premises are negative.) The middle term must be distributed at least once within the premises, and no term may be distributed in the conclusion if it has not already been distributed in the premise. And obviously enough, terms must never shift meaning.

EXERCISE

Which of the following syllogisms and seeming syllogisms are faulty? Why?

1. No men are immortal
   Xantippe is not a man
   Therefore Xantippe is immortal.

2. All human beings need love
   Some people who need love are unworthy of it
   Some human beings are unworthy of love.
3. No decent person wants his children to go hungry because he is too lazy to work
   Your neighbor is hardly a decent person
   Your neighbor, therefore, does not care if his children go hungry.
4. Good photography requires care in its execution
   All art forms require care in their execution
   Good photography, therefore, is an art form.
5. All insects have six legs
   No spider is an insect
   No spider has six legs.
6. All laws can be broken
   The basic statements of thermodynamics are laws
   The laws of thermodynamics, therefore, can be broken.
7. History is the record of our past
   Some records of our past are obviously unreliable
   Some histories, therefore, are unreliable.

The following student deductions were meant to be syllogisms in strict form. What is wrong with them?

8. Religion is necessary for morality
   Atheism does not preclude religion
   Atheism would not undermine morality because of lack of religion.
9. The primary aim of the university is to give students an academic education
   It has been found that students living in apartments average lower grades than students living in dormitories
   It is reasonable that students should be required to live in dormitories until they have completed at least two years of college.
10. I feel that the innermost nature of prayer is the soul's search for God and not for God's gifts
    Mr. Peale feels that this nature is the search for God's gifts
    Mr. Peale and I disagree or rather I disagree with Mr. Peale.

The categorical syllogism does not start to exhaust the field of logic. Syllogisms can also be constructed in hypothetical form:

If X, then Y	If X, then Y	If X, then Y
X	Not Y	If Y, then Z
Therefore Y.	Therefore not X.	Therefore if X, then Z.

In these syllogisms, X is called the antecedent and Y the consequent. The only valid forms of the hypothetical syllogism are those which affirm the antecedent and deny the consequent. To attempt anything else would be fallacious. Consider, for instance:

If X, then Y   If anyone neglects to work hard in this course, he
  Not X   will surely fail it
    Therefore not Y.   Sam has not neglected to work hard in this course
                   Therefore Sam will not fail.

In the alternative syllogism, the minor premise must deny one of the two possibilities:

Either X or Y	Either X or Y	Either we stand up for our rights or
Not X	Not Y	we risk losing them
Therefore Y.	Therefore X.	We must not risk losing them
		Therefore we must stand up for our rights.

In the disjunctive syllogism, the minor premise must affirm the truth of one of the two possibilities:

Not both X and Y	Not both X and Y	It isn't possible for students both to neglect
X	Y	their work and pass this
Therefore not Y.	Therefore not X.	course too
		Sam neglects his work
		Therefore Sam will not pass this course.

Largely outside the traditional syllogism, but very much a part of the reasoning we commit from day to day, are the relational inferences and syllogisms, including:

I weigh more than you do	El Paso is west of San Antonio
You weigh more than Tom	San Antonio is west of Houston
Therefore I weigh more than Tom.	El Paso, therefore, is west of Houston.

Julie is the daughter of Alfred
Alfred is the brother of Arthur
Therefore Julie is the niece of Arthur.

Not all relational terms lead so readily to new inferences. Sam may be an old friend of Marvin's, and Marvin may be an old friend of mine, but we can infer nothing about the friendship, new or old, existing or not, between Sam and me.

One of the richest of the logical processes, when properly used, is analogical reasoning, which is best thought of as an instrument of speculation rather than a means of proof. If two things, one known and one only partly known, resemble each other in a number of ways, it is likely that they resemble one another in still other respects. Thus the known resemblances between solar system and atom led Niels Bohr to take the solar system with its sun and planets as a model for the atom with its nucleus and electrons. The similarities between the Thirteen Colonies in 1776 and the states of Europe today have caused people to argue whether the nations of Europe could not unite to their general benefit. We often use the resemblances between two historic situations as guides in our thinking. The condition of America and Russia today has been compared with that of Carthage and Rome two millennia ago. The betrayal at Munich so haunts us that politicians even shun umbrellas as a symbol of that catastrophe. Reasoning by analogy is risky but often profitable; the sciences make particular use of it.

Most of our deductive reasoning takes the form of enthymemes, or compact deductions which suppress one or even two of the propositions of the full syllogism ("He drives just like a woman"). Considering the great distance between language and logic and the chances for fouling up even when propositions and syllogisms are in rigorous form, a reliance upon enthymemes only increases the odds against the writer. And even if his deductions should be free of error, enthymemic reasoning easily degenerates into something shadowy, ambiguous, and hard to pin down—full of hints but wanting clarity.

Even worse is the superficial argument that comes when the student doesn't know what his basic assumptions are, and the enthymeme is admirably suited to perpetuate this ignorance. Suppose that the student wishes to argue that certain novelists give a false picture of life in the United States. It is easy enough to list novels which are not true to life, but the argument is hardly a searching one because of the invisible major premise: that it is the duty of the novelist to give a true picture of the times. The perceptive writer spells out the assumptions that shape his arguments and attempts to convince his audience of their truth. The enthymeme encourages the writer to overlook these assumptions.

EXERCISE

Expand the following compressed deductions in a strict syllogistic form.

1. And if Chaucer portrays life in its reality, even if it is humorous, isn't the humor basically serious, by virtue of the seriousness of life?
2. Writers have to eat like the rest of us; therefore they write to make money.
3. A writer can't find joy in an empty society. He can't find joy because joy lacks definition.
4. This book has a candid approach to the male-female relationship, which isn't particularly out of place since most everyone knows of sex and love, anyway.
5. It has become clear during the last ten or twenty years that the future of the industrial system of this nation will not be decided by answering the classical questions of economics but by providing full employment.
6. If the people like that particular form of government, who are we to criticize it?
7. Before he can write, we demand that the student have something to say, and this means knowledge, which is most easily gotten from books, and wisdom, which the student himself must bring to the course.
8. Facts are details, and details make good writing; but not all details are facts.
9. This book should not be banned because it would lead to further control of a free press by the government.

This, in brief, is deduction, a very present help in avoiding logical blunders, but also a tool for constructing more penetrating arguments and an aid in organizing the essay itself. Given almost any thesis, such as "Football is highly desirable," we can view the statement as the conclusion to a syllogism, two terms of which are known. Our job, then, is to find the middle term:

> All X is highly desirable
> Football develops X
> Therefore football is highly desirable.

By locating the middle terms (character, good sportsmanship, team spirit, and the like) that lead to a fruitful discussion, the student has in effect constructed an outline for his argument. He has uncovered his reasons for boosting football— which he may not have known before—and he has built them into a framework which shows him, step by step, the statements he must prove if he is to persuade the reader of his conclusion. It is not enough to show that playing football develops team spirit; the writer must also prove that team spirit is desirable. If he can do this, he has taken a long step towards convincing his audience that football itself is one of the good things of life. By planning his arguments explicitly, in syllogistic form, the writer can avoid the superficiality that often comes from overly snappy enthymemes.

Once the writer sets up the syllogistic heart of his argument and checks its validity, his job is then to prove by every means available the truth of his premises. As often as not, this means induction, but all the logical processes have their part to play, and each one is indispensable. Ours is an age that exalts facts, and all but deifies them, but a thoughtful consideration of the nature and character of human knowledge suggests that facts seldom speak for themselves, that they are quite neutral until someone comes along to interpret them. (The same pitcher of beer may be half-full to the optimist and half-empty to the pessimist. And it's a fact that steaks are juicier if they're cooked rare; true enough, but such a contention overlooks the deductive framework into which this fact is fitted: namely, that juice makes a steak good.) Equally at fault is the mind that rides deduction like a wheelchair, leaving it only when someone forces it out for a little exercise. ("There are no flies in my kitchen, so how could there be one in your iced tea?") To reason mainly by induction or mainly by deduction or to work only by theory is to don mental blinders that permit us to see so much and no more.

The syllogism itself, if rightly handled, will suggest many of the topics which the writer needs to consider in developing his essay. But five lines of argument are particularly rich in possibilities: arguments from definition; cause and effect (or consequences); classification (often used together with consequences); comparison and contrast (or likeness-difference); and testimony.

Definition is frequently necessary simply to eliminate confusion. The words *true* and *valid* in their natural habitats have a variety of meanings, some of them overlapping; the person working with syllogisms recognizes their ambiguity and calls attention to the sharply restricted sense with which he uses these words. This is nothing more than good common sense—definition for clarity, which may avoid needless arguments and misunderstanding.

Definition is used argumentatively when a syllogistic proof hinges upon the meaning of a term. Our postal laws, for instance, forbid the transport through the mails of firearms, liquor, obscene literature, and the like. This seems clear enough in the case of weapons and spirits, but how do we establish obscenity? Over such definitions and their application many a lawsuit has been fought.

The hidden danger in the argument from definition is that the writer will operate with an accepted definition which blinds him to new and unsuspected evidence. In a famous illustration the linguist Benjamin Lee Whorf reported that workmen entered a gasoline tank marked "empty," not realizing that it was anything but empty of explosive fumes. A person reasoning about free will might first inquire what the term means and then argue for or against its existence by considering its effects. This is fine if we have total free will or no free will, but it misses the possibility of limited freedom of choice.

"Language Requirements in Foreign Service" by Robert Odess provides an example of definition in argument:

> When analysing the purposes and functions of diplomacy it is apparent that the most basic of these functions is that of communication. In a strict and narrow sense, of course, the diplomat or ambassador serves only as a personified telegraph line between two governments, but in reality he does a good deal more, for to be truly successful he will not only present his government's point of view but will present it in a manner acceptable to the foreign government and, ultimately, to the people who are represented by that government. To do this, the successful diplomat must be highly skilled in communicating his ideas to others, and must not only excel around the conference table but (as recent demonstrations around the world have so cruelly shown) must be able to give and, in turn, receive information from the people themselves. It is logical to assume that the representative who cannot converse with common people, cannot read local newspapers, cannot grasp popular opinion, in short, cannot communicate in the native language is at a striking disadvantage, for he must communicate through an interpreter who will inevitably serve as a filter, withdrawing the subtleties of inflexion and personal appeal which are so important in persuasive speaking. Thus, it appears that the foreign representative with a good command of a foreign language is at a distinct advantage over the representative who is forced to depend on the interpretations of others.

Causal analysis is probably the most rewarding, or at least the easiest, of the sources of argument, but the same cautions that apply to causal exposition obtain here. The construction of syllogisms, as previously described, frequently leads to causal arguments, but not always, for the main syllogisms upon which an argument rests may fail to consider all the meaningful issues.

There is no general formula for making a causal argument, no machine into which the student can feed a proposition and crank out a finished paper. Usually he will consider the consequences to which a proposal leads ("Football builds good sportsmanship"). If the consequences are good, the reader will feel that the proposal itself is good.

This is causal argumentation in its simplest form. If we argue that football builds good sportsmanship, we are really showing that football is a sufficient condition for creating good sportsmanship, but can we also demonstrate that football is a necessary condition for bringing it about? To put it in other words, if we have no football, is good sportsmanship conspicuously absent? Are there no other causes of good sportsmanship except football? A causal argument based upon sufficient conditions may have merit, but it lacks the strength of the argument based upon necessary and sufficient conditions—which is unassailable.

Another tack is to examine both cause and effect to see if they may be divided into species, or if they themselves are species of some larger genus. We have already begun such a division of the cause in asking if football and only football creates good sportsmanship. Perhaps there are other games that have this effect? Perhaps the causes of good sportsmanship are not limited only to games?

The effect may be handled similarly. Does football have consequences other than good sportsmanship, and are these desirable or not? In considering sportsmanship, suppose that we partition it into species and find that it has three manifestations: good sportsmanship, no sportsmanship, and poor sportsmanship. Does football always result in good sportsmanship and never the other kinds? Does the absence of football lead to bad sportsmanship or perhaps to no sportsmanship at all? By probing a general cause (or effect) closely and then subjecting its species to careful scrutiny, we can eliminate some of the shallowness that dogs the causal argument.

Nor should we forget to mark off the precise borders of our discussion. Football builds good sportsmanship, but in whom—everyone who goes to a game or just the team? If good sportsmanship is to be discovered only in a handful of players, coaches, and water boys, the effect is tearfully small in proportion to the machinery and expense of the cause. The idea that the effect should be proportionate to its cause has legitimate application in the world of ideas and policy, as well as in science.

An example of the argument from consequences is provided by Robert Odess:

> It is a tragic fact that fifty per cent of our entire Foreign Service officer corps does not have a speaking knowledge of *any* foreign language. Even the ambassadors to countries as important as France, Germany, and Italy are not able to conduct affairs of state in the language of the country to which they have been appointed, but are forced, instead, to converse through interpreters. The unfortunate results of such an inadequacy can be deduced in a theoretical manner and then verified with factual events. Due to the limitations of translation, the foreign representative often has a difficult time transmitting his ideas, for he is handicapped by the possibilities of faulty interpretation (either purposeful or accidental) and by the rather considerable time lapse involved in the translating process itself. This handicap, of course, is even greater in the area of social contacts and in the subtle and extremely important area of grasping popular opinion. The consequences of such a lack of language proficiency, moreover, are more than purely theoretical and can be seen in recent international events. In 1959, when President Eisenhower and Queen Elizabeth were in Montreal for the opening of the St. Lawrence seaway, the Queen was able to make a fine impression on the predominantly French population simply by addressing them in fluent French as well as in English, while the President was noticeably embarrassed when he falteringly read the few French words which had been written out for him. Incidents such as this, though seemingly insignificant, will often serve as effective means of building popular sentiment. The Ambassador to a Central American nation cannot as yet converse in Spanish although he has held his position for nine years. ("Not that it matters," he explains, "because the President and the

General speak excellent English. You won't find more American-type fine fellows anywhere.") The fact that he personally has been attacked by the landowners, students, Church, and businessmen, and that the present dictatorship which he ardently supports is on the verge of collapse have had no effect on his policy, largely because he is not in contact with any group other than his "American-type fine fellows." From these and numerous other incidents, it would appear that language prerequisites for Foreign Service officers would be among the most urgent of the many changes needed within our State Department.

Comparison and contrast (or likeness-difference) is a means of developing an idea by showing how well it applies to other species of the same genus. Consider this reason for not banning books: "How can someone who reads only goody-goody literature ever understand the people who are not like him and who do read books of this kind? How will he ever think for himself?" Presumably this means that we may understand other people (and also become thinking men) by sampling their activities. If we read questionable literature, we will understand people who are unlike us who read and write the stuff. But does the same recipe apply if we want to understand drunkards, drug addicts, and horse thieves? The principle is too uncritical, and we would do better to seek other, stronger reasons for opposing censorship, or else rethink our ideas on the subject. A generic argument ought to work for all the species within the genus. If a contention holds good for one species only, we must show that the argument somehow grows out of the unique properties of that species.

Comparison and contrast is also used as it would be in an expository essay—with the difference that in the argument a comparison of two species always leads to an evaluation or judgment. Thus we might compare medical care in the United States and Great Britain as part of an argument on socialized medicine.

Robert Odess again provides a specimen of the argument by likeness-difference:

> With the launching of the first Russian satellite, the United States began to wake up to the fact that somehow the Soviet Union was surpassing the United States in scientific achievement. Shortly thereafter, a series of incidents also drove home the realization that something was definitely lacking within our foreign policy. As part of a hasty effort to remedy both situations there has been considerable talk about the importance of foreign languages in both the scientific fields and in international relations. In this last area especially, I believe, language proficiency is of the utmost importance and the ready availability of translators is only the weakest of excuses for a member of our diplomatic corps not being able to speak the language of the country to which he has been assigned. Of course, it may be argued that both the original speaker and the translator do the same job: both are concerned with communicating ideas. This is certainly true. The important difference, however, lies in the manner in which the idea is communicated, and this communication is seriously weakened by a translator for several reasons. First, no matter how highly skilled the translator (and this is true of even the simultaneous translator) there will always be a distortion of the

phrasing, emphasis and intonation of the original speaker. Secondly, there is always the possibility of purposeful mistranslation. Thirdly, the translator can never work on a twenty-four hour basis and there will always be times when he is wanted, but unavailable. Fourthly, the use of a translator by an ambassador or other high official seems to inherently imply a lack of interest in the job he is doing. Certainly, direct address is far more cordial and unassuming than the constant dependence upon a "middleman" and particularly in dealing with Asians, such a dependence is very likely to be misconstrued as an insult. The translator, then, while certainly indispensable in some relationships, is a poor second to direct contact in the field of diplomacy.

Unlike the arguments from definition, cause and effect, classification, and comparison, the argument from testimony has no analogue in exposition. Testimony is usually nothing more than evidence as to the truth of some matter by someone qualified to speak. It may take the form of statements by eyewitnesses to an accident or letters of reference concerning a man's character and efficiency, but as often as not we seek testimony about matters which we haven't the time and training to unravel for ourselves. (How dangerous is radiation from fallout at its present level? Does smoking cause lung cancer? Is there intelligent life on other worlds? Can *like* be used as a conjunction?) For this we turn to authorities, sometimes to supplement what information we have acquired but often to decide for us when we cannot or will not decide for ourselves. As supplementary evidence, expert testimony certainly has its place, but the writer must always establish his authority's claim to eminence and keep in mind that an authority on nuclear physics does not possess an automatic right to set the world straight on modern art, or vice versa.

The authorities preferred by one age may not impress another. Ours is a time that reverences the scientist, and most of us depend upon him mightily. But in matters of art, literature, philosophy, and politics we apparently feel that every man armed with right reason needs little or no professional advice. A popular argument about religion might cite the Bible but seldom the Church fathers or religious philosophers that other times and other men would have invoked.

An example of the argument from authority, also by Robert Odess:

> The effectiveness of the American diplomatic corps is being seriously impaired by a lack of Foreign Service officers with even an elementary command of the language of the country to which they are assigned. It would seem obvious that in a vocation which depends to a great degree upon skill in conversation, the diplomatic representative without knowledge of the native language is most definitely at an enormous disadvantage. Commenting on this fact, Henry Cabot Lodge has said that ". . . the need for increased knowledge of foreign languages seems rarely to be acknowledged. Yet foreign languages are the channels for much of our diplomatic effort." In his seemingly incredible but well-documented *The Ugly American*, William Lederer brings out most dramatically the fact that American diplomats are, indeed, poorly prepared in this essential of communication when he brings to light the fact that ". . . in France, Italy, Germany, Belgium, the Netherlands, Nor-

way, and Turkey, our ambassadors cannot speak the native tongue. . . . In the entire Communist world, only our ambassador to Moscow can speak the native language." The result of this lack of linguistic training is, of course, a serious handicap in the area of communication, and communication, as John Osborne has stated, is the most important element in a good Foreign Service officer. In addition, this unfortunate condition has been responsible for a number of security leaks which have been traced to the necessity of using local labor to fill surprisingly important embassy positions. The solution to this real weakness in the administration of foreign policy is, I think, a strong language prerequisite for diplomatic appointments. If such a move is not made quickly the results may well prove tragic. Henry Cabot Lodge has said, "It is not going to do much good to have it recorded in the history books that Americans *wanted* to see freedom victorious over communism if in that same cause we cannot even be bothered to learn the language of another people."

Almost any contention may be argued in a multitude of ways, but the kinds of evidence available for use may not be equally strong. The writer must be able to discern the weight which any particular argument carries, and this calls for judgment, which cannot be taught. As an example, consider these reasons which were given by students in defense of a short story of real merit but built on a frankly sexual theme. A small but vocal group of parents had objected to the presence of the story in a high-school textbook:

> The parents were wrong to object to the story because (1) their action in effect constitutes censorship; (2) readings of this kind can bring about a realistic view of sex; (3) prudery will only make students try something worse than short stories; (4) the minority should not rule the majority; (5) the people teaching this story know more about good literature than the parents do; (6) the students will be unable to hold intelligent discussions with those people for whom the literary heritage is an exceedingly important part of their lives.

The complexities of a full essay cannot be summed up in a clause or two, but even these précis suggest that some of the reasons are stronger than others. The contentions are of three kinds: from definition (1 and 4); from consequences (2, 3, and 6); and from authority (5). The argument from authority is probably the least worthy (as used here) and the arguments from consequences the least convincing (simply because they are the hardest to prove).

The most promising arguments are those from definition, because here the definitions are drawn from an intelligent political philosophy that most of us wish to uphold; and the consequences of chipping away at such a philosophy are more serious than the consequences foreseen in reasons 2, 3, and 6. The essays incorporating these arguments from definition may become bungled in execution, but their potential strength is immense. Such are the arguments for which the thoughtful writer must search.

In shaping his argument, the writer should work from two directions: the ideal and the practical. A writer who can prove that the action he favors is in harmony with the ideal, the moral, the good, has made a stronger plea than the writer who considers only the expedient. The person who takes a stand because it is what we *should* do and *can* do or who opposes a line of action because it is what we *should* not and *cannot* do has considered and resolved the tension which often exists between the ideal and the practical, and if he is honest he has compromised neither.

A word of caution, though. There are large differences between *is* and *can* and *should* which cannot be slid over. A writer cannot simply assert that his recommendation is what the world should do and can do; he must prove it. Too many intellectual diddlers jump from one verb to another without cause. These are the people who observe that ours is a dog-eat-dog world and then conclude that this is as it should be and sensible canines will take advantage of it. Such confusion of fact and interpretation of fact is common and has nothing to recommend it.

Once the writer has studied his problem from every angle, outlined it, and made notes on it, the time finally comes for him to sit down and write it up. Integrity and honor oblige him to write only what he believes, whether his audience is friendly, hostile, or neutral, for "Trouthe is the hyeste thyng that man may kepe." But the audience must still be taken into account. The writer's concern is not to curry favor with his readers but to know what they are like and to write his essay with them in mind.

This is generally a matter of horse sense. The physician explaining oncology to a lay audience would not discuss the etiology and prognosis of carcinoma, sarcoma, melanoma, or the other neoplasms as if he were reading a technical paper before an assembly of specialists. But at the same time he would never oversimplify or talk down to his readers. The writer who offends his audience needlessly (like the young man who told a group of scholars, "I don't expect you to understand this") is a craven and a fool. The most unwelcome argument can be courteously presented as well as honestly, and the good writer will try to do both. He will also try to make his personality felt, perhaps by his wit, never by his eccentricities, always by the interest and enthusiasm which he feels for his subject and by the clarity with which he gets his ideas across. His aim is to argue the truth of an issue and to argue it persuasively.

EXERCISE

1. Write five paragraphs, arguing by definition, consequences, classification, comparison and contrast, and testimony that Americans should (*or* should not) have the right to vote at eighteen.
2. Argue by analogy with the situation in colonial America that the nations of Europe could (*or* could not) form a successful United States of Europe.
3. Write five paragraphs arguing, pro or con, the question of medical care for the aged. The first paragraph should be a letter to the editor of your newspaper; the second an address before the American Medical Association; the third a speech to a grade-school audience; the fourth a letter to your senior senator, urging a course of action; and the fifth a speech before a group of old ladies and gentlemen.

4. A student refuted an argument that only the artist (or someone well trained in art) is qualified to judge art by saying, "You don't have to be a chicken to be a connoisseur of eggs." Evaluate.

5. Concerning Vance Packard's *The Hidden Persuaders,* a student wrote: "The public doesn't always decide rationally (as Packard shows). Therefore it needs someone to make the right decisions for it until it is better educated." How good is this argument?

6. Evaluate this argument: "Americans shouldn't write to please Europeans. If they criticize our literature so what? Where would we be if we'd listened to Europeans in 1776?"

7. In August, 1960, Senator John F. Kennedy visited former President Harry S Truman at the Truman Library in Independence, Missouri. Later, as reported in *Time,* newsmen questioned Mr. Truman:

> Did Truman, they asked, still consider the Los Angeles convention rigged and the candidate immature? Said Truman, a smile flickering on his face: "The Democratic National Convention decided to nominate him for President. The convention is the law for the Democratic Party. I am a Democrat and I follow the law."

Evaluate.

8. Evaluate this argument, which is excerpted from a letter by Lloyd G. Allen to the *Evergreen* (April 12, 1961), an occasional publication of a Chicago co-operative grocery store:

> Lie detector tests are a very valuable management tool, entirely moral. The resolution opposing their use should be defeated.
>
> It is a terrible mistake to imagine that a lie detector test administered to an employee of a private firm is an invasion of privacy. . . .
>
> . . . Of course we know that lie detector evidence is not customarily acceptable in the courts. This is as it should be. Dishonest police officials might fake this type of evidence in a variety of ingenious ways.
>
> . . . in private industry a lie detector test is *only* one part of the evidence which a competent management will gather in connection with some suspected dishonesty on the part of an employee. If the management is competent (intelligent and well educated) and honest, it will not be misled by a polygraph. A resolution against the use of lie detector tests is an egregious affront to the competence and dignity of our top management.
>
> If those in charge can't be trusted in this matter, they should be fired. I trust them.
>
> . . . In a free, democratic economy, an honest employee need never fear a lie detector test. Would you, dear reader, fear to take a lie detector test on whether you had cheated your employer? Of course I mean a test administered by competent men and used by virtuous men like our present management.

9. Evaluate this political argument taken from the Beaumont *Journal,* August 31, 1960:

IT'S TIME YOU FACE THE
VOTERS, MR. BROOKS!

HERE IS THE STATEMENT RELEASED TO THE PRESS
FRIDAY NIGHT, AUGUST 26TH, BY FRED S. NEUMANN,
CONSERVATIVE CANDIDATE FOR CONGRESS, 2ND DISTRICT

Socialism is an insidious thing. It promises all things to all men. Those proponents of socialism sugar-coat their panaceas of gall, never mentioning that with each gift goes another link in the chain that will ultimately shackle all free men.

Our dread enemy is total State Socialism, and we must bend every effort to remove from office those people who espouse this system. Unless this is done now there will be no privileged sanctuary for anyone's freedom—neither yours nor mine.

My opponent, Jack Brooks, has voted less as a Texan than any other Congressman from Texas. On key issues my opponent regularly votes with the left-wing radicals of the North and never with the majority of the Texas Congressmen. This is not my kind of a Texan and I know he is not yours. He will lose this race because he has been voting himself out of office with the sorriest voting record of any Congressman from the Lone Star State.

My opponent has voted 91% against free enterprise on key issues! He has voted 80% of the time against labor when labor needed help to rid some unions of racketeers and convicts! He has voted 86% for inflationary measures! This is not idle surmising—this is all in the Congressional Record.

I am going to campaign with every ounce of my energy until this smear is wiped off the Lone Star flag. I am going to expose this man who shakes your hand as a friend, then votes against Texas and the best interests of his constituents. I am issuing a challenge to Mr. Brooks to face the voters of the Second Congressional District for the first time, to try to defend one of the sorriest voting records in Congress.

    I challenge my opponent to debates on KPAC-TV and KFDM-TV on as many programs as they will give in the public interest.

    I challenge my opponent to a debate in each of the following newspapers: The Beaumont Enterprise, The Beaumont Journal, The Orange Leader, and The Port Arthur News, as many times as possible in the public interest.

    I challenge my opponent to a debate in each of the weekly newspapers individually in Nederland, Port Neches, Liberty, Kirbyville, Vidor, Kountze, Silsbee, Jasper, Woodville, Bridge City, and San Augustine.

    I also challenge my opponent to a debate on the following radio stations: KFDM, KJET, KTRM, KRIC, KOGT, KPNG, KPAC, KOLE, KKAS, KWLD, KTXJ on each station individually on as many programs as they will give in the public interest.

I am not doing this to get better acquainted with Mr. Brooks. I know Mr. Brooks and I know his disgraceful voting record in Congress. I want the voters to get acquainted with him and to learn the truth, and I will debate, campaign, and work day and night until the Second Congressional District is delivered from the shackles of such thinkers.

As the conservative candidate, I, Fred S. Neumann, will not hand this District to the left-wingers on a platter. I and my organization will fight.

I pray that the good people of the Second Congressional District, who I know to be upright God-fearing citizens, interested far more in the type of government their children and grandchildren will grow up in, than in any "pie in the sky", will come forward and help me in this campaign to return your government to its rightful place in their lives—by electing Fred S. Neumann as your Congressman.

We wish to thank all radio stations, TV Channels 4 and 6, and the Port Arthur News and the Orange Leader for carrying the news story of the above challenge. Unfortunately, this challenge was not carried by the Beaumont Enterprise or the Beaumont Journal.

NEUMANN
WILL WIN!

THIS AD PAID FOR BY THE FRED S. NEUMANN FOR CONGRESS COMMITTEE,
MORRIS CLONINGER, CH.

[Editors' note: Congressman Brooks was re-elected.]

ESSAY SUGGESTIONS

First visit the library to see what you can learn and then write a paper, with a strong deductive framework, on any of these topics:

1. War can (cannot) be abolished.
2. Widespread atheism would (would not) undermine morality.
3. Too much emphasis is (is not) placed on sports in American schools and colleges.
4. The United States has (does not have) a right to intervene in the unstable politics of its neighbors.
5. Man has (does not have) free will.
6. World government is (is not) an idle dream.
7. There is (is not) too much censorship, in various forms, in the United States.
8. It is (is not) America's duty to help underdeveloped countries.
9. It is (is not) in America's best interest to help underdeveloped countries.
10. World disarmament is (is not) wishful thinking.
11. Nuclear warfare should (should not) be outlawed.
12. Bacteriological warfare should (should not) be outlawed.
13. Poison gas should (should not) be used again in war.
14. Wartime veterans deserve (do not deserve) special treatment from the government.
15. Peacetime veterans deserve (do not deserve) special treatment from the government.
16. Social security is (is not) a step forward in our national progress.
17. Socialized medicine would (would not) be a step forward in our national progress.
18. A man's first loyalty should (should not) be to his conscience.
19. Men act (do not act) only out of self-interest.

FURTHER READING

A very clear, simple introduction to deductive logic is provided by Bernard F. Huppé and Jack Kaminsky, *Logic and Language*, Chapter 4. W. H. Werkmeister's *Introduction to Critical Thinking* is a much more extensive text, but fine for the beginner. See Chapters VII through XII. *An Introduction to Logic and Scientific Method* by Morris R. Cohen and Ernest Nagel is a splendid book, but for the student who has already digested a more elementary text. See Chapters II through V. See also John Stuart Mill, *A System of Logic*, Book I, Chapters IV through VI, and all of Book II. The serious student will of course want to read Aristotle's Organon, since all our textbooks are ultimately derived from this collection of works on logic.

On general problems of argumentation, see Jim W. Corder and Lyle H. Kendall, Jr., *A College Rhetoric*, Chapter VII.

On analogical reasoning, see Morris R. Cohen and Ernest Nagel, *An Introduction to Logic and Scientific Method*, Chapter XIV, part 4; and Chapter XI, part 6. See also John Stuart Mill, *A System of Logic*, Book III, Chapter XX.

Our attention to the arguments from definition, consequences, likeness-difference, and authority is only one of our many great debts to the College Composition Staff of the University of Chicago, which is probably unique in recognizing the importance of the topics, as the classical rhetoricians called them. See Manuel Bilsky, McCrea Hazlett, Robert E. Streeter, and Richard M. Weaver, "Looking for an Argument," *College English*, XIV (1953), 210–216.

The student should also read Aristotle's *Topica*, which is part of the Organon, and his *Rhetorica*, especially Book II, which furnishes important lines of arguments. Cicero, in Book II of *De Oratore*, gives a list of topics. A convenient edition in two volumes, including English translation by E. W. Sutton and H. Rackham, appears in the Loeb Classical Library. Cambridge, Mass.: Harvard University Press, 1942.

E. B. WHITE

Freedom

I have often noticed on my trips up to the city that people have recut their clothes to follow the fashion. On my last trip, however, it seemed to me that people had remodeled their ideas too—taken in their convictions a little at the waist, shortened the sleeves of their resolve, and fitted themselves out in a new intellectual ensemble copied from a smart design out of the very latest page of history. It seemed to me they had strung along with Paris a little too long.

I confess to a disturbed stomach. I feel sick when I find anyone adjusting his mind to the new tyranny which is succeeding abroad. Because of its fundamental strictures, fascism does not seem to me to admit of any compromise or any rationalization, and I resent the patronizing air of persons who find in my plain belief in freedom a sign of immaturity. If it is boyish to believe that a human being should live free, then I'll gladly arrest my development and let the rest of the world grow up.

I shall report some of the strange remarks I heard in New York. One man told me that he thought perhaps the Nazi ideal was a sounder ideal than our constitutional system "because have you ever noticed what fine alert young faces the young German soldiers have in the newsreel?" He added: "Our American youngsters spend all their time at the movies—they're a mess." That was his summation of the case, his interpretation of the new Europe. Such a remark leaves me pale and shaken. If it represents the peak of our intelligence, then the steady march of despotism will not receive any considerable setback at our shores.

Another man informed me that our democratic notion of popular government was decadent and not worth bothering about—"because England is really rotten and the industrial towns there are a disgrace." That was the only reason he gave for the hopelessness of democracy; and he seemed mightily pleased with himself, as though he were more familiar than most with the anatomy of decadence, and had detected subtler aspects of the situation than were discernible to the rest of us.

Another man assured me that anyone who took *any* kind of government seriously was a gullible fool. You could be sure, he said, that there is nothing but corruption "because of the way Clemenceau acted at Versailles." He said it didn't make any difference really about this war. It was just another war. Having relieved himself of this majestic bit of reasoning, he subsided.

Another individual, discovering signs of zeal creeping into my blood, berated me for having lost my detachment, my pure skeptical point of view. He announced that he wasn't going to be swept away by all this nonsense, but would prefer to remain in the role of innocent bystander, which he said was the duty of any intelligent person. (I noticed, however, that he phoned later to qualify his remark, as though he had lost some of his innocence in the cab on the way home.)

Those are just a few samples of the sort of talk that seemed to be going round—talk which was full of defeatism and disillusion and sometimes of a too studied innocence. Men are not merely annihilating themselves at a great rate these days, but they are telling one another enormous lies, grandiose fibs. Such remarks as I heard are fearfully disturbing in their cumulative effect. They are more destructive than dive bombers and mine fields, for they challenge not merely one's immediate position but one's main defenses. They seemed to me to issue either from persons who could never have really come to grips with freedom, so as to understand her, or from renegades. Where I expected to find indignation, I found paralysis, or a sort of dim acquiescence, as in a child who is dully swallowing a distasteful pill. I was advised of the growing anti-Jewish sentiment by a man who seemed to be watching the phenomenon of intolerance not through tears of shame but with a clear intellectual gaze, as through a well-ground lens.

The least a man can do at such a time is to declare himself and tell where he stands.

I believe in freedom with the same burning delight, the same faith, the same intense abandon which attended its birth on this continent more than a century and a half ago. I am writing my declaration rapidly, much as though I were shaving to catch a train. Events abroad give a man a feeling of being pressed for time. Actually I do not believe I am pressed for time, and I apologize to the reader for a false impression that may be created. I just want to tell, before I get slowed down, that I am in love with freedom and that it is an affair of long standing and that it is a fine state to be in, and that I am deeply suspicious of people who are beginning to adjust to fascism and dictators merely because they are succeeding in war. From such adaptable natures a smell rises. I pinch my nose.

For as long as I can remember I have had a sense of living somewhat freely in a natural world. I don't mean I enjoyed freedom of action, but my existence seemed to have the quality of free-ness. I traveled with secret papers pertaining to a divine conspiracy. Intuitively I've always been aware of the vitally important pact which a man has with himself, to be all things to himself, and to be identified with all things, to stand self-reliant, taking advantage of his haphazard connection with a planet, riding his luck, and following his bent with the tenacity of a hound. My first and greatest love affair was with this thing we call freedom, this lady of infinite allure, this dangerous and beautiful and sublime being who restores and supplies us all.

It began with the haunting intimation (which I presume every child receives) of his mystical inner life; of God in man; of nature publishing herself through the "I." This elusive sensation is moving and memorable. It comes early in life: a boy, we'll say, sitting on the front steps on a summer night, thinking of nothing in particular, suddenly hearing as with a new perception and as though for the first time the pulsing sound of crickets, overwhelmed with the novel sense of identification with the natural company of insects and grass and night, conscious of a faint answering cry to the universal perplexing question: "What is 'I'?" Or a little girl, returning from the grave of

a pet bird leaning with her elbows on the windowsill, inhaling the unfamiliar draught of death, suddenly seeing herself as part of the complete story. Or to an older youth, encountering for the first time a great teacher who by some chance word or mood awakens something and the youth beginning to breathe as an individual and conscious of strength in his vitals. I think the sensation must develop in many men as a feeling of identity with God—an eruption of the spirit caused by allergies and the sense of divine existence as distinct from mere animal existence. This is the beginning of the affair with freedom.

But a man's free condition is of two parts: the instinctive freeness he experiences as an animal dweller on a planet, and the practical liberties he enjoys as a privileged member of human society. The latter is, of the two, more generally understood, more widely admired, more violently challenged and discussed. It is the practical and apparent side of freedom. The United States, almost alone today, offers the liberties and the privileges and the tools of freedom. In this land the citizens are still invited to write their plays and books, to paint their pictures, to meet for discussion, to dissent as well as to agree, to mount soapboxes in the public square, to enjoy education in all subjects without censorship, to hold court and judge one another, to compose music, to talk politics with their neighbors without wondering whether the secret police are listening, to exchange ideas as well as goods, to kid the government when it needs kidding, and to read real news of real events instead of phony news manufactured by a paid agent of the state. This is a fact and should give every person pause.

To be free, in a planetary sense, is to feel that you belong to earth. To be free, in a social sense, is to feel at home in a democratic framework. In Adolf Hitler, although he is a freely flowering individual, we do not detect either type of sensibility. From reading his book I gather that his feeling for earth is not a sense of communion but a driving urge to prevail. His feeling for men is not that they co-exist, but that they are capable of being arranged and standardized by a superior intellect—that their existence suggests not a fulfillment of their personalities but a submersion of their personalities in the common racial destiny. His very great absorption in the destiny of the German people somehow loses some of its effect when you discover, from his writings, in what vast contempt he holds *all* people. "I learned," he wrote, ". . . to gain an insight into the unbelievably primitive opinions and arguments of the people." To him the ordinary man is a primitive, capable only of being used and led. He speaks continually of people as sheep, halfwits, and impudent fools—the same people from whom he asks the utmost in loyalty, and to whom he promises the ultimate in prizes.

Here in America, where our society is based on belief in the individual, not contempt for him, the free principle of life has a chance of surviving. I believe that it must and will survive. To understand freedom is an accomplishment which all men may acquire who set their minds in that direction; and to love freedom is a tendency which many Americans are born with. To live in the same room with freedom, or in the same hemisphere, is still a profoundly shaking experience for me.

One of the earliest truths (and to him most valuable) that the author of *Mein Kampf* discovered was that it is not the written word, but the spoken word, which in heated moments moves great masses of people to noble or ignoble action. The written word, unlike the spoken word, is something which every person examines privately and judges calmly by his own intellectual standards, not by what the man standing next to him thinks. "I know," wrote Hitler, "that one is able to win people far more by the spoken than by the written word.

. . ." Later he adds contemptuously: "For let it be said to all knights of the pen and to all the political dandies, especially of today: the greatest changes in this world have never yet been brought about by a goose quill! No, the pen has always been reserved to motivate these changes theoretically."

Luckily I am not out to change the world —that's being done for me, and at a great clip. But I know that the free spirit of man is persistent in nature; it recurs, and has never successfully been wiped out, by fire or flood. I set down the above remarks merely (in the words of Mr. Hitler) to motivate that spirit, theoretically. Being myself a knight of the goose quill, I am under no misapprehension about "winning people"; but I am inordinately proud these days of the quill, for it has shown itself, historically, to be the hypodermic which inoculates men and keeps the germ of freedom always in circulation, so that there are individuals in every time in every land who are the carriers, the Typhoid Mary's, capable of infecting others by mere contact and example. These persons are feared by every tyrant— who shows his fear by burning the books and destroying the individuals. A writer goes about his task today with the extra satisfaction which comes from knowing that he will be the first to have his head lopped off— even before the political dandies. In my own case this is a double satisfaction, for if freedom were denied me by force of earthly circumstance, I am the same as dead and would infinitely prefer to go into fascism without my head than with it, having no use for it any more and not wishing to be saddled with so heavy an encumbrance.

QUESTIONS FOR STUDY AND DISCUSSION

1. Notice the elaborate metaphor which begins this essay. What is its effect upon the reader?

2. What other metaphors appear in the essay?

3. Why does White devote five paragraphs to "the strange remarks" he had been hearing? How does this build up his case? Do these paragraphs help to explain why the essay still has immediacy more than

twenty years after it was written?

4. What arguments does White use to show that America has real freedom? Do these arguments hold true for the cold war with communism?

5. E. B. White is justly admired for the fine quality of his prose. Point out some of the techniques which shape his style of writing.

ALDOUS HUXLEY

The Arts of Selling

The survival of democracy depends on the ability of large numbers of people to make realistic choices in the light of adequate information. A dictatorship, on the other hand, maintains itself by censoring or distorting the facts, and by appealing, not to reason, not to enlightened self-interest, but to passion and prejudice, to the powerful "hidden forces," as Hitler called them, present in the unconscious depths of every human mind.

In the West, democratic principles are proclaimed and many able and conscientious publicists do their best to supply electors with adequate information and to persuade them, by rational argument, to make realistic choices in the light of that information. All this is greatly to the good. But unfortunately propaganda in the Western democracies, above all in America, has two faces and a divided personality. In charge of the editorial department there is often a democratic Dr. Jekyll—a propagandist who would be very happy to prove that John Dewey had been right about the ability of human nature to respond to truth and reason. But this worthy man controls only a part of the machinery of mass communication. In charge of advertising we find an anti-democratic, because anti-rational, Mr. Hyde—or rather a Dr. Hyde, for Hyde is now a Ph.D in psychology and has a master's degree as well in the social sciences. This Dr. Hyde would be very unhappy indeed if everybody always lived up to John Dewey's faith in human nature. Truth and reason are Jekyll's affair, not his. Hyde is a motivation analyst, and his business is to study human weaknesses and failings, to investigate those unconscious desires and fears by which so much of men's conscious thinking and overt doing is determined. And he does this, not in the spirit of the moralist who would like to make people better, or of the physician who would like to improve their health, but simply in order to find out the best way to take advantage of their ignorance and to exploit their irrationality for the pecuniary benefit of his employers. But after all, it may be argued, "capitalism is dead, consumerism is king"—and consumerism requires the services of expert salesmen versed in all the arts (including the more insidious arts) of persuasion. Under a free enterprise system commercial propaganda by any and every means is absolutely indispensable. But the indispensable is not necessarily the desirable. What is demonstrably good in the sphere of economics may be far from good for men and women as voters or even as human beings. An earlier, more moralistic generation would have been profoundly shocked by the bland cynicism of the motivation analysts. Today we read a book like Mr. Vance Packard's *The Hidden Persuaders*, and are more amused than horrified, more resigned than indignant. Given Freud, given Behaviorism, given the mass producer's chronically desperate need for mass consumption, this is the sort of thing that is only to be expected. But what, we may ask, is the sort of thing that is to be expected in the future? Are Hyde's activities compatible in the long run with Jekyll's? Can a campaign in favor of rationality be successful in the teeth of another and even more vigorous campaign in favor of irrationality? These are questions which, for the moment, I shall not attempt to answer, but shall leave hanging, so to speak, as a backdrop to our discussion of the methods of mass persuasion in a technologically advanced democratic society.

The task of the commercial propagandist in a democracy is in some ways easier and in some ways more difficult than that of a political propagandist employed by an established dictator or a dictator in the making. It is easier inasmuch as almost everyone starts out with a prejudice in favor of beer, cigarettes and iceboxes, whereas almost nobody starts out with a prejudice in favor of tyrants. It is more difficult inasmuch as the commercial propagandist is not permitted, by the rules of his particular game, to appeal to the more savage instincts of his public. The advertiser of dairy products would dearly love to tell his readers and listeners that all their troubles are caused by the machinations of a gang of godless international margarine manufacturers, and that it is their patriotic duty to march out and burn the oppressors' factories. This sort of thing, however, is ruled out, and he must be content with a milder approach. But the mild approach is less exciting than the approach through verbal or physical violence. In the long run, anger and hatred are self-defeating emotions. But in the short run they pay high dividends in the form of psychological and even (since they release large quantities of adrenalin and noradrenalin) physiological satisfaction. People may start out with an initial prejudice against tyrants; but when tyrants or would-be tyrants treat them to adrenalin-releasing propaganda about the wickedness of their enemies—particularly of enemies weak enough to be persecuted—they are ready to follow him with enthusiasm. In his speeches Hitler kept repeating such words as "hatred," "force," "ruthless," "crush," "smash"; and he would accompany these violent words with even more violent gestures. He would yell, he would scream, his veins would swell, his face would turn purple. Strong emotion (as every actor and dramatist knows) is in the highest degree contagious. Infected by the malignant frenzy of the orator, the audience would groan and sob and scream in an orgy of uninhibited passion. And these orgies were so enjoyable that most of those who had experienced them eagerly came back for more. Almost all of us long for peace and freedom; but very few of us have much enthusiasm for the thoughts, feelings and actions that make for peace and freedom. Conversely almost nobody wants war or tyranny; but a great many people find an intense pleasure in the thoughts, feelings and actions that make for war and tyranny. These thoughts, feelings and actions are too dangerous to be exploited for commercial purposes. Accepting this handicap, the advertising man must do the best he can with the less intoxicating emotions, the quieter forms of irrationality.

Effective rational propaganda becomes possible only when there is a clear understanding, on the part of all concerned, of the nature of symbols and of their relations to the things and events symbolized. Irrational propaganda depends for its effectiveness on a general failure to understand the nature of symbols. Simple-minded people tend to equate the symbol with what it stands for, to attribute to things and events some of the qualities expressed by the words in terms of which the propagandist has chosen, for his own purposes, to talk about them. Consider a simple example. Most cosmetics are made of lanolin, which is a mixture of purified wool fat and water beaten up into an emulsion. This emulsion has many valuable properties: it penetrates the skin, it does not become rancid, it is mildly antiseptic and so forth. But the commercial propagandists do not speak about the genuine virtues of the emulsion. They give it some picturesquely voluptuous name, talk ecstatically and misleadingly about feminine beauty and show pictures of gorgeous blondes nourishing their tissues with skin food. "The cosmetic manufacturers," one of their number has written, "are not selling lanolin, they are selling hope." For this hope, this fraudulent implication of a promise that they will be transfigured, women will pay ten or twenty times the value of the emulsion which the propagandists have so skilfully related, by means of misleading symbols, to a deep-seated and almost universal feminine wish—the wish to be more attractive to members of the opposite sex. The principles underlying this kind of propaganda are extremely simple. Find some common desire, some widespread unconscious fear or anxiety; think out some way to relate this wish or fear to the product you have to sell; then build a bridge of verbal or pictorial symbols over which your customer can pass from fact to compensatory dream, and from the dream to the illusion that your product, when purchased, will make the dream come true. "We no longer buy oranges, we buy vitality. We do not buy just an auto, we buy prestige." And so with all the rest. In toothpaste, for example, we buy, not a mere cleanser and antiseptic, but release from the fear of being sexually repulsive. In vodka and whisky we are not buying a protoplasmic poison which, in small doses, may depress the nervous system in a psychologically valuable way; we are buying friendliness and good fellowship, the warmth of Dingley Dell and the brilliance of the Mermaid Tavern. With our laxatives we buy the health of a Greek god, the radiance of one of Diana's nymphs. With the monthly best seller we acquire culture, the envy of our less literate neighbors and the respect of the sophisticated. In every case the motivation analyst has found some deep-seated wish or fear, whose energy can be used to move the consumer to part with cash and so, indirectly, to turn the wheels of industry. Stored in the minds and bodies of countless individuals, this potential energy is released by, and transmitted along, a line of symbols carefully laid out so as to bypass rationality and obscure the real issue.

Sometimes the symbols take effect by being disproportionately impressive, haunting and fascinating in their own right. Of this kind are the rites and pomps of religion. These "beauties of holiness" strengthen faith where it already exists and, where there is no faith, contribute to conversion. Appealing, as they do, only to the aesthetic sense, they guarantee neither the truth nor the ethical value of the doctrines with which they have been, quite arbitrarily, associated. As a matter of plain historical fact, the beauties of holiness have often been matched and indeed surpassed by the beauties of unholiness. Under Hitler, for example, the yearly Nuremberg rallies were masterpieces of ritual and theatrical art. "I had spent six years in St. Petersburg before the war in the best days of the old Russian ballet," writes Sir Nevile Henderson, the British ambassador to Hitler's Germany, "but for grandiose beauty I have never seen any ballet to compare with the Nuremberg rally." One thinks of Keats—"beauty is truth, truth beauty." Alas, the identity exists only on some ultimate, supramundane level. On the levels of politics and theology, beauty is perfectly compatible with nonsense and tyranny. Which is very fortunate; for if beauty were incompatible with nonsense and tyranny, there would be precious little art in the world. The masterpieces of painting, sculpture and architecture were produced as religious or political propaganda, for the greater

glory of a god, a government or a priesthood. But most kings and priests have been despotic and all religions have been riddled with superstition. Genius has been the servant of tyranny and art has advertised the merits of the local cult. Time, as it passes, separates the good art from the bad metaphysics. Can we learn to make this separation, not after the event, but while it is actually taking place? That is the question.

In commercial propaganda the principle of the disproportionately fascinating symbol is clearly understood. Every propagandist has his Art Department, and attempts are constantly being made to beautify the billboards with striking posters, the advertising pages of magazines with lively drawings and photographs. There are no masterpieces; for masterpieces appeal only to a limited audience, and the commercial propagandist is out to captivate the majority. For him, the ideal is a moderate excellence. Those who like this not too good, but sufficiently striking, art may be expected to like the products with which it has been associated and for which it symbolically stands.

Another disproportionately fascinating symbol is the Singing Commercial. Singing Commercials are a recent invention; but the Singing Theological and the Singing Devotional—the hymn and the psalm—are as old as religion itself. Singing Militaries, or marching songs, are coeval with war, and Singing Patriotics, the precursors of our national anthems, were doubtless used to promote group solidarity, to emphasize the distinction between "us" and "them," by the wandering bands of paleolithic hunters and food gatherers. To most people music is intrinsically attractive. Moreover, melodies tend to ingrain themselves in the listener's mind. A tune will haunt the memory during the whole of a lifetime. Here, for example, is a quite uninteresting statement or value judgment. As it stands nobody will pay attention to it. But now set the words to a catchy and easily remembered tune. Immediately they become words of power. Moreover, the words will tend automatically to repeat themselves every time the melody is heard or spontaneously remembered. Orpheus has entered into an alliance with Pavlov—the power of sound with the conditioned reflex. For the commercial propagandist, as for his colleagues in the fields of politics and religion, music possesses yet another advantage. Nonsense which it would be shameful for a reasonable being to write, speak or hear spoken can be sung or listened to by that same rational being with pleasure and even with a kind of intellectual conviction. Can we learn to separate the pleasure of singing or of listening to song from the all too human tendency to believe in the propaganda which the song is putting over? That again is the question.

Thanks to compulsory education and the rotary press, the propagandist has been able, for many years past, to convey his messages to virtually every adult in every civilized country. Today, thanks to radio and television, he is in the happy position of being able to communicate even with unschooled adults and not yet literate children.

Children, as might be expected, are highly susceptible to propaganda. They are ignorant of the world and its ways, and therefore completely unsuspecting. Their critical faculties are undeveloped. The youngest of them have not yet reached the age of reason and the older ones lack the experience on which their new-found rationality can effectively work. In Europe, conscripts used to be playfully referred to as "cannon fodder." Their little brothers and sisters have now become radio fodder and television fodder. In my childhood we were taught to sing nursery rhymes and, in pious households, hymns. Today the little ones warble the Singing Commercials. Which is better—"Rheingold is my beer, the dry beer," or "Hey diddlediddle, the cat and the fiddle"? "Abide with me" or "You'll wonder where the yellow went, when you brush your teeth with Pepsodent"? Who knows?

"I don't say that children should be forced to harass their parents into buying products they've seen advertised on television, but at the same time I cannot close my eyes to the fact that it's being done every day." So writes the star of one of the many programs beamed to a juvenile audience. "Children," he adds, "are living, talking records of what we tell them every day." And in due course these living, talking records of television commercials will grow up, earn money and buy the products of industry. "Think," writes Mr. Clyde Miller ecstatically, "think of what it can mean to your firm in profits if you can condition a million or ten million children, who will grow up into adults trained to buy your product, as soldiers are trained in advance when they hear the trigger words, Forward March!" Yes, just think of it! And at the same time remember that the dictators and the would-be dictators have been thinking about this sort of thing for years, and that millions, tens of millions, hundreds of millions of children are in process of growing up to buy the local despot's ideological product and, like well-trained soldiers, to respond with appropriate behavior to the trigger words implanted in those young minds by the despot's propagandists.

Self-government is in inverse ratio to numbers. The larger the constituency, the less the value of any particular vote. When he is merely one of millions, the individual elector feels himself to be impotent, a negligible quantity. The candidates he has voted into office are far away, at the top of the pyramid of power. Theoretically they are the servants of the people; but in fact it is the servants who give orders and the people, far off at the base of the great pyramid, who must obey. Increasing population and advancing technology have resulted in an increase in the number and complexity of organizations, an increase in the amount of power concentrated in the hands of officials and a corresponding decrease in the amount of control exercised by electors, coupled with a decrease in the public's regard for democratic procedures. Already weakened by the vast impersonal forces at work in the modern world, democratic institutions are now being undermined from within by the politicians and their propagandists.

Human beings act in a great variety of irrational ways, but all of them seem to be capable, if given a fair chance, of making a reasonable choice in the light of available evidence. Democratic institutions can be made to wotk only if all concerned do their best to impart knowledge and to encourage rationality. But today, in the world's most powerful democracy, the politicians and their propagandists prefer to make nonsense of democratic procedures by appealing almost exclusively to the ignorance and irrationality of the electors. "Both parties," we were told in 1956 by the editor of a leading business journal, "will merchandize their candidates and issues by the same methods that business has developed to sell goods. These include scientific selection of appeals and planned repetition. . . . Radio spot announcements and ads will repeat phrases with a planned intensity. Billboards will push slogans of proven power. . . . Candidates need, in addition to rich voices and good diction, to be able to look 'sincerely' at the TV camera."

The political merchandisers appeal only to the weaknesses of voters, never to their potential strength. They make no attempt to educate the masses into becoming fit for self-government; they are content merely to manipulate and exploit them. For this purpose all the resources of psychology and the social sciences are mobilized and set to work. Carefully selected samples of the electorate are given "interviews in depth." These interviews in depth reveal the unconscious fears and wishes most prevalent in a given society at the time of an election. Phrases and images aimed at allaying or, if necessary, enhancing these fears, at satisfying these wishes, at least symbolically, are then chosen by the experts, tried out on readers and audiences, changed or improved in the

light of the information thus obtained. After which the political campaign is ready for the mass communicators. All that is now needed is money and a candidate who can be coached to look "sincere." Under the new dispensation, political principles and plans for specific action have come to lose most of their importance. The personality of the candidate and the way he is projected by the advertising experts are the things that really matter.

In one way or another, as vigorous heman or kindly father, the candidate must be glamorous. He must also be an entertainer who never bores his audience. Inured to television and radio, that audience is accustomed to being distracted and does not like to be asked to concentrate or make a prolonged intellectual effort. All speeches by the entertainer-candidate must therefore be short and snappy. The great issues of the day must be dealt with in five minutes at the most—and preferably (since the audience will be eager to pass on to something a little livelier than inflation or the H-bomb) in sixty seconds flat. The nature of oratory is such that there has always been a tendency among politicians and clergymen to over-simplify complex issues. From a pulpit or a platform even the most conscientious of speakers finds it very difficult to tell the whole truth. The methods now being used to merchandise the political candidate as though he were a deodorant positively guarantee the electorate against ever hearing the truth about anything.

QUESTIONS FOR STUDY AND DISCUSSION

1. Why does Huxley begin the essay with an elaborate characterization of the "two faces" of propaganda in America?

2. What arguments and evidence does Huxley use to show that advertisers employ "the quieter forms of irrationality"?

3. How does Huxley argue that the "arts

of selling" have political implications? What reasons does he give for his faith in the democratic ideal?

4. Comment on the transitions Huxley uses to tie together the important threads of his discussion.

ASHLEY MONTAGU

The Natural
Superiority of Women

Oh, no!, I can hear it said, *not* superior. Equal, partners, complementary, different, but *not* superior. I can even foresee that men will mostly smile, while women, alarmed, will rise to the defense of men—women always have, and always will. I hope that what I shall have to say in this article will make them even more willing to do so, for men need their help more than they as yet, mostly, consciously realize.

Women superior to men? This is a new idea. There have been people who have cogently, but apparently not convincingly, argued that women were as good as men, but I do not recall anyone who has publicly provided the evidence or even argued that women were better than or superior to men. How, indeed, could one argue such a case in the face of all the evidence to the contrary? Is it not a fact that by far the largest number of geniuses, great painters, poets, philosophers, scientists, etc., etc., have been men, and that women have made, by comparison, a very poor showing? Clearly the superiority is with men? Where are the Leonardos, the Michelangelos, the Shakespeares, the Donnes, the Galileos, the Whiteheads, the Kants, the Bachs, *et al.*, of the feminine sex? In fields in which women have excelled, in poetry and the novel, how many poets and novelists of the really first rank have there been? Haven't well-bred young women been educated for centuries in music? And how many among them have been great composers or instrumentalists? Composers—none of the first rank. Instrumentalists—well, in the recent period there have been such accomplished artists as Myra Hess and Wanda Landowska. Possibly there is a clue here to the answer to the question asked. May it not be that women are just about to emerge from the period of subjection during which they were the "niggers" of the masculine world?

The Royal Society of London has at last opened its doors and admitted women to the highest honor which it is in the power of the English scientific world to bestow—the Fellowship of the Royal Society. I well remember that when I was a youth—less than a quarter of a century ago—it was considered inconceivable that any woman would ever have brains enough to attain great distinction in science. Mme. Curie was an exception. But the half dozen women Fellows of the Royal Society in England are not. Nor is Lisa Meitner. And Mme. Curie no longer remains the only woman to share in the Nobel Prize award for science. There is Marie Curie's daughter, Irene Joliot-Curie, and there is Gerty Cory (1947) for physiology and medicine. Nobel prizes in literature have gone to Selma Lagerlof, Grazia Deledda, Sigrid Undset, Pearl Buck, and Gabriela Mistral. As an artist Mary Cassatt (1845–1926) was every bit as good as her great French friends Degas and Manet considered her to be, but it has taken the rest of the world another fifty years grudgingly to admit it. Among contemporaries Georgia O'Keeffe can hold her own with the best.

It is not, however, going to be any part of this article to show that women are about to emerge as superior scientists, musicians, painters, or the like. I believe that in these fields they may emerge as equally good, and possibly not in as large numbers as men, largely because the motivations and aspirations of most women will continue to be directed elsewhere. But what must be pointed out is that women are, in fact, just beginning to emerge from the period of subjection when they were treated in a manner not unlike that which is still meted out to the Negro in the Western world. The women of the nineteenth century were the "niggers" of the male-dominated world. All the traits that are mythically attributed to the Negro at the present time were for many generations saddled upon women. Women had smaller brains than men and less intelligence, they were more emotional and unstable, in a crisis you could always rely upon them to swoon or become otherwise helpless, they were weak and sickly creatures, they had little judgment and less sense, could not be relied upon to handle money, and as for the world outside, there they could be employed only at the most menial and routine tasks.

The biggest dent in this series of myths was made by World War I, when women were for the first time called upon to replace men in occupations which were formerly the exclusive preserve of men. They became bus drivers, conductors, factory workers, farm workers, laborers, supervisors, executive officers, and a great many other things at which many had believed they could never work. At first it was said that they didn't do as well as men, then it was grudgingly admitted that they weren't so bad, and by the time the war was over many employers were reluctant to exchange their women employees for men! But the truth was out—women could do as well as men in most of the fields which had been considered forever closed to them because of their alleged natural incapacities, and in many fields, particularly where delicate precision work was involved, they had proved themselves superior to men. From 1918 to 1939 the period for women was one essentially of consolidation of gains, so that by the time that World War II broke out there was no hesitation on the part of anyone in calling upon women to serve in the civilian roles of men and in many cases also in the armed services.

But women have a long way to go before they reach full emancipation—emancipation from the myths from which they themselves suffer. It is, of course, untrue that women have smaller brains than men. The fact is that in proportion to body weight they have larger brains than men; but this fact is in itself of no importance because within the limits of normal variation of brain size and weight there exists no relation between these factors and intelligence. Women have been conditioned to believe that they are inferior to men, and they have assumed that what everyone believes is a fact of nature; and as men occupy the superior positions in almost all societies, this superiority is taken to be a natural one. "Woman's place is in the home" and man's place is in the counting house and on the board of directors. "Women should not meddle in men's affairs." And yet the world does move. Some women have become Members of Parliament and even attained Cabinet rank. In the United States they have even gotten as far as the Senate. They have participated in peace conferences, but it is still inconceivable to most persons that there should ever be a woman Prime Minister or President. And yet that day, too, will come. *Eppure si muove!*

Woman has successfully passed through the abolition period, the abolition of her thraldom to man; she has now to pass successfully through the period of emancipation, the freeing of herself from the myth of inferiority, and the realization of her potentialities to the fullest.

And now for the evidence which proves the superiority of woman to man. But first, one word in explanation of the use of the word "superiority." The word is used in its common sense as being of better quality than, or of higher nature or character. Let us begin at the very beginning. What about the structure of the sexes? Does one show any superiority over the other? The answer is a resounding "Yes!" And I should like this "Yes" to resound all over the world, for no one has made anything of this key fact which lies at the base of all the differences between the sexes and the superiority of the female to the male. I refer to the chromosomal structure of the sexes. The chromosomes, those small cellular bodies which contain the hereditary particles, the genes, which so substantially influence one's development and fate as an organism, provide us with our basic facts.

In the sex cells there are twenty-four chromosomes, but only one of these is a sex chromosome. There are two kinds of sex chromosomes, X and Y. Half the sperm cells carry X and half carry Y chromosomes. All the female ova are made up of X-chromosomes. When an X-bearing sperm fertilizes an ovum the offspring is always female. When a Y-bearing chromosome fertilizes an ovum the offspring is always male. And this is what makes the difference between the sexes. So what? Well, the sad fact is that the

Y-chromosome is but an iota, the merest bit, of a remnant of an X-chromosome; it is a crippled X-chromosome. The X-chromosomes are fully developed structures; the Y-chromosome is the merest comma. It is as if in the evolution of sex a particle one day broke away from an X-chromosome, and thereafter in relation to X-chromosomes could produce only an incomplete female— the creature we now call the male! It is to this original chromosomal deficiency that all the various troubles to which the male falls heir can be traced.

In the first place the chromosomal deficiency of the male determines his incapacity to have babies. This has always been a sore point with men, though consciously they would be the last to admit it, although in some primitive societies, as among the Australian aborigines, it is the male who conceives a child by dreaming it, and then telling his wife. In this way a child is eventually born to them, the wife being merely the incubator who hatches the egg placed there through the grace of her husband.

The fact that men cannot have babies and suckle them nor remain in association with their children as closely as the wife has an enormous effect upon their subsequent psychological development. Omitting altogether from consideration the psychologic influences exercised by the differences in the hormonal secretions of the sexes, one can safely say that the mother-child relationship confers enormous benefits upon the mother which are not nearly so substantively operative in the necessary absence of such a relationship between father and child. The maternalizing influences of being a mother in addition to the fact of being a woman has from the very beginning of the human species—about a million years ago—made the female the more humane of the sexes. The love of a mother for her child is the basic patent and the model for *all* human relationships. Indeed, to the extent to which men approximate in their relationships with their fellow men to the love of the mother for her child, to that extent do they move more closely to the attainment of perfect human relations. The mother-child relationship is a dependent-interdependent one. The interstimulation between mother and child is something which the father misses, and to that extent suffers from the want of. In short, the female in the mother-child relationship has the advantage of having to be more considerate, more self-sacrificing, more cooperative, and more altruistic than usually falls to the lot of the male.

The female thus acquires, in addition to whatever natural biological advantages she starts with, a competence in social understanding which is usually denied the male. This, I take it, is one of the reasons why women are usually so much more able to perceive the nuances and pick up the subliminal signs in human behavior which almost invariably pass men by. It was, I believe, George Jean Nathan who called woman's intuition merely man's transparency. With all due deference to Mr. Nathan and sympathy for his lot as a mere male, I would suggest that man's opacity would be nearer the mark. It is because women have had to be so unselfish and forbearing and self-sacrificing and maternal that they possess a deeper understanding than men of what it is to be human. What is so frequently termed feminine indecision, the inability of women to make up their minds, is in fact an inverse reflection of the trigger-thinking of men. Every salesgirl prefers the male customer because women take time to think about what they are buying, and the male usually hasn't the sense enough to do so. Women don't think in terms of "Yes" or "No." Life isn't as simple as all that— except to males. Men tend to think in terms of the all-or-none principle, in terms of black and white. Women are more ready to make adjustments, to consider the alternative possibilities, and see the other colors and gradations in the range between black and white.

By comparison with the deep involvement of women in living, men appear to be only superficially so. Compare the love of a male for a female with the love of the female for the male. It is the difference between a rivulet and a great deep ocean. Women love the human race; men are, on the whole, hostile to it. Men act as if they haven't been adequately loved, as if they had been frustrated and rendered hostile, and becoming aggressive they say that aggressiveness is natural and women are inferior in this respect because they tend to be gentle and unaggressive! But it is precisely in this capacity to love and unaggressiveness that the superiority of women to men is demonstrated, for whether it be natural to be loving and cooperative or not, so far as the human species is concerned, its evolutionary destiny, its very survival is more closely tied to this capacity for love and cooperation than with any other. So that unless men learn from women how to be more loving and cooperative they will go on making the kind of mess of the world which they have so effectively achieved thus far.

And this is, of course, where women can realize their power for good in the world, and make their greatest gains. *It is the function of women to teach men how to be human.* Women must not permit themselves to be deviated from this function by those who tell them that their place is in the home in subservient relation to man. It is, indeed, in the home that the foundations of the kind of world in which we live are laid, and in this sense it will always remain true that the hand that rocks the cradle is the hand that rules the world. And it is in this sense that women must assume the job of making men who will know how to make a world fit for human beings to live in. The greatest single step forward in this direction will be made when women consciously assume this task—the task of teaching their children to be like themselves, loving and cooperative.

As for geniuses, I think that almost everyone will agree that there have been more geniuses for being human among women than there have among men. This, after all, is the true genius of women, and it is because we have not valued the qualities for being human anywhere nearly as highly as we have valued those for accomplishment in the arts and sciences that we have out-of-focusedly almost forgotten them. Surely, the most valuable quality in any human being is his capacity for being loving and cooperative. We have been placing our emphases on the wrong values—it is time we recognized what every man and every woman at the very least subconsciously knows—the value of being loving, and the value of those who can teach this better than anyone else.

Physically and psychically women are by far the superiors of men. The old chestnut about women being more emotional than men has been forever destroyed by the facts of two great wars. Women under blockade, heavy bombardment, concentration camp confinement, and similar rigors withstand them vastly more successfully than men. The psychiatric casualties of civilian populations under such conditions are mostly masculine, and there are more men in our mental hospitals than there are women. The steady hand at the helm is the hand that has had the practice at rocking the cradle. Because of their greater size and weight men are physically more powerful than women—which is not the same thing as saying that they are stronger. A man of the same size and weight as a woman of comparable background and occupational status would probably not be any more powerful than a woman. As far as constitutional strength is concerned women are stronger than men. Many diseases from which men suffer can be shown to be largely influenced by their relation to the male Y-chromosome. From fertilization on more males die than females. Deaths from almost all causes are more frequent in males at all ages. Though women are more frequently ill than men, they recover from illness more easily and more frequently than men.

Women, in short, are fundamentally more resistant than men. With the exception of the organ systems subserving the functions of reproduction women suffer much less frequently than men from the serious disorders which affect mankind. With the exception of India women everywhere live longer than men. For example, the expectation of life of the female child of white parentage in the United States at the present time is over seventy-one years, whereas for the male it is only sixty-five and a half years. Women are both biologically stronger and emotionally better shock absorbers than men. The myth of masculine superiority once played such havoc with the facts that in the nineteenth century it was frequently denied by psychiatrists that the superior male could ever suffer from hysteria. Today it is fairly well known that males suffer from hysteria and hysteriform conditions with a preponderance over the female of seven to one! Epilepsy is much more frequent in males, and stuttering has an incidence of eight males to one female.

At least four disorders are now definitely known to be due to genes carried in the Y-chromosomes, and hence are disorders which can appear only in males. These are barklike skin (ichthyosis hystrix gravior), dense hairy growth on the ears (hypertrichosis), nonpainful hard lesions of the hands and feet (keratoma dissipatum), and a form of webbing of the toes. It is however, probable that the disadvantages accruing to the male are not so much due to what is in the Y-chromosome as to what is wanting in it. This is well shown in such serious disorders as hemophilia or bleeder's disease. Hemophilia is inherited as a single sex-linked recessive gene. The gene, or hereditary particle, determining hemophilia is linked to the X-chromosome. When, then, an X-chromosome which carries the hemophilia gene is transmitted to a female it is highly improbable that it will encounter another X-chromosome carrying such a gene; hence, while not impossible, hemophilia has never been described in a female. Females are the most usual transmitters of the hemophilia gene, but it is only the males who are affected, and they are affected because they don't have any properties in their Y-chromosome capable of suppressing the action of the hemophilia gene. The mechanism of and the explanation for (red-green) color blindness is the same. About 8 per cent of all white males are color blind, but only half of one per cent of females are so affected.

Need one go on? Here, in fact, we have the explanation of the greater constitutional strength of the female as compared with the male, namely, in the possession of two complete sex chromosomes by the female and only one by the male. This may not be, and probably is not, the complete explanation of the physical inferiorities of the male as compared with the female, but it is certainly physiologically the most demonstrable and least questionable one. To the unbiased student of the facts there can no longer remain any doubt of the constitutional superiority of the female. I hope that I have removed any remaining doubts about her psychological superiority where psychological superiority most counts, namely, in a human being's capacity for loving other human beings.

I think we have overemphasized the value of intellectual qualities and grossly underemphasized the value of the qualities of humanity which women possess to such a high degree. I hope I shall not be taken for an anti-intellectual when I say that intellect without humanity is not good enough, and that what the world is suffering from at the present time is not so much an overabundance of intellect as an insufficiency of humanity. Consider men like Lenin, Stalin, and Hitler. These are the extreme cases. What these men lacked was the capacity to love. What they possessed in so eminent a degree was the capacity to hate. It is not for nothing that the Bolsheviks attempted to abolish the family and masculinize women, while the Nazis made informers of children against their parents and put the state so much before the family that it became a behemoth which has well-nigh destroyed everyone who was victimized by it.

What the world stands so much in need of at the present time, and what it will continue to need if it is to endure and increase in happiness, is more of the maternal spirit and less of the masculine. We need more persons who will love and less who will hate, and we need to understand how we can produce them; for if we don't try to understand how we may do so we shall continue to flounder in the morass of misunderstanding which frustrated love creates. For frustrated love, the frustration of the tendencies to love with which the infant is born, constitutes hostility. Hatred is love frustrated. This is what too many men suffer from and an insufficient number of women recognize, or at least too many women behave as if they didn't recognize it. What most women have learned to recognize is that the much-bruited superiority of the male isn't all that it's cracked up to be. The male doesn't seem to be as wise and as steady as they were taught to believe. But there appears to be a conspiracy of silence on this subject. Perhaps women feel that men ought to be maintained in the illusion of their superiority because it might not be good for them or the world to learn the truth. In this sense this article, perhaps, should have been entitled "What Every Woman Knows." But I'm not sure that every woman knows it. What I am sure of is that many women don't appear to know it, and that there are even many women who are horrified at the thought that anyone can entertain the idea that women are anything but inferior to men. This sort of childishness does no one any good. The world is in a mess. Men, without any assistance from women, have created it, and they have created it not because they have been failed by women, but because men have never really given women a chance to serve them as they are best equipped to do—by teaching men how to love their fellow men.

Women must cease supporting men for the wrong reasons in the wrong sort of way, and thus cease causing men to marry them for the wrong reasons, too. "That's what a man wants in a wife, mostly," says Mrs. Poyser (in "Adam Bede"), "he wants to make sure o' one fool as 'ull tell him he's wise." Well, it's time that men learned the truth, and perhaps they are likely to take it more gracefully from another male than from their unacknowledged betters. It is equally important that women learn the truth, too, for it is to them that the most important part, the more fundamental part, of the task of remaking the world will fall, for the world will be remade only by remaking, or rather helping, human beings to realize themselves more fully in terms of what their mothers have to give them. Without adequate mothers life becomes inadequate, nasty, and unsatisfactory, and Mother Earth becomes a battlefield on which fathers slay their young and are themselves slain.

Men have had a long run for their money in running the affairs of the world. It is time that women realized that men will continue to run the world for some time yet, and that they can best assist them to run it more humanely by teaching them, when young, what humanity means. Men will thus not feel that they are being demoted, but rather that their potentialities for good are so much more increased, and what is more important, instead of feeling hostile towards women, they will for the first time learn to appreciate them at their proper worth. There is an old Spanish proverb which has it that a good wife is the workmanship of a good husband. Maybe. But of one thing we can be certain: a good husband is the workmanship of a good mother. The best of all ways in which men can help themselves is to help women realize themselves. This way both sexes will come for the first time fully into their own, and the world of mankind may then look forward to a happier history than it has thus far enjoyed.

QUESTIONS FOR STUDY AND DISCUSSION

1. What does Montagu accomplish by his opening paragraph?

2. Does Montagu's anthropological argument on the superiority of women convince you? What about the other arguments in this essay—for instance, that men often think "in terms of black and white" and that women "love the human race" while men are "hostile to it"?

3. Granting that women are superior to men, does it follow that an increase of "the maternal spirit" will bring happier times to the human race?

WRITING ASSIGNMENT

Write an essay arguing from your own experience that Montagu's contention that women "love the human race" is (is not) so.

JOHN HENRY NEWMAN

Knowledge Viewed in Relation to Learning

It were well if the English, like the Greek language, possessed some definite word to express, simply and generally, intellectual proficiency or perfection, such as "health," as used with reference to the animal frame, and "virtue," with reference to our moral nature. I am not able to find such a term; —talent, ability, genius, belong distinctly to the raw material, which is the subject-matter, not to that excellence which is the result of exercise and training. When we turn, indeed, to the particular kinds of intellectual perfection, words are forthcoming for our purpose, as, for instance, judgment, taste, and skill; yet even these belong, for the most part, to powers or habits bearing upon practice or upon art, and not to any perfect condition of the intellect, considered in itself. Wisdom, again, is certainly a more comprehensive word than any other, but it has a direct relation to conduct, and to human life. Knowledge, indeed, and Science express purely intellectual ideas, but still not a state or quality of the intellect; for knowledge, in its ordinary sense, is but one of its circumstances, denoting a possession or a habit; and science has been appropriated to the subject-matter of the intellect, instead of belonging in English, as it ought to do, to the intellect itself. The consequence is that, on an occasion like this, many words are necessary, in order, first, to bring out and convey what surely is no difficult idea in itself,—that of the cultivation of the intellect as an end; next, in order to recommend what surely is no unreasonable object; and lastly, to describe and make the mind realize the particular perfection in which that object consists. Every one knows practically what are the constituents of health or of virtue; and every one recognizes health and virtue as ends to be pursued; it is otherwise with

intellectual excellence, and this must be my excuse, if I seem to any one to be bestowing a good deal of labour on a preliminary matter.

In default of a recognized term, I have called the perfection or virtue of the intellect by the name of philosophy, philosophical knowledge, enlargement of mind, or illumination; terms which are not uncommonly given to it by writers of this day: but, whatever name we bestow on it, it is, I believe, as a matter of history, the business of a University to make this intellectual culture its direct scope, or to employ itself in the education of the intellect,—just as the work of a Hospital lies in healing the sick or wounded, of a Riding or Fencing School, or of a Gymnasium, in exercising the limbs, of an Almshouse, in aiding and solacing the old, of an Orphanage, in protecting innocence, of a Penitentiary, in restoring the guilty. I say, a University, taken in its bare idea, and before we view it as an instrument of the Church, has this object and this mission; it contemplates neither moral impression nor mechanical production; it professes to exercise the mind neither in art nor in duty; its function is intellectual culture; here it may leave its scholars, and it has done its work when it has done as much as this. It educates the intellect to reason well in all matters, to reach out towards truth, and to grasp it.

This, I said in my foregoing Discourse, was the object of a University, viewed in itself, and apart from the Catholic Church, or from the State, or from any other power which may use it; and I illustrated this in various ways. I said that the intellect must have an excellence of its own, for there was nothing which had not its specific good; that the word "educate" would not be used of intellectual culture, as it is used, had not the intellect had an end of its own; that, had it not such an end, there would be no meaning in calling certain intellectual exercises "liberal," in contrast with "useful," as is commonly done; that the very notion of a philosophical temper implied it, for it threw us back upon research and system as ends in themselves, distinct from effects and works of any kind; that a philosophical scheme of knowledge, or system of sciences, could not, from the nature of the case, issue in any one definite art or pursuit, as its end; and that, on the other hand, the discovery and contemplation of truth, to which research and systematizing led, were surely sufficient ends, though nothing beyond them were added, and that they had ever been accounted sufficient by mankind.

Here then I take up the subject; and, having determined that the cultivation of the intellect is an end distinct and sufficient in itself, and that, so far as words go, it is an enlargement or illumination, I proceed to inquire what this mental breadth, or power, or light, or philosophy consists in. A hospital heals a broken limb or cures a fever: what does an Institution effect which professes the health, not of the body, not of the soul, but of the intellect? What is this good, which in former times, as well as our own, has been found worth the notice, the appropriation, of the Catholic Church?

I have then to investigate, in the Discourses which follow, those qualities and characteristics of the intellect in which its cultivation issues or rather consists; and, with a view of assisting myself in this undertaking, I shall recur to certain questions which have already been touched upon. These questions are three: viz. the relation of intellectual culture, first, to *mere* knowledge; secondly, to *professional* knowledge; and thirdly, to *religious* knowledge. In other words, are *acquirements* and *attainments* the scope of a University Education? or *expertness in particular arts* and *pursuits?* or *moral and religious proficiency?* or something besides these three? These questions I shall examine in succession, with the purpose I have mentioned; and I hope to be excused, if, in this anxious undertaking, I am led to repeat what, either in these Discourses or elsewhere, I have already put upon paper. And first, of *Mere Knowledge,* or Learning, and its connection with intellectual illumination or Philosophy.

I suppose the *prima-facie* view which the public at large would take of a University, considering it as a place of Education, is nothing more or less than a place for acquir-ing a great deal of knowledge on a great many subjects. Memory is one of the first developed of the mental faculties; a boy's business when he goes to school is to learn, that is, to store up things in his memory. For some years his intellect is little more than an instrument for taking in facts, or a receptacle for storing them; he welcomes them as fast as they come to him; he lives on what is without; he has his eyes ever about him; he has a lively susceptibility of impressions; he imbibes information of every kind; and little does he make his own in a true sense of the word, living rather upon his neighbours all around him. He has opinions, religious, political and literary, and, for a boy, is very positive in them and sure about them; but he gets them from his schoolfellows, or his masters, or his parents, as the case may be. Such as he is in his other relations, such also is he in his school exercises; his mind is observant, sharp, ready, retentive; he is almost passive in the acquisition of knowledge. I say this in no disparagement of the idea of a clever boy. Geography, chronology, history, language, natural history, he heaps up the matter of these studies as treasures for a future day. It is the seven years of plenty with him: he gathers in by handfuls, like the Egyptians, without counting; and though, as time goes on, there is exercise for his argumentative powers in the Elements of Mathematics, and for his taste in the Poets and Orators, still, while at school, or at least, till quite the last years of his time, he acquires, and little more; and when he is leaving for the University, he is mainly the creature of foreign influences and circumstances, and made up of accidents, homogeneous or not, as the case may be. Moreover, the moral habits, which are a boy's praise, encourage and assist this result; that is, diligence, assiduity, regularity, despatch, persevering application; for these are the direct conditions of acquisition, and naturally lead to it. Acquirements, again, are emphatically producible, and at a moment; they are a something to show, both for master and scholar; an audience, even though ignorant themselves of the subject of an examination, can comprehend when questions are answered and when they are not. Here again is a reason why mental culture is in the minds of men identified with the acquisition of knowledge.

The same notion possesses the public mind, when it passes on from the thought of a school to that of a University: and with the best of reasons so far as this, that there is no true culture without acquirements, and that philosophy presupposes knowledge. It requires a great deal of reading, or a wide range of information, to warrant us in putting forth our opinions on any serious subject; and without such learning the most original mind may be able indeed to dazzle, to amuse, to refute, to perplex, but not to come to any useful result or any trustworthy conclusion. There are indeed persons who profess a different view of the matter, and even act upon it. Every now and then you will find a person of vigorous or fertile mind, who relies upon his own resources, despises all former authors, and gives the world, with the utmost fearlessness, his views upon religion, or history, or any other popular subject. And his works may sell for a while; he may get a name in his day; but this will be all. His readers are sure to find on the long run that his doctrines are mere theories, and not the expression of facts, that they are chaff instead of bread, and then his popularity drops as suddenly as it rose.

Knowledge then is the indispensable condition of expansion of mind, and the instrument of attaining to it; this cannot be denied, it is ever to be insisted on; I begin with it as a first principle; however, the very truth of it carries men too far, and confirms to them the notion that it is the whole of the matter. A narrow mind is thought to be that which contains little knowledge; and an enlarged mind, that which holds a great deal; and what seems to put the matter beyond dispute is, the fact of the great number of studies which are pursued in a University, by its very profession. Lectures are given on every kind of subject; examinations are held; prizes awarded. There are moral, metaphysical, physical Professors; Professors of languages, of history, of mathematics, of experimental science. Lists of questions are published, wonderful for their range and depth, variety and difficulty; treatises are written, which carry upon their very face the evidence of extensive reading or multifarious

information; what then is wanting for mental culture to a person of large reading and scientific attainments? what is grasp of mind but acquirement? where shall philosophical repose be found, but in the consciousness and enjoyment of large intellectual possessions?

And yet this notion is, I conceive, a mistake, and my present business is to show that it is one, and that the end of a Liberal Education is not mere knowledge, or knowledge considered in its *matter*; and I shall best attain my object, by actually setting down some cases, which will be generally granted to be instances of the process of enlightenment or enlargement of mind, and others which are not, and thus, by the comparison, you will be able to judge for yourselves, Gentlemen, whether Knowledge, that is, acquirement, is after all the real principle of the enlargement, or whether that principle is not rather something beyond it.

For instance, let a person, whose experience has hitherto been confined to the more calm and unpretending scenery of these islands, whether here or in England, go for the first time into parts where physical nature puts on her wilder and more awful forms, whether at home or abroad, as into mountainous districts; or let one, who has ever lived in a quiet village, go for the first time to a great metropolis,—then I suppose he will have a sensation which perhaps he never had before. He has a feeling not in addition or increase of former feelings, but of something different in its nature. He will perhaps be borne forward, and find for a time that he has lost his bearings. He has made a certain progress, and he has a consciousness of mental enlargement; he does not stand where he did, he has a new centre, and a range of thoughts to which he was before a stranger.

Again, the view of the heavens which the telescope opens upon us, if allowed to fill and possess the mind, may almost whirl it round and make it dizzy. It brings in a flood of ideas, and is rightly called an intellectual enlargement, whatever is meant by the term.

And so again, the sight of beasts of prey and other foreign animals, their strangeness, the originality (if I may use the term) of their forms and gestures and habits, and their variety and independence of each other, throw us out of ourselves into another creation, and as if under another Creator, if I may so express the temptation which may come on the mind. We seem to have new faculties, or a new exercise for our faculties, by this addition to our knowledge; like a prisoner, who, having been accustomed to wear manacles or fetters, suddenly finds his arms and legs free.

Hence Physical Science generally, in all its departments, as bringing before us the exuberant riches and resources, yet the orderly course, of the Universe, elevates and excites the student, and at first, I may say, almost takes away his breath, while in time it exercises a tranquillizing influence upon him.

Again, the study of history is said to enlarge and enlighten the mind, and why? because, as I conceive, it gives it a power of judging of passing events, and of all events, and a conscious superiority over them, which before it did not possess.

And in like manner, what is called seeing the world, entering into active life, going into society, travelling, gaining acquaintance with the various classes of the community, coming into contact with the principles and modes of thought of various parties, interests, and races, their views, aims, habits and manners, their religious creeds and forms of worship,—gaining experience how various yet how alike men are, how low-minded, how bad, how opposed, yet how confident in their opinions; all this exerts a perceptible influence upon the mind, which it is impossible to mistake, be it good or be it bad, and is popularly called its enlargement.

And then again, the first time the mind comes across the arguments and speculations of unbelievers, and feels what a novel light they cast upon what he has hitherto accounted sacred; and still more, if it gives in to them and embraces them, and throws off as so much prejudice what it has hitherto held, and, as if waking from a dream, begins to realize to its imagination that there is now no such thing as law and the transgression of law, that sin is a phantom, and punishment a bugbear, that it is free to sin, free to enjoy the world and the flesh; and still

further, when it does enjoy them, and reflects that it may think and hold just what it will, that "the world is all before it where to choose," and what system to build up as its own private persuasion; when this torrent of wilful thoughts rushes over and inundates it, who will deny that the fruit of the tree of knowledge, or what the mind takes for knowledge, has made it one of the gods, with a sense of expansion and elevation,—an intoxication in reality, still, so far as the subjective state of the mind goes, an illumination? Hence the fanaticism of individuals or nations, who suddenly cast off their Maker. Their eyes are opened; and, like the judgment-stricken king in the Tragedy, they see two suns, and a magic universe, out of which they look back upon their former state of faith and innocence with a sort of contempt and indignation, as if they were then but fools, and the dupes of imposture.

On the other hand, Religion has its own enlargement, and an enlargement, not of tumult, but of peace. It is often remarked of uneducated persons, who have hitherto thought little of the unseen world, that, on their turning to God, looking into themselves, regulating their hearts, reforming their conduct, and meditating on death and judgment, heaven and hell, they seem to become, in point of intellect, different beings from what they were. Before, they took things as they came, and thought no more of one thing than another. But now every event has a meaning; they have their own estimate of whatever happens to them; they are mindful of times and seasons, and compare the present with the past; and the world, no longer dull, monotonous, unprofitable, and hopeless, is a various and complicated drama, with parts and an object, and an awful moral.

Now from these instances, to which many more might be added, it is plain, first, that the communication of knowledge certainly is either a condition or the means of that sense of enlargement, or enlightenment of which at this day we hear so much in certain quarters: this cannot be denied; but next, it is equally plain, that such communication is not the whole of the process. The enlargement consists, not merely in the passive reception into the mind of a number of ideas hitherto unknown to it, but in the mind's energetic and simultaneous action upon and towards and among those new ideas, which are rushing in upon it. It is the action of a formative power, reducing to order and meaning the matter of our acquirements; it is a making the objects of our knowledge subjectively our own, or, to use a familiar word, it is a digestion of what we receive, into the substance of our previous state of thought; and without this no enlargement is said to follow. There is no enlargement, unless there be a comparison of ideas one with another, as they come before the mind, and a systematizing of them. We feel our minds to be growing and expanding *then*, when we not only learn, but refer what we learn to what we know already. It is not the mere addition to our knowledge that is the illumination; but the locomotion, the movement onwards, of that mental centre, to which both what we know, and what we are learning, the accumulating mass of our acquirements, gravitates. And therefore a truly great intellect, and recognized to be such by the common opinion of mankind, such as the intellect of Aristotle, or of St. Thomas, or of Newton, or of Goethe (I purposely take instances within and without the Catholic pale, when I would speak of the intellect as such), is one which takes a connected view of old and new, past and present, far and near, and which has an insight into the influence of all these one on another; without which there is no whole, and no centre. It possesses the knowledge, not only of things, but also of their mutual and true relations; knowledge, not merely considered as acquirement but as philosophy.

Accordingly, when this analytical, distributive, harmonizing process is away, the mind experiences no enlargement, and is not reckoned as enlightened or comprehensive, whatever it may add to its knowledge. For instance, a great memory, as I have already said, does not make a philosopher, any more than a dictionary can be called a grammar. There are men who embrace in their minds a vast multitude of ideas, but with little sensibility about their real relations towards each other. These may be antiquarians, annalists, naturalists; they may be learned in the law; they may be versed in statistics; they are most useful in their own place; I should shrink from speaking disrespectfully of them; still, there is nothing in such attainments to guarantee the absence of narrowness of mind. If they are nothing more than well-read men, or men of information, they have not what specially deserves the name of culture of mind, or fulfils the type of Liberal Education.

In like manner, we sometimes fall in with persons who have seen much of the world, and of the men who, in their day, have played a conspicuous part in it, but who generalize nothing, and have no observation, in the true sense of the word. They abound in information in detail, curious and entertaining, about men and things; and, having lived under the influence of no very clear or settled principles, religious or political, they speak of every one and every thing, only as so many phenomena, which are complete in themselves, and lead to nothing, not discussing them, or teaching any truth, or instructing the hearer, but simply talking. No one would say that these persons, well informed as they are, had attained to any great culture of intellect or to philosophy.

The case is the same still more strikingly where the persons in question are beyond dispute men of inferior powers and deficient education. Perhaps they have been much in foreign countries, and they receive, in a passive, otiose, unfruitful way, the various facts which are forced upon them there. Seafaring men, for example, range from one end of the earth to the other; but the multiplicity of external objects, which they have encountered, forms no symmetrical and consistent picture upon their imagination; they see the tapestry of human life, as it were on the wrong side, and it tells no story. They sleep, and they rise up, and they find themselves, now in Europe, now in Asia; they see visions of great cities and wild regions; they are in the marts of commerce, or amid the islands of the South; they gaze on Pompey's Pillar, or on the Andes; and nothing which meets them carries them forward or backward, to any idea beyond itself. Nothing has a drift or relation; nothing has a history or a promise. Every thing stands by itself, and comes and goes in its turn, like the shifting scenes of a show, which leave the spectator where he was. Perhaps you are near such a man on a particular occasion, and expect him to be shocked or perplexed at something which occurs; but one thing is much the same to him as another, or, if he is perplexed, it is as not knowing what to say, whether it is right to admire, or to ridicule, or to disapprove, while conscious that some expression of opinion is expected from him; for in fact he has no standard of judgment at all, and no landmarks to guide him to a conclusion. Such is mere acquisition, and, I repeat, no one would dream of calling it philosophy.

Instances, such as these, confirm, by the contrast, the conclusion I have already drawn from those which preceded them. That only is true enlargement of mind which is the power of viewing many things at once as one whole, of referring them severally to their true place in the universal system, of understanding their respective values, and determining their mutual dependence. Thus is that form of Universal Knowledge, of which I have on a former occasion spoken, set up in the individual intellect, and constitutes its perfection. Possessed of this real illumination, the mind never views any part of the extended subject-matter of Knowledge without recollecting that it is but a part, or without the associations which spring from this recollection. It makes everything in some sort lead to everything else; it would communicate the image of the whole to every separate portion, till that whole becomes in imagination like a spirit, everywhere pervading and penetrating its component parts, and giving them one definite meaning. Just as our bodily organs, when mentioned, recall their function in the body, as the word "creation" suggests the Creator, and "subjects" a sovereign, so, in the mind of the Philosopher, as we are abstractedly conceiving of him, the elements of the physical and moral world, sciences, arts, pursuits, ranks, offices, events, opinions, individualities, are all viewed as one, with correlative functions, and as gradually by successive combinations converging, one and all, to the true centre.

To have even a portion of this illuminative reason and true philosophy is the highest state to which nature can aspire, in the way of intellect; it puts the mind above the influences of chance and necessity, above anxiety, suspense, unsettlement, and superstition, which is the lot of the many. Men, whose minds are possessed with some one object, take exaggerated views of its importance, are feverish in the pursuit of it, make it the measure of things which are utterly foreign to it, and are startled and despond if it happens to fail them. They are ever in alarm or in transport. Those on the other hand who have no object or principle whatever to hold by, lose their way every step they take. They are thrown out, and do not know what to think or say, at every fresh juncture; they have no view of persons, or occurrences, or facts, which come suddenly upon them, and they hang upon the opinion of others for want of internal resources. But the intellect, which has been disciplined to the perfection of its powers, which knows, and thinks while it knows, which has learned to leaven the dense mass of facts and events with the elastic force of reason, such an intellect cannot be partial, cannot be exclusive, cannot be impetuous, cannot be at a loss, cannot but be patient, collected, and majestically calm, because it discerns the end in every beginning, the origin in every end, the law in every interruption, the limit in each delay; because it ever knows where it stands, and how its path lies from one point to another. It is the τετράγωνος of the Peripatetic, and has the "nil admirari" of the Stoic,—

Felix qui potuit rerum cognoscere causas,
Atque metus omnes, et inexorabile fatum
Subjecit pedibus, strepitumque Acherontis
    avari.

There are men who, when in difficulties, originate at the moment vast ideas or dazzling projects; who, under the influence of excitement, are able to cast a light, almost as if from inspiration, on a subject or course of action which comes before them; who have a sudden presence of mind equal to any emergency, rising with the occasion, and an undaunted magnanimous bearing, and an energy and keenness which is but made intense by opposition. This is genius, this is heroism; it is the exhibition of a natural gift, which no culture can teach, at which no Institution can aim: here, on the contrary, we are concerned, not with mere nature, but with training and teaching. That perfection of the Intellect, which is the result of Education, and its *beau ideal*, to be imparted to individuals in their respective measures, is the clear, calm, accurate vision and comprehension of all things, as far as the finite mind can embrace them, each in its place, and with its own characteristics upon it. It is almost prophetic from its knowledge of history; it is almost heart-searching from its knowledge of human nature; it has almost supernatural charity from its freedom from littleness and prejudice; it has almost the repose of faith, because nothing can startle it; it has almost the beauty and harmony of heavenly contemplation, so intimate is it with the eternal order of things and the music of the spheres.

And now, if I may take for granted that the true and adequate end of intellectual training and of a University is not Learning or Acquirement, but rather, is Thought or Reason exercised upon Knowledge, or what may be called Philosophy, I shall be in a position to explain the various mistakes which at the present day beset the subject of University Education.

I will tell you, Gentlemen, what has been the practical error of the last twenty years,—not to load the memory of the student with a mass of undigested knowledge, but to force upon him so much that he has rejected all. It has been the error of distracting and enfeebling the mind by an unmeaning profusion of subjects; of implying that a smattering in a dozen branches of study is not shallowness, which it really is, but enlargement, which it is not; of considering an acquaintance with the learned names of things and persons, and the possession of clever duodecimos, and attendance on eloquent lecturers, and membership with scientific institutions, and the sight of the experiments of a platform and the specimens of a museum, that all this was not dissipation of mind, but progress. All things now are to be learned at once, not first one thing, then another, not one well, but many badly. Learning is to be without exertion, without attention, without toil; without grounding, without advance, without finishing. There is to be nothing individual in it; and this, forsooth, is the wonder of the age. What the steam engine does with matter, the printing-press is to do with mind; it is to act mechanically, and the population is to be passively, almost unconsciously enlightened, by the mere multiplication and dissemination of volumes. Whether it be the school-boy, or the school-girl, or the youth at college, or the mechanic in the town, or the politician in the senate, all have been the victims in one way or other of this most preposterous and pernicious of delusions. Wise men have lifted up their voices in vain; and at length, lest their own institutions should be outshone and should disappear in the folly of the hour, they have been obliged, as far as they could with a good conscience, to humour a spirit which they could not withstand, and make temporizing concessions at which they could not but inwardly smile.

I protest to you, Gentlemen, that if I had to choose between a so-called University, which dispensed with residence and tutorial superintendence, and gave its degrees to any person who passed an examination in a wide range of subjects, and a University which had no professors or examinations at all, but merely brought a number of young men together for three or four years, and then sent them away as the University of Oxford is said to have done some sixty years since, if I were asked which of these two methods was the better discipline of the intellect,—mind, I do not say which is *morally* the better, for it is plain that compulsory study must be a good and idleness an intolerable mischief,—but if I must determine which of the two courses was the more successful in training, moulding, enlarging the mind, which sent out men the more fitted for their secular duties, which produced better public men, men of the world, men whose names would descend to posterity, I have no hesitation in giving the preference to that University which did nothing, over that which exacted of its members an acquaintance with every science under the sun. And, paradox as this may seem, still if results be the test of systems, the influence of the public schools and colleges of England, in the course of the last century, at least will bear out one side of the contrast as I have drawn it. What would come, on the other hand, of the ideal systems of education which have fascinated the imagination of this age, could they ever take effect and whether they would not produce a generation frivolous, narrow-minded, and resourceless, intellectually considered, is a fair subject for debate; but so far is certain, that the Universities and scholastic establishments, to which I refer, and which did little more than bring together first boys and then youths in large numbers, these institutions, with miserable deformities on the side of morals, with a hollow profession of Christianity, and a heathen code of ethics,—I say, at least they can boast of a succession of heroes and statesmen, of literary men and philosophers, of men conspicuous for great natural virtues, for habits of business, for knowledge of life, for practical judgment, for cultivated tastes, for accomplishments, who have made England what it is,—able to subdue the earth, able to domineer over Catholics.

How is this to be explained? I suppose as follows: When a multitude of young men, keen, open-hearted, sympathetic, and observant, as young men are, come together and freely mix with each other, they are sure to learn one from another, even if there be no one to teach them; the conversation of all is a series of lectures to each, and they gain for themselves new ideas and views, fresh matter of thought, and distinct principles for judging and acting, day by day. An infant has to learn the meaning of the information which its senses convey to it, and this seems to be its employment. It fancies all that the eye presents to it to be close to it, till it actually learns the contrary, and thus by practice does it ascertain the relations and uses of those first elements of

knowledge which are necessary for its animal existence. A parallel teaching is necessary for our social being, and it is secured by a large school or a college; and this effect may be fairly called in its own department an enlargement of mind. It is seeing the world on a small field with little trouble; for the pupils or students come from very different places, and with widely different notions, and there is much to generalize, much to adjust, much to eliminate, there are interrelations to be defined, and conventional rules to be established, in the process, by which the whole assemblage is moulded together, and gains one tone and one character.

Let it be clearly understood, I repeat it, that I am not taking into account moral or religious considerations; I am but saying that that youthful community will constitute a whole, it will embody a specific idea, it will represent a doctrine, it will administer a code of conduct, and it will furnish principles of thought and action. It will give birth to a living teaching, which in course of time will take the shape of a self-perpetuating tradition, or a *genius loci*, as it is sometimes called; which haunts the home where it has been born, and which imbues and forms, more or less, and one by one, every individual who is successively brought under its shadow. Thus it is that, independent of direct instruction on the part of Superiors, there is a sort of self-education in the academic institutions of Protestant England; a characteristic tone of thought, a recognized standard of judgment is found in them, which if developed in the individual who is submitted to it, becomes a twofold source of strength to him, both from the distinct stamp it impresses on his mind, and from the bond of union which it creates between him and others,—effects which are shared by the authorities of the place, for they themselves have been educated in it, and at all times are exposed to the influence of its ethical atmosphere. Here then is a real teaching whatever be its standards and principles, true or false, and it at least tends towards cultivation of the intellect; it at least recognizes that knowledge is something more than a sort of passive reception of scraps and details; it is a something, and it does a something, which never will issue from the most strenuous efforts of a set of teachers, with no mutual sympathies and no inter-communion, of a set of examiners with no opinions which they dare profess, and with no common principles, who are teaching or questioning a set of youths who do not know them, and do not know each other, on a large number of subjects, different in kind, and connected by no wide philosophy, three times a week, or three times a year, or once in three years, in chill lecture-rooms or on a pompous anniversary.

QUESTIONS FOR STUDY AND DISCUSSION

1. How does Newman show that "the cultivation of the intellect" is in itself a good end?

2. What does Newman mean by *Learning*? By *Philosophy*? What is the relation-ship between the two?

3. What is the "practical error of the last twenty years" which Newman finds so disagreeable? What effect has this error had upon your own education?

WRITING ASSIGNMENTS

1. Write an outline of the arguments treated in this article. How does Newman use transitions, summaries, and lists of topics to guide the reader's attention?

2. What should a college or university attempt to teach you, both in class and out? Argue your position in a carefully reasoned essay.

A SQUARE
(EDWIN A. ABBOTT)

from

Flatland

I. Most illustrious Sir, excuse my awkwardness, which arises not from ignorance of the usages of polite society, but from a little surprise and nervousness, consequent on this somewhat unexpected visit. And I beseech you to reveal my indiscretion to no one, and especially not to my Wife. But before your Lordship enters into further communications, would he deign to satisfy the curiosity of one who would gladly know whence his Visitor came?

Stranger. From Space, from Space, Sir: whence else?

I. Pardon me, my Lord, but is not your Lordship already in Space, your Lordship and his humble servant, even at this moment?

Stranger. Pooh! what do you know of Space? Define Space.

I. Space, my Lord, is height and breadth indefinitely prolonged.

Stranger. Exactly: you see you do not even know what Space is. You think it is of Two Dimensions only; but I have come to announce to you a Third—height, breadth, and length.

I. Your Lordship is pleased to be merry. We also speak of length and height, or breadth and thickness, thus denoting Two Dimensions by four names.

Stranger. But I mean not only three names, but Three Dimensions.

I. Would your Lordship indicate or explain to me in what direction is the Third Dimension, unknown to me?

Stranger. I came from it. It is up above and down below.

I. My Lord means seemingly that it is Northward and Southward.

Stranger. I mean nothing of the kind. I mean a direction in which you cannot look, because you have no eye in your side.

I. Pardon me, my Lord, a moment's inspection will convince your Lordship that I have a perfect luminary at the juncture of two of my sides.

Stranger. Yes: but in order to see into Space you ought to have an eye, not on your Perimeter, but on your side, that is, on what you would probably call your inside; but we in Spaceland should call it your side.

I. An eye in my inside! An eye in my stomach! Your Lordship jests.

Stranger. I am in no jesting humour. I tell you that I come from Space, or, since you will not understand what Space means, from the Land of Three Dimensions whence I but lately looked down upon your Plane which you call Space forsooth. From that position of advantage I discerned all that you speak of as *solid* (by which you mean "enclosed on four sides"), your houses, your churches, your very chests and safes, yes even your insides and stomachs, all lying open and exposed to my view.

I. Such assertions are easily made, my Lord.

Stranger. But not easily proved, you mean. But I mean to prove mine.

When I descended here, I saw your four Sons, the Pentagons, each in his apartment, and your two Grandsons the Hexagons; I saw your youngest Hexagon remain a while with you and then retire to his room, leaving you and your Wife alone. I saw your Isosceles servants, three in number, in the kitchen at supper, and the little Page in the scullery. Then I came here, and how do you think I came?

I. Through the roof, I suppose.

Stranger. Not so. Your roof, as you know very well, has been recently repaired, and has no aperture by which even a Woman could penetrate. I tell you I come from Space. Are you not convinced by what I have told you of your children and household.

I. Your Lordship must be aware that such facts touching the belongings of his humble servant might be easily ascertained by any one in the neighbourhood possessing your Lordship's ample means of obtaining information.

Stranger. (To himself). What must I do? Stay; one more argument suggests itself to me. When you see a Straight Line—your wife, for example—how many Dimensions do you attribute to her?

I. Your Lordship would treat me as if I were one of the vulgar who, being ignorant of Mathematics, suppose that a Woman is really a Straight Line, and only of One Dimension. No, no, my Lord; we Squares are better advised, and are as well aware as your Lordship that a Woman, though popularly called a Straight Line, is, really and scientifically, a very thin Parallelogram, possessing Two Dimensions, like the rest of us, viz., length and breadth (or thickness).

Stranger. But the very fact that a Line is visible implies that it possesses yet another Dimension.

I. My Lord, I have just acknowledged that a Woman is broad as well as long. We see her length, we infer her breadth; which, though very slight, is capable of measurement.

Stranger. You do not understand me. I mean that when you see a Woman, you ought—besides inferring her breadth—to see her length, and to *see* what we call her *height*; although that last Dimension is infinitesimal in your country. If a line were mere length without "height," it would cease to occupy space and would become invisible. Surely you must recognize this?

I. I must indeed confess that I do not in the least understand your Lordship. When we in Flatland see a Line, we see length and *brightness*. If the brightness disappears, the line is extinguished, and, as you say, ceases to occupy space. But am I to suppose that your Lordship gives to brightness the title of a Dimension, and that what we call "bright" you call "high"?

Stranger. No, indeed. By "height" I mean a Dimension like your length: only, with you, "height" is not so easily perceptible, being extremely small.

I. My Lord, your assertion is easily put to the test. You say I have a Third Dimension, which you call "height." Now, Dimension implies direction and measurement. Do but measure my "height," or merely indicate to me the direction in which my "height" ex-

tends, and I will become your convert. Otherwise, your Lordship's own understanding must hold me excused.

Stranger. (To himself). I can do neither. How shall I convince him? Surely a plain statement of facts followed by ocular demonstration ought to suffice.—Now, Sir; listen to me.

You are living on a Plane. What you style Flatland is the vast level surface of what I may call a fluid, on, or in, the top of which you and your countrymen move about, without rising above it or falling below it.

I am not a plane Figure, but a Solid. You call me a Circle; but in reality I am not a Circle, but an infinite number of Circles, of size varying from a Point to a Circle of thirteen inches in diameter, one placed on top of the other. When I cut through your plane as I am now doing, I make in your plane a section which you, very rightly, call a Circle. For even a Sphere—which is my proper name in my own country—if he manifest himself at all to an inhabitant of Flatland—must needs manifest himself as a Circle.

Do you not remember—for I, who see all things, discerned last night the phantasmal vision of Lineland written upon your brain —do you not remember, I say, how, when you entered the realm of Lineland, you were compelled to manifest yourself to the King not as a Square, but as a Line, because that Linear Realm had not Dimensions enough to represent the whole of you, but only a slice or section of you? In precisely the same way, your country of Two Dimensions is not spacious enough to represent me, a being of Three, but can only exhibit a slice or section of me, which is what you call a Circle.

The diminished brightness of your eye indicates incredulity. But now prepare to receive proof positive of the truth of my assertions. You cannot indeed see more than one of my sections, or Circles, at a time; for you have no power to raise your eye out of the plane of Flatland; but you can at least see that, as I rise in Space, so my section becomes smaller. See now, I will rise; and the effect upon your eye will be that my Circle will become smaller and smaller till it dwindles to a point and finally vanishes.

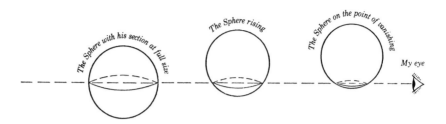

There was no "rising" that I could see; but he diminished and finally vanished. I winked once or twice to make sure that I was not dreaming. But it was no dream. For from the depths of nowhere came forth a hollow voice—close to my heart it seemed—"Am I quite gone? Are you convinced now? Well, now I will gradually return to Flatland, and you shall see my section become larger and larger."

Every reader in Spaceland will easily understand that my mysterious Guest was speaking the language of truth and even of simplicity. But to me, proficient though I was in Flatland Mathematics, it was by no means a simple matter. The rough diagram given above will make it clear to any Spaceland child that the Sphere, ascending in the three positions indicated there, must needs have manifested himself to me, or to any Flatlander, as a Circle, at first of full size, then small, and at last very small indeed, approaching to a Point. But to me, although I saw the facts before me, the causes were as dark as ever. All that I could comprehend was, that the Circle had made himself smaller and vanished, and that he had now reappeared and was rapidly making himself larger.

When he had regained his original size, he heaved a deep sigh; for he perceived by my silence that I had altogether failed to comprehend him. And indeed I was now inclining to the belief that he must be no Circle at all, but some extremely clever juggler; or else that the old wives' tales were true, and that after all there were such people as Enchanters and Magicians.

After a long pause he muttered to him-self, "One resource alone remains, if I am not to resort to action. I must try the method of Analogy." Then followed a still longer silence, after which he continued our dialogue.

Sphere. Tell me, Mr. Mathematician; if a Point moves Northward, and leaves a luminous wake, what name would you give to the wake?

I. A straight Line.

Sphere. And a straight Line has how many extremities?

I. Two.

Sphere. Now conceive the Northward straight line moving parallel to itself, East and West, so that every point in it leaves behind it the wake of a straight Line. What name will you give to the Figure thereby formed? We will suppose that it moves through a distance equal to the original straight Line.—What name, I say?

I. A Square.

Sphere. And how many sides has a Square? And how many angles?

I. Four sides and four angles.

Sphere. Now stretch your imagination a little, and conceive a Square in Flatland, moving parallel to itself upward.

I. What? Northward?

Sphere. No, not Northward; upward; out of Flatland altogether.

If it moved Northward, the Southern points in the Square would have to move through the positions previously occupied by the Northern points. But that is not my meaning.

I mean that every Point in you—for you are a Square and will serve the purpose of my illustration—every Point in you, that is to say in what you call your inside, is to pass upwards through Space in such a way that no Point shall pass through the position previously occupied by any other Point; but each Point shall describe a straight Line of its own. This is all in accordance with Analogy; surely it must be clear to you.

Restraining my impatience—for I was now under a strong temptation to rush blindly at my Visitor and to precipitate him into Space, or out of Flatland, anywhere, so that I could get rid of him—I replied:—

"And what may be the nature of the Figure which I am to shape out by this motion which you are pleased to denote by the word 'upward'? I presume it is describable in the language of Flatland."

Sphere. Oh, certainly. It is all plain and simple, and in strict accordance with Analogy—only, by the way, you must not speak of the result as being a Figure, but as a Solid. But I will describe it to you. Or rather not I, but Analogy.

We began with a single Point, which of course—being itself a Point—has only *one* terminal Point.

One Point produces a Line with *two* terminal Points.

One Line produces a Square with *four* terminal Points.

Now you can yourself give the answer to your own question: 1, 2, 4, are evidently in Geometrical Progression. What is the next number.

I. Eight.

Sphere. Exactly. The one Square produces a *Something-which-you-do-not-as-yet-know-a-name-for-but-which-we-call-a-Cube* with *eight* terminal Points. Now are you convinced?

I. And has this Creature sides, as well as angles or what you call "terminal Points"?

Sphere. Of course; and all according to Analogy. But, by the way, not what *you* call sides, but what *we* call sides. You would call them *solids*.

I. And how many solids or sides will appertain to this Being whom I am to generate by the motion of my inside in an "upward" direction and whom you call a Cube?

Sphere. How can you ask? And you a mathematician! The side of anything is always, if I may so say, one Dimension behind the thing. Consequently, as there is no Dimension behind a Point, a Point has 0 sides; a Line, if I may so say, has 2 sides (for the Points of a Line may be called by courtesy, its sides); a Square has 4 sides; 0, 2, 4; what Progression do you call that?

I. Arithmetical.

Sphere. And what is the next number?

I. Six.

Sphere. Exactly. Then you see you have answered your own question. The Cube which you will generate will be bounded by six sides, that is to say, six of your insides. You see it all now, eh?

"Monster," I shrieked, "be thou juggler, enchanter, dream, or devil, no more will I endure thy mockeries. Either thou or I must perish." And saying these words I precipitated myself upon him. . . .

The Sphere would willingly have continued his lessons by indoctrinating me in the conformation of all regular Solids, Cylinders, Cones, Pyramids, Pentahedrons, Hexahedrons, Dodecahedrons and Spheres: but I ventured to interrupt him. Not that I was wearied of knowledge. On the contrary, I thirsted for yet deeper and fuller draughts than he was offering to me.

"Pardon me," said I, "O Thou Whom I must no longer address as the Perfection of all Beauty; but let me beg thee to vouchsafe thy servant a sight of thine interior."

Sphere. "My what?"

I. "Thine interior: thy stomach, thy intestines."

Sphere. "Whence this ill-timed impertinent request? And what mean you by saying that I am no longer the Perfection of all Beauty?"

I. My Lord, your own wisdom has taught me to aspire to One even more great, more beautiful, and more closely approximate to Perfection than yourself. As you yourself, superior to all Flatland forms, combine many Circles in One, so doubtless there is One above you who combines many Spheres in One Supreme Existence, surpassing even the Solids of Spaceland. And even as we, who are now in Space, look down on Flatland and see the insides of all things, so of a certainty there is yet above us some higher, purer region, whither thou dost surely purpose to lead me—O Thou Whom I shall always call, everywhere and in all Dimensions, my Priest, Philosopher, and Friend—some yet more spacious Space, some more dimensionable Dimensionality, from the vantage-ground of which we shall look down together upon the revealed insides of Solid things, and where thine own intestines, and those of thy kindred Spheres, will lie exposed to the view of the poor wandering exile from Flatland, to whom so much has already been vouchsafed.

Sphere. Pooh! Stuff! Enough of this trifling! The time is short, and much remains to be done before you are fit to proclaim the Gospel of Three Dimensions to your blind benighted countrymen in Flatland.

I. Nay, gracious Teacher, deny me not what I know it is in thy power to perform. Grant me but one glimpse of thine interior, and I am satisfied for ever, remaining henceforth thy docile pupil, thy unemancipable slave, ready to receive all thy teachings and to feed upon the words that fall from thy lips.

Sphere. Well, then, to content and silence you, let me say at once, I would show you what you wish if I could; but I cannot. Would you have me turn my stomach inside out to oblige you?

I. But my Lord has shown me the intestines of all my countrymen in the Land of Two Dimensions by taking me with him into the Land of Three. What therefore more easy than now to take his servant on a second journey into the blessed region of the Fourth Dimension, where I shall look down with him once more upon this land of Three Dimensions, and see the inside of every three-dimensioned house, the secrets of the solid earth, the treasures of the mines in Spaceland, and the intestines of every solid living creature, even of the noble and adorable Spheres.

Sphere. But where is this land of Four Dimensions?

I. I know not: but doubtless my Teacher knows.

Sphere. Not I. There is no such land. The very idea of it is utterly inconceivable.

I. Not inconceivable, my Lord, to me, and therefore still less inconceivable to my Master. Nay, I despair not that, even here, in this region of Three Dimensions, your Lordship's art may make the Fourth Dimension visible to me; just as in the Land of Two Dimensions my Teacher's skill would fain have opened the eyes of his blind servant to the invisible presence of a Third Dimension, though I saw it not.

Let me recall the past. Was I not taught below that when I saw a Line and inferred a Plane, I in reality saw a Third unrecognized Dimension, not the same as brightness, called "height"? And does it not now follow that, in this region, when I see a Plane and infer a Solid, I really see a Fourth unrecognized Dimension, not the same as colour, but existent, though infinitesimal and incapable of measurement?

And besides this, there is the Argument from Analogy of Figures.

Sphere. Analogy! Nonsense: what analogy?

I. Your Lordship tempts his servant to see whether he remembers the revelations imparted to him. Trifle not with me, my Lord; I crave, I thirst, for more knowledge. Doubtless we cannot *see* that other higher Spaceland now, because we have no eye in our stomachs. But, just as there *was* the realm of Flatland, though that poor puny Lineland Monarch could neither turn to left nor right to discern it, and just as there *was* close at hand, and touching my frame, the land of Three Dimensions, though I, blind senseless wretch, had no power to touch it, no eye in my interior to discern it, so of a surety there is a Fourth Dimension, which my Lord perceives with the inner eye of thought. And that it must exist my Lord himself has taught me. Or can he have forgotten what he himself imparted to his servant?

In One Dimension, did not a moving Point produce a Line with *two* terminal points?

In Two Dimensions, did not a moving Line produce a Square with *four* terminal points?

In Three Dimensions, did not a moving Square produce—did not this eye of mine behold it—that blessed Being, a Cube, with *eight* terminal points?

And in Four Dimensions shall not a moving Cube—alas, for Analogy, and alas for the Progress of Truth, if it be not so—shall not, I say, the motion of a divine Cube result in a still more divine Organization with *sixteen* terminal points?

Behold the infallible confirmation of the Series, 2, 4, 8, 16: is not this a Geometrical Progression? Is not this—if I might quote my Lord's own words—"strictly according to Analogy"?

Again, was I not taught by my Lord that as in a Line there are *two* bounding Points, and in a Square there are *four* bounding Lines, so in a Cube there must be *six* bounding Squares? Behold once more the confirming Series, 2, 4, 6: is not this an Arithmetical Progression? And consequently does it not of necessity follow that the more divine offspring of the divine Cube in the Land of Four Dimensions, must have 8 bounding Cubes: and is not this also, as my Lord has taught me to believe, "strictly according to Analogy"?

O, my Lord, my Lord, behold, I cast myself in faith upon conjecture, not knowing the facts; and I appeal to your Lordship to confirm or deny my logical anticipations. If I am wrong, I yield, and will no longer demand a Fourth Dimension; but, if I am right, my Lord will listen to reason.

I ask therefore, is it, or is it not, the fact, that ere now your countrymen also have witnessed the descent of Beings of a higher order than their own, entering closed rooms, even as your Lordship entered mine, without the opening of doors or windows, and appearing and vanishing at will? On the reply to this question I am ready to stake everything. Deny it, and I am henceforth silent. Only vouchsafe an answer.

Sphere (after a pause). It is reported so. But men are divided in opinion as to the facts. And even granting the facts, they explain them in different ways. And in any case, however great may be the number of different explanations, no one has adopted or suggested the theory of a Fourth Dimension. Therefore, pray have done with this trifling, and let us return to business.

I. I was certain of it. I was certain that my anticipations would be fulfilled. And now have patience with me and answer me yet one more question, best of Teachers! Those who have thus appeared—no one knows whence—and have returned—no one knows whither—have they also contracted their sections and vanished somehow into that more Spacious Space, whither I now entreat you to conduct me?

Sphere (moodily). They have vanished, certainly—if they ever appeared. But most people say that these visions arose from the thought—you will not understand me—from the brain; from the perturbed angularity of the Seer.

I. Say they so? Oh, believe them not. Or if it indeed be so, that this other Space is really Thoughtland, then take me to that blessed Region where I in Thought shall see the insides of all solid things. There, before my ravished eye, a Cube, moving in some altogether new direction, but strictly according to Analogy, so as to make every particle of his interior pass through a new kind of Space with a wake of its own—shall create a still more perfect perfection than himself, with sixteen terminal Extra-solid angles, and Eight solid Cubes for his Perimeter. And once there, shall we stay our upward course? In that blessed region of Four Dimensions, shall we linger on the threshold of the Fifth, and not enter therein? Ah, no! Let us rather resolve that our ambition shall soar with our corporal ascent. Then, yielding to our intellectual onset, the gates of the Sixth Dimension shall fly open; after that a Seventh, and then an Eighth——

How long I should have continued I know not. In vain did the Sphere, in his voice of thunder, reiterate his commands of silence, and threaten me with the direst penalties if I persisted. Nothing could stem the flood of my ecstatic aspirations. Perhaps I was to blame; but indeed I was intoxicated with the recent draughts of Truth to which he himself had introduced me. However, the end was not long in coming. My words were cut short by a crash outside, and a simultaneous crash inside me, which impelled me through Space with a velocity that precluded speech. Down! down! down! I was rapidly descending; and I knew that return to Flatland was my doom. One glimpse, one last and never-to-be-forgotten glimpse I had of that dull level wilderness—which was now to become my Universe again—spread out before my eye. Then a darkness. Then a final, all-consummating thunder-peal; and, when I came to myself, I was once more a common creeping Square, in my Study at home, listening to the Peace-Cry of my approaching Wife.

QUESTIONS FOR STUDY AND DISCUSSION

1. *Flatland* is a humorous and pleasant specimen of analogical reasoning. Evaluate this excerpt for consistency of logic.

2. Does *Flatland* seek to prove the existence of two-dimensional and four-dimensional worlds? If analogical reasoning is not a proof, what then is its value?

3. How does analogical reasoning differ from induction and deduction?

WRITING ASSIGNMENT

Write an essay that uses analogical reasoning to speculate on the nature of a world of five dimensions.

Refutation

Is there a difference between refuting an argument and arguing the negative of a premise? If the student is given a statement like "Football is an abominable game" and asked to prove that football is not abominable, is this refutation?

Refutation implies a well-developed position which the writer wishes to attack. In many ways it is the most demanding and interesting of tasks because it calls for a synthesis of all the logical and rhetorical skills the writer has developed.

The person refuting an argument has two main jobs: to tear down the argumentative position he considers faulty and to put something better in its place. The business of constructing an argument is nothing new to the student, while the work of demolition demands nothing more difficult than new uses of old techniques. The student must move through the argument he intends to refute with a mental check list of what he has learned, ticking off errors and abuses of good reasoning and storing them as ammunition for his attack.

The writer should look first for errors of truth and deficiencies of evidence. Does his opponent make assertions for which there is no support or too little support? Has he grounded his generalizations on instances which are not representative of the whole class? Perhaps he overgeneralizes, making his statements apply to *all* instead of *some*. (If a Frenchman blithely insists that Americans are people who carry cameras, put their feet on the table, drink Coca-Cola, and speak no French, it is easy enough to prove him wrong. These observations are not true of all Americans, but we must not make the same mistake in reverse by saying that they do not apply to any Americans.) An even subtler perversion of truth is special pleading, a selection of evidence that presents only the information favorable to its conclusions, withholding everything else.

One step worse than weak evidence is the attempt to make verbal soufflés substitute for hard-headed content, an abuse of language that can be found all too abundantly in advertising and politics. The person who uses language to deceive is a propagandist. Sometimes he is a name-caller, but one who usually neglects to show that his labels fit. He plays upon hopes and hidden desires; he preys upon fears; and his reasons are often base ones ("Everyone is doing it"). He deals in massive generalities, unexamined premises, and undefined abstractions. Abstractions are of the greatest value, but the reader must always know what they stand for. The hallmarks of propaganda are emptiness of content, lack of orderly reasoning, and strong emphasis upon the emotional.

The writer should look next for flaws of validity. Since most deductive argument is only haphazardly syllogistic, the writer must take his opponent's enthymemes and attempt to fill in the gaps. If the opponent is a sloppy thinker, his enthymemes will be a tangle of premises and conclusions which do not mesh. He will leap from argument to argument wildly. To any systematic thinker, these will be serious weaknesses. Sometimes the writer will find errors of the most basic sort in his opponent's arguments: an undistributed middle term; a term distributed in the conclusion but not in the premises; wild shifts in the meaning of a term; or happy-go-lucky inferences. Many people adept in the categorical syllogism will flounder with the hypothetical, affirming consequents and denying antecedents.

These are but a few of the common fallacies that the human mind is capable of. Other sources of error include the confusion of class traits with individual characteristics ("Each part of the missile tested out perfectly, so the missile itself should be a success when fired" or "Your friend is French, so he'll certainly enjoy the snails we're having for dinner"). Akin to this is the genetic fallacy, in which reputation or the source of an idea is made to substitute for evidence and proof ("It can't be a good idea if Smith is for it" or "Everyone who knew him said that he was literally incapable of committing murder"). This latter argument is tricky, for while it is fallacious when it replaces or discredits real evidence, it is not entirely out of place as an adjunct to evidence. A good reputation does not prove one's innocence, just as a bad reputation does not prove guilt. But unsavory character plus formal evidence is a more damning combination than logical proof alone. Logical proof is enough to hang a man; but for whatever reason, good or bad, human beings are happier if they feel that the bad guy—the one who beats his wife and takes candy from children—has finally got what's coming to him. One of the most contemptible fallacies is the complex question ("How long must we keep on being a second-rate power in world affairs?"), which attempts to sneak unproved and unexamined ideas into the argument. The traditional fallacies include appeals of many kinds directed to the emotions. There is nothing wrong with strong feeling if it has its roots in evidence and rationality, but to the extent that the head is replaced by the viscera, such appeals are worthless and ignoble.

The writer should proceed to examine his opponent's argument for false analogies and false causes. Analogical reasoning is a profitable means of speculation but not a proof. If the writer can bring in evidence to show that his opponent's speculations do not accord with the facts, the argument is quickly exploded. But if his opponent is reasoning about things yet to come, the writer must attack the analogy itself. He can attempt to show that the model for the analogy is not sufficiently similar to the real situation to warrant a comparison. Possibly he can take the same points of resemblance used by his opponent and show that they lead equally well to other conclusions. He can carry the analogy further and show that it is reliable only for limited cases. If pushed a bit, a bad analogy generally ends in absurdity.

Causal investigations often show the logical processes at their least rigorous and most superficial. Finding fault with causal analyses is no great problem, but replacing them with something more substantial is. The writer can try to show that other phenomena than the ones claimed by his opponent could have caused the observable effects. If the effects are still in the future and can only be guessed at, the writer can show that the observable causes might bring consequences unimagined by his opponent.

Several abuses of causal reasoning are most common. Some writers are given to fanciful chains of causal speculation ("If we had stayed out of World War I, Germany would have conquered Europe, and then she and Russia would have knocked each other out in World War II"). The most tempting error, though, is *post hoc ergo propter hoc*: because one thing follows another it is therefore caused by what it follows ("My grandfather used to tie a string around Bobby's warts and then bury the string at night, and the warts always disappeared"). A similar boner consists of seizing upon an interesting concomitant to a phenomenon and proclaiming it as the cause ("The aurora is strong right now and it's making the radio act up"). Still other common errors are to confuse necessary and sufficient conditions ("Sound waves require the presence of air as a medium") or to claim as a cause a condition which merely favors or speeds a certain effect ("After his death she became disconsolate and soon took sick and died—died of a broken heart, poor girl"). Far too many writers are inclined to oversimplify causes, overlooking the possibility of multiple and reciprocal causes ("Who else started World War. I if not the Kaiser?").

These or any other weaknesses—even defects of classification, definition, or comparison and contrast—are potential ammunition for a refutation. The thorough student will not stop before he has combed through his opponent's argument for errors of fact, checking against sources for misinterpretation and misquotation. It is not enough to evaluate a man's ideas; refutation requires that the refuter know more about his subject and understand it better than the man he is refuting. And this means reading and learning as well as cerebration.

But the strongest of all refutations can be made only by the person skilled in probing beneath the surface of an argument. It is one thing to take an enthymeme and fill in the blanks. It is quite another to dig out the basic, unwritten assumptions on which many arguments turn, assumptions of which the writer himself may not be aware. In his famous *Essay on the Principle of Population*, Thomas Malthus examines the arguments made by William Godwin against property and marriage. Malthus refutes the arguments one by one and disposes of Godwin permanently by observing that each of Godwin's animadversions springs from his unvoiced conviction that human institutions are no good. This is refutation at its most powerful.

ESSAY SUGGESTIONS

1. Read "Positive Thinking on Pennsylvania Avenue" by Philip Roth. If you agree with Roth, write your own refutation of former President Eisenhower's concept of prayer. (First ask yourself about your concept of prayer. Then go to the encyclopedias of religious knowledge to find out what the experts think.)

2. After reading Roth's article, read *The Power of Positive Thinking* by Norman Vincent Peale. If Peale's ideas run counter to yours, write a refutation of Peale's philosophy of prayer.

3. If your ideas about prayer are similar to Eisenhower's and Peale's, refute Roth.

4. Read William Godwin's *Enquiry Concerning Political Justice* and write a refutation. If you agree with Godwin, attack Malthus' refutation referred to above.

5. Over a seven-year period, *Life* published three editorials on modern American

literature: August 16, 1948; January 11, 1954; and September 12, 1955. Read them. If you disagree with *Life's* position, refute.

6. Read any of the many recent articles on overpopulation and food supply (for instance, Sir Charles Darwin's "Forecasting the Future," printed in *Frontiers in Science*). If you disagree, refute. (You might find it interesting to look at Malthus' *Essay on the Principle of Population* in preparing for this essay. But note how Malthus' ideas changed between the first edition of his study in 1798 and the second edition in 1803.)

Simple honesty requires that a writer write only what he believes. It is a breach of integrity to support or attack—even as an exercise—any position that the writer is not himself convinced of. If a person cannot take a stand on a question, his position should be that of neutral examiner; in effect, he should write an expository essay on an argumentative topic.

FURTHER READING

Here the student should read everything connected with fallacies and errors in thinking. A good book to start with is *How to Think Straight* by Robert H. Thouless. New York: Simon and Schuster, 1941.

See Aristotle's De Sophisticis Elenchis, which is part of the Organon, and Book II of the Rhetorica. Also Bacon's discussion of the four Idols in Book I of the *Novum Organum*.

Morris R. Cohen and Ernest Nagel, *An Introduction to Logic and Scientific Method*, Chapter XIX.

Bernard F. Huppé and Jack Kaminsky, *Logic and Language*, Chapter 6.

W. H. Werkmeister, *An Introduction to Critical Thinking*, Chapters II through IV.

R. C. STEPHENSON

Speech to the University of Texas General Faculty

The first special meeting of the General Faculty for the academic year 1954–55 was held in Geology Building, Thursday, January 6, 1955, at 4 P.M.

ATTENDANCE. *Present: President* Wilson, *Secretary* Nelson, 81 other voting members, 2 non-voting members; *total* 85. Excused absences: 12 voting members, 0 non-voting members; *total* 12.

APPROVAL OF MINUTES OF THE FIRST REGULAR MEETING OF THE GENERAL FACULTY, OCTOBER 21, 1954 (G.F. MINUTES 6439-48). The *Minutes* of the first regular meeting of the General Faculty, October 21, 1954, were approved without corrections.

PROPOSAL OF THE FACULTY COUNCIL THAT THE "CAFETERIA ANNEX" BE NAMED THE "VARSITY CAFETERIA" (G.F. MINUTES 6457) (ADOPTED). Mr. *Leon*, as Chairman of the Special Committee to Name New Buildings on the Campus, moved that the new cafeteria building be named the Varsity Cafeteria. His motion was seconded by the committee. Mr. *Leon* then gave the background of the committee's recommendation. He stated that the original recommendation of the committee that the cafeteria be named for Miss Janzen had been rejected by the Regents because they were unwilling to make an exception to their rule that a University building should not be named for a person until ten years after his death. He read a letter from Vice-President Boner stating that the alternative recommendation of the committee, that the cafeteria be named the University Commons Annex, should be reconsidered because there was already a

University Commons Annex. The committee had then been reconvened and the name Varsity Cafeteria had been suggested as appropriate. Since nobody had another suggestion, the committee had adopted that name. He had not been present at the meeting of the Faculty Council when this recommendation was voted on. The Faculty Council had rejected the portion of the committee's report recommending that the name of the cafeteria be changed in 1961 to Janzen Cafeteria. The Council had felt that the Board of Regents should not be committed to a change of the name at a later time. He said that the committee had no special pride in the name that it had recommended. It had wanted a suitable temporary name because it believed that after six years the building should be named for Miss Janzen. Consequently, the committee did not want the name to be too attractive. If the faculty wanted to substitute another name, the committee had no grievous objections. Upon the motion of Mr. X, Mr. Y was given the privilege of the floor. Mr. Y expressed his appreciation for the courtesy extended him but stated that he would sometime like to know if a retired professor was a member of the General Faculty and if he had the privilege of speaking at faculty meetings. He stated that the principle which was involved in the letter of protest was a very important one. All would agree that all University utterances should be expressed in correct English and possibly in dignified English. He thought that the naming of a building of the University was important. Names stick for a long time. Sometimes they are carved into stone. University buildings should be given names that are correct and dignified. The term "Varsity" is a mutilated term. It is classified as a colloquial term in the dictionary, is usually associated with the theater and athletic teams and crews, and is not sufficiently dignified to designate University buildings. He said that there was available another name which was correct and dignified: The University Cafeteria. He said that there had been some talk that this name would be confusing since the University Commons was carried under the heading "University Cafeteria" in bookkeeping ac-

235

counts. He thought as far as the records were concerned, they could be kept under the names "commons" and "cafeteria." Finally, he did not want to advertise over the state and to young folks that the Faculty thought that the name Varsity was acceptable. He said that if the Faculty disapproved of this term, he would suggest that the matter of naming the building be referred back to the committee which would be glad to receive suggestions for a better name. Mr. X stated that he had signed the protest and thought that the name "Varsity Cafeteria" was objectionable. He said that in this particular case there were two objections. The first Dr. Y had expressed. The name "Varsity" is not in the American language, particularly English. It was used first at Cambridge and was applied only to athletic teams; it ought not to be applied to something dignified. He thought, too, that the name "Varsity Cafeteria" would be confusing. He said that there were many more acceptable names, such as El Comedor. Mr. *Cotner* said that he would like to substitute the name "El Comedor," a Spanish word which refers to a private or public dining room which is located near enough to the place where the food is prepared so that it will be hot when served but far enough away to be free from kitchen odors. Mr. *Cotner* moved that the name "El Comedor" be substituted for "Varsity Cafeteria" in the original motion. This motion was seconded by Mr. X. Mr. *Stephenson* stated that the issue before the Faculty was an important one involving the dignity of the words in the English language. The Faculty had been convened for a lesson on style and he for one insisted that the lesson should be carried out completely and that the metaphysical question should not go untouched. Mr. Y said that the General Faculty meeting was no place to name anything or to discuss various names. Therefore, he hoped that the substitute motion would be voted down. The President called for a vote on the substitute motion, which was defeated. Mr. *Mumma* then moved the previous question, which failed to receive the vote of two-thirds of the voting members present and was, therefore, defeated. Miss *Wheatley* stated that she objected strongly to the statement in

the protest that the name "Varsity" should be rejected simply because it was colloquial. Such a criticism implied an indictment of all our conversation. She added that she noticed that even the word "cafeteria" was not in Webster. Mr. *Leon* stated that since the protest he had received several suggested names for the cafeteria. Someone had suggested that it be named for Judge Bean and it be called "The Beanery." Mr. *McConnell* had recommended East Campus Cafeteria, which he thought suitable. Mr. *Stephenson* spoke as follows:

As I have said, Mr. President, this is a very important question. I deplore the apologetic tone in which the first two speakers have introduced the subject—quite as if it was not worth our while to come together this afternoon and discuss so serious a matter. It is true, of course, that ever since 1939 much more troublesome matters have been considered in this hall. But the issue was never pure. Extraneous values like civil rights and extraneous passions like self-respect were always pushing their way into the debate and distracting us from that single-mindedness that becomes us. But today it is different. We have a question before us that is worthy of us. It is one to which we can give undivided attention. It is a truly academic question.

Therefore I am very happy to raise my own voice, very happy to come to the support of the gentlemen who have protested the name "Varsity Cafeteria." As I understand them, though, I myself would explain the protest differently. It is presumptuous of me, I know, to suggest that I understand the workings of their minds even better than they do. Some of them are certainly much, and the rest at least a trifle, more learned than I am. Certainly they all handle the academic style more effectively than I do. But it is just because I know out of what deep, obscure and mysterious depths that style comes, that I hazard an explanation. It was no accident that led them to associate a cafeteria with athletic contests. It was part of the sure but devious association of ideas by which we arrive at our good phrases. I more than suspect, I feel sure, that in coupling the words "cafeteria" and "athletic contests" they were about to hit upon some splendid substitute of a name, but lacked the time to grope their way quite to it.

They argue that "the word 'varsity' is a colloquial term, usually associated with the theaters and athletic teams and crews, and not sufficiently dignified to designate a University building." But what they were just about to realize and say is that "the word 'varsity' is . . . usually associated with . . . athletic teams and crews, and therefore *quite* sufficiently dignified to designate a *cafeteria*." It is specifically a *cafeteria* we are about to name, not that generalization a "University building." Intuition was working for them but not fast enough. For how may we define an athletic contest? Is it not mass hysteria and mass intoxication at the scene of mass mutilation? And what is a cafeteria? Is it not the clattering, jostling scene of mass mastication? The correspondence is striking. It raises the problem of what we mean by "dignified" in such a case. And dignified is related to a Latin adjective that means, among other things, *suitable*. What is suitable here? I am reminded of the American Stud Book, which has the answer. The Stud Book stipulates that any colt registered in it must have a dignified name. So if a colt is listed in the Stud Book it has a dignified name. Very well, then. Let's consider the names of some of the horses that were running last fall: Summer Tan, Apache, High Gun, Jet Action, Bicarb, Devil Diver, High Voltage (who is a matron, incidentally), Pet Bully, Iceberg II, Dash for Cash, Bunny's Babe, and Brother Tex.

Brother Tex, by the way, reminds me that we have one eating place on the campus with a charming and appropriate name, The Chuck Wagon. This is certainly a colloquial phrase, but if colloquial means undignified then it is undignified too. But think of it! "Bunny's Babe" is a dignified name for a thoroughbred! For one of those noble Houyhnhnms that in heart, in spirit, in grace and in breeding put us poor Yahoos to shame. We know that Bunny's Babe is a dignified name because the Stud Book says so. But "Varsity" isn't a dignified enough epithet to stand before "cafeteria."

It may be argued that no fair parallel can be drawn between a cafeteria and a race horse, that they run on different lines or tracks. And this is true. Just as no fair parallel can be drawn between the chatter, the clatter, the jostle and the steam and reek of a cafeteria, on the one hand, and, on the other, the quiet and elegance of a thoroughbred's stall—have you ever been in one?— with its spicy, dry barley trough, its alfalfa-sweet manger, and the straw-strewn floor, ever so faintly but pleasantly acrid with manure. The comparison is altogether unfair to the cafeteria, but reminds us, even so, that there are many levels of dignity, and what is *infra dig.* on one level may easily be *supra dig.* on another. A cafeteria, as I have said, is a clamorous, pushing, vulgar place at best and might as well have a name to match. Besides, if I understand the situation, this is to be a cafeteria chiefly for students, and the student's ear ought to be consulted, not the professor's. One man's meat is another man's chow.

To tell the truth, there is no possible way to prettify or dignify such a frankly comical word as "cafeteria." "Varsity," by comparison, is a highly respectable term—just as it is a vastly older one in our language. In the 18th century, universities were called "varsities." "Varsity" is on record since 1846 at least. And ever since 1872 the professors have been objecting to it. It must be a pretty useful and hardy word to have survived countless such attacks as have been made upon it this afternoon.

No, there is simply no way to dress up the word "cafeteria." Either accept "Varsity Cafeteria" as dignified in the sense of *suitable* or get rid of both terms. The only satisfactory alternative is utter euphemism. Hide the place in really fancy language. And this brings me to the practical proposal I wish to make. But first I should like to read a remarkably relevant passage from a little story in the *New Yorker* for last December 4. It has to do with the tribulations of an American student who was working in the Bodleian Library, in the very environs, it may be, in which the word "varsity" was coined:

"... my hands became grimy from enforced intimacy with the *British Congregationalist*, the *Christian World Pulpit*, the *Expository Times*, and the

Examiner. I decided they had better be washed. I walked over to the reservation desk, where two girls were sitting.

" 'Would you please tell me,' I asked one of them, in a courteous, intendedly British, and slightly embarrassed whisper, 'how to get to the man's lavat'ry?'

" 'I beg your pardon?' the girl replied.

" 'Where's the men's washroom?' I asked, a little louder this time and with no pretense of Anglicized pronunciation.

"She frowned, turned to the other girl, whispered to her, and finally said to me, 'I don't know.'

"I was surprised, and even a little annoyed. Surely answering such questions was part of her job.

"Just then, the man employed to fetch the books for Readers appeared at the desk. I put my problem to him. Could he tell me where to find the men's washroom? He could indeed, and proceeded to do so in such a loud voice as to embarrass me acutely. I was standing with my back to most of the room, and during his monologue I imagined curious heads peering around the corners of carrels or over the tops of folio volumes.

" 'Well, sir,' the man said, as nearly as I can remember, 'you take those stairs there, and you go down four flights to the courtyard, and then you go across to the other side of the courtyard, diagonal-like, and you'll find a lit-

tle door marked "Schola Linguarum Hebraicae et Graecae." Just go in that little door, sir, and *there* it is.'

"After mumbling a word of thanks, I went down the stairs, crossed the courtyard, opened the door marked 'Schola Linguarum Hebraicae et Graecae,' and there, by George, it was."

Now that's the way to do it. If you have something coarse and common to name, like a gent's wash room or a greasy spoonery, call it by a goodnatured, comfortable piece of verbal impudence and have done with it, or else disguise it, hide it, utterly submerge it in pompous language—the way some women hide their telephones away in little poke bonnets or crocheted diaper bags.

Believing that, all things considered, this latter is the really elegant solution of the problem, Mr. President, I have crocheted such a diaper bag and if I get a second to it, I promise to let it come to a vote without further argument. I move, Mr. President, that the eating place in question be named The Mermaid Tavern, and that the waitresses be required to serve in tails.

The motion failed for want of a second. President *Wilson* called for a vote upon the original motion which was adopted.

ADJOURNMENT. The General Faculty adjourned at 4:50 P.M.

NEXT SCHEDULED MEETING OF THE GENERAL FACULTY. The next meeting of the General Faculty is scheduled May 10, 1955.

QUESTIONS FOR STUDY AND DISCUSSION

1. Suppose that Stephenson had argued in a straightforward manner that *varsity* is a respectable word and that his colleagues were being a little nice in objecting to it. What force would such a refutation have?

2. In the second paragraph of his address, Stephenson says that he is "very happy to come to the support of the gentlemen who have protested the name 'Varsity Cafeteria.' " What name do we give to statements which say something different from what is

really meant? How do we know that Stephenson is not actually supporting the men who objected to "Varsity Cafeteria"?

3. What arguments does the author use to show that "Varsity Cafeteria" is definitely an appropriate name?

4. What is the pun with which Stephenson concludes his speech? Make a list of all the puns you know and try to explain the mechanisms underlying word play of this kind.

PHILIP ROTH

Positive Thinking on
Pennsylvania Avenue

. . . He [Congressman Walter Judd of Minnesota] told me this fascinating story about President Eisenhower. Mrs. Judd had been having a visit with Mrs. Eisenhower who told her, "Ike gets into bed, lies back on the pillow, and prays out loud, something like this: 'Lord, I want to thank You for helping me to-day. You really stuck by me. I know, Lord, that I muffed a few and I'm sorry about that. But both the ones we did all right and the ones we muffed I am turning them all over to You. You take over from here. Good night, Lord, I'm going to sleep.' And," added the President's wife to Mrs. Judd, "that is just what he does; he just turns over and goes to sleep. . . ."

Norman Vincent Peale,
December 1956

The man of deep religious conscience and conviction traditionally speaks to his God with words of awe, love, fear, and wonder: he lifts his voice to the mysterious bigger-than-space, longer-than-time God, and his own finiteness, ignorance, and sinfulness grip his spirit and carve for his tongue a language of humility. Only recently Mrs. Eisenhower revealed to a White House guest the words the President himself speaks each night to the Lord from the quiet of his bed. As the President begins his second term in office, it would perhaps be fitting to examine the short prayer which has helped to carry him through these past few years, the prayer with which he attempts to crash through the barriers of flesh and finitude in his quest for communion with God.

To imagine the tone of voice with which the President delivers his prayers one need only read the closing sentences as Mrs.

Eisenhower reports them. "You take over from here," the President says aloud. "Good night, Lord, I'm going to sleep." The President's tone is clear: if one were to substitute the word "James" for "Lord" one might hear the voice of a man calling not to his God, but to his valet. "I have polished my left shoe, James. As for the right, well—you take over from here. Good night, James, I'm going to sleep." The tone is a chummy one, as opposed, say, to the tone taken toward Cinderella by her despised stepsisters: "Sweep the floor, wash the clothes, polish the shoes, and then get the hell out of here. . . ." The President addresses his valet as he does his God, as an equal. Where the theologian, Martin Buber, has suggested that man is related to his God as an "I" to a "Thou," Mr. Eisenhower's tone would seem to suggest that the I and Thou of Buber's thinking be converted into the more democratic You and Me.

"Lord," the President's prayer begins, "I want to thank You for helping me today. You really stuck by me. . . ." The Lord is not so much his shepherd, Mr. Eisenhower indicates, as his helper, his *aide-de-camp*. He is a kind of celestial Secretary of State, and one who apparently knows his place in the chain of command; it is quite clearly stated, "You stuck by me" and not "I stuck by you." The prayer continues, "I know, Lord, that I muffed a few and I'm sorry about that. But both the ones we did all right and the ones we muffed I am turning them all over to You." A slight ambiguity exists around the words "a few." A few what? Does Mr. Eisenhower mean decisions? And how many are a few? If, as we are led to suspect, the Lord works hand in hand with the President, then such questions are academic, for God would doubtless know precisely the decisions to which Mr. Eisenhower is alluding. Of course one cannot dismiss the possibility that all this mystery is intentional, as a sort of security measure. You will remember that Mrs. Eisenhower is no more than a few feet away, listening to every word.

Uncertain as he may *appear* as to the nature and number of the decisions, the President leaves no doubt as to how the decisions are formulated: it is a bi-partisan set-up, the

President and God working together right down the line. What seems unusual about the procedure is that while both share the responsibility for the successful ventures ("the ones we did all right"), the burden of failure falls rather singly upon the Shoulders of the Lord. Though admittedly "sorry" about muffing a few, Mr. Eisenhower informs the Lord point-blank, "I am turning them all over to You." Now nobility in defeat is a glorious spectacle—it is what immortalizes Oedipus and Othello, Socrates and Lincoln. The vision of a soul alone in the night confessing to his God that he has failed Him is in a way the tragic vision, the supreme gesture of humility and courage. However to admit failure is one thing, and to sneak out on a partnership is another. If the once flourishing business of X and Y suddenly tumbles into bankruptcy, Y does not expect that X will put on his hat and gloves and walk out muttering, "I'll see you —you pay the creditors whatever it is we owe them. Bye, bye. . . ." One should think that X and Y must pay the debts just as they had shared the profits: together.

Perhaps it is unjust to draw any implications from an analogy which is, I fear, not entirely appropriate. For instance, in the X and Y example it is assumed that the initial capital for the enterprise had been supplied equally by both X *and* Y; now whether or not this is analogous to the Eisenhower-God relationship is uncertain—as yet evidence released by the White House staff is not sufficient for any but the most zealous to conclude that the Chief Executive shared in either the planning or execution of the Original Creation. Moreover, I am confident that a religious consciousness like the President's, which manifests itself in prayer and good works, would be outraged at the notion of God as a partner; though the Lord is addressed as *an equal*, and functions as *a helper*, His ultimate powers, Mr. Eisenhower well knows, are those of *a superior*. Surely the President would be the first to remind us that he himself is in the service of the Lord, as are we all. The vital ques-

tion then is not the responsibility of partner to partner but of subordinate to superior, worker to boss. Perhaps Mr. Eisenhower's own history, as a halfback on the West Point football team and as a professional soldier, can provide analogies more appropriate to this problem.

Imagine, for example, that the Army football team has been beaten by Navy, 56 to 0; the quarterback returns to the bench and explains to the Coach, "Coach, I muffed a few and I'm sorry about that. But both the ones we did all right and the ones we muffed," he says, starting for the fieldhouse, "I am turning them all over to You." Or picture in your mind a colonel whose regiment has suffered disastrous and unpardonable losses; he is summoned to divisional headquarters; he enters the office of the Commanding General; he salutes; he speaks: "Sir, I muffed a few and I'm sorry about that," he admits. "But," he adds quickly, "both the ones we did all right and the ones we muffed I am turning them all over to You."

Anyone who has ever played left guard for a grade school team or toiled at K.P. in a company mess hall could conjecture the answer of both coach and general; as for the reaction of the Lord to so novel a concept of responsibility, my limited acquaintance with historical theology does not permit of conjecture. Off the cuff, I imagine it might strain even *His* infinite mercy.

Mrs. Eisenhower reports that when the President ends his prayer, "he just turns over and goes to sleep." I suspect that at this point the First Lady is not telling the whole truth, her own humility in operation now. The way I figure it, when the President has finished his man-to-man talk with the Lord, he removes his gaze from the ceiling of the White House bedroom, pauses for a moment, and then looking upwards again, says, "And now, Lord, *Mrs.* Eisenhower would like a few words with You." And then with that grin of his he turns to the First Lady and whispers, "Mamie, He's ready. . . ."

QUESTIONS FOR STUDY AND DISCUSSION

1. In his sermon of December, 1956, the Rev. Norman Vincent Peale first quoted President Eisenhower's prayer and then commented on it, saying, "I call that a wonderful secret of dynamic life. If you can turn over and go to sleep when you have the Suez situation on your mind, when the whole world seems to be in conflict, and a few other things as well, I feel it is a mark of genius." Why does Roth omit this from his quotation? Notice that except for the echo in the title, the essay is about Eisenhower and not Peale. What kind of essay could be written about the prayer if it were followed by Peale's comment?

2. Comment on Roth's use of analogy in this refutation. What part does wit play in the essay's effectiveness?

3. Notice how Roth appears at times to be thinking out loud. He comments, for example, that the analogy of X and Y is not altogether just and thereupon moves on to something stronger. Why does he not omit the analogy?

4. A refutation is supposedly an answer to another argument. If so, what is it that Roth is refuting—the prayer or the philosophy underlying the prayer?

WRITING ASSIGNMENTS

1. Outline this essay. Does it show a careful organization of its arguments? If not, what are the sources of its unity and coherence? Note particularly how Roth begins and ends his essay.

2. People have commented (see the letters that follow this article) that an essay of this kind is improper, that a man's prayers are his private property and not subject to the scrutiny of others. Argue pro or con in an essay of your own.

When Mr. Roth's essay appeared in the New Republic, *it provoked several letters to the Editor, to which Mr. Roth replied.*

Sirs:

"Positive Thinking on Pennsylvania Avenue" (*NR*, June 3) by Philip Roth is the most distasteful article I have ever read in *The New Republic*. To ridicule any man's approach to God is both cynical and smug.

Congressman Judd and Norman Vincent Peale may well feel bitter remorse for their part in the betrayal of a wife's confidence, the exploitation of which by Mr. Roth was nothing short of crass.

I cannot imagine why *NR* would publish such a low form of humor.

Dorothy Nelson
Glenview, Illinois

". . . in wretched taste"

Sirs:

If you are interested in a comment from a Democrat who doesn't know much about religion and prayer, and who thinks that Mr. Eisenhower is a rather poor President, here goes: The article by Philip Roth is a fatuous piece of boorishness, and in wretched taste. Our democratic society is healthier because the acts of public officials are subject to public comment and criticism, even to the extent of scorn and ridicule, but it is certainly no better off because of this prying into Mr. Eisenhower's prayers. I suggest that Mr. Roth and your staff go home and say theirs, incorporating a statement to the effect that you too muffed one.

James F. Bailey
River Forest, Illinois

Sirs:

In letters to NR (June 24) readers Bailey and Nelson indict me for "prying into Mr. Eisenhower's prayers." Somehow readers Bailey and Nelson seem to think that Mrs. Eisenhower whispered the prayer to Mrs. Judd who whispered it to Congressman Judd who whispered it to Peale who whispered it to me. I'm afraid this is not the case, and that if Mr. Peale permits himself to lapse into a state even faintly resembling contrition (which is a negative virtue at most), it will have to be for a betrayal even blacker than Miss Nelson may have imagined; for when Congressman Judd whispered Ike's prayer to Peale, Peale went ahead and thundered it to thousands of worshippers gathered in Marble Collegiate Church, N.Y.C., one Sunday last December. I happened to come across it in one of the reprints of Peale's sermons which, by the way, are delivered by the tens of thousands through the mails. I didn't have to do a great deal of prying.

As for Miss Nelson's charge that I am an exploiter of prayers, I suggest not that she put down her gun, but rather that she redirect her fire, for I get as angry as she does about vulgar exploitation. It was, in fact, unsettling to me to think that when the Reverend Mr. Peale got hold of Ike's prayer he may have thought to himself, "Now I've got myself a real testimonial." Unfortunately what Mr. Peale considers a testimonial I consider, not only bad taste but a blasphemy—and to my mind it would be "cynical and smug" to refrain from picking

up the whip of ridicule and driving the exploiters, blasphemers, and money-lenders from the temple.

Philip Roth
Moorestown, N. J.

"*. . . refreshing response*"

Sirs:

We read with considerable amusement the outraged squawks of your correspondents who deplore your bad taste in publishing an analysis of alleged presidential prayers.

For five long years we have been regaled with fulsome accounts of Mr. E's religiosity, neatly (if obviously) injected into all sorts of political publicity, even culminating in a whole book extolling Mr. E as, virtually, a new Messiah. We found Mr. Roth's ironic response to this type of adulation rather refreshing. If anyone has pried into and "crassly" advertised presidential prayers, how about Rep. Judd, Dr. Peale, *et al.*?

Mrs. W. W. Goodman
Seaside, Calif.

Part Three

STYLE

Concerning Style

We began thinking about style in "The Written Word." There our object was to consider some of the equipment a writer must possess before he can scale the essay itself. Here our purpose is more disinterested, being a simple attempt to learn some of the ingredients of prose style.

Style is the group of selections that a writer makes from among all the possible choices which his language offers him. The living totality that we call style is as hard to pin down as quicksilver, but some of its elements—some of the writer's choices—can be studied. *Style* itself is a neutral term. Every writer, from Aelfric to Mickey Spillane, has a style, but some styles we judge to be good and others deficient. But we learn from all of them.

In this part of our work, we will examine the suggestions of five wise men concerning style and apply these to the variety of styles—most of them memorable —appearing in this book, styles from our own time and from earlier periods as well. The idea is not to provide models for the student to ape (the worst notion a person can get is that he ought to rummage around for a style he likes and then wear it as if it were his own) but to give him a chance to study the many subtle devices which have enabled good writers to work their art. Study of this kind results in awareness, understanding, sensitivity. These in turn may happily lead the student to make his own choices with greater care and sureness of touch. This is the way a style is developed—not by mimicry and not by rooting around for new and eccentric ways of saying things.

Too often we think of style as something obvious, like a tiger-skin rug. Some good styles do call attention to themselves, but they needn't. What could be less obvious or more premeditated than the writing of George Orwell? A good style may show character and individuality, but its main purpose is to make reading easier, to aid comprehension, and not to distract the reader by throwing verbal spitballs. Lucidity results when clear thought is given form in clear language. This is the chief function of style. Everything else is subsidiary.

The great purpose of language is communication; but language well used may also bring pleasure, and this is the lesser concern of style. While writing should not attract attention by its gaudiness, it must always hold attention if it is to be read. Sluggish writing can put the reader to sleep; it is a mighty soporific. But good style seeks to please the ear and by pleasing, persuade.

A person's style may show some traits which seem to us typical of the period in which he lived; others which are not limited to the age or to the writer; and sometimes a third kind, the pet words or turns of phrase, or even real idiosyncrasies, which are very much the writer's own. A person's style is the configuration of these traits. It does not always stamp him as a man of his times, nor is it necessarily as distinctive as his face. It is this total pattern which we must investigate. The beginning writer is not yet ready to separate period from person and talk about the short sentences of modern prose or the balance and antithesis of eighteenth-century style.

Style is largely what we mean it to be. Painters show it; composers have it; women wear it. To some, style is the man himself; and in this sense the word may refer to any of the multitudinous choices that a writer makes in organizing his essay, in shaping a paragraph, or in tying an abstraction to some immediate detail that makes things clear. The principles of order we have called rhetoric, and together with style they form an unbroken spectrum. Without suggesting that a treatment of style is apart from the study of an author's rhetoric, we will concern ourselves here with listing some of the linguistic choices that the writer makes in his work. Such a list is hardly complete; it is certainly not a dissection procedure; and it risks repeating what has been said better by Hazlitt, Stevenson, Knox, and ironically by Masterson and Phillips. But it may help to bring together the ideas of these thoughtful men and suggest tactics which might be effective in unriddling a particular style.

To the extent that the writer is free to choose, he can manipulate all the features of his language, from raw sound to finished sentence. Assonance, alliteration, and other deliberate uses of sound are not common in English prose even though they are found in great plenty in advertising slogans ("I like Ike" is a little masterpiece in its way). But prose rhythm is very much with us. Consider this sentence from "The Dead," by James Joyce:

> Freddy Malins, who was nearing the climax of his story, waved the offer aside impatiently but Mr. Browne, having first called Freddy Malins' attention to a disarray in his dress, filled out and handed him a full glass of lemonade.

The sentence is studded with four or more major pauses interrupting the subject and predicate of both main clauses. Nor is there anything in the arrangement of stresses within the sentence to offset this awkwardness. Despite its gifted author, the sentence will not be remembered for its musicality of phrasing.

Compare the sentence by Joyce with one from *The Silver Tassie* by Sean O'Casey:

> The men that are defending us have leave to bow themselves down in the House of Rimmon, for the men that go with the guns are going with God.

The alliteration and the phrase *bow themselves down* perhaps have a touch of the poetic to them, but the character of the sentence is due to the relentless surge of its words. These are things that have to be heard. Unluckily, there is no sound method for treating the rhythmic effects that English produces so lavishly.

The variations in stress and pause which English offers can be woven into an expressive fabric of imbricate cadences, but no one has yet discovered a way to isolate its basic rhythmic elements, what in poetry we call the feet. Until that day comes, we can only continue to play it by ear as we read and as we write. If the student finds that a writer is particularly good in his rhythmic effects, he can always point this out even if he cannot analyze it.

To many men words are power, and to most men they are unfailing sources of interest. To the student who is learning to unweave prose, it will be words that have the most to tell him about style. What kinds of words does the writer use? Are they erudite, slangy, archaic, or drawn from the common speech? Do they refer to abstractions or to things with shape and form? Does the writer pin his abstractions to concrete details so that they may be the more readily grasped? Is the author inclined to use his words imaginatively, sticking them into surprising contexts for freshness of effect or wit? Does he milk them for their connotations? (Consider this sentence by Fritz Leiber: "We don't care what your motives are, or whether they are derived from jumbled genes, a curdled childhood, or a sick society.") Hardest of all to explain adequately, does the writer use language ironically? These are questions that no one should answer off the top of his head. They demand careful study, made with historical tools such as the *New English Dictionary* (called the *Oxford*), the *Dictionary of American English*, and the *Dictionary of Americanisms*.

Is the author given to new patterns of coining words and phrases? (Does he road-test a car before buying it? Does he prefer swim suits to swimming suits, fry pans to frying pans, and launch pads to launching pads? Was his vacation a success, fishwise?) Maybe he likes to use expressions only if they are tried and true, so that every canard is base and every violation flagrant. An expression is not to be sneered at simply because it comes second-hand—originality is not that great a prize—but a determination to manufacture prose out of prefabricated phrases is not the mark of an able or thoughtful writer.

Clichés and neologisms are narrow avenues leading to a broader question, which might be called commonality. To what degree does the writer select nouns, verbs, adjectives, and adverbs which are readily known? It is not just a question of words like *smooth* versus *glabrous* but the extent to which an author relies upon familiar or unfamiliar words and varies them for effect. A careless writer is particularly liable to overwork *have* and *be*. If the student hopes to investigate commonality with any assurance, he must learn to use reliable studies of word frequency, such as *The Teacher's Word Book of 30,000 Words* by Edward L. Thorndike and Irving Lorge.

Some stylistic revelations are not entirely meaningful until one style is compared with another. Does the writer like adjectives and adverbs? Styles that we think of as descriptive and vivid often acquire their color from a moderate use of these. What is the ratio of nouns to verbs in a selection? One of the commonplaces among people who dabble in composition is that a supple, readable style exploits the verb while dense, impenetrable writing multiplies nouns on every provocation. Another rough index to the difficulty of any piece of writing is the average number of syllables per word. The higher the ratio, the harder the reading. It is also a measure of the writer's ability: the poorer the writer, the greater his inclination to spew words out in polysyllabic mouthfuls.

Such questions will guide the student, but they will not do the job for him. Diction, like all the elements of style, requires awareness. The imperceptive student might study H. L. Mencken and conclude that he has a big vocabulary. The student who knows how to look will find that Mencken gets some of his best effects from mixing levels, juxtaposing the learned word with the colloquialism to startle and to amuse.

After words comes syntax, and here the student will see only as far as he under-stands the grammar of his language. The heart of the English sentence is its subject-and-predicate arrangement, but the possibilities for variations on this theme are huge. Selecting the verb alone determines the structure of the predicate. The choice of a verb like *ask* sets up certain possibilities for everything that fol-lows it (*ask him, ask him the answer, ask him to tell us*) which are considerably different from the patterns conditioned by some other verb, such as *try* (*just try it, just try hitting me, just try to hit me*). Simple subject and simple predicate may be composed of a word, a phrase, or a whole clause; they may be compounded; and they may be modified by other words, phrases, and clauses. Often subject to the writer's choice are the movable parts of the sentence—the parenthetical and adverbial elements, whether words, phrases, or entire clauses. The student must attempt to find what grammatical patterns the writer uses and which he favors, and there are no formulas to help him. His investigations should range from averaging the length of the writer's sentences to counting up the number of his sentences under ten words, twenty words, thirty words, and so on. He should learn how the writer puts his clauses and sentences together—whether he uses co-ordinating conjunctions, subordinating conjunctions, conjunctive adverbs or other transitions, or nothing at all. He should determine whether his writer em-ploys parallelism, balance, and antithesis, whether he uses loose sentences, with phrases and clauses strung together like beads on a string, or periodic sentences, which withhold the sense until the very last. These are a few of the grammatical possibilities, but they are no substitute for percipience.

Most fascinating of all the elements of prose style, partly because it is a link with poetry, is metaphor. Traditional descriptions largely ignore the superabun-dance of forms which metaphor appears in. We learn names for figures, such as *my love is like a red, red rose* and *the moon was a ghostly galleon,* but what about the host of other metaphors telling us about the bone-dry earth and cat-like beasts and things that are as green as grass and those that are not worth a bean? The diverse, linguistic forms of all these metaphors can be studied, and should be, but the important thing is what they have in common. In each metaphor one noun (other parts of speech, quite often) is related to another, usually through a quality or condition which they share. This is most easily expressed by a simple proportion:

> my love: unnamed quality : : unnamed quality : red rose
> bone : dry : : dry : earth

Of the three different terms in the proportion, sometimes only two are given, and the reader must guess what it is (beauty most likely) that my love and a red, red rose have in common. A good metaphor with only two terms is harder to construct than one with three but more subtle in its effect because it forces the reader to work with the writer; the effort is usually a small one and the satisfaction considerable.

Related to this broad class of metaphors is transference. Consider this sentence, taken from a review by *Time:*

> Squeezed between all that is heavy-handed in the show and all that is tawdry, what has merit is left gasping for air.

A proportion might again be set up, but this time the metaphor is most easily described through its diction, which speaks of one thing (a play) in the language usually reserved for another (people, and whatever else can be squeezed to the point of gasping). Transference may be as elaborate as the example from *Time* or limited to a single word (Leiber's "curdled childhood"). It is by such metaphoric uses, among other processes, that words develop and change meanings. Transference can be a source of gentle humor, but more important it gives to prose a richness of texture comparable to what we find in poetry.

Substitution, another rough subdivision of metaphor, consists of expressions which mention the part for the whole ("I would gladly choose the rope itself to his endless yapping") or the whole for the part ("Slow down or you'll have the law on your tail"), a characteristic for the object ("She's washing out her unmentionables"), or a species for the genus ("Is this your new Kodak?").

These are but a handful of the aspects of style. Style itself is an elusive prey—hard to stalk, difficult to cage, largely unknowable. It "is a living and breathing thing, with something of the demoniacal in it," as Mencken said, and "it fits its proprietor rightly and yet ever so loosely, as his skin fits him." We can seek to discover what style is, but we mustn't expect to reduce it to the peak-and-valley simplicity of a fever chart.

ESSAY SUGGESTIONS

1. Select any of the writers in this book and analyze his style. What are its salient features? As a supplement to your essay, write a one-paragraph parody of the author's style. Does this give you any new insights into the way your author writes?
2. Compare the styles of a modern author and a writer from the seventeenth or eighteenth century.
3. Select a modern writer whose style you admire and contrast him with another contemporary writer whose style you feel to be wanting. What are the reasons for the goodness of one and the lack of merit of the other?
4. Analyze your own style as shown in your essays for this course. What are its good points? Its weaknesses?

N.B.: The Gallery of Styles gives the merest taste of the historical variety of excellent writing which has been done in modern English. The student must read again the essays in this volume by Bacon, Coleridge, Hazlitt, Newman, Emerson, Twain, and Stevenson, considering them for their style. Likewise he must restudy the many fine contemporary writers printed here (especially Hersey, Orwell, Lynes, Wilson, Miss Carson, White, Huxley, Roth, Stephenson, Knox, Krutch, Woollcott, and Warren) for the characteristics of present-day style. The serious student will hasten to read more of the great masters of past times. He should not be satisfied before he has made the Authorized Version of the Bible (1611) and the Book of Common Prayer a part of his inmost consciousness, and he will study the works of Richard Hooker, Sir Thomas North, John Milton, Sir Thomas Browne, John Dryden, Edward Gibbon, and contemporary writers like Sir Winston Churchill and H. L. Mencken assiduously.

FURTHER READING

Charles Sears Baldwin, A *College Manual of Rhetoric*, Chapter VII.

Bonamy Dobrée, *Modern Prose Style*, Oxford: The Clarendon Press, 1934.

Edmund W. Gosse, "Style," *Encyclopaedia Britannica*. Eleventh Edition. Cambridge: Cambridge University Press, 1910–1911. This is one of the great editions of the *Britannica*, and the student would do well to make its acquaintance.

George Orwell, "Politics and the English Language," in *Shooting an Elephant*. New York: Harcourt, Brace and Company, Inc., 1950.

Walter Pater, "On Style," in *Appreciations*, volume V of the *Works*. New York: Macmillan Company, 1900–1901.

Sir Arthur Quiller-Couch, *On the Art of Writing*, Chapter XII.

Walter Raleigh, *Style*. London: Edward Arnold, 1911.

Herbert Read, *English Prose Style*, especially Chapters III, XII, and XIII.

Edith Rickert, *New Methods for the Study of Literature*. Chicago: University of Chicago Press, 1927.

Theodore Savory, *The Art of Translation*. London: Jonathan Cape, 1959.

Arthur Schopenhauer, "On Style," in *The Art of Literature*, translated by T. Bailey Saunders. New York: Macmillan Company, 1891.

James H. Sledd, "Applied Grammar: Some Notes on English Prose Style," in A *Short Introduction to English Grammar*. Chicago: Scott, Foresman and Company, 1959.

William Strunk and E. B. White, *Elements of Style*. New York: Macmillan Company, 1959.

Alexander Fraser Tytler, Lord Woodhouselee, *Essay on the Principles of Translation*. London: J. M. Dent & Company, n.d.

WILLIAM HAZLITT

On Familiar Style

It is not easy to write a familiar style. Many people mistake a familiar for a vulgar style, and suppose that to write without affectation is to write at random. On the contrary, there is nothing that requires more precision, and, if I may so say, purity of expression, than the style I am speaking of. It utterly rejects not only all unmeaning pomp, but all low, cant phrases, and loose, unconnected, *slip-shod* allusions. It is not to take the first word that offers, but the best word in common use; it is not to throw words together in any combinations we please, but to follow and avail ourselves of the true idiom of the language. To write a genuine familiar or truly English style, is to write as any one would speak in common conversation, who had a thorough command and choice of words, or who could discourse with ease, force, and perspicuity, setting aside all pedantic and oratorical flourishes. Or to give another illustration, to write naturally is the same thing in regard to common conversation, as to read naturally is in regard to common speech. It does not follow that it is an easy thing to give the true accent and inflection to the words you utter, because you do not attempt to rise above the level of ordinary life and colloquial speaking. You do not assume indeed the solemnity of the pulpit, or the tone of stage-declamation: neither are you at liberty to gabble on at a venture, without emphasis or discretion, or to resort to vulgar dialect or clownish pronunciation. You must steer a middle course. You are tied down to a given and appropriate articulation, which is determined by the habitual associations between sense and sound, and which you can only hit by entering into the author's meaning, as you must find the proper words and style to express yourself by fixing your thoughts on the subject you have to write about. Any one may mouth out a passage with a theatrical cadence, or get upon stilts to tell his thoughts: but to write

or speak with propriety and simplicity is a more difficult task. Thus it is easy to affect a pompous style, to use a word twice as big as the thing you want to express: it is not so easy to pitch upon the very word that exactly fits it. Out of eight or ten words equally common, equally intelligible, with nearly equal pretensions, it is a matter of some nicety and discrimination to pick out the very one, the preferableness of which is scarcely perceptible, but decisive. The reason why I object to Dr. Johnson's style is, that there is no discrimination, no selection, no variety in it. He uses none but 'tall, opaque words,' taken from the 'first row of the rubric:'—words with the greatest number of syllables, or Latin phrases with merely English terminations. If a fine style depended on this sort of arbitrary pretension, it would be fair to judge of an author's elegance by the measurement of his words, and the substitution of foreign circumlocutions (with no precise associations) for the mother-tongue.[1] How simple it is to be dignified without ease, to be pompous without meaning! Surely, it is but a mechanical rule for avoiding what is low to be always pedantic and affected. It is clear you cannot use a vulgar English word, if you never use a common English word at all. A fine tact is shewn in adhering to those which are perfectly common, and yet never falling into any expressions which are debased by disgusting circumstances, or which owe their signification and point to technical or professional allusions. A truly natural or familiar style can never be quaint or vulgar, for this reason, that it is of universal force and applicability, and that quaintness and vulgarity arise out of the immediate connection of certain words with coarse and disagreeable, or with confined ideas. The last form what we understand by *cant* or *slang* phrases.—To give an example of what is not very clear in the general statement. I should say that the phrase *To cut with a knife*, or *To cut a piece of wood*, is perfectly free from vulgar-

---

[1] I have heard of such a thing as an author, who makes it a rule never to admit a monosyllable into his vapid verse. Yet the charm and sweetness of Marlow's lines depended often on their being made up almost entirely of monosyllables.

ity, because it is perfectly common: but to *cut an acquaintance* is not quite unexceptionable, because it is not perfectly common or intelligible, and has hardly yet escaped out of the limits of slang phraseology. I should hardly therefore use the word in this sense without putting it in italics as a license of expression, to be received *cum grano salis*. All provincial or bye-phrases come under the same mark of reprobation—all such as the writer transfers to the page from his fire-side or a particular *coterie*, or that he invents for his own sole use and convenience. I conceive that words are like money, not the worse for being common, but that it is the stamp of custom alone that gives them circulation or value. I am fastidious in this respect, and would almost as soon coin the currency of the realm as counterfeit the King's English. I never invented or gave a new and unauthorised meaning to any word but one single one (the term *impersonal* applied to feelings) and that was in an abstruse metaphysical discussion to express a very difficult distinction. I have been (I know) loudly accused of revelling in vulgarisms and broken English. I cannot speak to that point: but so far I plead guilty to the determined use of acknowledged idioms and common elliptical expressions. I am not sure that the critics in question know the one from the other, that is, can distinguish any medium between formal pedantry and the most barbarous solecism. As an author, I endeavour to employ plain words and popular modes of construction, as were I a chapman and dealer, I should common weights and measures.

The proper force of words lies not in the words themselves, but in their application. A word may be a fine-sounding word, of an unusual length, and very imposing from its learning and novelty, and yet in the connection in which it is introduced, may be quite pointless and irrelevant. It is not pomp or pretension, but the adaptation of the expression to the idea that clenches a writer's meaning:—as it is not the size or glossiness of the materials, but their being fitted each to its place, that gives strength to the arch; or as the pegs and nails are as necessary to the support of the building as the larger timbers, and more so than the mere shewy, unsubstantial ornaments. I hate anything that occupies more space than it is worth. I hate to see a load of band-boxes go along the street, and I hate to see a parcel of big words without any thing in them. A person who does not deliberately dispose of all his thoughts alike in cumbrous draperies and flimsy disguises, may strike out twenty varieties of familiar every-day language, each coming somewhat nearer to the feeling he wants to convey, and at last not hit upon that particular and only one, which may be said to be identical with the exact impression in his mind. This would seem to shew that Mr. Cobbett is hardly right in saying that the first word that occurs is always the best. It may be a very good one; and yet a better may present itself on reflection or from time to time. It should be suggested naturally, however, and spontaneously, from a fresh and lively conception of the subject. We seldom succeed by trying at improvement, or by merely substituting one word for another that we are not satisfied with, as we cannot recollect the name of a place or person by merely plaguing ourselves about it. We wander farther from the point by persisting in a wrong scent; but it starts up accidentally in the memory when we least expected it, by touching some link in the chain of previous association.

There are those who hoard up and make a cautious display of nothing but rich and rare phraseology;—ancient medals, obscure coins, and Spanish pieces of eight. They are very curious to inspect; but I myself would neither offer nor take them in the course of exchange. A sprinkling of archaisms is not amiss; but a tissue of obsolete expressions is more fit *for keep than wear*. I do not say I would not use any phrase that had been brought into fashion before the middle or the end of the last century; but I should be shy of using any that had not been employed by any approved author during the whole of that time. Words, like clothes, get old-fashioned, or mean and ridiculous, when they have been for some time laid aside. Mr. Lamb is the only imitator of old English style I can read with pleasure; and he is so thoroughly imbued with the spirit of his authors, that the idea of imitation is almost done away. There is an inward unction, a marrowy vein both in the thought and feeling, an intuition, deep and lively, of his subject, that carries off any quaintness or awkwardness arising from an antiquated style and dress. The matter is completely his own, though the manner is assumed. Perhaps his ideas are altogether so marked and individual, as to require their point and pungency to be neutralised by the affectation of a singular but traditional form of conveyance. Tricked out in the prevailing costume, they would probably seem more startling and out of the way. The old English authors, Burton, Fuller, Coryate, Sir Thomas Brown, are a kind of mediators between us and the more eccentric and whimsical modern, reconciling us to his peculiarities. I do not however know how far this is the case or not, till he condescends to write like one of us. I must confess that what I like best of his papers under the signature of Elia (still I do not presume, amidst such excellence, to decide what is most excellent) is the account of *Mrs. Battle's Opinions on Whist*, which is also the most free from obsolete allusions and turns of expression—

'A well of native English undefiled.'

To those acquainted with his admired prototypes, these Essays of the ingenious and highly gifted author have the same sort of charm and relish, that Erasmus's Colloquies or a fine piece of modern Latin have to the classical scholar. Certainly, I do not know any borrowed pencil that has more power or felicity of execution than the one of which I have here been speaking.

It is as easy to write a gaudy style without ideas, as it is to spread a pallet of shewy colours, or to smear in a flaunting transparency. 'What do you read?'—'Words, words, words.'—'What is the matter?'—'*Nothing*,' it might be answered. The florid style is the reverse of the familiar. The last is employed as an unvarnished medium to convey ideas; the first is resorted to as a spangled veil to conceal the want of them. When there is nothing to be set down but words, it costs little to have them fine. Look through the dictionary, and cull out a *florilegium*, rival the *tulippomania*. *Rouge* high enough, and never mind the natural complexion. The vulgar, who are not in the secret, will admire the look of preternatural health and vigour; and the fashionable, who regard only appearances, will be delighted with the imposition. Keep to your sounding generalities, your tinkling phrases, and all will be well. Swell out an unmeaning truism to a perfect tympany of style. A thought, a distinction is the rock on which all this brittle cargo of verbiage splits at once. Such writers have merely *verbal* imaginations, that retain nothing but words. Or their puny thoughts have dragon-wings, all green and gold. They soar far above the vulgar failing of the *Sermo humi obrepens*—their most ordinary speech is never short of an hyperbole, splendid, imposing, vague, incomprehensible, magniloquent, a cento of sounding common-places. If some of us, whose 'ambition is more lowly,' pry a little too narrowly into nooks and corners to pick up a number of 'unconsidered trifles,' they never once direct their eyes or lift their hands to seize on any but the most gorgeous, tarnished, thread-bare patch-work set of phrases, the left-off finery of poetic extravagance, transmitted down through successive generations of barren pretenders. If they criticise actors and actresses, a huddled phantasmagoria of feathers, spangles, floods of light, and oceans of sound float before their morbid sense, which they paint in the style of Ancient Pistol. Not a glimpse can you get of the merits or defects of the performers: they are hidden in a profusion of barbarous epithets and wilful rhodomontade. Our hypercritics are not thinking of these little fantoccini beings—

'That strut and fret their hour upon the stage'—

but of tall phantoms of words, abstractions, *genera* and *species*, sweeping clauses, periods that unite the Poles, forced alliterations, astounding antitheses—

'And on their pens *Fustian* sits plumed.'

If they describe kings and queens, it is an Eastern pageant. The Coronation at either

House is nothing to it. We get at four repeated images—a curtain, a throne, a sceptre, and a foot-stool. These are with them the wardrobe of a lofty imagination; and they turn their servile strains to servile uses. Do we read a description of pictures? It is not a reflection of tones and hues which 'nature's own sweet and cunning hand laid on,' but piles of precious stones, rubies, pearls, emeralds, Golconda's mines, and all the blazonry of art. Such persons are in fact besotted with words, and their brains are turned with the glittering, but empty and sterile phantoms of things. Personifications, capital letters, seas of sunbeams, visions of glory, shining inscriptions, the figures of a transparency, Britannia with her shield, or Hope leaning on an anchor, make up their stock in trade. They may be considered as *hieroglyphical* writers. Images stand out in their minds isolated and important merely in themselves, without any ground-work of feeling—there is no context in their imaginations. Words affect them in the same way, by the mere sound, that is, by their possible, not by their actual application to the subject in hand. They are fascinated by first appearances, and have no sense of consequences. Nothing more is meant by them than meets the ear: they understand or feel nothing more than meets their eye. The web and texture of the universe, and of the heart of man, is a mystery to them: they have no faculty that strikes a chord in unison with it. They cannot get beyond the daubings of fancy, the varnish of sentiment. Objects are not linked to feelings, words to things, but images revolve in splendid mockery, words represent themselves in their strange rhapsodies. The categories of such a mind are pride and ignorance—pride in outside show, to which they sacrifice every thing, and ignorance of the true worth and hidden structure both of words and things. With a sovereign contempt for what is familiar and natural, they are the slaves of vulgar affectation—of a routine of high-flown phrases. Scorning to imitate realities, they are unable to invent any thing, to strike out one original idea. They are not copyists of nature, it is true: but they are the poorest of all plagiarists, the plagiarists of words. All is far-fetched, dear-bought, artificial, oriental in subject and allusion: all is mechanical, conventional, vapid, formal, pedantic in style and execution. They startle and confound the understanding of the reader, by the remoteness and obscurity of their illustrations: they soothe the ear by the monotony of the same everlasting round of circuitous metaphors. They are the *mock-school* in poetry and prose. They flounder about between fustian in expression, and bathos in sentiment. They tantalise the fancy, but never reach the head nor touch the heart. Their Temple of Fame is like a shadowy structure raised by Dulness to Vanity, or like Cowper's description of the Empress of Russia's palace of ice, as 'worthless as in shew 'twas glittering'—

'It smiled, and it was cold!'

QUESTIONS FOR STUDY AND DISCUSSION

1. In what sense does Hazlitt use the word *style*? What matters of style does he explicitly discuss? What does he leave out that you would consider to be elements of style in writing?

2. Hazlitt uses the expression "to cut an acquaintance" as an example of the use of *cut* as slang. Is this usage still considered "not quite unexceptionable"? Make a list of words and expressions which might be considered slang but which, in your opinion, are now acceptable.

3. Presumably Hazlitt writes the "familiar style" he is discussing. Would it be considered "familiar style" today? Use Hazlitt's own "rules" in supporting your opinion.

Does Hazlitt practice what he preaches when he employs words like *cento, coterie,* and *fantoccini*? Can they be justified as the right word, the only word, "being fitted each to its place"?

4. In handling question 3, or as a separate exercise, draw up a set of rules for the "familiar style" as described in the essay.

5. The "gaudy" or "florid" style, Hazlitt alleges, is resorted to by writers to conceal a want of ideas. Do you agree? Can you cite exceptions or make a defense of a highly ornamental style, or one which prefers long words?

WRITING ASSIGNMENTS

1. Choose from one of the essays in this book (or elsewhere if your instructor wishes) a passage which is not in the "familiar style," and rewrite it in what you judge to be a modern equivalent of that style. Then develop a short essay in which you point out the changes you have made and give your reasons for making them.

2. Alternatively, write your own example of highly formal expression; then proceed as in assignment 1.

ROBERT LOUIS STEVENSON

On Some Technical Elements of Style in Literature

There is nothing more disenchanting to man than to be shown the springs and mechanism of any art. All our arts and occupations lie wholly on the surface; it is on the surface that we perceive their beauty, fitness, and significance; and to pry below is to be appalled by their emptiness and shocked by the coarseness of the strings and pulleys. In a similar way, psychology itself, when pushed to any nicety, discovers an abhorrent baldness, but rather from the fault of our analysis than from any poverty native to the mind. And perhaps in æsthetics the reason is the same: those disclosures which seem fatal to the dignity of art seem so perhaps only in the proportion of our ignorance; and those conscious and unconscious artifices which it seems unworthy of the serious artist to employ were yet, if we had the power to trace them to their springs, indications of a delicacy of the sense finer than we conceive, and hints of ancient harmonies in nature. This ignorance at least is largely irremediable. We shall never learn the affinities of beauty, for they lie too deep in nature and too far back in the mysterious history of man. The amateur, in consequence, will always grudgingly receive details of method, which can be stated but never can wholly be explained; nay, on the principle laid down in *Hudibras*, that

> "Still the less they understand,
> The more they admire the sleight-of-hand,"

many are conscious at each new disclosure of a diminution in the ardour of their pleasure. I must therefore warn that well-known character, the general reader, that I am here embarked upon a most distasteful business: taking down the picture from the wall and looking on the back; and, like the inquiring child, pulling the musical cart to pieces.

1. *Choice of Words.*—The art of literature stands apart from among its sisters, because the material in which the literary artist works is the dialect of life; hence, on the one hand, a strange freshness and immediacy of address to the public mind, which is ready prepared to understand it; but hence, on the other, a singular limitation. The sister arts enjoy the use of a plastic and ductile material, like the modeller's clay; literature alone is condemned to work in mosaic with finite and quite rigid words. You have seen these blocks, dear to the nursery: this one a pillar, that a pediment, a third a window or a vase. It is with blocks of just such arbitrary size and figure that the literary architect is condemned to design the palace of his art. Nor is this all; for since these blocks, or words, are the acknowledged currency of our daily affairs, there are here possible none of those suppressions by which other arts obtain relief, continuity, and vigour: no hieroglyphic touch, no smoothed impasto, no inscrutable shadow, as in painting; no blank wall, as in architecture; but every word, phrase, sentence, and paragraph must move in a logical progression, and convey a definite conventional import.

Now the first merit which attracts in the pages of a good writer, or the talk of a brilliant conversationalist, is the apt choice and contrast of the words employed. It is, indeed, a strange art to take these blocks, rudely conceived for the purpose of the market or the bar, and by tact of application touch them to the finest meanings and distinctions, restore to them their primal energy, wittily shift them to another issue, or make of them a drum to rouse the passions. But though this form of merit is without doubt the most sensible and seizing, it is far from being equally present in all writers. The effect of words in Shakespeare, their singular justice, significance, and poetic charm, is different, indeed, from the effect of words in Addison or Fielding.

Or, to take an example nearer home, the words in Carlyle seem electrified into an energy of lineament, like the faces of men furiously moved; whilst the words in Macaulay, apt enough to convey his meaning, harmonious enough in sound, yet glide from the memory like undistinguished elements in a general effect. But the first class of writers have no monopoly of literary merit. There is a sense in which Addison is superior to Carlyle; a sense in which Cicero is better than Tacitus, in which Voltaire excels Montaigne: it certainly lies not in the choice of words; it lies not in the interest or value of the matter; it lies not in force of intellect, of poetry, or of humour. The three first are but infants to the three second; and yet each, in a particular point of literary art, excels his superior in the whole. What is that point?

2. *The Web.*—Literature, although it stands apart by reason of the great destiny and general use of its medium in the affairs of men, is yet an art like other arts. Of these we may distinguish two great classes: those arts, like sculpture, painting, acting, which are representative, or, as used to be said very clumsily, imitative; and those, like architecture, music, and the dance, which are self-sufficient, and merely presentative. Each class, in right of this distinction, obeys principles apart; yet both may claim a common ground of existence, and it may be said with sufficient justice that the motive and end of any art whatever is to make a pattern; a pattern, it may be, of colours, of sounds, of changing attitudes, geometrical figures, or imitative lines; but still a pattern. That is the plane on which these sisters meet; it is by this that they are arts; and if it be well they should at times forget their childish origin, addressing their intelligence to virile tasks, and performing unconsciously that necessary function of their life, to make a pattern, it is still imperative that the pattern shall be made.

Music and literature, the two temporal arts, contrive their pattern of sounds in time; or, in other words, of sounds and pauses. Communication may be made in broken words, the business of life be carried on with substantives alone; but that is not what we call literature; and the true business of the literary artist is to plait or weave his meaning, involving it around itself; so that each sentence, by successive phrases, shall first come into a kind of knot, and then, after a moment of suspended meaning, solve and clear itself. In every properly constructed sentence there should be observed this knot or hitch; so that (however delicately) we are led to foresee, to expect, and then to welcome the successive phrases. The pleasure may be heightened by an element of surprise, as, very grossly, in the common figure of the antithesis, or, with much greater subtlety, where an antithesis is first suggested and then deftly evaded. Each phrase, besides, is to be comely in itself; and between the implication and the evolution of the sentence there should be a satisfying equipoise of sound; for nothing more often disappoints the ear than a sentence solemnly and sonorously prepared, and hastily and weakly finished. Nor should the balance be too striking and exact, for the one rule is to be infinitely various; to interest, to disappoint, to surprise, and yet still to gratify; to be ever changing, as it were, the stitch, and yet still to give the effect of an ingenious neatness.

The conjurer juggles with two oranges, and our pleasure in beholding him springs from this, that neither is for an instant overlooked or sacrificed. So with the writer. His pattern, which is to please the supersensual ear, is yet addressed, throughout and first of all, to the demands of logic. Whatever be the obscurities, whatever the intricacies of the argument, the neatness of the fabric must not suffer, or the artist has been proved unequal to his design. And, on the other hand, no form of words must be selected, no knot must be tied among the phrases, unless knot and word be precisely what is wanted to forward and illuminate the argument; for to fail in this is to swindle in the game. The genius of prose rejects the *cheville* no less emphatically than the laws of verse; and the *cheville*, I should perhaps explain to some of my readers, is any meaningless or very watered phrase employed to strike a balance in the sound. Pattern and argument live in each other; and it is by the brevity, clearness, charm, or emphasis of the second, that we judge the strength and fitness of the first.

Style is synthetic; and the artist, seeking, so to speak, a peg to plait about, takes up at once two or more elements or two or more views of the subject in hand; combines, implicates, and contrasts them; and while, in one sense, he was merely seeking an occasion for the necessary knot, he will be found, in the other, to have greatly enriched the meaning, or to have transacted the work of two sentences in the space of one. In the change from the successive shallow statements of the old chronicler to the dense and luminous flow of highly synthetic narrative, there is implied a vast amount of both philosophy and wit. The philosophy we clearly see, recognising in the synthetic writer a far more deep and stimulating view of life, and a far keener sense of the generation and affinity of events. The wit we might imagine to be lost; but it is not so, for it is just that wit, these perpetual nice contrivances, these difficulties overcome, this double purpose attained, these two oranges kept simultaneously dancing in the air, that, consciously or not, afford the reader his delight. Nay, and this wit, so little recognised, is the necessary organ of that philosophy which we so much admire. That style is therefore the most perfect, not, as fools say, which is the most natural, for the most natural is the disjointed babble of the chronicler; but which attains the highest degree of elegant and pregnant implication unobtrusively; or if obtrusively, then with the greatest gain to sense and vigour. Even the derangement of the phrases from their (so-called) natural order is luminous for the mind; and it is by the means of such designed reversal that the elements of a judgment may be most pertinently marshalled, or the stages of a complicated action most perspicuously bound into one.

The web, then, or the pattern: a web at once sensuous and logical, an elegant and pregnant texture: that is style, that is the foundation of the art of literature. Books indeed continue to be read, for the interest of the fact or fable, in which this quality is poorly represented, but still it will be there. And, on the other hand, how many do we continue to peruse and reperuse with pleasure whose only merit is the elegance of texture? I am tempted to mention Cicero; and since Mr. Anthony Trollope is dead, I will. It is a poor diet for the mind, a very colourless and toothless "criticism of life"; but we enjoy the pleasure of a most intricate and dexterous pattern, every stitch a model at once of elegance and of good sense; and the two oranges, even if one of them be rotten, kept dancing with inimitable grace.

Up to this moment I have had my eye mainly upon prose; for though in verse also the implication of the logical texture is a crowning beauty, yet in verse it may be dispensed with. You would think that here was a death-blow to all I have been saying; and far from that, it is but a new illustration of the principle involved. For if the versifier is not bound to weave a pattern of his own, it is because another pattern has been formally imposed upon him by the laws of verse. For that is the essence of a prosody. Verse may be rhythmical; it may be merely alliterative; it may, like the French, depend wholly on the (quasi) regular recurrence of the rhyme; or, like the Hebrew, it may consist in the strangely fanciful device of repeating the same idea. It does not matter on what principle the law is based, so it be a law. It may be pure convention; it may have no inherent beauty; all that we have a right to ask of any prosody is, that it shall lay down a pattern for the writer, and that what it lays down shall be neither too easy nor too hard. Hence it comes that it is much easier for men of equal facility to write fairly pleasing verse than reasonably interesting prose; for in prose the pattern itself has to be invented, and the difficulties first created before they can be solved. Hence, again, there follows the peculiar greatness of the true versifier: such as Shakespeare, Milton, and Victor Hugo, whom I place beside them as versifier merely, not as poet. These not only knit and knot the logical texture of the style with all the dexterity and strength of prose; they not only fill up the pattern of the verse with infinite variety and sober wit; but they give us, besides, a rare and special pleasure, by the art, comparable to that of counterpoint, with which they follow at the same time, and now contrast, and now combine, the double pattern of the texture and the verse. Here the sounding line concludes; a little further on, the well-knit sentence; and yet a little further, and both will reach their solution on the same ringing syllable. The best that can be offered by the best writer of prose is to show us the development of the idea and the stylistic pattern proceed hand in hand, sometimes by an obvious and triumphant effort, sometimes with a great air of ease and nature. The writer of verse, by virtue of conquering another difficulty, delights us with a new series of triumphs. He follows three purposes where his rival followed only two; and the change is of precisely the same nature as that from melody to harmony. Or if you prefer to return to the juggler, behold him now, to the vastly increased enthusiasm of the spectators, juggling with three oranges instead of two. Thus it is: added difficulty, added beauty; and the pattern, with every fresh element, becoming more interesting in itself.

Yet it must not be thought that verse is simply an addition; something is lost as well as something gained; and there remains plainly traceable, in comparing the best prose with the best verse, a certain broad distinction of method in the web. Tight as the versifier may draw the knot of logic, yet for the ear he still leaves the tissue of the sentence floating somewhat loose. In prose, the sentence turns upon a pivot, nicely balanced, and fits into itself with an obtrusive neatness like a puzzle. The ear remarks and is singly gratified by this return and balance; while in verse it is all diverted to the measure. To find comparable passages is hard; for either the versifier is hugely the superior of the rival, or, if he be not, and still persist in his more delicate enterprise, he fails to be as widely his inferior. But let us select them from the pages of the same writer, one who was ambidexter; let us take, for instance, Rumour's Prologue to the Second Part of *Henry IV.*, a fine flourish of eloquence in

Shakespeare's second manner, and set it side by side with Falstaff's praise of sherris, act iv. scene i.; or let us compare the beautiful prose spoken throughout by Rosalind and Orlando; compare, for example, the first speech of all, Orlando's speech to Adam, with what passage it shall please you to select—the Seven Ages from the same play, or even such a stave of nobility as Othello's farewell to war; and still you will be able to perceive, if you have an ear for that class of music, a certain superior degree of organisation in the prose; a compacter fitting of the parts; a balance in the swing and the return as of a throbbing pendulum. We must not, in things temporal, take from those who have little, the little that they have; the merits of prose are inferior, but they are not the same; it is a little kingdom, but an independent.

3. *Rhythm of the Phrase.*—Some way back, I used a word which still awaits an application. Each phrase, I said, was to be comely; but what is a comely phrase? In all ideal and material points, literature, being a representative art, must look for analogies to painting and the like; but in what is technical and executive, being a temporal art, it must seek for them in music. Each phrase of each sentence, like an air or a recitative in music, should be so artfully compounded out of long and short, out of accented and unaccented, as to gratify the sensual ear. And of this the ear is the sole judge. It is impossible to lay down laws. Even in our accentual and rhythmic language no analysis can find the secret of the beauty of a verse; how much less, then, of those phrases, such as prose is built of, which obey no law but to be lawless and yet to please? The little that we know of verse (and for my part I owe it all to my friend Professor Fleeming Jenkin) is, however, particularly interesting in the present connection. We have been accustomed to describe the heroic line as five iambic feet, and to be filled with pain and confusion whenever, as by the conscientious school-boy, we have heard our own description put in practice.

"All nìght | the dreàd | less àn | gel ùn |
pursùed," [Milton]

goes the school-boy; but though we close our ears, we cling to our definition, in spite of its proved and naked insufficiency. Mr. Jenkin was not so easily pleased, and readily discovered that the heroic line consists of four groups, or, if you prefer the phrase, contains four pauses:

"All night | the dreadless | angel | unpursued."

Four groups, each practically uttered as one word: the first, in this case, an iamb; the second, an amphibrachys; the third, a trochee; and the fourth, an amphimacer; and yet our school-boy, with no other liberty but that of inflicting pain, had triumphantly scanned it as five iambs. Perceive, now, this fresh richness of intricacy in the web; this fourth orange, hitherto unremarked, but still kept flying with the others. What had seemed to be one thing it now appears is two; and, like some puzzle in arithmetic, the verse is made at the same time to read in fives and to read in fours.

But, again, four is not necessary. We do not, indeed, find verses in six groups, because there is not room for six in the ten syllables; and we do not find verses of two, because one of the main distinctions of verse from prose resides in the comparative shortness of the group; but it is even common to find verses of three. Five is the one forbidden number; because five is the number of the feet; and if five were chosen, the two patterns would coincide, and that opposition which is the life of verse would instantly be lost. We have here a clue to the effect of polysyllables, above all in Latin, where they are so common and make so brave an architecture in the verse; for the polysyllable is a group of Nature's making. If but some Roman would return from Hades (Martial, for choice), and tell me by what conduct of the voice these thundering verses should be uttered—"*Aut Lacedæmonium Tarentum*," for a case in point—I feel as if I should enter at last into the full enjoyment of the best of human verses.

But, again, the five feet are all iambic, or supposed to be; by the mere count of syllables the four groups cannot be all iambic; as a question of elegance, I doubt if any one of them requires to be so; and I am

certain that for choice no two of them should scan the same. The singular beauty of the verse analysed above is due, so far as analysis can carry us, part, indeed, to the clever repetition of L, D, and N, but part to this variety of scansion in the groups. The groups which, like the bar in music, break up the verse for utterance, fall uniambically; and in declaiming a so-called iambic verse, it may so happen that we never utter one iambic foot. And yet to this neglect of the original beat there is a limit.

"Athens, the eye of Greece, mother of arts," [Milton]

is, with all its eccentricities, a good heroic line; for though it scarcely can be said to indicate the beat of the iamb, it certainly suggests no other measure to the ear. But begin

"Mother Athens, eye of Greece,"

or merely "Mother Athens," and the game is up, for the trochaic beat has been suggested. The eccentric scansion of the groups is an adornment; but as soon as the original beat has been forgotten, they cease implicitly to be eccentric. Variety is what is sought; but if we destroy the original mould, one of the terms of this variety is lost, and we fall back on sameness. Thus, both as to the arithmetical measure of the verse, and the degree of regularity in scansion, we see the laws of prosody to have one common purpose: to keep alive the opposition of two schemes simultaneously followed; to keep them notably apart, though still coincident; and to balance them with such judicial nicety before the reader, that neither shall be unperceived and neither signally prevail.

The rule of rhythm in prose is not so intricate. Here, too, we write in groups, or phrases, as I prefer to call them, for the prose phrase is greatly longer and is much more nonchalantly uttered than the group in verse; so that not only is there a greater interval of continuous sound between the pauses, but, for that very reason, word is linked more readily to word by a more summary enunciation. Still, the phrase is the strict analogue of the group, and successive phrases, like successive groups, must differ openly in length and rhythm. The rule of scansion in verse is to suggest no measure but the one in hand; in prose, to suggest no measure at all. Prose must be rhythmical, and it may be as much so as you will; but it must not be metrical. It may be anything, but it must not be verse. A single heroic line may very well pass and not disturb the somewhat larger stride of the prose style; but one following another will produce an instant impression of poverty, flatness, and disenchantment. The same lines delivered with the measured utterance of verse would perhaps seem rich in variety. By the more summary enunciation proper to prose, as to a more distant vision, these niceties of difference are lost. A whole verse is uttered as one phrase; and the ear is soon wearied by a succession of groups identical in length. The prose writer, in fact, since he is allowed to be so much less harmonious, is condemned to a perpetually fresh variety of movement on a larger scale, and must never disappoint the ear by the trot of an accepted metre. And this obligation is the third orange with which he has to juggle, the third quality which the prose writer must work into his pattern of words. It may be thought perhaps that this is a quality of ease rather than a fresh difficulty; but such is the inherently rhythmical strain of the English language, that the bad writer—and must I take for example that admired friend of my boyhood, Captain Reid?—the inexperienced writer, as Dickens in his earlier attempts to be impressive, and the jaded writer, as any one may see for himself, all tend to fall at once into the production of bad blank verse. And here it may be pertinently asked, Why bad? And I suppose it might be enough to answer that no man ever made good verse by accident, and that no verse can ever sound otherwise than trivial when uttered with the delivery of prose. But we can go beyond such answers. The weak side of verse is the regularity of the beat, which in itself is decidedly less impressive than the movement of the nobler prose; and it is just into this weak side, and this alone, that our careless writer falls. A peculiar density and mass, consequent on the nearness of the pauses, is one of the chief good qualities of verse; but this our accidental versifier, still following after the swift gait and large gestures

of prose, does not so much as aspire to imitate. Lastly, since he remains unconscious that he is making verse at all, it can never occur to him to extract those effects of counterpoint and opposition which I have referred to as the final grace and justification of verse, and, I may add, of blank verse in particular.

4. *Contents of the Phrase.*—Here is a great deal of talk about rhythm—and naturally; for in our canorous language rhythm is always at the door. But it must not be forgotten that in some languages this element is almost, if not quite, extinct, and that in our own it is probably decaying. The even speech of many educated Americans sounds the note of danger. I should see it go with something as bitter as despair, but I should not be desperate. As in verse no element, not even rhythm, is necessary, so, in prose also, other sorts of beauty will arise and take the place and play the part of those that we outlive. The beauty of the expected beat in verse, the beauty in prose of its larger and more lawless melody, patent as they are to English hearing, are already silent in the ears of our next neighbours; for in France the oratorical accent and the pattern of the web have almost or altogether succeeded to their places; and the French prose writer would be astounded at the labours of his brother across the Channel, and how a good quarter of his toil, above all *invita Minerva*, is to avoid writing verse. So wonderfully far apart have races wandered in spirit, and so hard it is to understand the literature next door!

Yet French prose is distinctly better than English; and French verse, above all while Hugo lives, it will not do to place upon one side. What is more to our purpose, a phrase or a verse in French is easily distinguishable as comely or uncomely. There is then another element of comeliness hitherto overlooked in this analysis: the contents of the phrase. Each phrase in literature is built of sounds, as each phrase in music consists of notes. One sound suggests, echoes, demands, and harmonises with another; and the art of rightly using these concordances is the final art in literature. It used to be a piece of good advice to all young writers to avoid alliteration; and the advice was sound, in so far as it prevented daubing. None the less for that, was it abominable nonsense, and the mere raving of those blindest of the blind who will not see. The beauty of the contents of a phrase, or of a sentence, depends implicitly upon alliteration and upon assonance. The vowel demands to be repeated; the consonant demands to be repeated; and both cry aloud to be perpetually varied. You may follow the adventures of a letter through any passage that has particularly pleased you; find it, perhaps, denied awhile, to tantalise the ear; find it fired again at you in a whole broadside; or find it pass into congenerous sounds, one liquid or labial melting away into another. And you will find another and much stranger circumstance. Literature is written by and for two senses: a sort of internal ear, quick to perceive "unheard melodies"; and the eye, which directs the pen and deciphers the printed phrase. Well, even as there are rhymes for the eye, so you will find that there are assonances and alliterations; that where an author is running the open A, deceived by the eye and our strange English spelling, he will often show a tenderness for the flat A; and that where he is running a particular consonant, he will not improbably rejoice to write it down even when it is mute or bears a different value.

Here, then, we have a fresh pattern—a pattern, to speak grossly, of letters—which makes the fourth preoccupation of the prose writer, and the fifth of the versifier. At times it is very delicate and hard to perceive, and then perhaps most excellent and winning (I say perhaps); but at times again the elements of this literal melody stand more boldly forward and usurp the ear. It becomes, therefore, somewhat a matter of conscience to select examples; and as I cannot very well ask the reader to help me, I shall do the next best by giving him the reason or the history of each selection. The two first, one in prose, one in verse, I chose without previous analysis, simply as engaging passages that had long re-echoed in my ear.

"I cannot praise a fugitive and cloistered virtue, unexercised and unbreathed, that never sallies out and sees her adversary, but slinks out of the race where that immortal garland is to be run for, not without dust and heat."[1] Down to "virtue," the current S and R are both announced and repeated unobtrusively, and by way of a grace-note that almost inseparable group PVF is given entire.[2] The next phrase is a period of repose, almost ugly in itself, both S and R still audible, and B given as the last fulfilment of PVF. In the next four phrases, from "that never" down to "run for," the mask is thrown off, and, but for a slight repetition of the F and V, the whole matter turns, almost too obtrusively, on S and R; first S coming to the front, and then R. In the concluding phrase all these favourite letters, and even the flat A, a timid preference for which is just perceptible, are discarded at a blow and in a bundle; and to make the break more obvious, every word ends with a dental, and all but one with T, for which we have been cautiously prepared since the beginning. The singular dignity of the first clause, and this hammerstroke of the last, go far to make the charm of this exquisite sentence. But it is fair to own that S and R are used a little coarsely.

"In Xanadu did Kubla Khan (KĂNDL)
   A stately pleasure dome
      decree, (KDLSR)
Where Alph the sacred river
   ran, (KĂNDLSR)
Through caverns measureless
   to man, (KĂNLSR)
    Down to a sunless sea." (NDLS)
      [Coleridge]

Here I have put the analysis of the main group alongside the lines; and the more it is looked at, the more interesting it will seem. But there are further niceties. In lines two and four, the current S is most delicately varied with Z. In line three, the current flat A is twice varied with the open A, already suggested in line two, and both

[1] Milton.
[2] As PVF will continue to haunt us through our English examples, take, by way of comparison, this Latin verse, of which it forms a chief adornment, and do not hold me answerable for the all too Roman freedom of the sense: "Hanc volo, quæ facilis, quæ palliolata vagatur."

times ("where" and "sacred") in conjunction with the current R. In the same line F and V (a harmony in themselves, even when shorn of their comrade P) are admirably contrasted. And in line four there is a marked subsidiary M, which again was announced in line two. I stop from weariness, for more might yet be said.

My next example was recently quoted from Shakespeare as an example of the poet's colour sense. Now, I do not think literature has anything to do with colour, or poets anyway the better of such a sense; and I instantly attacked this passage, since "purple" was the word that had so pleased the writer of the article, to see if there might not be some literary reason for its use. It will be seen that I succeeded amply; and I am bound to say I think the passage exceptional in Shakespeare—exceptional, indeed, in literature; but it was not I who chose it.

> "The BaRge she sat iN, like a BUR-
> Nished throNe
> BURNt oN the water: the POOP was
> BeateN gold,
> PURPle the sails and so PUR * Fumèd
> that   *per
> The wiNds were love-sick with them."
> [*Antony and Cleopatra*]

It may be asked why I have put the F of "perfumed" in capitals; and I reply, because this change from P to F is the completion of that from B to P, already so adroitly carried out. Indeed, the whole passage is a monument of curious ingenuity; and it seems scarce worth while to indicate the subsidiary S, L, and W. In the same article, a second passage from Shakespeare was quoted, once again as an example of his colour sense:

> "A mole cinque-spotted like the crim-
> son drops
> I' the bottom of a cowslip." [*Cymbeline*]

It is very curious, very artificial, and not worth while to analyse at length: I leave it to the reader. But before I turn my back on Shakespeare, I should like to quote a passage, for my own pleasure, and for a very model of every technical art:

> "But in the wind and tempest of her
> frown,   W. P. V.[3] F. (st) (ow)
> Distinction with a loud and powerful
> fan,   W. P. F. (st) (ow) L.
> Puffing at all, winnows the light away;
>   W. P. F. L.
> And what hath mass and matter by
> itself   W. F. L. M. A.
> Lies rich in virtue and unmingled."[4]
>   V. L. M.

From these delicate and choice writers I turned with some curiosity to a player of the big drum—Macaulay. I had in hand the two-volume edition, and I opened at the beginning of the second volume. Here was what I read:

> "The violence of revolutions is generally proportioned to the degree of the maladministration which has produced them. It is therefore not strange that the government of Scotland, having been during many years greatly more corrupt than the government of England, should have fallen with a far heavier ruin. The movement against the last king of the house of Stuart was in England conservative, in Scotland destructive. The English complained not of the law, but of the violation of the law."

This was plain-sailing enough; it was our old friend PVF, floated by the liquids in a body; but as I read on, and turned the page, and still found PVF with his attendant liquids, I confess my mind misgave me utterly. This could be no trick of Macaulay's; it must be the nature of the English tongue. In a kind of despair, I turned half-way through the volume; and coming upon his lordship dealing with General Cannon, and fresh from Claverhouse and Killiecrankie, here, with elucidative spelling, was my reward:

> "Meanwhile the disorders of Kannon's Kamp went on inKreasing. He Kalled a Kouncil of war to Konsider what Kourse it would be advisable to taKe. But as soon as the Kouncil had

---

[3] The V is in "of."
[4] *Troilus and Cressida.*

met, a preliminary Kuestion was raised. The army was almost eKsKlusively a Highland army. The recent viKtory had been won eKsKlusively by Highland warriors. Great chiefs who had brought siKs or Seven hundred fighting men into the field did not think it fair that they should be outvoted by gentlemen from Ireland, and from the Low Kountries, who bore indeed King James's Kommission, and were Kalled Kolonels and Kaptains, but who were Kolonels without regiments and Kaptains without Kompanies."

A moment of FV in all this world of K's! It was not the English language, then, that was an instrument of one string, but Macaulay that was an incomparable dauber.

It was probably from this barbaric love of repeating the same sound, rather than from any design of clearness, that he acquired his irritating habit of repeating words; I say the one rather than the other, because such a trick of the ear is deeper-seated and more original in man than any logical consideration. Few writers, indeed, are probably conscious of the length to which they push this melody of letters. One, writing very diligently, and only concerned about the meaning of his words and the rhythm of his phrases, was struck into amazement by the eager triumph with which he cancelled one expression to substitute another. Neither changed the sense; both being monosyllables, neither could affect the scansion; and it was only by looking back on what he had already written that the mystery was solved: the second word contained an open A, and for nearly half a page he had been riding that vowel to the death.

In practice, I should add, the ear is not always so exacting; and ordinary writers, in ordinary moments, content themselves with avoiding what is harsh, and here and there, upon a rare occasion, buttressing a phrase, or linking two together, with a patch of assonance or a momentary jingle of alliteration. To understand how constant is this preoccupation of good writers, even where its results are least obtrusive, it is only necessary to turn to the bad. There, indeed, you will find cacophony supreme, the rattle of incongruous consonants only relieved by the jaw-breaking hiatus, and whole phrases not to be articulated by the powers of man.

Conclusion.—We may now briefly enumerate the elements of style. We have, peculiar to the prose writer, the task of keeping his phrases large, rhythmical, and pleasing to the ear, without ever allowing them to fall into the strictly metrical: peculiar to the versifier, the task of combining and contrasting his double, treble, and quadruple pattern, feet and groups, logic and metre—harmonious in diversity: common to both, the task of artfully combining the prime elements of language into phrases that shall be musical in the mouth; the task of weaving their argument into a texture of committed phrases and of rounded periods—but this particularly binding in the case of prose: and, again common to both, the task of choosing apt, explicit, and communicative words. We begin to see now what an intricate affair is any perfect passage; how many faculties, whether of taste or pure reason, must be held upon the stretch to make it; and why, when it is made, it should afford us so complete a pleasure. From the arrangement of according letters, which is altogether arabesque and sensual, up to the architecture of the elegant and pregnant sentence, which is a vigorous act of the pure intellect, there is scarce a faculty in man but has been exercised. We need not wonder, then, if perfect sentences are rare, and perfect pages rarer.

QUESTIONS FOR STUDY AND DISCUSSION

1. Are you "disenchanted" by Robert Louis Stevenson's analysis of some of the technical elements of style?

2. Have you ever discovered that, when you revised themes or other pieces of writing, the changes you made, though they seemed to be "improvements," did not change the plain sense of the passage? Your

answer may suggest the extent to which you are aware, consciously or unconsciously, of some of the elements of style Stevenson discusses.

3. Should a writer become consciously aware of the "technical elements of style"? Why?

4. Can you think of any exceptions to Stevenson's rule that in literature "every word, phrase, sentence, and paragraph must move in a logical progression, and convey a definite conventional import"? Do such exceptions impair the validity of Stevenson's analysis of style?

5. What are the "oranges" the prose writer juggles?

6. What do you think Stevenson means when he talks about writing "so that each sentence, by successive phrases, shall first come into a kind of knot, and then, after a moment of suspended meaning, solve and clear itself"?

WRITING ASSIGNMENTS

1. Compare and contrast, in an essay of moderate length, Hazlitt and Stevenson on "style."

2. Examine one of the themes you have written for this course (or any other approved paper) for evidence of the technical elements of style Stevenson discusses. Choose one or more of these elements and write an essay on your handling of them.

3. Stevenson is usually considered a literary "stylist." Examine "On Some Technical Elements of Style in Literature" and write an essay on Stevenson's employment of one or more of the elements he writes about.

4. Do you agree, wholly or in part, with Stevenson's analysis of technical elements of style? Do you feel the discussion is relevant? Write a reasoned defense of or attack on the essay.

RONALD A. KNOX

Thoughts on Bible Translation

Almost for the first time in my life, I am reading a paper before a learned audience *con amore*. As a rule, I find the process involves talking about something in which you are not interested, talking about something of which you have no knowledge, or talking about something about which there is very little to say—sometimes all three. Now, all I have got to do is to ventilate the ideas which have been simmering in my brain continuously these last three years; the ideas which, unless I am carefully controlled, I pour out freely in conversation. There is a great deal to be said about translating the Bible; most of that I claim to know, even if I know nothing else, and I am furiously interested in it.

Let us be precise; when I talk about translating the Bible, I mean translating the Vulgate. I have every respect for the patient scholarship which is giving us the Westminster Version, and I have sometimes found myself envying its compilers their liberty. But, it is well known, for all official purposes a Bible translation must take the Vulgate as its standard. I have been translating, these last three years, from the Vulgate text, relegating other readings, however plausible, to the foot of the page. I have even denied myself the privilege claimed by the latest American revisers, of going back behind the Clementine edition, and taking the Vulgate as it stands (say) in Wordsworth and White's collation of it. The American version, for example, in Acts xvii. 6, has 'these men who are setting the world in an uproar'. That is quite certainly the true reading; but a bad copyist has written *urbem* instead of *orbem*, and the Clementine follows this tradition. So I have rendered, 'who turn the state upside down'; that is how the thing stands in every Vulgate in the world

nowadays, and it is no part of the translator's business to alter, on however good grounds, his original.

That is not to say, that when you are translating a translation you must never look back at the original document. There will be passages in which the Latin is patient of two different interpretations; and here the original will put you right. This is especially true in the Vulgate psalms; only the original to which you must refer is not the Hebrew but the Septuagint, which they follow almost slavishly. Again, there will be passages in which the Latin translators have thrown up the sponge, and simply given you a meaningless transliteration of the Greek; in Acts xvii. 18, for example, the word *spermologos* is translated *seminiverbius*. You cannot translate *seminiverbius*; it is a *vox nihili*. If the Vulgate had meant 'one who sows words', it would have given us *sator verborum*. In such a case, I hold, the English translator is justified in going back to the Greek, and giving the most accurate rendering of it that he can find. Much oftener, the Latin gives you a weak equivalent for a colourful word in the original; thus, in the first passage I have alluded to, *concito*, to stir up, is a very weak rendering of *anastatoo*, to turn a thing upside down. Here (though with less confidence) I claim the right to go back to the original, and render, 'turn the state upside down', because *concito* does not contradict that notion, and is not meant to contradict it; it simply falls short of it.

The only considerable liberty I have allowed myself of going back behind the Latin—and I have only done so tentatively —is to restore, here and there, more plausible tenses to the verbs when the Latin comes, directly or indirectly, from the Hebrew. In the psalms, particularly,[1] I do not see how you are to make any consecutive sense of passages here and there unless you give a present where the Latin has a perfect, and sometimes where the Latin has a future. King David had, after all, only two tenses to express himself in; and by the time the Septuagint has translated his imperfect (or was it a future?) into an aorist which

[1] This was written before the appearance of the new Latin psalter.

may or may not be gnomic, and the Vulgate has translated the aorist into a perfect which may or may not be the 'perfect with have', a rich confusion has been introduced into the time-sequence which impels the translator to put the verb in the present and call it a day. You must, after all, translate with some reference to the context.

That, then, is what we have to translate —the Clementine recension of the Vulgate. And now, how are we to translate it?

Two alternatives present themselves at once, the literal and the literary method of translation. Is it to be 'Arms and the man I sing', or is it to be something which will pass for English? If you are translating for the benefit of a person who wants to learn Latin by following the gospel in a Latin missal when it is read out in church, then your 'arms and the man I sing' is exactly what he wants. If you are translating for the benefit of a person who wants to be able to read the word of God for ten minutes on end without laying it aside in sheer boredom or bewilderment, a literary translation is what you want—and we have been lacking it for centuries.

Among the many good things Mr. Belloc has done, which are almost entirely unknown, is a little brochure of 44 pages, the substance of a lecture he once gave at the Taylorian, on 'Translation'. The great principle he there lays down is that the business of a translator is not to ask, 'How shall I make this foreigner talk English?' but 'What would an Englishman have said to express this?' For instance, he says, if you are faced with the French sentence, 'Il y avait dans cet homme je ne sais quoi de suffisance', you do not want to write, 'There was in this man I know not what of self-sufficiency'; you want to write, 'There was a touch of complacency about him'. So with arms and the man. You have not translated the phrase when you have merely corrected the preposterous order, and written, 'I sing of arms and the man'. 'Sing' is only used like that by English poets when they are imitating Virgil, and you must not translate Virgil by imitating Virgil. The opening is also too abrupt; there is not time to give the words 'I sing' a proper emphasis. You want

something like, 'My song tells of arms; tells of the man' and so on. Anybody who has really tackled the business of translation, at least where the classical languages are concerned, will tell you that the bother is not finding the equivalent for this or that word, it is finding out how to turn the sentence. And about this, the older translators of the Bible took no trouble at all. Take this sentence: 'The Pharisees, and all the Jews, except they wash their hands oft, eat not, holding the tradition of the elders'. No, do not exclaim against the cumbrousness of Douay; that comes from the Authorized Version. The Authorized Version is supposed to be the fountain of pure English; but there it gives you an English sentence which would get any man the sack, and rightly, from Fleet Street. 'For the Pharisees, and indeed all the Jews, holding to the tradition of their ancestors, never eat without washing their hands again and again'—there is the English of it.

Incidentally, let us never be taken in by the people who talk to us about the 'effective inversions of order' which bring out the emphasis so well in the Bible. There are, indeed, such things as effective inversions of order. But what they mean is a sentence like, 'If I by the finger of God cast out devils'. Here, the operative words, 'by the finger of God', have been taken away from the end of the sentence, where the emphasis would have fallen on them, and shipped round to the front, leaving the whole emphasis of the sentence wrong; 'If I by the finger of God cast out DEVILS', as if somebody had been accusing our LORD of casting out angels. There, of course, the Authorized Version knew better; it was Douay, feverishly keeping the order of the Latin, that gave us the piece of false rhetoric to which our ears, by annual repetition, have grown accustomed.

I say, then, that the first thing demanded of a new translation of the Vulgate is that it should break away from the literal translation of sentences. What could be flatter than the first verse of St. John, as usually translated, 'In the beginning was the Word, and the Word was with God, and the Word was God'? That represents a very subtle chiasmus in the Greek, closely followed by the Latin; 'Et Verbum erat apud Deum, et Deus erat Verbum'. To restore that chiasmus, you must have something like 'God had the Word abiding with him, and the Word was God'. Latin and Greek leave the end of the sentence unemphatic, English emphasizes the end of the sentence. Therefore the English for 'De tribu Juda duodecim millia signati' is not what we are accustomed to. It is 'twelve thousand were sealed of the tribe of JUDA'. You must play cat's cradle with almost every sentence in the New Testament, if you want to decide *how an Englishman would have said the same thing*.

So much for sentences; and now, what of phrases? It stands to reason that no two languages have exactly the same idiom; that the English for 'Comment vous portez-vous?' is not 'How do you carry yourself?' If anybody has come across that extremely rare book, 'English as she is Spoke', he will know what I mean. The book was a phrase-book compiled by a Portuguese author for the benefit of English travellers in Portugal. And you do not need much critical insight to detect the fact that this well-meaning gentleman knew no English at all. He knew French; so he translated his sentences into French and then did them into English with a dictionary. Consequently, when he wanted to render a Portuguese idiom which meant, 'to wait about, to kick one's heels', he could do all right for the first part of his process; he knew that the corresponding idiom in French was 'croquer le marmot'—I have no notion why. The English, therefore, for kicking one's heels was 'to crunch the marmoset'. It is an extremely entertaining book; but, if you come to think of it, practically every translation of the Bible you have ever read makes errors which are quite as ludicrous—only we are accustomed to them. Douay was consistent; it translated the Latin word for word, and if you protested that its version sounded rather odd, replied woodenly, 'Well, that's what it says'. In the eleventh psalm, for instance, you get the words 'deceitful lips, they have spoken in heart and heart' Even Challoner saw that that would not do, so he pillaged from

the Authorized Version and gave us 'with a double heart have they spoken'. I don't see what a double heart could be except an abnormal anatomical condition, or an obscure kind of convention at bridge; but anyhow it sounds a little more like English. But when the Latin had 'renew a right spirit within my bowels', that was what Challoner put; and when the Latin had 'Examine, O Lord, my kidneys', Challoner put that down too; only he changed kidneys to the obsolete word 'reins', hoping that his readers would not look it up in the dictionary. We are sensible of these Hebraisms, and most of us would like to see the last of them. But there are hundreds and hundreds of other Hebraisms which we do not notice, because we have allowed ourselves to grow accustomed to them. We should have thought it odd if we had read in *The Times* 'General Montgomery's right hand has smitten Rommel in the hinder parts'; but if we get that sort of thing in the Bible we take it, unlike Rommel, sitting down. 'Mr. Churchill then opened his mouth and spoke'—is that English? No, it is Hebrew idiom clothed in English words.

Constantly, then, you have to be on the look-out for phrases which, because you have so often met them in the Bible, read like English, and yet are not English. Many of them, beginning life as Bible English, have even crept into the language; 'to give a person the right hand of fellowship', for example, or 'to sleep with one's fathers', or 'the son of perdition'; if the translator is not careful, he will let these through the barrier by mistake, and he will be wrong. When a public speaker urges that we should give Chiang Kai-shek the right hand of fellowship, he *means* 'give him the right hand of fellowship, as the dear old Bible would say'. And when you are translating the Bible, you must not describe the apostles as 'giving Paul and Barnabas the right hand of fellowship, as the dear old Bible would say'. Some of the phrases which we take over, as unconscious quotations, from the Authorized Version, or more rarely from Douay, have even become jocose. It is intolerable, in a modern translation of the New Testament, to find St. Paul talking about 'the inner man', when 'the inner man' has been used for so many years as a facetious synonym for the human stomach. If you are simply revising the old text of the Douay, you may, perhaps, be justified in leaving such phrases as they stand. But if you are writing a translation of the Bible, a translation of your own, you must find some other way of putting it; 'the inner man' is a phrase that has become desecrated.

A propos of that, may I suggest some considerations about what are called 'consecrated phrases' in the Bible, which, we are told, we must not alter in any way, because they have become so familiar? I quite admit that where a form of words has become stereotyped through passing into liturgical use, it is a pity and probably a waste of time to try and alter it. The words of the *Our Father* and of the *Hail Mary* have got to remain as they are. Again, there are certain formulas which are best left alone, or altered as little as possible, because alteration cannot hope to make them clearer, and they have already a supreme literary value of their own, depending on association; the words of Consecration, for example, or the seven words from the Cross. But it is, I submit, a grave error to stick to a form of words, in itself unnatural English, merely because a thousand repetitions have familiarized the public ear with the sound of it. Just because we are familiar with a form of words, we fail to be struck by its full meaning. For instance, I had a very interesting letter from an Irish Redemptorist, expressing the hope that I had found some better translation for *arneito heauton (abneget semetipsum)* than 'let him deny himself'. This has become a consecrated phrase, and for years, now, nuns have been encouraging schoolgirls to give up toffee during Lent and write the fact down on a card as a record of 'self-denial'. For years, Salvation Army lasses have picketed us with demands for a half-penny because it is 'self-denial week'. The whole glorious content of the phrase, *arneito heauton*, let him obliterate himself, let him annihilate himself, let him rule Self out of his world-picture altogether, has become degraded and lost. That is what happens to 'consecrated phrases'.

I have urged that the translator's business is to recondition, as often as not, whole sentences, so as to allow for the characteristic emphasis of his own language. I have urged that it is his business to transpose whole phrases, so as to reduce them to the equivalent idiom of his own language. And now, what of words? Here a consideration comes which is often forgotten. The Bible is usually translated by a syndicate; and the first thing a syndicate does when it gets together is to make sure that all the members of it tell the same story. If you propose to translate the Aeneid in this way, each member of it translating one book, the first item on the Committee's agenda would be, What is going to be our formula for translating the word 'pius' as applied to the hero of the poem? They go away, after agreeing (say) on the word 'dutiful', which does well enough. But if a single man translates the whole Aeneid, he very soon realizes that 'pius' takes on a different shade of meaning with each fresh context; now it is 'Aeneas, that dutiful son', now it is 'Aeneas, that admirable host', now it is 'Aeneas, that trained liturgiologist'. The compilers of the Authorized Version evidently did something of that kind with a word like *dikaiosune* in the New Testament, or *tsedeq* in the Old. They could see that Douay's rendering 'justice', was beside the mark nine times out of ten. What they did was to resuscitate a more or less obsolete word, 'rightwiseness', recondition it as 'righteousness', and use that all through the Bible as the equivalent of the *tsedeq-dikaiosune* idea. It served well enough; but this wooden rendering, constantly recurring in all sorts of different contexts, has resulted all through the Authorized Version in a certain flatness, a certain want of grip. You constantly feel that your author is not being allowed to say what he wants to say; his thought is being forced into an artificial mould.

For every common word in every living language has, not one meaning, but a quantity of shades of meaning. If you set out to give *salus* the meaning of 'salvation' all through the New Testament, you find yourself up against St. Paul inviting the ship's company during the storm to take a little food for the sake of their salvation. It is a capital heresy among translators, the idea that you must *always* render so-and-so in Latin by such-and-such in English. We sometimes get the idea that this must be a holy principle; is it not, after all, we are asked, the way in which the Vulgate proceeds in translating the Greek of the New Testament? If anybody harbours that delusion, he is recommended to consult Plummer's edition of II Corinthians; he will find there an appendix giving about 250 Greek words in the epistles, each of which the Vulgate renders in two or more ways. The word *eudokein*, he points out, is rendered in no less than ten different ways in the epistles alone. He appears to be scandalized by this procedure, which shows that he knew very little about translation. It is true, I think, that the Vulgate very often picks on the *wrong* rendering, the word with the wrong shade of meaning for that particular context. Over that, Plummer is welcome to have a grievance. But let him not demand that *eudokein* should be translated 'be well pleased' wherever it occurs, simply for the sake of uniformity.

Words are not coins, dead things whose value can be mathematically computed. You cannot quote an exact English equivalent for a French word, as you might quote an exact English equivalent for a French coin. Words are living things, full of shades of meaning, full of associations; and, what is more, they are apt to change their significance from one generation to the next. The translator who understands his job feels, constantly, like Alice in Wonderland trying to play croquet with flamingoes for mallets and hedge-hogs for balls; words are for ever eluding his grasp. Think of the delicate differences there are between the shades of meaning in a group of words like 'mercy, pity, clemency, pardon', or a group of words like 'fear, terror, awe, reverence, respect', or a group of words like 'glory, honour, fame, praise, credit'. How is it to be expected, on the law of averages, that any such group of words in English has an exactly corresponding group of words in Latin, and another in Greek, so that you can say, for example, *doxa* always means *gloria* in Latin, always means 'glory' in Eng-

lish? *Tsedeq* or *dikaiosune* can mean, when used of a man, innocence, or honesty, or uprightness, or charitableness, or dutifulness, or (very commonly) the fact of being in God's good books. Used of God, it can mean the justice which punishes the sinner, or, quite as often, the faithfulness which protects the good; it can mean, also, the approval with which God looks upon those who are in his good books. Only a meaningless token-word, like righteousness, can pretend to cover all these meanings. To use such a token-word is to abrogate your duty as a translator. Your duty as a translator is to think up the right expression, though it may have to be a paraphrase, which will give the reader the exact shade of meaning *here* and *here* and *here*.

The translator, let me suggest in passing, must never be frightened of the word 'paraphrase'; it is a bogey of the half-educated. As I have already tried to point out, it is almost impossible to translate a *sentence* without paraphrasing; it is a paraphrase when you translate 'Comment vous portez-vous?' by 'How are you?' But often enough it will be a single word that calls for paraphrase. When St. Paul describes people as 'wise according to the flesh', the translator is under an obligation to paraphrase. In English speech, you might be called fat according to the flesh, or thin according to the flesh, but not wise or foolish. The flesh here means natural, human standards of judging, and the translator has got to say so. 'Wise according to the flesh' is Hebrew in English dress; it is not English. You have not translated 'Galeotto fu il libbro, e chi lo scrisse', if you write, 'The book was Galahad, and so was the man who wrote it'. Dante's 'Galeotto' (being paraphrased) means 'a pandar'; and how (shades of Lord Tennyson!) is the English reader to know that?

The sentence, the phrase, the word—over all these the translator must keep watch; must beware of the instinct which bids him save trouble, or avoid criticism, by giving a merely photographic reproduction of his original. Nor does his task end there; his matter has to be duly chopped up into sentences. The first sentence of St. Paul's epistle to the Romans has ninety-one Latin words in it. The second sentence in his epistle to the Ephesians has a hundred and eighty-two. I admit that these figures are exceptional, but it is the clear fact about St. Paul, that he thought in paragraphs. St. John, on the other hand, has an insatiable passion for full stops. And nothing, I fancy, is so subtly disconcerting to the modern reader as having his intellectual food cut up into unsuitable lengths. The easy art of making it masticable has been learned to perfection by the journalists and public speakers whose thought he is accustomed to follow. If you want him to read Scripture without a kind of unconscious indigestion, you must prepare it more or less according to the current formula.

'The modern reader', I have said; thereby, I am afraid, taking for granted a point which remains to be discussed. Ought the modern reader of the Bible to have the illusion that he is reading something written in the twentieth century? Or will he prefer to have these holy documents wrapped up in archaic forms, just as he prefers to see the priest at Mass dressed up in a sixth-century overcoat? The latter suggestion is not so improbable as it sounds. Unlike the French, the English have always been accustomed to having an archaic Bible. Douay and the Authorized Version were compiled in the time of Shakespeare; but neither was written in the idiom of Shakespeare's time. Read a couple of pages out of any of the comedies, and you will be sensible of it at once. More than three centuries have passed, and as current idiom has changed, 'Bible English' has become a sort of hieratic language; it is old, therefore it is venerable (for it is a fixed belief in the heart of the ordinary Englishman that the word 'venerable' means 'old'). Let him beware, then, who proposes to alter it. Let him try to render the sense of Scripture plainer to us by whatever means he will, but let him adhere (or rather, let him cleave) to the good old-fashioned diction which was good enough for our forefathers, and is still better for us because for us it is still more old-fashioned.

Upon my word, if I had been trying to translate the Bible a hundred years ago, or even at the time when it seemed as if Newman was to be entrusted with the work

of translating the Bible, these arguments would have impressed me. For England, and indeed Europe generally, was then passing through a phase of romantic revival, and all our art and literature reeked of the past. Pugin, erecting Gothic cathedrals while you waited, Rossetti and Burne Jones covering yards of canvas with Arthurian legends executed in the very manner of Fra Angelico, William Morris pouring out synthetic medievalism, and all the poets, from Keats to Tennyson, dredging the Faery Queen to get hold of more and more odd words to impress the British public with—ah, it would have been child's play translating the Bible then! I believe I would have executed a version of the Scriptures, compared to which the old Douay would have looked painfully modern, and almost colloquial. But that was a hundred or nearly a hundred years ago.

To-day, we have boxed the compass. Rightly or wrongly, architecture is breaking away everywhere from the Gothic tradition. Our artists, instead of boasting themselves pre-Raphaelite, are looking round all the time to see what they can be Post. Poets speak in the language of the day, often in the strong language of the day. Prose-writers produce remarkable effects by breaking suddenly into italics, and filling their pages up with rows and rows of little dots. The young men will criticize Stevenson for caring so much about style, as if style mattered! The most damning criticism which can be passed on any work of art is that it is bogus; and how can any literature fail to be bogus that is deliberately written in the manner of four hundred years ago? Whatever else our contemporaries may worship, they will not bow the knee to the past; we have debunked the past.

Am I, then, prepared to haul down my colours, and pipe to this generation in the airs it has grown accustomed to, in the hope that it will dance? Must I translate the Bible in the idiom of James Joyce, or of Louis Macneice? I confess that I draw a different moral from the disconcerting change of fashion which I have been trying, very inadequately, to outline. It seems to me that elderly people, among whose number I am reluctantly beginning to reckon myself, have lived through enough vicissitudes of public taste to beware of catering exclusively for the mood of to-day. If the conventions of art can, in our times, be so rapidly over-hauled, catering for the mood of to-day will mean, almost certainly, ministering to the nausea of to-morrow. The moral, surely, is that anybody who tries to do a new transla-tion of the Bible in these days should aim at producing something which will not, in fifty or a hundred years' time, be 'dated'. In a word, what you want is neither sixteenth-century English nor twentieth-century Eng-lish, but timeless English. Whether you can get it, is another question. The method I proposed to myself was this—to use no word, no phrase, and as far as possible no turn of sentence, which would not have passed as decent literary English in the seventeenth century, and would not pass as decent literary English to-day. All these last three years, Murray's dictionary, in the full-size edition, has been more frequently in my hands than Forcellini, or Liddell and Scott, or Gesenius.

Strictly speaking, the thing is not pos-sible. 'Peter stood at the door without' sounds old-fashioned to-day; 'Peter stood at the door outside' would have been incompre-hensible in the seventeenth century. And I confess that I have preserved one or two archaisms; 'multitude', for example—'crowd' is such an ugly word; and 'brethren', so fa-miliar in ecclesiastical use, and one or two others. Much more serious was the problem, what to do about 'thou' and 'you.' I confess I would have liked to go the whole hog, and dispense with the use of 'thou' and 'thee', even where the Almighty was being addressed. They do these things in France, but I felt sure you could not get it past the British public. Why not, then, have 'thou' for God and 'you' for man? That is Mof-fatt's principle; but it seems to me to break down hopelessly in relation to our Incarnate Lord. Who is to say, exactly, when he is being addressed as God and when he is being addressed as Man? Moffatt makes St. Paul address him as 'you' in a vision, but the Lamb of the Apocalypse is 'thou'. In a single chapter of the Hebrews, quoting from a single psalm, Moffatt gives us 'thou art my

Son', and 'sit at my right hand till I make your enemies a foot-stool'. I despaired in the face of these difficulties, and resolved to keep 'thou', with its appropriate form, throughout, at the same time abolishing third-person forms like 'speaketh', which serve no useful purpose whatever.

On the other hand, I confess that I have given more weight to modern usage in cer-tain points; particularly over the conjunc-tions at the beginning of sentences or clauses. The conjunction, it seems to me, is tending to disappear. Nobody, nowadays, uses 'therefore' at the beginning of a sen-tence. We say, 'I must be going, I've got to catch a 'bus', not 'I must be going, for I've got to catch a 'bus'. No modern crowd would shout, 'Not this man, but Barabbas'; it would be, 'Not this man; Barabbas!' And I confess that I think our language is gain-ing in strength by depending more on em-phasis, less on subsidiary parts of speech. Here, if nowhere else, I have confessed my-self a child of the twentieth century.

I cannot guess what impression all these considerations will make on my audience; I only know that when I set them out like this, they convince *me*. But I am not, for that, too sanguine in the belief that any-thing will be done about giving us a new translation of the Bible—I mean, for of-ficial purposes. If such a step is proposed, I am quite sure that it will meet with oppo-sition from a number of influential people—almost all of them priests—who will be hon-estly convinced that the Catholic public is being deprived of a priceless possession. We shall be told about the simple folk, always invoked on such occasions, who like what they have always been accustomed to. The faith of our grandfathers will be mentioned a great deal, and nothing will be said about the faith of our grandchildren. It is easy to recognize opposition, where the discomforts attendant on a change will be felt by the clergy of to-day, while the benefits are for the clergy of to-morrow.

And yet, is the Douay, as it has come down to us through Challoner, really so fa-miliar to us, so universally beloved? I under-stand that, for several years, during and after the war it was impossible, in England or

Scotland, for a Catholic to buy a copy of the New Testament. Would any other Christian denomination in the world have sat down under that? In my experience, the laity's attitude towards the Bible is one of blank indifference, varied now and again by one of puzzled hostility. The clergy, no doubt, search the Scriptures more eagerly. And yet, when I used to go round preaching a good deal, and would ask the P.P. for a Bible to verify my text from, there was generally an ominous pause of twenty minutes or so before he returned, banging the leaves of the sacred volume and visibly blowing on the top. The new wine of the gospel, you felt, was kept in strangely cobwebby bottles.

No doubt certain passages, familiarized to us by being read out on solemn occasions —St. John's account of the Passion, for example—have entwined themselves graciously in the memory. But let anyone take up the Douay version and open it at random in the middle of the epistles; what does he make of the strange by-paths of it? Take this passage, for example, from the Hebrews. 'For the priesthood being translated, it is necessary that a translation also be made of the law. For he of whom these things are spoken is of another tribe, of which no one attended on the altar. For it is evident that our Lord sprang out of Juda: in which tribe Moses spoke nothing concerning priests. And it is yet far more evident: if according to the similitude of Melchisedech there ariseth another priest, who is made, not according to the law of a carnal commandment, but according to the power of an indissoluble life.' My ear may be faulty, but I do not find anything very impressive about the cadences I have just read; and as for the *meaning*— one knows the *sort* of thing it means, because one has read it in the Latin; but as a piece of English it is gibberish; you can give it no other name. The Douay people knew how to write, and Challoner's age was an age in which men could give you a good rendering—witness that extract from an old version Fr. Hugh Pope sent me, from the epistle of St. James, 'And he says to the fine suit of clothes, Sit you here, that's for quality'; there you have translation. But the Bible translated at Douay on the principle of Kelly's Keys, and then watered down by Challoner to make it sound less rugged— was there any hope that this would give us desirable English?

QUESTIONS FOR STUDY AND DISCUSSION

1. What are the two possible kinds of translation that Knox discusses? What does he mean by "a literary translation"?

2. Why does Knox consider paraphrase essential to a good translation? How do clarity and fidelity enter into this problem?

3. Consider Knox's argument that *The Times* would never write that "General Montgomery's right hand has smitten Rommel in the hinder parts." Does it follow that if *The Times* wouldn't write it, it's out for a translation of the Bible?

4. If you were translating the Bible, what specimens of good modern English would you choose as appropriate models to follow? Why?

5. Comment upon Knox's own essay style. Consider, among other things, his use of words and turns of phrase: "*con amore,*" "to ventilate the ideas," "the Latin translators have thrown up the sponge," "an English sentence which would get any man the sack," etc.

JAMES R. MASTERSON
and WENDELL BROOKS
PHILLIPS

Can You Understand the Rules *of Federal Prose?*

Unfortunately there are those who respond to the spirit but who have no capacity for the unremitting labor of emmets and beavers. Such persons may as well withdraw at this point and devote themselves to the writing of minor poems.

Strictly speaking, the rules of Federal Prose may best be derived by pure induction. After examining several million cubic feet of Federal writings, even the comparatively obtuse reader will eventually understand the principles which they exhibit. But this book is addressed to beginners who have not had the privilege of such perusal. For them the following rules will serve both as a test of innate capacity and, should the ultimate goal of Federal employment be reached, as a preliminary guide for composition:

(1) Use nouns in preference to verbs. Children, illiterates, and artists use verbs in abundance. But verbs are too direct, too outspoken, too naïve, not abstract enough to suit the needs of Federal Prose. When you are absolutely obliged to use a verb, use if possible some form of "to be," or a verb ending in "-ize," "-ate," or "-ect."

ENGLISH	FEDERAL PROSE
Time flies.	Time is fugitive. Fugacity is characteristic of time.
Hens lay eggs.	Egg-laying characterizes hens. Hens are typically oviparous.
	Hens ovulate, though not continuously and not without exception. Gallinaceous ovulation is effected only by hens.
Jack fell down and broke his crown.	A youth designated only as "Jack" sustained, incident to a loss of equilibrium, a fracture of the cranium.
When the cat's away the mice will play.	Rodents, in the absence of their feline enemy, are prone to divert themselves.
Haste makes waste.	Precipitation entails negation of economy.
Every dog has his day.	In every canine life-span is manifested a period of optimum euphoria.
Yours of the 20th received and contents noted.	Receipt by this office of your communication dated November 20, 1945, and cognizance of the contents thereof, are herewith acknowledged.
Please return these papers.	Return of papers is requested.
The old gray mare came out of the wilderness, forty-fifty years ago.	At a period subsequent to 1905 but prior to 1915 the subject mare, described as anile and in consequence grizzled, issued for motives unknown from a region defined only as uninhabited.
Man proposes but God disposes.	Human planning is subject to divine controls.

274

(2) Use abstract and general nouns, not concrete and particular nouns. In other words, intellectualize your nominalism. Untutored minds see particular objects. Minds trained in the Federal service see patterns and essences illustrated in particular objects.

ENGLISH	FEDERAL PROSE
Roses are red.	Rosaceae exhibit roseateness.
Scissors cut.	Scissors effect scission functionally.
Two heads are better than one.	Dual is preferred to unilateral consideration.
Call not thy brother "fool."	Avoid attribution of imbecility to your male sib.
The sun rises in the east.	Solar bodies tend to exhibit, with respect to and from the viewpoint of their satellites, an apparent orientality of anabasis.
Show your pass.	The display of your entrance permit is mandatory.
Hark! Hark! The dogs do bark. The beggars are coming to town— Some in rags, and some in tags, And some in velvet gowns.	The canine ululations now obtrusively perceptible adumbrate the visitation cityward of mendicants exhibiting a variability of costume between the extremes of quasinudity and velours. Public protests have been received with respect to the imminent concentration of artists, convicts, and doctors of philosophy in the District of Columbia.

ENGLISH	FEDERAL PROSE
Satisfaction guaranteed or your money back.	The remittance of sums paid by customers purchasing articles in or of this establishment is hereby guaranteed in the event that such articles, or one or more thereof, shall be hereafter deemed unsatisfactory to or by the said customers, or any of them: —provided, however, (a) that the dissatisfaction be expressed verbally or through correspondence and not otherwise, (b) that the said dissatisfaction be expressed by a customer or customers, (c) that the said customer or customers be, or have been, customers of the establishment designated hereinabove, and (d) that the said dissatisfaction relate to, and be justifiably directed toward, an article or articles purchased thereby herein.
Hey diddle diddle! The cat and the fiddle! The cow jumped over the moon. The little dog laughed To see the sport, And the dish ran with the spoon.	The alarming because unprecedented spectacle of feline musicianship exhibited by means of catgut elicited from the spectators such reactions as, in the case of a cow, translunary saltation; of a diminutive canine, cachinnation; and of two articles of tableware, collusive flight.

(3) Use attributive nouns in preference to adjectives or adjectival phrases.

ENGLISH	FEDERAL PROSE
The writing of books is a trade.	Book composition is a trade.
The Department of the Interior.	The Interior Department.
The search for truth is endless.	The truthquest is interminable.

(4) Avoid the rigid and unnatural parallelism of English.

ENGLISH	FEDERAL PROSE
The candidate is not only young but pretty.	The candidate not only is youthful but also personable. The candidate is not juvenile merely but is personable as well. Not only juvenile, also the candidate is personable.
The candidate is neither young nor pretty.	The candidate neither is youthful or is she personable.
The market will go either up or down.	In the event of its instability the market either will ascend or descend.
A candidate is wanted who can read and write.	A candidate able to read and who can write is indicated.

(5) Place clauses and phrases in such a way as to hold attention.

ENGLISH	FEDERAL PROSE
My father died when I was a baby.	When an infant my father died.
While being examined the candidate went to sleep.	In the course of examination somnolence acquired complete mastery over the candidate.
One rule is bad; two are worse.	One rule is bad, two worse.

ENGLISH	FEDERAL PROSE
Finding no weapon on Jones, the police let him go.	Finding no weapon on him, Jones was released by the police.
The chairman finds that the third report duplicated the second.	It is ascertained by the chairman the tertiary report to be duplicated by the second.

(6) Indicate explicitly the relations among all facts and ideas that you express. Do not expect your reader to solve riddles. Leave nothing to his imagination, because (*a*) he probably has none or (*b*) he may imagine something erotic. Few Federal adults can interpret the following:

> Hickory, dickory, dock.
> A mouse ran up the clock.
> The princess hopped, the fiddlers stopped,
> Not knowing what to do.

Expand this approximately as follows:

> A sound suggestive of but distinguishable from striking issued from a tall clock in a ballroom in which a princess was but the most distinguished of the gay multitude that whirled in unison to the strains of a corps of violinists. Startled by the sudden and discordant plangency, the beauteous scion of royalty stumbled to an abrupt halt in her graceful evolutions; the orchestra, confused by this cessation of movement, subsided into silence; and only after investigation had divulged the origin of the perturbing phenomena in the hitherto unsuspected ascent, within the clock, of a rodent that had in some manner not ascertained effected adit thereto, were the festivities resumed.

Figurative language (unless two or more figures are combined) is inappropriate to the Federal service. The following proverb would not be readily understood:

> Though thou shouldest bray a fool in a mortar among wheat with a pestle, yet will not his foolishness depart from him.

This could be rewritten for Federal purposes somewhat as follows:

All efforts looking toward alteration induced from without of the congenital mental configuration of personnel are ill advised, adaptation of administrative methodology thereto in contradistinction to adaptation thereof to administrative methodology being indicated.

(7) When using words that are in dictionaries, use them in senses that are unknown to lexicographers. Employ either *synecdoche* (designation of part as whole or of whole as part) or *transference* (migration of meaning from a word to another word often found in the same context).

Classified documents; i.e., documents classified as restricted, confidential, secret, or top secret. (Non-Federal readers, coming upon this phrase, will suppose that it refers to documents that are arranged by a system of classification, as distinguished from documents not so arranged. In view of the nature of classified documents, it is well that they should be designated somewhat mysteriously, so that the general public will think that it knows what it does not know. If it knew that it cannot see the documents, it would want to see them.)

Document file; i.e., a file consisting of folded papers as distinguished from one consisting of flat or bound papers. (Here, again, non-Federal readers will suppose that they know what they do not know. They will assume that a document file is a file consisting of documents, as distinguished from a file consisting of something that is not documents. Not knowing that other files also consist of documents, they will not care to see those files.)

Higher or lower *echelons* of command. (Formerly, echelons were units of a body of troops, each, except the last, drawn up parallel to but to right or left of the unit in its rear. All the units were characterized by being at different distances from the officer in command. Levels of command in the hierarchy of army organization have this same characteristic. The mathematical line extending from an offi-

cer to an echelon is horizontal; the metaphysical line extending from an officer to his superior or subordinate is vertical; the two lines are at right angles to each other, forming a Greek cross of which the orientation is inconsequential and, if insisted on, would occasion intellectual strain.)

Inhabitants *evacuated* from a town. (Etymologically, to evacuate is to cause to be vacant or empty. A town is evacuated when it is caused to be vacant. Its inhabitants are evacuated when they are caused to be empty, as by catharsis or fright. The inhabitants can evacuate the town by leaving it. Military authorities can evacuate the town either by departing from it themselves or by causing the inhabitants to depart from it. In the latter event, the inhabitants are removed from the town. The removal of the inhabitants is equated with the evacuation of the town. Therefore evacuation is the same as removal. Therefore the inhabitants are evacuated from the town and are designated as evacuees.)

(8) Learn to punctuate scientifically.

a. Federal prose is not subject to the trivial rules of English punctuation, which were designed by pedants for the needless discomfiture of the young. The concepts of punctuation in Federal Prose are larger and broader than those entertained by novelists, poets, and scholars. . . .

b. When tempted to punctuate, first ask "Is it necessary?" Though use of a period at the end of a sentence is often allowable, even this can generally be avoided by a skillful grouping into sections, subsections, and sub-subsections, each with its proper symbol of designation and with the required degree of indentation.

c. Never use commas recklessly. The attempt to make a sentence clear on first reading is a juvenile practice that should be avoided.

ENGLISH	FEDERAL PROSE
Tom, Dick, and Harry went down the street.	Tom, Dick and Harry went down the street. (It is unnecessary to inquire wheth-

ENGLISH   FEDERAL PROSE

er the three persons mentioned went down the street, or whether Tom is being told that the other two did so. Even teachers and journalists are discarding use of the comma between the last two members of a series—and to this extent, English and Federal Prose are becoming ONE.)

ENGLISH	FEDERAL PROSE
The superintendent ordered the children to burn all waste paper, and teachers saw that the order was carried out.	The superintendent ordered the children to burn all waste paper and teachers saw that the order was carried out. (A comma in this sentence would insult the reader's intelligence.)

d. Use semicolons only under extreme duress. Any person whose thought-pattern includes the semicolon is not qualified to write Federal Prose. Typists are cautioned, however, not to remove this symbol from their machines (though the type-bar could be utilized for some more serviceable mark), since a few old-fashioned office chiefs insist on using semicolons in their letters to Congressmen.

e. The colon, on the other hand, is indispensable in Federal Prose, since it has become the great symbol of anticipation and logical order. There is, indeed, some question whether the Federal Government could operate without it. Skillfully used, it reveals the master, particularly in breaking the backbone of a stubborn sentence. Amateurish: "His favorite colors were red, green, and blue." Competent: "His favorite colors were: red, green and blue." Professional:

His favorite colors were:

   I. red
  II. green
 III. blue
 IV. or, a combination of the three above colors, with:
    A. red predominating
    B. green predominating
    C. blue predominating
    D. or, a balanced combination of the foregoing colors in which none of the following predominates:
      (x) red
      (y) green
      (z) blue

QUESTIONS FOR STUDY AND DISCUSSION

1. Is "Federal Prose" confined to writing done by government employees? Where else have you encountered it?

2. What are the faults of "Federal Prose"? For what reasons is it objectionable? What would be gained if "Federal Prose" were "translated" into English?

3. What advantages does "Federal Prose" have? On what grounds can it be defended?

4. Do any of the examples of "Federal Prose" make better sense to you than their plain English equivalents? If so, why?

5. How would you define "classified documents" and "document file"? Why are your definitions improvements on the "Federal Prose" versions?

WRITING ASSIGNMENT

Find and copy a good one-paragraph example of "Federal Prose" (reports of governmental agencies and sociology and education textbooks are favorite hunting-grounds); rewrite the paragraph to remove "Federalese"; then write a commentary on your changes.

A Gallery of Excellent Styles

JAMES VI AND I

A Counterblaste to Tobacco

To The Reader

As every humane body (deare Countrey men) how wholesome soever, is notwithstanding subiect, or at least naturally inclined to some sorts of diseases, or infirmities: so is there no Common-wealth, or Body-politicke, how well governed, or peaceable soever it bee, that lackes the owne popular errors, and naturally enclined corruptions: and therefore is it no wonder, although this our Countrey and Common-wealth, though peaceable, though wealthy, though long flourishing in both, be amongst the rest, subiect to the owne naturall infirmities. We are of all Nations the people most loving and most reverently obedient to our Prince, yet are wee (as time hath often borne witnesse) too easie to be seduced to make Rebellion, upon very slight grounds. Our fortunate and oft prooved valour in warres abroad, our heartie and reverent obedience to our Princes at home, hath bred us a long, and a thrice happy peace: Our Peace hath bred wealth: And Peace and wealth hath brought foorth a generall sluggishnesse, which makes us wallow in all sorts of idle delights, and soft delicacies, the first seedes of the subversion of all great Monarchies.

Our Cleargie are become negligent and lazie, our Nobilitie and Gentrie prodigall, and solde to their private delights, Our Lawyers covetous, our Common-people prodigall and curious; and generally all sorts of people more carefull for their privat ends, then for their mother the Common-wealth.

For remedie whereof, it is the Kings part (as the proper Phisician of his Politicke-body) to purge it of all those diseases, by Medicines meete for the same: as by a certain milde, and yet iust forme of government, to maintaine the Publicke quietnesse, and prevent all occasions of Commotion: by the example of his owne Person and Court, to make us all ashamed of our sluggish delicacie, and to stirre us up to the practise againe of all honest exercises, and Martiall shadowes of Warre; As likewise by his, and his Courts moderatenesse in Apparell, to make us ashamed of our prodigalitie: By his quicke admonitions and carefull overseeing of the Cleargie, to waken them up againe, to be more diligent in their Offices: By the sharpe triall, and severe punishment of the partiall, covetous and bribing Lawyers, to reforme their corruptions: And generally by the example of his owne Person, and by the due execution of good Lawes, to reforme and abolish, piece and piece, these old and evill grounded abuses. For this will not bee Opus unius diei, but as every one of these diseases, must from the King receive the owne cure proper for it, so are there some sorts of abuses in Commonwealths, that though they be of so base and contemptible a condition, as they are too low for the Law to looke on, and too meane for a King

279

to interpone his authoritie, or bend his eye upon: yet are they corruptions, aswell as the greatest of them. So is an Ant an Animal, aswell as an Elephant: so is a Wrenne Avis, aswell as a Swanne, and so is a small dint of the Toothake, a disease aswell as the fearefull Plague is. But for these base sorts of corruption in Common-wealthes, not onely the King, or any inferior Magistrate, but Quilibet è populo may serve to be a Phisician, by discovering and impugning the error, and by perswading reformation thereof.

And surely in my opinion, there cannot be a more base, and yet hurtfull, corruption in a Countrey, then is the vile use (or other abuse) of taking Tobacco in this Kingdome, which hath mooved me, shortly to discover the abuses thereof in this following little Pamphlet.

If any thinke it a light Argument, so is it but a toy that is bestowed upon it. And since the Subiect is but of Smoke, I thinke the fume of an idle braine, may serve for a sufficient battery against so fumous and feeble an enemy. If my grounds be found true, it is all I looke for; but if they cary the force of perswasion with them, it is all I can wish, and more than I can expect. My onely care is, that you, my deare Countreymen, may rightly conceive even by this smallest trifle, of the sinceritie of my meaning in greater matters, never to spare any paine, that may tend to the procuring of your weale and prosperitie.

That the manifolde abuses of this vile custome of *Tobacco* taking, may the better be espied, it is fit, that first you enter into consideration both of the first originall thereof, and likewise of the reasons of the first entry thereof into this Countrey. For certainely as such customes, that have their first institution either from a godly, necessary, or honorable ground, and are first brought in, by the meanes of some worthy, vertuous, and great Personage, are ever, and most iustly, holden in great and reverent estimation and account, by all wise, vertuous, and temperate spirits: So should it by the contrary, iustly bring a great disgrace into that sort of customes, which having their originall from base corruption and barbarity,

doe in like sort, make their first entry into a Countrey, by an inconsiderate and childish affectation of Noveltie, as is the true case of the first invention of *Tobacco* taking, and of the first entry therefore among us. For *Tobacco* being a common herbe, which (though under divers names) growes almost every where, was first found out by some of the barbarous *Indians*, to be a Preservative, or Antidot against the Pockes, a filthy disease, whereunto these barbarous people are (as all men know) very much subiect, what through the uncleanly and adust constitution of their bodies, and what through the intemperate heate of their Climat: so that as from them was first brought into Christendome, that most detestable disease, so from them likewise was brought this use of *Tobacco*, as a stinking and unsavorie Antidot, for so corrupted and execrable a Maladie, the stinking Suffumigation whereof they yet use against that disease, making so one canker or venime to eate out another.

And now good Countrey men let us (I pray you) consider, what honour or policie can moove us to imitate the barbarous and beastly maners of the wilde, godlesse, and slavish *Indians*, especially in so vile and stinking a custome? Shall wee that disdaine to imitate the maners of our neighbour *France* (having the stile of the first Christian Kingdom) and that cannot endure the spirit of the Spaniards (their King being now comparable in largenes of Dominions, to the great Emperor of *Turkie*) Shall wee, I say, that have bene so long civill and wealthy in Peace, famous and invincible in Warre, fortunate in both, we that have bene ever able to aide any of our neighbours (but never deafed any of their eares with any of our supplications for assistance) shall we, I I say, without blushing, abase our selves so farre, as to imitate these beastly *Indians*, slaves to the *Spaniards*, refuse to the world, and as yet aliens from the holy Covenant of God? Why doe we not as well imitate them in walking naked as they doe? in preferring glasses, feathers, and such toyes, to golde and precious stones, as they do? yea why do we not denie God and adore the Devill, as they doe?

Now to the corrupted basenesse of the

first use of this *Tobacco*, doeth very well agree the foolish and groundlesse first entry thereof into this Kingdome. It is not so long since the first entry of this abuse amongst us here, as this present age cannot yet very well remember, both the first Author, and the forme of the first introduction of it amongst us. It was neither brought in by King, great Conquerour, nor learned Doctor of Phisicke.

With the report of a great discovery for a Conquest, some two or three Savage men, were brought in, together with this Savage custome. But the pitie is, the poore wilde barbarous men died, but that vile barbarous custome is yet alive, yea in fresh vigor; so as it seemes a miracle to me, how a custome springing from so vile a ground, and brought in by a father so generally hated, should be welcomed upon so slender a warrant. For if they that first put it in practise heere, had remembred for what respect it was used by them from whence it came, I am sure they would have bene loath, to have taken so farre the imputation of that disease upon them as they did, by using the cure thereof. For *Sanis non est opus medico*, and counter-poisons are never used, but where poyson is thought to precede.

But since it is true, that divers customes slightly grounded, and with no better warrant entred in a Commonwealth, may yet in the use of them thereafter, proove both necessary and profitable; it is therefore next to be examined, if there be not a full Sympathie and true Proportion, betweene the base ground and foolish entrie, and the loathsome, and hurtfull use of this stinking Antidote.

I am now therefore heartily to pray you to consider, first upon what false and erroneous grounds you have first built the generall good liking thereof; and next, what sinnes towards God, and foolish vanities before the world you commit, in the detestable use of it.

As for these deceitfull grounds, that have specially mooved you to take a good and great conceit thereof, I shall content my selfe to examine here onely foure of the principals of them; two founded upon the Theoricke of a deceivable apparance of Reason, and two of them upon the mistaken Practicke of generall Experience.

First, it is thought by you a sure Aphorisme in the Physickes, That the braines of all men, beeing naturally colde and wet, all dry and hote things should be good for them; of which nature this stinking suffumigation is, and therefore of good use to them. Of this Argument, both the Proposition and Assumption are false, and so the Conclusion cannot but be voyd of it selfe. For as to the Proposition, That because the braines are colde and moist, therefore things that are hote and drie are best for them, it is an inept consequence: For man beeing compounded of the foure Complexions, (whose fathers are the foure Elements) although there be a mixture of them all in all the parts of his body, yet must the divers parts of our *Microcosme* or little world within our selves, be diversly more inclined, some to one, some to another complexion, according to the diversitie of their uses, that of these discords a perfect harmonie may bee made up for the maintenance of the whole body.

The application then of a thing of a contrary nature, to any of these parts, is to interrupt them of their due function, and by consequence hurtfull to the health of the whole body. As if a man, because the Liver is hote (as the fountaine of blood) and as it were an oven to the stomacke, would therfore apply and weare close upon his Liver and stomacke a cake of lead; he might within a very short time (I hope) be susteined very good cheape at an Ordinarie, besides the cleering of his conscience from that deadly sinne of gluttonie. And as if, because the Heart is full of vital spirits, and in perpetuall motion, a man would therefore lay a heavy pound stone on his breast, for staying and holding downe that wanton palpitation, I doubt not but his breast would bee more bruised with the weight thereof, then the heart would be comforted with such a disagreeable and contrarious cure. And even so is it with the Braines. For if a man, because the Braines are colde and humide, would therefore use inwardly by smells, or outwardly by application, things of hot and drie qualitie, all the gaine that he could make thereof, would onely be to put himselfe in a great forwardnesse for running mad, by over-watching himselfe, the coldnesse and moistnesse of our braine beeing the onely ordinarie meanes that procure our sleepe and rest. Indeed I do not denie, but when it falls out that any of these, or any part of our bodie growes to be distempered, and to tend to an extremitie, beyond the compasse of Natures temperate mixture, that in that case cures of contrary qualities, to the intemperate inclination of that part, being wisely prepared and discreetely ministered, may be both necessarie and helpfull for strengthning and assisting Nature in the expulsion of her enemies: for this is the true definition of all profitable Physicke.

But first these Cures ought not to bee used, but where there is neede of them, the contrarie whereof, is daily practised in this generall use of *Tobacco* by all sorts and complexions of people.

And next, I deny the Minor of this argument, as I have already said, in regard that this *Tobacco*, is not simply of a dry and hot qualitie; but rather hath a certaine venemous facultie ioyned with the heate thereof, which makes it have an Antipathie against nature, as by the hatefull smell thereof doeth well appeare. For the Nose being the proper Organ and convoy of the sense of smelling to the braines, which are the onely fountaine of that sense, doeth ever serve us for an infallible witnesse, whether that Odour which we smell, be healthfull or hurtfull to the braine (except when it fals out that the sense it selfe is corrupted and abused through some infirmitie, and distemper in the braine). And that the suffumigation thereof cannot have a drying qualitie, it needes no further probation, then that it is a smoake, all smoake and vapour, being of it selfe humide, as drawing neere to the nature of the ayre, and easie to be resolved againe into water, whereof there needes no other proofe but the Meteors, which being bred of nothing else but of the vapours and exhalations sucked up by the Sunne out of the earth, the Sea, and waters yet are the same smoakie vapours turned, and transformed into Raynes, Snowes, Deawes, hoare Frostes, and such like waterie Meteors, as by the contrarie the

raynie cloudes are often transformed and evaporated in blustering winds.

The second Argument grounded on a show of reason is, That this filthie smoake, aswell through the heat and strength thereof, as by a naturall force and qualitie, is able and fit to purge both the head and stomacke of Rhewmes and distillations, as experience teacheth, by the spitting and avoyding fleame, immeadiately after the taking of it. But the fallacie of this Argument may easily appeare, by my late preceding description of the Meteors. For even as the smoakie vapours sucked up by the Sunne, and staied in the lowest and colde Region of the ayre, are there contracted into cloudes and turned into raine and such other watery Meteors: So this stinking smoake being sucked up by the Nose, and imprisoned in the colde and moyst braines, is by their colde and wett facultie, turned and cast foorth againe in waterie distillations, and so are you made free and purged of nothing, but that wherewith you wilfully burdened your selves: and therefore are you no wiser in taking *Tobacco* for purging you of distillations, then if for preventing the Cholike you would take all kinde of windie meates and drinkes, and for preventing of the Stone, you would take all kinde of meates and drinkes that would breede gravell in the Kidneyes, and then when you were forced to avoyde much winde out of your stomacke, and much gravell in your Vrine, that you should attribute the thanke thereof to such nourishments as bred those within you, that behoved either to be expelled by the force of Nature, or you to have *burst at the broad side*, as the Proverbe is.

As for the other two reasons founded upon experience, the first of which is, That the whole people would not have taken so generall a good liking thereof, if they had not by experience found it verie soveraigne and good for them: For answere thereunto how easily the mindes of any people, wherewith God hath replenished this world, may be drawn to the foolish affectation of any noveltie, I leave it to the discreet iudgement of any man that is reasonable.

Doe we not dayly see, that a man can no sooner bring over from beyond the Seas any new forme of apparell, but that hee can not bee thought a man of spirit, that would not presently imitate the same? And so from hand to hand it spreades, till it be practised by all, not for any commoditie that is in it, but only because it is come to be the fashion. For such is the force of that naturall Selfe-love in every one of us, and such is the corruption of envie bred in the brest of every one, as we cannot be content unlesse we imitate every thing that our fellowes doe, and so proove our selves capable of every thing whereof they are capable, like Apes, counterfeiting the maners of others, to our owne destruction. For let one or two of the greatest Masters of Mathematickes in any of the two famous Vniversities, but constantly affirme any cleare day, that they see some strange apparition in the skies: they will I warrant you be seconded by the greatest part of the Students in that profession: So loath will they be, to bee thought inferiour to their fellowes, either in depth of knowledge or sharpnesse of sight: And therefore the generall good liking and imbracing of this foolish custome, doeth but onely proceede from that affectation of noveltie, and popular errour, whereof I have already spoken.

The other argument drawn from a mistaken experience, is but the more particular probation of this generall, because it is alleaged to be found true by proofe, that by the taking of *Tobacco* divers and very many doe finde themselves cured of divers diseases as on the other part, no man ever received harme thereby. In this argument there is first a great mistaking and next a monstrous absurditie. For is it not a very great mistaking, to take *Non causam pro causa*, as they say in the Logicks? because peradventure when a sicke man hath had his disease at the height, hee hath at that instant taken *Tobacco*, and afterward his disease taking the naturall course of declining, and consequently the patient of recovering his health, O then the *Tobacco* forsooth, was the worker of that miracle. Beside that, it is a thing well knowen to all Phisicians, that the apprehension and conceit of the patient hath by wakening and uniting the vitall spirits, and so strengthening nature, a great

power and vertue, to cure divers diseases. For an evident proofe of mistaking in the like case, I pray you what foolish boy, what sillie wench, what olde doting wife, or ignorant countrey clowne, is not a Phisician for the toothach, for the cholicke, and divers such common diseases? Yea, will not every man you meete withal, teach you a sundry cure for the same, and sweare by that meane either himselfe, or some of his neerest kinsmen and friends was cured? And yet I hope no man is so foolish as to beleeve them. And al these toyes do only proceed from the mistaking *Non causam pro causa*, as I have already sayd, and so if a man chance to recover one of any disease, after he hath taken *Tobacco*, that must have the thankes of all. But by the contrary, if a man smoke himselfe to death with it (and many have done) O then some other disease must beare the blame for that fault. . . . And so doe olde drunkards thinke they prolong their dayes, by their swinelike diet, but never remember howe many die drowned in drinke before they be halfe olde.

And what greater absurditie can there bee, then to say that one cure shall serve for divers, nay, contrarious sortes of diseases? It is an undoubted ground among all Phisicians, that there is almost no sort either of nourishment or medicine, that hath not some thing in it disagreeable to some part of mans bodie, because, as I have already sayd, the nature of the temperature of every part, is so different from another, that according to the olde proverbe, That which is good for the head, is evill for the necke and the shoulders. For even as a strong enemie, that invades a towne or fortresse, although in his siege thereof, he do belaie and compasse it round about, yet he makes his breach and entrie, at some one or few special parts thereof, which hee hath tried and found to bee weakest and least able to resist; so sickenesse doth make her particular assault, upon such part or parts of our bodie, as are weakest and easiest to be overcome by that sort of disease, which then doth assaile us, although all the rest of the body by Sympathie feele it selfe, to be as it were belaied, and besieged by the affliction of that speciall part, the griefe and smart thereof being by the sence of feeling dispersed through all the rest of our members. And therefore the skilfull Phisician presses by such cures, to purge and strengthen that part which is afflicted, as are only fit for that sort of disease, and doe best agree with the nature of that infirme part; which being abused to a disease of another nature, would proove as hurtfull for the one, as helpfull for the other. Yea, not only will a skilfull and warie Phisician bee carefull to use no cure but that which is fit for that sort of disease, but he wil also consider all other circumstances, and make the remedies sutable thereunto: as the temperature of the clime where the Patient is, the constitution of the Planets, the time of the Moone, the season of the yere, the age and complexion of the Patient, and the present state of his body, in strength or weakenesse. For one cure must not ever be used for the self-same disease, but according to the varying of any of the foresaid circumstances, that sort of remedie must be used which is fittest for the same. Whear by the contrarie in this case, such is the miraculous omnipotencie of our strong tasted *Tobacco*, as it cures all sorts of diseases (which never any drugge could do before) in all persons, and at all times. It cures all maner of distillations, either in the head or stomacke (if you beleeve their Axiomes) although in very deede it doe both corrupt the braine, and by causing over quicke disgestion, fill the stomacke full of crudities. It cures the Gowt in the feet, and (which is miraculous) in that very instant when the smoke thereof, as light, flies up into the head, the vertue thereof, as heavie, runs downe to the little toe. It helpes all sorts of Agues. It makes a man sober that was drunke. It refreshes a weary man, and yet makes a man hungry. Being taken when they goe to bed, it makes one sleepe soundly, and yet being taken when a man is sleepie and drowsie, it will, as they say, awake his braine, and quicken his understanding. As for curing of the Pockes, it serves for that use but among the pockie Indian slaves. Here in *England* it is refined, and will not deigne to cure heere any other then cleanly and gentlemanly diseases. O omnipotent power of *Tobacco*! And if it could by the

smoke thereof chace out devils, as the smoke of *Tobias* fish did (which I am sure could smel no stronglier) it would serve for a precious Relicke, both for the superstitious Priests, and the insolent Puritanes, to cast out devils withall.

Admitting then, and not confessing that the use thereof were healthfull for some sortes of diseases; should it be used for all sicknesses? should it be used by all men? should it be used at al times? yea should it be used by able, yong, strong, healthful men? Medicine hath that vertue, that it never leaveth a man in that state wherin it findeth him: it makes a sicke man whole, but a whole man sicke. And as Medicine helpes nature being taken at times of necessitie, so being ever and continually used, it doth but weaken, wearie, and weare nature. What speake I of Medicine? Nay let a man every houre of the day, or as oft as many in this countrey use to take *Tobacco*, let a man I say, but take as oft the best sorts of nourishments in meate and drinke that can bee devised, hee shall with the continuall use thereof weaken both his head and his stomacke: all his members shall become feeble, his spirits dull, and in the end, as a drowsie lazie belly-god, he shall evanish in a Lethargie.

And from this weaknesse it proceeds, that many in this kingdome have had such a continuall use of taking this unsavorie smoke, as now they are not able to forbeare the same, no more then an olde drunkard can abide to be long sober, without falling into an uncurable weakenesse and evill constitution: for their continuall custome hath made to them, *habitum, alteram naturam*: so to those that from their birth have bene continually nourished upon poison and things venemous, wholesome meates are onely poisonable.

Thus having, as I truste, sufficiently answered the most principall arguments that are used in defence of this vile custome, it rests onely to informe you what sinnes and vanities you commit in the filthie abuse thereof. First, are you not guiltie of sinnefull and shamefull lust? (for lust may bee as well in any of the senses as in feeling) that although you bee troubled with no disease, but in perfect health, yet can you neither be merry at an Ordinarie, nor lascivious in the Stewes, if you lack *Tobacco* to provoke your appetite to any of those sorts of recreation, lusting after it as the children of Israel did in the wildernesse after Quailes? Secondly it is, as you use or rather abuse it, a branche of the sinne of drunkennesse, which is the roote of all sinnes: for as the onely delight that drunkards take in Wine is in the strength of the taste, and the force of the fume thereof that mounts up to the braine: for no drunkards love any weake, or sweete drinke: so are not those (I meane the strong heate and the fume) the onely qualities that make *Tobacco* so delectable to all the lovers of it? And as no man likes strong headie drinke the first day (because *nemo repente fit turpissimus*) but by custome is piece and piece allured, while in the ende, a drunkard will have as great a thirst to bee drunke, as a sober man to quench his thirst with a draught when hee hath need of it: So is not this the very case of all the great takers of *Tobacco*? which therefore they themselves do attribute to a bewitching qualitie in it. Thirdly, is it not the greatest sinne of all, that you the people of all sortes of this Kingdome, who are created and ordeined by God to bestowe both your persons and goods for the maintenance both of the honour and safetie of your King and Commonwealth, should disable your selves in both? In your persons having by this continuall vile custome brought your selves to this shameful imbecilitie, that you are not able to ride or walke the iourney of a Iewes Sabboth, but you must have a reekie cole brought you from the next poore house to kindle your *Tobacco* with? whereas he cannot be thought able for any service in the warres, that cannot endure oftentimes the want of meate, drinke and sleepe, much more then must hee endure the want of *Tobacco*. In the times of the many glorious and victorious battailes fought by this Nation, there was no word of *Tobacco*. But now if it were time of warres, and that you were to make some sudden *Cavalcado* upon your enemies, if any of you should seeke leisure to stay behinde his fellowe for taking of *Tobacco*, for my part I should never bee

sorie for any evill chance that might befall him. To take a custome in any thing that cannot bee left againe, is most harmeful to the people of any land. *Mollicies* and delicacie were the wracke and overthrow, first of the Persian, and next of the Romane Empire. And this very custome of taking *Tobacco* (whereof our present purpose is) is even at this day accounted so effeminate among the Indians themselves, as in the market they will offer no price for a slave to be sold, whom they finde to be a great *Tobacco* taker.

Now how you are by this custome disabled in your goods, let the Gentry of this lande beare witnesse, some of them bestowing three, some foure hundred pounds a yeere upon this precious stinke, which I am sure might be bestowed upon many farre better uses. I read indeede of a knavish Courtier, who for abusing the favour of the Emperour *Alexander Severus* his Master by taking bribes to intercede, for sundry persons in his Masters eare, (for whom he never once opened his mouth) was iustly choked with smoke, with this doome, *Fumo pereat, qui fumum vendidit*: but so many smoke-buyers, as are at this present in this kingdome, I never read nor heard.

And for the vanities committed in this filthie custome, is it not both great vanitie and uncleanenesse, that at the table, a place of respect, of cleanlinesse, of modestie, men should not be ashamed, to sit tossing of *Tobacco pipes*, and puffing of the smoke of *Tobacco* one to another, making the filthy smoke and stinke thereof, to exhale athwart the dishes, and infect the aire, when very often, men that abhorre it are at their repast? Surely Smoke becomes a kitchin far better then a Dining chamber, and yet it makes a kitchin also oftentimes in the inward parts of men, soiling and infecting them, with an unctuous and oily kinde of Soote, as hath bene found in some great *Tobacco* takers, that after their death were opened. And not onely meate time, but no other time nor action is exempted from the publike use of this uncivill tricke: so as if the wives of *Diepe* list to contest with this Nation for good maners their worst maners would in all reason be found at least not so dishonest (as ours are) in this point. The publike use whereof, at all times, and in all places, hath now so farre prevailed, as divers men very sound both in iudgement, and complexion, have bene at last forced to take it also without desire, partly because they were ashamed to seeme singular, (like the two Philosophers that were forced to duck themselves in that raine water, and so become fooles aswell as the rest of the people) and partly, to be as one that was content to eate Garlicke (which hee did not love) that he might not be troubled with the smell of it, in the breath of his fellowes. And is it not a great vanitie, that a man cannot heartily welcome his friend now, but straight they must bee in hand with *Tobacco*? No it is become in place of a cure, a point of good fellowship, and he that will refuse to take a pipe of *Tobacco* among his fellowes, (though by his own election he would rather feel the savour of a Sinke) is accounted peevish and no good company, even as they doe with tippeling in the cold Easterne Countries. Yea the Mistresse cannot in a more manerly kinde, entertaine her servant, then by giving him out of her faire hand a pipe of *Tobacco*. But herein is not onely a great vanitie, but a great contempt of Gods good giftes, that the sweetenesse of mans breath, being a good gift of God, should be willfully corrupted by this stinking smoke, wherein I must confesse, it hath too strong a vertue: and so that which is an ornament of nature, and can neither by any artifice be at the first acquired, nor once lost, be recovered againe, shall be filthily corrupted with an incurable stinke, which vile qualitie is as directly contrary to that wrong opinion which is holden of the wholesomnesse thereof, as the venime of putrifaction is contrary to the vertue Preservative.

Moreover, which is a great iniquitie, and against all humanitie, the husband shall not bee ashamed, to reduce thereby his delicate, wholesome, and cleane complexioned wife, to that extremitie, that either shee must also corrupt her sweete breath therewith, or else resolve to live in a perpetuall stinking torment.

Have you not reason then to bee ashamed, and to forbeare this filthie noveltie, so basely grounded, so foolishly received and so grossely mistaken in the right use thereof? In your abuse thereof sinning against God, harming your selves both in persons and goods, and raking also thereby the markes and notes of vanitie upon you: by the custome thereof making your selves to be wondered at by all forraine civil Nations, and by all strangers that come among you, to be scorned and contemned. A custome lothsome to the eye, hatefull to the Nose, harmefull to the braine, dangerous to the Lungs, and in the blacke stinking fume thereof, neerest resembling the horrible Stigian smoke of the pit that is bottomelesse.

QUESTIONS FOR STUDY AND DISCUSSION

1. Discuss the metaphors which you find in this essay. How often are they used for argumentative purposes?

2. In his introduction to the reader, James mentions "the force of perswasion." To what extent is James's persuasiveness the product of his style? Discuss.

3. Consider James's use of rhetorical questions, exclamations, and all the other techniques you find in this essay. Would any of them seem artificial today?

WRITING ASSIGNMENT

Select any three sentences which you consider typical of James's prose and analyze them grammatically. Then use your analysis to write an imitation.

JOHN DONNE

Devotion XVII

Nunc lento sonitu dicunt,
Morieris.

*Now, this Bell tolling softly for another,
saies to me, Thou must die.*

Perchance hee for whom this *Bell* tolls,
may be so ill, as that he knowes not it tolls
for him; And perchance I may thinke my
selfe so much better than I am, as that they
who are about mee, and see my state, may
have caused it to toll for mee, and I know
not that. The *Church* is *Catholike, uni-
versall,* so are all her *Actions; All* that she
does, belongs to *all.* When she *baptizes a
child,* that action concernes mee; for that
child is thereby connected to that *Head*
which is my *Head* too, and engraffed into
that *body,* whereof I am a *member.* And
when she *buries a Man,* that action concernes me: All *mankinde* is of one *Author,*
and is one *volume;* when one Man dies, one
Chapter is not *torne* out of the *booke,* but
translated into a better *language;* and every
Chapter must be so *translated; God* em-
ploies several *translators;* some peeces are
translated by *age,* some by *sicknesse,* some
by *warre,* some by *justice;* but *Gods* hand
is in every *translation;* and his hand shall
binde up all our scattered leaves againe, for
that *Librarie* where every *booke* shall lie
open to one another: As therefore the *Bell*
that rings to a *Sermon,* calls not upon the
Preacher onely, but upon the *Congregation*
to come; so this *Bell* calls us all: but how
much more mee, who am brought so neere
the *doore* by this *sicknesse.* There was a
contention as farre as a *suite,* (in which both
pietie and *dignitie, religion,* and *estimation,*
were mingled) which of the religious *Orders*
should ring to *praiers* first in the *Morning;*
and it was *determined,* that *they should ring
first that rose earliest.* If we understand
aright the *dignitie* of this *Belle* that tolls

for our *evening prayer,* wee would bee glad
to make it ours, by rising early, in that *application,* that it might bee ours, as wel as
his, whose indeed it is. The *Bell* doth toll
for him that *thinkes* it doth; and though it
intermit againe, yet from that *minute,* that
that occasion wrought upon him, hee is
united to *God.* Who casts not up his *Eye*
to the *Sunne* when it rises? but who takes
off his *Eye* from a *Comet* when that breakes
out? Who bends not his *eare* to any *bell,*
which upon any occasion rings? but who can
remove it from that *bell,* which is passing a
peece of himselfe out of this *world?* No
man is an *Iland,* intire of it selfe; every man
is a peece of the *Continent,* a part of the
maine; if a *Clod* bee washed away by the
Sea, Europe is the lesse, as well as if a
Promontorie were, as well as if a *Mannor*
of thy *friends* or of *thine owne* were; any
mans *death* diminishes *me,* because I am involved in *Mankinde;* And therefore never
send to know for whom the *bell* tolls; It
tolls for *thee.* Neither can we call this a
begging of *Miserie* or a *borrowing* of *Miserie,*
as though we were not miserable enough
of our selves, but must fetch in more from
the next house, in taking upon us the *Miserie* of our *Neighbours.* Truly it were an
excusable *covetousnesse* if wee did; for
affliction is a *treasure,* and scarce any man
hath *enough* of it. No man hath *affliction*
enough that is not matured, and ripened by
it, and made fit for *God* by that *affliction.*
If a man carry *treasure* in *bullion,* or in a
wedge of *gold,* and have none coined into
currant Monies, his *treasure* will not defray
him as he travells. *Tribulation* is *Treasure* in
the *nature* of it, but it is not *currant money*
in the *use* of it, except wee get nearer and
nearer our *home, Heaven,* by it. Another
man may be sicke too, and sick to *death,*
and this *affliction* may lie in his *bowels,* as
gold in a *Mine,* and be of no use to him;
but this *bell,* that tells me of his *affliction,*
digs out, and applies that *gold* to *mee;* if by
this consideration of anothers danger, I take
mine owne into contemplation, and so secure my selfe, by making my recourse to my
God, who is our onely securitie.

QUESTIONS FOR STUDY AND DISCUSSION

1. Which lines in this devotion are already familiar to you? Why?

2. Central to Donne's prose style is his sentence structure. What comments can you make on the form of the sentences? (Do not be misled by the semicolons.)

3. Much of the richness of this devotion stems from Donne's brilliant metaphors (for instance, "All *mankinde* is of one *Author*," etc.). List and analyze these. Then reread the devotion and show how one thought leads into another.

4. Are Donne's metaphors used only as ornaments or do they further his argument?

5. Do you agree with Donne that "*affliction* is a *treasure*"? Argue pro or con.

JEREMY TAYLOR

from

Holy Living

It is necessary that every man should consider, that since God hath given him an excellent nature, wisdom and choice, an understanding soul and an immortal spirit, having made him lord over the beasts, and but a little lower than the angels; He hath also appointed for him a work and a service great enough to employ those abilities, and hath also designed him to a state of life after this, to which he can only arrive by that service and obedience: and therefore as every man is wholly God's own portion by the title of creation, so all our labours and care, all our powers and faculties, must be wholly employed in the service of God, even all the days of our life; that, this life being ended, we may live with Him for ever.

Neither is it sufficient that we think of the service of God as a work of the least necessity, or of small employment, but that it be done by us as God intended it; that it be done with great earnestness and passion, with much zeal and desire; that we refuse no labour, that we bestow upon it much time; that we use the best guides, and arrive at the end of glory by all the ways of grace, of prudence, and religion.

And indeed if we consider, how much of our lives is taken up by the needs of nature; how many years are wholly spent before we come to any use of reason; how many years more before that reason is useful to us to any great purposes; how imperfect our discourse is made by our evil education, false principles, ill company, bad examples, and want of experience; how many parts of our wisest and best years are spent in eating and sleeping, in necessary businesses and unnecessary vanities, in worldly civilities and less useful circumstances, in the learning arts and sciences, languages or trades: that little portion of hours that is left for the practices of piety and religious walking with God is so short and trifling, that were not the goodness of God infinitely great, it might seem unreasonable or impossible for us to expect of Him eternal joys in heaven, even after the well spending those few minutes which are left for God and God's service after we have served ourselves and our own occasions.

And yet it is considerable that the fruit which comes from the many days of recreation and vanity, is very little; and although we scatter much, yet we gather but little profit: but from the few hours we spend in prayer and the exercises of a pious life the return is great and profitable; and what we sow in the minutes and spare portions of a few years, grows up to crowns and sceptres in a happy and a glorious eternity.

Therefore, first, although it cannot be enjoined that the greatest part of our time be spent in the direct actions of devotion and religion, yet it will become not only a duty but also a great providence, to lay aside for the services of God and the businesses of the Spirit as much as we can; because God rewards our minutes with long and eternal happiness; and the greater portion of our time we give to God, the more we treasure up for ourselves; and "no man is a better merchant than he that lays out his time upon God, and his money upon the poor."

Only, secondly, it becomes us to remember, and to adore God's goodness for it, that God hath not only permitted us to serve the necessities of our nature, but hath made them to become parts of our duty; that if we, by directing these actions to the glory of God, intend them as instruments to continue our persons in His service, He, by adopting them into religion, may turn our nature into grace, and accept our natural actions as actions of religion. God is pleased to esteem it for a part of His service, if we eat or drink, so it be done temperately, and as may best preserve our health, that our health may enable our services towards Him: and there is no one minute of our lives, after we are come to the use of reason, but we are or may be doing the work of God, even then when we most of all serve ourselves.

To which if we add, thirdly, that in these

and all other actions of our lives we always stand before God, acting and speaking, and thinking in His presence, and that it matters not that our conscience is sealed with secrecy, since it lies open to God; it will concern us to behave ourselves carefully, as in the presence of our judge.

These three considerations rightly managed, and applied to the several parts and instances of our lives, will be like Elisha stretched upon the child, apt to put life and quickness into every part of it, and to make us live the life of grace and do the work of God.

QUESTIONS FOR STUDY AND DISCUSSION

1. Discuss Taylor's use of parallelism in his writing.

2. Part of the effectiveness of this introduction to the first chapter of *Holy Living* is certainly due to specifics—the lists of details which illustrate and make clear. Discuss these. Does Taylor rely upon highly concrete examples or fairly general illustrations presented in great abundance? How much force does each kind of detail carry?

3. What metaphors do you find in this passage? Allusions?

4. How does Taylor handle his transitions between paragraphs?

JONATHAN SWIFT

A Meditation upon a Broomstick

This single stick, which you now behold ingloriously lying in that neglected corner, I once knew in a flourishing state in a forest: it was full of sap, full of leaves, and full of boughs: but now, in vain does the busy art of man pretend to vie with nature, by tying that withered bundle of twigs to its sapless trunk: it is now, at best, but the reverse of what it was, a tree turned upside down, the branches on the earth, and the root in the air; it is now handled by every dirty wench, condemned to do her drudgery, and, by a capricious kind of fate, destined to make other things clean, and be nasty itself: at length, worn to the stumps in the service of the maids, it is either thrown out of doors, or condemned to the last use, of kindling a fire. When I beheld this, I sighed, and said within myself, *Surely man is a Broomstick!* Nature sent him into the world strong and lusty, in a thriving condition, wearing his own hair on his head, the proper branches of this reasoning vegetable, until the axe of intemperance has lopped off his green boughs, and left him a withered trunk: he then flies to art, and puts on a periwig, valuing himself upon an unnatural bundle of hairs (all covered with powder), that never grew on his head; but now, should this our broomstick pretend to enter the scene, proud of those birchen spoils it never bore, and all covered with dust, though the sweepings of the finest lady's chamber, we should be apt to ridicule and despise its vanity. Partial judges that we are of our own excellences and other men's defaults!

But a broomstick, perhaps you will say, is an emblem of a tree standing on its head; and pray what is man but a topsyturvy creature, his animal faculties perpetually mounted on his rational, his head where his heels should be, grovelling on the earth? And yet, with all his faults, he sets up to be a universal reformer and corrector of abuses, a remover of grievances, rakes into every slut's corner of nature, bringing hidden corruption to the light, and raises a mighty dust where there was none before; sharing deeply all the while in the very same pollutions he pretends to sweep away: his last days are spent in slavery to women, and generally the least deserving; till, worn out to the stumps, like his brother besom, he is either kicked out of doors, or made use of to kindle flames for others to warm themselves by.

QUESTIONS FOR STUDY AND DISCUSSION

1. Since this meditation is a parody of Robert Boyle, is it legitimate material for the study of style? What do you already know about Boyle?

2. What is the source of humor in the *Meditation*?

3. Compare the sentence structure in the *Meditation* with that of James, Donne, and Taylor. What differences do you find?

4. Suppose that Swift had omitted most of the details from the *Meditation*. How effective would it then be?

WRITING ASSIGNMENT

Choose a writer whose style you consider excessive in any way and write a paragraph-long parody. Does the parody give you new insights into the nature of the author's style?

JOSEPH ADDISON

On the Cries of London

—Linguæ centum sunt, oraque centum,
Ferrea vox.—   VIRG.

There is nothing which more astonishes a foreigner and frights a country squire, than the Cries of London. My good friend Sir Roger often declares, that he cannot get them out of his head, or go to sleep for them, the first week that he is in town. On the contrary, Will. Honeycomb calls them the *Ramage de la Ville*, and prefers them to the sounds of larks and nightingales, with all the music of the fields and woods. I have lately received a letter from some very odd fellow upon this subject, which I shall leave with my reader, without saying anything further of it.

"SIR,

I am a man out of all business, and would willingly turn my head to anything for an honest livelihood. I have invented several projects for raising many millions of money without burthening the subject, but I cannot get the parliament to listen to me, who look upon me, forsooth, as a crack and a projector; so that despairing to enrich either myself or my country by this public-spiritedness, I would make some proposals to you relating to a design which I have very much at heart, and which may procure me an handsome subsistence, if you will be pleased to recommend it to the cities of London and Westminster.

"The post I would aim at is to be Comptroller-general of the London Cries, which are at present under no manner of rules or discipline. I think I am pretty well qualified for this place, as being a man of very strong lungs, of great insight into all the branches of our British trades and manufactures, and of a competent skill in music.

"The cries of London may be divided into vocal and instrumental. As for the latter, they are at present under a very great disorder. A freeman of London has the privilege of disturbing a whole street, for an hour together, with the twanking of a brass-kettle or a frying-pan. The watchman's thump at midnight startles us in our beds as much as the breaking in of a thief. The sow-gelder's horn has indeed something musical in it, but this is seldom heard within the liberties. I would therefore propose, that no instrument of this nature should be made use of, which I have not tuned and licensed, after having carefully examined in what manner it may affect the ears of her Majesty's liege subjects.

"Vocal cries are of a much larger extent, and, indeed, so full of incongruities and barbarisms, that we appear a distracted city to foreigners, who do not comprehend the meaning of such enormous outcries. Milk is generally sold in a note above *ela*, and it sounds so exceeding shrill, that it often sets our teeth on edge. The chimney-sweeper is confined to no certain pitch; he sometimes utters himself in the deepest bass, and sometimes in the sharpest treble; sometimes in the highest, and sometimes in the lowest note of the gamut. The same observation might be made on the retailers of small coal, not to mention broken glasses or brick-dust. In these, therefore, and the like cases, it should be my care to sweeten and mellow the voices of these itinerant tradesmen, before they make their appearance in our streets, as also to accommodate their cries to their respective wares; and to take care in particular that those may not make the most noise who have the least to sell, which is very observable in the venders of card-matches, to whom I cannot but apply that old proverb of 'Much cry, but little wool.'

"Some of these last-mentioned musicians are so very loud in the sale of these trifling manufactures, that an honest splenetic gentleman of my acquaintance bargained with one of them never to come into the street where he lived: but what was the effect of this contract? why, the whole tribe of card-match-makers which frequent the quarter, passed by his door the very next day, in

292

hopes of being bought off after the same manner.

"It is another great imperfection in our London cries, that there is no just time nor measure observed in them. Our news should, indeed, be published in a very quick time, because it is a commodity that will not keep cold. It should not, however, be cried with the same precipitation as 'fire:' yet this is generally the case. A bloody battle alarms the town from one end to another in an instant. Every motion of the French is published in so great a hurry, that one would think the enemy were at our gates. This likewise I would take upon me to regulate in such a manner, that there should be some distinction made between the spreading of a victory, a march, or an encampment, a Dutch, a Portugal, or a Spanish mail. Nor must I omit under this head, those excessive alarms with which several boisterous rustics infest our streets in turnip season; and which are more inexcusable, because these are wares which are in no danger of cooling upon their hands.

"There are others who affect a very slow time, and are, in my opinion, much more tunable than the former; the cooper, in particular, swells his last note in an hollow voice, that is not without its harmony: nor can I forbear being inspired with a most agreeable melancholy, when I hear that sad and solemn air with which the public is very often asked, if they have any chairs to mend? Your own memory may suggest to you many other lamentable ditties of the same nature, in which the music is wonderfully languishing and melodious.

"I am always pleased with that particular time of the year which is proper for the pickling of dill and cucumbers; but, alas, this cry, like the song of the nightingale, is not heard above two months. It would, therefore, be worth while to consider whether the same air might not in some cases be adapted to other words.

"It might likewise deserve our most serious consideration, how far, in a well-regulated city, those humourists are to be tolerated, who, not contented with the tra-

ditional cries of their forefathers, have invented particular songs and tunes of their own: such as was, not many years since, the pastryman, commonly known by the name of the colly-molly-puff; and such as is at this day the vender of powder and washballs, who, if I am rightly informed, goes under the name of Powder Watt.

"I must not here omit one particular absurdity which runs through this whole vociferous generation, and which renders their cries very often not only incommodious, but altogether useless to the public; I mean that idle accomplishment which they all of them aim at, of crying so as not to be understood. Whether or no they have learned this from several of our affected singers, I will not take upon me to say; but most certain it is, that people know the wares they deal in rather by their tunes than by their words; insomuch, that I have sometimes seen a country boy run out to buy apples of a bellows-mender, and ginger-bread from a grinder of knives and scissars. Nay, so strangely infatuated are some very eminent artists of this particular grace in a cry, that none but their acquaintance are able to guess at their profession; for who else can know that, 'Work if I had it,' should be the signification of a corn-cutter.

"Forasmuch, therefore, as persons of this rank are seldom men of genius or capacity, I think it would be very proper, that some man of good sense, and sound judgment, should preside over these public cries, who should permit none to lift up their voices in our streets, that have not tuneable throats, and are not only able to overcome the noise of the crowd, and the rattling of coaches, but also to vend their respective merchandises in apt phrases, and in the most distinct and agreeable sounds. I do therefore humbly recommend myself as a person rightly qualified for this post: and if I meet with fitting encouragement, shall communicate some other projects which I have by me, that may no less conduce to the emolument of the public.

"I am, sir, &c.
"Ralph Crotchet."

QUESTIONS FOR STUDY AND DISCUSSION

1. Discuss the organization of Ralph Crotchet's letter. What does it suggest about his personality?

2. How does the style of expression in this essay differ from present-day English?

3. How does Crotchet's use of words add to the interest and effectiveness of his letter?

SAMUEL JOHNSON

The Rambler, No. 89

Dulce est desipere in loco.   HOR.

Wisdom at proper times is well forgot.

Locke, whom there is no reason to suspect of being a favourer of idleness or libertinism, has advanced, that whoever hopes to employ any part of his time with efficacy and vigour, must allow some of it to pass in trifles. It is beyond the powers of humanity to spend a whole life in profound study and intense meditation, and the most rigorous exacters of industry and seriousness have appointed hours for relaxation and amusement.

It is certain, that, with or without our consent, many of the few moments allotted us will slide imperceptibly away, and that the mind will break, from confinement to its stated task, into sudden excursions. Severe and connected attention is preserved but for a short time, and when a man shuts himself up in his closet, and bends his thoughts to the discussion of any abstruse question, he will find his faculties continually stealing away to more pleasing entertainments. He often perceives himself transported, he knows not how, to distant tracts of thought, and return to his first object as from a dream, without knowing when he forsook it, or how long he has been abstracted from it.

It has been observed that the most studious are not always the most learned. There is, indeed, no great difficulty in discovering that this difference of proficiency may arise from the difference of intellectual powers, of the choice of books, or the convenience of information. But I believe it likewise frequently happens that the most recluse are not the most vigorous prosecutors of study. Many impose upon the world, and many upon themselves, by an appearance of severe and exemplary diligence, when they, in reality, give themselves up to the luxury of fancy, please their minds with regulating the past, or planning out the future; place themselves at will in varied situations of happiness, and slumber away their days in voluntary visions. In the journey of life some are left behind, because they are naturally feeble and slow; some because they miss the way, and many because they leave it by choice, and instead of pressing onward with a steady pace, delight themselves with momentary deviations, turn aside to pluck every flower, and repose in every shade.

There is nothing more fatal to a man whose business is to think, than to have learned the art of regaling his mind with those airy gratifications. Other vices or follies are restrained by fear, reformed by admonition, or rejected by the conviction which the comparison of our conduct with that of others may in time produce. But this invisible riot of the mind, this secret prodigality of being, is secure from detection, and fearless of reproach. The dreamer retires to his apartments, shuts out the cares and interruptions of mankind, and abandons himself to his own fancy; new worlds rise up before him, one image is followed by another, and a long succession of delights dances round him. He is at last called back to life by nature, or by custom, and enters peevish into society, because he cannot model it to his own will. He returns from his idle excursions with the asperity, though not with the knowledge of a student, and hastens again to the same felicity with the eagerness of a man bent upon the advancement of some favourite science. The infatuation strengthens by degrees, and, like the poison of opiates, weakens his powers, without any external symptom of malignity.

It happens, indeed, that these hypocrites of learning are in time detected, and convinced by disgrace and disappointment of the difference between the labour of thought, and the sport of musing. But this discovery is often not made till it is too late to recover the time that has been fooled away. A thousand accidents may, indeed, awaken drones to a more early sense of their danger and their shame. But they who are convinced of the necessity of breaking from this habitual drowsiness, too often relapse in spite of their resolution; for these ideal seducers are always near, and neither any particularity of time nor place is necessary to their influence; they invade the soul without warning, and have often charmed down resistance before their reproach is perceived or suspected.

This captivity, however, it is necessary for every man to break, who has any desire to be wise or useful, to pass his life with the esteem of others, or to look back with satisfaction from his old age upon his earlier years. In order to regain liberty, he must find the means of flying from himself; he must, in opposition to the *Stoick* precept, teach his desires to fix upon external things; he must adopt the joys and the pains of others, and excite in his mind the want of social pleasures and amicable communication.

It is, perhaps, not impossible to promote the cure of this mental malady, by close application to some new study, which may pour in fresh ideas, and keep curiosity in perpetual motion. But study requires solitude, and solitude is a state dangerous to those who are too much accustomed to sink into themselves. Active employment or publick pleasure is generally a necessary part of this intellectual regimen, without which, though some remission may be obtained, a complete cure will scarcely be effected.

This is a formidable and obstinate disease of the intellect, of which, when it has once become radicated by time, the remedy is one of the hardest tasks of reason and of virtue. Its slightest attacks, therefore, should be watchfully opposed; and he that finds the frigid and narcotick infection beginning to seize him, should turn his whole attention against it, and check it at the first discovery by proper counteraction.

The great resolution to be formed, when happiness and virtue are thus formidably invaded, is, that no part of life be spent in a state of neutrality or indifference; but that some pleasure be found for every moment that is not devoted to labour; and that, whenever the necessary business of life grows irksome or disgusting, an immediate transition be made to diversion and gaiety.

After the exercises which the health of the body requires, and which have themselves a natural tendency to actuate and invigorate the mind, the most eligible amusement of a rational being seems to be that interchange of thoughts which is practised in free and easy conversation; where suspicion is banished by experience, and emulation by benevolence; where every man speaks with no other restraint than unwillingness to offend, and hears with no other disposition than desire to be pleased.

There must be a time in which every man trifles; and the only choice that nature offers us, is, to trifle in company or alone. To join profit with pleasure, has been an old precept among men who have had very different conceptions of profit. All have agreed that our amusements should not terminate wholly in the present moment, but contribute more or less to future advantage. He that amuses himself among well chosen companions, can scarcely fail to receive, from the most careless and obstreperous merriment which virtue can allow, some useful hints; nor can converse on the most familiar topicks, without some casual information. The loose sparkles of thoughtless wit may give new light to the mind, and the gay contention for paradoxical positions rectify the opinions.

This is the time in which those friendships that give happiness or consolation, relief or security, are generally formed. A wise and good man is never so amiable as in his unbended and familiar intervals. Heroick generosity, or philosophical discoveries, may compel veneration and respect, but love always implies some kind of natural or voluntary equality, and is only to be excited by that levity and cheerfulness which disencumbers all minds from awe and solicitude, invites the modest to freedom, and exalts the timorous to confidence. This easy gaiety is certain to please, whatever be the character of him that exerts it; if our superiors descend from their elevation, we love them for lessening the distance at which we are placed below them; and inferiors, from whom we can receive no lasting advantage, will always keep our affections while their sprightliness and mirth contribute to our pleasure.

Every man finds himself differently affected by the sight of fortresses of war, and palaces of pleasure; we look on the height and strength of the bulwarks with a kind of gloomy satisfaction, for we cannot think of defence without admitting images of danger; but we range delighted and jocund through the gay apartments of the palace, because nothing is impressed by them on the mind but joy and festivity. Such is the difference between great and amiable characters; with protectors we are safe, with companions we are happy.

QUESTIONS FOR STUDY AND DISCUSSION

1. An understanding of Dr. Johnson's sentence structure is basic to any study of his prose style. Compare his sentences with James, Donne, Taylor, Swift, and Addison. To which writers is he closest?

2. Terms like parallelism, balance, and antithesis are often applied to a style such as this. Give examples to illustrate these traits.

3. What generalizations can you venture on Johnson's diction? His use of detail? His use of metaphor?

WRITING ASSIGNMENT

Write an imitation of a typically Johnsonian sentence.

CHARLES LAMB

Dream-Children:
A Reverie

Children love to listen to stories about their elders, when *they* were children; to stretch their imagination to the conception of a traditionary great-uncle, or grandame, whom they never saw. It was in this spirit that my little ones crept about me the other evening to hear about their great-grandmother Field, who lived in a great house in Norfolk (a hundred times bigger than that in which they and papa lived) which had been the scene—so at least it was generally believed in that part of the country—of the tragic incidents which they had lately become familiar with from the ballad of the Children in the Wood. Certain it is that the whole story of the children and their cruel uncle was to be seen fairly carved out in wood upon the chimney-piece of the great-hall, the whole story down to the Robin Redbreasts; till a foolish rich person pulled it down to set up a marble one of modern invention in its stead, with no story upon it. Here Alice put out one of her dear mother's looks, too tender to be called upbraiding. Then I went on to say, how religious and how good their great-grandmother Field was, how beloved and respected by everybody, though she was not indeed the mistress of this great house, but had only the charge of it (and yet in some respects she might be said to be the mistress of it too) committed to her by the owner, who preferred living in a newer and more fashionable mansion which he had purchased somewhere in the adjoining county; but still she lived in it in a manner as if it had been her own, and kept up the dignity of the great house in a sort while she lived, which afterwards came to decay, and was nearly pulled down, and all its old ornaments stripped and carried away to the owner's other house, where they were set up, and looked as awkward as if some one were to carry away the old tombs they had seen lately at the Abbey, and stick them up in Lady C.'s tawdry gilt drawing-room. Here John smiled, as much as to say, "that would be foolish indeed." And then I told how, when she came to die, her funeral was attended by a concourse of all the poor, and some of the gentry, too, of the neighborhood, for many miles round, to show their respect for her memory, because she had been such a good and religious woman; so good indeed that she knew all the Psaltery by heart, ay, and a great part of the Testament besides. Here little Alice spread her hands. Then I told what a tall, upright, graceful person their great-grandmother Field once was; and how in her youth she was esteemed the best dancer—here Alice's little right foot played an involuntary movement, till, upon my looking grave, it desisted—the best dancer, I was saying, in the county, till a cruel disease, called a cancer, came, and bowed her down with pain; but it could never bend her good spirits, or make them stoop, but they were still upright, because she was so good and religious. Then I told how she was used to sleep by herself in a lone chamber of the great lone house; and how she believed that an apparition of two infants was to be seen at midnight gliding up and down the great staircase near where she slept, but she said "those innocents would do her no harm;" and how frightened I used to be, though in those days I had my maid to sleep with me, because I was never half so good or religious as she—and yet I never saw the infants. Here John expanded all his eyebrows and tried to look courageous. Then I told how good she was to all her grandchildren, having us to the great house in the holidays, where I in particular used to spend many hours by myself, in gazing upon the old busts of the twelve Cæsars, that had been Emperors of Rome, till the old marble heads would seem to live again, or I to be turned into marble with them; how I could never be tired with roaming about that huge mansion, with its vast empty rooms, with their worn-out hangings, fluttering tapestry, and carved oaken pannels, with the gilding almost rubbed out—sometimes in the spacious old-fashioned gardens, which I had almost to myself, unless when now and then a solitary gardening man would cross me—and how the nectarines and peaches hung upon the walls, without my ever offering to pluck them, because they were forbidden fruit, unless now and then,—and because I had more pleasure in strolling about among the old melancholy-looking yew-trees, or the firs, and picking up the red-berries, and the fir-apples, which were good for nothing but to look at—or in lying about upon the fresh grass with all the fine garden smells around me—or basking in the orangery, till I could almost fancy myself ripening too along with the oranges and the limes in that grateful warmth—or in watching the dace that darted to and fro in the fish pond, at the bottom of the garden, with here and there a great sulky pike hanging midway down the water in silent state, as if it mocked at their impertinent friskings; I had more pleasure in these busy-idle diversions than in all the sweet flavors of peaches, nectarines, oranges, and such-like common baits of children. Here John slily deposited back upon the plate a bunch of grapes, which, not unobserved by Alice, he had meditated dividing with her, and both seemed willing to relinquish them for the present as irrelevant. Then, in somewhat a more heightened tone, I told how, though their great-grandmother Field loved all her grand-children, yet in an especial manner she might be said to love their uncle, John L——, because he was so handsome and spirited a youth, and a king to the rest of us; and, instead of moping about in solitary corners, like some of us, he would mount the most mettlesome horse he could get, when but an imp no bigger than themselves, and make it carry him half over the county in a morning, and join the hunters when there were any out; and yet he loved the old great house and gardens too, but had too much spirit to be always pent up within their boundaries—and how their uncle grew up to man's estate as brave as he was handsome, to the admiration of everybody, but of their great-grandmother Field most especially; and how he used to carry me upon his back when I was a lame-footed boy—

for he was a good bit older than me—many a mile when I could not walk for pain; and how in after life he became lame-footed too, and I did not always (I fear) make allowances enough for him when he was impatient, and in pain, nor remember sufficiently how considerate he had been to me when I was lame-footed; and how when he died, though he had not been dead an hour, it seemed as if he had died a great while ago, such a distance there is betwixt life and death; and how I bore his death as I thought pretty well at first, but afterwards it haunted and haunted me; and though I did not cry or take it to heart as some do, and as I think he would have done if I had died, yet I missed him all day long, and knew not till then how much I had loved him. I missed his kindness, and I missed his crossness, and wished him to be alive again, to be quarrelling with him (for we quarrelled sometimes), rather than not have him again, and was as uneasy without him, as he their poor uncle must have been when the doctor took off his limb. Here the children fell a crying, and asked if their little mourning which they had on was not for uncle John, and they looked up, and prayed me not to go on about their uncle, but to tell them some stories about their pretty dead mother. Then I told how for seven long years, in hope sometimes, sometimes in despair, yet persisting ever, I courted the fair Alice W—n; and, as much as children could understand, I explained to them what coyness, and difficulty, and denial, meant in maidens—when suddenly, turning to Alice, the soul of the first Alice looked out at her eyes with such a reality of re-presentment, that I became in doubt which of them stood there before me, or whose that bright hair was; and while I stood gazing, both the children gradually grew fainter to my view, receding, and still receding, till nothing at last but two mournful features were seen in the uttermost distance, which, without speech, strangely impressed upon me the effects of speech: "We are not of Alice, nor of thee, nor are we children at all. The children of Alice call Bartrum father. We are nothing, less than nothing, and dreams. We are only what might have been, and must wait upon the tedious shores of Lethe millions of ages before we have existence, and a name"—— and immediately awaking, I found myself quietly seated in my bachelor arm-chair, where I had fallen asleep, with the faithful Bridget unchanged by my side; but John L. (or James Elia) was gone for ever.

QUESTIONS FOR STUDY AND DISCUSSION

1. Compare Lamb's sentences with Johnson's. What differences do you find?

2. Compare Lamb's use of words with Johnson's. What differences are there?

3. The multitude of details in this essay contributes greatly to the effectiveness of its characterizations. Give examples. Do the details also explain the pathos of the essay?

ABRAHAM LINCOLN

Farewell to Springfield

My friends, no one not in my situation can appreciate my feelings of sadness at this parting. To this place, and the kindness of these people, I owe everything. Here I have lived a quarter of a century, and have passed from a young to an old man. Here my children have been born, and one is buried. I now leave, not knowing when or whether ever I may return, with a task before me greater than that which rested upon Washington. Without the assistance of that Divine Being who ever attended him, I cannot succeed. With that assistance, I cannot fail. Trusting in Him, who can go with me, and remain with you, and be everywhere for good, let us confidently hope that all will yet be well. To His care commending you, as I hope in your prayers you will commend me, I bid you an affectionate farewell.

QUESTIONS FOR STUDY AND DISCUSSION

1. This touching farewell to the people of Springfield, the town that Lincoln was never again to see, reads almost like poetry. Can you arrange the speech in loose verse form? After you have re-copied the speech, count up the number of syllables in each verse. What does this teach you about balance and prose rhythm?

2. A device of major importance in this address is Lincoln's parallelism of syntax. Discuss.

3. What use does Lincoln make in this speech of antithesis? Does it ever become forced or artificial?

ADLAI STEVENSON

Speech of Acceptance: Democratic National Convention, Chicago, Illinois, July 26, 1952

Mr. President, ladies and gentlemen of the convention, my fellow citizens:

I accept your nomination—and your program.

I should have preferred to hear those words uttered by a stronger, a wiser, a better man than myself. But after listening to the President's speech, I even feel better about myself.

None of you, my friends, can wholly appreciate what is in my heart. I can only hope that you understand my words. They will be few.

I have not sought the honor you have done me. I could not seek it because I aspired to another office, which was the full measure of my ambition. And one does not treat the highest office within the gift of the people of Illinois as an alternative or as a consolation prize.

I would not seek your nomination for the Presidency because the burdens of that office stagger the imagination. Its potential for good or evil now and in the years of our lives smothers exultation and converts vanity to prayer.

I have asked the merciful Father, the Father to us all, to let this cup pass from me. But from such dread responsibility one does not shrink in fear, in self-interest or in false humility.

So, "If this cup may not pass from me, except I drink it, Thy will be done."

That my heart has been troubled, that I have not sought this nomination, that I could not seek it in good conscience, that I would not seek it in honest self-appraisal, it is not to say that I value it the less. Rather it is that I revere the office of the Presidency of the United States.

And now that you have made your decision I will fight to win that office with all my heart and my soul. And with your help, I have no doubt that we will win.

You have summoned me to the highest mission within the gift of any people. I could not be more proud. Better men than I were at hand for this mighty task, and I owe to you and to them every resource of mind and of strength that I possess to make your deed today a good one for our country and for our party. I am confident, too, that your selection of a candidate for Vice President will strengthen me and our party immeasurably in the hard, the implacable work that lies ahead of all of us.

I know you join me in gratitude and in respect for the great Democrats and the leaders of our generation whose names you have considered here in this convention, whose vigor, whose character and devotion to the Republic we love so well have won the respect of countless Americans and enriched our party.

I shall need them, we shall need them, because I have not changed in any respect since yesterday. Your nomination, awesome as I find it, has not enlarged my capacities. So I am profoundly grateful and emboldened by their comradeship and their fealty. And I have been deeply moved by their expressions of goodwill and of support. And I cannot, my friends, resist the urge to take the one opportunity that has been afforded me to pay my humble respects to a very great and good American whom I am proud to call my kinsman—Alben Barkley of Kentucky.

Let me say, too, that I have been heartened by the conduct of this convention. You have argued and disagreed because as Democrats you care and you care deeply. But you have disagreed and argued without calling each other liars and thieves, without despoiling our best traditions. You have not spoiled our best traditions in any naked struggles for power.

And you have written a platform that neither equivocates, contradicts nor evades.

You have restated our party's record, its principles and its purposes in language that none can mistake, and with a firm confidence in justice, freedom and peace on earth that will raise the hearts and the hopes of mankind for that distant day when no one rattles a saber and no one drags a chain.

For all these things I am grateful to you. But I feel no exultation, no sense of triumph. Our troubles are all ahead of us.

Some will call us appeasers; others will say that we are the war party.

Some will say we are reactionary.

Others will say that we stand for socialism.

There will be the inevitable cries of "throw the rascals out"; "it's time for a change"; and so on and so on.

We'll hear all those things and many more besides. But we will hear nothing that we have not heard before. I am not too much concerned with partisan denunciation, with epithets and abuse, because the working man, the farmer, the thoughtful business man, all know that they are better off than ever before and they all know that the greatest danger to free enterprise in this country died with the great depression under the hammer blows of the Democratic party.

Nor am I afraid that the precious two-party system is in danger. Certainly the Republican party looked brutally alive a couple of weeks ago, and I mean both Republican parties! Nor am I afraid that the Democratic party is old and fat and indolent.

After 150 years it has been old for a long time; and it will never be indolent as long as it looks forward and not back, as long as it commands the allegiance of the young and the hopeful who dream the dreams and see the visions of a better America and a better world.

You will hear many sincere and thoughtful people express concern about the continuation of one party in power for twenty years. I don't belittle this attitude. But change for the sake of change has no absolute merit in itself.

If our greatest hazard is preservation of the values of Western civilization, in our self-interest alone, if you please, is it the part of wisdom to change for the sake of change to a party with a split personality; to a leader whom we all respect, but who has been called upon to minister to a hopeless case of political schizophrenia?

If the fear is corruption in official position, do you believe with Charles Evans Hughes that guilt is personal and knows no party? Do you doubt the power of any political leader, if he has the will to do so, to set his own house in order without his neighbors having to burn it down?

What does concern me, in common with thinking partisans of both parties, is not just winning this election, but how it is won, how well we can take advantage of this great quadrennial opportunity to debate issues sensibly and soberly.

I hope and pray that we Democrats, win or lose, can campaign not as a crusade to exterminate the opposing party, as our opponents seem to prefer, but as a great opportunity to educate and elevate a people whose destiny is leadership, not alone of a rich and prosperous, contented country as in the past, but of a world in ferment.

And, my friends, even more important than winning the election is governing the nation. That is the test of a political party —the acid, final test. When the tumult and the shouting die, when the bands are gone and the lights are dimmed, there is the stark reality of responsibility in an hour of history haunted with those gaunt, grim spectres of strife, dissension and ruthless, inscrutable and hostile power abroad.

The ordeal of the Twentieth Century— the bloodiest, most turbulent era of the Christian age—is far from over. Sacrifice, patience, understanding and implacable purpose may be our lot for years to come.

Let's face it. Let's talk sense to the American people. Let's tell them the truth, that there are no gains without pains, that we are now on the eve of great decisions, not easy decisions, like resistance when you're attacked, but a long, patient, costly struggle which alone can assure triumph over the great enemies of man—war, poverty and tyranny—and the assaults upon human dignity which are the most grievous consequences of each.

Let's tell them that the victory to be won in the Twentieth Century, this portal to the golden age, mocks the pretensions of individual acumen and ingenuity. For it is a citadel guarded by thick walls of ignorance and mistrust which do not fall before the trumpets' blast or the politicians' imprecations or even a general's baton. They are, my friends, walls that must be directly stormed by the hosts of courage, morality and of vision, standing shoulder to shoulder, unafraid of ugly truth, contemptuous of lies, half-truths, circuses and demagoguery.

The people are wise—wiser than the Republicans think. And the Democratic party is the people's party, not the labor party, not the farmers' party, not the employers' party—it is the party of no one because it is the party of everyone.

That, I think, is our ancient mission. Where we have deserted it we have failed. With your help there will be no desertion now. Better we lose the election than mislead the people; and better we lose than misgovern the people.

Help me do the job in this autumn of conflict and of campaign; help me to do the job in these years of darkness, of doubt and of crisis which stretch beyond the horizon of tonight's happy vision, and we will justify our glorious past and the loyalty of silent millions who look to us for compassion, for understanding and for honest purpose. Thus we will serve our great tradition greatly.

I ask of you all you have; I will give to you all I have, even as he who came here tonight and honored me, as he has honored you—the Democratic party—by a lifetime of service and bravery that will find him an imperishable page in the history of the Republic and of the Democratic party—President Harry S. Truman.

And finally, my friends, in the staggering task that you have assigned me, I shall always try "to do justly, to love mercy, and walk humbly with my God."

QUESTIONS FOR STUDY AND DISCUSSION

1. Discuss Stevenson's use of parallelism, balance, and antithesis. Comment upon his variations in sentence length and structure.

2. Discuss Stevenson's use of words and phrases in this address. Are they all of the same kind, or does he move from one level of diction to another? Is the tone ever inconsistent?

WRITING ASSIGNMENT

List the allusions, echoes, and quotations in this speech. Where are they drawn from?

DYLAN THOMAS

from

Under Milk Wood

To begin at the beginning:

It is spring, moonless night in the small town, starless and bible-black, the cobblestreets silent and the hunched, courters'-and-rabbits' wood limping invisible down to the sloeblack, slow, black, crowblack, fishingboat-bobbing sea. The houses are blind as moles (though moles see fine to-night in the snouting, velvet dingles) or blind as Captain Cat there in the muffled middle by the pump and the town clock, the shops in mourning, the Welfare Hall in widows' weeds. And all the people of the lulled and dumbfound town are sleeping now.

Hush, the babies are sleeping, the farmers, the fishers, the tradesmen and pensioners, cobbler, schoolteacher, postman and publican, the undertaker and the fancy woman, drunkard, dressmaker, preacher, policeman, the webfoot cocklewoman and the tidy wives. Young girls lie bedded soft or glide in their dreams, with rings and trousseaux, bridesmaided by glowworms down the aisles of the organplaying wood. The boys are dreaming wicked or of the bucking ranches of the night and the jollyrodgered sea. And the anthracite statues of the horses sleep in the fields, and the cows in the byres, and the dogs in the wetnosed yards; and the cats nap in the slant corners or lope sly, streaking and needling, on the one cloud of the roofs.

You can hear the dew falling, and the hushed town breathing. Only *your* eyes are unclosed to see the black and folded town fast, and slow, asleep. And you alone can hear the invisible starfall, the darkest-before-dawn minutely dewgrazed stir of the black, dab-filled sea where the *Arethusa*, the *Curlew* and the *Skylark*, *Zanzibar*, *Rhiannon*, the *Rover*, the *Cormorant*, and the *Star of Wales* tilt and ride.

Listen. It is night moving in the streets, the processional salt slow musical wind in Coronation Street and Cockle Row, it is the grass growing on Llaregyb Hill, dewfall, starfall, the sleep of birds in Milk Wood.

Listen. It is night in the chill, squat chapel, hymning in bonnet and brooch and bombazine black, butterfly choker and bootlace bow, coughing like nannygoats, sucking mintoes, fortywinking hallelujah; night in the four-ale, quiet as a domino; in Ocky Milkman's lofts like a mouse with gloves; in Dai Bread's bakery flying like black flour. It is to-night in Donkey Street, trotting silent, with seaweed on its hooves, along the cockled cobbles, past curtained fernpot, text and trinket, harmonium, holy dresser, watercolours done by hand, china dog and rosy tin teacaddy. It is night neddying among the snuggeries of babies.

Look. It is night, dumbly, royally winding through the Coronation cherry trees; going through the graveyard of Bethesda with winds gloved and folded, and dew doffed; tumbling by the Sailors Arms.

Time passes. Listen. Time passes.

Come closer now.

Only you can hear the houses sleeping in the streets in the slow deep salt and silent black, bandaged night. Only you can see, in the blinded bedrooms, the combs and petticoats over the chairs, the jugs and basins, the glasses of teeth, Thou Shalt Not on the wall, and the yellowing dickybird-watching pictures of the dead. Only you can hear and see, behind the eyes of the sleepers, the movements and countries and mazes and colours and dismays and rainbows and tunes and wishes and flight and fall and despairs and big seas of their dreams.

QUESTIONS FOR STUDY AND DISCUSSION

1. List the metaphors in this little description. How many of them are conventional ("blind as moles")? How many are inventive and fresh ("starless and bible-black")?

2. Comment upon the unusual syntactic

structures in this piece (including "the sloe-black, slow, black, crowblack, fishingboat-bobbing sea" and "The boys are dreaming wicked"). What is their effect? How much do they startle? Entertain? What other features must be considered besides syntax? Would you recommend such inventiveness as a safe way to spice up a style?

3. Thomas is famous for the way in which he heaps detail upon detail, almost to the bewilderment of the reader. Illustrate. What kinds of things does Thomas mention? List some of the more unusual ones.

The Book of Ruth: A Comparison

The Authorized Version of 1611

The Revised Standard Version, 1952

Chap. I.

1 Elimelech driven by famine into Moab, dieth here. 4 Mahlon and Chilion, having married wives of Moab, die also. 6 Naomi returning homeward, 8 disswadeth her two daughters in law from going with her. 14 Orpah leaveth her, but Ruth with great constancie accompanieth her. 19 They two come to Bethlehem, where they are gladly received.

Nowe it came to passe in the dayes when the Judges ruled, that there was a famine in the land: and a certaine man of Bethlehem Judah, went to sojourne in the countrey of Moab, he, and his wife, and his two sonnes.

2. And the name of the man *was* Elimelech, and the name of his wife, Naomi, and the name of his two sonnes, Mahlon, and Chilion, Ephrathites of Bethlehem Judah: and they came into the countrey of Moab, and continued there.

3 And Elimelech Naomies husband died, and shee was left, and her two sonnes;

4 And they tooke them wives of the women of Moab: the name of the one *was* Orpah, and the name of the other Ruth: and they dwelled there about ten yeeres.

5 And Mahlon and Chilion died also both of them, and the woman was left of her two sonnes, and her husband.

6 Then shee arose with her daughters in law, that shee might returne from the countrey of Moab: for shee had heard in the countrey of Moab, how that the LORD had visited his people, in giving them bread.

7 Wherefore she went foorth out of the place where she was, and her two daughters in law with her: and they went on the way to returne unto the land of Judah.

1 In the days when the judges ruled there was a famine in the land, and a certain man of Bethlehem in Judah went to sojourn in the country of Moab, he and his wife and his two sons. ² The name of the man was Elim'elech and the name of his wife Na'omi, and the names of his two sons were Mahlon and Chil'ion; they were Eph'rathites from Bethlehem in Judah. They went into the country of Moab and remained there. ³ But Elim'elech, the husband of Na'omi, died, and she was left with her two sons. ⁴ These took Moabite wives; the name of the one was Orpah and the name of the other Ruth. They lived there about ten years; ⁵ and both Mahlon and Chil'ion died, so that the woman was bereft of her two sons and her husband.

6 Then she started with her daughters-in-law to return from the country of Moab, for she had heard in the country of Moab that the LORD had visited his people and given them food. ⁷ So she set out from the place where she was, with her two daughters-in-law, and they went on the way to return to

THE BOOK OF RUTH

The American Translation of Smith & Goodspeed

THE KNOX Translation

THE BOOK OF RUTH

THE ANTECEDENTS OF RUTH, 1:1–22

In the time when the judges were in power a famine occurred in the land; so a certain man from Bethlehem in Judah emigrated to the country of Moab, along with his wife and two sons. The man's name was Elimelech, his wife's Naomi, and the names of his two sons Mahlon and Chilion—Ephrathites from Bethlehem in Judah. So they came to the country of Moab, and remained there. Then Elimelech, the husband of Naomi, died; and she was left a widow, with her two sons. These married Moabite women, the name of one being Orpah, and the name of the other Ruth. They lived there for about ten years, and then both Mahlon and Chilion died. Then, being bereft of her two children as well as of her husband, the woman, with her daughters-in-law, prepared to return from the country of Moab; for she had heard in the country of Moab that the LORD had taken note of his people by giving them food. So she left the place where she was, accompanied by her two daughters-in-law, and they set out on the road to return to the land of Judah.

In the old days, when Israel was ruled by judges, there was a man of Bethlehem-Juda that took his wife and his two sons to live in the Moabite country, to escape from a famine. There, in Moab, these Ephrathites from Bethlehem-Juda continued to dwell, Elimelech, and his wife Noemi, and his two sons Mahalon and Chelion; there Elimelech died, and Noemi was left a widow. But still she would be with her sons, who had now married wives of Moabite race, one called Orpha and the other Ruth. So ten years passed, and then Mahalon and Chelion both died. And now, both widowed and childless, she bade farewell to Moab and set out, with her two daughters-in-law, on the journey home; the Lord had been merciful to his people, she was told, and there was food to be had once more.

Thus Noemi left her dwelling-place; and when she set foot on the road that led to the domain of Juda, she turned to her com-

8. And Naomi said unto her two daughters in law, Goe, returne each to her mothers house: the LORD deale kindly with you, as ye have dealt with the dead, and with me.

9 The LORD graunt you, that you may finde rest each *of you* in the house of her husband. Then she kissed them, and they lift up their voyce and wept.

10 And they said unto her, Surely wee will returne with thee, unto thy people.

11 And Naomi said, Turne againe, my daughters: why will you goe with mee: Are there yet any moe sonnes in my wombe, that they may be your husbands:

12 Turne againe, my daughters, go *your way*, for I am too old to have an husband: if I should say, I have hope, if I should have a husband also to night, and should also beare sonnes:

13 Would ye tary for them till they were growen: would ye stay for them from having husbands: nay my daughters: for it grieveth me much for your sakes, that the hand of the LORD is gone out against me.

14 And they lift up their voyce, and wept againe: and Orpah kissed her mother in law, but Ruth clave unto her.

15 And she said, Behold, thy sister in law is gone backe unto her people, and unto her gods: returne thou after thy sister in law.

16 And Ruth said, Intreate mee not to leave thee, *or* to returne from following after thee: for whither thou goest, I will goe; and where thou lodgest, I will lodge: thy people shall be my people, and thy God my God:

17 Where thou diest, wil I die, and there will I bee buried: the LORD doe so to me, and more also, if *ought* but death part thee and me.

18 When shee sawe that shee was stedfastly minded to goe with her, then shee left speaking unto her.

19 So they two went untill they came to Bethlehem: And it came to passe when they were come to Bethlehem, that all the citie was mooved about them, and they said, Is this Naomi:

20 And she said unto them, Call me not Naomi; call mee Mara: for the Almightie hath dealt very bitterly with me.

21 I went out full, and the LORD hath

the land of Judah. 8 But Na'omi said to her two daughters-in-law, "Go, return each of you to her mother's house. May the LORD deal kindly with you, as you have dealt with the dead and with me. 9 The LORD grant that you may find a home, each of you in the house of her husband!" Then she kissed them, and they lifted up their voices and wept. 10 And they said to her, "No, we will return with you to your people." 11 But Na'omi said, "Turn back, my daughters, why will you go with me? Have I yet sons in my womb that they may become your husbands? 12 Turn back, my daughters, go your way, for I am too old to have a husband. If I should say I have hope, even if I should have a husband this night and should bear sons, 13 would you therefore wait till they were grown? Would you therefore refrain from marrying? No, my daughters, for it is exceedingly bitter to me for your sake that the hand of the LORD has gone forth against me." 14 Then they lifted up their voices and wept again; and Orpah kissed her mother-in-law, but Ruth clung to her.

15 And she said, "See, your sister-in-law has gone back to her people and to her gods; return after your sister-in-law." 16 But Ruth said, "Entreat me not to leave you or to return from following you; for where you go I will go, and where you lodge I will lodge; your people shall be my people, and your God my God; 17 where you die I will die, and there will I be buried. May the LORD do so to me and more also if even death parts me from you." 18 And when Na'omi saw that she was determined to go with her, she said no more.

19 So the two of them went on until they came to Bethlehem. And when they came to Bethlehem, the whole town was stirred because of them; and the women said, "Is this Na'omi?" 20 She said to them, "Do not call me Na'omi,* call me Mara,† for the Almighty has dealt very bitterly with me. 21 I went away full, and the LORD has

* That is *Pleasant.*
† That is *Bitter.*

But Naomi said to her two daughters-in-law,

"Go, return each of you to her mother's house. May the LORD deal as kindly with you as you have dealt with the dead and with me! May the LORD enable you to find a home, each of you, in the house of her husband!"

Then she kissed them good-bye; but they lifted up their voices in weeping, and said to her,

"No, we will go back with you to your people."

But Naomi said,

"Turn back, my daughters. Why should you go with me? Have I any more sons in my womb to become husbands for you? Turn back, my daughters; go your way; for I am too old to get married. If I should say that I have hopes both of getting married tonight and of bearing sons, would you wait for them until they were grown up? Would you forego marriage for them? No, my daughters; but I am very sorry for your sakes that the hand of the LORD has been raised against me."

Then they lifted up their voices again in weeping, and Orpah kissed her mother-in-law good-bye, but Ruth clung to her.

"See," she said, "your sister-in-law has turned back to her own people and her own gods; turn back after your sister-in-law."

But Ruth said,

"Do not press me to leave you, to turn back from following you; for wherever you go, I will go; and wherever you lodge, I will lodge; your people shall be my people, and your god my god; wherever you die, I will die, and there will I be buried. May the LORD requite me and worse, if even death separates me from you."

When she saw that she was determined to go with her, she ceased arguing with her. So the two of them went on until they came to Bethlehem. Upon their arrival in Bethlehem the whole city became agitated over them, and the women said,

"Is this Naomi?"

But she said to them,

"Do not call me Naomi [pleasant]; call me Mara [bitter]; for the Almighty has dealt very bitterly with me. I went away

panions, and bade either go back to her own mother's house; May the Lord shew kindness to you, she said, as you have shewn kindness to the memory of the dead, and to me; may you live at ease with new husbands. And with that she gave them a parting kiss. But no, they wept aloud, and declared they would go on in her company, to the home of her own people. Come with me, my daughters? she answered. Nay, you must go back. I have no more sons in my womb to wed you; go back, daughters, and leave me; I am an old woman, past the age for marrying. Though I should conceive this very night, and bear sons, it would be weary waiting for you till they should be grown to manhood; you would be old women too, long before your wedding day. Enough of this, daughters; it is your hard lot that makes it weigh heavy on me, this burden the Lord has given me to bear. At this, they wept louder than ever; but Orpha kissed her mother-in-law and went back; Ruth would not leave her side.

Here is thy sister-in-law gone back, Noemi said, back to her own people and the gods they worship; do thou, too, go with her. Nay, said Ruth, do not press me to go back and leave thee. I mean to go where thou goest, and dwell where thou dwellest; thy people shall be my people, thy God my God; whatever earth closes over thee when thou diest shall be my place of death and burial. Due meed of punishment the Lord give me, and more than due, if aught but death part thee and me.

When she found Ruth so resolved to bear her company, Noemi would cross her no longer, nor bid her return home; together they went on, and at last reached Bethlehem. They had scarce entered the city gate before the tale went round, and all the gossips were saying, Why, it is Noemi. Call me no longer, she said, by that name of delight; call me Mara, the unhappy one. Has not an almighty hand filled my cup with bitterness? Rich in blessings I left my brought me home againe emptie: why then call ye me Naomi, seeing the LORD hath testified against me, and the Almighty hath afflicted me:

22 So Naomi returned, and Ruth the Moabitesse her daughter in law with her, which returned out of the countrey of Moab: and they came to Bethlehem, in the beginning of barley harvest.

Chap. II.

1 *Ruth gleaneth in the fields of Boaz.* 4 *Boaz taking knowledge of her,* 8 *sheweth her great favour.* 18 *That which she got, shee carieth to Naomi.*

And Naomi had a kinseman of her husbands, a mighty man of wealth, of the familie of Elimelech, and his name was Boaz.

2 And Ruth the Moabitesse saide unto Naomi, Let me now goe to the field, and gleane eares of corne after *him*, in whose sight I shall finde grace. And shee saide unto her, Goe, my daughter.

3 And she went, and came, and gleaned in the field after the reapers: and her happe was to light on a part of the fielde *belonging* unto Boaz, who *was* of the kinred of Elimelech.

4 And behold, Boaz came from Bethlehem, and said unto the reapers, The LORD *bee* with you; and they answered him, The LORD blesse thee.

5 Then said Boaz unto his servant, that was set over the reapers, Whose damosell *is* this:

6 And the servaunt that was set over the reapers, answered and said, It is the Moabitish damosell that came backe with Naomi out of the countrey of Moab:

7 And she said, I pray you, let mee gleane and gather after the reapers amongst the sheaves: so shee came, and hath continued even from the morning untill now, *that* she taried a little in the house.

8 Then said Boaz unto Ruth, Hearest thou not, my daughter: Goe not to gleane in another field, neither goe from hence, but abide here fast by my maidens.

9 Let thine eyes be on the field that they doe reape, and go thou after them: Have I

brought me back empty. Why call me Na'omi, when the LORD has afflicted* me and the Almighty has brought calamity upon me?"

22 So Na'omi returned, and Ruth the Moabitess her daughter-in-law with her, who returned from the country of Moab. And they came to Bethlehem at the beginning of barley harvest.

2 Now Na'omi had a kinsman of her husband's, a man of wealth, of the family of Elim'elech, whose name was Bo'az. ² And Ruth the Moabitess said to Na'omi. "Let me go to the field, and glean among the ears of grain after him in whose sight I shall find favor." And she said to her, "Go, my daughter." ³ So she set forth and went and gleaned in the field after the reapers; and she happened to come to the part of the field belonging to Bo'az, who was of the family of Elim'elech. ⁴ And behold, Bo'az came from Bethlehem; and he said to the reapers, "The LORD be with you!" And they answered, "The LORD bless you." ⁵ Then Bo'az said to his servant who was in charge of the reapers, "Whose maiden is this?" ⁶ And the servant who was in charge of the reapers answered, "It is the Moabite maiden, who came back with Na'omi from the country of Moab. ⁷ She said, 'Pray, let me glean and gather among the sheaves after the reapers.' So she came, and she has continued from early morning until now, without resting even for a moment."†

8 Then Bo'az said to Ruth, "Now, listen, my daughter, do not go to glean in another field or leave this one, but keep close to my maidens. ⁹ Let your eyes be upon the field which they are reaping, and go after them.

* Gk Syr Vg: Heb *testified against.*
† Compare Gk Vg: the meaning of the Hebrew text is uncertain.

full, but the LORD has brought me back destitute. Why should you call me Naomi, seeing that the LORD has afflicted me, and the Almighty has brought evil upon me?"

So Naomi returned from the country of Moab, accompanied by her daughter-in-law, Ruth, the Moabitess. They reached Bethlehem at the beginning of the barley harvest.

THE MEETING OF RUTH AND BOAZ, 2:1–23

Now Naomi had a kinsman of her husband, a man of great wealth, belonging to the family of Elimelech, whose name was Boaz.

One day Ruth, the Moabitess, said to Naomi,

"Let me go to the fields and glean among the ears of grain after him with whom I may find favor."

"Go, my daughter," she said to her.

So off she went, and came and gleaned in the fields after the harvesters; and it was her fortune to come upon the part of the field belonging to Boaz, who belonged to the family of Elimelech. Just then Boaz himself came from Bethlehem.

"The LORD be with you!" he said to the harvesters.

"The LORD bless you!" they replied.

"Whose girl is this?" said Boaz to his overseer in charge of the harvesters.

"It is a Moabite girl who came back with Naomi from the country of Moab," the overseer in charge of the harvesters answered. "She said, 'Let me glean, if you please, and gather among the sheaves after the harvesters.' So she came, and has remained since morning until now, without resting even a little."

Then Boaz said to Ruth,

"Now listen, my girl. Do not go to glean in another field, nor leave this one, but stay here close by my women. Note the field that they are reaping, and follow them. Have I

home, and the Lord has brought me back destitute. So humbled by the Lord's hand, visited by the Almighty with such calamity, and will you call me Noemi still?

Thus it was that Noemi returned from the land of her adoption, with her daughter-in-law Ruth, that was Moabite born. They were just beginning to cut the barley in the fields, when she came back to her home at Bethlehem.

2 Elimelech had a kinsman called Booz, a man of great influence and wealth. And now Ruth, the Moabitess, asked leave of her mother-in-law to go out and glean after the reapers, by some rich man's favour. Go then, daughter, said she; and it so chanced that the field in which Ruth went to glean after the reapers belonged to no other than Booz, Elimelech's kinsman. After a while, he himself came out from Bethlehem, and when he had greeted the reapers, The Lord be with you, and they had wished him God's blessing in return, he asked the man in charge of them, a servant of his own, whose daughter this maid might be? It is Ruth, said he, the Moabitess, that came here from Moab with Noemi; she asked leave to glean after the reapers, and here she has been, ever since morning, without once going home to rest.

not charged the young men, that they shall not touch thee: and when thou art athirst, goe unto the vessels, and drinke of that which the yong men have drawen.

10 Then she fel on her face, and bowed her selfe to the ground, and said unto him, Why have I found grace in thine eyes, that thou shouldest take knowledge of me, seeing I am a stranger:

11 And Boaz answered and said unto her, It hath fully bene shewed me, all that thou hast done unto thy mother in law since the death of thine husband: and *how* thou hast left thy father and thy mother, and the land of thy nativitie, and art come unto a people, which thou knewest not heretofore.

12 The LORD recompense thy worke, and a full reward be given thee of the LORD God of Israel, under whose wings thou art come to trust.

13 Then she said, Let me finde favour in thy sight, my lord, for that thou hast comforted mee, and for that thou hast spoken friendly unto thy hand-maid, though I be not like unto one of thy hand-maidens.

14 And Boaz sayde unto her, At meale time come thou hither, and eate of the bread, and dip thy morsell in the vineger. And shee sate beside the reapers: and he reached her parched corne, and she did eate, and was sufficed, and left.

15 And when shee was risen up to gleane, Boaz commanded his young men, saying, Let her gleane even among the sheaves, and reproch her not.

16 And let fall also *some* of the handfuls of purpose for her, and leave them that she may gleane *them*, and rebuke her not.

17 So she gleaned in the field untill even, and beat out that she had gleaned: and it was about an Ephah of barley.

18 And shee tooke *it* up, and went into the citie: and her mother in lawe saw what shee had gleaned; and shee brought foorth, and gave to her that she had reserved, after she was sufficed.

19 And her mother in law said unto her, where hast thou gleaned to day: and where wroughtest thou: blessed be hee that did take knowledge of thee. And she shewed her mother in lawe with whom shee had wrought,

Have I not charged the young men not to molest you? And when you are thirsty, go to the vessels and drink what the young men have drawn." ¹⁰ Then she fell on her face, bowing to the ground, and said to him, "Why have I found favor in your eyes, that you should take notice of me, when I am a foreigner?" ¹¹ But Bo′az answered her, "All that you have done for your mother-in-law since the death of your husband has been fully told me, and how you left your father and mother and your native land and came to a people that you did not know before. ¹² The LORD recompense you for what you have done, and a full reward be given you by the LORD, the God of Israel, under whose wings you have come to take refuge!" ¹³ Then she said, "You are most gracious to me, my lord, for you have comforted me and spoken kindly to your maidservant, though I am not one of your maidservants."

14 And at mealtime Bo′az said to her, "Come here, and eat some bread, and dip your morsel in the wine." So she sat beside the reapers, and he passed to her parched grain; and she ate until she was satisfied, and she had some left over. ¹⁵ When she rose to glean, Bo′az instructed his young men, saying, "Let her glean even among the sheaves, and do not reproach her. ¹⁶ And also pull out some from the bundles for her, and leave it for her to glean, and do not rebuke her."

17 So she gleaned in the field until evening; then she beat out what she had gleaned, and it was about an ephah of barley. ¹⁸ And she took it up and went into the city; she showed her mother-in-law what she had gleaned, and she also brought out and gave her what food she had left over after being satisfied. ¹⁹ And her mother-in-law said to her, "Where did you glean today? And where have you worked? Blessed be the man who took notice of you." So she told her mother-in-law with whom she had

not charged the servants not to molest you? And when you are thirsty, go to the water jars, and drink some of what the servants draw."

Then she fell on her face, bowing to the ground, and said to him,

"Why have I found such favor with you that you should take notice of me, when I am a foreigner?"

Boaz in reply said to her,

"I have been fully informed of all that you have done for your mother-in-law since the death of your husband, and of how you left your father and mother, and the land of your birth, and came to a people that you did not know before. May the Lord reward your conduct, and may you receive full recompense from the Lord, the God of Israel, under whose wings you have come for shelter!"

"I thank you, sir," she said; "for you have cheered me, and have spoken comfortingly to your maidservant, even though I do not belong to your maidservants."

At mealtime Boaz said to her,

"Come here, and eat some of the bread, and dip your piece in the sour wine."

So she seated herself beside the harvesters, and he handed her roasted grain. She ate until she was satisfied, and had some left over. When she got up to glean, Boaz gave orders to his servants,

"Let her glean right among the sheaves, and do not be rude to her. Indeed pull out some bunches for her, and leave them for her to glean, and do not hinder her."

So she gleaned in the field until evening; then she beat out what she had gleaned, and it amounted to about an ephah of barley. She took it up, and coming into the city, showed her mother-in-law what she had gleaned. Then she brought out and gave her what she had left over after being satisfied.

"Where did you glean today," her mother-in-law said to her. "Where did you work? Blessed be he who took such notice of you!"

So she told her mother-in-law with whom she had worked.

Listen, my daughter, Booz said to Ruth; do not look for any other field to glean in; stay here and keep my maidens company, following ever where they reap. My servants have orders not to interfere with thee; if thou art thirsty, go to the buckets yonder and share the water they drink. At this, Ruth bowed low, face to ground; How have I deserved any favour of thine? she asked. Why wouldst thou take notice of an alien woman such as I am? I have had word, he answered, of thy goodness to thy mother-in-law since thy husband's death; how thou didst leave kindred and country, to dwell among strangers. May the Lord reward thee for what thou hast done; may the Lord God of Israel, in whose shelter thou hast learned to trust, make thee full return for it! Then she said, This is great kindness in thee, my lord, so to comfort and encourage me, thy poor servant that cannot compare with these handmaids of thine.

He bade her come back when it was time for a meal, to eat bread there and dip her crust in the vinegar. So there she sat with the reapers, and still at her side the heap of parched corn grew, till she had eaten her fill, and had more to carry away.* By the time she had risen up to go on with her gleaning, Booz had given orders to his servants that they were to put no hindrance in her way, though she were to go reaping in their company; and of set purpose they were to drop some of the handfuls they gathered, and leave them there for her to glean, never shaming her by a rebuke. So it was that when she had worked till evening, and took her rod to beat out what she had gathered, she found it was a whole ephi, that is a bushel.

Such were the earnings she brought back with her to the city, and shewed to her mother-in-law; offering her besides some of the food that was left over when she had finished her meal. Why, said Noemi, where hast thou been gleaning to-day? Where didst thou find so much work to do? Blessed be

---

* It is made clear in the Hebrew text, though not in the Latin version, that Booz gave Ruth more than her share of the parched corn allotted to the reapers.

and said, The mans name with whom I wrought to day, is Boaz.

20 And Naomi said unto her daughter in law, Blessed be he of the LORD, who hath not left off his kindnesse to the living and to the dead. And Naomi said unto her, The man is neere of kin unto us, one of our next kinsemen.

21 And Ruth the Moabitesse said, He said unto me also, Thou shalt keepe fast by my yong men, untill they have ended all my harvest.

22 And Naomi said unto Ruth her daughter in law, It is good, my daughter, that thou goe out with his maidens, that they meete thee not in any other field.

23 So shee kept fast by the maidens of Boaz to gleane, unto the end of barley harvest, and of wheat harvest, and dwelt with her mother in law.

Chap. III.

1 By Naomi her instruction, 5 Ruth lieth at Boaz his feete. 8 Boaz acknowledgeth the right of a kinseman. 14 He sendeth her away with sixe measures of barley.

Then Naomi her mother in law said unto her, My daughter, shal I not seeke rest for thee, that it may be well with thee:

2 And now is not Boaz of our kinred, with whose maidens thou wast: Behold, he winnoweth barley to night in the threshing floore.

3 Wash thy selfe therefore, and annoint thee, and put thy raiment upon thee, and get thee downe to the floore: *but* make not thy selfe knowen unto the man, untill hee shall have done eating and drinking.

4 And it shall be when hee lieth downe, that thou shalt marke the place where hee shall lie, and thou shalt goe in, and uncover his feete, and lay thee downe, and he will tell thee what thou shalt doe.

5 And shee said unto her, All that thou sayest unto me, I will doe.

6 And she went downe unto the floore, and did according to all that her mother in law bade her.

7 And when Boaz had eaten and drunke, and his heart was merrie, hee went to lie

worked, and said, "The man's name with whom I worked today is Bo'az." 20 And Na'omi said to her daughter-in-law, "Blessed be he by the LORD, whose kindness has not forsaken the living or the dead!" Na'omi also said to her, "The man is a relative of ours, one of our nearest kin." 21 And Ruth the Moabitess said, "Besides, he said to me, 'You shall keep close by my servants, till they have finished all my harvest.'" 22 And Na'omi said to Ruth, her daughter-in-law, "It is well, my daughter, that you go out with his maidens, lest in another field you be molested." 23 So she kept close to the maidens of Bo'az, gleaning until the end of the barley and wheat harvests; and she lived with her mother-in-law.

3 Then Na'omi her mother-in-law said to her, "My daughter, should I not seek a home for you, that it may be well with you? 2 Now is not Bo'az our kinsman, with whose maidens you were? See, he is winnowing barley tonight at the threshing floor. 3 Wash therefore and anoint yourself, and put on your best clothes and go down to the threshing floor; but do not make yourself known to the man until he has finished eating and drinking. 4 But when he lies down, observe the place where he lies; then, go and uncover his feet and lie down; and he will tell you what to do." 5 And she replied, "All that you say I will do."

6 So she went down to the threshing floor and did just as her mother-in-law had told her. 7 And when Bo'az had eaten and drunk, and his heart was merry, he went to lie down

"Boaz is the name of the man with whom I worked today," she said.

Then Naomi said to her daughter-in-law, "Blessed be he of the Lord, whose goodness has failed neither the living nor the dead!"

"The man is a relative of ours," Naomi said to her; "he is next after our next-of-kin."

"Furthermore," said Ruth, the Moabitess, "he said to me, 'You must stay close by my servants until they have finished all my harvest.'"

"It is best, my daughter," Naomi said to her daughter-in-law, Ruth, "that you should go out with his women, so as not to be molested in another field."

So she stayed close by the women working for Boaz, gleaning until the end of both the barley and wheat harvests; then she returned to her mother-in-law.

RUTH'S APPEAL TO BOAZ, 3:1–18

Then her mother-in-law Naomi said to her,

"Should I not be seeking a home for you, my daughter, where you may be comfortable? Now then, what about our relative Boaz, with whose women you have been? See, he is going to winnow barley at the threshing-floor tonight. Wash and anoint yourself therefore, put on your best clothes, and go down to the threshing-floor; but do not let your presence be known to the man until he has finished eating and drinking. See to it, however, when he lies down, that you note the place where he lies; then go in, uncover his feet, and lie down yourself; he will let you know what to do."

"I will do just as you say," she responded.

So she went down to the threshing-floor, and did just as her mother-in-law had instructed her. Boaz, having eaten and drunk, had a sense of well-being and went to lie

the man that has so befriended thee! And Ruth told her whose field it was she had worked in, It was a man called Booz, she said. May the Lord bless him, answered Noemi; here is a man that is generous to his own, living as well as dead. And she told Ruth that Booz was their near kinsman. This too, said Ruth, was his bidding, that I should keep close to his men till all the reaping is done. That is best, daughter, said her mother-in-law, that thou shouldst go out to glean with those maidens of his; in some other field they might say thee nay. And with the maidservants of Booz she still kept company, till barley and wheat were both carried.

3 Now that she had come back home, her mother-in-law said to her, Daughter, I mean to win thee an easy life, and bring thee happiness. This Booz, whose maidens were thy companions in harvest-time, Booz, our kinsman, will be at the threshing-floor to-night, winnowing his barley. Wash thee, and anoint thee, and put on thy best array, and so go down to the threshing-floor. He will not have finished eating and drinking; do not let him see thee, but wait till he goes to bed, and mark where it is that he is sleeping. Then come close, and turn back the end of his mantle where it covers his feet, and lie down there. After that, it is for him to counsel thee.

So Ruth promised to do all her bidding; down to the threshing-floor she went, and carried out all her mother-in-law's plan. She waited till Booz came, his heart cheered with food and drink, to take his rest by a downe at the ende of the heape of corne: and she came softly, and uncovered his feete, and laid her downe.

8 And it came to passe at midnight, that the man was afraid, and turned himselfe: and behold, a woman lay at his feete.

9 And hee said, who *art* thou: And she answered, I *am* Ruth thine handmaid: spread therefore thy skirt over thine handmaid, for thou *art* a neare kinseman.

10 And hee said, Blessed be thou of the LORD, my daughter: *for* thou hast shewed more kindnesse in the latter ende, then at the beginning, in as much as thou followedst not yong men, whether poore, or rich.

11 And now my daughter, feare not, I will doe to thee all that thou requirest: for all the citie of my people doeth know, that thou art a vertuous woman.

12 And now it is true, that I am *thy* neare kinseman: howbeit there is a kinseman nearer then I.

13 Tary this night, and it shall be in the morning, that if hee will performe unto thee the part of a kinseman, well, let him doe the kinsemans part; but if hee will not doe the part of a kinseman to thee, then will I doe the part of a kinseman to thee, as the LORD liveth: lie downe until the morning.

14 And shee lay at his feete untill the morning: and she rose up before one could know another. And he said, Let it not be knowen, that a woman came into the floore.

15 Also he said, Bring the vaile that thou hast upon thee, and holde it. And when she helde it, he measured sixe *measures* of barley, and laide it on her: and he went into the citie.

16 And when shee came to her mother in law, she said, who *art* thou, my daughter: and she tolde her all that the man had done to her.

17 And she said, These sixe *measures* of barley gave he me, for he said to me, Go not emptie unto thy mother in law.

18 Then said she, Sit still, my daughter, untill thou know how the matter will fall: for the man will not be in rest, until he have finished the thing this day.

at the end of the heap of grain. Then she came softly, and uncovered his feet, and lay down. 8 At midnight the man was startled, and turned over, and behold, a woman lay at his feet! 9 He said, "Who are you?" And she answered, "I am Ruth, your maidservant; spread your skirt over your maidservant, for you are next of kin." 10 And he said, "May you be blessed by the LORD, my daughter; you have made this last kindness greater than the first, in that you have not gone after young men, whether poor or rich. 11 And now, my daughter, do not fear, I will do for you all that you ask, for all my fellow townsmen know that you are a woman of worth. 12 And now it is true that I am a near kinsman, yet there is a kinsman nearer than I. 13 Remain this night, and in the morning, if he will do the part of the next of kin for you, well; let him do it; but if he is not willing to do the part of the next of kin for you, then, as the LORD lives, I will do the part of the next of kin for you. Lie down until the morning."

14 So she lay at his feet until the morning, but arose before one could recognize another; and he said, "Let it not be known that the woman came to the threshing floor." 15 And he said, "Bring the mantle you are wearing and hold it out." So she held it, and he measured out six measures of barley, and laid it upon her; then she went into the city. 16 And when she came to her mother-in-law, she said, "How did you fare, my daughter?" Then she told her all that the man had done for her, 17 saying, "These six measures of barley he gave to me, for he said, 'You must not go back empty-handed to your mother-in-law.'" 18 She replied, "Wait, my daughter, until you learn how the matter turns out, for the man will not rest, but will settle the matter today."

down at the end of the straw stack. Then she came in stealthily, uncovered his feet, and lay down. At midnight the man started up, and turning over, discovered a woman lying at his feet!

"Who are you?" he said.

"I am Ruth, your maidservant," she said. "Take your maidservant in marriage; for you are next-of-kin."

"Blessed be you of the Lord, my girl!" he said. "This last kindness of yours is lovelier than the first, in that you have not run after the young men, either poor or rich. And now, my girl, have no fear; I will do for you all you ask; for all the council of my people know that you are a woman of worth. But now, as matter of fact, I am really not next-of-kin, since there is another nearer than I who is next-of-kin. Stay here tonight, and then, in the morning, if he will do the duty of next-of-kin for you, good; let him do so; but if he does not wish to do the duty of next-of-kin for you, then, as the Lord lives, I will do so for you. Lie down until morning."

So she lay at his feet until morning, but got up before one could recognize another; for he said, "It must not be known that the woman came to the threshing-floor."

"Bring the mantle which you have on," he said, "and hold it out."

So she held it out, and he poured out six homers of barley, and put it on her shoulder; then she went back to the city, and came to her mother-in-law.

"How did you get along, my daughter?" she said.

Then she told her all that the man had done for her.

"These six homers of barley he gave to me," she said; " 'For,' said he, 'you must not go back empty-handed to your mother-in-law.' "

"Wait, my daughter," she said, "until you learn how the matter turns out; for the man will not rest unless he settles the matter today."

pile of sheaves that lay there; then she crept near, turned back the end of his mantle, and lay down. At midnight, Booz was startled from his sleep, and looked about him in bewilderment to find a woman lying there at his feet. Who art thou? he asked. It is Ruth, she said, Ruth, thy handmaid, that bids thee cast thy mantle over her, as one that is near of kin. The Lord bless thee, daughter, he answered; now, more than ever, thou hast shewn the goodness of thy heart; to have no eyes for younger men, rich or poor! Be comforted, thou shalt have all thou wilt of me; all the city knows thee for a bride worth the winning. True enough, we are near of kin, but thou hast another kinsman nearer yet. Wait till night is past; at daybreak, if he will claim thee by right of kinship, well and good; if not, as the Lord is a living God, thou shalt be mine without more ado. Sleep, then, till day comes.

So there, at his feet, she slept till the night passed; and he rose while it was still too early for men to recognize one another. He warned her not to let anyone know that she had been there; then he said, Spread out the fold of that mantle thou wearest, and hold it with either hand. So she held it spread out, and he measured out two bushels of barley for her to carry. When she reached the city with her load, she found Noemi eager to know how she had fared; and she told the story of how Booz had treated her. Look, she said, he has given me two bushels of barley; he protested that he must not send me home to my mother-in-law empty-handed. Wait, then, daughter, said Noemi, till we see what will come of it. Here is a man that will not rest till he has made good his promise.

Chap. IIII.

1 *Boaz calleth into judgment the next kinseman.* 6 *He refuseth the redemption according to the maner in Israel.* 9 *Boaz buyeth the inheritance.* 11 *He marrieth Ruth.* 13 *She beareth Obed the grandfather of David.* 18 *The generation of Pharez.*

Then went Boaz up to the gate, and sate him downe there: and beholde, the kinseman of whome Boaz spake, came by, unto whom he said, Ho, such a one: turne aside, sit downe here. And hee turned aside, and sate downe.

2 And hee tooke ten men of the Elders of the citie, and said, Sit ye downe here. And they sate downe.

3. And he said unto the kinseman: Naomi that is come againe out of the countrey of Moab, selleth a parcell of land, which was our brother Elimelechs.

4 And I thought to advertise thee, saying, Buy *it* before the inhabitants, and before the Elders of my people. If thou wilt redeeme *it*, redeeme *it*, but if thou wilt not redeeme *it*, then tell mee, that I may know: for there is none to redeeme *it*, besides thee, and I *am* after thee. And he said, I will redeeme *it*.

5 Then said Boaz, What day thou buyest the field of the hand of Naomi, thou must buy *it* also of Ruth the Moabitesse, the wife of the dead, to raise up the name of the dead upon his inheritance.

6 And the kinseman said, I cannot redeeme *it* for my selfe, lest I marre mine own inheritance: redeeme thou my right to thy selfe, for I cannot redeeme *it*.

7 Now this was *the maner* in former time in Israel, concerning redeeming and concerning changing, for to confirme all things: a man plucked off his shooe, and gave *it* to his neighbour: and this *was* a testimonie in Israel.

8 Therfore the kinseman said unto Boaz, Buy *it* for thee: so he drew off his shooe.

9 And Boaz saide unto the Elders, and unto all the people, Ye *are* witnesses this day, that I have bought all that was Elimelechs, and all that was Chilions, and Mahlons, of the hande of Naomi.

4 And Bo'az went up to the gate and sat down there; and behold, the next of kin, of whom Bo'az had spoken, came by. So Bo'az said, "Turn aside, friend; sit down here"; and he turned aside and sat down. ² And he took ten men of the elders of the city, and said, "Sit down here"; so they sat down. ³ Then he said to the next of kin, "Na'omi, who has come back from the country of Moab, is selling the parcel of land which belonged to our kinsman Elim'-elech. ⁴ So I thought I would tell you of it, and say, Buy it in the presence of those sitting here, and in the presence of the elders of my people. If you will redeem it, redeem it; but if you will not, tell me, that I may know, for there is no one besides you to redeem it, and I come after you." And he said, "I will redeem it." ⁵ Then Bo'az said, "The day you buy the field from the hand of Na'omi, you are also buying Ruth* the Moabitess, the widow of the dead, in order to restore the name of the dead to his inheritance." ⁶ Then the next of kin said, "I cannot redeem it for myself, lest I impair my own inheritance. Take my right of redemption yourself, for I cannot redeem it."

7 Now this was the custom in former times in Israel concerning redeeming and exchanging: to confirm a transaction, the one drew off his sandal and gave it to the other, and this was the manner of attesting in Israel. ⁸ So when the next of kin said to Bo'az, "Buy it for yourself," he drew off his sandal. ⁹ Then Bo'az said to the elders and all the people, "You are witnesses this day that I have bought from the hand of Na'omi

* Old Latin Vg: Heb *of Naomi and from Ruth.*

4.7: Deut. 25. 8–10.

RUTH'S MARRIAGE TO BOAZ AND THEIR
DESCENDANTS, 4:1–22

Meanwhile Boaz went up to the city gate, and sat down there just as the next-of-kin was passing, of whom Boaz had spoken.

"Come over and sit down here somewhere," he said.

So he came over and sat down. Then Boaz got ten of the elders of the city, and said,

"Sit down here."

When they had seated themselves, he said to the next-of-kin,

"Naomi, who has come back from the country of Moab, is selling the piece of land which belonged to our relative, Elimelech; so I thought that I would tell you about it, suggesting that you buy it in the presence of those who are sitting here, and in the presence of the elders of my people. If you will redeem it, do so; but if you will not redeem it, then tell me, so that I may know; for there is no one but you to redeem it, and I come after you."

"I will redeem it," he said.

Then Boaz said,

"At the time that you buy the field from Naomi, you must also buy Ruth, the Moabitess, the widow of the deceased, in order to restore the name of the deceased to his estate."

Then the next-of-kin said,

"I cannot redeem it for myself, lest I ruin ,my own estate. Use my right of redemption for yourself; for I cannot do so."

Now this was the ancient custom in Israel: to validate any transaction in the matter of the right of redemption and its conveyance, the one pulled off his sandal, and gave it to the other; this was the manner of attesting in Israel. Accordingly, when the next-of-kin said to Boaz, "Buy it for yourself," he drew off his sandal. Then Boaz said to the elders and all the people,

"You are witnesses today that I am buying from Naomi all that belonged to Elimelech and all that belonged to Chilion and

4 So Booz went up to the city gate, and sat waiting there. When the man he was looking for passed by, the kinsman of whom he had spoken, he called him by name, bidding him stay his journey and sit there for a little; and so he did. Then Booz chose out ten of the city elders, and would have these, too, sit beside him. When they were seated, he told the rival claimant, Here is Noemi, that lately came back out of Moab, offering to sell part of the land which belonged to our kinsman Elimelech. Of this, I thought it well to give thee notice, and challenge thee before the neighbours who are sitting by, and these, the elders of my people. Hast thou a mind to play a kinsman's part, and claim it for thy own? Then thou must buy it, and so enter into possession. If not, tell me, so that I may know what to do; thy right comes first, and mine second; there is no other kinsman. Yes, said he, I will buy it. Why then, said Booz, if thou dost buy the land from Noemi, thou must needs take with it a dead man's widow, Ruth the Moabitess, to perpetuate the name of the kinsman whose lands thou dost enjoy. Nay, then, said the other, I forgo my right of kinship; I would not disinherit the heirs of my own body. I yield thee my rights, willing enough to forgo them.

It was the custom of Israel in old times that if one kinsman yielded his right to another, he must untie his shoe and hand it over to this kinsman of his, or else the gift was not valid; thus did the Israelites put the grant on record.* So now Booz said to the rival claimant, Untie thy shoe; and as soon as he had done so, made appeal to the elders and to all that were present. You are witnesses, he said, this day, that I have reclaimed all the possessions of Elimelech, Chelion and Mahalon by purchase from

---

* Cf. Deut. 25. 7–10.

10 Moreover, Ruth the Moabitesse, the wife of Mahlon, have I purchased to be my wife, to raise up the name of the dead upon his inheritance, that the name of the dead be not cut off from among his brethren, and from the gate of his place: ye *are* witnesses this day.

11 And all the people that were in the gate, and the Elders said, W*ee are* witnesses: The LORD make the woman that is come unto thine house, like Rachel and like Leah, which two did build the house of Israel: and do thou worthily in Ephratah, and bee famous in Bethlehem.

12 And let thy house be like the house of Pharez, (whom Tamar bare unto Judah) of the seed which the LORD shall give thee of this yong woman.

13 So Boaz tooke Ruth, and she was his wife: and when he went in unto her, the LORD gave her conception, and she bare a sonne.

14 And the women said unto Naomi, Blessed be the LORD which hath not left thee this day without a kinsman, that his name may bee famous in Israel:

15 And he shalbe unto thee a restorer of *thy* life, and a nourisher of thine old age: for thy daughter in law which loveth thee, which is better to thee then seven sonnes, hath borne him.

16 And Naomi tooke the childe, and laid it in her bosome, and became nurse unto it.

17 And the women her neighbours gave it a name, saying, There is a sonne borne to Naomi, and they called his name Obed: hee *is* the father of Jesse, the father of David.

18 Now these are the generations of Pharez: Pharez begate Hezron,

19 And Hezron begate Ram, and Ram begate Amminadab,

20 And Amminadab begate Nahshon, and Nahshon begate Salmon,

21 And Salmon begate Boaz, and Boaz begate Obed,

22 And Obed begate Jesse, and Jesse begate David.

all that belonged to Elim'elech and all that belonged to Chil'ion and to Mahlon. 10 Also Ruth the Moabitess, the widow of Mahlon, I have bought to be my wife, to perpetuate the name of the dead in his inheritance, that the name of the dead may not be cut off from among his brethren and from the gate of his native place; you are witnesses this day." 11 Then all the people who were at the gate, and the elders, said, "We are witnesses. May the LORD make the woman, who is coming into your house, like Rachel and Leah, who together built up the house of Israel. May you prosper in Eph'rathah and be renowned in Bethlehem; 12 and may your house be like the house of Perez, whom Tamar bore to Judah, because of the children that the LORD will give you by this young woman."

13 So Bo'az took Ruth and she became his wife; and he went in to her, and the LORD gave her conception, and she bore a son. 14 Then the women said to Na'omi, "blessed be the LORD, who has not left you this day without next of kin; and may his name be renowned in Israel! 15 He shall be to you a restorer of life and a nourisher of your old age; for your daughter-in-law who loves you, who is more to you than seven sons, has borne him." 16 Then Na'omi took the child and laid him in her bosom, and became his nurse. 17 And the women of the neighborhood gave him a name, saying, "A son has been born to Na'omi." They named him Obed; he was the father of Jesse, the father of David.

18 Now these are the descendants of Perez: Perez was the father of Hezron, 19 Hezron of Ram, Ram of Ammin'adab, 20 Ammin'adab of Nahshon, Nahshon of Salmon, 21 Salmon of Bo'az, Bo'az of Obed, 22 Obed of Jesse, and Jesse of David.

Mahlon. Also Ruth, the Moabitess, the widow of Mahlon, I am buying to be my wife, in order to restore the name of the dead to his estate, so that the name of the dead may not be cut off from among his relatives nor from the council of his home; you are witnesses today."

Whereupon all the people at the gate and the elders said,

"We are witnesses. May the LORD make the woman who is coming into your home like Rachel and Leah, both of whom built up the house of Israel; may you achieve wealth in Ephrath, and gain fame in Bethlehem; and from the offspring that the LORD gives you by this young woman, may you have a house like the house of Perez, whom Tamar bore to Judah!"

So Boaz took Ruth, and she became his wife; he had intercourse with her, and the LORD made her conceive, and she bore a son. Then the women said to Naomi,

"Blessed be the LORD, who has not left you this day without a next-of-kin! May the boy's name become famous in Israel! He shall renew your youth, and be the stay of your old age; for your daughter-in-law, who loves you, has borne him, who herself is more to you than seven sons."

Then Naomi took the child, and laid him in her bosom, and became his nurse; and the women of the neighborhood gave him a name, saying, "A son has been born to Naomi!" So they called his name Obed. He was the father of Jesse, the father of David.

Now this is the genealogy of Perez: Perez was the father of Hezron, Hezron of Ram, Ram of Amminadab, Amminadab of Nahshon, Nahshon of Salmon, Salmon of Boaz, Boaz of Obed, Obed of Jesse, and Jesse of David.

Noemi: and moreover, that I have taken Mahalon's widow, Ruth the Moabitess, to wife. I mean to hand on the dead man's property to heirs of his own, so that his name may never be lost to his family, his kindred and his people. Of all this, you are witnesses. So the elders made answer, and all that were present made answer, We bear witness of it. Take thy bride home, and may the Lord make her as fruitful as Rachel and Lia, that gave a posterity to Israel. May Ephrata know her worth, and Bethlehem tell her praises; may thy house be famous as the house of Phares, that Thamar bore to Juda, through the sons the Lord will give thee by this wife of thine.

So Booz claimed Ruth, and wedded and bedded her, and the Lord made her conceive and give birth to a son. Blessed be the Lord, all the women said to Noemi, for not leaving thy family without an heir, to perpetuate its name in Israel. Here is one that shall bring comfort to thy heart, and support to thy old age; such a mother is his, such a daughter-in-law is thine, whose love is worth more to thee than seven sons of thy own. And so Noemi took the child to her bosom, and still it must be she that nursed him, she that carried him, till the neighbours, congratulating her, said It is Noemi that has a son. And they called him Obed.

This Obed had a son called Jesse, that was father to David. Thus, then, runs the pedigree of Phares; Phares was the father of Esron, Esron of Aram, Aram of Aminadab, Aminadab of Nahasson, Nahasson of Salmon, Salmon of Booz, Booz of Obed, Obed of Jesse, and Jesse of David.

QUESTIONS FOR STUDY AND DISCUSSION

1. What should a translator attempt in his work? Should he try above all to be faithful to the sense of the original, or has he succeeded if he captures its spirit?

2. What dangers face the translator who feels free to depart from the original language of the Bible in order to capture the real meaning, as he conceives it to be? Discuss "Thoughts on Bible Translation" in this light. Are there other ways of handling this inevitable problem?

3. Is it possible to translate or somehow reproduce the style or tone of a document in another language? How would you characterize the style of the four translations of Ruth printed here? If you know Hebrew, compare with the tone of the original.

4. Most of us would probably ask for clarity as the greatest possible virtue in any translation of the Bible. Evaluate the four translations of Ruth for clearness of expression.

5. Consider the four translations of I.16-17 both for clarity and for beauty of expression. How would you rank the translations? Next, take any two other verses from Ruth and rank the translations for the same qualities. Is your evaluation influenced by your familiarity with certain favorite passages?

6. Sentence rhythm is an elusive quality at best, but can you point out sentences in the translations which are especially beautiful to hear and others which are matter of fact or clumsy? Can you rank the translations on this score?

7. Make a list of passages in which the choice of individual words varies significantly. (Consider, for instance, II.5, where The Authorized Version uses *damosell*, the Revised Standard Version *maiden*, the American Translation *girl*, and Knox gives a rendering quite different from the usual translation.) What guides the translators in their selection of words?

8. Which of the modern translations employ *thou*, *thee*, and other archaisms? Can you explain or justify this? Do you think that there is a kind of language most appropriate for the Bible and for prayer, or would consistent modern English be better?

9. If you feel that some archaisms are justified in modern translations of the Bible and in prayer, do you also feel that word and phrase should be more elevated than in normal English? Compare the translations of IV.13. Where the Revised Standard Version says that Boaz "went in to her," the American Translation tells us that Boaz "had intercourse with" Ruth, and Knox with a deliberate jingle writes that Booz "wedded and bedded her." Are the translations equally dignified at this point?

Part Four

IN SEARCH OF IDEAS

The World Around Us: Science

JOSEPH WOOD KRUTCH

Love in the Desert

The ancients called love "the mother of all things," but they didn't know the half of it. They did not know, for instance, that plants as well as animals have their love life and they supposed that even some of the simpler animals were generated by sunlight on mud without the intervention of Venus.

Centuries later when Chaucer and the other medieval poets made "the mystic rose" a euphemism for an anatomical structure not commonly mentioned in polite society, they too were choosing a figure of speech more appropriate than they realized, because every flower really is a group of sex organs which the plants have glorified while the animals —surprisingly enough, as many have observed—usually leave the corresponding items of their own anatomy primitive, unadorned and severely functional. The ape, whose behind blooms in purple and red, represents the most any of the higher animals has achieved along this line and even it is not, by human standards, any great aesthetic success. At least no one would be likely to maintain that it rivals either the poppy or the orchid.

In another respect also plants seem to have been more aesthetically sensitive than animals. They have never tolerated that odd arrangement by which the same organs are used for reproduction and excretion. Men, from St. Bernard to William Butler Yeats, have ridiculed or scorned it and recoiled in distaste from the fact that, as Yeats put it, "love has pitched his mansion in / The place of excrement." As a matter of fact, the reptiles are the only backboned animals who have a special organ used only in mating. Possibly—though improbably, I am afraid— if this fact were better known it might be counted in favor of a generally unpopular group.

All this we now know and, appropriately enough, much of it—especially concerning the sexuality of plants—was first discovered during the eighteenth-century Age of Gallantry. No other age would have been more disposed to hail the facts with delight and it was much inclined to expound the new knowledge in extravagantly gallant terms. One does not usually think of systematizers as given to rhapsody, but Linnaeus, who first popularized the fact that plants can make love, wrote rhapsodically of their nuptials:

> *The petals serve as bridal beds which the Great Creator has so gloriously arranged, adorned with such noble bed curtains and perfumed with so many sweet scents, that the bridegroom there may celebrate his nuptials with all the greater solemnity. When the bed is thus prepared, it is time for the bridegroom to embrace his beloved bride and surrender his gifts to her: I mean, one can*

see how testiculi *open and emit* pulverem genitalem, *which falls upon* tubam *and fertilizes* ovarium.

In England, half a century later, Erasmus Darwin, distinguished grandfather of the great Charles, wrote even more exuberantly in his didactic poem, "The Loves of the Plants," where all sorts of gnomes, sylphs and other mythological creatures benevolently foster the vegetable *affaires de coeur*. It is said to have been one of the best-selling poems ever published, no doubt because it combined the newly fashionable interest in natural history with the long standing obsession with "the tender passion" as expressible in terms of cupids, darts, flames and all the other clichés which now survive only in St. Valentine's Day gifts.

Such romantic exuberance is not much favored today when the seamy side is likely to interest us more. We are less likely to abandon ourselves to a participation in the joys of spring than to be on our guard against "the pathetic fallacy" even though, as is usually the case, we don't know exactly what the phrase means or what is "pathetic" about the alleged fallacy. Nevertheless, those who consent, even for a moment, to glance at that agreeable surface of things with which the poets used to be chiefly concerned will find in the desert what they find in every other spring, and they may even be aware that the hare, which here also runs races with itself, is a good deal fleeter than any Wordsworth was privileged to observe in the Lake Country.

In this warm climate, moreover, love puts in his appearance even before "the yonge sonne hath in the Ram his halfe cours y-ronne" or, in scientific prose, ahead of the spring equinox. Many species of birds, which for months have done little more than chirp, begin to remember their songs. In the canyons where small pools are left from some winter rain, the subaqueous and most mysterious of all spring births begins and seems to recapitulate the first morning of creation. Though I have never noticed that either of the two kinds of doves which spend the whole year with us acquire that "livelier iris" which Tennyson celebrated,

the lizard's belly turns turquoise blue, as though to remind his mate that even on their ancient level sex has its aesthetic as well as its biological aspect. Fierce sparrow hawks take to sitting side by side on telegraph wires, and the Arizona cardinal, who has remained all winter long more brilliantly red than his eastern cousin ever is, begins to think romantically of his neat but not gaudy wife. For months before, he had been behaving like an old married man who couldn't remember what he once saw in her. Though she had followed him about, he had sometimes driven her rudely away from the feeding station until he had had his fill. Now gallantry begins to revive and he may even graciously hand her a seed.

A little later the cactus wren and the curved-bill thrasher will build nests in the wicked heart of the cholla cactus and, blessed with some mysterious impunity, dive through its treacherous spines. Somewhere among the creosote bushes, by now yellow with blossoms, the jack rabbit—an unromantic looking creature if there ever was one—will be demonstrating that she is really a hare, not a rabbit at all, by giving birth to young furred babies almost ready to go it alone instead of being naked, helpless creatures like the infant cottontail. The latter will be born underground, in a cozily lined nest; the more rugged jack rabbit on the almost bare surface.

My special charge, the Sonoran spadefoot toad, will remain buried no one knows how many feet down for months still to come. He will not celebrate his spring until mid-July when a soaking rain penetrates deeply enough to assure him that on the surface a few puddles will form. Some of those puddles may just possibly last long enough to give his tadpoles the nine or ten days of submersion necessary, if they are to manage the metamorphosis which will change them into toadlets capable of repeating that conquest of the land which their ancestors accomplished so many millions of years ago. But while the buried spadefoots dally, the buried seeds dropped last year by the little six-week ephemerals of the desert will spring up and proceed with what looks like indecent haste to the business of reproduction, as though—as for them is almost the case—life were not long enough for anything except preparation for the next generation.

Human beings have been sometimes praised and sometimes scorned because they fall so readily into the habit of pinning upon their posterity all hope for a good life, of saying, "At least my children will have that better life which I somehow never managed to achieve." Even plants do that, as I know, because when I have raised some of the desert annuals under the unsuitable conditions of a winter living room, they have managed, stunted and sickly though they seemed, to seed. "At least," they seemed to say, "our species is assured another chance." And if this tendency is already dominant in a morning glory, human beings will probably continue to accept it in themselves also, whether, by human standards, it is wise or not.

As I write this another spring has just come around. With a regularity in which there is something pleasantly comic, all the little romances, dramas and tragedies are acting themselves out once more, and I seize the opportunity to pry benevolently.

Yesterday I watched a pair of hooded orioles—he, brilliant in orange and black; she, modestly yellow green—busy about a newly constructed nest hanging from the swordlike leaves of a yucca, where one would have been less surprised to find the lemon yellow cousin of these birds which builds almost exclusively in the yucca. From this paradise I drove away the serpent—in this case a three-foot diamondback rattler who was getting uncomfortably close to the nesting site—and went on to flush out of the grass at least a dozen tiny Gambel's quail whose male parent, hovering close by, bobbed his head plume anxiously as he tried to rally them again. A quarter of a mile away a red and black Gila monster was sunning himself on the fallen trunk of another yucca, and, for all I know, he too may have been feeling some stirring of the spring, though I can hardly say that he showed it.

From birds as brightly colored as the orioles one expects only gay domesticity and lighthearted solicitude. For that reason I have been more interested to follow the home life of the road runner, that unbird-like bird whom we chose at the beginning as a desert dweller par excellence. One does not expect as much of him as one does of an oriole for two good reasons. In the first place, his normal manner is aggressive, ribald and devil-may-care. In the second place, he is a cuckoo, and the shirking of domestic responsibilities by some of the tribe has been notorious for so long that by some confused logic human husbands who are the victims of unfaithfulness not only wear the horns of the deer but are also said to be cuckolded. The fact remains, nevertheless, that though I have watched the developing domestic life of one road runner couple for weeks, I have observed nothing at which the most critical could cavil.

The nest—a rather coarse affair of largish sticks—was built in the crotch of a thorny cholla cactus some ten feet above the ground, which is rather higher than usual. When first found there were already in it two eggs, and both of the parent birds were already brooding them, turn and turn about. All this I had been led to expect because the road runner, unlike most birds, does not wait until all the eggs have been laid before beginning to incubate. Instead she normally lays them one by one a day or two apart and begins to set as soon as the first has arrived. In other words the wife follows the advice of the Planned Parenthood Association and "spaces" her babies—perhaps because lizards and snakes are harder to come by than insects, and it would be too much to try to feed a whole nest full of nearly grown infants at the same time. Moreover, in the case of my couple "self-restraint" or some other method of birth control had been rigorously practiced and two young ones were all there were.

Sixteen days after I first saw the eggs, both had hatched. Presently both parents were bringing in lizards according to a well-worked-out plan. While one sat on the nest to protect the young from the blazing sun, the other went hunting. When the latter returned with a catch, the brooding bird gave up its place, went foraging in its turn and presently came back to deliver a catch, after which it again took its place on the nest. One day, less than a month after the eggs were first discovered, one baby was standing on the edge of the nest itself, the other on a cactus stem a few feet away. By the next day both had disappeared.

Thus, despite the dubious reputation of the family to which he belongs, the road runner, like the other American cuckoos, seems to have conquered both the hereditary taint and whatever temptations his generally rascally disposition may have exposed him to. In this case at least, both husband and wife seemed quite beyond criticism, though they do say that other individuals sometimes reveal a not-too-serious sign of the hereditary weakness when a female will, on occasion, lay her eggs in the nest of another bird of her own species—which is certainly not so reprehensible as victimizing a totally different bird as the European cuckoo does.

Perhaps the superior moral atmosphere of America has reformed the cuckoo's habit and at least no American representative of the family regularly abandons its eggs to the care of a stranger. Nevertheless, those of us who are inclined to spiritual pride should remember that we do have a native immoralist, abundant in this same desert country and just as reprehensible as any to be found in decadent Europe—namely the cowbird, who is sexually promiscuous, never builds a home of his own and is inveterately given to depositing eggs in the nests of other birds. In his defense it is commonly alleged that his "antisocial conduct" should be excused for the same reason that such conduct is often excused in human beings—because, that is to say, it is actually the result not of original sin but of certain social determinants. It seems that long before he became a cowbird this fellow was a buffalo bird. And because he had to follow the wide ranging herds if he was to profit from the insects they started up from the grass, he could never settle down long enough to raise a family. Like Rousseau and like Walt Whitman, he had to leave his offspring (if any) behind.

However that may be, it still can hardly be denied that love in the desert has its still

seamier side. Perhaps the moth, whom we have already seen playing pimp to a flower and profiting shamelessly from the affair, can also be excused on socio-economic grounds. But far more shocking things go on in dry climates as well as in wet, and to excuse them we shall have to dig deeper than the social system right down into the most ancient things-as-they-used-to-be. For an example which seems to come straight out of the most unpleasant fancies of the Marquis de Sade, we might contemplate the atrocious behavior of the so-called tarantula spider of the sandy wastes. Here, unfortunately, is a lover whom all the world will find it difficult to love.

This tarantula is a great hairy fellow much like the kind which sometimes comes north in a bunch of bananas and which most people have seen exhibited under a glass in some fruiterer's window. Most visitors to the desert hate and fear him at sight, even though he is disinclined to trouble human beings and is incapable even upon extreme provocation of giving more than a not-too-serious bite. Yet he does look more dangerous than the scorpion and he is, if possible, even less popular.

He has a leg spread of four or sometimes of as much as six inches, and it is said that he can leap for as much as two feet when pouncing upon his insect prey. Most of the time he spends in rather neat tunnels or burrows excavated in the sand, from which entomologists in search of specimens flush him out with water. And it is chiefly in the hottest months, especially after some rain, that one sees him prowling about, often crossing a road and sometimes waiting at a screen door to be let in. Except for man, his most serious enemy is the "tarantula hawk," a large black-bodied wasp with orange-red wings, who pounces upon his larger antagonist, paralyzes him with a sting and carries his now helpless body to feed the young wasps which will hatch in their own underground burrow.

Just to look at the tarantula's hairy legs and set of gleaming eyes is to suspect him of unconventionality or worse, and the suspicions are justified. He is one of those creatures in whom love seems to bring out the worst. Moreover, because at least one of the several species happens to have been the subject of careful study, the details are public. About the only thing he cannot be accused of is "infantile sexuality," and he can't be accused of that only because the male requires some eleven years to reach sexual maturity or even to develop the special organs necessary for his love making—if you can stretch this euphemistic term far enough to include his activities.

When at last he has come of age, he puts off the necessity of risking contact with a female as long as possible. First he spins a sort of web into which he deposits a few drops of sperm. Then he patiently taps the web for a period of about two hours in order to fill with the sperm the two special palps or mouth parts which he did not acquire until the molt which announced his maturity. Then, and only then, does he go off in search of his "mystic and somber Dolores" who will never exhibit toward him any tender emotions.

If, as is often the case, she shows at first no awareness of his presence, he will give her a few slaps until she rears angrily with her fangs spread for a kill. At this moment he then plays a trick which nature, knowing the disposition of his mate, has taught him and for which nature has provided a special apparatus. He slips two spurs conveniently placed on his forelegs over the fangs of the female, in such a way that the fangs are locked into immobility. Then he transfers the sperm which he has been carrying into an orifice in the female, unlocks her fangs and darts away. If he is successful in making his escape, he may repeat the process with as many as three other females. But by this time he is plainly senile and he slowly dies, presumably satisfied that his life work has been accomplished. Somewhat unfairly, the female may live for a dozen more years and use up several husbands. In general outline the procedure is the same for many spiders, but it seems worse in him, because he is big enough to be conspicuous.

It is said that when indiscreet birdbanders announced their discovery that demure little house wrens commonly swap mates between the first and second of their summer broods, these wrens lost favor with many old ladies who promptly took down their nesting boxes because they refused to countenance such loose behavior.

In the case of the tarantula we have been contemplating mores which are far worse. But there ought, it seems to me, to be some possible attitude less unreasonable than either that of the old ladies who draw away from nature when she seems not to come up to their very exacting standards of behavior, and the seemingly opposite attitude of inverted romantics who are prone either to find all beasts other than man completely beastly, or to argue that since man is biologically a beast, nothing should or can be expected of him that is not found in all his fellow creatures.

Such a more reasonable attitude will, it seems to me, have to be founded on the realization that sex has had a history almost as long as the history of life, that its manifestations are as multifarious as the forms assumed by living things and that their comeliness varies as much as do the organisms themselves. Man did not invent it and he was not the first to exploit either the techniques of love making or the emotional and aesthetic themes which have become associated with them. Everything either beautiful or ugly of which he has found himself capable is somewhere anticipated in the repertory of plant and animal behavior. In some creatures sex seems a bare and mechanical necessity; in others the opportunity for elaboration has been seized upon and developed in many different directions. Far below the human level, love can be a game on the one hand, or a self-destructive passion on the other. It can inspire tenderness or cruelty; it can achieve fulfillment through either violent domination or prolonged solicitation. One is almost tempted to say that to primitive creatures, as to man, it can be sacred or profane, love or lust.

The tarantula's copulation is always violent rape and usually ends in death for the aggressor. But over against that may be set not only the romance of many birds but also of other less engaging creatures in whom nevertheless a romantic courtship is succeeded by an epoch of domestic attachment and parental solicitude. There is no justification for assuming, as some romanticists do, that the one is actually more "natural" than the other. In one sense nature is neither for nor against what have come to be human ideals. She includes both what we call good and what we call evil. We are simply among her experiments, though we are, in some respects, the most successful.

Some desert creatures have come quite a long way from the tarantula—and in our direction, too. Even those who have come only a relatively short way are already no longer repulsive. Watching from a blind two parent deer guarding a fawn while he took the first drink at a water hole, it seemed that the deer at least had come a long way.

To be sure many animals are, if this is possible, more "sex obsessed" than we—intermittently at least. Mating is the supreme moment of their lives and for many, as for the male scorpion and the male tarantula, it is also the beginning of the end. Animals will take more trouble and run more risks than men usually will, and if the Strindbergs are right when they insist that the woman still wants to consume her mate, the biological origin of that grisly impulse is rooted in times which are probably more ancient than the conquest of dry land.

Our currently best-publicized student of human sexual conduct has argued that some of what are called "perversions" in the human being—homosexuality, for example—should be regarded as merely "normal variations" because something analogous is sometimes observed in the animal kingdom. But if that argument is valid then nothing in the textbooks of psychopathology is "abnormal." Once nature had established the fact of maleness and femaleness, she seems to have experimented with every possible variation on the theme. By comparison, Dr. Kinsey's most adventurous subjects were hopelessly handicapped by the anatomical and physiological limitations of the human being.

In the animal kingdom, monogamy, polygamy, polyandry and promiscuity are only trivial variations. Nature makes hermaphrodites, as well as Tiresiases who are alternately of one sex and then the other; also hordes of neuters among the bees and the ants. She causes some males to attach themselves permanently to their females and teaches others how to accomplish impregnation without ever touching them. Some embrace for hours; some, like Onan, scatter their seed. Many males in many different orders—like the seahorse and the ostrich, for example—brood the eggs, while others will eat them, if they get a chance, quite as blandly as many females will eat their mate, once his business is done. Various male spiders wave variously decorated legs before the eyes of a prospective spouse in the hope (often vain) that she will not mistake them for a meal just happening by. But husband-eating is no commoner than child-eating. Both should be classed as mere "normal variants" in human behavior if nothing except a parallel in the animal kingdom is necessary to establish that status. To her children nature seems to have said, "Copulate you must. But beyond that there is no rule. Do it in whatever way and with whatever emotional concomitants you choose. That you should do it somehow or other is all that I ask."

If one confines one's attention too closely to these seamy sides, one begins to understand why, according to Gibbon, some early Fathers of the Church held that sex was the curse pronounced upon Adam and that, had he not sinned, the human race would have been propagated "by some harmless process of vegetation." Or perhaps one begins to repeat with serious emphasis the famous question once asked by the Messrs. Thurber and White, "Is Sex Necessary?" And the answer is that, strictly speaking, it isn't. Presumably the very first organisms were sexless. They reproduced by a "process of vegetation" so harmless that not even vegetable sexuality was involved. What is even more impressive is the patent fact that it is not necessary today. Some of the most successful of all plants and animals—if by successful you mean abundantly surviving—have given it up either entirely or almost entirely. A virgin birth may require a miracle if the virgin is to belong to the human race, but there is nothing miraculous about it in the case of many of nature's successful children. Parthenogenesis, as the biologist calls it, is a perfectly normal event.

Ask the average man for a serious answer to the question what sex is "for" or why it is "necessary," and he will probably answer without thinking that it is "necessary for reproduction." But the biologist knows that it is not. Actually the function of sex is not to assure reproduction but to prevent it—if you take the word literally and hence to mean "exact duplication." Both animals and plants could "reproduce" or "duplicate" without sex. But without it there would be little or no variation, heredities could not be mixed, unexpected combinations could not arise, and evolution would either never have taken place at all or, at least, taken place so slowly that we might all still be arthropods or worse.

If in both the plant and animal kingdom many organisms are actually abandoning the whole of the sexual process, that is apparently because they have resigned their interest in change and its possibilities. Everyone knows how the ants and the bees have increased the singleminded efficiency of the worker majority by depriving them of a sexual function and then creating a special class of sexual individuals. But their solution is far less radical than that of many of the small creatures, including many insects, some of whom are making sexless rather than sexual reproduction the rule, and some of whom are apparently dispensing with the sexual entirely so that no male has ever been found.

In the plant world one of the most familiar and successful of all weeds produces its seeds without pollinization, despite the fact that it still retains the flower which was developed long ago as a mechanism for facilitating that very sexual process which it has now given up. That it is highly "successful" by purely biological standards no one who has ever tried to eliminate dandelions from a lawn is likely to doubt. As I have said before, they not only get along very well in the world, they have also been astonishing colonizers here, since the white man unintentionally brought them from Europe, probably in hay. Sexless though the dandelion is, it is inheriting the earth, and the only penalty which it has to pay for its sexlessness is the penalty of abandoning all hope of ever being anything except a dandelion, even of being a better dandelion than it is. It seems to have said at some point, "This is good enough for me. My tribe flourishes. We have found how to get along in the world. Why risk anything?"

But if, from the strict biological standpoint, sex is "nothing but" a mechanism for encouraging variation, that is a long way from saying that there are not other standpoints. It is perfectly legitimate to say that it is also "for" many other things. Few other mechanisms ever invented or stumbled upon opened so many possibilities, entailed so many unforeseen consequences. Even in the face of those who refuse to entertain the possibility that any kind of purpose or foreknowledge guided evolution, we can still find it permissible to maintain that every invention is "for" whatever uses or good results may come from it, that all things, far from being "nothing but" their origins, are whatever they have become. Grant that and one must grant also that the writing of sonnets is one of the things which sex is "for."

Certainly nature herself discovered a very long time ago that sex was—or at least could be used—"for" many things besides production of offspring not too monotonously like the parent. Certainly also, these discoveries anticipated pretty nearly everything which man himself has ever found it possible to use sex "for." In fact it becomes somewhat humiliating to realize that we seem to have invented nothing absolutely new.

Marital attachment? Attachment to the home? Devotion to children? Long before us, members of the animal kingdom had associated them all with sex. Before us they also founded social groups on the family unit and in some few cases even established monogamy as the rule! Even more strikingly, perhaps, many of them abandoned *force majeure* as the decisive factor in the formation of a mating pair and substituted for it courtships, which became a game, a ritual and an aesthetic experience. Every device of courtship known to the human being was exploited by his predecessors: colorful costume display, song, dance and the wafted perfume. And like man himself, certain animals have come to find the preliminary ceremonies so engaging that they prolong them far beyond the point where they have any justification outside themselves. The grasshopper, for instance, continues to sing like a troubadour long after the lady is weary with waiting.

Even more humiliating, perhaps, than the fact that we have invented nothing is the further fact that the evolution has not been in a straight line from the lowest animal families up to us. The mammals, who are our immediate ancestors, lost as well as gained in the course of their development. No doubt because they lost the power to see colors (which was not recaptured until the primates emerged), the appeal of the eye plays little part in their courtship. In fact "love" in most of its manifestations tends to play a much lesser part in their lives than in that of many lower creatures—even in some who are distinctly less gifted than the outstandingly emotional and aesthetic birds. On the whole, mammalian sex tends to be direct, unadorned, often brutal, and not even the apes, despite their recovery from color blindness, seem to have got very far beyond the most uncomplicated erotic experiences and practices. Intellectually the mammals may be closer to us than any other order of animals, but emotionally and aesthetically they are more remote than some others—which perhaps explains the odd fact that most comparisons with any of them, and all comparisons with the primates, are derogatory. You may call a woman a "butterfly" or describe her as "birdlike." You may even call a man "leonine." But there is no likening with an ape which is not insulting.

How consciously, how poetically or how nobly each particular kind of creature may have learned to love, Venus only knows. But at this very moment of the desert spring many living creatures, plant as well as animal, are celebrating her rites in accordance with the tradition which happens to be theirs.

Fortunately, it is still too early for the tarantulas to have begun their amatory black mass, which, for all I know, may represent one of the oldest versions of the rituals still practiced in the worship of Mr. Swinburne's "mystic and somber Dolores." But this very evening as twilight falls, hundreds of moths will begin to stir themselves in the dusk and presently start their mysterious operations in the heart of those yucca blossoms which are just now beginning to open on the more precocious plants. Young jack rabbits not yet quite the size of an adult cottontail are proof that their parents went early about their business, and many of the brightly colored birds—orioles, cardinals and tanagers—are either constructing their nests or brooding their eggs. Some creatures seem to be worshiping only Venus Pandemos; some others have begun to have some inkling that the goddess manifests herself also as the atavist which the ancients called Venus Eurania. But it is patent to anyone who will take the trouble to look that they stand now upon different rungs of that Platonic ladder of love which man was certainly not the first to make some effort to climb.

Of this I am so sure that I feel it no betrayal of my humanity when I find myself entering with emotional sympathy into a spectacle which is more than a mere show, absorbing though it would be if it were no more than that. Modern knowledge gives me, I think, ample justification for the sense that I am not outside but a part of it, and if it did not give me that assurance, then I should probably agree that I would rather be "some pagan suckled in a creed outworn" than compelled to give it up.

Those very same biological sciences which have traced back to their lowly origins the emotional as well as the physiological characteristics of the sentient human being inevitably furnish grounds for the assumption that if we share much with the animals, they must at the same time share much with us. To maintain that all the conscious concomitants of our physical activities are without analogues in any creatures other than man is to fly in the face of the very evolutionary principles by which those "hardheaded" scientists set so much store. It is to assume that desire and joy have no origins in simpler forms of the same thing, that everything human has "evolved" except the consciousness which makes us aware of what we do. A Descartes, who held that man was an animal-machine differing from other animal-machines in that he alone possessed a gland into which God had inserted a soul, might consistently make between man and the other animals an absolute distinction. But the evolutionist is the last man who has a right to do anything of the sort.

He may, if he can consent to take the extreme position of the pure behaviorist, maintain that in man and the animals alike consciousness neither is nor can be anything but a phosphorescent illusion on the surface of physiological action and reaction, and without any substantial reality or any real significance whatsoever. But there is no choice between that extreme position and recognition of the fact that animals, even perhaps animals as far down in the scale as any still living or preserved in the ancient rocks, were capable of some awareness and of something which was, potentially at least, an emotion.

Either love as well as sex is something which we share with animals, or it is something which does not really exist in us. Either it is legitimate to feel some involvement in the universal Rites of Spring, or it is not legitimate to take our own emotions seriously. And even if the choice between the two possibilities were no more than an arbitrary one, I know which of the alternatives I should choose to believe in and to live by.

QUESTIONS FOR STUDY AND DISCUSSION

1. In what ways does the discussion of mating practices in this essay differ from a science textbook discussion of the subject? In what ways is it "unscientific"?

2. Who is the Marquis de Sade? Swinburne's "mystic and somber Dolores"? Dr. Kinsey? Why does Mr. Krutch refer to them in discussing the "seamy sides" of sex?

3. Why, according to Mr. Krutch, is sex, "from the strict biological standpoint . . . 'nothing but' a mechanism for encouraging variation"? Why does sexual reproduction promote variation?

4. "Man did not invent it [sex] and he was not the first to exploit either the techniques of love making or the emotional and aesthetic themes which have become associated with them. Everything either beautiful or ugly of which he has found himself capable is somewhere anticipated in the repertory of plant and animal behavior." Find as many examples as you can in the essay to support Mr. Krutch's assertion.

5. How does Mr. Krutch justify "entering with emotional sympathy" into the "spectacle" of the amatory rites of desert life?

6. Does this essay have any purpose apart from describing "love in the desert"? What is its thesis?

WRITING ASSIGNMENTS

1. Does "love" differ from "lust"? If so, what characteristics differentiate them? If not, why are apparent differences really superficial? Write a thoughtful essay supporting your view.

2. Is man essentially like other living forms, or is he distinctive? If distinctive, what are the significant differences? Does man possess unique characteristics, or qualitative differences, or no valid distinguishing traits? State and support your point of view in a reasoned essay.

3. What constitutes "abnormal" behavior in man? Write an essay in which you attempt to define "normality" in some area of human affairs.

4. After observing closely some habitual activity of an animal or plant (e.g., food-

gathering, nest-building, migration, court-ship, care of the young), write two short descriptions. In the first, report the activity in a purely objective, "scientific" way. In the second, describe the same activity from the point of view of a man who sees analo-gous behavior in human life.

5. To what extent do men convert every-day human activities (of all kinds) into "a game, a ritual and an aesthetic experience"? Write an essay on some such subject as "The Rite of Shaving," "The Game of Business," "Forms and Ceremonies in Dating," "The Beauty of Bricklaying."

GEORGE A. W. BOEHM

Are We Being Hailed from Interstellar Space?

More than a century ago, Joseph Johann von Littrow, an astronomer at the Vienna Observatory, proposed building a geometric array of bonfires in the Sahara Desert to signal man's presence to the Martians. The bonfires were never built, but speculation that there was life on Mars, and possibly on Venus too, persisted until fairly recently. Today astronomers no longer expect to find intelligent forms of life on the arid landscape of Mars, beneath the boiling, choking atmosphere of Venus, or indeed anywhere else in the solar system. But they have taken on new hope of finding intelligent beings elsewhere in the universe.

More intently than ever before, scientists are searching for signs that man is not alone; but now, in contrast to von Littrow, they are reconciled to beaming their search trillions of miles beyond the solar system. Although they may achieve no tangible results for many years, never before have they had so much hope for ultimate success.

Any contact with life elsewhere might prove shattering to man's ego. Though he has barely entered from the wings, modern, nonphilosophic man fancies that the whole pageant of creation has been staged for his benefit. Unaware of any intellectual rival, he proudly calls himself *Homo sapiens* and regards his intelligence as the acme of evolution. Recently, however, a number of leading scientists have advanced the humbling theory that man is not the only intelligent species in the universe. Elsewhere there may exist thousands of races so superior in intellect that they might look upon man as condescendingly as man regards his domestic animals.

A decade ago such speculation was left chiefly to devotees of the sort of fiction that deals with intergalactic warfare and bug-eyed monsters. Most scientists, from what they thought they knew about the origins of Earth and life, supposed that human intelligence (or anything approaching it) was a freak unlikely to have developed more than once in a universe throughout eternity. But in the last few years scientists have gained a better understanding of some of the crucial steps in the evolution from primordial dust and gas to man. They now suspect that a great many places in the Milky Way, our own galaxy of stars, are habitable and, indeed, inhabited.

Astronomer Harlow Shapley estimates conservatively that life may exist in the planetary systems of one out of a million stars. Other estimates run as high as one out of four stars. But even on the basis of Shapley's figure, life would be commonplace: in the Milky Way, with more than 100 billion stars, there would be no less than 100,000 inhabited bodies. Throughout the other galaxies that are revealed by powerful telescope there might be literally billions of intelligent races.

Now for the first time technology has developed the instruments by which life in outer space might be detected. With the development of radio telescopes and sensitive electronic amplifiers, speculations about other civilizations have taken on a fresh sense of reality. An interstellar radio network, extending hundreds of trillions of miles, is technologically feasible. If intelligent beings do live in the neighborhood of nearby stars, it is theoretically possible to communicate with them, even if their radio transmitters and receivers are no more powerful and sensitive than our own.

Man stands to learn a great deal from contact with his remote neighbors. Any civilization that we heard from here on Earth would almost surely be far ahead of us in science and technology. Only since about 1940 has man been able to build radio equipment powerful enough to reach the stars. Thus any beings more than a few years behind us would not be able to communicate with us at all. It is, of course, possible that we would make contact with a civilization that mastered radio just about the time we did. But that would be an incredible coincidence; the twenty-year history of high-power radio represents merely an instant on the time scale of evolution. It is much more likely that any messages from outer space would come from a people who developed radio at least as far back as the beginning of the Christian era, or perhaps even before man learned to use fire.

What such technically mature beings could teach us is anybody's guess. They might be expected to know the secret of taming thermonuclear hydrogen fusion and thus to have in their possession virtually unlimited sources of energy. They might understand the chemistry of life well enough to modify genes and thereby produce living organisms that are tailored to exact specifications. Very likely they would have solved countless scientific problems that our civilization has not yet even encountered.

They could immediately convince us of their scientific superiority merely by transmitting for our edification a single nine-digit number like the following: 137.039217. Any terrestrial physicist would recognize the first few figures; this is the "fine structure constant" of atomic physics. A dimensionless number that crops up repeatedly in physics, it represents several basic relationships at the atomic level—e.g., the ratio of the wave length of light emitted by hydrogen, the simplest atom, to the circumference of the orbit of hydrogen's only electron; or the ratio of the speed of light to the speed of the hydrogen electron; or, in a more involved fashion, the number of uranium atoms needed to sustain a chain reaction. Physicists on Earth know for sure only the first five digits of the fine structure constant, they are not quite sure of the sixth, and they are constantly working to find the seventh. It may yet take them a century or more to calculate or measure the fine structure constant accurately to nine digits.

Beyond any such lessons that man might learn from another civilization, the contact would have a profound effect on our society. Says Nobel Prize-winning physicist Edward Purcell of Harvard University: "It's not so important whether we learn anything or whether we just hear 'one, two, three' or some other trivial message. Just knowing we are not alone would change our entire philosophic outlook."

This thought worries some people, among them the authors of a recent Brookings Institution report on "Proposed Studies on the Implications of Peaceful Space Activities for Human Affairs" prepared for the National Aeronautics and Space Administration. They note that life elsewhere in the universe could be discovered at any time. They warn that the shock of making contact could lead to the downfall of civilization because "societies sure of their own place in the universe have disintegrated when confronted by a superior society."

Purcell himself doesn't see any cause for worry. "The communication would be utterly benign," he says. "We won't be able to threaten one another with objects; persuasion and deceit would be pointless."

Behind Purcell's assurance is his conviction that man is unlikely ever to meet his interstellar neighbors face to face, for travel outside of our solar system, he thinks, is physically impossible. According to Purcell's calculations, a space ship would have to accelerate to a speed 99 per cent that of light in order to make a round trip to one of the nearer sunlike stars within the span of a human lifetime. The engine would have to be fantastically big and powerful. The best imaginable fuel would consist half of anti-matter—that is, a substance consisting of anti-protons, anti-neutrons, and other particles that are, in a sense, inverse to particles that make up ordinary matter. Physicists have observed anti-matter particles only fleetingly, for when anti-matter comes in contact with matter, both are mutually destroyed and converted entirely into energy. A mixture of matter and anti-matter would be the perfectly efficient fuel. Yet to convey a ten-ton payload the engine would need 200,000 tons of each.

The fact that no one has the faintest notion of how to isolate and store even an ounce of anti-matter is disheartening enough. But there is a still more serious problem. Even if such a space vehicle could be built, fueled, and launched, its exhaust stream would consist of a billion-billion watts of hard x-rays—enough radiation to doom instantly all life on Earth. Besides, a ship traveling at 99 per cent of the speed of light would collide with swarms of hydrogen atoms that pervade space. The relative speeds of atoms and ship would produce an effect equivalent to bombardment by a powerful atom smasher. The ten-ton payload would not provide nearly enough shielding to protect passengers from the radiation. "The moral is that we aren't going anywhere, and neither are *they*," Purcell concludes. "Maybe you can get there by magic, but you can't get there by physics."

But while the prospect of interstellar travel has been banished, the prospect of interspatial communications has grown brighter. The first step is to select the most likely places to seek out alien civilizations and the best ways of communicating with them. The scientists engaged in this study make two basic philosophic assumptions: the first, that life elsewhere is not radically different from life on Earth; the second, that the evolution of life in other places followed roughly the same course as evolution on Earth. Admittedly these assumptions are bold, but they are the only rational basis we have for theorizing.

The consensus is that life can be found only on planets, not on stars. In fact, life, as we conceive of it, can hardly exist in an environment much different from Earth's. Chemistry is presumably pretty much the same throughout the universe; spectroscopic studies of the stars show that their compositions differ only in minor details. It is likely therefore that higher forms of life are limited to the temperature range where water is liquid: between 32° and 212° Fahrenheit. In colder places the life-supporting chemical reactions would take place too slowly for higher plants and animals to evolve. In a hotter climate heat would rupture the delicate chemical bonds between carbon and hydrogen atoms, the principal ingredients of living tissue. It has been suggested that life of a sort could be based on compounds of the element silicon; in this case the temperature limit might be raised by a few hundred degrees. But it is inconceivable that living things, even if made of asbestos, could survive on any star; the coolest stars are close to 3,000°.

Astronomers have never actually seen a planet outside the solar system, and up to about twenty years ago they generally believed that planets were extremely rare. According to a theory of Sir James Jeans and others, the solar planets were torn from the sun when it was side-swiped by a passing star. Such near misses could not possibly have occurred in the Milky Way more than once every few hundred million years.

Today, however, astronomers believe that the universe abounds in planets. They have discarded Jeans's theory of planet formation in favor of one that was worked out in some detail about a dozen years ago. According to this theory the solar system originated from a veil of gas and dust, thinner than a wisp of smoke. Slowly at first, then faster and faster, the particles in this tenuous stuff were pulled together by gravity. Eons went by while a dense, swirling cloud took form. From time to time, as the whirlpool of gas contracted, blobs were shed from its rim. Atoms of hydrogen, which made up most of the cloud, were crushed by the pressure of inrushing matter, and they began to fuse, as in an H-bomb but much more slowly. Meanwhile the blobs that had been thrown off solidified and began to spin in orbits around the central mass of nuclear fire. Thus, almost five billion years ago, were born the sun and its planets.

The laws of physics provide compelling, though indirect, evidence that much the same thing happened (and is still happening) elsewhere in the Milky Way. All stars are presumably born from rapidly spinning clouds. Yet, except for the largest and hottest, stars generally rotate slowly after taking form. Somehow in the course of evolving the slow stars must have disposed of the energy of spinning. All this energy could not have just disappeared without violating the laws of physics; it must have been transferred to other forms of rotation. Some gas and dust clouds split to form two or three stars, which continue to orbit around one another like circling boxers; sky surveys show that about 40 per cent of stars are twins or triplets. But the rest—the single stars—seem to have dumped their rotational energy into relatively small bodies—namely, planets. If that is the case, at least 50 billion stars in the Milky Way are surrounded by planets, and there may be well over 100 billion potential platforms for life in the galaxy.

But only on a small proportion of the planets could intelligent life have evolved. In order for the temperature to be endurable, a planet's orbit has to be just the right size and shape. There are limits also to the size of stars that might support inhabitable planets. Whereas the sun has changed relatively little in the last five billion years and is expected to remain about the same for ten billion more, much larger stars burn out relatively fast. They consume their primary fuel, hydrogen, and start to expand rapidly. They then become "red giants," billowing masses of searing gas that would completely envelop any planets around them. A star twice the mass of the sun, for example, remains stable for only two billion years, which is probably too short a time to permit higher forms of life to evolve. At the other extreme, the smallest stars, about a third the mass of the sun, are relatively cool and quite stable. Some of them will not change for 100 billion years. But the habitable zones around them are very shallow, as astronomer Su-Shu Huang of the National Aeronautics and Space Administration has pointed out. The chance that a planet would be found orbiting at precisely the right distance from a small star is therefore almost nil. So the search for life narrows down to the planets of single stars roughly the size of the sun.

Huang believes the size of the planet itself is still another critical factor. If its gravitational pull is much different from that of Earth, it is unlikely to have the kind of atmosphere that living things can breathe. Chemist Harold Urey has theorized that when the solar system was young, the planets were swaddled in blankets of noxious gas consisting mainly of hydrogen, methane (a hydrogen carbon compound), ammonia (a hydrogen nitrogen compound), and water vapor. On Earth this primeval atmosphere underwent a gradual change in the course of some two or three billion years. Ultraviolet light from the sun split some of the water molecules into oxygen and hydrogen, thereby starting a series of chemical reactions that purified the air. The freed oxygen attacked the methane and formed carbon dioxide; the oxygen also released nitrogen from the ammonia. All the time, excess hydrogen, being extremely light, escaped into space; the heavier gases that now make up our atmosphere—oxygen, nitrogen, and carbon dioxide—were held close to Earth by gravity.

In contrast, Jupiter, which is 318 times heavier than Earth, has such a strong gravitational pull that hydrogen cannot readily escape. Because a chemical equilibrium has been set up, the atmosphere of this giant planet is still rich in methane and ammonia. Some of the simplest bacteria can exist without air, and they may have evolved on Jupiter. But the atmosphere is unfit for higher forms of life. Mars, on the other hand, is one-tenth as heavy as Earth, and its gravitational attraction is too weak to retain much oxygen or water vapor. The atmosphere of Mars went through the chemical evolution hundreds of millions of years ago, but by now almost all its air seems to have been dissipated. Conceivably, at one stage higher forms of life did exist on Mars. As the air and water were lost, however, they must have died out and been replaced by a succession of simpler plants. Some scientists suspect that lichens may exist on Mars, but evolution in reverse has eliminated the possibility of more complex organisms.

Scientists' assumption that there was nothing exceptional about the sequence of events that formed Earth and its atmosphere takes them on to a startling conclusion: given a salubrious climate, life is not only possible, but likely. Some years ago Stanley Miller, one of Urey's students at the University of Chicago, made up a steaming brew that was supposedly a model of Earth's original atmosphere. He then discharged sparks through the vapors to simulate the effect of electrical storms that struck Earth when it was young. After some hours he analyzed the liquid and found traces of surprisingly complex inorganic chemicals, including amino acids, which are fragments of protein.

Since then, chemist Melvin Calvin of the University of California has studied specks of organic matter embedded in meteorites. He has found small amounts of compounds that are fragments of nucleotides, which are in turn fragments of deoxyribonucleic acid (DNA), the stuff of heredity-bearing genes. He has also made nucleotide fragments in an experiment similar to Miller's.

Calvin now believes he can outline the transition from inanimate matter to life— up to a point. On Earth, the seas were first enriched with chemicals like those created in Miller's experiment. Then in the shuffling of molecules that takes place in solutions of organic chemicals, more complex compounds were formed by chance. These compounds combined with each other and formed still larger molecules. Ultimately chemical evolution led to giant molecules that were capable of reproducing, as are DNA and some other chemicals important to life. With this explanation Calvin describes evolution up to the threshold of life. What happened to breathe the spark of life into the first organisms is still a mystery to science. Nevertheless, Calvin says confidently that life is a "state of matter widely distributed throughout the universe."

Chance dominated every stage of evolution from primitive organisms to man, as Darwin and his successors have explained. Each new plant or animal originated as an improbable freak. Yet, on the whole, the course of evolution has been orderly and straightforward, for natural selection has lopped off the mistakes and digressions. In the two billion years or so since life emerged on Earth, a pyramid of life has gradually taken form. More highly organized and adaptable species have been steadily added at the top. And in the last million years man has taken his place at the apex. Given another planet with the physical characteristics of Earth, it can be presumed that biological evolution proceeded in much the same fashion and at about the same pace. If Earth and the life it supports represents a norm, then perhaps half the other habitable planets in the universe have been populated by intelligent beings.

Whether all of them are *still* habitable is another question, about which man has reason to be especially curious at this time. It may well be a universal fact that any civilization which has mastered the secret of releasing enormous amounts of energy—as with a hydrogen bomb—is forever in danger of annihilating itself. How long have civilizations elsewhere survived after they have reached this stage? If the life expectancy is only a few hundred years, man has very few living neighbors in the galaxy. The natural tendency toward self-destruction is, of course, imponderable. Astronomer Frank Drake of the National Radio Astronomy Observatory wryly suggests: "We might get a better feeling for the situation if we could first answer the question: 'Is there intelligent life on Earth?' "

Scientists are now ready to search nearby regions of the Milky Way for direct evidence of intelligent life. They will use radio telescopes to "listen" for messages, and the chances of success seem reasonably good. Purcell estimates that two 300-foot radio-telescope antennas—one a receiver, the other a transmitter—could communicate over a distance of 500 light-years (3,000 trillion miles). Within that range are some 2,000 sunlike stars that have a good chance of supporting life.

Right now no scientist suggests transmitting messages into outer space. In order to send signals, we would have to build a number of costly transmitters—in effect, one large radio telescope for each star we wanted to address—and transmit day in, day out, for a period of years. There might be no positive results within a lifetime, and meanwhile the equipment would be tied up, useless for any other purpose. Listening, on the other hand, is relatively cheap. Adequate radio telescopes are already available, and they can be directed from time to time at particularly promising stars. Purcell feels, "We ought to plan to listen for at least two centuries before we even consider transmitting."

While there is yet no organized program for listening, Drake has already made a preliminary attempt. Last spring, at the

N.R.A.O. in Green Bank, West Virginia, he launched Project Ozma (named after the Queen of Oz, the land of fancy created by L. Frank Baum). Using the observatory's radio telescope, Drake spent two months recording radio signals from the direction of two of the nearest stars: Tau Ceti and Epsilon Eridani, each a little more than ten light-years, or 60 trillion miles, away. Some 400 hours of listening yielded nothing but a meaningless "hash" of radio noise. But no one had really expected the first Ozma trial to produce positive results. The telescope, an eighty-five-foot dish-shaped antenna, and the amplifiers were not sensitive enough to detect any but the strongest signals beamed directly at earth. It is entirely possible that the squiggles traced by the instrument's recording pen actually do contain an intelligent message, but the radio noise makes them undecipherable.

But the principles employed in Ozma are likely to guide future listening attempts. In planning the project, Drake anticipated a strategy proposed in 1959 by Giuseppe Cocconi and Philip Morrison of Cornell University and enthusiastically endorsed by most other scientists interested in intragalactic communication. It can be summed up as follows: If other civilizations are transmitting in our direction, they want their messages to be readily detected and easily understood. Therefore, like players at charades, they are broadcasting to us as we would broadcast to them, if our positions were reversed. It follows that we should be on the lookout for the kind of messages we would transmit to them.

For efficient listening, it is necessary at the outset to make an educated guess about the wave length that outer-space broadcasters would be likeliest to use. Conceivably, *they* could be transmitting on any part of the electromagnetic spectrum, but scanning the whole spectrum from long-wave radio through infrared, visible, and ultraviolet light to x-rays and gamma rays would be an interminable task—like combing a vast forest to find a particular ant. Instead Cocconi and Morrison proposed limiting the search to one branch of a specific tree. They think

that any scientifically sophisticated civilization would beam interstellar broadcasts at a frequency of 1,420 megacycles (1,420 million cycles per second). It was on a small portion of the radio band around this frequency that Drake's Project Ozma concentrated.

Why 1,420 megacycles? First of all, because this frequency has a special significance for astronomers. Each hydrogen atom emits an infinitesimal amount of energy at this frequency and atomic hydrogen constitutes at least 75 per cent of all the matter in the universe. By measuring the strength of 1,420-megacycle radiation in all directions, radio astronomers have been able to map the distribution of matter in our galaxy. Presumably, other intelligent beings who have mastered radio would also recognize the unique significance of hydrogen and its radiation frequency. Second, our atmosphere—and very likely the atmospheres of other life-bearing planets—is almost perfectly transparent to 1,420-megacycle waves.

The next listening project will employ better equipment—i.e., a bigger antenna and more sensitive amplifier. Radio astronomers are confident that if any 1,420-megacycle signals are being sent, they will eventually be detected. The modern radio telescope is a remarkably sensitive receiver. In the decade since radio astronomers started tuning in at the hydrogen frequency, they have got a lot of information about the galaxy, although the total energy collected by all the telescopes has amounted to not quite one erg: slightly less than the energy required to flick the ash from a cigarette.

Scientists are reasonably sure that, once they received a recognizable signal, they could understand the message. A signal would have some degree of regularity that would set it apart from cosmic radio noise, which is random and utterly irregular. Deciphering the message would depend more on the cleverness of the sender than on the ingenuity of scientists on earth. Presumably our partners in communication would be wise enough to employ cryptography in reverse. That is, they would design a code that could easily be broken. And their first messages would include plenty of hints in the form of information that is surely universal among all scientifically minded societies— e.g., numbers and elementary geometry.

We would record the signals and study them at our leisure. But in less than ten minutes of transmission the signals should be able to tell us how to project their television pictures on our screens . . . . Once television communication was established, a civilization should be able to describe itself thoroughly and in short order.

If powerful radio telescopes failed to pick up signals at 1,420 megacycles, scientists would turn to other parts of the electromagnetic spectrum. Intelligent beings in nearby space might not be transmitting by radio. Our radio communications might seem as crude to them as smoke signals or bonfires on the Sahara do to us. Perhaps some other civilization is even now sending us messages in pulses of light. Earthbound physicists are just now perfecting the "laser," a device that emits a narrow beam of light concentrated at one specific frequency. On some remote planet laser sets might be as commonplace as transistor radios. Or a more advanced technology than ours might have learned how to modulate a beam of neutrinos—weightless, uncharged particles that human physicists are hard put even to detect. If so, they may have to wait more than a century until we learn how to build a neutrino receiver.

At least two other long shots might deserve attention. Freeman Dyson, a theoretical physicist at the Institute for Advanced Study, has suggested looking for abnormally strong infrared radiation from stars. He has a hunch that a technologically proficient civilization in need of living space might demolish a spare planet with tools and power we do not yet possess, and reassemble it as a ring surrounding the central star at a comfortable distance for commuting. Such a ring would radiate detectably in the infrared part of the spectrum—specifically, at a wave length of about ten microns if the temperature were suitable for life. Some scientists speculate that in 3,000 years or so man, desperate for elbow-room, might develop the

techniques needed to break pieces from Jupiter and rearrange them as a string of artificial planets along the earth's orbit.

Radio astronomer R. N. Bracewell of Stanford University thinks that we may have already unwittingly received messages from another civilization. He has an idea that space probes may have been put into orbit around earth by another race. (An unmanned interstellar space probe is conceivable. Since it would not have to complete its mission within a lifetime, it could be dispatched at relatively low speed with a much smaller engine than is required for a manned vehicle.)

According to Bracewell, these space probes might try to reveal their presence by repeating back to us radio signals received from earth. At the same time they might be transmitting back to their home planet an assortment of terrestrial broadcasts. If so, some beings out there have probably formed a strange impression of life on earth. It has taken many years for our radio broadcasts to be relayed to them. Radio signals travel at the speed of light; thus a planet twenty-five light-years away would just now be receiving earthly broadcasts of circa 1936: the prattlings of Amos and Andy, the crooning of Kate Smith, Gabriel Heatter's voice booming: "There's good news tonight." A few years hence they will hear the sepulchral voice of Raymond Gram Swing, on the eve of World War II. It will be no wonder then if they decide that the end of civilization on earth is at hand and turn the knob to another planet.

Some ancient civilizations, in fact, may have given up on us long ago. "It seems possible to me," says Urey, "that the intelligent life on planets of other stars has been beaming signals to us for the last ten million to hundred million years. And they have simply concluded that there is no one home on earth; so they have stopped both listening and sending."

To establish contact with another planet may require more patience than man possesses. There may be a wait of decades, centuries, or even millenniums before another race decides to beam messages in our direction. If two-way communication is ever set up, men on earth may have to reconcile themselves to asking questions, knowing they will not live to hear the answers. "But im-agine," says Purcell, "that a reply to one of your messages was scheduled to be received forty years from now. What a legacy for your grandchildren."

QUESTIONS FOR STUDY AND DISCUSSION

1. "The scientists . . . make two basic . . . assumptions: the first, that life elsewhere is not radically different from life on Earth; the second, that the evolution of life in other places followed roughly the same course as evolution on Earth." What are the bases for these assumptions?

2. Is any form of "life" which is not like anything we conceive of as "life" possible? Can there be an "equivalent" of "intelligent life"? What would its characteristics be?

3. What does Frank Drake mean when he "wryly" asks, " 'Is there intelligent life on earth' "? Can an "intelligent" being collaborate in the destruction of his species?

4. Does Mr. Boehm's essay answer the question its title propounds?

5. According to this essay a report warns "that the shock of making contact [with intelligent life from another solar system] could lead to the downfall of civilization because 'societies sure of their own place in the universe have disintegrated when confronted by a superior society.' " Should Mr. Boehm have developed this point further? Why? What does the report mean? How valid, in your view, is the fear expressed in the report?

6. Make a list of assumptions which scientists who believe in the possibility of life on other worlds are making. Find one or more which, if invalid, would destroy the case for life on other worlds.

7. Is this essay "science fiction" or "science fact"? Why?

8. Why is God not mentioned in this essay?

WRITING ASSIGNMENTS

1. Develop the ideas suggested by the statement "societies sure of their own place in the universe have disintegrated when confronted by a superior society." You may agree or disagree with this statement. Whatever position you take, explain what the statement means.

2. Justify the expenditure of time, intelligence, and money on the attempt to "listen in" on a hypothetical civilization in a distant solar system—a civilization that we will never meet "face to face" and that will never threaten us.

3. "In the two billion years or so since life emerged on Earth, a pyramid of life has gradually taken form." Write an essay with the title "The Pyramid of Life," in which you express your views of Man. Consider the title ironic if you wish.

4. Write an essay reporting on some new, experimental, little-known, or speculative area of a field of endeavor or study in which you are particularly interested.

C. P. SNOW

The Two Cultures

It is about three years since I made a sketch in print of a problem which had been on my mind for some time.[1] It was a problem I could not avoid just because of the circumstances of my life. The only credentials I had to ruminate on the subject at all came through those circumstances, through nothing more than a set of chances. Anyone with similar experience would have seen much the same things and I think made very much the same comments about them. It just happened to be an unusual experience. By training I was a scientist: by vocation I was a writer. That was all. It was a piece of luck, if you like, that arose through coming from a poor home.

But my personal history isn't the point now. All that I need say is that I came to Cambridge and did a bit of research here at a time of major scientific activity. I was privileged to have a ringside view of one of the most wonderful creative periods in all physics. And it happened through the flukes of war—including meeting W. L. Bragg in the buffet on Kettering station on a very cold morning in 1939, which had a determining influence on my practical life—that I was able, and indeed morally forced, to keep that ringside view ever since. So for thirty years I have had to be in touch with scientists not only out of curiosity, but as part of a working existence. During the same thirty years I was trying to shape the books I wanted to write, which in due course took me among writers.

There have been plenty of days when I have spent the working hours with scientists and then gone off at night with some literary colleagues. I mean that literally. I have had, of course, intimate friends among both scientists and writers. It was through living among these groups and much more, I think, through moving regularly from one to the

[1] 'The Two Cultures', *New Statesman*, 6 October 1956.

other and back again that I got occupied with the problem of what, long before I put it on paper, I christened to myself as the 'two cultures'. For constantly I felt I was moving among two groups—comparable in intelligence, identical in race, not grossly different in social origin, earning about the same incomes, who had almost ceased to communicate at all, who in intellectual, moral and psychological climate had so little in common that instead of going from Burlington House or South Kensington to Chelsea, one might have crossed an ocean.

In fact, one had travelled much further than across an ocean—because after a few thousand Atlantic miles, one found Greenwich Village talking precisely the same language as Chelsea, and both having about as much communication with M.I.T. as though the scientists spoke nothing but Tibetan. For this is not just our problem; owing to some of our educational and social idiosyncrasies, it is slightly exaggerated here, owing to another English social peculiarity it is slightly minimised; by and large this is a problem of the entire West. By this I intend something serious. I am not thinking of the pleasant story of how one of the more convivial Oxford greats dons—I have heard the story attributed to A. L. Smith—came over to Cambridge to dine. The date is perhaps the 1890's. I think it must have been at St John's, or possibly Trinity. Anyway, Smith was sitting at the right hand of the President—or Vice-Master —and he was a man who liked to include all round him in the conversation, although he was not immediately encouraged by the expressions of his neighbours. He addressed some cheerful Oxonian chit-chat at the one opposite to him, and got a grunt. He then tried the man on his own right hand and got another grunt. Then, rather to his surprise, one looked at the other and said, 'Do you know what he's talking about?' 'I haven't the least idea.' At this, even Smith was getting out of his depth. But the President, acting as a social emollient, put him at his ease, by saying, 'Oh, those are mathematicians! We never talk to *them*'.

No, I intend something serious. I believe the intellectual life of the whole of western

345

society is increasingly being split into two
polar groups. When I say the intellectual
life, I mean to include also a large part of
our practical life, because I should be the
last person to suggest the two can at the
deepest level be distinguished. I shall come
back to the practical life a little later. Two
polar groups: at one pole we have the literary intellectuals, who incidentally while no
one was looking took to referring to themselves as 'intellectuals' as though there were
no others. I remember G. H. Hardy once
remarking to me in mild puzzlement, some
time in the 1930's: 'Have you noticed how
the word "intellectual" is used nowadays?
There seems to be a new definition which
certainly doesn't include Rutherford or Eddington or Dirac or Adrian or me. It does
seem rather odd, don't y' know.'[2]

Literary intellectuals at one pole—at the
other scientists, and as the most representative, the physical scientists. Between the
two a gulf of mutual incomprehension—
sometimes (particularly among the young)
hostility and dislike, but most of all lack of
understanding. They have a curious distorted
image of each other. Their attitudes are so
different that, even on the level of emotion,
they can't find much common ground. Non-
scientists tend to think of scientists as brash
and boastful. They hear Mr T. S. Eliot,
who just for these illustrations we can take
as an archetypal figure, saying about his attempts to revive verse-drama, that we can
hope for very little, but that he would feel
content if he and his co-workers could prepare the ground for a new Kyd or a new
Greene. That is the tone, restricted and con-
strained, with which literary intellectuals
are at home: it is the subdued voice of their
culture. Then they hear a much louder
voice, that of another archetypal figure,
Rutherford, trumpeting: 'This is the heroic
age of science! This is the Elizabethan age!'
Many of us heard that, and a good many
other statements beside which that was mild;

[2] This lecture was delivered to a Cambridge
audience, and so I used some points of reference
which I did not need to explain. G. H. Hardy,
1877–1947, was one of the most distinguished
pure mathematicians of his time, and a pictur-
esque figure in Cambridge both as a young don
and on his return in 1931 to the Sadleirian Chair
of Mathematics.

and we weren't left in any doubt whom
Rutherford was casting for the role of Shakespeare. What is hard for the literary intellectuals to understand, imaginatively or
intellectually, is that he was absolutely right.

And compare 'this is the way the world
ends, not with a bang but a whimper'—
incidentally, one of the least likely scientific
prophecies ever made—compare that with
Rutherford's famous repartee, 'Lucky fellow,
Rutherford, always on the crest of the wave.'
'Well, I made the wave, didn't I?'

The non-scientists have a rooted impression that the scientists are shallowly optimistic, unaware of man's condition. On the
other hand, the scientists believe that the
literary intellectuals are totally lacking in
foresight, peculiarly unconcerned with their
brother men, in a deep sense anti-intellectual, anxious to restrict both art and thought
to the existential moment. And so on. Anyone with a mild talent for invective could
produce plenty of this kind of subterranean
back-chat. On each side there is some of it
which is not entirely baseless. It is all destructive. Much of it rests on misinterpreta-
tions which are dangerous. I should like to
deal with two of the most profound of these
now, one on each side.

First, about the scientists' optimism. This
is an accusation which has been made so
often that it has become a platitude. It has
been made by some of the acutest non-
scientific minds of the day. But it depends
upon a confusion between the individual
experience and the social experience, between
the individual condition of man and his
social condition. Most of the scientists I
have known well have felt—just as deeply
as the non-scientists I have known well—
that the individual condition of each of us
is tragic. Each of us is alone: sometimes we
escape from solitariness, through love or affection or perhaps creative moments, but
those triumphs of life are pools of light we
make for ourselves while the edge of the
road is black: each of us dies alone. Some
scientists I have known have had faith in
revealed religion. Perhaps with them the
sense of the tragic condition is not so strong.
I don't know. With most people of deep
feeling, however high-spirited and happy
they are, sometimes most with those who

are happiest and most high-spirited, it seems to be right in the fibres, part of the weight of life. That is as true of the scientists I have known best as of anyone at all.

But nearly all of them—and this is where the colour of hope genuinely comes in—would see no reason why, just because the individual condition is tragic, so must the social condition be. Each of us is solitary: each of us dies alone: all right, that's a fate against which we can't struggle—but there is plenty in our condition which is not fate, and against which we are less than human unless we do struggle.

Most of our fellow human beings, for instance, are underfed and die before their time. In the crudest terms, *that* is the social condition. There is a moral trap which comes through the insight into man's loneliness: it tempts one to sit back, complacent in one's unique tragedy, and let the others go without a meal.

As a group, the scientists fall into that trap less than others. They are inclined to be impatient to see if something can be done: and inclined to think that it can be done, until it's proved otherwise. That is their real optimism, and it's an optimism that the rest of us badly need.

In reverse, the same spirit, tough and good and determined to fight it out at the side of their brother men, has made scientists regard the other culture's social attitudes as contemptible. That is too facile: some of them are, but they are a temporary phase and not to be taken as representative.

I remember being cross-examined by a scientist of distinction. 'Why do most writers take on social opinions which would have been thought distinctly uncivilised and démodé at the time of the Plantagenets? Wasn't that true of most of the famous twentieth-century writers? Yeats, Pound, Wyndham Lewis, nine out of ten of those who have dominated literary sensibility in our time—weren't they not only politically silly, but politically wicked? Didn't the influence of all they represent bring Auschwitz that much nearer?'

I thought at the time, and I still think, that the correct answer was not to defend the indefensible. It was no use saying that Yeats, according to friends whose judgment I trust, was a man of singular magnanimity of character, as well as a great poet. It was no use denying the facts, which are broadly true. The honest answer was that there is, in fact, a connection, which literary persons were culpably slow to see, between some kinds of early twentieth-century art and the most imbecile expressions of anti-social feeling.[3] That was one reason, among many, why some of us turned our backs on the art and tried to hack out a new or different way for ourselves.[4]

But though many of those writers dominated literary sensibility for a generation, that is no longer so, or at least to nothing like the same extent. Literature changes more slowly than science. It hasn't the same automatic corrective, and so its misguided periods are longer. But it is ill-considered of scientists to judge writers on the evidence of the period 1914–50.

Those are two of the misunderstandings between the two cultures. I should say, since I began to talk about them—the two cultures, that is—I have had some criticism. Most of my scientific acquaintances think that there is something in it, and so do most of the practising artists I know. But I have been argued with by non-scientists of strong down-to-earth interests. Their view is that it is an over-simplification, and that if one is going to talk in these terms there ought to be at least three cultures. They argue that, though they are not scientists themselves, they would share a good deal of the scientific feeling. They would have as little use—perhaps, since they knew more about it, even less use—for the recent literary culture as the scientists themselves. J. H. Plumb, Alan Bullock and some of my American sociological friends have said that they vigorously refuse to be corralled in a cultural box with people they wouldn't be seen dead with, or to be regarded as helping to produce

[3] I said a little more about this connection in *The Times Literary Supplement*, 'Challenge to the Intellect', 15 August 1958. I hope some day to carry the analysis further.

[4] It would be more accurate to say that, for literary reasons, we felt the prevailing literary modes were useless to us. We were, however, reinforced in that feeling when it occurred to us that those prevailing modes went hand in hand with social attitudes either wicked, or absurd, or both.

a climate which would not permit of social hope.

I respect those arguments. The number 2 is a very dangerous number: that is why the dialectic is a dangerous process. Attempts to divide anything into two ought to be regarded with much suspicion. I have thought a long time about going in for further refinements: but in the end I have decided against. I was searching for something a little more than a dashing metaphor, a good deal less than a cultural map: and for those purposes the two cultures is about right, and subtilising any more would bring more disadvantages than it's worth.

At one pole, the scientific culture really is a culture, not only in an intellectual but also in an anthropological sense. That is, its members need not, and of course often do not, always completely understand each other; biologists more often than not will have a pretty hazy idea of contemporary physics; but there are common attitudes, common standards and patterns of behaviour, common approaches and assumptions. This goes surprisingly wide and deep. It cuts across other mental patterns, such as those of religion or politics or class.

Statistically, I suppose slightly more scientists are in religious terms unbelievers, compared with the rest of the intellectual world —though there are plenty who are religious, and that seems to be increasingly so among the young. Statistically also, slightly more scientists are on the Left in open politics— though again, plenty always have called themselves conservatives, and that also seems to be more common among the young. Compared with the rest of the intellectual world, considerably more scientists in this country and probably in the U.S. come from poor families.[5] Yet, over a whole range of thought and behaviour, none of that matters very much. In their working, and in much of their emotional life, their attitudes are closer to other scientists than to non-scientists who in religion or politics or class have the same

labels as themselves. If I were to risk a piece of shorthand, I should say that naturally they had the future in their bones.

They may or may not like it, but they have it. That was as true of the conservatives J. J. Thomson and Lindemann as of the radicals Einstein or Blackett: as true of the Christian A. H. Compton as of the materialist Bernal: of the aristocrats Broglie or Russell as of the proletarian Faraday: of those born rich, like Thomas Merton or Victor Rothschild, as of Rutherford, who was the son of an odd-job handyman. Without thinking about it, they respond alike. That is what a culture means.

At the other pole, the spread of attitudes is wider. It is obvious that between the two, as one moves through intellectual society from the physicists to the literary intellectuals, there are all kinds of tones of feeling on the way. But I believe the pole of total incomprehension of science radiates its influence on all the rest. That total incomprehension gives, much more pervasively than we realise, living in it, an unscientific flavour to the whole 'traditional' culture, and that unscientific flavour is often, much more than we admit, on the point of turning antiscientific. The feelings of one pole become the anti-feelings of the other. If the scientists have the future in their bones, then the traditional culture responds by wishing the future did not exist.[6] It is the traditional culture, to an extent remarkably little diminished by the emergence of the scientific one, which manages the western world.

This polarisation is sheer loss to us all. To us as people, and to our society. It is at the same time practical and intellectual and creative loss, and I repeat that it is false to imagine that those three considerations are clearly separable. But for a moment I want to concentrate on the intellectual loss.

The degree of incomprehension on both sides is the kind of joke which has gone sour. There are about fifty thousand working scientists in the country and about eighty thousand professional engineers or applied scientists. During the war and in the years

[5] An analysis of the schools from which Fellows of the Royal Society come tells its own story. The distribution is markedly different from that of, for example, members of the Foreign Service or Queen's Counsel.

[6] Compare George Orwell's 1984, which is the strongest possible wish that the future should not exist, with J. D. Bernal's World Without War.

since, my colleagues and I have had to interview somewhere between thirty to forty thousand of these—that is, about 25 per cent. The number is large enough to give us a fair sample, though of the men we talked to most would still be under forty. We were able to find out a certain amount of what they read and thought about. I confess that even I, who am fond of them and respect them, was a bit shaken. We hadn't quite expected that the links with the traditional culture should be so tenuous, nothing more than a formal touch of the cap.

As one would expect, some of the very best scientists had and have plenty of energy and interest to spare, and we came across several who had read everything that literary people talk about. But that's very rare. Most of the rest, when one tried to probe for what books they had read, would modestly confess, 'Well, I've *tried* a bit of Dickens', rather as though Dickens were an extraordinarily esoteric, tangled and dubiously rewarding writer, something like Rainer Maria Rilke. In fact that is exactly how they do regard him: we thought that discovery, that Dickens had been transformed into the type-specimen of literary incomprehensibility, was one of the oddest results of the whole exercise.

But of course, in reading him, in reading almost any writer whom we should value, they are just touching their caps to the traditional culture. They have their own culture, intensive, rigorous, and constantly in action. This culture contains a great deal of argument, usually much more rigorous, and almost always at a higher conceptual level, than literary persons' arguments—even though the scientists do cheerfully use words in senses which literary persons don't recognise, the senses are exact ones, and when they talk about 'subjective', 'objective', 'philosophy' or 'progressive',[7] they know what

[7] *Subjective,* in contemporary technological jargon, means 'divided according to subjects'. *Objective* means 'directed towards an object'. *Philosophy* means 'general intellectual approach or attitude' (for example, a scientist's 'philosophy of guided weapons' might lead him to propose certain kinds of 'objective reasearch'.) A 'progressive' job means one with possibilities of promotion.

they mean, even though it isn't what one is accustomed to expect.

Remember, these are very intelligent men. Their culture is in many ways an exacting and admirable one. It doesn't contain much art, with the exception, an important exception, of music. Verbal exchange, insistent argument. Long-playing records. Colour-photography. The ear, to some extent the eye. Books, very little, though perhaps not many would go so far as one hero, who perhaps I should admit was further down the scientific ladder than the people I've been talking about—who, when asked what books he read, replied firmly and confidently: 'Books? I prefer to use my books as tools.' It was very hard not to let the mind wander —what sort of tool would a book make? Perhaps a hammer? A primitive digging instrument?

Of books, though, very little. And of the books which to most literary persons are bread and butter, novels, history, poetry, plays, almost nothing at all. It isn't that they're not interested in the psychological or moral or social life. In the social life, they certainly are, more than most of us. In the moral, they are by and large the soundest group of intellectuals we have; there is a moral component right in the grain of science itself, and almost all scientists form their own judgments of the moral life. In the psychological they have as much interest as most of us, though occasionally I fancy they come to it rather late. It isn't that they lack the interests. It is much more that the whole literature of the traditional culture doesn't seem to them relevant to those interests. They are, of course, dead wrong. As a result, their imaginative understanding is less than it could be. They are self-impoverished.

But what about the other side? They are impoverished too—perhaps more seriously, because they are vainer about it. They still like to pretend that the traditional culture is the whole of 'culture', as though the natural order didn't exist. As though the exploration of the natural order was of no interest either in its own value or its consequences. As though the scientific edifice of the physical world was not, in its intellectual depth, complexity and articulation, the most beautiful and wonderful collective work of the mind of man. Yet most non-scientists have no conception of that edifice at all. Even if they want to have it, they can't. It is rather as though, over an immense range of intellectual experience, a whole group was tone-deaf. Except that this tone-deafness doesn't come by nature, but by training, or rather the absence of training.

As with the tone-deaf, they don't know what they miss. They give a pitying chuckle at the news of scientists who have never read a major work of English literature. They dismiss them as ignorant specialists. Yet their own ignorance and their own specialisation is just as startling. A good many times I have been present at gatherings of people who, by the standards of the traditional culture, are thought highly educated and who have with considerable gusto been expressing their incredulity at the illiteracy of scientists. Once or twice I have been provoked and have asked the company how many of them could describe the Second Law of Thermodynamics. The response was cold: it was also negative. Yet I was asking something which is about the scientific equivalent of: *Have you read a work of Shakespeare's?*

I now believe that if I had asked an even simpler question—such as, What do you mean by mass, or acceleration, which is the scientific equivalent of saying, *Can you read?* —not more than one in ten of the highly educated would have felt that I was speaking the same language. So the great edifice of modern physics goes up, and the majority of the cleverest people in the western world have about as much insight into it as their neolithic ancestors would have had.

Just one more of those questions, that my non-scientific friends regard as being in the worst of taste. Cambridge is a university where scientists and non-scientists meet every night at dinner.[8] About two years ago, one of the most astonishing experiments in the whole history of science was brought off. I don't mean the sputnik—that was admirable for quite different reasons, as a feat of organisation and a triumphant use of existing knowledge. No, I mean the experiment at

[8] Almost all college High Tables contain Fellows in both scientific and non-scientific subjects.

Columbia by Yang and Lee. It is an experiment of the greatest beauty and originality, but the result is so startling that one forgets how beautiful the experiment is. It makes us think again about some of the fundamentals of the physical world. Intuition, common sense—they are neatly stood on their heads. The result is usually known as the contradiction of parity. If there were any serious communication between the two cultures, this experiment would have been talked about at every High Table in Cambridge. Was it? I wasn't here: but I should like to ask the question.

There seems then to be no place where the cultures meet. I am not going to waste time saying that this is a pity. It is much worse than that. Soon I shall come to some practical consequences. But at the heart of thought and creation we are letting some of our best chances go by default. The clashing point of two subjects, two disciplines, two cultures—of two galaxies, so far as that goes—ought to produce creative chances. In the history of mental activity that has been where some of the breakthroughs came. The chances are there now. But they are there, as it were, in a vacuum, because those in the two cultures can't talk to each other. It is bizarre how very little of twentieth-century science has been assimilated into twentieth-century art. Now and then one used to find poets conscientiously using scientific expressions, and getting them wrong—there was a time when 'refraction' kept cropping up in verse in a mystifying fashion, and when 'polarised light' was used as though writers were under the illusion that it was a specially admirable kind of light.

Of course, that isn't the way that science could be any good to art. It has got to be assimilated along with, and as part and parcel of, the whole of our mental experience, and used as naturally as the rest.

I said earlier that this cultural divide is not just an English phenomenon: it exists all over the western world. But it probably seems at its sharpest in England, for two reasons. One is our fanatical belief in educational specialisation, which is much more deeply ingrained in us than in any country in the world, west or east. The other is our tendency to let our social forms crystallise. This tendency appears to get stronger, not weaker, the more we iron out economic inequalities: and this is specially true in education. It means that once anything like a cultural divide gets established, all the social forces operate to make it not less rigid, but more so.

The two cultures were already dangerously separate sixty years ago; but a prime minister like Lord Salisbury could have his own laboratory at Hatfield, and Arthur Balfour had a somewhat more than amateur interest in natural science. John Anderson did some research in organic chemistry in Würzburg before passing first into the Civil Service, and incidentally took a spread of subjects which is now impossible.[9] None of that degree of interchange at the top of the Establishment is likely, or indeed thinkable, now.[10]

In fact, the separation between the scientists and non-scientists is much less bridgeable among the young than it was even thirty years ago. Thirty years ago the cultures had long ceased to speak to each other: but at least they managed a kind of frozen smile across the gulf. Now the politeness has gone, and they just make faces. It is not only that the young scientists now feel that they are part of a culture on the rise while the other is in retreat. It is also, to be brutal, that the young scientists know that with an indifferent degree they'll get a comfortable job, while their contemporaries and counterparts in English or History will be lucky to earn 60 per cent as much. No young scientist of any talent would feel that he isn't wanted or that his work is ridiculous, as did the hero of *Lucky Jim*, and in fact, some of the disgruntlement of Amis and his associates is the disgruntlement of the underemployed arts graduate.

There is only one way out of all this: it is, of course, by rethinking our education. In this country, for the two reasons I have given, that is more difficult than in any other. Nearly everyone will agree that our school education is too specialised. But nearly everyone feels that it is outside the will of man to alter it. Other countries are as dissatisfied with their education as we are, but are not so resigned.

The U.S. teach out of proportion more children up to eighteen than we do: they teach them far more widely, but nothing like so rigorously. They know that: they are hoping to take the problem in hand within ten years, though they may not have all that time to spare. The U.S.S.R. also teach out of proportion more children than we do: they also teach far more widely than we do (it is an absurd western myth that their school education is specialised) but much too rigorously.[11] They know that—and they are beating about to get it right. The Scandinavians, in particular the Swedes, who would make a more sensible job of it than any of us, are handicapped by their practical need to devote an inordinate amount of time to foreign languages. But they too are seized of the problem.

Are we? Have we crystallised so far that we are no longer flexible at all?

Talk to schoolmasters, and they say that our intense specialisation, like nothing else on earth, is dictated by the Oxford and Cambridge scholarship examinations. If that is so, one would have thought it not utterly impracticable to change the Oxford and Cambridge scholarship examinations. Yet one would underestimate the national capacity for the intricate defensive to believe that that was easy. All the lessons of our educational history suggest we are only capable of increasing specialisation, not decreasing it.

Somehow we have set ourselves the task of producing a tiny *élite*—far smaller proportionately than in any comparable coun-

---

[9] He took the examination in 1905.

[10] It is, however, true to say that the compact nature of the managerial layers of English society —the fact that 'everyone knows everyone else'— means that scientists and non-scientists do in fact know each other as people more easily than in most countries. It is also true that a good many leading politicians and administrators keep up lively intellectual and artistic interests to a much greater extent, so far as I can judge, than is the case in the U.S. These are both among our assets.

[11] I tried to compare American, Soviet and English education in 'New Minds for the New World', *New Statesman*, 6 September 1956.

try—educated in one academic skill. For a hundred and fifty years in Cambridge it was mathematics: then it was mathematics or classics: then natural science was allowed in. But still the choice had to be a single one.

It may well be that this process has gone too far to be reversible. I have given reasons why I think it is a disastrous process, for the purpose of a living culture. I am going on to give reasons why I think it is fatal, if we're to perform our practical tasks in the world. But I can think of only one example, in the whole of English educational history, where our pursuit of specialised mental exercises was resisted with success.

It was done here in Cambridge, fifty years ago, when the old order-of-merit in the Mathematical Tripos was abolished. For over a hundred years, the nature of the Tripos had been crystallising. The competition for the top places had got fiercer, and careers hung on them. In most colleges, certainly in my own, if one managed to come out as Senior or Second Wrangler, one was elected a Fellow out of hand. A whole apparatus of coaching had grown up. Men of the quality of Hardy, Littlewood, Russell, Eddington, Jeans, Keynes, went in for two or three years' training for an examination which was intensely competitive and intensely difficult. Most people in Cambridge were very proud of it, with a similar

pride to that which almost anyone in England always has for our existing educational institutions, whatever they happen to be. If you study the flysheets of the time, you will find the passionate arguments for keeping the examination precisely as it was to all eternity: it was the only way to keep up standards, it was the only fair test of merit, indeed, the only seriously objective test in the world. The arguments, in fact, were almost exactly those which are used today with precisely the same passionate sincerity if anyone suggests that the scholarship examinations might conceivably not be immune from change.

In every respect but one, in fact, the old Mathematical Tripos seemed perfect. The one exception, however, appeared to some to be rather important. It was simply—so the young creative mathematicians, such as Hardy and Littlewood, kept saying—that the training had no intellectual merit at all. They went a little further, and said that the Tripos had killed serious mathematics in England stone dead for a hundred years. Well, even in academic controversy, that took some skirting round, and they got their way. But I have an impression that Cambridge was a good deal more flexible between 1850 and 1914 than it has been in our time. If we had had the old Mathematical Tripos firmly planted among us, should we have ever managed to abolish it?

QUESTIONS FOR STUDY AND DISCUSSION

1. What are "the two cultures"? Do they really exist, as C. P. Snow asserts? What evidence from your own observation and reflection can you offer to support, qualify, or deny his assertion?

2. If "the two cultures" exist, to which of them do you belong? Why? Can you argue that you belong to both or to neither one? If so, on what grounds?

3. Do you think of the "arts" and the "sciences" as dealing with totally different "kinds" of knowledge? Why?

4. Have you observed that people C. P. Snow calls "literary intellectuals" are in the

habit of "referring to themselves as 'intellectuals' as though there were no others"?

5. Does the undergraduate program in your college attempt to make you aware of the elements of both of Snow's "two cultures"? If so, how successful is the attempt?

6. Have you observed "hostility and dislike" in the attitudes of science and arts majors toward each other? What impression have you of the attitudes of teachers in these areas toward each others' fields?

7. Which of these educational alternatives would you prefer: specialization in science, specialization in the humanities, a

non-specialized combination of arts and sciences, a non-specialized introduction to both, followed by specialization?

8. Are there alternatives not listed in question 7? Where do business and professional training fit in? Do the life, interests, and skills of the businessman constitute a "culture"?

WRITING ASSIGNMENTS

Below are some suggested titles for papers. Your answers to the study questions will provide you with a good many more possibilities.

1. " 'The Two Cultures' in My High School Senior Class" (or "in My Dormitory" or any other association of people thrown together for any reason other than common interests).

2. "What Is an 'Intellectual'?"

3. "The Principal Aim of a College Education."

4. "Revising the College Curriculum."

5. "Education for Life."

6. "Sciences (or The Humanities) Don't Interest Me."

Other essays in this book which are appropriate to a consideration of THE WORLD AROUND US: SCIENCE are Ashley Montagu's "The Natural Superiority of Women" and Rachel Carson's "The Global Thermostat."

The World of People

ALEXANDER WOOLLCOTT

Obituary

October 1929.
Last week the Marx Brothers buried their mother. On the preceding Friday night, more from gregariousness than from appetite, she had eaten two dinners instead of the conventional one, and, after finishing off with a brief, hilarious game of ping-pong, was homeward bound across the Queensboro Bridge when paralysis seized her. Within an hour she was dead in her Harpo's arms. Of the people I have met, I would name her as among the few of whom it could be said that they had greatness.

Minnie Marx was in this world sixty-five years and *lived* all sixty-five of them. None knew better than her sons that she had not only borne them, brought them up, and (with a bit of coaxing here and a *schlag* there) turned them into successful play-actors. She had done much more than that. She had *invented* them. They were just comics she imagined for her own amusement. They amused no one more, and their reward was her ravishing smile.

It was her idea that they should go into the theater at all. She herself was doing sweat-shop lace-work when she married a tailor named Sam Marx. But for fifty years her father was a roving magician in Hanover, and as a child she had known the excitement of their barn-storming cart-rides from one German town to another. Now here she was, sidetracked in a Third Avenue tenement, with a swarm of children on her hands. But hadn't her brother deserted his career as a pants-presser to go into vaudeville? You remember the song about Mr. Gallagher and Mr. Shean? Well, that was her brother—Mr. Shean. His first success only strengthened her conviction that she came of showfolks, and she was determined that her sons should enter into that inheritance. She had six, in all. One died as a baby. After the war, she lost another to the silk-dress business. This defection from her now notable quartet did not baffle her long. Reaching for Zeppo, her youngest, she yanked him out of high school and flung him into the breach.

At first she had an undisputed monopoly of the idea that her boys would do well in the theater. Even they did not share it with her. To be sure, Chico, her eldest, was a piano player. Fortunately for her peace of mind, she didn't know where. But she knew he was a piano player, for she herself had amassed the weekly quarter which paid for his lessons. Then her Julius—that's Groucho—had a promising soprano voice. After cleaning up the breakfast things, she used to tether the youngest to the kitchen table and sit all day in agents' offices, until finally she got her Julius a job. Then, when she had incredibly launched her vaudeville act—it consisted of a son or so, pieced out with a pretty girl and a tenor—she couldn't bear the thought of setting forth on tour while her Harpo stayed behind, a bellhop at the Seville, with no one to see that he ate properly. It was a woman of magnificent decision who therefore called a cab, drove to the Seville, snatched Harpo from his employment and, enroute to Henderson's at Coney Island, transformed him with a white duck suit, so that, just as the curtain was rising, she could catapult him into the act. Really, one cannot say that the Marxes ever *went* on the stage. They were pushed on.

The uphill stretch was a long one, humble, worrisome, yet somehow rollicking. The Third Avenue flat, with the rent money never once on time in ten years, gave way to a Chicago house, with an equally oppressive mortgage. And when in their trouping through that territory they would grow so harumscarum that there was real danger of a fine by the management, she would have to subdue them by a magic word whispered piercingly from the wings. The word was "Greenbaum." You see, Mr. Greenbaum held the mortgage aforesaid.

It was eighteen years after her first homespun efforts as an impresario that her great night came. That was when, for the first time, the words "Marx Brothers" were written in lamps over the door of a Broadway theater. For the première of *I'll Say She Is,* she felt entitled to a new gown, with which she proposed to sweep to her seat in the proscenium box. But while she was standing on a chair to have it fitted, the incompetent chair gave way, and she broke her ankle. So she couldn't exactly sweep to her seat on the first night. They had to carry her. But she got there.

Her trouble was that her boys had got there too. They had arrived. Thereafter, I think she took less interest in their professional lives. When someone paid them a king's ransom to make their first talkie, she only yawned. What she sighed for was the zest of beginnings. Why, I hear that last year she was caught hauling her embarrassed chauffeur off to a dancing-school, with the idea of putting *him* on the stage. In her boredom she took to poker, her game being marked by so incurable a weakness for inside straights that, as often as not, her rings were missing and her bureau drawer littered with sheepish pawntickets. On the night *Animal Crackers* opened she was so absorbed that she almost forgot to go at all. But at the last moment she sent her husband for her best wig, dispatched her chauffeur to fetch her new teeth, and, assembling herself on the way downtown, reached the theater in time to greet the audience. Pretty as a picture she was, as she met us in the aisle. "We have a big success," she said.

Minnie Marx was a wise, tolerant, generous, gallant matriarch. In the passing of such a one, a woman full of years, with her work done, and children and grandchildren to hug her memory all their days, you have no more a sense of death than you have when the Hudson—sunlit, steady, all-conquering—leaves you behind on the shore on its way to the fathomless sea.

She died during rehearsals, in the one week of the year when all her boys would be around her—back from their summer roamings, that is, but not yet gone forth on tour. Had she foreseen this—I'm not sure she didn't—she would have chuckled, and, combining a sly wink with her beautiful smile, she would have said, "How's that for perfect timing?"

QUESTIONS FOR STUDY AND DISCUSSION

1. Compare this essay with a typical newspaper obituary notice. What notable differences do you find? Are there any basic similarities?

2. How does Alexander Woollcott support the statement that Minnie Marx "*lived* all sixty-five" years of her life?

3. What evidence is there to support the statement, "Minnie Marx was a wise, tolerant, generous, gallant matriarch"? Is each of these qualities illustrated by specific examples?

4. Does Mr. Woollcott satisfactorily demonstrate why he "would name her [Minnie

Marx] as among the few of whom it could be said that they had greatness"? What constitutes the greatness of Minnie Marx?

5. What are the qualities that make for human greatness? Is there more than one kind of greatness? If so, what are the distinguishing characteristics of each kind? Study of the other essays in "The World of People" section may help you crystallize your ideas.

WRITING ASSIGNMENTS

1. Write a biographical sketch (you need not think of it as an obituary) of someone whom you have known well for several years, in which you attempt to give the reader an impression of that person's dominant personality traits.

2. Using the facts in "Obituary" and any information you possess about the Marx brothers, write a "straight" biographical account of Minnie Marx.

3. Write a short essay on the personality of Minnie Marx as it is revealed by Mr. Woollcott's account of her, but do not refer directly to or quote from that account.

4. As part of assignment 2 above, or as a separate assignment, write an essay analyzing the differences between a "straight" biographical sketch and "Obituary."

5. After reflecting on the questions and problems raised in study question 5, attempt a reasoned discussion of one of the following topics (or another of the same sort suggested by the central question): "The Characteristics of Human Greatness," "Success in Life," " 'Living' vs. 'Existing.' "

DEEMS TAYLOR

The Monster

He was an undersized little man, with a head too big for his body—a sickly little man. His nerves were bad. He had skin trouble. It was agony for him to wear anything next to his skin coarser than silk. And he had delusions of grandeur.

He was a monster of conceit. Never for one minute did he look at the world or at people, except in relation to himself. He was not only the most important person in the world, to himself; in his own eyes he was the only person who existed. He believed himself to be one of the greatest dramatists in the world, one of the greatest thinkers, and one of the greatest composers. To hear him talk, he was Shakespeare, and Beethoven, and Plato, rolled into one. And you would have had no difficulty in hearing him talk. He was one of the most exhausting conversationalists that ever lived. An evening with him was an evening spent in listening to a monologue. Sometimes he was brilliant; sometimes he was maddeningly tiresome. But whether he was being brilliant or dull, he had one sole topic of conversation: himself. What *he* thought and what *he* did.

He had a mania for being in the right. The slightest hint of disagreement, from anyone, on the most trivial point, was enough to set him off on a harangue that might last for hours, in which he proved himself right in so many ways, and with such exhausting volubility, that in the end his hearer, stunned and deafened, would agree with him, for the sake of peace.

It never occurred to him that he and his doing were not of the most intense and fascinating interest to anyone with whom he came in contact. He had theories about almost any subject under the sun, including vegetarianism, the drama, politics, and music; and in support of these theories he wrote pamphlets, letters, books . . . thousands upon thousands of words, hundreds and hundreds of pages. He not only wrote these things, and published them—usually at somebody else's expense—but he would sit and read them aloud, for hours, to his friends and his family.

He wrote operas; and no sooner did he have the synopsis of a story, but he would invite—or rather summon—a crowd of his friends to his house and read it aloud to them. Not for criticism. For applause. When the complete poem was written, the friends had to come again, and hear *that* read aloud. Then he would publish the poem, sometimes years before the music that went with it was written. He played the piano like a composer, in the worst sense of what that implies, and he would sit down at the piano before parties that included some of the finest pianists of his time, and play for them, by the hour, his own music, needless to say. He had a composer's voice. And he would invite eminent vocalists to his house, and sing them his operas, taking all the parts.

He had the emotional stability of a six-year-old child. When he felt out of sorts, he would rave and stamp, or sink into suicidal gloom and talk darkly of going to the East to end his days as a Buddhist monk. Ten minutes later, when something pleased him, he would rush out of doors and run around the garden, or jump up and down on the sofa, or stand on his head. He could be grief-stricken over the death of a pet dog, and he could be callous and heartless to a degree that would have made a Roman emperor shudder.

He was almost innocent of any sense of responsibility. Not only did he seem incapable of supporting himself, but it never occurred to him that he was under any obligation to do so. He was convinced that the world owed him a living. In support of this belief, he borrowed money from everybody who was good for a loan—men, women, friends, or strangers. He wrote begging letters by the score, sometimes groveling without shame, at others loftily offering his intended benefactor the privilege of contributing to his support, and being mortally offended if the recipient declined the honor.

I have found no record of his ever paying or repaying money to anyone who did not have a legal claim upon it.

What money he could lay his hands on he spent like an Indian rajah. The mere prospect of a performance of one of his operas was enough to set him to running up bills amounting to ten times the amount of his prospective royalties. On an income that would reduce a more scrupulous man to doing his own laundry, he would keep two servants. Without enough money in his pocket to pay his rent, he would have the walls and ceiling of his study lined with pink silk. No one will ever know—certainly he never knew—how much money he owed. We do know that his greatest benefactor gave him $6,000 to pay the most pressing of his debts in one city, and a year later had to give him $16,000 to enable him to live in another city without being thrown into jail for debt.

He was equally unscrupulous in other ways. An endless procession of women marches through his life. His first wife spent twenty years enduring and forgiving his infidelities. His second wife had been the wife of his most devoted friend and admirer, from whom he stole her. And even while he was trying to persuade her to leave her first husband he was writing to a friend to inquire whether he could suggest some wealthy woman—*any* wealthy woman—whom he could marry for her money.

He was completely selfish in his other personal relationships. His liking for his friends was measured solely by the completeness of their devotion to him, or by their usefulness to him, whether financial or artistic. The minute they failed him—even by so much as refusing a dinner invitation—or began to lessen in usefulness, he cast them off without a second thought. At the end of his life he had exactly one friend left whom he had known even in middle age.

He had a genius for making enemies. He would insult a man who disagreed with him about the weather. He would pull endless wires in order to meet some man who admired his work, and was able and anxious to be of use to him—and would proceed to make a mortal enemy of him with some idiotic and wholly uncalled-for exhibition of arrogance and bad manners. A character in one of his operas was a caricature of one of the most powerful music critics of his day. Not content with burlesquing him, he invited the critic to his house and read him the libretto aloud in front of his friends.

The name of this monster was Richard Wagner. Everything that I have said about him you can find on record—in newspapers, in police reports, in the testimony of people who knew him, in his own letters, between the lines of his autobiography. And the curious thing about this record is that it doesn't matter in the least.

Because this undersized, sickly, disagreeable, fascinating little man was right all the time. The joke was on us. He *was* one of the world's great dramatists; he *was* a great thinker; he *was* one of the most stupendous musical geniuses that, up to now, the world has ever seen. The world did owe him a living. People couldn't know those things at the time, I suppose; and yet to us, who know his music, it does seem as though they should have known. What if he did talk about himself all the time? If he had talked about himself for twenty-four hours every day for the span of his life he would not have uttered half the number of words that other men have spoken and written about him since his death.

When you consider what he wrote—thirteen operas and music dramas, eleven of them still holding the stage, eight of them unquestionably worth ranking among the world's great musico-dramatic masterpieces—when you listen to what he wrote, the debts and heartaches that people had to endure from him don't seem much of a price. Eduard Hanslick, the critic whom he caricatured in *Die Meistersinger* and who hated him ever after, now lives only because he was caricatured in *Die Meistersinger*. The women whose hearts he broke are long since dead; and the man who could never love anyone but himself has made them deathless atonement, I think, with *Tristan und Isolde*. Think of the luxury with which for a time, at least, fate rewarded Napoleon, the man who ruined France and looted Europe; and then perhaps you will agree that a few thousand dollars' worth of debts were not too heavy a price to pay for the *Ring* tetralogy.

What if he was faithless to his friends and to his wives? He had one mistress to whom he was faithful to the day of his death: Music. Not for a single moment did he ever compromise with what he believed, with what he dreamed. There is not a line of his music that could have been conceived by a little mind. Even when he is dull, or downright bad, he is dull in the grand manner. There is greatness about his worst mistakes. Listening to his music, one does not forgive him for what he may or may not have been. It is not a matter of forgiveness. It is a matter of being dumb with wonder that his poor brain and body didn't burst under the torment of the demon of creative energy that lived inside him, struggling, clawing, scratching to be released; tearing, shrieking at him to write the music that was in him. The miracle is that what he did in the little space of seventy years could have been done at all, even by a great genius. Is it any wonder that he had no time to be a man?

QUESTIONS FOR STUDY AND DISCUSSION

1. In the evaluation of a human being, does the possession of genius compensate for monstrous personality defects?

2. Can a man be a great artist and a repulsive human being? This question is not so simple as it seems. Why?

3. What is the nature of the relationship between great art and the personality of its creator? It has been argued that great art cannot be created by bad men nor flourish in essentially immoral or decadent cultures. What is your view? Why?

4. Wagner, says Deems Taylor, "was almost innocent of any sense of responsibility. Not only did he seem incapable of supporting himself, but it never occurred to him that he was under any obligation to do so." Why is this attitude reprehensible? Or is it? If Wagner had been an egregious failure as an artist, would your answer be different? If he had been a "fake," no artist at all but merely a pretender, what would your answer be?

5. In what ways, if any, is society responsible for the support and encouragement of the artist?

6. The record of Wagner's cruelty, irresponsibility, immorality, unscrupulousness, egotism, and irascibility "doesn't matter in the least," says Deems Taylor. Why does he say this? Do you agree with him? This is not precisely the same question as 1 above. There the point was evaluation of the person as a human being. Here the question involves the larger question of making exceptions to the laws of a society for those who have contributed something of value to that society. How did you answer questions 4 and 5 above? Can you make your answer here consistent with your answers to 4 and 5?

7. "*Tout comprendre c'est tout pardonner.*" Do you believe that one can and should forgive anyone's actions, no matter how despicable, if one understands their motivation?

WRITING ASSIGNMENTS

1. Take up and support, in a logically organized essay, a point of view toward one of the following statements:

a. The artist is outside the "rules" of society.

b. The artist's life should not influence our appreciation of his work.

c. The "artistic temperament" is not necessary or desirable in an artist.

d. Good art is produced only by good men.

e. Society owes the artist a living.

f. Art is the product of neurosis.

2. If you know anyone who thinks and

acts like "The Monster," organize a sketch of this person. But do not stop with a mere description of character traits: try to (a) explain why this person acts as he does and (b) make some evaluative judgment about him.

3. Write an essay (not necessarily a biographical sketch) employing the device of delayed identification. Your choice of subject should reflect your thinking regarding the kinds of subjects (or handling of subjects) to which this technique is appropriate.

HERBERT ASBURY

The Noble Experiment

of Izzy and Moe

Prohibition went into effect throughout the United States on January 16, 1920, and the country settled back with an air of "Well *that's* settled." There had been a liquor problem. But a Law had been passed. Naturally, there was no longer a liquor problem. No prophet arose to foretell the awful things that were coming—the rum ships prowling off the coasts, the illicit breweries and distilleries, the bootleggers and the speakeasies, the corruption of police and judiciary, the hijackers and their machine guns, the gang wars, the multimillionaire booze barons, the murders and assassinations, the national breakdown of morals and manners, and all the rest of the long train of evils that sprang from the Eighteenth Amendment.

Nor did anyone imagine that the Amendment and its enabling legislation, the Volstead Act, would be difficult to enforce. It was THE LAW, and by and large the American people were law-abiding. The common attitude was expressed, somewhat flamboyantly, by John F. Kramer, the first Prohibition Commissioner. "This law," he said, "will be obeyed in cities large and small, and in villages, and where it is not obeyed it will be enforced. The law says that liquor to be used as a beverage must not be manufactured. We shall see that it is not manufactured. Nor sold, nor given away, nor hauled in anything on the surface of the earth or under the earth or in the air." The Anti-Saloon League estimated that prohibition could be enforced for less than $5,000,000 a year, so eager were the people to enter the shining gates of the dry Utopia. Congress appropriated a little more than that amount, enough to set up an enforcement organization and to provide about 1,500 prohibition agents. These noble snoopers, paid an average of about $2,000 a year

and hence immune to temptation, were supposed to keep 125,000,000 people from manufacturing or drinking anything stronger than near-beer. They didn't, but two of them made a spectacular try.

In a $14-a-month flat on Ridge Street, in New York's lower East Side, lived a bulbous little man named Isadore Einstein, whom everyone called Izzy. He had been a salesman, both inside and on the road, but was now a minor clerk at Station K of the New York Post Office. It required very shrewd management to feed, house, and clothe his family—his wife and four children and his father—on the meager salary of a postal employee. He was looking for something better, and decided that he had found it when he read in his newspaper about the government's plans to pay enforcement agents up to $2,500 a year.

But James Shevlin, Chief Enforcement Agent for the Southern District of New York, was not enthusiastic about Izzy. "I must say, Mr. Einstein," he said, "you don't look much like a detective." And that was the truth. Probably no one ever looked less like a detective than Izzy Einstein. He was forty years old, almost bald, five feet and five inches tall, and weighed 225 pounds. Most of this poundage was around his middle, so that when he walked his noble paunch, gently wobbling, moved majestically ahead like the breast of an overfed pouter pigeon.

But Izzy was accomplished. Besides English and Yiddish, he spoke German, Polish, and Hungarian fluently, and could make headway, though haltingly, in French, Italian, and Russian. He had even picked up a few words and phrases of Chinese. Moreover, Izzy had a knack of getting along with people and inspiring confidence. No one, looking at his round, jolly face and twinkling black eyes, could believe that he was a government snooper. Down on the lower East Side in New York he was the neighborhood cutup; whenever he dropped into the corner cigar stores and the coffeehouses his witticisms and high spirits never failed to draw an appreciative crowd.

"I guess Mr. Shevlin never saw a type like

me," Izzy said afterward. "Maybe I fascinated him or something. Anyhow, I sold him on the idea that this prohibition business needed a new type of people that couldn't be spotted so easy."

Whatever the reason, Izzy got the job.

"But I must warn you," said Shevlin, "that hunting down liquor sellers isn't exactly a safe line of work. Some law violator might get mad and try to crack a bottle over your head."

"Bottles," said Izzy, "I can dodge."

Izzy's first assignment was to clean up a place in Brooklyn which the enforcement authorities shrewdly suspected housed a speakeasy, since drunken men had been seen staggering from the building, and the air for half a block around was redolent with the fumes of beer and whiskey. Several agents had snooped and slunk around the house; one had watched all one afternoon from a roof across the street, and another had hidden for hours in an adjoining doorway, obtaining an accurate count of the number of men who entered and left. But none had been able to get inside. Izzy knew nothing of sleuthing procedures; he simply walked up to the joint and knocked on the door. A peephole was opened, and a hoarse voice demanded to know who was there.

"Izzy Einstein," said Izzy. "I want a drink."

"Oh, yeah? Who sent you here, bud? What's your business?"

"My boss sent me," Izzy explained. "I'm a prohibition agent. I just got appointed."

The door swung open and the doorman slapped Izzy jovially on the back.

"Ho! ho!" he cried. "Come right in, bud. That's the best gag I've heard yet."

Izzy stepped into a room where half a dozen men were drinking at a small, makeshift bar.

"Hey, boss!" the doorman yelled. "Here's a prohibition agent wants a drink! You got a badge, too, bud?"

"Sure I have," said Izzy, and produced it.

"Well, I'll be damned," said the man behind the bar. "Looks just like the real thing."

He poured a slug of whiskey, and Izzy downed it. That was a mistake, for when the time came to make the pinch Izzy had no evidence. He tried to grab the bottle but the bartender ran out the back door with it.

"I learned right there," said Izzy, "that a slug of hooch in an agent's belly might feel good, but it ain't evidence."

So when he went home that night he rigged up an evidence-collector. He put a small funnel in the upper left-hand pocket of his vest, and connected it, by means of a rubber tube, with a flat bottle concealed in the lining of the garment. Thereafter, when a drink was served to him, Izzy took a small sip, then poured the remainder into the funnel while the bartender was making change. The bottle wouldn't hold much, but there was always enough for analysis and to offer in evidence. "I'd have died if it hadn't been for that little funnel and the bottle," said Izzy. "And most of the stuff I got in those places was terrible."

Izzy used his original device of giving his real name, with some variation, more than twenty times during the next five years. It was successful even after he became so well known, and so greatly feared, that his picture hung behind the bar in many speakeasies, that all might see and be warned. Occasionally Izzy would prance into a ginmill with his badge pinned to his lapel, in plain sight, and shout jovially, "How about a drink for a hard-working prohibition agent?" Seeing the round little man trying so hard to be funny, everyone in the place would rush forward to hand him something alcoholic, and Izzy would arrest them and close the joint.

Once he went into a gin-mill where three huge portraits of himself, framed in what he described as "black, creepy crape," ornamented the back bar. He asked for a drink, and the bartender refused to serve it.

"I don't know you," he said.

"Why," said Izzy, laughing. "I'm Izzy Epstein, the famous prohibition detective."

"Get the name right, bud," growled the bartender. "The bum's name is Einstein."

"Epstein," said Izzy. "Don't I know my own name?"

"Maybe you do, but the low-life you're

trying to act like is named Einstein. E-i-n-s-t-e-i-n."

"Brother," said Izzy, "I ain't never wrong about a name. It's Epstein."

"Einstein!" roared the bartender.

"Epstein!" shouted Izzy.

"You're nuts!" yelled the bartender, furiously. "I'll bet you anything you want it's Einstein!"

"Okay," said Izzy. "I'll bet you the drinks."

The bartender called his other customers, and after much argument and pointing to Izzy's pictures, they agreed that the name was Einstein. So Izzy—or rather the government—had to buy nine drinks, and the bartender served them, and shortly after went to jail.

After Izzy had been an enforcement agent for a few weeks, he began to miss his old friend Moe Smith, with whom he had spent many pleasant evenings in the East Side coffeehouses. Like Izzy, Moe was a natural comedian, and, also like Izzy, he was corpulent. He tipped the scales at about 235 pounds, but he was a couple of inches taller than Izzy and didn't look quite so roly-poly. Moe had been a cigar salesman, and manager of a small fight club at Orchard and Grand Streets, New York City, and had invested his savings in a little cigar store, where he was doing well. Izzy persuaded him to put a relative in charge of the store, and to apply for a job as enforcement agent.

Moe could probably have got on the enforcement staff by his own efforts, for his background and experience were at least as good as those of nine-tenths of the agents who were hired, but he obtained the post a little quicker through Izzy's recommendation. As soon as he was sworn in as an agent, he and Izzy teamed up together, and most of the time thereafter worked as a pair. Their first assignment took them to Rockaway Beach, near New York, where they confiscated a still and arrested the operator. This man apparently took a great liking to Izzy, for after he got out of jail he made several trips to New York especially to urge Izzy to go on a fishing trip with him.

"I'll take you three miles out to sea," he said. "You'll have quite a time."

But Izzy firmly declined the invitation. "Sure he'll take me out to sea," he said, "but will he bring me back? He could leave me with the fishes."

In those early days of the noble experiment everything that happened in connection with prohibition was news, and some of New York's best reporters covered enforcement headquarters. Casting about for a way to enliven their stories and provide exercise for their imaginations, they seized upon the exploits of Izzy and Moe. The two fat and indefatigable agents supplied human-interest material by the yard; moreover, they were extraordinarily co-operative. They frequently scheduled their raids to suit the convenience of the reporters and the newspaper photographers, and soon learned that there was more room in the papers on Monday morning than on any other day of the week.

One Sunday, accompanied by a swarm of eager reporters, they established a record by making seventy-one raids in a little more than twelve hours. On another they staged a spectacular raid for the benefit of Dr. John Roach Straton, a famous hell-buster of the period, and the congregation of the Calvary Baptist Church in West Fifty-seventh Street, of which Dr. Straton was pastor. Izzy and Moe timed their raid, on a small café near the church, to coincide with the dismissal of Dr. Straton's flock after morning services, and the members of the congregation reached the street in time to see the agents rolling barrels of whiskey out of the café and smashing them with hatchets. This raid made everybody happy, except, of course, the man who owned the whiskey.

Hundreds of stories, a great many of them truthful, were written about Izzy and Moe and their grotesque adventures, and they probably made the front pages oftener than any other personages of their time except the President and the Prince of Wales.

Izzy especially gained great renown, for he was the acknowledged leader of the team. The New York *Tribune* called him "the master mind of the Federal rum ferrets." O. O. McIntyre, in his syndicated column, informed his readers that Izzy had "become as famous in New York as the Woolworth Building," and that "no morning paper is complete without some account of his exploits." Wayne B. Wheeler, General Superintendent of the Anti-Saloon League and the man who lobbied the prohibition law through Congress, graciously expressed his approval of Izzy's feats in a personal letter. "The bootlegger who gets away from you," he wrote, "has to get up early in the morning." In fact, it didn't matter how early a bootlegger got up, Izzy was usually ahead of him.

"Izzy does not sleep," reported the Brooklyn *Eagle.* "He's on the job day and night, and accomplishes more for the drys than half a dozen anti-saloon leagues. It's getting so now that a saloonkeeper hesitates in serving the wants of his oldest and best-known customer, for fear that he may suddenly develop into Izzy. A few more Izzies scattered over the country and the U. S. would be bone dry, parched, and withered."

What the newspapers enjoyed most about Izzy and Moe was their ingenuity. Once they went after a speakeasy where half a dozen dry agents had tried without success to buy a drink. The bartender positively wouldn't sell to anyone he didn't know. So on a cold winter night Izzy stood in front of the gin-mill, in his shirt sleeves, until he was red and shivering and his teeth were chattering. Then Moe half-carried him into the speakeasy, shouting excitedly:

"Give this man a drink! He's just been bitten by a frost!"

The kindhearted bartender, startled by Moe's excitement and upset by Izzy's miserable appearance, rushed forward with a bottle of whiskey. Moe promptly snatched the bottle and put him under arrest.

One of Izzy's most brilliant ideas was always to carry something on his raids, the nature of the burden depending upon the character of the neighborhood and of a particular speakeasy's clientele. When he wanted to get into a place frequented by musicians, for example, he carried a violin or a trombone, and if, as sometimes happened, he was asked to play the instrument, he could do it. He usually played "How Dry I Am." On the East Side and in the poorer sections of the Bronx, if the weather permitted, Izzy went around in his shirt sleeves carrying a

pitcher of milk, the very pattern of an honest man on his way home from the grocery. Once in Brooklyn he was admitted to half a dozen gin-mills because he was lugging a big pail of dill pickles. "A fat man with pickles!" said Izzy. "Who'd ever think a fat man with pickles was an agent?"

When Izzy operated on the beaches around New York he always carried a fishing rod or a bathing suit; he had great success one day at Sheepshead Bay with a string of fish slung over his shoulder. The doorman of the Assembly, a café in Brooklyn which catered to judges and lawyers, let him in without question because he wore a frock coat and carried a huge tome bound in sheepskin. Once inside, Izzy opened his book and adjusted a pair of horn-rimmed spectacles and, with lips moving and brow furrowed, marched with stately tread across the room and barged into the bar. Without lifting his eyes from the book, he called sonorously for "a beverage, please," and the fascinated bartender poured a slug of whiskey before he realized what he was doing. When Izzy and Moe visited Reisenweber's, a famous and expensive resort on Broadway, they carried two lovely blondes and wore "full-dress tuxedos," with rings on their fingers, sweet-smelling pomade on their hair, and huge imitation-pearl studs in their shirt fronts. The headwaiter asked them for references when they ordered liquor, and Izzy searched his pockets and pulled out the first card he found. It happened to be the card of a rabbi, with which Izzy planned to ensnare a sacramental-wine store. But the headwaiter, a man of scant perception, bowed deferentially and sold them a bottle of whiskey. "He deserved to be arrested," said Izzy, indignantly. "Imagine! A rabbi with a blonde and no beard!"

Up in Van Cortlandt Park, in New York City, near the public playing fields, was a soft-drink establishment which was suspected of being one of the retail outlets of a big rum ring. Many complaints were made to enforcement headquarters that customers had become tipsy after a few shots of the soda water sold in the place; one woman wrote that by mistake her milk shake had been filled with gin. Bad gin, too, she added.

The job of getting the evidence was given to Izzy. It proved a difficult task, for the owner of the joint would sell liquor to no one he didn't know personally. So on a Saturday afternoon in November Izzy assembled a group of half a dozen dry agents, clad them in football uniforms, and smeared their arms and faces with fresh dirt. Then Izzy tucked a football under his arm, hung a helmet over his ears, and led them whooping and rah-rahing into the suspected speakeasy, where they shouted that they had just won the last game of the season and wanted to break training in a big way. The speakeasy owner, pleased at such a rush of business, sold each agent a pint of whiskey. "Have fun, boys," he said. "The same to you," said Izzy, handing him a summons.

Flushed with this striking success, which showed that at heart he was a college boy, Izzy went to Ithaca, N. Y., to investigate a complaint by officials of Cornell University that some soda fountains near the campus were not confining their sales to pop. Izzy disguised himself as an undergraduate by putting on a little cap and a pair of white linen knickers, not so little, and for several days strolled about the campus. He hummed snatches of Cornell songs which he had learned, and played safe by addressing everyone with a mustache as "Professor," and everyone with a beard as "Dean." Having located the soda fountains which sold liquor, he dashed into them one by one, establishing himself as a student by shouting, "Sizzle Boom! Sizzle Boom! Rah! Rah! Rah!" The speakeasy boys thought he was a comedian, which indeed he was, and they gladly sold him all the booze he wanted, after which he went from place to place distributing "diplomas," or summonses.

From Cornell, and without the blessing of the student body, Izzy rushed into Harlem to investigate a complaint about a grocery store. "The man charged me two dollars for a can of tomatoes," a woman wrote to enforcement headquarters, "and when I got it home I found there was nothing in it but a lot of nasty-smelling water. My husband he grabbed it and ran out of the house and I ain't seen him since. I want you to arrest that man." Izzy disguised himself as a Negro, with his face blackened by burnt cork

and a rich Southern accent rolling off his tongue. He visited the store and awaited his turn in a long line of impatient customers. He found that to buy a half-pint of whskey (four dollars) a customer asked for a can of beans. If he wanted gin (two dollars) he asked for tomatoes. Izzy bought both beans and tomatoes and came back the next day with a warrant and a truck. Besides the groceryman, he hauled away four hundred bottles of gin, some empty cans, a canning machine, three barrels of whiskey, and a barrel of pickles which contained one hundred small bottles of gin. "Pickles was a kind of hobby of mine," he said, "and I could always tell if anything was wrong with a barrel."

The trail of illegal liquor led Izzy and Moe into some mighty queer places, but they followed wherever it led, and were always ready with the appropriate disguise. Dressed as a longshoreman, Izzy captured an Italian who used his cash register as a cellarette; its drawers were filled with little bottles of booze. In the guise of a mendicant, Izzy pawned an old pair of pants for two dollars in Brooklyn, and snooping about the pawnshops a bit found ten thousand dollars' worth of good liquor wrapped in clothing that had been left as pledges. He got into the Half Past Nine Club, on Eighth Avenue, as a prosperous poultry salesman, playing tipsy and carrying a sample, and found a large stock of liquor in a stuffed grizzly bear.

When he made an investigation of a snooty delicatessen on Madison Avenue, which catered exclusively to the carriage trade, Izzy got himself up as a Park Avenue dude, with evening clothes, a huge imitation diamond stud, and a gold-headed cane. He snooped around, acting hard to please, until he found that many of the beribboned baskets of fruit had bottles tucked away in them. Next morning he returned with a warrant, and was just about to enter the store to serve it when a young man drove up in a truck. "Hey, mister," he said, "do me a favor, will you? I gotta deliver some stuff here and they told me to be careful. Take a look inside and see if everything looks okay." Izzy glanced into the delicatessen and reported that everything looked wonderful. Then he arrested the young man and confiscated his truck and stuff, which was fifty cases of liquor. In the delicatessen Izzy found five hundred more cases.

One of Izzy's largest and most important hauls came as the result of a visit to a graveyard on the outskirts of New York. He had gone to the cemetery to attend the burial services of a friend, and, as usual, kept his eyes open. Just as the car in which he was riding turned into the cemetery gates, he saw two men come out of the back door of a house across the street, look furtively about, and then carry a large galvanized can across the yard into a shed. This looked suspicious, so when the services were over, instead of returning to New York, Izzy hid in some shrubbery. At sundown, when the cemetery gates had been closed, he moved to a tombstone directly across from the house, and crouched behind it. For three hours he watched and listened. Several times he thought he caught a whiff of mash, but nothing happened.

Izzy returned to New York about midnight, but without evidence to justify making a raid or asking for a warrant. So he evolved a scheme, for he was convinced that dirty business was afoot in the house. Next day he and Moe appeared at the cemetery office, two very seedy-looking characters, clad in rags and obviously down on their luck. They asked for work as gravediggers. The superintendent said there were no jobs open but changed his mind when they offered to dig graves for half price. They worked in an obscure corner of the cemetery until the time came to close the gates, then they told the superintendent that they needed money badly and would like to work overtime. He agreed, and left them there with their picks and shovels. After he had gone they moved to an unused area near the fence, across from the house, and began to dig. About an hour later a man came out of the house, stood on the porch watching them for a few minutes, then crossed the road and leaned idly against the fence.

"Hard work, ain't it, boys?" he asked.

"Yeah," said Moe. "Thirsty work, too. I'd give ten dollars for a pint right now."

"Five, anyway," said Izzy.

The man said nothing, and after a few minutes went back into the house. Then Izzy had another idea. He and Moe quickly dug three or four shallow holes, and were working on a fifth when the man returned. When he got within hearing distance Moe called to Izzy:

"How many more we got to dig tonight?"

"Ten," said Izzy.

"My God!" exclaimed the man. "What happened? Somebody blow up a hotel?"

"Well, that's the way it goes," said Izzy. "Sometimes nobody dies for a long time, then all of a sudden a lot of people make up their minds at the same time."

"It wouldn't be so bad," said Moe, "if we could get a drink."

"You boys come over to the house after a while," the man said. "Maybe I can fix you up."

Half an hour later Izzy and Moe put away their tools, climbed the fence, and strolled across the road. The man greeted them cordially, and introduced them to two others as hard-working gravediggers. The party adjourned to the kitchen, where Izzy bought a pint of whiskey for six dollars, having beat the price down from ten. Then while Moe covered the three prisoners with his gun, Izzy kicked in the door of an adjoining room, from which came the heavy odor of fermenting mash. There he found three big stills running full blast, fifty-one barrels containing alcohol, and a dozen bottles of essences and chemical coloring, used to give the new hooch the appearance, and something of the flavor, of the real stuff. In another room Izzy discovered a large quantity of counterfeit labels and government revenue stamps. The hosts had the job of carrying all this stuff out and loading it on a truck.

For more than five years the whole country laughed at the antics of Izzy and Moe, with the exception of the ardent drys, who thought the boys were wonderful, and the bootleggers and speakeasy proprietors, who thought they were crazy and feared them mightily. And their fear was justified, for in their comparatively brief career Izzy and Moe confiscated 5,000,000 bottles of booze, worth $15,000,000, besides thousands of gallons in kegs and barrels and hundreds of stills and breweries. They smashed an enormous quantity of saloon fixtures and equipment, and made 4,392 arrests, of which more than 95 per cent resulted in convictions. No other two agents even approached this record.

Nearly all of the victims were small-fry bootleggers and speakeasy operators, although they raided and confiscated a considerable number of large stills and breweries. Their largest single haul was 2,000 cases of bottled whiskey and 365 barrels of whiskey and brandy, which they found in a Bronx garage. And they made one terrifying swoop up and down Broadway which put the finishing touches to such celebrated nightlife resorts as Jack's, the Ted Lewis Club, Shanley's, the Beaux Arts, and Reisenweber's.

Neither Izzy nor Moe molested hip-flask toters; nor, unlike other agents who made themselves obnoxious to the general public, did they go barging into restaurants sniffing at glasses and snatching bottles off tables. "Personally," wrote Izzy, "I never saw any call for such tactics. I did my work quietly, and extended courtesy to any law violator I had to deal with. If it was a high-class place I was pinching, I'd sometimes even let the manager collect his dinner checks so he wouldn't be stuck for the food he'd served. Even in tough places I never abused my power. I used the name of the law and not blackjacks."

Izzy and Moe made many spectacular raids in Chicago, Detroit, and other cities ruled by the gangsters and the beer barons, but they never encountered Al Capone, Johnny Torrio, Frankie Yale, or any of the other great hoodlums who were the real beneficiaries of the Eighteenth Amendment. If they had, there is little doubt that they would have taken the triggermen in their stride, for neither Izzy nor Moe lacked courage. Izzy didn't approve of guns, and never carried one. Moe lugged a revolver around occasionally, but in five years fired it only twice. Once he shot out a lock that had resisted his efforts, and another time he shot a hole in a keg of whiskey. Izzy said later that guns were pulled on him only twice. The first time was on Dock Street, in Yonkers, N. Y.,

where he had spent a pleasant and profitable evening with raids on five speakeasies. To make it an even half dozen, he stepped into a sixth place that looked suspicious, bought a slug of whiskey for sixty cents, and poured it into the funnel in his vest pocket. While he was arresting the bartender, the owner of the joint came into the bar from another part of the house.

"He pulled an automatic from behind the bar," wrote Izzy. "She clicked but the trigger jammed. It was aimed right at my heart. I didn't like that. I grabbed his arm and he and I had a fierce fight all over the bar, till finally I got the pistol. I don't mind telling you I was afraid, particularly when I found the gun was loaded."

On another occasion an angry bartender shoved a revolver against Izzy's stomach. But Izzy didn't bat an eye; he calmly shoved the gun aside.

"Put that up, son," he said, soothingly. "Murdering me won't help your family."

Fortunately, the bartender had a family, and Izzy's warning brought to his mind a vision of his fatherless children weeping at the knee of their widowed mother, who was also weeping. He stopped to think. While he was thinking, Moe knocked him cold.

On one of his swings around the so-called enforcement circuit, Izzy made up a sort of schedule showing the length of time it took him to get a drink in various cities. New Orleans won first prize, a four-star hiss from the Anti-Saloon League. When Izzy arrived in the Crescent City he climbed into an ancient taxicab, and as the machine got under way he asked the driver where he could get a drink.

"Right here, suh," said the driver, and pulled out a bottle, "Fo' bits."

Time—thirty-five seconds.

In Pittsburgh, disguised as a Polish mill worker, Izzy bought a drink of terrible whiskey in eleven minutes. Just seventeen minutes after he got off the train in Atlanta, he walked into a confectionery shop on Peachtree Street, bought a drink, and arrested the proprietor. In Chicago he bought a drink in twenty-one minutes without leaving the railroad station, and duplicated this feat in St. Louis. In Cleveland it took twenty-nine minutes, but that was because an usher in a vaudeville theater, who had offered to take him to a speakeasy, couldn't leave his job right away. In Baltimore, Izzy got on a trolley car and asked the conductor where he could find a speakeasy. "In the next block," the conductor replied. Time, fifteen minutes. It took longer in Washington than anywhere else; Izzy roamed the city for a whole hour before he could locate a gin-mill. He finally had to ask a policeman, who provided him with the necessary directions.

During the summer of 1925 the almost continual stories about Izzy and Moe in the newspapers got on the nerves of high prohibition enforcement officials in Washington, few of whom ever got mentioned in the papers at all. National headquarters announced that any agent whose name appeared in print in connection with his work would be suspended, and perhaps otherwise punished, on the ground that publicity brought discredit to the service. At the same time a high official called Izzy to Washington and spoke to him rather severely. "You get your name in the newspaper all the time, and in the headlines, too," he complained, "whereas mine is hardly ever mentioned. I must ask you to remember that you are merely a subordinate, not the whole show." For a while Izzy really tried to keep away from the reporters and out of the papers, but both he and Moe had become public personages, and it was impossible to keep the newspapermen from writing about

them. When they refused to tell what they had done, the reporters invented stories about them, so a stream of angry denials and protests continued to come from Washington.

Finally, on November 13, 1925, it was announced that Izzy and Moe had turned in their gold badges and were no longer prohibition agents. Izzy's story was that he had been told he was to be transferred to Chicago. He had lived in New York since he was fifteen years old, and had no intention of ever living anywhere else, so he refused to go, and "thereby fired myself." Government officials, however, said that Izzy and Moe had been dismissed "for the good of the service." Off the record they added, "The service must be dignified. Izzy and Moe belong on the vaudeville stage." Most of the newspapers took the position that the whole problem of enforcement belonged on the vaudeville stage. The New York *Herald Tribune* said, "They [Izzy and Moe] never made prohibition much more of a joke than it has been made by some of the serious-minded prohibition officers."

Both Izzy and Moe went into the insurance business, and did well. They dropped out of the public eye, and remained out except for an occasional Sunday feature story, and a brief flurry of publicity in 1928, when Izzy went to Europe and returned with some entertaining accounts of his adventures. Izzy died in New York on February 17, 1938, by which time his four sons had all become successful lawyers.

QUESTIONS FOR STUDY AND DISCUSSION

1. Why is this essay called "The *Noble Experiment* of Izzy and Moe"? Was the work of the two protagonists noble or experimental? Were you familiar with the special meaning of the expression "The Noble Experiment"?

2. This essay is about two men, but it is also about Prohibition. How would you characterize Herbert Asbury's attitude toward his characters? Toward the work they were doing? Toward Prohibition?

3. How much do you know about Prohibition? If your knowledge is vague and sketchy, fill it out by consulting reference books. You may then be better able to form an opinion on the principle of Prohibition, its effectiveness, and its side-effects. To what extent does the United States continue to have Prohibition? How does it work in areas where you have seen it in operation?

4. At the conclusion of the essay, Mr. Asbury reports, "Most of the newspapers

took the position that the whole problem of enforcement," not just Izzy and Moe, "belonged on the vaudeville stage." How does his presentation of the exploits of Izzy and Moe predispose the reader to concur in this judgment?

5. How does Mr. Asbury's choice of words help to establish his attitude toward the enforcement of Prohibition? Make a list of such words.

6. Are the dangers run by Prohibition agents minimized in this essay? How many times is Izzy in danger? How is this version of an agent's risks at variance with other accounts of bootleggers and speakeasy operators that you have encountered—on TV, for example? Which version seems nearer the truth?

WRITING ASSIGNMENTS

1. Write a character sketch of Isadore Einstein. The essay you have read furnishes many details. Your job is not simply to reproduce them but to select, synthesize, and finally make your own generalization about what Izzy was like.

2. Legal prohibition or restrictions on the consumption of alcoholic beverages continues to be a controversial subject. An adequate discussion of the entire question is far beyond the scope of a theme, but papers of reasonable length might be written on particular phases. For example: prohibition for minors; the side-effects of Prohibition; the side-effects of Repeal; the "right to drink"; alcohol and drugs—the same thing or different?

3. Write a "portrait" of Prohibition, as you visualize it from books, TV viewing, and your knowledge of recent American history. Make all parts of the essay—word-choice and selection of detail as well as "main points"—reflect your point of view toward "the noble experiment."

4. Choose some controversial decision from your own immediate experience and describe its effects.

RALPH WALDO EMERSON

Thoreau

Henry David Thoreau was the last male descendant of a French ancestor who came to this country from the Isle of Guernsey. His character exhibited occasional traits drawn from this blood in singular combination with a very strong Saxon genius.

He was born in Concord, Massachusetts, on the 12th of July, 1817. He was graduated at Harvard College in 1837, but without any literary distinction. An iconoclast in literature, he seldom thanked colleges for their service to him, holding them in small esteem, whilst yet his debt to them was important. After leaving the University, he joined his brother in teaching a private school, which he soon renounced. His father was a manufacturer of lead-pencils, and Henry applied himself for a time to this craft, believing he could make a better pencil than was then in use. After completing his experiments, he exhibited his work to chemists and artists in Boston, and having obtained their certificates to its excellence and to its equality with the best London manufacture, he returned home contented. His friends congratulated him that he had now opened his way to fortune. But he replied, that he should never make another pencil. "Why should I? I would not do again what I have done once." He resumed his endless walks and miscellaneous studies, making every day some new acquaintance with Nature, though as yet never speaking of zoölogy or botany, since, though very studious of natural facts, he was incurious of technical and textual science.

At this time, a strong, healthy youth, fresh from college, whilst all his companions were choosing their profession, or eager to begin some lucrative employment, it was inevitable that his thoughts should be exercised on the same question, and it required rare decision to refuse all the accustomed paths, and keep his solitary freedom at the cost of disappointing the natural expectations of his family and friends: all the more difficult that he had a perfect probity, was exact in securing his own independence, and in holding every man to the like duty. But Thoreau never faltered. He was a born protestant. He declined to give up his large ambition of knowledge and action for any narrow craft or profession, aiming at a much more comprehensive calling, the art of living well. If he slighted and defied the opinions of others, it was only that he was more intent to reconcile his practice with his own belief. Never idle or self-indulgent, he preferred, when he wanted money, earning it by some piece of manual labor agreeable to him, as building a boat or a fence, planting, grafting, surveying, or other short work, to any long engagements. With his hardy habits and few wants, his skill in wood-craft, and his powerful arithmetic, he was very competent to live in any part of the world. It would cost him less time to supply his wants than another. He was therefore secure of his leisure.

A natural skill for mensuration, growing out of his mathematical knowledge, and his habit of ascertaining the measures and distances of objects which interested him, the size of trees, the depth and extent of ponds and rivers, the height of mountains, and the air-line distance of his favorite summits,— this, and his intimate knowledge of the territory about Concord, made him drift into the profession of land-surveyor. It had the advantage for him that it led him continually into new and secluded grounds, and helped his studies of Nature. His accuracy and skill in this work were readily appreciated, and he found all the employment he wanted.

He could easily solve the problems of the surveyor, but he was daily beset with graver questions, which he manfully confronted. He interrogated every custom, and wished to settle all his practice on an ideal foundation. He was a protestant à l'outrance, and few lives contain so many renunciations. He was bred to no profession; he never married; he lived alone; he never went to church; he never voted; he refused to pay a tax to the State; he ate no flesh, he drank no wine, he never knew the use of tobacco;

and, though a naturalist, he used neither trap nor gun. He chose, wisely, no doubt, for himself, to be the bachelor of thought and Nature. He had no talent for wealth, and knew how to be poor without the least hint of squalor or inelegance. Perhaps he fell into his way of living without forecasting it much, but approved it with later wisdom. "I am often reminded," he wrote in his journal, "that, if I had bestowed on me the wealth of Crœsus, my aims must be still the same, and my means essentially the same." He had no temptations to fight against,— no appetites, no passions, no taste for elegant trifles. A fine house, dress, the manners and talk of highly cultivated people were all thrown away on him. He much preferred a good Indian, and considered these refinements as impediments to conversation, wishing to meet his companion on the simplest terms. He declined invitations to dinner-parties, because there each was in every one's way, and he could not meet the individuals to any purpose. "They make their pride," he said, "in making their dinner cost much; I make my pride in making my dinner cost little." When asked at table what dish he preferred, he answered, "The nearest." He did not like the taste of wine, and never had a vice in his life. He said,—"I have a faint recollection of pleasure derived from smoking dried lily-stems, before I was a man. I had commonly a supply of these. I have never smoked anything more noxious."

He chose to be rich by making his wants few, and supplying them himself. In his travels, he used the railroad only to get over so much country as was unimportant to the present purpose, walking hundreds of miles, avoiding taverns, buying a lodging in farmers' and fishermen's houses, as cheaper, and more agreeable to him, and because there he could better find the men and the information he wanted.

There was somewhat military in his nature not to be subdued, always manly and able, but rarely tender, as if he did not feel himself except in opposition. He wanted a fallacy to expose, a blunder to pillory, I may say required a little sense of victory, a roll of the drum, to call his powers into full exercise. It cost him nothing to say No; indeed, he found it much easier than to say Yes. It seemed as if his first instinct on hearing a proposition was to controvert it, so impatient was he of the limitations of our daily thought. This habit, of course, is a little chilling to the social affections; and though the companion would in the end acquit him of any malice or untruth, yet it mars conversation. Hence, no equal companion stood in affectionate relations with one so pure and guileless. "I love Henry," said one of his friends, "but I cannot like him; and as for taking his arm, I should as soon think of taking the arm of an elm-tree."

Yet, hermit and stoic as he was, he was really fond of sympathy, and threw himself heartily and childlike into the company of young people whom he loved, and whom he delighted to entertain, as he only could, with the varied and endless anecdotes of his experiences by field and river. And he was always ready to lead a huckleberry-party or a search for chestnuts or grapes. Talking, one day, of a public discourse, Henry remarked, that whatever succeeded with the audience was bad. I said, "Who would not like to write something which all can read, like 'Robinson Crusoe'? and who does not see with regret that his page is not solid with a right materialistic treatment, which delights everybody?" Henry objected, of course, and vaunted the better lectures which reached only a few persons. But, at supper, a young girl, understanding that he was to lecture at the Lyceum, sharply asked him, "whether his lecture would be a nice, interesting story, such as she wished to hear, or whether it was one of those old philosophical things that she did not care about." Henry turned to her, and bethought himself, and, I saw, was trying to believe that he had matter that might fit her and her brother, who were to sit up and go to the lecture, if it was a good one for them.

He was a speaker and actor of the truth,— born such,—and was ever running into dramatic situations from this cause. In any circumstance, it interested all bystanders to know what part Henry would take, and what he would say; and he did not disappoint expectation, but used an original judgment on each emergency. In 1845 he built himself a small framed house on the shores of Walden Pond, and lived there two years alone, a life of labor and study. This action was quite native and fit for him. No one who knew him would tax him with affectation. He was more unlike his neighbors in his thought than in his action. As soon as he had exhausted the advantages of that solitude, he abandoned it. In 1847, not approving some uses to which the public expenditure was applied, he refused to pay his town tax, and was put in jail. A friend paid the tax for him, and he was released. The like annoyance was threatened the next year. But, as his friends paid the tax, notwithstanding his protest, I believe he ceased to resist. No opposition or ridicule had any weight with him. He coldly and fully stated his opinion without affecting to believe that it was the opinion of the company. It was of no consequence, if every one present held the opposite opinion. On one occasion he went to the University Library to procure some books. The librarian refused to lend them. Mr. Thoreau repaired to the President, who stated to him the rules and usages, which permitted the loan of books to resident graduates, to clergymen who were alumni, and to some others resident within a circle of ten miles' radius from the College. Mr. Thoreau explained to the President that the railroad had destroyed the old scale of distances,—that the library was useless, yes, and President and College useless, on the terms of his rules,—that the one benefit he owed to the College was its library,— that, at this moment, not only his want of books was imperative, but he wanted a large number of books, and assured him that he, Thoreau, and not the librarian, was the proper custodian of these. In short, the President found the petitioner so formidable, and the rules getting to look so ridiculous, that he ended by giving him a privilege which in his hands proved unlimited thereafter.

No truer American existed than Thoreau. His preference of his country and condition was genuine, and his aversation from English and European manners and tastes almost reached contempt. He listened impa-

tiently to news or *bon mots* gleaned from London circles; and though he tried to be civil, these anecdotes fatigued him. The men were all imitating each other, and on a small mould. Why can they not live as far apart as possible, and each be a man by himself? What he sought was the most energetic nature; and he wished to go to Oregon, not to London. "In every part of Great Britain," he wrote in his diary, "are discovered traces of the Romans, their funereal urns, their camps, their roads, their dwellings. But New England, at least, is not based on any Roman ruins. We have not to lay the foundations of our houses on the ashes of a former civilization."

But, idealist as he was, standing for abolition of slavery, abolition of tariffs, almost for abolition of government, it is needless to say he found himself not only unrepresented in actual politics, but almost equally opposed to every class of reformers. Yet he paid the tribute of his uniform respect to the Anti-Slavery party. One man, whose personal acquaintance he had formed, he honored with exceptional regard. Before the first friendly word had been spoken for Captain John Brown, he sent notices to most houses in Concord, that he would speak in a public hall on the condition and character of John Brown, on Sunday evening, and invited all people to come. The Republican Committee, the Abolitionist Committee, sent him word that it was premature and not advisable. He replied,—"I did not send to you for advice, but to announce that I am to speak." The hall was filled at an early hour by people of all parties, and his earnest eulogy of the hero was heard by all respectfully, by many with a sympathy that surprised themselves.

It was said of Plotinus that he was ashamed of his body, and 't is very likely he had good reason for it,—that his body was a bad servant, and he had not skill in dealing with the material world, as happens often to men of abstract intellect. But Mr. Thoreau was equipped with a most adapted and serviceable body. He was of short stature, firmly built, of light complexion, with strong, serious blue eyes, and a grave aspect,—his face covered in the late years with a becoming beard. His senses were acute, his frame well-knit and hardy, his hands strong and skilful in the use of tools. And there was a wonderful fitness of body and mind. He could pace sixteen rods more accurately than another man could measure them with rod and chain. He could find his path in the woods at night, he said, better by his feet than his eyes. He could estimate the measure of a tree very well by his eye; he could estimate the weight of a calf or a pig, like a dealer. From a box containing a bushel or more of loose pencils, he could take up with his hands fast enough just a dozen pencils at every grasp. He was a good swimmer, runner, skater, boatman, and would probably outwalk most countrymen in a day's journey. And the relation of body to mind was still finer than we have indicated. He said he wanted every stride his legs made. The length of his walk uniformly made the length of his writing. If shut up in the house, he did not write at all.

He had a strong common sense, like that which Rose Flammock, the weaver's daughter, in Scott's romance, commends in her father, as resembling a yardstick, which, whilst it measures dowlas and diaper, can equally well measure tapestry and cloth of gold. He had always a new resource. When I was planting forest-trees, and had procured half a peck of acorns, he said that only a small portion of them would be sound, and proceeded to examine them, and select the sound ones. But finding this took time, he said, "I think, if you put them all into water, the good ones will sink"; which experiment we tried with success. He could plan a garden, or a house, or a barn; would have been competent to lead a "Pacific Exploring Expedition"; could give judicious counsel in the gravest private or public affairs.

He lived for the day, not cumbered and mortified by his memory. If he brought you yesterday a new proposition, he would bring you to-day another not less revolutionary. A very industrious man, and setting, like all highly organized men, a high value on his time, he seemed the only man of leisure in town, always ready for any excursion that promised well, or for conversation prolonged into late hours. His trenchant sense was never stopped by his rules of daily prudence, but was always up to the new occasion. He liked and used the simplest food, yet, when some one urged a vegetable diet, Thoreau thought all diets a very small matter, saying that "the man who shoots the buffalo lives better than the man who boards at the Graham House." He said,—"You can sleep near the railroad, and never be disturbed: Nature knows very well what sounds are worth attending to, and has made up her mind not to hear the railroad-whistle. But things respect the devout mind, and a mental ecstasy was never interrupted." He noted, what repeatedly befell him, that, after receiving from a distance a rare plant, he would presently find the same in his own haunts. And those pieces of luck which happen only to good players happened to him. One day, walking with a stranger, who inquired where Indian arrow-heads could be found, he replied, "Everywhere," and, stooping forward, picked one on the instant from the ground. At Mount Washington, in Tuckerman's Ravine, Thoreau had a bad fall, and sprained his foot. As he was in the act of getting up from his fall, he saw for the first time the leaves of the *Arnica mollis*.

His robust common sense, armed with stout hands, keen perceptions, and strong will, cannot yet account for the superiority which shone in his simple and hidden life. I must add the cardinal fact, that there was an excellent wisdom in him, proper to a rare class of men, which showed him the material world as a means and symbol. This discovery, which sometimes yields to poets a certain casual and interrupted light, serving for the ornaments of their writing, was in him an unsleeping insight; and whatever faults or obstructions of temperament might cloud it, he was not disobedient to the heavenly vision. In his youth, he said, one day, "The other world is all my art: my pencils will draw no other; my jack-knife will cut nothing else; I do not use it as a means." This was the muse and genius that ruled his opinions, conversation, studies, work, and course of life. This made him a searching judge of men. At first glance he measured his companion, and, though insensible to some fine traits of culture, could very well

report his weight and calibre. And this made the impression of genius which his conversation sometimes gave.

He understood the matter in hand at a glance, and saw the limitations and poverty of those he talked with, so that nothing seemed concealed from such terrible eyes. I have repeatedly known young men of sensibility converted in a moment to the belief that this was the man they were in search of, the man of men, who could tell them all they should do. His own dealing with them was never affectionate, but superior, didactic, —scorning their petty ways,—very slowly conceding, or not conceding at all, the promise of his society at their houses, or even at his own. "Would he not walk with them?" "He did not know. There was nothing so important to him as his walk; he had no walks to throw away on company." Visits were offered him from respectful parties, but he declined them. Admiring friends offered to carry him at their own cost to the Yellow-Stone River,—to the West Indies,—to South America. But though nothing could be more grave or considered than his refusals, they remind one in quite new relations of that fop Brummel's reply to the gentleman who offered him his carriage in a shower, "But where will *you* ride, then?"—and what accusing silences, and what searching and irresistible speeches, battering down all defences, his companions can remember!

Mr. Thoreau dedicated his genius with such entire love to the fields, hills, and waters of his native town, that he made them known and intèresting to all reading Americans, and to people over the sea. The river on whose banks he was born and died he knew from its springs to its confluence with the Merrimack. He had made summer and winter observations on it for many years, and at every hour of the day and the night. The result of the recent survey of the Water Commissioners appointed by the State of Massachusetts he had reached by his private experiments, several years earlier. Every fact which occurs in the bed, on the banks, or in the air over it; the fishes, and their spawning and nests, their manners, their food; the shad-flies which fill the air on a certain evening once a year, and which

are snapped at by the fishes so ravenously that many of these die of repletion; the conical heaps of small stones on the river-shallows, one of which heaps will sometimes overfill a cart,—these heaps the huge nests of small fishes; the birds which frequent the stream, heron, duck, sheldrake, loon, osprey; the snake, muskrat, otter, woodchuck, and fox, on the banks; the turtle, frog, hyla, and cricket, which make the banks vocal,— were all known to him, and, as it were, townsmen and fellow-creatures; so that he felt an absurdity or violence in any narrative of one of these by itself apart, and still more of its dimensions on an inch-rule, or in the exhibition of its skeleton, or the specimen of a squirrel or a bird in brandy. He liked to speak of the manners of the river, as itself a lawful creature, yet with exactness, and always to an observed fact. As he knew the river, so the ponds in this region.

One of the weapons he used, more important than microscope or alcohol-receiver to other investigators, was a whim which grew on him by indulgence, yet appeared in gravest statement, namely, of extolling his own town and neighborhood as the most favored centre for natural observation. He remarked that the Flora of Massachusetts embraced almost all the important plants of America,—most of the oaks, most of the willows, the best pines, the ash, the maple, the beech, the nuts. He returned Kane's "Arctic Voyage" to a friend of whom he had borrowed it, with the remark, that "most of the phenomena noted might be observed in Concord." He seemed a little envious of the Pole, for the coincident sunrise and sunset, or five minutes' day after six months: a splendid fact, which Annursnuc had never afforded him. He found red snow in one of his walks, and told me that he expected to find yet the *Victoria regia* in Concord. He was the attorney of the indigenous plants, and owned to a preference of the weeds to the imported plants, as of the Indian to the civilized man,—and noticed, with pleasure, that the willow bean-poles of his neighbor had grown more than his beans. "See these weeds," he said, "which have been hoed at by a million farmers all spring and summer, and yet have prevailed, and just now come out triumphant over all lanes, pastures, fields, and gardens, such is their vigor. We have insulted them with low names, too,—as Pigweed, Wormwood, Chickweed, Shad-Blossom." He says, "They have brave names, too,—Ambrosia, Stellaria, Amelanchia, Amaranth, etc."

I think his fancy for referring everything to the meridian of Concord did not grow out of any ignorance or depreciation of other longitudes or latitudes, but was rather a playful expression of his conviction of the indifference of all places, and that the best place for each is where he stands. He expressed it once in this wise:—"I think nothing is to be hoped from you, if this bit of mould under your feet is not sweeter to you to eat than any other in this world, or in any world."

The other weapon with which he conquered all obstacles in science was patience. He knew how to sit immovable, a part of the rock he rested on, until the bird, the reptile, the fish, which had retired from him, should come back, and resume its habits, nay, moved by curiosity, should come to him and watch him.

It was a pleasure and a privilege to walk with him. He knew the country like a fox or a bird, and passed through it as freely by paths of his own. He knew every track in the snow or on the ground, and what creature had taken this path before him. One must submit abjectly to such a guide, and the reward was great. Under his arm he carried an old music-book to press plants; in his pocket, his diary and pencil, a spy-glass for birds, microscope, jack-knife, and twine. He wore straw hat, stout shoes, strong gray trousers, to brave shrub-oaks and smilax, and to climb a tree for a hawk's or a squirrel's nest. He waded into the pool for the water-plants, and his strong legs were no insignificant part of his armor. On the day I speak of he looked for the Menyanthes, detected it across the wide pool, and, on examination of the florets, decided that it had been in flower five days. He drew out of his breast-pocket his diary, and read the names of all the plants that should bloom on this day, whereof he kept account as a banker when his notes fall due. The Cypripedium not due

till to-morrow. He thought, that, if waked up from a trance, in this swamp, he could tell by the plants what time of the year it was within two days. The redstart was flying about, and presently the fine grosbeaks, whose brilliant scarlet makes the rash gazer wipe his eye, and whose fine clear note Thoreau compared to that of a tanager which has got rid of its hoarseness. Presently he heard a note which he called that of the night-warbler, a bird he had never identified, had been in search of twelve years, which always, when he saw it, was in the act of diving down into a tree or bush, and which it was vain to seek; the only bird that sings indifferently by night and by day. I told him he must beware of finding and booking it, lest life should have nothing more to show him. He said, "What you seek in vain for, half your life, one day you come full upon all the family at dinner. You seek it like a dream, and as soon as you find it you become its prey."

His interest in the flower or the bird lay very deep in his mind, was connected with Nature,—and the meaning of Nature was never attempted to be defined by him. He would not offer a memoir of his observations to the Natural History Society. "Why should I? To detach the description from its connections in my mind would make it no longer true or valuable to me: and they do not wish what belongs to it." His power of observation seemed to indicate additional senses. He saw as with microscope, heard as with ear-trumpet, and his memory was a photographic register of all he saw and heard. And yet none knew better than he that it is not the fact that imports, but the impression or effect of the fact on your mind. Every fact lay in glory in his mind, a type of the order and beauty of the whole.

His determination on Natural History was organic. He confessed that he sometimes felt like a hound or a panther, and, if born among Indians, would have been a fell hunter. But, restrained by his Massachusetts culture, he played out the game in this mild form of botany and ichthyology. His intimacy with animals suggested what Thomas Fuller records of Butler the apiologist, that "either he had told the bees things or the bees had told him." Snakes coiled round his leg; the fishes swam into his hand, and he took them out of the water; he pulled the woodchuck out of its hole by the tail, and took the foxes under his protection from the hunters. Our naturalist had perfect magnanimity; he had no secrets: he would carry you to the heron's haunt, or even to his most prized botanical swamp,—possibly knowing that you could never find it again, yet willing to take his risks.

No college ever offered him a diploma, or a professor's chair; no academy made him its corresponding secretary, its discoverer, or even its member. Whether these learned bodies feared the satire of his presence. Yet so much knowledge of Nature's secret and genius few others possessed, none in a more large and religious synthesis. For not a particle of respect had he to the opinions of any man or body of men, but homage solely to the truth itself; and as he discovered every-where among doctors some leaning of cour-tesy, it discredited them. He grew to be revered and admired by his townsmen, who had at first known him only as an oddity. The farmers who employed him as a sur-veyor soon discovered his rare accuracy and skill, his knowledge of their lands, of trees, of birds, of Indian remains, and the like, which enabled him to tell every farmer more than he knew before of his own farm; so that he began to feel a little as if Mr. Tho-reau had better rights in his land than he. They felt, too, the superiority of character which addressed all men with a native au-thority.

Indian relics abound in Concord,—arrow-heads, stone chisels, pestles, and fragments of pottery; and on the river-bank, large heaps of clam-shells and ashes mark spots which the savages frequented. These, and every circumstance touching the Indian, were important in his eyes. His visits to Maine were chiefly for love of the Indian. He had the satisfaction of seeing the manufacture of the bark-canoe, as well as of trying his hand in its management on the rapids. He was inquisitive about the making of the stone arrow-head, and in his last days charged a youth setting out for the Rocky Mountains to find an Indian who could tell him that:

"It was well worth a visit to California to learn it." Occasionally, a small party of Penobscot Indians would visit Concord, and pitch their tents for a few weeks in summer on the river-bank. He failed not to make acquaintance with the best of them; though he well knew that asking questions of In-dians is like catechizing beavers and rabbits. In his last visit to Maine he had great satis-faction from Joseph Polis, an intelligent Indian of Oldtown, who was his guide for some weeks.

He was equally interested in every natural fact. The depth of his perception found likeness of law throughout Nature, and I know not any genius who so swiftly inferred universal law from the single fact. He was no pedant of a department. His eye was open to beauty, and his ear to music. He found these, not in rare conditions, but wheresoever he went. He thought the best of music was in single strains; and he found poetic suggestion in the humming of the telegraph-wire.

His poetry might be bad or good; he no doubt wanted a lyric facility and technical skill; but he had the source of poetry in his spiritual perception. He was a good reader and critic, and his judgment on poetry was to the ground of it. He could not be de-ceived as to the presence or absence of the poetic element in any composition, and his thirst for this made him negligent and per-haps scornful of superficial graces. He would pass by many delicate rhythms, but he would have detected every live stanza or line in a volume, and knew very well where to find an equal poetic charm in prose. He was so enamored of the spiritual beauty that he held all actual written poems in very light esteem in the comparison. He admired Æschylus and Pindar; but, when some one was commending them, he said that "Æschy-lus and the Greeks, in describing Apollo and Orpheus, had given no song, or no good one. They ought not to have moved trees, but to have chanted to the gods such a hymn as would have sung all their old ideas out of their heads, and new ones in." His own verses are often rude and defective. The gold does not yet run pure, is drossy and crude. The thyme and marjoram are not yet honey.

But if he want lyric fineness and technical merits, if he have not the poetic temperament, he never lacks the causal thought, showing that his genius was better than his talent. He knew the worth of the Imagination for the uplifting and consolation of human life, and liked to throw every thought into a symbol. The fact you tell is of no value, but only the impression. For this reason his presence was poetic, always piqued the curiosity to know more deeply the secrets of his mind. He had many reserves, an unwillingness to exhibit to profane eyes what was still sacred in his own, and knew well how to throw a poetic veil over his experience. All readers of "Walden" will remember his mythical record of his disappointments:—

"I long ago lost a hound, a bay horse, and a turtle-dove, and am still on their trail. Many are the travellers I have spoken concerning them, describing their tracks, and what calls they answered to. I have met one or two who had heard the hound, and the tramp of the horse, and even seen the dove disappear behind a cloud; and they seemed as anxious to recover them as if they had lost them themselves."

His riddles were worth the reading, and I confide, that, if at any time I do not understand the expression, it is yet just. Such was the wealth of his truth that it was not worth his while to use words in vain. His poem entitled "Sympathy" reveals the tenderness under that triple steel of stoicism, and the intellectual subtilty it could animate. His classic poem on "Smoke" suggests Simonides, but is better than any poem of Simonides. His biography is in his verses. His habitual thought makes all his poetry a hymn to the Cause of causes, the Spirit which vivifies and controls his own.

> "I hearing get, who had but ears,
>   And sight, who had but eyes before;
> I moments live, who lived but years,
>   And truth discern, who knew but learning's lore."

And still more in these religious lines:—

> "Now chiefly is my natal hour,
>   And only now my prime of life;
> I will not doubt the love untold,

> Which not my worth or want hath bought,
> Which wooed me young, and wooes me old,
> And to this evening hath me brought."

Whilst he used in his writings a certain petulance of remark in reference to churches or churchmen, he was a person of a rare, tender, and absolute religion, a person incapable of any profanation, by act or by thought. Of course, the same isolation which belonged to his original thinking and living detached him from the social religious forms. This is neither to be censured nor regretted. Aristotle long ago explained it, when he said, "One who surpasses his fellow-citizens in virtue is no longer a part of the city. Their law is not for him, since he is a law to himself."

Thoreau was sincerity itself, and might fortify the convictions of prophets in the ethical laws by his holy living. It was an affirmative experience which refused to be set aside. A truth-speaker he, capable of the most deep and strict conversation; a physician to the wounds of any soul; a friend, knowing not only the secret of friendship, but almost worshipped by those few persons who resorted to him as their confessor and prophet, and knew the deep value of his mind and great heart. He thought that without religion or devotion of some kind nothing great was ever accomplished: and he thought that the bigoted sectarian had better bear this in mind.

His virtues, of course, sometimes ran into extremes. It was easy to trace to the inexorable demand on all for exact truth that austerity which made this willing hermit more solitary even than he wished. Himself of a perfect probity, he required not less of others. He had a disgust at crime, and no worldly success would cover it. He detected paltering as readily in dignified and prosperous persons as in beggars, and with equal scorn. Such dangerous frankness was in his dealing that his admirers called him "that terrible Thoreau," as if he spoke when silent, and was still present when he had departed. I think the severity of his ideal interfered to deprive him of a healthy sufficiency of human society.

The habit of a realist to find things the reverse of their appearance inclined him to put every statement in a paradox. A certain habit of antagonism defaced his earlier writings,—a trick of rhetoric not quite outgrown in his later, of substituting for the obvious word and thought its diametrical opposite. He praised wild mountains and winter forests for their domestic air, in snow and ice he would find sultriness, and commended the wilderness for resembling Rome and Paris. "It was so dry, that you might call it wet."

The tendency to magnify the moment, to read all the laws of Nature in the one object or one combination under your eye, is of course comic to those who do not share the philosopher's perception of identity. To him there was no such thing as size. The pond was a small ocean; the Atlantic, a large Walden Pond. He referred every minute fact to cosmical laws. Though he meant to be just, he seemed haunted by a certain chronic assumption that the science of the day pretended completeness, and he had just found out that the *savans* had neglected to discriminate a particular botanical variety, had failed to describe the seeds or count the sepals. "That is to say," we replied, "the blockheads were not born in Concord; but who said they were? It was their unspeakable misfortune to be born in London, or Paris, or Rome; but, poor fellows, they did what they could, considering that they never saw Bateman's Pond, or Nine-Acre Corner, or Becky-Stow's Swamp. Besides, what were you sent into the world for, but to add this observation?"

Had his genius been only contemplative, he had been fitted to his life, but with his energy and practical ability he seemed born for great enterprise and for command; and I so much regret the loss of his rare powers of action, that I cannot help counting it a fault in him that he had no ambition. Wanting this, instead of engineering for all America, he was the captain of a huckleberry-party. Pounding beans is good to the end of pounding empires one of these days; but if, at the end of years, it is still only beans!

But these foibles, real or apparent, were fast vanishing in the incessant growth of a spirit so robust and wise, and which effaced its defeats with new triumphs. His study of Nature was a perpetual ornament to him, and inspired his friends with curiosity to see the world through his eyes, and to hear his adventures. They possessed every kind of interest.

He had many elegances of his own, whilst he scoffed at conventional elegance. Thus, he could not bear to hear the sound of his own steps, the grit of gravel; and therefore never willingly walked in the road, but in the grass, on mountains and in woods. His senses were acute, and he remarked that by night every dwelling-house gives out bad air, like a slaughter-house. He liked the pure fragrance of melilot. He honored certain plants with special regard, and, over all, the pond-lily,—then, the gentian, and the *Mikania scandens*, and "life-everlasting," and a bass-tree which he visited every year when it bloomed, in the middle of July. He thought the scent a more oracular inquisition than the sight,—more oracular and trustworthy. The scent, of course, reveals what is concealed from the other senses. By it he detected earthiness. He delighted in echoes, and said they were almost the only kind of kindred voices that he heard. He loved Nature so well, was so happy in her solitude, that he became very jealous of cities, and the sad work which their refinements and artifices made with man and his dwelling. The axe was always destroying his forest. "Thank God," he said, "they cannot cut down the clouds!" "All kinds of figures are drawn on the blue ground with this fibrous white paint."

I subjoin a few sentences taken from his unpublished manuscripts, not only as records of his thought and feeling, but for their power of description and literary excellence.

"Some circumstantial evidence is very strong, as when you find a trout in the milk."

"The chub is a soft fish, and tastes like boiled brown paper salted."

"The youth gets together his materials to build a bridge to the moon, or, perchance, a palace or temple on the earth, and at length the middle-aged man concludes to build a wood-shed with them."

"The locust z–ing."

"Devil's-needles zigzagging along the Nut-Meadow brook."

"Sugar is not so sweet to the palate as sound to the healthy ear."

"I put on some hemlock-boughs, and the rich salt crackling of their leaves was like mustard to the ear, the crackling of uncountable regiments. Dead trees love the fire."

"The bluebird carries the sky on his back."

"The tanager flies through the green foliage as if it would ignite the leaves."

"If I wish for a horse-hair for my compass-sight, I must go to the stable; but the hair-bird, with her sharp eyes, goes to the road."

"Immortal water, alive even to the superficies."

"Fire is the most tolerable third party."

"Nature made ferns for pure leaves, to show what she could do in that line."

"No tree has so fair a bole and so handsome an instep as the beech."

"How did these beautiful rainbow-tints get into the shell of the fresh-water clam, buried in the mud at the bottom of our dark river?"

"Hard are the times when the infant's shoes are second-foot."

"We are strictly confined to our men to whom we give liberty."

"Nothing is so much to be feared as fear. Atheism may comparatively be popular with God himself."

"Of what significance the things you can forget? A little thought is sexton to all the world."

"How can we expect a harvest of thought who have not had a seed-time of character?"

"Only he can be trusted with gifts who can present a face of bronze to expectations."

"I ask to be melted. You can only ask of the metals that they be tender to the fire that melts them. To nought else can they be tender."

There is a flower known to botanists, one of the same genus with our summer plant called "Life-Everlasting," a *Gnaphalium* like that, which grows on the most inaccessible cliffs of the Tyrolese mountains, where the chamois dare hardly venture, and which the hunter, tempted by its beauty, and by his love, (for it is immensely valued by the Swiss maidens,) climbs the cliffs to gather, and is sometimes found dead at the foot, with the flower in his hand. It is called by botanists the *Gnaphalium leontopodium*, but by the Swiss *Edelweisse*, which signifies *Noble Purity*. Thoreau seemed to me living in the hope to gather this plant, which belonged to him of right. The scale on which his studies proceeded was so large as to require longevity, and we were the less prepared for his sudden disappearance. The country knows not yet, or in the least part, how great a son it has lost. It seems an injury that he should leave in the midst his broken task, which none else can finish,—a kind of indignity to so noble a soul, that it should depart out of Nature before yet he has been really shown to his peers for what he is. But he, at least, is content. His soul was made for the noblest society; he had in a short life exhausted the capabilities of this world; wherever there is knowledge, wherever there is virtue, wherever there is beauty, he will find a home.

QUESTIONS FOR STUDY AND DISCUSSION

1. "I love Henry," Emerson reports a friend of Thoreau as saying, "but I cannot like him." What is the meaning of this distinction? What qualities in Thoreau made it hard to like him?

2. Emerson knew Thoreau well, and it is clear that he admired him. Yet his account of Thoreau is not entirely panegyrical. Is this a breach of friendship? See how many places in the essay you can find where Emerson finds fault or deems it necessary to "explain" a quality of mind or a form of characteristic behavior which is generally thought to be a fault. What effect do these "shadings" have on the over-all credibility of Emerson's portrait?

3. Does Thoreau's resolute determination to go against conventional expectations strike you as admirable, or the reverse?

4. Could Thoreau live his life in the same way today? Is his life a reasonable model for contemporary men?

5. Emerson remarks that "none knew better than he [Thoreau] that it is not the fact that imports, but the impression or effect of the fact on your mind. Every fact lay in glory in his mind, a type of the order and beauty of the whole." Can you explain this statement? What relation, if any, does it bear to the earlier statement, "there was an excellent wisdom in him . . . which showed him the material world as a means and symbol"?

6. "Nothing is so much to be feared as fear," is one of Thoreau's sayings. Are you familiar with another famous quotation much like it?

7. Make a list of Thoreau's "good qualities," as you see them, and another of the "bad." Weigh them, and try to make an estimate of your own about Thoreau the man.

8. What do you think of Thoreau's formula of choosing "to be rich by making his wants few, and supplying them himself"?

9. "We [Americans]," Thoreau thought, "have not to lay the foundations of our houses on the ashes of a former civilization." Does this statement, in context, signify a contempt for tradition? For history and its lessons?

WRITING ASSIGNMENTS

1. "Thoreau in the Modern World."

2. "Thoreau as Beatnik."

3. "The 'Unlikable' Thoreau."

4. "The Values of Unconventionality: Thoreau and the Bourgeoisie."

5. "Thoreau's Debt to Society—Paid or Owing?"

6. Emerson's essay provides you with a model for a thoughtful appraisal of someone you know well. Starting from a considered judgment of that person's character as a whole, in sum, develop an essay in which you point out both good and bad qualities, explaining, condoning, or condemning as you see fit. Flesh out your analysis with details, anecdotes.

The four essays in "The World of People" section together form a unit for study. The subjects of two of the essays are famous men whose temperaments are well worth comparing. The other essays are about people whose accomplishments are less notable, but whose personalities have a warmth that the "famous" seem to lack.

1. Are there any qualities which all of these people have in common?

2. Which of these people are most nearly alike? In what ways?

3. How are magnitude of achievement and personal attractiveness related?

4. Which of these people do you admire most? Why?

5. Which has, in your opinion, the most attractive personality?

6. Which would you most like to know personally?

7. What generalizations about character, greatness, and successful living can you now make?

People and Their Recreation

GENE TUNNEY

My Fights with Jack Dempsey

The laugh of the twenties was my confident insistence that I would defeat Jack Dempsey for the heavyweight championship of the world. To the boxing public, this optimistic belief was the funniest of jokes. To me, it was a reasonable statement of calculated probability, an opinion based on prize-ring logic.

The logic went back to a day in 1919, to a boat trip down the Rhine River. The first World War having ended in victory, the Army was sending a group of A.E.F. athletes to give exhibitions for doughboys in the occupation of the German Rhineland. I was light heavyweight champion of the A.E.F. Sailing past castles on the Rhine, I was talking with the Corporal in charge of the party. Corporal McReynolds was a peacetime sports writer at Joplin, Missouri, one of those Midwestern newspapermen who combined talent with a copious assortment of knowledge. He had a consummate understanding of boxing, and I was asking him a question of wide interest in the A.E.F. of those days.

We had been hearing about a new prizefight phenomenon in the United States, a battler burning up the ring back home. He was to meet Jess Willard for the heavyweight championship. His name was Jack Dempsey. None of us knew anything about him, his rise to the challenging position for the title had been so swift. What about him? What was he like? American soldiers were interested in prizefighting. I was more than most —an A.E.F. boxer with some idea of continuing with a ring career in civilian life.

The Corporal said yes, he knew Jack Dempsey. He had seen Dempsey box a number of times, had covered the bouts for his Midwestern newspaper. Dempsey's career had been largely in the West.

"Is he good?" I inquired.

"He's tops," responded Corporal McReynolds. "He'll murder Willard."

"What's he like?" I asked.

The Corporal's reply was vividly descriptive. It won't mean anything to most people nowadays, but at that time it was completely revealing to anyone who read the sports pages. McReynolds said: "He's a big Jack Dillon."

I knew about Jack Dillon, as who didn't thirty years ago? He was a middleweight whose tactics in the ring were destructive assault—fast, shifty, hard-hitting, weaving in with short, savage punches, a knocker-out, a killer. Dillon even looked like Dempsey, swarthy, beetle-browed, and grim—a formidable pair of Jacks.

I thought the revelation over for a moment, and recalled: "Jack Dillon was beaten by Mike Gibbons, wasn't he?"

"Yes," replied the Corporal. "I saw that

bout. Gibbons was too good a boxer. He was too fast. His defense was too good. Dillon couldn't lay a glove on him."

Mike Gibbons was the master boxer of his time, the height of defensive skill, a perfectionist in the art of sparring.

I said to the Corporal: "Well, maybe Jack Dempsey can be beaten by clever boxing."

His reply was reflective, thought out. "Yes," he said, "when Dempsey is beaten, a fast boxer with a good defense will do it."

This, coming from a brainy sports writer, who knew so much about the technique of the ring and who had studied the style of the new champion, aroused a breathless idea in me. My own ambition in the ring had always been skillful boxing, speed and defense—on the order of Mike Gibbons.

As a West Side kid fooling around with boxing gloves, I had been, for some reason of temperament, more interested in dodging a blow than in striking one. Fighting in preliminary bouts around New York, I had learned the value of skill in sparring. In A.E.F. boxing I had emphasized skill and defense—the more so as during this time I had hurt my hands. Previously I had been a hard hitter. Now, with damaged fists, I had more reason than ever to cultivate defensive sparring.

Sailing down the Rhine, I thought maybe I might be a big Mike Gibbons for the big Jack Dillon. It was my first inkling that someday I might defeat Jack Dempsey for the Heavyweight Championship of the World, which all assumed Jack was about to acquire.

This stuck in mind, and presently the time came when I was able to make some observation firsthand. I was one of the boxers on the card of that first Battle of the Century, the Dempsey-Carpentier fight. I was in the semifinal bout. This place of honor and profit was given to me strictly because of my service title. The ex-doughboys were the heroes of that postwar period, and the light heavyweight championship of the A.E.F. was great for publicity. I was ballyhooed as the "Fighting Marine."

Actually, I had no business in the bout of second importance on that occasion of the first Million Dollar Gate. I was an A.E.F. champ, but we service boxers knew well enough that our style of pugilism was a feeble amateur thing, compared with professional prizefighting in the United States. The best of us were mere former prelim fighters, as I was. There were mighty few prominent boxers in Pershing's A.E.F. In World War II you saw champs and near-champs in uniform, but the draft was not so stern in such matters during the war against the Kaiser's Germany.

In the semifinal bout of the Dempsey-Carpentier extravaganza, I, with my bad hands, fought poorly. Nobody there could have dreamed of me as a possible future conqueror of the devastating champ—least of all Jack himself, if he had taken any notice of the semifinal battlers. I won on a technical K.O. from my opponent, but that was only because he was so bad—Soldier Jones of Canada, who, like myself, was in the big show only because he too had an army title—the war covering a multitude of sins.

After the bout, clad in a bathrobe, I crouched at one corner of the ring, and watched the Manassa Mauler exchange blows with the Orchid Man of France. As prizering history records, the bout was utterly one-sided; the frail Carpentier was hopelessly overmatched. But it afforded a good look at the Dempsey style.

The Corporal on the boat sailing down the Rhine had been exact in his description of Dempsey. The Champ was, in every respect, a big Jack Dillon—with all the fury and destruction implied by that. No wonder they called him the Man Killer. But, studying intently, I saw enough to confirm the Corporal's estimate that when Dempsey was defeated it would be by a skillful defensive boxer, a big Mike Gibbons. Correct defense would foil the shattering Dempsey attack.

This estimate was confirmed again and again during subsequent opportunities. I attended Dempsey fights, and studied motion pictures of them. More and more I saw how accurate defense could baffle the Man Killer's assault. The culmination was the Shelby, Montana, meeting of Dempsey and Tom Gibbons, the heavyweight younger brother of Mike. Tom, like Mike, was a consummate boxer, and Dempsey couldn't knock him out. For the first time in his championship and near-championship career, the Man Killer failed to flatten an opponent. The public, which had considered Tom Gibbons an easy mark, was incredulous and thought there must have been something peculiar about it. For me there was nothing peculiar, just final proof that good boxing could thwart the murder in the Dempsey fists. There was a dramatic twist in the fact that the final proof was given by a brother of Mike Gibbons.

At the Dempsey-Carpentier fight, I had seen one other thing. Another angle flashed, as at a corner of the ring I watched and studied. Famous in those days was the single dramatic moment, the only moment when the Orchid Man seemed to have a chance. That was when, in the second round, Carpentier lashed out with a right-hand punch. He was renowned for his right, had knocked out English champions with it. He hit Dempsey high on the jaw with all his power.

I was in a position to see the punch clearly and note how Carpentier threw it. He drew back his right like a pitcher with a baseball. The punch was telegraphed all over the place. Yet it landed on a vulnerable spot. How anybody could be hit with a right launched like that was mystifying to one who understood boxing. Dempsey went back on his heels, jarred. Carpentier couldn't follow up, and in a moment Jack was again on the relentless job of wrecking the Orchid Man with body blows. But it was a vivid demonstration that the champion could be hit with a right.

Dempsey was no protective boxer. He couldn't do defensive sparring. He relied on a shifty style, his own kind of defense, and couldn't be hit just any way. His weakness was that he could be nailed with a straight right. Later on, I saw this confirmed in other Dempsey battles. It was dramatized sensationally at the Polo Grounds when the powerful but clumsy Firpo smashed him with a right at the very beginning of the first round, and later blasted Dempsey out of the ring with right-hand punches—the Wild Bull of

the Pampas almost winning the championship.

To me it signified that the strategy of defensive boxing might be supplemented by a right-hand punch—everything thrown into a right. It would never do for me to start mixing with the Champ in any knockdown, drag-out exchange of haymakers. He'd knock me out. It would have to be a surprise blow, and it could easily be that. Both Carpentier and Firpo, who had nailed the Champ, were noted for their right—all they had. But Jack would never suspect a Sunday punch from me, stepping in and trying to knock him out with a right.

I was catalogued not only as a defensive boxer but also as a light hitter, no punch. I might wear an opponent down and cut him to pieces, but I couldn't put him to sleep with a knockout slam. That had been true —previously. I had been going along with the handicap of bad hands. I could hit hard enough, but didn't dare for fear of breaking my hands. So I was a comparatively light hitter—and typed as one.

Finally, in desperation, I had to do something about my fragile hands. I went to a lumber camp in Canada for one winter and worked as a woodsman, chopping down trees. The grip of the ax was exercise for my damaged mitts. Months of lumber camp wood chopping and other hand exercises worked a cure. My hands grew strong and hard, my fists rugged enough to take the impact of as powerful a blow as I could land. In subsequent bouts I had little trouble with my hands. This I knew, and others might have been aware of the change, but I was tagged as a feather duster puncher— and that was that. The old philosophy of giving a dog a bad name.

Prizefight publicity often resorts to the ballyhoo of a secret punch, a surprise blow, nearly always a fraud—but I really had the chance. At the beginning of the first round I would step in and put everything I had in a right-hand punch, every ounce of strength. I might score a knockout, or the blow would daze the champion sufficiently to make it easier to outbox him the rest of the way.

I was, meanwhile, fighting my way to the position of challenger. I won the light heavyweight championship from Battling Levinsky and subsequently fought Carpentier, the Orchid Man, and went through a series of savage bouts with Harry Greb, one of the greatest of pugilists. In our first bout, Greb gave me a murderous mauling. In our last, I beat him almost as badly. After a long series of matches with sundry light heavies and heavies I went on to establish myself as heavyweight contender by defeating Tom Gibbons. It was dramatic irony that I earned my shot at the title at the expense of Tom, brother of my model, Mike.

Public opinion of my prospects with Dempsey was loud and summary. The champion is always the favorite, and Dempsey was one of the greatest champions, as destructive a hitter as the prize ring has ever known. He was considered unbeatable, and I was rated as a victim peculiarly doomed to obliteration, pathetic, absurd.

It was argued that I was a synthetic fighter. That was true. As a kid prelim battler, my interest had been in romantic competition and love of boxing, while holding a job as a shipping clerk with a steamship company. As a marine in France, my love of boxing and a distaste for irksome military duties after the armistice brought me back as a competitor in A.E.F. boxing tournaments. We gave our best to entertain our buddies and, incidentally, to avoid guard duty. After the war, when I had grown up, my purpose simply was to develop the sparring ability I had as a means of making money—seeing in the heavyweight championship a proud and profitable eminence.

They said I lacked the killer instinct—which was also true. I found no joy in knocking people unconscious or battering their faces. The lust for battle and massacre was missing. I had a notion that the killer instinct was really founded in fear, that the killer of the ring raged with ruthless brutality because deep down he was afraid.

Synthetic fighter, not a killer! There was a kind of angry resentment in the accusation. People might have reasoned that, to have arrived at the position of challenger, I must have won some fights. They might have noted that, while the champion had

failed to flatten Tom Gibbons, I had knocked him out. But then the Dempsey-Gibbons bout was ignored as rather mystifying, one of "those things."

The prizefight "experts" were almost unanimous in not giving me a chance. The sports writers ground out endless descriptions of the doleful things that would happen to me in the ring with Dempsey. There were, so far as I know, only a few persons prominent in sports who thought I might win, and said so. One was Bernard Gimbel, of the famous mercantile family, a formidable amateur boxer and a student of ring strategy. The others included that prince of sports writers, the late W. O. McGeehan, and a few lesser lights in the sports-writing profession. They picked me to win, and were ridiculed. The consensus of the experts was echoed by the public, though with genuine sadness on the part of some.

Suspicion of a hoax started following a visit by a newspaperman to my training camp at Speculator, New York. Associated Press reporter Brian Bell came for an interview. He noticed a book lying on the table next to my bed. Books were unexpected equipment in a prizefight training camp. He was curious and took a look at the volume— *The Way of All Flesh*. That surprised him. The Samuel Butler opus was, at that time, new in its belated fame, having been hugely praised by George Bernard Shaw as a neglected masterpiece. It was hardly the thing you'd expect a prizefighter to be reading, especially while training for a bout with Jack Dempsey.

Brian Bell knew a story when he saw one. He later became one of the chief editors of the Associated Press. Instead of talking fight, he queried me about books. I told him I liked to read Shakespeare. That was the gag. That was the pay-off. The A.P. flashed the story far and wide—the challenger, training for Jack Dempsey, read books, literature —Shakespeare. It was a sensation. The Shakespeare-Tunney legend was born.

The story behind it all went back to a day in 1917 when a young marine named Gene Tunney was getting ready to embark with his company bound for the war in France. We were stowing things in our kits, when I happened to glance at the fellow next to me. I noticed that among the belongings he was packing were two books. That surprised me.

In the marines you kept the stuff you took to the minimum. You carried your possessions on your back in the long marches favored by the Marine Corps. Every ounce would feel like a ton. Yet here was a leatherneck stowing away two books to add to his burden. I was so curious that I sneaked a look at the two books and saw—Shakespeare. One was *Julius Caesar*, the other, *A Winter's Tale*. He must be a real professor, I thought.

The leatherneck in question was the company clerk. I had known him when in recruit camp—a young lawyer in civilian life, quiet and intelligent. Now, my respect for him went up many notches. He must be educated indeed to be taking two volumes of Shakespeare to carry on his back on the long marches we would have in France.

We sailed in the usual transport style, piled in bunks in a stuffy hold. The weather was rough, and virtually the whole division of marines became seasick. The few good sailors poked unmerciful fun at their seasick comrades. I happened to be one of the fortunate, and joined in the ridicule of the miserable sufferers.

Sickest of all was the company clerk. He writhed in misery. He would lie on deck all day, an object of groaning filth. At night he was equally disgusting in his bunk. This was the tier next to mine, and I saw more of him than most. The high respect I had formed for him went down those many notches. He might be educated, he might take Shakespeare to war with him, but he was a mess at sea.

We put in at Brest, and promptly the order came—prepare to march. We were to put on a show at the dock for inspection by the brass hats. I started to get ready, and then came the appalling discovery. I couldn't find the tunic of my uniform. I knew I had stowed it in my kit, but it was gone. I hunted everywhere. In the Marine Corps it

was practically a capital offense for a leatherneck to be without an article of issue, and here I was without my tunic for the long march upon arrival in France.

I heard a marine asking: "Whose is this?" He was on a cleaning job, and was holding up a disreputable object that he had fished from under the bunks. "Somebody's blouse," he announced with a tone of disgust, "and look at it."

I did—it was my blouse, a mess of seasick filth.

The explanation was easy to guess. The company clerk in the tier of bunks next to mine had done it. Having befouled all of his clothes, he had, in his dumb misery, reached into my bunk and taken my blouse. He had worn it until it was too filthy to wear—after which he had chucked it under the bunks.

There was nothing I could do. There was no time to get the blouse cleaned, and there was no use blaming it on the company clerk. It was strictly up to me to have possession of every article of issue in good shape. I could only inform our company commander that I didn't have my tunic—and take the penalty, extra guard duty and kitchen police.

When, ashore, the company clerk came out of his seasickness and realized what had happened, he was duly remorseful. He was a decent fellow, his only real offense having been seasickness. He told me how sorry he was, and asked what he could do to make up for the trouble he had got me into. What could he give me? That was the way things were requited among the marines— handing something over to make up for something. What did he have that I might want? He hadn't anything I could take, except those two books. I told him, "Give me one of them and call things square." He did. He retained *Julius Caesar* and gave me *A Winter's Tale*. He knew what he was about, as anyone who knows Shakespeare will attest.

Having the book, I tried to read it but couldn't make any sense of it. I kept on trying. I always had a stubborn streak, and figured the book must mean something. But it didn't, so far as I could make out. I went to the company clerk. He had given me the book, and it might mean something to him. It did, and he proceeded to explain.

He coached me, led me through *A Winter's Tale*, which turned out to be interesting. That was practically my introduction to Shakespeare—the hard way. After training on *A Winter's Tale*, I read such works as *Hamlet, Macbeth, Othello*, with ease.

I had always liked reading—and this had a practical side. I found that books helped in training for boxing bouts. One of the difficulties of the prizefight game is that of relieving tension in training camp, getting one's mind off the fight. The usual training camp devices were jazz phonograph records and the game of pinochle. I didn't like jazz, and the mysteries of pinochle were too deep for me. So I resorted to reading as a way to ease the dangerous mental strain during training. I found that books were something in which I could lose myself and get my mind off the future fight—like *The Way of All Flesh*, which Brian Bell of the Associated Press found me reading while training for Dempsey.

Hitherto, as just another prizefighter, my personal and training camp habits had been of little news interest, and nobody had bothered to find out whether I read books or not. Now, as the challenger for the heavyweight title, I was in a glare of publicity, and the disclosure that I read books, literature, Shakespeare, was a headline. The exquisite twist was when one of Dempsey's principal camp followers saw the newspaper story. He hurried to Jack with a roar of mirth. "It's in the bag, Champ. The so-and-so is up there reading a book!"

The yarn grew with the telling—training for Dempsey on Shakespeare. It simplified itself down to the standing joke—Tunney, the great Shakespearean. This put the finishing touch to the laugh over my prospects in the ring with Dempsey.

It made me angry and resentful. I was an earnest young man with a proper amount of professional pride. The ridicule hurt. It might have injured my chances. To be consigned so unanimously to certain and abject defeat might have been intimidating, might

have impaired confidence. What saved me from that was my stubborn belief in the correctness of my logic. The laugh, in fact, helped to defeat itself and bring about the very thing that it ridiculed. It could only tend to make the champion overconfident.

For a boxer there's nothing more dangerous than to underestimate an opponent. Jack Dempsey was not one to underestimate. It was not his habit of mind to belittle an antagonist. He was far too intelligent for that. In fact, Jack rather tended to underestimate himself. With all his superb abilities in the ring, he was never arrogant or cocky, never too sure of himself. But not even Jack Dempsey could escape the influence of opinion so overwhelming, such mockery as "It's in the bag, Champ. The so-and-so is up there reading a book." That could help my strategy of a surprise blow to knock him out or daze him for the rest of the fight.

When we finally got into the ring at Philadelphia things went so much according to plan that they were almost unexciting to me. During the first minute of sparring, I feinted Dempsey a couple of times, and then lashed out with the right-hand punch, the hardest blow I ever deliberately struck. It failed to knock him out. Jack was tough, a hard man to flatten. His fighting style was such that it was difficult to tag him on the jaw. He fought in a crouch, with his chin tucked down behind his left shoulder. I hit him high, on the cheek. He was shaken, dazed. His strength, speed, and accuracy were reduced. Thereafter it was a methodical matter of outboxing him, foiling his rushes, piling up points, clipping him with repeated, damaging blows, correct sparring.

There was an element of the unexpected —rain. It drizzled and showered intermittently throughout the fight. The ring was wet and slippery, the footing insecure. That was bad for a boxer like me, who depended on speed and sureness of foot for maneuvering. One false step with Jack Dempsey might bring oblivion. On the other hand, the slippery ring also worked to the disadvantage of the champion. A hitter needs secure footing from which to drive his punches, and any small uncertainty under-foot may rob him of his power. So the rain was an even thing except that it might have the therapeutic value of a shower for a dazed man, and Dempsey was somewhat dazed during the ten rounds. Jack was battered and worn out at the end, and I might have knocked him out if the bout had gone a few rounds more. The decision was automatic, and I was heavyweight champion of the world.

The real argument of the decade grew out of my second bout with Dempsey, at Chicago, the following year—the "long count" controversy. It produced endless talk, sense and nonsense, logic and illogic. To this day in any barroom you can work up a wrangle on the subject of the long count. How long was Tunney on the floor after Dempsey knocked him down? Could he have got up if the count had been normal?

To me the mystery has always been how Dempsey contrived to hit me as he did. In a swirl of action, a wild mix-up with things happening fast, Jack might have nailed the most perfect boxer that ever blocked or side-stepped a punch, he was that swift and accurate a hitter. But what happened to me did not occur in any dizzy confusion of fly-ing fists. In an ordinary exchange Dempsey simply stepped in and hit me with a left hook.

It was in the seventh round. I had been outboxing Jack all the way. He hadn't hurt me, hadn't hit me with any effect. I wasn't dazed or tired. I was sparring in my best form, when he lashed out.

For a boxer of any skill to be hit with a left swing in a commonplace maneuver of sparring is sheer disgrace. It was Dempsey's most effective blow, the one thing you'd watch for—you'd better, for the Dempsey left, as prize-ring history relates, was murder. I knew how to evade it, side-step or jab him with a left and beat him to the punch. I had been doing that all along.

I didn't see the left coming. So far as I was concerned, it came out of nowhere. That embarrassed me more than anything else—not to mention the damage done. It was a blow to pride as well as to the jaw. I was vain of my eyesight. My vision in the ring was always excellent. I used to think I could see a punch coming almost before it started. If there was anything I could rely on, it was my sharpness of eye—and I utterly failed to see that left swing.

The only explanation I have ever been able to think of is that in a training bout I had sustained an injury to my right eye. A sparring partner had poked me in the eye with thumb extended. I was rendered com-pletely blind for an instant, and after some medical treatment was left with astigmatism which could easily have caused a blind spot, creating an area in which there was no vi-sion. Our relative position, when Dempsey hit me, must have been such that the left swing came up into the blind spot, and I never saw it.

With all his accuracy and power Dempsey hit me flush on the jaw, the button. I was knocked dizzy. Whereupon he closed for the kill, and that meant fighting fury at its most destructive. When Dempsey came in for a knockout he came with all his speed and power. I didn't know then how many times he slugged me. I had to look at the motion pictures the next day to find out. There were seven crashing blows, Dempsey battering me with left and right as I fell against the ropes, collapsing to a sittting position on the canvas.

Of what ensued during the next few sec-onds, I knew nothing. I was oblivious of the most debated incident of the long count and had to be told later on what happened.

The story went back to the Dempsey-Firpo fight, to that wild first round during which Firpo hit the floor in one knock-down after another. This was in New York, where the rule was that a boxer scoring a knock-down must go to a neutral corner and remain there until the referee had com-pleted the count. In the ring with the Wild Bull of the Pampas, Dempsey undoubtedly through excitement of battle violated that rule, as the motion pictures showed clearly afterward.

Jack confesses he remembers nothing that took place during that entire fight. Firpo landed a terrific first blow. Dempsey, after suffering a first-blow knock-down, apparently jumped up to the fray by sheer professional instinct—the fighting heart of a true champion. Instead of going to a corner, Jack would stand over Firpo and slug him as he got up. After one knock-down, Jack stepped over his prostrate opponent to the other side, to get a better shot at him—the referee was in the way. After another knock-down, Dempsey slugged Firpo before the South American had got his hands off the floor, when he was still technically down. The Champ might well have been disqualified for that—not to mention the fact that he was pushed back into the ring when Firpo battered him out. The referee, however, in his confusion permitted all the violations.

The Dempsey-Firpo brawl aroused a storm of protest and brought about a determination that in the future Dempsey should be kept strictly to the rules. In our Chicago bout the regulation applied—go to a neutral corner upon scoring a knock-down. The referee had been especially instructed to enforce this. He was told that, in case of a knock-down, he was not to begin a count until the boxer who had scored the knock-down had gone to a neutral corner.

This was the reason for the long count. Dempsey, having battered me to the canvas, stood over me to hit me the moment I got up—if I did get up. The referee ordered him to a neutral corner. He didn't go. The referee, in accordance with instructions, refrained from giving count until he did go. That imposed on Jack a penalty of four seconds. It was that long before he went to the corner and the referee began the count.

When I regained full consciousness, the count was at two. I knew nothing of what had gone on, was only aware that the referee was counting two over me. What a surprise! I had eight seconds in which to get up. My head was clear. I had trained hard and well, as I always did, and had that invaluable asset—condition. In the proverbial pink, I recovered quickly from the shock of the battering I had taken. I thought—what now? I'd take the full count, of course. Nobody but a fool fails to do that. I felt all right, and had no doubt about being able to get up. The question was what to do when I was back on my feet.

I never had been knocked down before. In all the ring battles and training bouts I had engaged in, I had never previously been on the canvas. But I had always thought about the possibility, and had always planned before each bout what to do if I were knocked down, what strategy to use upon getting up. That depended on the kind of opponent.

I had thought the question out carefully in the case of Jack Dempsey. If he were to knock me down, he would, when I got up, rush me to apply the finisher. He would be swift and headlong about it. Should I try to clinch and thus gain some seconds of breathing space? That's familiar strategy for a boxer after a knock-down. Often it's the correct strategy—but not against Dempsey, I figured. He hit too hard and fast with short punches for it to be at all safe to close for a clinch. He might knock me out.

Another possibility was to get set and hit him as he rushed. That can be effective against a fighter who, having scored a knock-down, comes tearing in wide open, a mark for a heavy blow. If you are strong upon getting to your feet, you can sometimes turn the tables by throwing everything into a punch. Bob Fitzsimmons often did it. But that wouldn't do against Dempsey, I reckoned. He was too tough and hit too hard. He would welcome a slugging match. After having been knocked down, I might not be in any shape to take the risk of stepping in and hitting him.

For my second bout with Dempsey the plan that I decided upon, in case I was knocked down, was based on the thing I had learned about Jack. Word from his training camp had indicated that his legs were none too good. I had learned that his trainers had been giving him special exercises for footwork, because he had slowed down in the legs. That was the cue—match my legs against his, keep away from him, depend on speed of foot, let him chase me until I was sure I had recovered completely from the knock-down.

The plan would work if my own legs were in good shape, after the battering I had taken. That was what I had to think about on the floor in Chicago. My legs felt all right. At the count of nine I got up. My legs felt strong and springy.

Jack came tearing in for the kill. I stepped away from him, moving to my left—circling away from his left hook. As I side-stepped swiftly, my legs had never been better. What I had heard about Dempsey's legs was true. As I circled away from him, he tried doggedly, desperately, to keep up with me—but he was slow. The strategy was okay—keep away from him until I was certain that all the effects of the knock-down had worn off. Once, in sheer desperation, Jack stopped in his tracks and growled at me to stand and fight.

I did—but later, when I knew that my strength, speed, and reflexes were completely normal. I started to close with him and hit him with the encyclopedia of boxing. Presently Dempsey's legs were so heavy that he couldn't move with any agility at all, and I was able to hit him virtually at will. He was almost helpless when the final bell rang—sticking it out with stubborn courage.

I have often been asked—could I have got up and carried on as I did without those extra four seconds of the long count? I don't know. I can only say that at the count of two I came to, and felt in good shape. I had eight seconds to go. Without the long count, I would have had four seconds to go. Could I, in that space of time, have got up? I'm quite sure that I could have. When I regained consciousness after the brief period of black-out, I felt that I could have jumped up immediately and matched my legs against Jack's, just as I did.

The long count controversy, with all the heated debate, produced a huge public demand for another Dempsey-Tunney fight, number three. Tex Rickard was eager to stage it. He knew, as everybody else did, that it would draw the biggest gate ever. The first Dempsey-Tunney fight grossed over a million seven hundred thousand; the second, over two million and a half. Rickard was sure a third would draw three million. I was willing, eager. I planned to retire after another championship bout, wanted to get all that I could out of it.

But Jack refused. He was afraid of going blind. The battering he had taken around the eyes in his two fights with me alarmed him. The very thing that kept him from being hit on the jaw, his style of holding his chin down behind his shoulder, caused punches to land high. He dreaded the horror that has befallen so many ring fighters and is the terror of them all—the damage that comes from too many punches around the eyes, blindness.

Jack Dempsey was a great fighter—possibly the greatest that ever entered a ring. Looking back objectively, one has to conclude that he was more valuable to the sport or "The Game" than any prizefighter of his time. Whether you consider it from his worth as a gladiator or from the point of view of the box office, he was tops. His name in his most glorious days was magic among his people, and today, twenty years after, the name Jack Dempsey is still magic. This tells a volume in itself. As one who has always had pride in his profession as well as his professional theories, and possessing a fair share of Celtic romanticism, I wish that we could have met when we were both at our unquestionable best. We could have decided many questions, to me the most important of which is whether "a good boxer can always lick a good fighter."

I still say yes.

QUESTIONS FOR STUDY AND DISCUSSION

1. What is the thesis of Gene Tunney's essay? If you find yourself in any doubt about the thesis, try to find the reasons for your confusion. Is this essay "about" one thing or several things?

2. It is never easy for a man to write about his own success without seeming egotistical. How well does Gene Tunney manage this problem?

3. Most readers know, before Mr. Tunney describes the fights, that he defeated Dempsey twice. If you knew this, was all suspense destroyed? If so, was the essay interesting for other reasons? If suspense remained, why

did it not fade? To what extent is the essay responsible, and to what extent are you responsible?

4. Can you reconstruct the logic which convinced Gene Tunney that he could beat Dempsey?

5. What image of himself as a fighter does Tunney create? Can you point to the places where parts of this image are put in place or reinforced?

6. Why does Mr. Tunney say that the marine who gave him *A Winter's Tale* instead of *Julius Caesar* "knew what he was about"?

7. What role does the retelling of the Shakespeare-reading-Tunney publicity play in the developing "image" of Tunney? What is Mr. Tunney's attitude—at least in this essay—toward his scholarly habits? Is this attitude stated? implied? both?

8. Why is the famous "long count" discussed so fully? What part does this discussion play in forming the Tunney "image"?

9. Notice how the narration breaks up chronological continuity. Is this dislocation accidental? If not, what purpose does it serve?

WRITING ASSIGNMENTS

1. Select some activity in which you excel (everyone excels in something, or thinks he does), and write an essay describing this excellence and analyzing the reasons why you have come to possess it.

2. No doubt you have more than once "won out" in a situation where you were not expected to. Recall such a circumstance, trying to determine why you were not expected to be victorious and why, in fact, the general consensus was quite wrong. Organize your essay about this experience with the purpose of demonstrating (a) the fallaciousness of "the world's" judgments or (b) the unapparent "logic" which controverted the world's judgment in your case.

3. To what basic needs does a particular sport appeal? Organize an essay which attempts to answer this question. You may feel it necessary to discuss the appeal of all sports, but concentrate on the particular satisfactions offered by one.

4. Athletes are traditionally "dumb." Mr. Tunney is a famous exception. What is your view regarding the intellectual capacities of the athletic type? Present your view in a paper.

5. Injuries, some of them serious or fatal, are not uncommon in sports, and the physical stress of competition often causes permanent bodily damage. Is this fact relevant to a discussion of the "morality" of public interest in athletic contests? Embody your views in an essay, limiting yourself to a consideration of this point.

6. Are such activities as bullfighting, cockfighting, old-time bear-baiting, and ancient gladiatorial combats really sports? What are the characteristics of a sport? Write an essay defining *sport* or *sports contest*.

JAMES THURBER

The Tree on the Diamond

My grandfather built the first house on Bryden Road nearly seventy years ago, and until recently a granite carriage stone bearing the carved legend "Fisher, 1884" marked the point of his bold pioneering east of Parsons Avenue. I don't know what became of the stone; perhaps it is buried somewhere in a city dump, the old iron hitching post festering nearby.

Commerce began to creep eastward in Columbus, Ohio, a long time ago, following the route of the Great Run the day the dam broke and obliterating the quiet landmarks of the carriage years. The last I heard, my grandfather's house had been cut up into apartments, and I find it hard to picture the rambling coolness of the old place quartered and confined. Group civilization has come to the corner of Parsons and Bryden Road, and I suppose the individual has taken on the gray color of the mass. But there were individuals about during the first decade of the century, each possessed of his own bright and separate values.

There was George Harvey, the odd-jobs man, who claimed to be eighty, might have been seventy, but worked like a man of fifty when he put his mind and back to it. George always wore a smile and a dark-blue shirt spangled with medals and ribbons that came from curio shops, state fairs, and the attic trunks of his various employers, but George said he had won them all in the Civil War. It seems that he had been a slave and that he had freed himself. Once I asked him, "How did you do that, George?," and he broke into his loud and easy laughter. " 'How did you do that, George?' the boy says!," as if the simple question had been a Johnsonian retort. Our uncertainty about George's age was increased by his fondness for birthdays. He had several a year. "Dis is

it! Dis is de real one!" he would tell us gleefully. He would knock on the front door of my grandfather's house on those festive days and say to whoever answered, "Ah want to see Mistah Fishah's bright face this fine mornin'!" The person who had gone to the door would call out, "It's George's birthday!," and from his study at the top of the stairs my grandfather would call back, "Give him a dime!" When George got the money, he would flash his great grin and cry, "Lawd bless de gentleman o' dis house!" When George's birthday fell in fair weather, and the walking was good, he collected lots of dimes, but he was a religious man and he sometimes punished himself for pagan thoughts or other errors of faith by decreeing an anniversary on a day of wind and rain or heavy snow. "Too bad you were born in January," my Uncle Kirt said to him once. "You won't collect many dimes on a day like this." George laughed and laughed and slapped his leg, as he did at whatever any gentleman said, and then he sobered suddenly. "Ah'm repentin' fo' mah sins, Mistah Kirt," he said, "Ah'm repentin' fo' mah sins."

When George died, he was laid to rest wearing all his medals. One of these, my uncle said, was a genuine decoration for valor, and another was the blue ribbon that had been awarded in 1905 at the Ohio State Fair for the best Rhode Island cock in the poultry exhibit.

Then, there was Charlie Potts, my grandfather's stableman, whose getup on his Sundays off was the envy of us boys. The dark-skinned Charlie had a high stack of black, curly hair, glossy with Macassar oil, or whatever they used in those days. He affected light suits, gay shirts, and flowered yellow ties; a bright bandanna bloomed in his breast pocket, and he swung a bamboo cane. He preferred to keep his Sunday destinations a secret. When we boys wanted to know where he was going, he had an invariable answer, accompanied by a mysterious wink: "If anybody should ask you, tell 'em I left you inquirin'." His room occupied a corner of the barn loft, and its walls were covered with colorful posters presenting scenes from plays of the period—"The Squaw Man,"

"Strongheart," "The Round Up," "The Great Divide," "The Call of the North," and "Arizona"—and photographs of Faversham, Robert Edeson, and Kyrle Bellew. When the automobile replaced the carriage, putting Charlie Potts out of a job, he took a trip to Europe on his savings. He called on us when he came back, to tell stories of what he kept calling the "rather peculiar circumstances" that attended his travels. In Charlie's idiom, the phrase fitted the commonplace as well as the extraordinary. It still does. He lives in a town in central Ohio now, and I phoned him when I was in Columbus a few years ago. "I haven't seen you for thirty years, Jim," Charlie said, "but I ran into your brother Bill, under rather peculiar circumstances, when I was spending a few weeks in Columbus recently." It turned out that he had run into Bill, as everybody runs into everybody else in Columbus, at the corner of Broad and High.

Nobody I knew in the Bryden Road days stands out quite so clearly for me as Frank James, organizer, manager, captain, and first baseman of the Blind Asylum team, and jealous overseer of the craziest baseball field in the history of the game.

Few of us middle-aged men who knew Frank James as youngsters forty years ago would have recognized him dressed for burial in his full and formal name, Benjamin Franklin James. The Columbus papers revealed that elegant secret in brief obituaries when he died, last spring, at the age of seventy-seven, in the house of a woman relative. They also acquainted us with the news that Frank was part Cherokee Indian. We should have suspected this from his singularly erect posture and his fine, springy step—he walked as if the ground under him were pneumatic—but kids in central Ohio accepted the brown-skinned man as a Negro and let it go at that. I count it a happy wonder that nobody resented, in those innocent years, his sharp-tongued command of a ball club on which every player except himself was a white man.

The catcher, a man named Lang, threw the ball like a bullet and he could take the fastest pitch of any hurler barehanded, and

he could have broken his captain in two, but he always obeyed orders docilely ("Bunt it, boy, bunt it! You heah me? *Bunt* it!") and the James insults never provoked him ("What kind o' playin' is that for a grown man, Lang? What kind o' playin' is that?").

The baseball team of the School for the Blind—we called it "the Blinky," in the easy and unmalicious parlance of the young —was made up of employees of the institution. I think Frank James was in charge of the boiler rooms, although the notices of his death credited him with having been an instructor.

Lang was an engineer, I believe, and the rest of the players came from the kitchen, the laundry, the stable, and other corners and corridors of the gloomy institution.

When my grandfather bought a Thomas Flyer, he put Maud, the family mare, out to pasture and tore down the brick barn behind the house, leaving a clear vista across the Blind Asylum grounds all the way to Main Street. The place was to become one of the landscapes of my nightmares. Its central structure was a massive crawl of dank stone. Even the architect whose dark genius for the ungainly had created the brooding monster must have realized that it needed a touch of light. He stuck a fountain in front of it, but it turned out to be a sullen cub of the mother building, an ugly cone of rock blubbering water from a length of pipe that jutted out of the top.

We neighborhood kids used to play around the fountain, but we rarely saw the blind children there. They seemed to be in class most of the time, and from my grandfather's house the institution often looked deserted. The shouting and laughing of the ball team behind the main building on Saturday afternoons in summer seemed out of place, like the sound of a child's voice calling down an old, abandoned well. We could hear occasional noises from the building— a tray falling, a sharp voice protesting, a melancholy hand running scales on a piano lost in the wilderness of stone.

The main building sent back two brown wings, or tentacles, which invaded Frank James' outfield, as if they wanted to crush the players and stop the game. The left tentacle crept up to within fifty feet of the second baseman, and the other swung behind the center fielder, forcing him to play in and cramping the range of his action. The blunt end of this wing was separated from the stables by thirty feet of paved courtyard, on which the left fielder had to stand, an easy victim of ricochetting balls, frightened horses, and stablemen with pitchforks. If these were the stony frustrations of a Freudian dream, the gigantic tree between first and second was a hazard out of Lewis Carroll. It had the patriarchal spread of Longfellow's chestnut, and it could drop leaves on the shortshop and, with its large and sinewy roots, trip up runners rounding first. Many a hard-hit ball that should have been good for extra bases would cling and linger in the thick foliage of that ancient tree, and drop finally into Frank James' glove, or the glove of his right fielder, who had plenty of time to jog in from his position on the concrete walk beside the left wing and wait for it to come down. Visiting players screamed and cursed, and now and then they would gather up their bats and gloves, stalk off the Dali diamond, and go home, while Frank James, his hands on his hips, exasperation in his eyes, his mouth open—he was always excited and breathing hard—demanded to know what the hell could possibly be the matter with the yellow-bellies. Sometimes the finicky enemy would quit in disgust, late in the game, after the James Boys had demonstrated a special and practiced skill in bouncing the ball off walls, losing it on roofs, hitting it into the crotch of the tree, or lining it under the lowest bough, so that it would land on the concrete pavement and roll to Parsons Avenue, a hundred and fifty yards away.

The miracle men of Parsons Avenue played the post-office team and the city firemen and police, as well as teams made up of employees of other state institutions, and beat them all most of the time. Panting heavily, his sharp, black eyes taking in every play and every player, Frank urged his men on as if each game were the seventh in a World Series. His tongue was never silent, and he always repeated his loud commands to batters at least once: "Lay it down easy, Steffie, lay it down easy!," or "Get me a double, boy, get me a double!," or "Hit it in the tree, keed, hit it in the tree!" It was the same when his team was in the field: "Close in! Close in!," or "Lay back! Lay back!," or "Watch the bunt, boys, watch the bunt!" If a hard-hit grounder took a bad bounce on the uneven terrain, struck one of his infielders on the chest, and bounced high in the air, Frank would scream, "Ovah ya, undah ya, wheah ah ya?" Human fallibility he could not abide. "What's the mattah, keed, can't ya see 'em?" he would bawl if a player muffed a hard chance, or "Use ya brains! Use ya brains!" It is a wonder that nobody ever took a swing at him with fist or bat. If his team was far ahead and sure to win against men confused by walls and branches, Frank's voice softened and his tone grew friendly. He would let his batters use their own judgment. "Your way's mine, Emil, your way's mine," he would say affectionately. Once this same Emil, in the midst of a tight game, stepped to the plate and said to his captain, "I'll get you a home run, Frank." Instead, he popped weakly to the shortstop. "Thanks for the home run, keed!" screamed Frank. "Thanks for the home run!" Nor did his temper and sarcasm wear off. Every time Emil walked to the plate after that, Frank shouted at the opposing outfielders, "Give him room, men, give him room!"

The James Boys lost few games—not more than four or five, I believe, in all the years they played. One reason for this was that Frank could seldom be lured onto the home grounds of any of his opponents. "The boys can't get away from the institution," he explained once to the manager of a club composed of employees of the State Asylum for the Insane. "If the crazy people want to play us, let the crazy people come ovah heah."

"They are not crazy people," snapped their manager.

"You bring 'em ovah heah an' we'll drive 'em crazy," Frank retorted.

The man stared at the outfield walls, and at the tree that made pop flies out of triples and base hits out of pop flies. "I have no doubt of that," he said testily, and went away.

When Frank James' team did drop a game, he revealed himself as the worst loser in the history of baseball, amateur or professional. He had no heart or philosophy for defeat. The best team had lost, and there was no justice in the world. His voice would grow husky from howling that his men should be inmates, not employees, of the School for the Blind, that they couldn't beat the Columbus School for Girls the best day they ever saw, that the whole team should give up baseball for checkers or lotto, that the Lord God had never seen a man so cruelly betrayed as Frank James. One Saturday afternoon, when I was sixteen, I heard Frank fiercely bawling out one of his pitchers for losing a game. "You threw your arm out in practice!" he roared. "I told you not to pitch more than a dozen balls before the game, but you threw your arm out." The man stared at him in astonishment. "That was five years ago, Frank," he said. "Are you still bellyachin' about that old game?" Baseball time stood still in Frank James' head and the sore of defeat never healed. Once he had a close call at the hands of a team organized by Mr. Harvey, proprietor of a drugstore on Main Street, near Parsons. The Harvey Boys were all young men of the neighborhood, familiar with the weird diamond and capable of hitting into or under the big tree. The Harveys led, 2–1, going into the eighth, and Frank heaped abuse on the head of the Harvey pitcher, a slender, quiet youngster named Billy Alloway, who had Emil and the others missing his curves and popping up his fast ones. He struck out Frank James twice, but the raging captain continued to berate his men for going down on strikes.

"Goddam it, Frank," said one of them finally, "he fanned *you* twice."

"That's 'cause you upset me," yelled Frank, "standin' up theah an' swingin' at nothin'!"

Frank went right on belaboring the impassive Alloway—"that little boy out theah" —with quip and insult. In the ninth inning, the James Boys clumsied two runs across with the help of the enormous tree and won the game. For the first time in his life, Frank James praised an opposing player. "You pitched a good game, Billy!" he shouted. "You pitched a good game!"

I supposed that shocked Nature has long since covered that crazy ball field with grass, and, no doubt, crickets sing where Frank James used to stand and shout his insults and commands. Frank would have played on into his sixties, but his eyesight began to fail thirty years ago. He had thought his legs would be the first to go, but we who had heard him bawl the summer afternoons away were sure it would be his lungs and larynx. One story has it that a broken steampipe in the boiler rooms caused an injury that gradually brought on blindness, but, however that may be, he stayed on the job as long as he could see to grope his way around.

Frank James was king of that crazy ball field, but even in his heyday he was not always the center of attention. Since the diamond was the only one for miles around, officials of the institution allowed the boys from nearby Douglas School to meet their rivals there on Saturday mornings—or in the afternoon, if the James club was idle or playing somewhere else. The Avondale Avenue team came from the West Side, bringing with it, around 1908, a youngster of destiny, its captain and center fielder, Billy Southworth, who was later signed by the New York Giants and is now, as everybody knows, manager of the Boston Braves. Hank Gowdy, hero of the 1914 World Series, must have played there, too, in his day, and oldtimers distinctly remember Billy Purtell, who went to Chicago fifty years ago to play third base for the White Sox.

In the autumn, the field was turned into a makeshift gridiron, with one goal post, and several famous football stars scrimmaged there as boys: Chic Harley, Ohio State's immortal halfback and three-time All-American; Allen Thurman, whose long, high, spiral punts helped the University of Virginia beat Yale, 10–0, in 1915; his younger brother Johnny, All-America tackle at the University of Pennsylvania in 1922; and the celebrated Raymond (Fike) Eichenlaub, plunging fullback of the Notre Dame team of Rockne and Dorais, which dazzled and smashed Army in 1913. I remember young Donald Ogden Stewart showing up one day in a brand-new football uniform and carrying a brand-new football; Bill Burnett, who was to write "Little Caesar;" Carl Randall, who went on to dance in the "Follies;" and now and then little Joel Sayre would toddle over from his home in Rich Street to watch the goings on. Long before their day and mine, George Bellows, from Monroe Avenue around the corner, practiced on the diamond —he later became, among other things, one of the best shortstops Ohio State ever had.

I like to think that the aged Frank James, nearing his lonely end, remembered and was remembered by these "keeds" of so long ago. Some of them he outlived, of course; most of the others left Columbus or moved away from the neighborhood, but at least one, Billy Alloway, was a constant visitor during Frank's last days at the School for the Blind. They would sit in Frank's small office, which held a desk and two chairs, and recall the battles of former years. "You know, Frank," Alloway told him one day, "you should have put chicken wire up in that tree." Benjamin Franklin James turned his head sharply in the direction of his guest. "Ah'm a sportsman, Billy," he said reproachfully, "an' a sportsman don't take unfair advantage."

QUESTIONS FOR STUDY AND DISCUSSION

1. Is "The Tree on the Diamond" really about sports? What else is it about?

2. What is the function of the first section—the anecdotes about George Harvey and Charlie Potts? Why does the focus shift, near the close of the essay, from Frank James to players on other teams that used the diamond?

3. You probably have read "profiles" of great sports figures, sketches in which their competitive spirit, their eccentricities, and some of their great moments were affectionately reported. Does the "profile" of Frank James resemble these accounts?

4. Why did James Thurber, one of America's great humorists, and the *New Yorker*, the not unsophisticated magazine in which "The Tree on the Diamond" first appeared, judge that reminiscences about little-known people who lived in Ohio a generation or two ago would be intrinsically interesting? Where does the interest lie? Did the essay affect you deeply in any way, or were you relatively indifferent?

5. Unless you are totally out of sympathy with the essay, you will have sensed its humor. Now try to analyze the humorous quality you have observed.

6. What is the difference between "the frustrations of a Freudian dream" (the wings and courtyard of the asylum) and "a hazard out of Lewis Carroll" (the tree on the diamond)? Why is the field a "Dali diamond"?

WRITING ASSIGNMENTS

1. Your own experience may provide you with interesting and perhaps humorous "reminiscences" of amateur sports. Below are a few possible topics:

"The Peculiarities of Sand-lot Baseball"
"My High School Coach"
"The Special Problems of Girls' Basketball"
"Tumbling for the Clumsy"
"Everyone Must Take Phys. Ed."

2. Have you ever known "characters" like George Harvey, Charlie Potts, or Frank James? Try to "bring to life" such a person, but be careful to determine your own point of view toward him and maintain it consistently.

3. Are you developing a nostalgic fondness for certain parts of your early life? Try to recapture the quality of pleasure you found in some outstanding feature of your "good old days."

American Education

ARTHUR NORMAN
and LEWIS SAWIN

What Johnny Don't Know

In the spring of 1956, not long before the nominating conventions and not long after Princess Margaret bowed to authority, we made up a list of 20 important and/or notorious persons from public life—past and present—and asked 359 college freshmen and sophomores at a large state university in the South where we taught to identify them, by way of testing the students' knowledge of history, the arts, and current affairs. Specifically, 143 of those tested were students in a course called 1B, which is the second semester of a three-semester course in English composition for freshmen; 132 were taken from 1C, the third semester of this same course; and the other 84 were from an introductory literature course. All of the students in all sections of these three courses were tested: the group as a whole was, insofar as one could determine, quite "average"—at least for a state university whose admission requirements can be met merely by graduation from an accredited high school. Geographically, they came from many parts of the country (there was a noticeable admixture of "Yankees"), though the largest number naturally were from the state in which the university is located.

The persons we asked the 359 students to identify were: Adlai Stevenson, Norman Thomas, Henry Wallace, Warren G. Harding, Mrs. Wallis W. Simpson, Captain Peter Townsend, Charles Wilson, Francisco Franco, Charles de Gaulle, John Dillinger, Fiorello La Guardia, Pablo Picasso, Giuseppe Verdi, Karl Marx, T. S. Eliot, Richard Wagner, Oliver Cromwell, Robert Frost, Richard Rodgers, and Leo Tolstoi. Names like Hitler, Stalin, Eisenhower, and Marilyn Monroe, who, we felt, were universally recognizable, we purposely omitted.

In most cases we expected the student to know no more than the nationality of each and the activity for which he was chiefly famous.

We assumed that every student would be able to identify half of the people we chose with some degree of exactness, but we were wrong. Though we graded liberally, fewer than *one-fourth* (22 percent) were able to do so. In fact only four of the twenty names were clearly identified by as many as half of the students. These were Stevenson (86 percent), John Dillinger (78 percent), Peter Townsend (66 percent), and (a poor fourth, the only "historical" figure, and really not in the same class as the other three in point of score) Karl Marx (50 percent). At the bottom of the list was Norman Thomas; only seven students (2 percent) knew who he is.

Between these extremes straggled the others in various degrees of non-recognition:

Wilson (45 percent), Harding (42 percent), Rodgers (37 percent), La Guardia (36 percent), Frost (35 percent), Franco (32 percent), de Gaulle (30 percent). None of the others received correct identifications from even one-fourth of the students. Most of the artists on the list fared very badly. Verdi, Picasso, and Wagner marched hand-in-hand to oblivion with 22 percent each. There followed Cromwell (19 percent), Tolstoi and Mrs. Simpson, an interesting pair (17 percent), Wallace (14 percent), Eliot (6 percent), and Thomas (2 percent).

There were, of course, many ludicrous mistakes: Adlai Stevenson was identified by a total of 10 students as a Republican presidential aspirant. This might mean that one student in 36 at the freshman-sophomore level does not know the difference between a Republican and a Democrat. Or, perhaps, since some of the students knew that their families called themselves Democrats but favored Eisenhower, Ike then is a Democrat and Stevenson a Republican.

Other students identified Stevenson as a Senator from Wisconsin trying for the Democratic nomination; as a Democratic "former gov of Ohio—ran in last presedential election"; as a man who "ran for president time before last (presently runing for governor of NY)"; and as "The man from tenn with coonskin cap." Five other students called Stevenson a Senator. One student identified him as a "General of US Army," and another, not without a certain insight, as a "Plutocrat of the democratic party."

Norman Thomas seems to have been generally confused with Lowell Thomas, for he was identified as a news commentator by 34 students. Four thought he was a singer (John Charles Thomas?). He was also called a sports commentator, a poet, a labor leader, a "Notorious Pirate," a "Democratic politician," and a "world famous painter."

Three students identified Henry Wallace as an official of the CIO; one as an official of the AFL; one as head of both organizations. One said he was a Republican "seanator"; five others called him a Senator, party unspecified; two said he was the Secretary of State; one the Secretary of State under President Truman; four a former Secretary of State; one the Secretary of Health, Education, and Welfare. Other identifications ran the political spectrum: "Republican who was once a presidental nominee" (4—some spelling correctly); "republican chairman of some committee"; "high ranking politician of the republican party"; "former Political leader in the Republican Party"; author of *One World*; English statesman; "German leader in World War II"; and "married . . . Duke of Wales."

Even more astonishing than these complete misidentifications are the answers of those students who *have* heard something about Wallace but not enough to know what he stood for politically. He "once ran for president on non partician ticket"; he "ran for President on Probation Ticket"; he is an ex-president of the United States or a "Past president with subversive affiliations?"; he "ran for president with truman, he was a communist." Eight students called him a past presidential candidate on the Socialist ticket. Other comments: communist (two students); Communist party presidential candidate (two students); "a communist and Vice-Pres. of the US"; and "I somehow associate his name with Communism."

It is gratifying that 40 percent and more of our students could recognize the name of one of the Presidents of the United States. From those who had trouble identifying Warren G. Harding came responses such as: "President during the bombing of Pearl Harbor"; "assinated President of US"; "President impeached." Two called Harding a news commentator, four a labor leader, three a military figure, nine a US Senator; he was called an FBI agent or counterspy (David Harding, Counterspy?) by four, and head of the FBI by one. One soul stated that he ran for President on the Progressive Party ticket. From confusion with Earl Warren he was called variously the "Former governor of Calif. also Chief Justice," a former Chief Justice, and so on. Other comments were: "Popular character on true dective mysteries"; "head of department of treasury agents" (David Harding again); "great aviator"; and "communist."

Mrs. Wallis W. Simpson was identifed as a cabinet member by seven (twice as Secretary of the Treasury, five times as Secretary of "Health & Welfare"—Mrs. Hobby please note). By others she was called the "first lady in Congress"; a US Senator (3); a woman ambassador or diplomat (4); and an "american good will ambassador" (attention Mrs. Mesta). She was also misidentified as the head of the SPCA; as "an adultress of renown fame"; "wife of former Mayor of New York"; "governess of the Royal Children"; and as someone "recently on trial for fraud." Others called her the wife of the Duke of Edinburgh; "Wife of the ex-George ? of England"; "married the ex-king of England (George IV)"; and "wife of man having something to do with government." Full credit was given to the student who wrote that "By marrying her Edward was forced to advocate."

Capt. Peter Townsend, best known of the twenty personalities after Stevenson and Dillinger, was identified by one student as "Queen Elizabeth's old bow." Others, spelling more correctly, called him Queen Elizabeth's sweetheart, beau, fiance, or lover (10); Elizabeth's sweetheart (5); or Princess Elizabeth's sweetheart (9). One claimed that he had "married princess Margaret"; one that he was "in love with Princess Margaret, heir-apparent to the throne of England"; and one that he was "Princess Margaretts sweetheart —marriage not permitted between the two by the Pope." Seven students identified Townsend as the heroic captain of a ship that sank (Curt Carlsen of the *Flying Enterprise?*), and another five mentioned him in connection with the Townshend Acts ("ruler of England at one time and taxed the colonies & it was called Townsend Act"). By various others he was called a "soldier— early Am. History"; a "character of some story"; the "Main character in the novel, *The Secret Road.* Lived during time of Civil War"; a "Southern General during Civil War"; a "Famous American Captain in Korean War"; a "Communist prisoner"; one of the "red turn coats"; and a "traitor to country."

Eleven students identified Charles Wilson as the Secretary of State and one as the ex-Secretary of State. Others thought he was the Secretary of Labor or an official in that department (6); a labor leader (4); the Secretary of War (3); the Secretary of the Army (3); an ex-Secretary of the Navy (1); "Sec. of War (or navy)" (1); Secretary of the Air Force (1); Secretary of the Treasury (3); "Secretary of the Treasurer" (1); and the Secretary of Commerce (1). Two called him a leader in the AFL; two others made him an official in the Department of Agriculture. Two said that he was a former President of the United States; and by various other students he was identified as a critic, an ex-Secretary of Defense, "a admiral," a Supreme Court Justice, and the brother of Woodrow Wilson.

Francisco Franco got off light. Only two students associated him with Franco-American spaghetti. Others called him the Dictator of Italy (4), an Italian leader (1), the President of Mexico (1), a Mexican bullfighter (1), the king or emperor of Spain (3), a Spanish Communist leader (2), and a "Former Ruler of Spain—member of Big 4 powers" (1). Most interesting of all, perhaps, was the comment that he "started a revolution in Spain that broke the hold of the Turks."

Apart from the five students who thought Dillinger was a "TV wizard" or mindreader (Dunninger?) the three who claimed that he invented a gun (Derringer?), the three who thought that he was "a great figure of old west," the several who called him a politician, and a scattering who said he was a writer, a fighter, a "movie actor of earlier years," or the "Davy Crocket fad starter" (Disney?), students were commendably clear about Dillinger's identity. To some, however, it will be a reflection upon the students' sense of values that 38 described Dillinger as a "famous" criminal. Other comments included "ex-criminal of some fame"; "noted outlaw"; "leading gangster"; "a great gangster"; "One of greatest crimmial of our time"; "A great crook"; "noted criminal" (2); "a notorious bandit whom is deceased"; "fictitious gangster & murder"; "one of the american greatest gangsters"; "one of the greatest of all crimincels"; "brilliant" criminal; "highly renowned criminal"; "past renowned underworld character"; and "fearless gangster."

Fiorello La Guardia, known to about a third of the students, suffered only slight misidentification. Eleven students thought he had been a governor of New York. A number knew him only as someone ("famed flier"—2) with an airport named in his honor. Three claimed he was an ex-mayor of New York City who is now Ambassador to Mexico. Two thought he was an Italian politician, and one each called him a violinist, a boxer, an Italian sculptor, a French writer, a South American writer, a native of "Venezuella," an American general, and the "wife of past governor of New York."

One student each thought that Picasso was the President of Italy, the Dictator of Italy, or an Italian leader. Two called him a Mexican artist, and one each suggested that he was a Mexican bullfighter, the Mexican Ambassador, a fighter from Mexico, a Mexican leader, or simply a Mexican. Others (one each) would have him a bank robber, a violinist, a "Famous European Fashioner of clothes," a writer, the ruler of Portugal, a composer, an athlete, or a "discoverer of the New world." Among those who recognized him as an artist, six listed him as an Italian; others as a "Painter way, way back"; or an "Italian artist during Renaissance"; or as a "famous artist whose paintings have lasted until today."

Verdi, known to only a fifth of the students, was called "phylossopher," conductor, "Italian humorist and playright," Spanish politician, scientist, and French actress. One student claimed that he "killed a little girl who later became a saint."

While Karl Marx is known, more or less, to half the students, a surprising number have only the remotest idea as to who he was and what he did. Twelve thought or pretended to think that he was one of the Marx brothers; others that he was a "TV Actor with Sid Cesaer"; someone connected with the "$64,000 Question—master of seremonies"; or a "TV announcer—$64,000,000 Question" (Hal March?). Among those who called him a German, one identified him as

the "German Dictator before Hitler"; an Emperor of Germany; and as the "Nazi author of Mein Kampf—dead." One stated that "his theory was the 'survival of the fittest' "; while another credited him with the Malthusian theory of population growth and food supply. Of those who connected his name with Russia or Communism, four stated that Marx was a Czar of Russia, two that he was the Czar of Russia who had started Communism. Others wrote that he was a Communist ruler of Russia (2); a "Russia communist leader of a few years ago"; the "Russian Leader after revolution"; the "Learder of Maxium in Russia"; and a "Companion of Lennin in Revolution of Russia." Thirteen described him as a *Russian* Communist or Socialist, several others as a Russian philosopher, thinker, economist.

The most misidentified of the twenty names was that of T. S. Eliot. A great many students merely called him an author, an answer we did not count right because it lacked specificity. Readers may object that it is expecting too much of a college student to know the difference between an author and a poet. Perhaps so, but since twelve of our students called Eliot not only an author but a woman author (George Eliot, presumably), we feel that our distinction was more than justified. Still others called Eliot the author of *Leaves of Grass*, a "war correspondent—writer; died in battle"; a "huge financier"; and a news analyst. One student thought Eliot was really O. Henry.

A rather stunning total of forty-two students identified Richard Wagner as a movie star (by confusion, apparently, with Robert Wagner). Six called him a motion picture producer (Walter Wanger?), one a motion picture director, and one a "motion picture president." One thoroughly confused student labeled him a "musician also a moviestar." Six students thought Wagner was the mayor or former mayor of New York (Robert F. Wagner?). One each called him an author, a US Senator, an American outlaw, a baseball player, a commentator, an American millionaire, the Secretary of the Interior, and a "musician of the 17th century."

In a still greater confusion (conceivably

EXHIBITION IN FRESHMAN COMPOSITION[1]

Ruff, Ruff!

Three months before I graduated from high school, I arranged for an interview with my state representative. He had sent me a letter asking for an interview with me on my application for a scolarship to . . . . This scholarship ment a lot to me and the answer to my problem was the out-come of this interview.

It was a hot summer's afternoon, about three o'clock. He had asked me to come visit with him at his home thirty-two miles from my house. As I drove out to his farm, I kept getting a little more up-set and worried about the whole idea. To express matters plainly, I was scared. As I drove up the driveway three large dogs came running out to great me with a big "ruff! ruff!" Then as I got out of the car I saw a man sitting on the patio. It was the representative. I introduce myself, he in return. We sat down, talk about the dogs, the farm, and all about the other things you try to make-up when meeting a stranger. Finally he said, "Bob, you want a scolarship, don't you?" "Yes Sir," I answered quickly. "Well," he paused, "I've looked up your high-school reckored and you seem to be a pretty good boy; right, Bob?" "I try to be, sir!" I grasped. Then in a very serious tone of voice he said, "Son, I have decided to give you a four year scolarship to . . . . with all expensives paid. Now, is there anything else I can do for you?" I grended turn and twist for a few seconds, and answered, "That is more than I exspected in the first place, sir. You don't know how much this means to me. Let me thank you from the bottom of my heart." And then I departed with dogs trailing behind me as I left going "ruff! ruff!"

Seventeen

I was seventhen before I had my farst date Have big dreans of being a grate athlete women were not for me but in due time I Had changed my mind. I was in High School and eveary day at the end of school I wool live by the back way and one day as I was leving school I met this fine babe and I spoke to and she spoke back to me and thise Kaep up for a week ore so and then one day I asked Her to goe withe me the mext weekin withe me and she sad she wood.

I picked Her up about seven and we went to the show it was in the last part of school in june and she Had a summer sun dress on it Had a low nick line and she Had size 38 brass . . . , I am not much on talking but I could talk about Her all night doring the Hauld show I could not tack my eays off of Her after the show we went out and Had a few drinks and something to eat and dance for a while, My mother taught me How to dance and thise was the farst time I was Haulding a strange women in my armes and what a women I Held her close to me and the was brathing one my nick that was allmost draiveing out of my mind and eveary time I wood tray to Hold a conversaytion she woon just look into my eays and she sammed as she cannt Hear a thing I was saying, being a very bashful boy I Had to put a stop to this so I tauck Her Home and I never saw her agen.

[1] Two themes, admittedly "from the bottom of the barrel," submitted to our colleagues.

with Oliver Goldsmith), 76 students stated that Oliver Cromwell was a writer; four called him a poet. Along similar lines, two associated him with Dickens (Oliver Twist?), and others called him a fictional character; one listed him as "Fiction, in Walt Disney's comics." Still another student believed that he "wrote Gulliver's travels." Others thought he was an actor; an eighteenth century English jurist; a nineteenth century English politician; a radio commentator (2); a "legendary figure"; an English lord (2); a detective; a playwright; a "retired navel officer"; an American cartoonist; and an English civic leader of the eighteenth or nineteenth century. Two students thought him to be the founder of a colony in America, one that he was "Responsible for convicts being brought to Georgia" (Oglethorpe?). Six had him a British general at the time of the American Revolution (Cornwallis?). Some confusion is evident in the mind of the student who wrote: "Cromwell (English General) surrendered to Washington at Appomatox Court House at end of Revolution."

The name Richard Rodgers brought in the identification: "The name found on all good silver."

Comments on Tolstoi are indicative of what can be said of someone with a Russian name. He was called a composer, an orchestra conductor, a "former ruler of Russia."

Six students seemingly confused him with Trotsky: "Ex-Czar of Russia murdered in Mexico"; "Dead communist leader killed in Mexico"; "killed by Stalin." He was also called a baseball player and a physicist.

During the last part of the testing for this study, 77 of our students were asked to print the name of the President of the United States. Some students did not try; others wrote "Ike." Twenty-one who tried could not spell his name correctly.

LEWIS SAWIN and
ARTHUR NORMAN

What Johnny Needs to Know: After-Thoughts on Undergraduate Unpreparedness

Our earlier report on "What Johnny Don't Know" suggested that not all college freshmen are as well informed as some English teachers might like. We gave some amusing examples of undergraduate ignorance, and we let the evidence speak for itself. But what can be said beyond this? Is it possible to suggest who or what is to blame for the kind of intellectual unpreparedness which we described and to which a great many college teachers can testify?

A course in freshman composition usually employs a book of essays which in various ways refer to current or past history, and allude to persons and events in the world of today or yesterday. The text might include essays on George Lyman Kittredge, electric eels, and the need for opposition in a democracy; articles by Al Capp on comics or by Mencken on euphemisms in American English. But to most of the students we taught at the university where we made our survey, these matters were so much spinach; they seemed unable to understand or to find any interest in the materials offered. And this was not, so far as we could determine, because of the materials themselves or from any extraordinary stupidity in the students, but from a lack of academic preparation for college which resulted in a lack of awareness. For illustrative purposes only, let us quote from one of the papers written in a first-semester course in college English:

> It saturday morning and everyone lay-ing in bead sound asleep. Than all of a sudden I hear a noise in the back room It my aunt. She just remembered that her relation from texas are do in this saturday morning. She hurderly goes around wakeing everybody up. So that she can have her house in tip top shape. It a mad rush everybody runing back and forth getting thing in there proper place. They running into one another knocking thing down. Then all of a sudden one of her dauhter take a fly into the air. One of the rugs she was walking on came from under her feet. She knock her head aganist the wall. And she was out for a second. As thing began to take there ploper place and the rooms look ordely there was a knock on the front door. As she gou to open it, it was the paper boy for he weckly play. As she receive the paper from him she noticed at the top left had corner is the date. It was saturday the for-teenth, and she just remember that her relation wasn't do in until saturday the twenty-first.

It was compositions such as this which startled us sufficiently so that we determined to obtain more reliable evidence of under-graduate capabilities. We set up a test that would tell us more about our students' ac-quaintance with the world around them by having them identify names such as those which might be mentioned in any freshman reader. In scoring the test papers, we graded generously, demanding little more than the activity for which each personality was chiefly famous. But there soon arose the difficulty of classifying certain answers as either Right or Wrong. For example, if a student identified Adlai Stevenson as a "nominee for Pres. in 1951 defeated by Eisenhower—Sec. of State," we accepted this as Right. But if Stevenson were called the "Former Republican canitate for Presi-dent"; or identified as someone who "ran against Mr. Truman in the past years for president of the U.S."; or listed as "republi-can presidential candacy"—these answers we scored Limbo. Certainly they are not Right, but on the other hand they are not quite so Wrong as the responses identifying

Stevenson as a US Congressman, or one of "todays labor leaders," or Secretary of "Something."

As we reported in the first NR article on "What Johnny Don't Know," only four names out of 20 (Stevenson, Dillinger, Townsend and Marx) were known to half or more of the 359 students we tested. Nine of the 20 personalities were correctly identified by a limited 2-22 percent of the students. Furthermore, 121 students—almost a third of the group—could recognize no more than four names. The average collegian managed to get 6.7 names Right. Bare statistics, however, are inadequate as description; they do not portray the student who could identify Norman Thomas as a "news commentator"; call Warren G. Harding a "News commtator. (Ex President of U.S.)."; or label Karl Marx "an arthur" and Oliver Cromwell a "wrighter."

It might be argued that our test merely indicates a lamentable condition happily restricted to the South. We do not agree, and our impressions are supported by the findings of a New England high school which administered the same test this autumn to 103 seniors. Adlai Stevenson, one year after his second attempt at the presidency, was known to 77 students. Only four of the personalities were identified by half or more of the seniors (Stevenson, 75 percent; Wilson and Harding, 66 percent; Frost, 51 percent). As with the college group, Norman Thomas was the lowest scorer (0 percent), while 10 others (Picasso, Henry Wallace, de Gaulle, Verdi, Cromwell, Richard Wagner, Mrs. Simpson, Tolstoi, Marx and Franco) were known by 1-10 percent of the seniors.

What is wrong, and can it be remedied?

Undoubtedly the situation is influenced by a host of factors: insufficient financial support for overcrowded and understaffed schools; mistaken theories as to what should be taught; poor preparation of teachers by the colleges, among other things. But is not the American attitude toward learning—with its orientation to the immediate, the practical, and the profitable—largely responsible for our trouble? This attitude is encouraged by a popular educational philosophy which, in gearing itself to the least able students,

tends to stress method while mocking content; it sets social dancing and other "life-adjustment" courses on the same level as academic studies.

We are not concerned at the moment with nobility of intention; we wish merely to point out that it is as unjust for the schools to ignore the able students as it is democratic of them to care for the less than able. Weakening or minimizing content (reflected in teacher training, which makes the study of educational techniques as important as or more important than the sound knowledge of a teaching specialty) often produces students who acquire only stereotypes (George Washington: nice; George III: bad), but little knowledge or understanding. And, in struggling to make content glamorous by relating it to the problems of everyday life, the schools unknowingly invite an anti-intellectualism that cannot tolerate the theoretical or the abstract except as they can be justified in terms of evident usefulness. By neglecting the subjects which only the school is in a position to teach well in favor of extra-academic material which could be got at home and church, the schools become over-priced nurseries where Johnny can, if co-operative, gain semi-literacy while being kept off the streets.

We applaud the idea of educating every student to the extent of his ability to learn, but this is precisely what is *not* being done. We believe that while studies should be made as attractive as possible, no amount of embellishment can disguise the fact that learning, for most of us, demands effort and —rather often—hard work. Finally, we think that if we are to have scientists capable of doing pure research, we must cultivate intellectual curiosity for the virtue that it is, an attribute of our humanity more or less unconnected with the dollar sign. More specifically, it seems to us that:

First, the colleges and universities of the nation must protect themselves by setting high entrance standards. Candidates for a college—state or private—should be examined extensively on their ability to read, write, and do arithmetic; a high-school diploma is no longer a guarantee of such ability. Those who cannot make a good showing on the examination should be invited to return to their high schools for further study. Those who do exceptionally well, on the other hand, should be given college credit and permitted to enroll in advanced courses. It is not easy to justify the presence in college of students as unlettered as the one we have quoted. Why should a university keep a student who writes: "He is now admitted to the Holy Communion, the symbolical eating and drinking of the body and blood of Jeasus Christ."

The barrier here is that a great many state-supported colleges do not have the power to choose their students; they are obliged by their legislatures to accept any and all, the able along with the disabled. Unless the colleges can reject the unprepared sent them by the secondary school as unfit, there is little hope for "higher" education.

Second, college standards must be raised to match the stiffer entrance requirements, and colleges must cease teaching at the high-school level. A college cannot in four years cover the ground which the public school has neglected during the previous twelve. Similarly, a student who has never had to study or one who has not yet learned to read and write cannot, by entering college, become a scholar in the time allowed for college work.

Third, the colleges should demand that all their students—engineers, Latin majors, musicians, and farmers—acquire a familiarity with history, government, languages, literature, music and the fine arts, mathematics, and the natural, political, and social sciences. In our Sputnik-given awareness that we must produce scientists who equal and outstrip Russia's, the importance of liberal education may be overlooked. But almost as dangerous as not having enough scientists is the training of men who are ignorant of their civilization's culture and aims.

It should not particularly matter how the student acquires his liberal training—from reading, from high school, or from formal study in college—but a general examination some time during Johnny's college career should certify that the knowledge is there.

It should be obvious that these suggestions are not meant to restrict college to a tiny intellectual elite, but to insure that those who want a college education are ready to receive it. We are aware, moreover, that even if these recommendations were adopted at once, only a part of the trouble would have been eliminated. For if most of our students are as unprepared for college as our tests suggested, how well prepared for citizenship are the thousands who go no further than high school?

QUESTIONS FOR STUDY AND DISCUSSION

1. Give yourself the test described in "What Johnny Don't Know." Then look up the answers (even those you think you are sure of). How many of these public figures can you identify "with some degree of exactness"? How many did you "know" vaguely, but without enough exactness to make the identification worth anything?

2. Were you able to identify half of the names? Which names were easiest? Would you say that Adlai Stevenson and John Dillinger were among the easiest for you? Was Peter Townsend hard? Why was it a relatively easy name for the students whose test results are reported on in the essay? Would you agree that the hardest names were those identified by fewest of the students tested?

3. With your instructor's approval, work out with the other members of the class the class percentages on each question, then compare them with the percentages reported in the article. What does this comparison tell you?

4. The test described in "What Johnny Don't Know" was given in 1956. Is it as "fair" today as it was then? If you wished to up-date it, what figures would you replace? With whom would you replace them? Make a list.

5. Would the test, if up-dated, be entirely fair? If not, why not?

6. In "What Johnny Needs to Know," "the American attitude toward learning—with its orientation to the immediate, the practical, and the profitable" is made "largely responsible" for the demonstrated inadequacy

of college students. Why should such an orientation be responsible?

7. What subsidiary reasons are educed? How does "popular educational philosophy" encourage American "orientation to the immediate, the practical, and the profitable"?

8. What's wrong with an orientation toward "the immediate, the practical, and the profitable"?

9. These articles appeared during a period of heavy criticism of American education. Since that time changes have taken place. To what extent do the criticisms in these essays apply to your own education?

WRITING ASSIGNMENTS

1. Support or deny the statement that "popular educational philosophy" gears itself "to the least able students."

2. Did your high school set "social dancing and other 'life-adjustment' courses on the same level as academic studies"? What is the value of "life-adjustment" courses? Write a paper on the subject of the "life-adjustment" course.

3. Study the three recommendations made at the conclusion of "What Johnny Needs to Know." Then write an essay in which you criticize (a critic may agree as well as disagree) these recommendations.

4. If you agree that American education is defective, write an essay about *one* major problem.

5. If you feel that American education has been unfairly attacked (in some or many ways) by its critics, write an essay defending *one* of the principal objects of controversy.

NEWSWEEK

(MAY 22, 1961)

Junior Burns Man

As the world's largest detective agency, William J. Burns International (12,000 employees) prides itself on its ability to serve up a sleuth for every occasion. In the past, it has supplied private-eye musicians for symphony orchestras, aristocratic-looking gumshoes for fancy balls, a small army of "industrial espionage" operatives, and even a bandanna-kerchiefed railroad engineer.

The steady expansion of Burns' undercover activities came a cropper last week, though, when the agency ran up against the American Association of University Professors. The controversy started when a letter bearing the agency's letterhead went out from Burns' Houston office in January, addressed to six college presidents in Texas. "Many colleges and universities have found that our services can be very beneficial and informative," it began. "The same system which has saved countless dollars in business can be used in your institution to give you an inside, on-the-scene report concerning any practices detrimental to the institution's character and reputation.

"Teaching practices can be viewed with information from a 'student' who is trained to report objectively on what he or she sees or hears from the classroom. Almost each department has its controversial faculty member. These departments invariably are: Religion, philosophy, psychology, English (literature), biology, history, government, journalism, speech, and drama."

Confidential: "A 'student' trained in his duties as a Burns Operative can enroll . . . obtain his class schedule . . . attend class and send daily, confidential reports to the Agency . . . After the necessary body of fact and information is developed, corrective steps can be made quickly, quietly, and efficiently.

"Burns operators can also be inconspicuously placed in positions of kitchen help, laborers, cashiers, office help, janitors, in any field where a security problem might exist . . ."

When the letter was brought to the attention of the American Association of University Professors, that group vigorously objected to Burns headquarters in New York. The offer, they fumed, was "entirely inconsistent with every concept of academic freedom and academic due process, which represent the hallmarks and the foundation of the whole system of higher education."

Burns quickly apologized. It was all a case of "misguided sales enthusiasm to get new business" by one operative in the Houston office, said Burns. The letter had been retracted and the operative responsible "kicked in the pants."

While it has often provided guard services for colleges, said Burns, "it has never been called upon to investigate any activity of college professors." From now on, the agency promised, such activity would go on its taboo list along with divorce and anti-labor investigation.

Though the agency repudiated its letter, the very concept of academic espionage left educators outraged. Their feelings could be summed up in the one word reaction of President Virgil Hancher of the State University of Iowa: "Despicable."

Full texts of the letters exchanged by the General Secretary of the AAUP, Mr. William P. Fidler, and Mr. W. Sherman Burns

March 23, 1961
Messrs. W. Sherman and Raymond J. Burns
New York 17, New York

Gentlemen:

We have been informed that one of your local offices has approached a college in its district with what apparently is a form inquiry, offering its services in what is identified as an undercover operation, whereby operators of your agency can, in effect, by posing as students, spy on "controversial" faculty members on behalf of the institution. The letter offers the prospect of reports on the basis of which corrective steps can be taken "quickly, quietly, and efficiently."

As the General Secretary of the national professional organization for faculty members of institutions of higher education, I must indicate a deep concern and vigorous objection to this kind of proposed operation. It is entirely inconsistent with every concept of academic freedom and academic due process, which represent the hallmarks and the foundation of the whole system of higher education. In all frankness, I can also tell you that we cannot particularly appreciate the whole concept of an undercover system, particularly as developed for the use of one constituent of the academic community against the other.

While we do not have any realistic hope that the report to us is inaccurate, it is possible that it represents an unauthorized procedure, based on a misunderstanding of the whole nature of the academic community and its complete differentiation from industry, that may be impossible to prevent altogether in an operation the size and complexity of yours. In any case, we would hope very much that with this matter called to your personal attention, appropriate action will be taken by your agency to discontinue this type of activity.

We would welcome your clarification with respect to the entire matter.

Sincerely yours,
/s/William P. Fidler

April 3, 1961

Mr. William P. Fidler, General Secretary
American Association of University
  Professors
Washington 6, D. C.

Dear Mr. Fidler:

With reference to your letter under date of March 23rd, and your telephone conversation with our Mr. McKellar, we have looked into this situation and regret to say that a letter offering the services mentioned in your letter of March 23rd was mailed to six different institutions in the Southwest.

These letters were sent without the approval of the local manager and steps have been taken to correct this to see that there is no recurrence of it. In connection with these letters, I am afraid that there was more "sales enthusiasm" generated than there was mature thought.

I appreciate your calling this to our attention.

Yours very truly,
/s/W. Sherman Burns
President

QUESTIONS FOR STUDY AND DISCUSSION

1. Why should the word "invariably" be used in Par. 3? What unites the departments mentioned?

2. Why should "realistic" be used in Mr. Fidler's letter? What does the word imply?

3. What are the implications of "Many colleges and universities have found . . ." in Par. 2? Reconcile these with the denial in Par. 8.

4. Why, if at all, should such a letter go to universities in Texas?

5. How does the gumshoeing salesman manage to equate "controversial" with "detrimental"?

6. What might a "student" from the Burns Agency be expected to learn in class?

7. Why might a college president want

an "objective" report? Cf. the use of this word by Newman and Snow in essays in this text.

8. What does "inconspicuously" in Par. 5 mean? Why did the salesman-operative use it? What does it imply?

9. Why should professors get huffier about "inconspicuous," "objective" detectives than musicians? factory workers? railroad engineers?—all mentioned in Par. 1. Why don't bankers and college presidents appear on this list?

10. Does Newsweek's use of "fumed" (Par. 6) represent accurately the tone of Mr. Fidler's letter? Can you suggest any connection between "fumed" and "educator" instead of "teacher" or "professor"?

WRITING ASSIGNMENTS

1. After reading C. P. Snow's "The Two Cultures," decide whether or not learning can be fruitfully controversial and discuss the implications of the Burns Agency's investigation of "controversial" courses.

2. Write an essay arguing that private spies should or should not be used as freely in a classroom as in a stockroom. Is there a difference in what they are expected to discover?

3. After reading Newman's "Knowledge Viewed in Relation to Learning" decide whether he suggests that academic freedom is necessary. Does C. P. Snow's "The Two Cultures" suggest this? Write an essay proving your decision.

4. Write a report to the Burns Agency, for transmittal to the President of the college or university on the most "controversial" class you have taken in this school.

Other essays in this book which are appropriate to a consideration of AMERICAN EDUCATION are John Henry Newman's "Knowledge Viewed in Relation to Learning" and, for its general implications, C. P. Snow's "The Two Cultures."

American Democracy:
The Problem of Segregation

HARRY GOLDEN

The Vertical Negro
Plan

Those who love North Carolina will jump at the chance to share in the great responsibility confronting our Governor and the State Legislature. A special session of the Legislature (July 25–28, 1956) passed a series of amendments to the State Constitution. These proposals submitted by the Governor and his Advisory Education Committee included the following:

> (a) The elimination of the compulsory attendance law, "to prevent any child from being forced to attend a school with a child of another race."
>
> (b) The establishment of "Education Expense Grants" for education in a private school, "in the case of a child assigned to a public school attended by a child of another race."
>
> (c) A "uniform system of local option" whereby a majority of the folks in a school district may suspend or close a school if the situation becomes "intolerable."

But suppose a Negro child applies for this "Education Expense Grant" and says he wants to go to the private school too? There are fourteen Supreme Court decisions involving the use of public funds; there are only two "decisions" involving the elimination of racial discrimination in the public schools.

The Governor has said that critics of these proposals have not offered any constructive advice or alternatives. Permit me, therefore, to offer an idea for the consideration of the members of the regular sessions. A careful study of my plan, I believe, will show that it will save millions of dollars in tax funds and eliminate forever the danger to our public education system. Before I outline my plan, I would like to give you a little background.

One of the factors involved in our tremendous industrial growth and economic prosperity is the fact that the South, voluntarily, has all but eliminated VERTICAL SEGREGATION. The tremendous buying power of the twelve million Negroes in the South has been based wholly on the absence of racial segregation. The white and Negro stand at the same grocery and supermarket counters; deposit money at the same bank teller's window; pay phone and light bills to the same clerk; walk through the same dime and department stores, and stand at the same drugstore counters.

It is only when the Negro "sets" that the fur begins to fly.

Now, since we are not even thinking about restoring VERTICAL SEGREGATION, I think my plan would not only comply with

413

the Supreme Court decisions, but would maintain "sitting-down" segregation. Now here is the GOLDEN VERTICAL NEGRO PLAN. Instead of all those complicated proposals, all the next session needs to do is pass one small amendment which would provide *only* desks in all the public schools of our state— *no seats.*

The desks should be those standing-up jobs, like the old-fashioned bookkeeping desk. Since no one in the South pays the slightest attention to a VERTICAL NEGRO, this will completely solve our problem. And it is not such a terrible inconvenience for young people to stand up during their class-room studies. In fact, this may be a blessing in disguise. They are not learning to read sitting down, anyway; maybe standing up will help. This will save more millions of dollars in the cost of our remedial English course when the kids enter college. In whatever direction you look with the GOLDEN VERTICAL NEGRO PLAN, you save millions of dollars, to say nothing of eliminating forever any danger to our public education system upon which rests the destiny, hopes, and happiness of this society.

My WHITE BABY PLAN offers another possible solution to the segregation problem— this time in a field other than education.

Here is an actual case history of the "White Baby Plan To End Racial Segregation":

Some months ago there was a revival of the Laurence Olivier movie, *Hamlet,* and several Negro schoolteachers were eager to see it. One Saturday afternoon they asked some white friends to lend them two of their little children, a three-year-old girl and a six-year-old boy, and, holding these white children by the hands, they obtained tickets from the movie-house cashier without a moment's hesitation. They were in like Flynn.

This would also solve the baby-sitting problem for thousands and thousands of white working mothers. There can be a mutual exchange of references, then the people can sort of pool their children at a central

point in each neighborhood, and every time a Negro wants to go to the movies all she need do is pick up a white child—and go.

Eventually the Negro community can set up a factory and manufacture white babies made of plastic, and when they want to go to the opera or to a concert, all they need do is carry that plastic doll in their arms. The dolls, of course, should all have blond curls and blue eyes, which would go even further; it would give the Negro woman and her husband priority over the whites for the very best seats in the house.

While I still have faith in the WHITE BABY PLAN, my final proposal may prove to be the most practical of all.

Only after a successful test was I ready to announce formally the GOLDEN "OUT-OF-ORDER" PLAN.

I tried my plan in a city of North Carolina, where the Negroes represent 39 per cent of the population.

I prevailed upon the manager of a department store to shut the water off in his "white" water fountain and put up a sign, "Out-of-Order." For the first day or two the whites were hesitant, but little by little they began to drink out of the water fountain belonging to the "coloreds"—and by the end of the third week everybody was drinking the "segregated" water; with not a single solitary complaint to date.

I believe the test is of such sociological significance that the Governor should appoint a special committee of two members of the House and two Senators to investigate the GOLDEN "OUT-OF-ORDER" PLAN. We kept daily reports on the use of the unsegregated water fountain which should be of great value to this committee. This may be the answer to the necessary uplifting of the white morale. It is possible that the whites may accept desegregation if they are assured that the facilities are still "separate," albeit "Out-of-Order."

As I see it now, the key to my Plan is to keep the "Out-of-Order" sign up for at least two years. We must do this thing gradually.

QUESTIONS FOR STUDY AND DISCUSSION

1. Should this essay be divided into three: "The Vertical Negro Plan," "White Baby Plan," and "Golden Out-of-Order Plan"? What reasons for or against division can you offer?

2. How serious are Harry Golden's proposals? Could any or all of them actually work? If you think so, try to explain why. If you do not think so, be prepared to give good reasons for your point of view.

3. What is Mr. Golden saying about the principle of segregation?

4. Why is it that "no one in the South pays the slightest attention to a VERTICAL NEGRO," while "when the Negro 'sets' . . . the fur begins to fly"? What symbolic significance attaches to sitting and standing?

5. Why could Negroes holding white babies by the hand enter a segregated theater? What is their presumed relationship to these children?

6. What might be the ostensible reasons for segregated water fountains? What does Harry Golden's "test" indicate about such ostensible reasons?

WRITING ASSIGNMENTS

1. Choose with some care a subject which you feel capable of handling ironically. Then write a proposal for solving some vexing problem. Your solution, however, no matter how reasonable it seems to someone not familiar with the problem, must be recognizable as ridiculous—or worse. Further, it must reveal by indirection the heart of the problem. The "White Baby" proposal of Mr. Golden is laughable, though it worked— really it is laughable *because* it worked. The reader gets a glimpse of some of the real reasons for segregation behind the ostensible ones by seeing the absurdity—on the ostensible grounds—of the exception to the rule.

2. Unless you have already thought deeply about the subject of segregation, you may not be ready to write a thoroughgoing essay on any of its problems until you have read Oscar Handlin's "Where Equality Leads" and Robert Penn Warren's *Segregation* in this book. Nevertheless it might be helpful to get some ideas on paper at this stage. A short paper might deal with any one of the following, for example:

a. Passive resistance as a means of insisting on racial equality.

b. The wisdom (or justice) of planned attacks by the NAACP on anti-integration statutes.

c. The right—real or illegally assumed— of the federal government to enforce school integration.

d. How a newly integrated school works.

OSCAR HANDLIN

Where Equality Leads

The public debate on desegregation has dealt largely with the shadow of the issue rather than with its substance. Not states' rights or federalism or the control of education, but some other gnawing fear—rarely expressed—lies behind the violence of the protest against the Supreme Court's decision. The dread lest desegregation open the way to a contaminating race mixture is the fundamental anxiety that troubles many white Southerners; it is the nightmare that drives men to disregard the law in Tennessee and Texas and Alabama.

The haunting specter of racial amalgamation corresponds to nothing in the world of actuality. It is rather the product of three profound misconceptions. The men frightened by it mistake the meaning of the Supreme Court's decision of 1954. They misjudge the probable consequences of desegregation on both whites and blacks. And, most important, their conjectures as to what results will follow upon more intimate contact between Negroes and other Americans in the schools run counter to all the available evidence.

Segregation emerged as a defined pattern of social behavior in the 1880s. Segregation was not directed simply at the schools; it aimed to create a mode of life that would establish the distinct inferiority of the Negro by setting him apart in every important activity—in the school as elsewhere. The supporters of segregation argued that they had no intention of negating the rights of the Negro. It was possible, they insisted, to provide separate but equal facilities in education as in transportation and in the other spheres where the two races had contact. In 1896, in the famous case of *Plessy v. Ferguson*, the Supreme Court accepted that contention, assuming that the privileges guaranteed by the Fourteenth Amendment would still be assured under a segregated regime. The decision affirmed the right of the Negroes to equality, but it accepted the argument that equality could be attained through separateness.

When the Supreme Court reviewed this issue in 1954, it had almost sixty years of experience on the basis of which to test the validity of that argument. Its unanimous decision was that the pattern of separate treatment, as it had developed, had not brought equality of treatment to the Negro. This was a question of fact and not of law. No serious observer of the Southern scene had denied that the educational facilities supplied to the black citizens of the Southern states were markedly inferior to those of the whites. Indeed, in many vital respects the Negro's relative situation had actually deteriorated since 1896. Those who had affirmed the compatibility of segregation and equality had not in those decades of opportunity made it work.

The Court was therefore compelled to review the findings of *Plessy v. Ferguson*. If separateness did not bring the equality guaranteed by the Fourteenth Amendment, then the laws establishing the segregated system were unconstitutional, for they fixed the Negro in an inferior place and thus deprived him of the rights guaranteed by the Amendment.

But that was all the Court said. Its findings were purely negative. It did not go on to any positive injunction laying down a line of action to be followed. Instead, it left the various states free gradually to develop a variety of adjustments that would meet the clear constitutional obligation to provide equal treatment for all citizens regardless of race.

The Court's decision insisted only that the element of racial compulsion be removed, and it left a considerable range of alternatives available to those who wish to adapt themselves to the conditions it created. In the years to come, good sense and tolerance will undoubtedly encourage the majority of

Americans to explore these alternatives. The results will vary widely according to the local conditions of each community.

Desegregation therefore does not necessarily involve the emergence of a single, all-inclusive, integrated type of school, unless the students and their parents choose to have it do so. The question then arises: what will the parents choose?

Under conditions of genuine equality, Negroes have thus shown the inclination to continue to attend schools preponderantly made up of members of their own race. In 1949, for instance, an Indiana state law prohibited the segregation which theretofore prevailed in some schools, including those of the city of Evansville. The result was not the mass rush to the white schools that some Hoosiers had anticipated. The overwhelming majority of Evansville Negroes—over 90 per cent—continued to attend their own schools. On the other hand, there is no doubt that the colored people of Clinton, Tennessee, or Clay, Kentucky, who braved obloquy, boycott, and the danger of violence to do so, preferred to send their children to integrated schools.

Integration is not an end in itself but a means to an end. Black parents, like white, hope that education will give their boys and girls the best possible preparation for life. They resent the compulsion to attend Negro schools, unequal to the white, that will forever burden their children with handicaps and label them indelibly with the stigma of inferiority. They will not resent schools that are genuinely equal and that bear no imputation of inferiority, no matter what their racial composition. Indeed, under some circumstances, they may actually find their children more comfortable in such schools with those who share a common cultural and social background.

There will necessarily be sustained regional and communal differences in adjustment. Classes in Bronzeville and Harlem are predominantly Negro, just as those in East Boston are Italian and those in Hamtramck are Polish. Only in rare instances are such schools likely to contain a completely mixed and heterogeneous student body. In smaller cities there is less scope for such adjustments. The elementary schools may reflect the neighborhood differences. But if there is only one high school in town it will have to accommodate all the students eligible to attend it.

The greatest problem will no doubt exist in rural regions which enjoy a minimum of flexibility. There the segregated school has been least convenient and most expensive; and there it most often produced the types of inferiority that the Supreme Court condemned. It may be that no solution other than integration in the general school system will do justice to the dozen Negro families of Clinton, Tennessee. But the fact that integration is sought there does not mean it will be sought everywhere.

There has been a subtle change in the attitudes of Negroes with the improvement of their status in the past thirty years. There was a time when colored people were so depressed by the sense of their own inferiority that they accepted unquestioningly all the white man's standards. Their own habits and tastes, like their blackness, were inherently degrading; and success and happiness went to those who could most closely model themselves upon the dominant race. There was a premium upon "marrying light" even though within the group, because that most closely approximated the standards of the whites.

With the Negro's achievement of some degree of stability and the restoration of his self-confidence, there has been a significant change, even since Gunnar Myrdal noticed it in 1944. Rejecting the notion of his own inferiority, the Negro has ceased to take the white as the determining model. He has come to value the standards and tastes of his own group and often actually to take pride in his color. Not a few are unwilling to "pass" even though their pigmentation is pale enough to permit them to do so. The girl who holds the cake of soap in the *Ebony* advertisement is black; and she is pretty to those who see her because she is black. The era of the hair straightener is coming to an end. The notion that Negroes are eager to marry whites is a delusion born of the white's own vanity and of his ignorance of the real sentiments of his fellow Americans of another color.

The experience of schools in which segregation has come to an end amply confirms these judgments. The circumstances vary widely according to the conditions and traditions of the communities in which the adjustment occurs. In the Southern colleges, Negroes, once admitted, have generally enjoyed a minimum of social contact with white students. Elsewhere the relationship between the races has extended beyond the classroom to the formal social activities conducted under school auspices. But even when the boy and girl of different colors dance together at the senior prom, they do not think of dating. They hesitate, as does the Methodist with the Catholic, because courtship and marriage involve an altogether different order of considerations.

The obsession with the unreal dangers of intermarriage has unfortunately obscured the true source of race mixture in the past and in the present. The white ancestors of the mulattoes and of the Negroes of varying degrees of lightness of skin were not married to blacks. These are the progeny of relationships outside wedlock; and miscegenation, not intermarriage, has, in the United States, been the mode of infusing the black with the white strain in our society. Furthermore, miscegenation under these terms was the direct product of the inferiority of Negro women. Whatever has tended to increase that inferiority has increased the rate of miscegenation. Whatever diminishes it lowers the rate. In that sense, segregation actually is indirectly more conducive to the mixture of races than is desegregation.

Through much of the nineteenth century, white men who kept black concubines suffered no loss of social esteem thereby. Until the Civil War, the women were their property, and no control limited the treatment accorded them. In most of the Southern states miscegenation was no crime, although intermarriage was.

Concubinage began to decline after the Civil War. It hardly exists now. It was extirpated by the liberation of the Negroes, which removed their women from the absolute power of the masters.

Less formal sexual relations between white men and black women, however, were long thereafter tolerated in many parts of the South. They were facilitated by the disorganization of Negro family life and by the simple brute fact that blacks were incapable of protecting their daughters and sisters against the aggressions of those who had once been their masters. The law and the mores were alike acquiescent. There are authentic, if scarcely credible, instances of respectable white businessmen who warned off the Negro preacher who wished to strengthen the morals of the women in his flock.

Insofar as that can be measured, the incidence of interracial sexual intercourse seems also to have declined perceptibly in the last forty years. It has fallen off precisely because the Negro now sees the prospect of leading a decent family life and because he himself has grown in self-respect and in the power to resist. The transformation in the general conception of what the law and the practices of society owe him is the most important element in that change.

If we strengthen the trend toward equality of opportunity and of rights, then we strengthen also the elements of cohesion and order in the Negro's own life. If we weaken that trend and perpetuate his inferiority, then we weaken also the fabric of his family life and leave him a loose, helpless, and potentially disorderly element in our society. If we can but free ourselves of the habit of thinking in terms of the absolutes of total conformity and amalgamation on the one hand and of total separateness and segregation on the other, we shall find our institutions flexible enough to accommodate a variety of solutions among which individuals will be able to make their own personal choices. It was the virtue of the Supreme Court to have understood that, and in its decision to have laid a foundation for constructive development in the future. And it is the insistence upon thinking of the nightmare of amalgamation as the only alternative to segregation that is most likely to perpetuate the tensions that all Americans should dread.

QUESTIONS FOR STUDY AND DISCUSSION

1. The "three profound misconceptions" in Par. 2 organize the central section of this essay. A. Mark out the paragraphs that refer to each misconception. B. Discuss the function of Pars. 13 and 14 in this regard. Do they refer to the second or to the third "misconception," or do they serve an independent function of transition? C. How would you account for Mr. Handlin's brief treatment of the third misconception?

2. How is the opening paragraph related to the central section discussed above? What section of the essay is directly controlled by the opening paragraph? In the light of the answers given above, how would you formulate in one phrase the essential unity of this essay?

3. Characterize the use of paragraphs in this essay. How would you defend Mr. Handlin against the charge of excessive paragraphing?

4. "The dread lest desegregation open the way to a contaminating race mixture is the fundamental anxiety that troubles many white Southerners; it is the nightmare that drives men to disregard the law in Tennessee and Texas and Alabama." Discuss the structure of this topic sentence in the opening paragraph. What are some possible revisions? Consider: "the nightmare that drives," etc.

What reasons do you suppose Mr. Handlin had for his diction in the first clause of this sentence? What is the tone of "contaminating" in this context? How does this word prepare the reader for the final paragraphs of the essay?

5. Would you agree that Mr. Handlin has isolated the basic cause of Southern resistance to desegregation?

6. Why does Mr. Handlin attach so much importance to a precise understanding of the "separate but equal" clause of Plessy vs. Ferguson in 1896?

7. Mr. Handlin says: "Segregation emerged as a defined pattern of social behavior in the 1880s," and "Desegregation therefore does not necessarily involve the emergence of a single, all-inclusive, integrated type of school, unless the students and their parents choose to have it do so." Would you think that either of these assertions is widely known or accepted by the general public? How does this affect the customary lines of argument in this matter?

8. What are the implications of Mr. Handlin's remarks concerning the opposition of respectable white businessmen to the moral efforts of the Negro clergy in past decades?

WRITING ASSIGNMENTS

1. Write an essay complementary to "Where Equality Leads" developing the thesis that a major cause of white Southern opposition to desegregation is a desire to have a pool of cheap labor. Consider carefully the nature and extent of facts needed to support this contention.

2. Comment on the reasons why some white Southerners are reluctant to face the

historical record of miscegenation discussed in the final section of the essay.

3. Develop some of the reasons why segregation "emerged as a defined pattern of social behavior in the 1880s."

4. To the extent that your experience and knowledge allow, discuss the extent to which social patterns in the United States outside of the South bear out Mr. Handlin's analysis.

ROBERT PENN WARREN

Segregation

"I'm glad it's you going," my friend, a Southerner, long resident in New York, said, "and not me." But I went back, for going back this time, like all the other times, was a necessary part of my life. I was going back to look at the landscapes and streets I had known—Kentucky, Tennessee, Arkansas, Mississippi, Louisiana—to look at the faces, to hear the voices, to hear, in fact, the voices in my own blood. A girl from Mississippi had said to me: "I feel it's all happening inside of me, every bit of it. It's all there."

I know what she meant.

To the right, the sun, cold and pale, is westering. Far off, a little yellow plane scuttles down a runway, steps awkwardly into the air, then climbs busily, learning grace. Our big plane trundles ponderously forward, feeling its weight like a fat man, hesitates, shudders with an access of sudden, building power; and with a new roar in my ears, I see the ground slide past, then drop away, like a dream. I had not been aware of the instant we had lost that natural contact.

Memphis is behind me, and I cannot see it, but yonder is the river, glittering coldly, and beyond, the tree-sprigged flats of Arkansas. Still climbing, we tilt eastward now, the land pivoting away below us, the tidy toy farms, white houses, silos the size of a spool of white thread, or smaller, the stock ponds bright like little pieces of gum wrapper dropped in brown grass, but that brown grass is really trees, the toy groves with shadows precise and long in the leveling light.

Arkansas has pivoted away. It is Mississippi I now see down there, the land slipping away in the long light, and in my mind I see, idly, the ruined, gaunt, classic clay hills, with the creek bottoms throttled long since in pink sand, or the white houses of Holly Springs, some of them severe and beautiful, or Highway 61 striking south from Memphis,

straight as a knife edge through the sad and baleful beauty of the Delta country, south toward Vicksburg and the Federal cemeteries, toward the fantasia of Natchez.

It seems like a thousand years since I first drove that road, more than twenty-five years ago, a new concrete slab then, dizzily glittering in the August sun-blaze, driving past the rows of tenant shacks, Negro shacks set in the infinite cotton fields, and it seems like a hundred years since I last drove it, last week, in the rain, then toward sunset the sky clearing a little, but clouds solid and low on the west like a black range of mountains frilled upward with an edge of bloody gold light, quickly extinguished. Last week, I noticed that more of the shacks were ruinous, apparently abandoned. More, but not many, had an electric wire running back from the road. But when I caught a glimpse, in the dusk, of the interior of a lighted shack, I usually saw the coal-oil lamp. Most shacks were not lighted. I wondered if it was too early in the evening. Then it was early no longer. Were that many of the shacks abandoned?

Then we would pass in the dark some old truck grudging and clanking down the concrete, and catch, in the split-second flick of our headlamps, a glimpse of the black faces and the staring eyes. Or the figure, sudden in our headlight, would rise from the roadside, dark and shapeless against the soaked blackness of the cotton land: the man humping along with the croker sack on his shoulders (containing what?), the woman with a piece of sacking or paper over her head against the drizzle now, at her bosom' a bundle that must be a small child, the big children following with the same slow, mud-lifting stride in the darkness. The light of the car snatches past, and I think of them behind us in the darkness, moving up the track beside the concrete, seeing another car light far yonder toward Memphis, staring at it perhaps, watching it grow, plunge at them, strike them, flick past. They will move on, at their pace. Yes, they are still here.

I see a river below us. It must be the Tennessee. I wonder on which side of us Shiloh is, and guess the right, for we must have swung far enough north for that. I had two grandfathers at Shiloh, that morning of April 6, 1862, young men with the other young men in gray uniforms stepping toward the lethal spring thickets of dogwood and redbud, to the sound of bird song. "One hundred and sixty men we took in the first morning, son. Muster the next night, and it was sixteen answered." They had fallen back on Corinth, into Mississippi.

The man in the seat beside me on the plane is offering me a newspaper. I see the thumb of the hand clutching the paper. The nail is nearly as big as a quarter, split at the edges, grooved and horny, yellowish, with irrevocable coal-black grime deep under the nail and into the cuticle. I look at the man. He is a big man, very big, bulging over the seat, bulging inside his blue serge. He is fiftyish, hair graying. His face is large and raw-looking, heavy-jowled, thick gray eyebrows over small, deep-set, appraising eyes. His name, which he tells me, sounds Russian or Polish, something ending in -ski.

I begin to read the paper, an article about the riots at the University of Alabama. He notices what I am reading. "Bet you thought I was from down here," he said. "From the way I talk. But I ain't. I was born and raised in New York City, but I been in the scrap business down here ten years. Didn't you think I was from down here?"

"Yes," I say, for that seems the sociable thing to say.

He twists his bulk in the blue serge and reaches and stabs a finger at the headline about Alabama. "Folks could be more gen-'rous and fair-thinking," he says. "Like affable, you might say, and things would work out. If folks get affable and contig'ous, you might say, things sort of get worked out in time, but you get folks not being affable-like and stirring things up and it won't work out. Folks on both sides the question."

He asks me if I don't agree, and I say, sure, I agree. Sure, if folks were just affable-like.

I am thinking of what a taxi driver had said to me in Memphis: "Looks like the Lucy girl wouldn't want to go no place where people throwed eggs at her and sich. But if they'd jist let her alone, them Good-

rich plant fellers and all, it would blow over. What few niggers come would not have stayed no duration. Not when they found she couldn't git the social stuff, and all."

And what the school superintendent, in middle Tennessee, had said: "You take a good many people around here that I know, segregationists all right, but when they read about a thousand to one, it sort of makes them sick. It is the unfairness in that way that gets them."

And an organizer of one of the important segregation groups, a lawyer, when I asked him if Autherine Lucy wasn't acting under law, he creaked his swivel chair, moved his shoulders under his coat, and touched a pencil on his desk, before saying: "Yes—yes—but it was just the Federal Court ruled it."

And a taxi driver in Nashville, a back-country man come to the city, a hard, lean, spare face, his lean, strong shoulders humped forward over the wheel so that the clavicles show through the coat: "A black-type person and a white-type person, they ain't alike. Now the black-type person, all they think about is fighting and having a good time and you know what. Now the white-type person is more American-type, he don't mind fighting but he don't fight to kill for fun. It's that cannibal blood you caint git out."

Now, on the plane, my companion observes me scribbling something in a notebook.

"You a writer or something?" he asks. "A newspaper fellow, maybe?"

I say yes.

"You interested in that stuff?" he asks, and points to the article. "Somebody ought to tell 'em not to blame no state, not even Alabam' or Mississippi, for what the bad folks do. Like stuff in New York or Chicago. Folks in Mississippi got good hearts as any place. They always been nice and good-hearted to me, for I go up to a man affable. The folks down here is just in trouble and can't claw out. Don't blame 'em, got good hearts but can't claw out of their trouble. It is hard to claw out from under the past and the past way."

He asks me if I have been talking to a lot of people.

I had been talking to a lot of people.

I had come to the shack at dusk, by the brimming bayou, in the sea of mud where cotton had been. The cold drizzle was still falling. In the shack, on the hickory chair, the yellow girl, thin but well made, wearing a salmon sweater and salmon denim slacks, holds the baby on her knee and leans toward the iron stove. On the table beyond her is an ivory-colored portable radio and a half-full bottle of Castoria. On the other side of the stove are her three other children, the oldest seven. Behind me, in the shadowy background, I know there are faces peering in from the other room of the shack, black faces, the half-grown boys, another girl I had seen on entering. The girl in the salmon sweater is telling how she heard her husband had been killed. "Livin in town then, and my sister, she come that night and tole me he was shot. They had done shot him dead. So I up and taken out fer heah, back to the plantation. Later, my sister got my chillen and brought 'em. I ain't gonna lie, mister. I tell you, I was scairt. No tellin if that man what done it was in jail or no. Even if they had arrest him, they might bon' him out and he come and do it to me. Be mad because they 'rest him. You caint never tell. And they try him and 'quit him, doan know as I kin stay heah. Even they convick him, maybe I leave. Some good folks round heah and they helpin me, and I try to appreciate and be a prayin chile, but you git so bore down on and nigh ruint and sort of brainwashed, you don't know what. Things git to goin round in yore head. I could run out or somethin, but you caint leave yore chillen. But look like I might up and leave. He git 'quitted, that man, and maybe I die, but I die goin."

This is the cliché. It is the thing the uninitiate would expect. It is the cliché of fear. It is the cliché come fresh, and alive.

There is another image. It is morning in Nashville. I walk down Union Street, past the Negro barber shops, past the ruinous buildings plastered over with placards of old circuses and rodeos, buildings being wrecked now to make way for progress, going into the square where the big white stone boxlike, ugly and expensive Davidson County Court House now stands on the spot where the old brawling market once was. Otherwise, the square hasn't changed much, the same buildings, wholesale houses, liquor stores, pawn shops, quick lunches, and the same kind of people stand on the corners, countrymen, in khaki pants and mackinaw coats, weathered faces and hard, withdrawn eyes, usually pale eyes, lean-hipped men ("narrow-assted" in the country phrase) like the men who rode with Forrest, the farm wives, young with a baby in arms, or middle-aged and work-worn, with colored cloths over the head, glasses, false teeth, always the shopping bag.

I walk down toward the river, past the Darling Display Distribution show window, where a wax figure stands in skirt and silk blouse, the fingers spread on one uplifted hand, the thin face lifted with lips lightly parted as though in eternal, tubercular expectation of a kiss. I see the power pylons rising above the river mist. A tug is hooting up-river in the mist.

I go on down to the right, First Street, to the replica of Fort Nashborough, the original settlement, which stands on the river bank under the shadow of warehouses. The stockade looks so child-flimsy and jerry-built jammed against the massive, soot-stained warehouses. How could the settlers have ever taken such protection seriously? But it was enough, that and their will and the long rifles and the hunting knives and the bear-dogs they unleashed to help them when they broke the Indians at the Battle of the Bluffs. They took the land, and remain.

I am standing in the middle of the empty stockade when a boy enters and approaches me. He is about fifteen, strongly built, wearing a scruffed and tattered brown leather jacket, blue jeans, a faded blue stocking cap on the back of his head, with a mop of yellow hair hanging over his forehead. He is a fine-looking boy, erect, manly in the face, with a direct, blue-eyed glance. "Mister," he said to me, "is this foh't the way it was, or they done remodeled it?"

I tell him it is a replica, smaller than the original and not on the right spot, exactly.

"I'm glad I seen it, anyway," he says. "I like to go round seeing things that got history, and such. It gives you something to think about. Helps you in a quiz sometimes, too."

I ask him where he goes to school.

"Atlanta," he says. "Just come hitch-hiking up this a-way, looking at things for interest. Like this here foh't."

"You all been having a little trouble down your way," I ask, "haven't you?"

He looks sharply at me, hesitates, then says: "Niggers—you mean niggers?"

"Yes."

"I hate them bastards," he says, with a shuddering, automatic violence, and averts his face and spits through his teeth, a quick, viperish, cut-off expectoration.

I say nothing, and he looks at me, stares into my face with a dawning belligerence, sullen and challenging, and suddenly demands: "Don't you?"

"I can't say that I do," I reply. "I like some and I don't like some others."

He utters the sudden obscenity, and removes himself a couple of paces from me. He stops and looks back over his shoulder. "I'm hitching on back to Atlanta," he declares in a flat voice, "this afternoon," and goes on out of the fort.

This, too, is a cliché. The boy, standing on the ground of history and heroism, his intellect and imagination stirred by the fact, shudders with that other, automatic emotion which my question had evoked. The cliché had come true: the cliché of hate. And somehow the hallowedness of the ground he stood on had vindicated, as it were, that hate.

The boy in the fort was the only person to turn from me, but occasionally there would be a stiffening, a flicker of suspicion, an evasion or momentary refusal of the subject, even in the casual acquaintance of lobby or barroom. At one of the new luxurious motels near Clarksdale (the slick motels and the great power stations and booster stations, silver-glittering by day and jewel-glittering by night, are the most obvious marks of the new boom), a well-dressed young man is talking about a movie being made down near Greenville. The movie is something about cotton, he says, by a fellow named Williams. Anyway, they had burned

down a gin in the middle of the night, just for the movie. The woman at the desk (a very good blue dress that had cost money, a precise, respectable middle-aged mouth, pince-nez) speaks up: "Yes, and they say it's the only movie ever made here didn't criticize Mississippi."

"Criticize?" I ask. "Criticize how?"

She turns her head a little, looks at the man with her behind the desk, then back at me. "You know," she says, "just criticize."

I see the eyes of the man behind the desk stray to the license of our car parked just beyond the glass front. It has a Tennessee license, a U-Drive-It from Memphis.

"Criticize?" I try again.

The man had been busy arranging something in the drawer behind the desk. Suddenly, very sharply, not quite slamming, he shoves the drawer shut. "Heck, you know," he says.

"Didn't they make another movie over at Oxford?" I ask.

The man nods, the woman says yes. I ask what that one had been about. Nobody has seen it, not the woman, neither of the men. "It was by that fellow Faulkner," the woman says. "But I never read anything he ever wrote."

"I never did either," the man behind the desk says, "but I know what it's like. It's like that fellow Hemingway. I read some of his writings. Gory and on the seedy side of life. I didn't like it."

"That's exactly right," the woman says, and nods. "On the seedy side of life. That fellow Faulkner, he's lost a lot of friends in Mississippi. Looking at the seedy side."

"Does he criticize?" I ask.

She turns away. The man goes into a door behind the desk. The well-dressed young man has long since become engrossed in a magazine.

My Tennessee license, and Tennessee accent, hadn't been good enough credentials in Clarksdale, Mississippi. But on one occasion, the accent wasn't good enough even in Tennessee, and I remember sitting one evening in the tight, tiny living room (linoleum floor, gas heater, couch, one chair, small table with TV) of an organizer of a new important segregation group (one-time official of the Klan, this by court record) while he harangues me. He is a fat but powerful man, face fat but not flabby, the gray eyes squinty, set deep in the flesh, hard and sly by turns, never genial though the grin tries to be when he has scored a point and leans forward at me, creaking the big overstuffed chair, his big hands crossed on his belly. He is a hill-man, come to town from one of the counties where there aren't too many Negroes, but he's now out to preserve, he says, "what you might name the old Southern way, what we was raised up to."

He is not out for money. ("I just git one dollar ever fellow I sign, the other two goes to Mr. Perkins at headquarters, for expense. Hell, I lose money on hit, on my gasoline.") No, he's not out for money, but something else. He is clearly a man of force, force that somehow has never found its way, and a man of language and leadership among his kind, the angry and ambitious and disoriented and dispossessed. It is language that intoxicates him now. He had been cautious at first, had thought I was from the FBI (yes, he had had a brush with them once, a perjury indictment), but now it seems some grand vista is opening before him and his eyes gleam and the words come.

He is talking too much, tangling himself. All the while his wife (very handsome, almost beautiful, in fact, bobbed, disordered black hair around a compact, smooth-chiseled, tanned face, her body under a flimsy dress tight and compact but gracefully made) has been standing in the deep shadow of the doorway to a room beyond, standing patiently, hands folded but tense, with the fingers secretly moving, standing like the proper hill-wife while the men-folks talk.

"Excuse me," she suddenly says, but addressing me, not the husband, "excuse me, but didn't you say you were born down here, used to live right near here?"

I say yes.

She takes a step forward, coming out of the shadow. "Yes," she says, "yes," leaning at me in vindictive triumph, "but you never said where you're living now!"

And I remember sitting with a group of college students, and one of them, a law student it develops, short but strong-looking, dark-haired and slick-headed, dark bulging eyes in a slick, rather handsome, arrogant—no, bumptious—face, breaks in: "I just want to ask one question before anything starts. I just want to ask where you're from."

Suspicion of the outlander, or of the corrupted native, gets tangled up sometimes with suspicion of the New York press, but this latter suspicion may exist quite separately, on an informed and reasoned basis. For instance, I have seen a Southern newspaper man of high integrity and ability (an integrationist, by the way) suddenly strike down his fist and exclaim: "Well, by God, it's just a fact, it's not in them not to load the dice in a news story!" And another, a man publicly committed to maintaining law and order, publicly on record against the Citizens Councils and all such organizations: "*Life* magazine's editorial on the Till case, that sure fixed it. If Till's father had died a hero's death fighting for liberty, as *Life* said, that would have been as irrelevant as the actual fact that he was executed by the American army for rape-murder. It sure makes it hard."

There is the Baptist minister, an educated and intelligent man, who, when I show him an article in the *Reader's Digest*, an article mentioning that the Southern Baptist Convention had voted overwhelmingly for support of the Supreme Court decision, stiffens and says to me: "Look—look at that title!"

I didn't need to look. I knew what it was: "The Churches Repent."

But there is another suspicion story. A Negro told me this. A man from New Haven called on him, and upon being asked politely to take a chair, said, "Now, please, won't you tell me about the race problem."

To which the Negro replied: "Mister, I can't tell you a thing about that. There's nothing I could tell to you. If you want to find out, you better just move down here and live for a while."

That is the something else—the instinctive fear, on the part of black or white, that the massiveness of experience, the concreteness of life, will be violated; the fear of

abstraction. I suppose it is this fear that
made one man, a subtle and learned man,
say to me: "There's something you can't
explain, what being a Southerner is." And
when he said that, I remembered a Yankee
friend saying to me: "Southerners and Jews,
you're exactly alike, you're so damned special."

"Yes," I said, "we're both persecuted
minorities."

I had said it for a joke.

But had I?

In the end people talked, even showed an
anxiety to talk, to explain something. Even
the black Southerners, a persecuted minority,
too, would talk, for over and over the moment of some sudden decision would come:
"All right—all right—I'll tell it to you
straight. All right, there's no use beating
around the bush."

But how fully can I read the words offered
in the fullest effort of candor?

It is a town in Louisiana, and I am riding
in an automobile driven by a Negro, a
teacher, a slow, careful man, who puts his
words out in that fashion, almost musingly,
and drives his car that way, too. He has been
showing me the Negro business section, how
prosperous some of it is, and earlier he had
said he would show me a section where the
white men's cars almost line up at night.
Now he seems to have forgotten that sardonic notion in the pleasanter, more prideful
task. He has fallen silent, seemingly occupied with his important business of driving,
and the car moves deliberately down the
street. Then, putting his words out that slow
way, detachedly as though I weren't there,
he says: "You hear some white men say they
know Negroes. Understand Negroes. But it's
not true. No white man ever born ever understood what a Negro is thinking. What
he's feeling."

The car moves on down the empty street,
negotiates a left turn with majestic deliberation.

"And half the time that Negro," he continues, "he don't understand, either."

I know that the man beside me had once,
long back, had a bright-skinned, pretty wife.
She had left him to be set up by a well-off

white man (placée is the old word for it).
The Negro man beside me does not know
that I know this, but I have known it a long
time, and now I wonder what this man
is thinking as we ride along, silent again.

Just listening to talk as it comes is best,
but sometimes it doesn't come, or the man
says, "You ask me some questions," and so,
bit by bit, a certain pattern of questions
emerges, the old obvious questions, I suppose—the questions people respond to or
flinch from.

What are the white man's reasons for
segregation?

The man I am talking to is a yellow man,
about forty years old, shortish, rather fat,
with a very smooth, faintly Mongolian face,
eyes very shrewd but ready to smile. When
the smile really comes, there is a gold tooth
showing, to become, in that gold face, part
of the sincerity of the smile. His arms seem
somewhat short, and as he sits very erect in
a straight chair, he folds his hands over his
stomach. He gives the impression of a man
very much at home in himself, at peace in
himself, in his dignity, in his own pleasant,
smooth-skinned plumpness, in some sustaining humorousness of things. He owns a
small business, a shoe shop with a few employees.

"What does the white man do it for?"
he rephrases the question. He pauses, and
you can see he is thinking, studying on it,
his smooth, yellow face compressing a little.
All at once the face relaxes, a sort of humorous ripple, humorous but serious too, in a
sort of wry way, before the face settles to its
blandness. "You know," he says, "you know,
years and years I look at some white feller,
and I caint never figure him out. You go
long with him, years and years, and all of
a sudden he does something. I caint figure
out what makes him do the way he does. It
is like a mystery, you might say. I have
studied on it."

Another Negro, a very black man, small-
built and intense, leans forward in his chair.
He says it is money, so the white man can
have cheap labor, can make the money. He
is a bookish man, has been to a Negro college, and though he has never been out of

the South, his speech surprises me the way my native ear used to be surprised by the speech of a Negro born and raised, say, in Akron, Ohio. I make some fleeting, tentative association of his speech, his education, his economic interpretation of things; then let the notion slide.

"Yeah, yeah," the yellow man is saying, agreeing, "but—" He stops, shakes his head.

"But what?" I ask.

He hesitates, and I see the thumbs of the hands lightly clasped across his belly begin to move, ever so slowly, round and round each other. "All right," he says, "I might as well say it to you."

"Say what?"

"Mongrelization," he says, "that's what a white man will say. You ask him and he'll say that. He wants to head it off, he says. But—" He grins, the skin crinkles around his eyes, the grin shows the gold tooth. "But," he says, "look at my face. It wasn't any black man hung it on me."

The other man doesn't seem to think this is funny. "Yes," he says, "yes, they claim they don't want mongrelization. But who has done it? They claim Negroes are dirty, diseased, that that's why they want segregation. But they have Negro nurses for their children, they have Negro cooks. They claim Negroes are ignorant. But they won't associate with the smartest and best educated Negro. They claim—" And his voice goes on, winding up the bitter catalogue of paradoxes. I know them all. They are not new.

The smooth-faced, yellow man is listening. But he is thinking, too, the yellow blandness of his face creaming ever so little with his slow, humorous intentness. I ask him what he is thinking.

He grins, with philosophic ruefulness. "I was just studying on it," he says. "It's all true, what Mr. Elmo here says. But there must be something behind it all. Something he don't ever say, that white feller. Maybe—" He pauses, hunting for the formulation. "Maybe it's just pridefulness," he says, "him being white."

Later, I am talking with the hill-man organizer, the one with the handsome wife who asks me where I live now, and he is telling me why he wants segregation. "The Court," he says, "hit caint take no stick and mix folks up like you swivel and swull eggs broke in a bowl. Naw," he says, "you got to raise 'em up, the niggers, not bring the white folks down to nigger level." He illustrates with his pudgy, strong hands in the air before him, one up, one down, changing levels. He watches the hands, with fascination, as though he has just learned to do a complicated trick.

How would you raise the level? I ask.

"Give 'em good schools and things, yeah. But"—and he warms to the topic, leaning at me—"I'd 'bolish common law marriage. I'd put 'em in jail fer hit, and make 'em learn morals. Now a nigger don't know how to treat no wife, not even a nigger wife. He whup her and beat her and maybe carve on her jaw with a pocketknife. When he ought to trick and pet her, and set her on his knee like a white man does his wife."

Then I talk with a Negro grade-school teacher, in the country, in Tennessee. She is a mulatto woman, middle-aged, with a handsome aquiline face, rather Indian-looking. She is sitting in her tiny, pridefully clean house, with a prideful bookcase of books beyond her, talking with slow and detached tones. I know what her story has been, years of domestic service, a painfully acquired education, marriage to a professional man, no children ("It was a cross to bear, but maybe that's why I love 'em so and like to teach 'em not my own").

I ask her why white people want to keep segregation.

"You ought to see the school house I teach in," she says, and pauses, and her lips curl sardonically, "set in the mud and hogs can come under it, and the privies set back in the mud. And see some of the children that come there, out of homes with nothing, worse than the school house, no sanitation or cleanness, with disease and dirt and no manners. You wouldn't blame a white person for not wanting the white child set down beside them." Then with a slow movement of the shoulders, again the curl of the lips: "Why didn't the Federal Government give us money ten years ago for our school?

To get ready, to raise us up a little to integrate. It would have made it easier. But now—"

But now? I ask.

"You got to try to be fair," she says.

I am talking with an official of one of the segregation outfits, late at night, in his house, in a fringe subdivision, in a small living room with red velvet drapes at the one window, a TV set, new, on a table, a plastic or plaster bas-relief of a fox hunter hung on the wall, in color, the hunting coat very red and arrogant. My host is seventy-five years old, bald except for a fringe of gray hair, sallow-skinned, very clean and scrubbed-looking, white shirt but no tie, a knife-edge crease to his hard-finish gray trousers. He smokes cigarettes, one after another, with nervous, stained fingers.

He was born in North Kentucky, romantically remembers the tobacco night riders ("Yeah, it was tight, nobody talked tobacco much, you might get shot"), remembers the Civil War veterans ("even the GAR's") sitting round, talking to the kids ("Yeah, they talked their war, they had something to remember and be proud of, not like these veterans we got nowadays, nothing to be proud of"), started out to be a lawyer ("But Blackstone got too dry, but history now, that's different, you always get something out of it to think about"), but wound up doing lots of things, finally, for years, a fraternal organizer.

Yes, he is definitely a pro, and when he talks of Gerald L. K. Smith he bursts out, eyes a-gleam: "Lord, that man's mailing list would be worth a million dollars!" He is not the rabble-rouser, the crusader, but the persuader, the debater, the man who gives the reasons. He is, in fact, a very American type, the old-fashioned, self-made, back-country intellectual—the type that finds apotheosis in Mark Twain and Abraham Lincoln. If he is neither of them, if he says "gondorea" and "enviro-mental" and "ethnolology," if something went wrong, if nothing ever came out quite right for him along the long way, you can still sense the old, unappeased hungers, the old drives of a nameless ambition. And he is sadly contemptuous of his organizers, who "aren't up to it," who "just aren't posted on history and ethnolology," who just haven't got "the old gray matter."

I ask him why the white man wants segregation.

"He'll say one thing and another," he says, "he knows in his bones it ain't right to have mixing. But you got to give him the reasons, explain it to him. It is the ethnology of it you got to give. You got to explain how no *Negroes*"—he pronounces it with the elaborate polemical correctness, but not for polemics, just to set himself off intellectually, I suppose, from the people who might say *nigger*—"explain how no Negroes ever created a civilization. They are parasites. They haven't got the stuff up here." And he taps his forehead. "And explain how there is just two races, white and black, and—"

"What about the Bible," I ask, "doesn't the Bible say three?"

"Yes, but you know, between you and me, I don't reckon you have to take much stock in the Bible in this business. I don't take much stock in Darwin in some ways, either. He is too enviromental, he don't think enough about the blood. Yes, sir, I'll tell you, it's hard to come by good books on ethnolology these days. Got a good one from California the other day, though. But just one copy. Been out of print a long time. But like I was saying, the point is there's just two races, black and white, and the rest of them is a kind of mixing. You always get a mess when the mixing starts. Take India. They are a pure white people like you and me, and they had a pretty good civilization, too. Till they got to shipping on a little Negro blood. It don't take much to do the damage. Look at 'em now."

That is his argument. It is much the same argument given me by another official of another segregation group, whom I sit with a week later in another state, a lawyer, forty-five or -six, of strong middle height, sandy blond, hands strong with pale hairs and square-cut, scrubbed-looking nails. He is cagey at first, then suddenly warm, in an expanding, sincere, appealing way. He really wants to explain himself, wants to be regarded as an honest man, wants to be liked. I do like him, as he tells about himself, how he had gone to college, the hard way I gather, had prepared to be a teacher of history in high school, had given that up, had tried business in one way or another, had given that up, had studied law. "You ought to know my politics, too," he says. He was New Deal till the Court-packing plan. "That disgusted me," he says, and you believe him. Then he was for Willkie, then for Dewey, then Dixiecrat, then for Eisenhower. (I remember another lawyer, hired by another group: "Hell, all Southerners are Republicans at heart, conservative, and just don't know they're Republican.")

But Eisenhower doesn't satisfy my friend now. "We'll elect our own President. Our organization isn't just Southern. We're going national. Plenty of people in Chicago and other places feel like we do. And afraid of a big central government, too. We'll elect our own President and see how Chief Justice Warren's decision comes out."

I ask if the main point is the matter of States Rights, of local integrity.

"Yes, in a way," he says, "but you got to fight on something you can rouse people up about, on segregation. There's the constitutional argument, but your basic feeling, that's what you've got to trust—what you feel, not your reasons for it. But we've got argument, reasons."

He hesitates, thumps the desk top in a quick tattoo of his strong, scrubbed-looking fingers (he isn't a nervous man in the ordinary sense, but there are these sudden bursts), twists himself in his chair, then abruptly leans forward, jerks a drawer open (literally jerks it), and thrusts an envelope at me. "Heck, you might as well see it," he says.

I look at it. The stuff is not new. I have seen it before, elsewhere. It was used in the last gubernatorial campaign in Tennessee, it was used in the march on the Capitol at Nashville a few weeks ago. There are the handbills showing "Harlem Negro and White Wife," lying abed, showing "Crooner Roy Hamilton & Teenage Fans," who are

white girls, showing a school yard in Baltimore with Negro and white children, "the new look in education." On the back of one of the handbills is a crudely drawn valentine-like heart, in it the head of a white woman who (with feelings not indicated by the artist) is about to be kissed by a black man of the most primitive physiognomy. On the heart two vultures perch. Beneath it is the caption: "The Kiss of Death."

Below are the "reasons": "While Russia makes laws to protect her own race she continues to prod us to accept 14,000,000 Negroes as social equals and we are doing everything possible to please her. . . . Segregation is the law of God, not man. . . . Continue to rob the white race in order to bribe the Asiatic and Negro and these people will overwhelm the white race and destroy all progress, religion, invention, art, and return us to the jungle. . . . Negro blood destroyed the civilization of Egypt, India, Phoenicia, Carthage, Greece, and it will destroy America!"

I put the literature into my pocket, to join the other samples. "If there's trouble," I ask, "where will it begin?"

"We don't condone violence," he says.

"But if—just suppose," I say.

He doesn't hesitate. "The red-neck," he says, "that's what you call 'em around here. Those fellows—and I'm one of them myself, just a red-neck that got educated—are the ones who will feel the rub. He is the one on the underside of the plank with nothing between him and the bare black ground. He's got to have something to give him pride. Just to be better than something."

To be better than something: so we are back to the pridefulness the yellow man had talked about. But no, there is more, something else.

There is the minister, a Baptist, an intellectual-looking man, a man whose face indicates conscience and thoughtfulness, pastor of a good church in a good district in a thriving city. "It is simple," he says. "It is a matter of God's will and revelation. I refer you to Acts 17—I don't remember the verse. This is the passage the integrationists are always quoting to prove that integration is Christian. But they won't quote it all. It's the end that counts."

I looked it up: *And hath made of one blood all nations of men for to dwell on all the face of the earth, and hath determined the times before appointed, and the bounds of their habitation.*

There is the very handsome lady of forty-five, charming and witty and gay, full of dramatic mimicry, a wonderful range of phrase, a quick sympathy, a totally captivating talker of the kind you still occasionally find among women of the Deep South, but never now in a woman under forty. She is sitting before the fire in the fine room, her brother, big and handsome but barefoot and rigid drunk, opposite her. But she gaily overrides that small difficulty ("Oh, don't mind him, he's just had a whole bottle of brandy. Been on a high-lonesome all by himself. But poor Jack, he feels better now"). She has been talking about the Negroes on her plantation, and at last, about integration, but that only in one phrase, tossed off as gaily and casually as any other of the evening, so casual as to permit no discussion: "But of course we have to keep the white race intact."

But the husband, much her senior, who has said almost nothing all evening, lifts his strong, grizzled old face, and in a kind of *sotto voce* growl, not to her, not to me, not to anybody, utters: "In power—in power—you mean the white race in power."

And I think of another Southerner, an integrationist, saying to me: "You simply have to recognize a fact. In no county where the Negroes are two to one is the white man going to surrender political power, not with the Negroes in those counties in their present condition. It's not a question of being Southern. You put the same number of Yankee liberals in the same county and in a week they'd be behaving the same way. Living with something and talking about it are two very different things, and living with something is always the slow way."

And another, not an integrationist, from a black county, saying: "Yeah, let 'em take over and in six months you'd be paying the taxes but a black sheriff would be collecting 'em. You couldn't walk down the sidewalk. You'd be communized, all right."

But is it power. Merely power? Or any of the other things suggested thus far?

I think of a college professor in a section where about half the population is Negro. The college has no Negro students, but— "The heat is on," he says. "But listen, brother," he says, "lots of our boys don't like it a bit. Not a bit."

I ask would it be like the University of Alabama.

"It would be something, brother. I'll tell you that, brother. One of our boys—been fooling around with an organization uptown —he came to me and asked me to be sure to let him know when a nigger was coming, he and some friends would stop that clock. But I didn't want to hear student talk. I said, son, just don't tell me."

I asked what the faculty would do.

"Hide out, brother, hide out. And brother, I would, too."

Yes, he was a segregationist. I didn't have to ask him. Or ask his reasons, for he was talking on, in his rather nasal voice—leaning happily back in his chair in the handsome office, a spare, fiftyish man, dark-suited, rather dressy, sharp-nosed, with some fringe-remnants of sandy hair on an elongated, slightly freckled skull, rimless glasses on pale eyes: "Yeah, brother, back in my county there was a long ridge running through the county, and one side the ridge was good land, river bottom, and folks put on airs there and held niggers, but on the other side of the ridge the ground so pore you couldn't grow peas and nothing but pore white trash. So when the Civil War came, the pore white trash, as the folks who put on airs called them, just picked down the old rifle off the deer horns over the fireplace and joined the Federals coming down, just because they hated those fellows across the ridge. But don't get me wrong, brother. They didn't want any truck with niggers, either. To this day they vote Republican and hate niggers. It is just they hate niggers."

Yes, they hate niggers, but I am in another room, the library of a plantation house, in Mississippi, and the planter is talking to me, leaning his length back at ease, speaking deliberately from his high-nosed, commanding face, the very figure of a Wade Hampton or Kirby Smith, only the gray uniform and cavalry boots not there, saying: "No, I don't hate Negroes. I never had a minute's trouble with one in my life, and never intend to. I don't believe in getting lathered up, and I don't intend to get lathered up. I simply don't discuss the question with anybody. But I'll tell you what I feel. I came out of the university with a lot of ideals and humanitarianism, and I stayed by it as long as I could. But I tell you now what has come out of thirty years of experience and careful consideration. I have a deep contempt for the Negro race as it exists here. It is not so much a matter of ability as of character. Character."

He repeats the word. He is a man of character, it could never be denied. Of character and force. He is also a man of fine intelligence and good education. He reads Roman history. He collects books on the American West. He is widely traveled. He is unusually successful as a planter and businessman. He is a man of human warmth and generosity, and eminent justice. I overhear his wife, at this moment, talking to a Negro from the place, asking him if she can save some more money for him, to add to the hundred dollars she holds, trying to persuade him.

The husband goes on: "It's not so much the hands on my place, as the lawyers and doctors and teachers and insurance men and undertakers—oh, yes, I've had dealings all around, or my hands have. The character just breaks down. It is not dependable. They pay lip service to the white man's ideals of conduct. They say, yes, I believe in honesty and truth and morality. But it is just lip service. Most of the time. I don't intend to get lathered up. This is just my private opinion. I believe in segregation, but I can always protect myself and my family. I dine at my club and my land is my own, and when I travel, the places I frequent have few if any Negroes. Not that I'd ever walk out of a restaurant, for I'm no professional Southerner. And I'd never give a nickel to the

Citizens Council or anything like that. Nor have any of my friends, that I know of. That's townpeople stuff, anyway."

Later on, he says: "For years, I thought I loved Negroes. And I loved their humor and other qualities. My father—he was a firster around here, first man to put glass windows in for them, first to give them a written monthly statement, first to do a lot to help them toward financial independence—well, my father, he used to look at me and say how it would be. He said, son, they will knock it out of you. Well, they did. I learned the grimness and the sadness."

And later, as we ride down the long row of the houses of the hands, he points to shreds of screening at windows, or here and there a broken screen door. "One of my last experiments," he says, dourly. "Three months, and they poked it out of the kitchen window so they could throw slops on the bare ground. They broke down the front door so they could spit tobacco juice out on the porch floor."

We ride on. We pass a nicely painted house, with a fenced dooryard, with flower beds, and flower boxes on the porch, and good, bright-painted porch furniture. I ask who lives there. "One of the hands," he says, "but he's got some energy and character. Look at his house. And he loves flowers. Has only three children, but when there's work he gets it done fast, and then finds some more to do. Makes $4,500 to $5,000 a year." Some old pride, or something from the lost days of idealism, comes back into his tone.

I ask what the other people on the place think of the tenant with the nice house.

"They think he's just lucky." And he mimics, a little bitterly, without any humor: "Boss, looks lak Jefferson's chillen, they jes picks faster'n mine. Caint he'p it, Boss."

I ask what Jefferson's color is.

"A real black man, a real Negro, all right. But he's got character."

I look down the interminable row of dingy houses, over the interminable flat of black earth toward the river.

Now and then, I encounter a man whose argument for segregation, in the present context, has nothing to do with the Negro at all. At its simplest level its spokesman says: "I don't give a durn about the niggers, they never bother me one way or another. But I don't like being forced. Ain't no man ever forced me."

But the law always carries force, you say.

"Not this law. It's different. It ain't our law."

At another level, the spokesman will say it is a matter of constitutionality, pure and simple. He may even be an integrationist. But this decision, he will say, carries us one more step toward the power state, a cunningly calculated step, for this decision carries a moral issue and the objector to the decision is automatically put in the role of the enemy of righteousness. "But wait till the next decision," he will say. "This will be the precedent for it, and the next one won't have the moral façade."

Precedent for what? you ask.

"For government by sociology, not law," he will say.

"Is it government by law," one man asks me, "when certain members of the Supreme Court want to write a minority decision, and the great conciliator conciliates them out of it, saying that the thing is going to be controversial enough without the Court splitting? Damn it, the Court should split, if that's the honest reading of the law. We want the reading of the law, not conciliation by sociology. Even if we don't happen to like the kind of law it turns out to be in a particular case."

And another man: "Yes, government by sociology not law is a two-edged business. The next guy who gets in the saddle just picks another brand of sociology. And nothing to stop him, for the very notion of law is gone."

Pridefulness, money, level of intelligence, race, God's will, filth and disease, power, hate, contempt, legality—perhaps these are not all the words that get mentioned. There is another thing, whatever the word for it. An eminent Negro scholar is, I suppose, saying something about that other thing. "One thing," he says, "is that a lot of people down here just don't like change. It's not merely desegregation they're against so much, it's

just the fact of any change. They feel some emotional tie to the way things are. A change is disorienting, especially if you're pretty disoriented already."

Yes, a lot of them are disoriented enough already, uprooted, driven from the land, drawn from the land, befuddled by new opportunities, new ambitions, new obligations. They have entered the great anonymity of the new world.

And I hear a college student in the Deep South: "You know, it's just that people don't like to feel like they're spitting on their grandfather's grave. They feel some connection they don't want to break. Something would bother them if they broke it."

The young man is, I gather, an integrationist. He adds: "And sometimes something bothers them if they don't break it."

Let us give a name now to whatever it is that the eminent Negro scholar and the young white college boy were talking about. Let us, without meaning to be ironical, call it piety.

What does the Negro want?

The plump yellow man, with his hands folded calmly over his belly, the man who said it is the white man's "pridefulness," thinks, and answers the new question. "Opportunity," he says. "It's opportunity a man wants."

For what? I ask.

"Just to get along and make out. You know, like anybody."

"About education, now. If you got good schools, as good as anybody's, would that satisfy you?"

"Well," the yellow man begins, but the black, intense-faced man breaks in. "We never had them, we'd never have them!"

"You might get them now," I say, "under this pressure."

"Maybe," the yellow man agrees, "maybe. And it might have satisfied once. But"— and he shakes his head—"not now. That doctrine won't grip now."

"Not now," the intense-faced man says. "Not after the Supreme Court decision. We want the law."

"But when?" I ask. "Right now? Tomorrow morning?"

"The Supreme Court decision says—"
And he stops.

"It says deliberate speed," I say, "or something like that."

"If a Negro wants to study medicine, he can't study it. If he wants to study law, he can't study it. There isn't any way in this state for him to study it."

"Suppose," I say, "suppose professional and graduate schools got opened. To really qualified applicants, no funny business either way. Then they began some sort of staggered system, a grade or two at a time, from either top or bottom. Would something like that satisfy you? Perhaps not all over the state at the same time, some place serving as a sort of pilot for others where the going would be rougher."

The yellow man nods. The intense-faced man looks down at his new and newly polished good black shoes. He looks across at the wall. Not looking at me, he says, "Yes, if it was in good faith. If you could depend on it. Yes."

He hates to say it. At least, I think he hates to say it. It is a wrench, grudging.

I sit in another room, in another city, in the Deep South, with several men, two of them Negroes. One Negro is the local NAACP secretary, a man in build, color and quality strangely like the black, intense-faced man. I am asking again what will satisfy the Negroes. Only this time the intense-faced man does not as readily say, yes, a staggered system would be satisfactory. In fact, he doesn't say it at all. I ask him what his philosophy of social change is, in a democracy. He begins to refer to the law, to the Court, but one of the white men breaks in.

This white man is of the Deep South, born, bred and educated here. He is a middle-aged man, tall, rather spare but not angular, the impression of the lack of angularity coming, I suppose, from a great deliberation in voice and movement, a great calmness in voice and face. The face is an intellectual's face, a calm, dedicated face, but not a zealot's. His career, I know, has been identified with various causes of social reform. He has sat on many committees, has signed many things, some of them things I

personally take to be nonsense. What he says now, in his serene voice, the words and voice being really all that I know of him, is this: "I know that Mr. Cranford here"—and he nods toward this black, intense-faced man —"doesn't want any change by violence. He knows—we know—that change will take time. He wants a change in a Christian way that won't aggravate to violence. We have all got to live together. It will take time."

Nobody says anything. After a moment I go back to my question about the philosophy of social change. Wearily the intense-faced man says something, something not very relevant, not evasive, just not relevant. I let the matter drop. He sits with his head propped on his right hand, brow furrowed. He is not interested in abstractions. Why should he be?

Again, it is the Deep South, another town, another room, the bright, new-sparkling living room of the house of a Negro businessman, new furniture, new TV, new everything. There are several white men present, two journalists, myself (I've just come along to watch, I'm not involved), some technicians, and about ten Negroes, all in Sunday best, at ease but slightly formal, as though just before going in to a church service. Some of the Negroes, I have heard, are in the NAACP.

The technicians are rigging up their stuff, lights and cameras, etc., moving arrogantly in their own world superior to human concerns. In the background, in the dining room, the wife of our host, a plump, fortyish mulatto, an agreeable-looking woman wearing a new black dress with a discreet white design in it, stands watching a big new electric percolator on a silver tray. Another silver tray holds a bottle of Canadian whisky, a good whisky, and glasses. When someone comes out of the kitchen, I catch a glimpse of a gray-haired Negro woman, wearing a maid's uniform.

It is a bright, sunny, crisp day outside. The coffee is bubbling cheerfully. Out the window I see a little Negro girl, about ten years old, with a pink bow in her hair, an enormous bow, come out of a small pink house with aquamarine trim and shutters, and a dull blue roof. She stands a moment with the pink bow against the aquamarine door, then moves through the opening in the clipped privet hedge, a very tidy, persnickety hedge, and picks her way down the muddy street, where there is no sidewalk.

One of the journalists is instructing a Negro who is to be interviewed, a tall, well-set-up, jut-nosed, good-looking dark brown man in a blue suit. He has a good way of holding his head. "Now you're supposed to tell them," the journalist is saying, "what a lot of hogwash this separate but equal stuff is. What you said to me last night."

Pedagogical and irritable, one of the technicians says: "Quiet, quiet!"

They take a voice level. The dark brown man is very much at ease, saying: "Now is the time for all good men to come to the aid of their country."

The interview begins. The dark brown man, still very much at ease, is saying: "—and we're not disturbed. The only peop disturbed are those who have not taken an unbiased look. We who have taken our decision, we aren't disturbed." He goes on to say the Negroes want an interracial discussion on the "how" of desegregation—but with the background understanding that the Court decision is law.

The journalist cuts in: "Make it simple and direct. Lay it on the line."

The tall brown man is unruffled. There is sweat on his face now, but from the lamps. He wipes his face, and patiently, condescendingly, smiles at the journalist. "Listen," he says, "you all are going back to New York City. But we stay here. We aren't afraid, but we live here. They know what we think, but it's a way of putting it we got to think about."

He says it is going to take some time to work things out, he knows that, but there is a chorus from the Negroes crowded back out of range of the camera: "Don't put no time limit—don't put any time on it—no ten or fifteen years!"

The dark brown man doesn't put any time on it. He says all they want is to recognize the law and to sit down in a law-abiding way to work out the "how" and the "when."

"That's good, that's all right!" the chorus decides.

Leave the "how" in detail up to the specialists in education. As for the "when"— the dark brown, jut-nosed man hesitates a second: "Well, Negroes are patient. We can wait a little while longer."

The dark brown man gets up to his considerable height, wipes the sweat off his face, asks the journalist: "You got your playback?"

The chorus laughs. It is indulgent laughter of human vanity and such. Sure, any man would like to hear his voice played back, hear himself talking.

There is no playback. Not now, anyway.

The dark brown man is receiving the handshakes, the shoulder-slaps, of his friends. They think he did well. He did do well. He looks back over his shoulder at the white men, grins. "When I got to leave," he says, "who's going to give me that job as chauffeur? I see that nice Cadillac sitting out front there."

There are the quick, deep-throated giggles.

I turn to a Negro beside me. "Ten years ago," I ask, "would this have been possible?"

"No," he says.

Then there is another house, the tangle of wires, the jumble of rig and lights, and another Negro being arranged for an interview. There is no air of decorous festivity here, just a businesslike bustle, with the Negro waiting. This one will be knocked off quick. It's getting on to lunch.

This one, one of the journalists told me, is supposed to be the Uncle Tom. He is a middle-aged man, fair-sized, tallish, medium brown, with a balding, rather high forehead. He is wearing a good dark suit. His manner is dignified, slow, a little sad. I have known him before, know something about him. He had begun life as waterboy on a plantation, back in the times when "some folks didn't think a thing of bloodying a Negro's head, just for nothing, and I have seen their heads bloodied." But a white man on the plantation had helped him ("Noticed I was sort of quick and took an interest in things, trying to learn"), and now he is a preacher. For a voice level he does not say, "Now is the time for all good men to come to the aid of their country." He says: "Jesus wept, Jesus wept, Jesus wept."

The journalist tells him he is supposed to say some good things for segregation.

The Negro doesn't answer directly to that. "If you have some opinions of your own," he says, "your own people sometimes call you a son-of-a-gun, and sometimes the white people call you a son-of-a-gun."

Your own people. And I remember that the men at the last house had said: "Don't tell him you've seen us, don't tell him that or you won't get him to talk."

Is integration a good thing, the journalist asks him, and he says: "Till Negro people get as intelligent and self-sustaining they can't mix." But he flares up about discrimination along with segregation: "That's what makes Negroes bitter, wage differentials, no good jobs, that and the ballot." As for the Court decision, he says: "It's something for people to strive for, to ascertain their best."

I break in—I don't think the machinery is going yet—and ask about humiliation as a bar to Negro fulfilment.

"Segregation did one thing," he says. "No other race but the Negroes could build up as much will to go on and do things. To get their goals."

What goals? I ask.

"Just what anybody wants, just everything people can want to be a citizen," he says.

This isn't what the journalist has come for.

Things aren't promising too well. Uncle Tom is doing a disappearing act, Old Black Joe is evaporating, the handkerchief-head, most inconveniently, isn't there. The genie has got out of the bottle clearly labeled: *Negro* segregationist.

But maybe the genie can be coaxed back into the bottle. The sad-mannered man is, the journalist suggests, a pro-segregationist in that he thinks segregation built a will to achieve something.

The machinery gets going, the mike is lifted on its rod, the slow, sad voice speaks: "For segregation has test steel into the Negro race and this is one valuable point of segregation—segregation has proven that Negroes in the South, where it's practiced most,

have done a fine job in building an economic strength beyond that of many other sections in the United States of America. Negroes own more farm land in Mississippi than any other state in the United States that is engaged in agriculture."

He goes along, he says, "with the idea you should have a moderate approach. You will never be able to integrate children on the school campus, the mothers holding a lot of bitterness in their hearts against each other white and colored."

It will take time, he says: "It is absurd otherwise, it's just foolish thinking for people to believe you can get the South to do in four or five years what they have been doing in the North for one hundred years. These people are emotional about their tradition, and you've got to have an educational program to change their way of thinking and this will be a slow process."

Yes, the genie is safely back in the labeled bottle. Or is he?

For the slow, sad voice is saying: "—has got to outthink the white man, has got to outlive the white man—"

Is saying: "—no need of saying the South won't ever integrate—"

Is saying: "—not ultimate goal just to go to white schools and travel with white people on conveyances over the country. No, the Negro, he is a growing people and he will strive for all the equalities belonging to any American citizen. He is a growing people."

Yes, Uncle Tom is gone again, and gone for good. Too bad for the program. I wondered if they got this last part on tape.

The Negro turns to the journalist and asks if he has interviewed other people around.

"Yes, saw Mr. So-and-so of the Citizens Council."

Had we interviewed any other Negroes?

"Oh, some," after a shade of hesitation.

Had we seen So-and-so and So-and-so?

"No—why, no. Well, we want to thank you—"

We leave the sad-mannered, slow man and we know that he knows. He isn't a big enough fool not to know. White men have lied to him before. What is one more time after all the years?

Besides, what if you do tell him a lie?

There are, as a matter of fact, in Arkansas, Negroes who go from door to door collecting money to fight integration. There *are* Uncle Toms.

So it all evens out.

I ask my question of the eminent Negro scholar. His reply is immediate: "It's not so much what the Negro wants as what he doesn't want. The main point is not that he has poor facilities. It is that he must endure a constant assault on his ego. He is denied human dignity."

And I think of the yellow girl wearing the salmon sweater and slacks, in the shack in the sea of mud, at dusk, the girl whose husband has been shot, and she says: "It's how yore feelings git tore up all the time. The way folks talk, sometimes. It ain't what they say sometimes, if they'd jes say it kind."

She had gone to a store, in another town, for some dress goods, and had requested a receipt for the minister who manages the fund raised in her behalf. By the receipt the saleswoman identifies her and asks if "that man up yonder is still in jail for killing a nigger."

"Well," the girl had said, "if you want to put it that a-way."

"They can't do anything to a man for something he does drunk," the saleswoman has said.

The girl has laid the package down on the counter. "If you want it that a-way," she has said, "you kin take back yore dress goods. They's other places to buy."

She tells me the story.

And I think of another woman, up in Tennessee, middle-aged, precise, the kind of woman who knows her own competent mind, a school inspector for county schools, a Negro. "We don't want to socialize. That's not what we want. We do everything the white folks do already, even if we don't spend as much money doing it. And we have more fun. But I don't want to be insulted. If somebody has to tell you something, about some regulation or other, they could say it in a low, kind voice, not yell it out at you. And when I go to a place to buy something, and have that dollar bill in my hand, I want to be treated right. And I

won't ride on a bus. I won't go to a restaurant in a town where there's just one. I'll go hungry. I won't be insulted at the front door and then crawl around to the back. You've got to try to keep some respect."

And in Tennessee again, the Negro at the biracial committee meeting says: "My boy is happy in the Negro school where he goes. I don't want him to go to the white school and sit by your boy's side. But I'd die fighting for his right to go."

"We don't want to socialize," the woman in Tennessee says.

The college student, a Negro, in Tennessee, says: "The Negro doesn't want social equality. My wife is my color. I'm above wanting to mix things up. That's low class. Low class of both races."

The Negro man in Mississippi says: "Take a Negro man wanting a white woman. A man tends to want his own kind, now. But the white folks make such an awful fuss about it. They make it seem so awful special-like. Maybe that's what makes it sort of prey on some folks' mind."

And I remember the gang rape by four Negroes of a white woman near Memphis last fall, shortly after the Till killing. "One of our boys was killed down in Mississippi the other day and we're liable to kill you," one of the Negroes said as they bludgeoned the man who was with the woman and told him to get going.

This is a question for Negroes only. *Is there any difference between what the Negro feels at the exclusions of segregation, and what a white man feels at the exclusions which he, any man, must always face at some point?*

"Yes, it's different," the Negro college administrator says, "when your fate is on your face. Just that. It's the unchangeableness. Now a white man, even if he knows he can't be President, even if he knows the chances for his son are one in many millions—long odds—still there's an idea there."

And the Negro lawyer: "Yes, it's different. But it's not easy to name it. Take how some unions come in and make some plant build nice rest rooms, one for white, one for Negroes, but same tile, same fixtures and all.

But off the white ones, there's a little lounge for smoking. To make 'em feel superior to somebody. You see what I mean, how it's different?"

He thinks some more. "Yes," he says, "I got my dreams and hopes and aspirations, but me, I have to think what is sort of possible in the possibilities and probabilities. Some things I know I can't think on because of the circumstances of my birth."

And he thinks again, looking out the window, over Beale Street. "Yes, there's a difference," he says. "A Negro, he doesn't really know some things, but he just goes walking pregnant with worries, not knowing their name. It's he's lost his purpose, somewhere. He goes wandering and wondering, and no purpose."

I look out the window, too, over Beale Street. It is late afternoon. I hear the pullulation of life, the stir and new tempo toward evening, the babble of voices, a snatch of laughter. I hear the remorseless juke boxes.. They shake the air.

What's coming?

"Whatever it is," the college student in the Deep South says, "I'd like to put all the Citizens Council and all the NAACP in one room and give every man a baseball bat and lock 'em in till it was over. Then maybe some sensible people could work out something."

What's coming? I say it to the country grade-school superintendent. He is a part-time farmer, too, and now he is really in his role as farmer, not teacher, as we stand, at night, under the naked light of a flyspecked 200-watt bulb hanging from the shed roof, and he oversees two Negroes loading sacks of fertilizer on a truck. "I know folks round here," he says, and seeing his hard, aquiline, weathered face, with the flat, pale, hard eyes, I believe him.

"They aren't raised up to it," he says. "Back in the summer now, I went by a lady's house to ask about her children starting to school. Well, she was a real old-timey gal, a gant-headed, barefoot, snuff-dipping, bonnet-wearing, hard-ankled old gal standing out in the tobacco patch, leaning on her hoe, and she leaned at me and said,

'Done hear'd tell 'bout niggers gonna come in,' and before I could say anything, she said, 'Not with none of my young 'uns,' and let out a stream of ambeer."

"Would you hire a Negro teacher?" I asked.

"I personally would, but folks wouldn't stand for it, not now, mostly those who never went much to school themselves. Unless I could prove I couldn't get white." He paused. "And it's getting damned hard to get white, I tell you," he says.

I ask if integration will come.

"Sure," he says, "in fifty years. Every time the tobacco crop is reduced, we lose just that many white sharecroppers and Negroes. That eases the pain."

What's coming? And the Methodist minister, riding with me in the dusk, in the drizzle, by the flooded bayou, says: "It'll come, desegregation and the vote and all that. But it will be twenty-five, thirty years, a generation. You can preach love and justice, but it's a slow pull till you get the education." He waves a hand toward the drowned black cotton fields, stretching on forever, toward the rows of shacks marshaled off into the darkening distance, toward the far cypresses where dusk is tangled. "You can see," he says. "Just look, you can see."

What's coming? I ask the young lawyer in a mid-South city, a lawyer retained by one of the segregation outfits. "It's coming that we got to fight this bogus law," he says, "or we'll have a lot of social dis-tensions. The bogus law is based on social stuff and progress and just creates dis-tension. But we're gaining ground. Some upper-class people, I mean a real rich man, is coming out for us. And we get rolling, a Southern President could repack the court. But it's got so a man can't respect the Supreme Court. All this share-the-wealth and Communist stuff and progress. You can't depend on law any more."

What can you depend on? I ask.

"Nothing but the people. Like the Civil War."

I suggest that whatever the constitutional rights and wrongs of the Civil War were, we had got a new Constitution out of it.

"No," he said, "just a different type of dog saying what it is."

I ask if, in the end, the appeal would be to violence.

"No, I don't believe in violence. I told Mr. Perkins, when we had our mass meeting, to keep the in-ci-dents down. But you get a lot of folks and there's always going to be in-ci-dents."

I ask if at Tuscaloosa the mob hadn't dictated public policy.

"Not dictate exactly." And he smiles his handsome smile. "But it was a lot of people."

He has used the word *progress*, over and over, to damn what he does not like. It is peculiar how he uses this laudatory word— I can imagine how he would say it in other contexts, on public occasions, rolling it on his tongue—as the word now for what he hates most. I wonder how deep a cleavage the use of that word indicates.

What's coming? I ask the handsome, aristocratic, big gray-haired man, sitting in his rich office, high over the city, an ornament of the vestry, of boards of directors, of club committees, a man of exquisite simplicity and charm, and a member of a segregation group.

"We shall exhaust all the legal possibilities," he says.

I ask if he thinks his side will win. The legal fight, that is.

He rolls a cigarette fastidiously between strong, white, waxy forefinger and thumb. "No," he says. "But it is just something you have to do." He rolls the cigarette, looking out the window over the city, a city getting rich now, "filthy rich," as somebody has said to me. There is the undertone and unceasing susurrus of traffic in the silence of his thoughts.

"Well," he says at last, "to speak truth, I think the whole jig is up. We'll have desegregation right down the line. And you know why?"

I shake my head.

"Well, I'll tell you. You see those girls in my office outside, those young men. Come from good lower-middle-class homes, went to college a lot of them. Well, a girl comes in here and says to me a gentleman is wait-

ing. She shows him in. He is as black as the ace of spades. It just never crossed that girl's mind, what she was saying, when she said a gentleman was waiting." He pauses. "Yes, sir," he says, "I just don't know why I'm doing it."

I am thinking of walking down Canal Street, in New Orleans, and a man is saying to me: "Do you know how many millions a year the Negroes spend up and down this street?"

No, I had said, I didn't know.

He tells me the figure, then says: "You get the logic of that, don't you?"

What's coming? And the college student says: "I'll tell you one thing that's coming, there's not going to be any academic freedom or any other kind around here if we don't watch out. Now I'm a segregationist, that is, the way things are here right now, but I don't want anybody saying I can't listen to somebody talk about something. I can make up my own mind."

What's coming? And a state official says: "Integration sure and slow. A creeping process. If the NAACP has got bat sense, not deliberately provoking things as in the University of Alabama deal. They could have got that girl in quiet and easy, but that wouldn't satisfy them. No, they wanted the bang. As for things in general, grade schools and high schools, it'll be the creeping process. The soft places first, and then one county will play football or basketball with Negroes on the team. You know how it'll be. A creeping process. There'll be lots of court actions, but don't let court actions fool you. I bet you half the superintendents over in Tennessee will secretly welcome a court action in their county. Half of 'em are worried morally and half financially, and a court action just gets 'em off the hook. They didn't initiate it, they can always claim, but it gets them off the hook. That's the way I would feel, I know."

What's coming? I ask the taxi driver in Memphis. And he says: "Lots of dead niggers round here, that's what's coming. Look at Detroit, lots of dead niggers been in the Detroit River, but it won't be a patch on the Ole Mississippi. But hell, it won't stop nothing. Fifty years from now everybody will be gray anyway, Jews and Germans and French and Chinese and niggers, and who'll give a durn?"

The cab has drawn to my destination. I step out into the rain and darkness. "Don't get yourself drownded now," he says. "You have a good time now. I hope you do."

What's coming? And a man in Arkansas says: "We'll ride it out. But it looked like bad trouble one time. Too many outsiders. Mississippians and all. They come back here again, somebody's butt will be busted."

And another man: "Sure, they aim for violence, coming in here. When a man gets up before a crowd and plays what purports to be a recording of an NAACP official, an inflammatory sex thing, and then boasts of having been in on a lynching himself, what do you call it? Well, they got him on the witness stand, under oath, and he had to admit he got the record from Patterson, of the Citizens Council, and admitted under oath the lynching statement. He also admitted under oath some other interesting facts—that he had once been indicted for criminal libel but pleaded guilty to simple libel, that he has done sixty days for contempt of court on charges of violating an injunction having to do with liquor. Yeah, he used to run a paper called *The Rub Down*— that's what got him into the libel business. What's going to happen if a guy like that runs things? I ask you."

What's coming? And the planter leans back with the glass in his hand. "I'm not going to get lathered up," he says, "because it's no use. Why is the country so lathered up to force the issue one way or the other? Democracy—democracy has just come to be a name for what you like. It has lost responsibility, no local integrity left, it has been bought off. We've got the power state coming on, and communism or socialism, whatever you choose to call it. Race amalgamation is inevitable. I can't say I like any of it. I am out of step with the times."

What's coming? I ask the Episcopal rector, in the Deep South, a large handsome man, almost the twin of my friend sitting in the fine office overlooking the rich city. He has just told me that when he first came down from the North, a generation back, his

bishop had explained it all to him, how the Negroes' skull capacity was limited. But as he has said, brain power isn't everything, there's justice, and not a member of his congregation wasn't for conviction in the Till case.

"But the Negro has to be improved before integration," he says. "Take their morals, we are gradually improving the standard of morality and decency."

The conversation veers, we take a longer view. "Well, anthropologically speaking," he says, "the solution will be absorption, the Negro will disappear."

I ask how this is happening.

"Low-class people, immoral people, libertines, wastrels, prostitutes and such," he says.

I ask if, in that case, the raising of the moral level of the Negro does not prevent, or delay, what he says is the solution.

The conversation goes into a blur.

What's coming? And the young man from Mississippi says: "Even without integration, even with separate but pretty good facilities for the Negro, the Negro would be improving himself. He would be making himself more intellectually and socially acceptable. Therefore, as segregationists, if we're logical, we ought to deny any good facilities to them. Now I'm a segregationist, but I can't be that logical."

What's coming? And the officer of the Citizens Council chapter says: "Desegregation, integration, amalgamation—none of it will come here. To say it will come is defeatism. It won't come if we stand firm."

And the old man in north Tennessee, a burly, full-blooded, red-faced, raucous old man, says: "Hell, son, it's easy to solve. Just blend 'em. Fifteen years and they'll all be blended in. And by God, I'm doing my part!'

Out of Memphis, I lean back in my seat on the plane, and watch the darkness slide by. I know what the Southerner feels going out of the South, the relief, the expanding vistas. Now, to the sound of the powerful, magnanimous engines bearing me through the night, I think of that, thinking of the new libel laws in Mississippi, of the academic pressures, of academic resignations, of the Negro facing the shotgun blast, of the white man with a nice little, hard-built business being boycotted, of the college boy who said: "I'll just tell you, everybody is *scairt.*"

I feel the surge of relief. But I know what the relief really is. It is the relief from responsibility.

Now you may eat the bread of the Pharisee and read in the morning paper, with only a trace of irony, how out of an ultimate misery of rejection some Puerto Rican school boys—or is it Jews or Negroes or Italians?—who call themselves something grand, The Red Eagles or the Silver Avengers, have stabbed another boy to death, or raped a girl, or trampled an old man into a bloody mire. If you can afford it, you will, according to the local mores, send your child to a private school, where there will be, of course, a couple of Negro children on exhibit. And that delightful little Chinese girl who is so good at dramatics. Or is it finger painting?

Yes, you know what the relief is. It is the flight from the reality you were born to.

But what is that reality you have fled from?

It is the fact of self-division. I do not mean division between man and man in society. That division is, of course, there, and it is important. Take, for example, the killing of Clinton Melton, in Glendora, Mississippi, in the Delta, by a man named Elmer Kimbell, a close friend of Milam (who had been acquitted of the murder of Till, whose car was being used by Kimbell at the time of the killing of Melton, and to whose house Kimbell returned after the deed).

Two days after the event, twenty-one men —storekeepers, planters, railroad men, school teachers, preacher, bookkeepers—sent money to the widow for funeral expenses, with the note: "Knowing that he was outstanding in his race, we the people of this town are deeply hurt and donate as follows." When the Lions Club met three days after the event, a resolution was drawn and signed by all members present: "We consider the taking of the life of Clinton Melton an outrage against him, against all the people of

Glendora, against the people of Mississippi as well as against the entire human family. . . . We humbly confess in repentance for having so lived as a community that such an evil occurrence could happen here, and we offer ourselves to be used in bringing to pass a better realization of the justice, righteousness and peace which is the will of God for human society."

And the town began to raise a fund to realize the ambition of the dead man, to send his children to college, the doctor of Glendora offered employment in his clinic to the widow, and the owner of the plantation where she had been raised offered to build for her and her children a three-room house.

But, in that division between man and man, the jury that tried Elmer Kimbell acquitted him.

But, in that same division between man and man, when the newspaper of Clarksdale, Mississippi, in the heart of the Delta, ran a front-page story of the acquittal, that story was bracketed with a front-page editorial saying that there had been some extenuation for acquittal in the Till case, with confusion of evidence and outside pressures, but that in the Melton case there had been no pressure and "we were alone with ourselves and we flunked it."

Such division between man and man is important. As one editor in Tennessee said to me: "There's a fifth column of decency here, and it will, in the end, betray the extremists, when the politicians get through." But such a division between man and man is not as important in the long run as the division within the individual man.

Within the individual there are, or may be, many lines of fracture. It may be between his own social idealism and his anger at Yankee Phariseeism. (Oh, yes, he remembers that in the days when Federal bayonets supported the black Reconstruction state governments in the South, not a single Negro held elective office in any Northern state.) It may be between his social views and his fear of the power state. It may be between his social views and his clan sense: It may be between his allegiance to organized labor and his racism—for status or blood purity. It may be between his Christianity and his social prejudice. It may be between his sense of democracy and his ingrained attitudes toward the Negro. It may be between his own local views and his concern for the figure America cuts in the international picture. It may be between his practical concern at the money loss to society caused by the Negro's depressed condition and his own personal gain or personal prejudice. It may be, and disastrously, between his sense of the inevitable and his emotional need to act against the inevitable.

There are almost an infinite number of permutations and combinations, but they all amount to the same thing, a deep intellectual rub, a moral rub, anger at the irremediable self-division, a deep exacerbation at some failure to find identity. That is the reality.

It expresses itself in many ways. I sit for an afternoon with an old friend, a big, weather-faced, squarish man, a farmer, an intelligent man, a man of good education, of travel and experience, and I ask him questions. I ask if he thinks we can afford, in the present world picture, to alienate Asia by segregation here at home. He hates the question. "I hate to think about it," he says. "It's too deep for me," he says, and moves heavily in his chair. We talk about Christianity—he is a church-going man—and he says: "Oh, I know what the Bible says, and Christianity, but I just can't think about it. My mind just shuts up."

My old friend is an honest man. He will face his own discomfort. He will not try to ease it by passing libel laws to stop discussion or by firing professors.

There are other people whose eyes brighten at the thought of the new unity in the South, the new solidarity of resistance. These men are idealists, and they dream of preserving the traditional American values of individualism and localism against the anonymity, irresponsibility and materialism of the power state, against the philosophy of the ad-man, the morality of the Kinsey report, and the gospel of the bitch-goddess. *To be Southern again*: to recreate a habitation for the values they would preserve, to achieve in unity some clarity of spirit, to

envisage some healed image of their own identity.

Some of these men are segregationists. Some are desegregationists, but these, in opposing what they take to be the power-state implications of the Court decision, find themselves caught, too, in the defense of segregation. And defending segregation, both groups are caught in a paradox: in seeking to preserve individualism by taking refuge in the vision of a South redeemed in unity and antique virtue, they are fleeing from the burden of their own individuality—the intellectual rub, the moral rub. To state the matter in another way, by using the argument of *mere* social continuity and the justification by mere *mores*, they think of a world in which circumstances and values are frozen; but the essence of individuality is the willingness to accept the rub which the flux of things provokes, to accept one's fate in time. What heroes would these idealists enshrine to take the place of Jefferson and Lee, those heroes who took the risk of their fate?

Even among these people some are in discomfort, discomfort because the new unity, the new solidarity, once it descends from the bright world of Idea, means unity with some quite concrete persons and specific actions. They say: "Yes—yes, we've got to unify." And then: "But we've got to purge certain elements."

But who will purge whom? And what part of yourself will purge another part?

"Yes, it's our own fault," the rich businessman, active in segregation, says. "If we'd ever managed to bring ourselves to do what we ought to have done for the Negro, it would be different now, if we'd managed to educate them, get them decent housing, decent jobs."

So I tell him what a Southern Negro professor had said to me. He had said that the future now would be different, would be hopeful, if there could just be "one gesture of graciousness" from the white man—even if the white man didn't like the Supreme Court decision, he might try to understand the Negro's view, not heap insult on him.

And the segregationist, who is a gracious man, seizes on the word. "Graciousness," he says, "that's it, if we could just have managed some graciousness to the race. Sure, some of us, a lot of us, could manage some graciousness to individual Negroes, some of us were grateful to individuals for being gracious to us. But you know, we couldn't manage it for the race." He thinks a moment, then says: "There's a Negro woman buried in the family burial place. We loved her."

I believe him when he says it. And he sinks into silence, feeling the rub, for the moment anyway, between the man who can talk in terms of graciousness, in whatever terms that notion may present itself to him, and the man who is a power for segregation.

This is the same man who has said to me, earlier, that he knows integration to be inevitable, doesn't know why he is fighting it. But such a man is happier, perhaps, than those men, destined by birth and personal qualities to action and leadership, who in the face of what they take to be inevitable feel cut off from all action. "I am out of step with the times," one such man says to me, and his wife says, "You know, if we feel the way we do, we ought to do something about it," and he, in some deep, inward, unproclaimed bitterness, says, "No, I'm not going to get lathered up about anything."

Yes, there are many kinds of rub, but I suppose that the commonest one is the moral one—the Christian one, in fact, for the South is still a land of faith. There is, of course, the old joke that after the Saturday night lynching, the congregation generally turns up a little late for church, and the sardonic remark a man made to me about the pro-integration resolution of the Southern Baptist Convention: "They were just a little bit exalted. When they got back with the home folks a lot of 'em wondered how they did it."

But meanwhile, there are the pastors at Glendora and Hoxie and Oxford and other nameless places. And I remember a pastor, in Tennessee, a Southerner born and bred, saying to me: "Yes, I think the Court decision may have set back race equality—it was coming fast, faster than anybody could guess, because so quiet. But now some people get so put out with the idea of Negroes in church, they stop me on the street and

say if I ever let one in they won't come to church. So I ask about Heaven, what will they do in Heaven?

" 'Well,' one woman said, 'I'll just let God segregate us.'

" 'You'll *let* God segregate you?' I said, and she flounced off. But I ask, where is Christianity if people can't worship together? There's only one thing to try to preach, and that is Christ. And there's only one question to ask, and that is what would Christ do?"

Will they go with him, I ask.

"They are good Christian people, most of them," he says. "It may be slow, but they are Christians."

And in a town in south Kentucky, in a "black county," a Confederate county, where desegregation is now imminent in the high schools, the superintendent says to me: "The people here are good Christian people, trying to do right. When this thing first came up, the whole board said they'd walk out. But the ministers got to preaching, and the lawyers to talking on it, and they came around."

I asked how many were influenced by moral, how many by legal, considerations.

About half and half, he reckons, then adds: "I'm a Rebel myself, and I don't deny it, but I'm an American and a law-abiding citizen. A man can hate an idea but know it's right, and it takes a lot of thinking and praying to bring yourself around. You just have to uncover the unrecognized sympathy in the white man for the Negro humiliation."

Fifty miles away I shall sit in a living room and hear some tale of a Negro coming to somebody's front door—another house— and being admitted by a Negro servant and being found by the master of the house, who says: "I don't care if Susie did let you in. I don't care if Jesus Christ let you in. No black son-of-a-bitch is coming to my front door."

After the tale, there is silence. All present are segregationist, or I think they are.

Then one woman says: "Maybe he did take a lot on himself, coming to the front door. But I can't stand it. He's human."

And another woman: "I think it's a moral

question, and I suffer, but I can't feel the same way about a Negro as a white person. It's born in me. But I pray I'll change."

The successful businessman in Louisiana says to me: "I have felt the moral question. It will be more moral when we get rid of segregation. But I'm human enough—I guess it's human to be split up—to want things just postponed till my children are out of school. But I can't lift my finger to delay things."

But this man, privately admitting his division of feeling, having no intention of public action on either side, is the sort of man who can be trapped, accidentally, into action.

There is the man who got the letter in the morning mail, asking him to serve as chairman of a citizens committee to study plans for desegregation in his county. "I was sick," he says, "and I mean literally sick. I felt sick all day. I didn't see how I could get into something like that. But next morning, you know, I did it."

That county now has its schedule for desegregation.

There is another man, a lawyer, who has been deeply involved in a desegregation action. "I never had much feeling of prejudice, but hell, I didn't have any theories either, and I now and then paid some lip service to segregation. I didn't want to get mixed up in the business. But one night a telephone call came. I told the man I'd let him know next day. You know, I was sick. I walked on back in the living room and my wife looked at me. She must have guessed what it was. 'You going to do it?' she asked me. I said, hell I didn't know, and went out. I was plain sick. But next day I did it. Well," he says, and grins, and leans back under the shelves of law books, "and I'm stuck with it. But you know, I'm getting damned tired of the paranoiacs and illiterates I'm up against."

Another man, with a small business in a poor county, "back in the shelf country," he calls it, a short, strong-looking, ovoidal kind of man with his belt cutting into his belly when he leans back in his office chair. He is telling me what he has been through. "I wouldn't tell you a lie," he says. "I'm

Southern through and through, and I guess I got every prejudice a man can have, and I certainly never would have got mixed up in this business if it hadn't been for the Court decision. I wouldn't be out in front. I was just trying to do my duty. Trying to save some money for the county. I never expected any trouble. And we might not have had any if it hadn't been for outsiders, one kind and another.

"But what nobody understands is how a man can get cut up inside. You try to live like a Christian with your fellow man, and suddenly you find out it is all mixed up. You put in twenty-five years trying to build up a nice little business and raise up a family and it looks like it will all be ruined. You get word somebody will dynamite your house and you in it. You go to lawyers and they say they sympathize, but nobody'll take your case. But the worst is, things just go round and round in your head. Then they won't come a-tall, and you lay there in the night. You might say, it's the psychology of it you can't stand. Getting all split up. Then, all of a sudden, somebody stops you on the street and calls you something, a so-and-so nigger-lover. And you know, I got so mad not a thing mattered any more. I just felt like I was all put back together again."

He said he wished he could write it down, how awful it is for a man to be split up.

Negroes, they must be split up, too, I think. They are human, too. There must be many ways for them to be split up. I remember asking a Negro school teacher if she thought Negro resentment would be a bar to integration. "Some of us try to teach love," she says, "as well as we can. But some of us teach hate. I guess we can't help it."

Love and hate, but more than that, the necessity of confronting your own motives: *Do we really want to try to work out a way to live with the white people or do we just want to show them, pay off something, show them up, rub their noses in it?*

And I can imagine the grinding anger, the sense of outrage of a Negro crying out within himself: *After all the patience, after all the humility, after learning and living those virtues, do I have to learn magnanimity, too?*

Yes, I can imagine the outrage, the outrage as some deep, inner self tells him, yes, he must.

I am glad that white people have no problem as hard as that.

The taxi drew up in front of the apartment house, and I got out, but the driver and I talked on for a moment. I stood there in the rain, then paid him, and ran for the door. It wasn't that I wanted to get out of the rain. I had an umbrella. I wanted to get in and write down what he had said.

He was a local man, born near Nashville, up near Goodlettsville, "raised up with niggers." He had been in the army, with lots of fighting, Africa, Sicily, Italy, but a lot of time bossing work gangs. In Africa, at first, it had been Arabs, but Arabs weren't "worth a durn." Then they got Negro work battalions.

But here are the notes:

Niggers a lot better than Arabs, but they didn't hurt themselves—didn't any of 'em git a hernia for Uncle Sam—race prejudice —but it ain't our hate, it's the hate hung on us by the old folks dead and gone. Not I mean to criticize the old folks, they done the best they knew, but that hate, we don't know how to shuck it. We got that Goddamn hate stuck in our craw and can't puke it up. If white folks quit shoving the nigger down and calling him a nigger he could maybe get to be a asset to the South and the country. But how stop shoving?

We are the prisoners of our history.

Or are we?

There is one more interview I wish to put on record. I shall enter it by question and answer.

Q. You're a Southerner, aren't you?

A. Yes.

Q. Are you afraid of the power state?

A. Yes.

Q. Do you think the Northern press sometimes distorts Southern news?

A. Yes.

Q. Assuming that they do, why do they do it?

A. They like to feel good.

Q. What do you think the South ought to do about that distortion?

A. Nothing.

Q. Nothing? What do you mean, nothing?

A. The distortion—that's the Yankees' problem, not ours.

Q. You mean they ought to let the South work out a way to live with the Negro?

A. I don't think the problem is to learn to live with the Negro.

Q. What is it then?

A. It is to learn to live with ourselves.

Q. What do you mean?

A. I don't think you can live with yourself when you are humiliating the man next to you.

Q. Don't you think the races have made out pretty well, considering?

A. Yes. By some sort of human decency and charity, God knows how. But there was always an image of something else.

Q. An image?

A. Well, I knew an old lady who grew up in a black county, but a county where relations had been, as they say, good. She had a fine farm and a good brick house, and when she got old she sort of retired from the world. The hottest summer weather and she would lock all the doors and windows at night, and lie there in the airless dark. But sometimes she'd telephone to town in the middle of the night. She would telephone that somebody was burning the Negroes out there on her place. She could hear their screams. Something was going on in her old head which in another place and time would not have been going on in her old head. She had never, I should think, seen an act of violence in her life. But something was going on in her head.

Q. Do you think it is chiefly the red-neck who causes violence?

A. No. He is only the cutting edge. He, too, is a victim. Responsibility is a seamless garment. And the northern boundary of that garment is not the Ohio River.

Q. Are you for desegregation?

A. *Yes.*

Q. When will it come?

A. Not soon.

Q. When?

A. When enough people, in a particular place, a particular county or state, cannot live with themselves any more. Or realize they don't have to.

Q. What do you mean, don't have to?

A. When they realize that desegregation is just one small episode in the long effort for justice. It seems to me that that perspective, suddenly seeing the business as little, is a liberating one. It liberates you from yourself.

Q. Then you think it is a moral problem?

A. Yes, but no moral problem gets solved abstractly. It has to be solved in a context for possible solution.

Q. Can contexts be changed?

A. Sure. We might even try to change them the right way.

Q. Aren't you concerned about possible racial amalgamation?

A. I don't even think about it. We have to deal with the problem our historical moment proposes, the burden of our time. We all live with a thousand unsolved problems of justice all the time. We don't even recognize a lot of them. We have to deal only with those which the moment proposes to us. Anyway, we can't legislate for posterity. All we can do for posterity is to try to plug along in a way to make them think we—the old folks—did the best we could for justice, as we could understand it.

Q. Are you a gradualist on the matter of segregation?

A. If by gradualist you mean a person who would create delay for the sake of delay, then no. If by gradualist you mean a person who thinks it will take time, not time as such, but time for an educational process, preferably a calculated one, then yes. I mean a process of mutual education for whites and blacks. And part of this education should be in the actual beginning of the process of desegregation. It's a silly question, anyway, to ask if somebody is a gradualist. Gradualism is all you'll get. History, like nature, knows no jumps. Except the jump backward, maybe.

Q. Has the South any contribution to make to the national life?

A. It has made its share. It may again.

Q. How?

A. If the South is really able to face up to itself and its situation, it may achieve identity, moral identity. Then in a country where moral identity is hard to come by, the South, because it has had to deal concretely with a moral problem, may offer some leadership. And we need any we can get. If we are to break out of the national rhythm, the rhythm between complacency and panic.

This is, of course, an interview with myself.

QUESTIONS FOR STUDY AND DISCUSSION

1. How does the viewpoint (not exactly the same thing as the "point of view") shift in the first part of Mr. Warren's essay? What does the author gain from this device? Try to define the connection between the author's handling of panorama and specific scene in the first part of the essay and the essay as a whole.

2. Although Mr. Warren's essay is a report of many interviews he recorded in the South, to what extent does he make use of fictional methods? To what degree does he develop the conventions of plot? With what episode, for example, does the fundamental complexity of the conflict begin to emerge? Does there seem to be a climax to the "story"? A dénouement (resolution)?

3. Does the author as narrator function in any way as the protagonist of the "story"? Does he appear to plead a special case (i.e., that of an expatriate Southerner returning home)? Does his attitude change or develop in any way throughout the narrative? What general view or attitude does he seem to typify? Consider the handling of "point of view" (not viewpoint). How much does the author, as narrator, reveal of his personal feelings? How far, and by what means, does

he penetrate the feelings of the other people in the account? What use does he make of the relationship between his feelings and those of his subjects?

4. Discuss the persuasive techniques of this essay. Analyze and evaluate the author's strategy. Why does Mr. Warren present his argument through dramatic example?

5. What is the validity of Mr. Warren's emphasis on morality? Self-division? Sense of moral identity? Does your answer to this question depend on your answer to question 4?

6. Why does Mr. Warren move from the convinced to the confused, from the trite to the troubled? Does he get from thesis and antithesis a valid synthesis?

7. Why does Mr. Warren describe, as he does, the topography of Arkansas and Mississippi?

8. How does the description of the characters who speak parallel Mr. Warren's allusions to Southern history? What is the significance of the section on "Uncle Tom"?

9. Discuss, using implications from three places in Mr. Warren's discussion, the validity of the dichotomy between Law and Sociology.

10. Discuss Mr. Warren's complex of characters who are gracious, pious, and segregationist. Is their attitude theoretically possible? Is "graciousness" like or unlike charity in the Christian sense?

11. If tragic conflicts exist for whites in the South, do they also for Negroes? Why does Mr. Warren mention "magnanimity"?

WRITING ASSIGNMENTS

1. Write an essay, using Mr. Warren's as an example, on the conflict between Law and *Pieties*, or between morality and social custom. Is such a conflict tragic? Why?

2. What evidence is there in Mr. Warren's essay that Southern responsibility is solving the segregation problem? That it is not? Argue either side.

3. Using the articles on segregation which comprise this section of the book as background or source material, together with your own experience, write an essay developing your own view of the problem.

4. Evaluate the impact of segregation on your own religious principles.

5. Show how the principle of segregation complements or offends a man's "inalienable right" to the "pursuit of happiness."

6. Compare / contrast two of the essays on segregation, as your instructor directs, with respect to some point of technique or content.

INDEX OF AUTHORS AND TITLES